AQA Certificat Physics (iGCSE)

Level 1/2

SCIENCE

Jim Breithau

Margaret Cros

Brian Turner

Editor

Lawrie Ryan

Nelson Thornes

Published in 2012 by:
Nelson Thornes Ltd
Delta Place
27 Bath Road
CHELTENHAM
GL53 7TH
United Kingdom

12 13 14 15 16 / 10 9 8 7 6 5 4 3 2

A catalogue record for this book is available from the British Library.

ISBN 978 1 4085 1712 3

Cover photograph: iStockphoto

Page make-up by Wearset Ltd, Boldon, Tyne and Wear

Printed and bound in Spain by GraphyCems

Physics

Contents

Welcome to AQA Level 1/2 Certificate in Physics

Learning objectives

Each topic begins with statements of key content that you should know by the end of the lesson.

This book has been written for you by the people who will be marking your exams, very experienced teachers and subject experts. It covers everything you need to know for your exams and is packed full of features to help you achieve the very best that you can.

Figure 1 Many diagrams are as important for you to learn as the text, so make sure you revise them carefully.

Key words are highlighted in the text. You can look them up in the glossary at the back of the book if you are not sure what they mean.

Examiner's tip

Hints from the examiners who will mark your exams, giving you important advice on things to remember and what to watch out for.

Practical

This feature helps you become familiar with key practicals. It may be a simple introduction, a reminder or the basis for a practical in the classroom.

Did you know ... ?

There are lots of interesting and often strange facts about science. This feature tells you about many of them.

Summary questions

These questions give you the chance to test whether you have learned and understood everything in the topic. If you get any wrong, go back and have another look. They are designed to be increasingly challenging.

links

Links will tell you where you can find more information about what you are learning and how different topics link up.

And at the end of each chapter you will find ...

Summary questions

These will test you on what you have learned throughout the whole chapter, helping you to work out what you have understood and where you need to go back and revise.

Activity

An activity is linked to a main lesson and could be a discussion or task in pairs, in groups or by yourself.

AQA Examination-style questions

These questions are examples of the types of question you will answer in your actual exam, so you can get lots of practice during your course.

Maths skills

This feature highlights the maths skills that you will need for your Science exams with short, visual explanations.

Key points

At the end of the topic are the important points that you must remember. They can be used to help with revision and summarising your knowledge.

P1.1 Distance–time graphs

Learning objectives

After this topic, you should know:

- how a distance–time graph can tell us if an object is stationary or moving at constant speed
- what the gradient of the line on a distance–time graph can tell us
- how to use the equation for constant speed.

Figure 1 Capturing the land speed record

Examiner's tip

Be careful when plotting points on a graph grid. Make a clear point or a small cross, not a 'blob' – you will lose marks if you make a large 'blob'.

Did you know ...?

- A cheetah is faster than any other animal. It can run about 30 metres every second – but only for about 20 seconds! This is nearly as fast as a vehicle travelling at 70 miles per hour (mph).
- The land speed record at present is 763 mph, which is more than Mach 1, the speed of sound. The Bloodhound Project is aiming to set a new record of 1000 mph.

Some motorways have marker posts every kilometre. If you are a passenger in a car on a motorway, you can use these posts to check the speed of the car. You need to time the car as it passes each post. The table below shows some measurements made on a car journey.

Distance (metres, m)	0	1000	2000	3000	4000	5000	6000
Time (seconds, s)	0	40	80	120	160	200	240

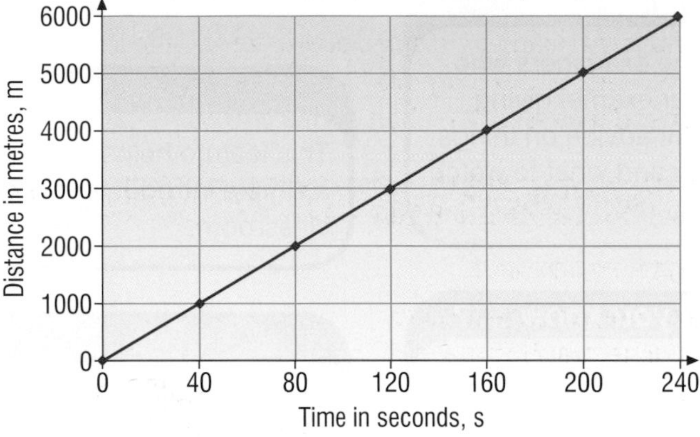

Figure 2 A distance–time graph

Look at the readings plotted on a graph of distance against time in Figure 2.

The graph shows that:

- the car took 40 s to go from each marker post to the next. So its speed was **constant** (or uniform).
- the car went a distance of 25 metres every second (= 1000 metres ÷ 40 seconds). So its speed was 25 metres per second.

If the car had travelled faster, it would have gone further than 1000 metres every 40 seconds. So the line on the graph would have been **steeper**. In other words, the **gradient** of the line would have been greater.

The gradient of a line on a distance–time graph represents speed.

Speed

For an object moving at **constant speed**, we can calculate its speed using the equation:

$$\textbf{speed in metres per second, m/s} = \frac{\textbf{distance travelled in metres, m}}{\textbf{time taken in seconds, s}}$$

The scientific unit of speed is the metre per second, usually written as metre/second or m/s.

This equation can also be used to calculate the **average speed** of an object whose speed varies. For example, if a motorist in a traffic queue took 50 s to travel a distance of 300 m, the car's average speed was 6.0 m/s (= 300 m ÷ 50 s).

Speed in action

Long-distance vehicles are fitted with recorders called **tachographs.** These can check that their drivers don't drive for too long. Look at the distance–time graphs in Figure 3 for three lorries, X, Y and Z, on the same motorway.

- X went fastest because it travelled furthest in the same time.
- Y travelled more slowly than X. From the graph, you can see it travelled 30 000 metres in 1250 seconds. So its speed was:

  distance ÷ time = 30 000 m ÷ 1250 s = 24 m/s.

- Z travelled the least distance. It stopped for some of the time. Its speed was zero during this time. When it was moving its speed was also less than that of X or Y.

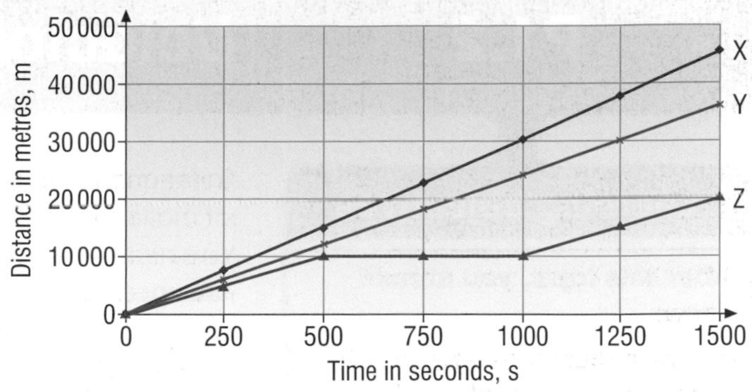

Figure 3 Comparing distance–time graphs

Maths skills

Rearranging the speed formula

If two of the three quantities are known, the third can be found. It may help to use the speed formula triangle below:

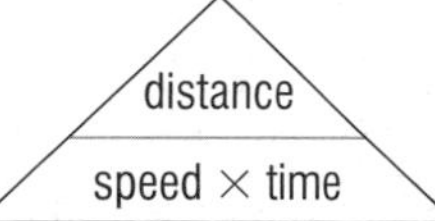

Cover up the unknown quantity and the triangle tells you how to use the other two known quantities.

Practical

Be a distance recorder!

Take the measurements needed to plot distance–time graphs for a person:

- walking
- running
- riding a bike.

Remember that you must always label the graph axes, which includes units.

- Work out the average speeds.

Figure 4 Measuring distance

Examiner's tip

Always convert time into seconds in these calculations if it is given in minutes or hours.

Summary questions

1 a For an object travelling at constant speed:
   i What can you say about the distance it travels every second?
   ii What can you say about the gradient of its distance–time graph?
 b Look at the distance–time graphs in Figure 3.
   i Calculate the speed of X.
   ii How long did Z stop for?
   iii Calculate the **average** speed of Z, using the total distance Z travels in its journey.

2 A vehicle on a motorway travels 1800 m in 60 seconds. Calculate:
 a the average speed of the vehicle in m/s
 b how far it would travel in 300 seconds if it continued travelling at this speed
 c how long it would take to travel a distance of 3300 m at this speed.

3 A car on a motorway travels a certain distance *d* in six minutes at a speed of 21 m/s. A coach takes seven minutes to travel the same distance. Calculate the distance *d* and the speed of the coach.

Key points

- **The distance–time graph for any object that is**
  - **stationary is a horizontal line**
  - **moving at constant speed is a straight line that slopes upwards.**
- **The gradient of a distance–time graph for an object represents the object's speed.**
- **Speed, m/s, = $\dfrac{\text{distance travelled, m}}{\text{time taken, s}}$**

P1.2 Velocity and acceleration

Learning objectives

After this topic, you should know:

- the difference between speed and velocity
- the difference between vectors and scalars
- how to calculate the acceleration of an object
- the difference between acceleration and deceleration.

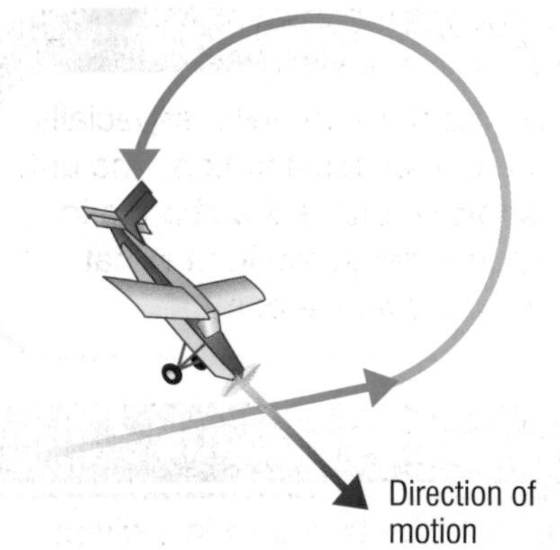

Figure 1 Speed and velocity

In fairground rides that throw you round and round, your speed and direction of motion keep changing. We use the word **velocity** for speed in a given direction. An exciting ride would be one that changes your velocity often and unexpectedly!

Velocity is speed in a given direction.

- An object moving steadily round in a circle has a constant speed. Its direction of motion changes continuously as it goes round so its velocity is not constant.
- Two moving objects can have the same speed but different velocities. For example, a car travelling north at 30 m/s on a motorway has the same speed as a car travelling south at 30 m/s. But their velocities are not the same because they are moving in opposite directions.

An object that travels at constant velocity travels at a constant speed without changing its direction. It therefore travels in a straight line in a certain direction. We use the word **displacement** for the distance moved in a certain direction.

Figure 2 You experience plenty of changes in velocity on a corkscrew ride!

Displacement is distance in a certain direction.

For example, the displacement of a car that travels 20 km on a straight motorway due north is 20 km due north. A car travelling the same distance in the opposite direction would have a displacement of 20 km due south.

Vectors and scalars

As well as velocity and displacement, many other physical quantities are directional. Physical quantities that are directional are called **vectors**. Other examples of vectors later in this book include acceleration, force, momentum, weight and gravitational field strength.

Physical quantities that are not directional are called **scalars**. Examples include speed, distance, time, mass, energy and power.

The size of a quantity is its **magnitude**. A vector has magnitude (i.e. size) as well as a direction. A scalar has magnitude only.

Acceleration

A car maker claims their new car 'accelerates more quickly than any other new car'. A rival car maker is not pleased by this claim and issues a challenge. Each car in turn is tested on a straight track with a velocity recorder fitted.

The results are shown in the table:

Time from a standing start (seconds, s)	0	2	4	6	8	10
Velocity of car X (metres per second, m/s)	0	5	10	15	20	25
Velocity of car Y (metres per second, m/s)	0	6	12	18	18	18

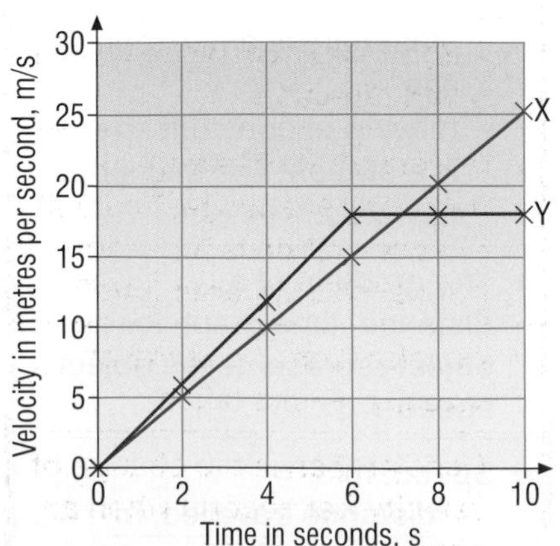

Figure 3 Velocity–time graph

Which car has a greater **acceleration**? The results are plotted on the velocity–time graph in Figure 3. You can see the velocity of Y goes up from zero faster than the velocity of X does. So Y accelerates more in the first 6 seconds.

The acceleration of an object is its change of velocity per second. The unit of acceleration is the metre per second squared, abbreviated to m/s^2.

Any object with a changing velocity is accelerating. We can work out its acceleration using the equation:

$$\textbf{Acceleration} \text{ (metres per second squared, m/s}^2) = \frac{\textbf{change in velocity} \text{ in metres per second, m/s}}{\textbf{time taken for the change} \text{ in seconds, s}}$$

For an object that accelerates steadily from an initial velocity u to a final velocity v,

its change of velocity = final velocity – initial velocity = $v - u$.

Therefore, we can write the equation for acceleration as:

$$\textbf{acceleration, } a = \frac{v - u}{t}$$

where:
v = the final velocity in metres per second,
u = the initial velocity in metres per second,
t = time taken in seconds.

Maths skills

Worked example

In Figure 3, the velocity of Y increases from 0 to 18 m/s in 6 seconds. Calculate its acceleration.

Solution

Change of velocity = $v - u$ = 18 m/s – 0 m/s = 18 m/s
Time taken, t = 6 s

$$\text{Acceleration, } a = \frac{\text{change in velocity in metres per second, m/s}}{\text{time taken for the change in seconds, s}}$$

$$= \frac{v - u}{t} = \frac{18\,\text{m/s}}{6\,\text{s}} = \mathbf{3\,m/s^2}$$

Deceleration

A car decelerates when the driver brakes. We use the term **deceleration** or **negative acceleration** for any situation where an object slows down.

Summary questions

1 a What is the difference between speed and velocity?
  b A car on a motorway is travelling at a constant speed of 30 m/s when it overtakes a lorry travelling at a speed of 22 m/s. If both vehicles maintain their speeds, how far ahead of the lorry will the car be after 300 s?

2 The velocity of a car increased from 8 m/s to 28 m/s in 16 s without change of direction. Calculate its acceleration.

3 The driver of a car increased the speed of the car as it joined the motorway. It then travelled at constant velocity before slowing down as it left the motorway at the next junction.
  a i When did the car decelerate?
    ii When was the acceleration of the car zero?
  b When the car joined the motorway, it accelerated from a speed of 7.0 m/s for 10 s at an acceleration of 2.0 m/s^2. What was its speed at the end of this time?

Maths skills

We can write an equation for velocity as:

$$\textbf{velocity, } v = \frac{s}{t}$$

where
v is the velocity in metres per second,
s is the displacement in metres, and
t is the time in seconds.

Note: Speed and velocity may also be described in kilometres per hour (km/h).

As 1000 m = 1 km and 3600 s = 1 hour, then a speed of 1 km/h is equal to 1000 m ÷ 3600 s = 0.278 m/s.

Examiner's tip

Be careful with units, especially the unit of acceleration. The unit is **m/s^2 –** that is the change in speed measured in **m/s** that occurs every second.

Key points

- Velocity is speed in a given direction.
- A vector is a physical quantity that has a direction as well as a magnitude.
- A scalar is a physical quantity that has a magnitude only and does not have a direction.
- Displacement is distance in a given direction.
- Acceleration is change of velocity per second. The unit of acceleration is the metre per second squared (m/s^2).
- Acceleration = change of velocity ÷ time taken.
- Deceleration is the change of velocity per second when an object slows down.

P1.3 More about velocity–time graphs

Learning objectives

After this topic, you should know:

- what a horizontal line on a velocity–time graph tells us
- how to tell from a velocity–time graph if an object is accelerating or decelerating
- what the area under a velocity–time graph tells us.

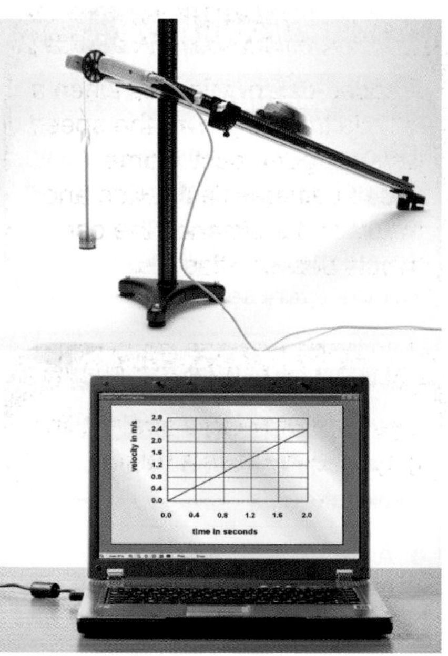

Figure 2 Measuring motion using a computer

Investigating acceleration

We can use a motion sensor linked to a computer to record how the velocity of an object changes. Figure 1 shows how we can do this, using a trolley as the moving object. The computer can also be used to display the measurements as a velocity–time graph.

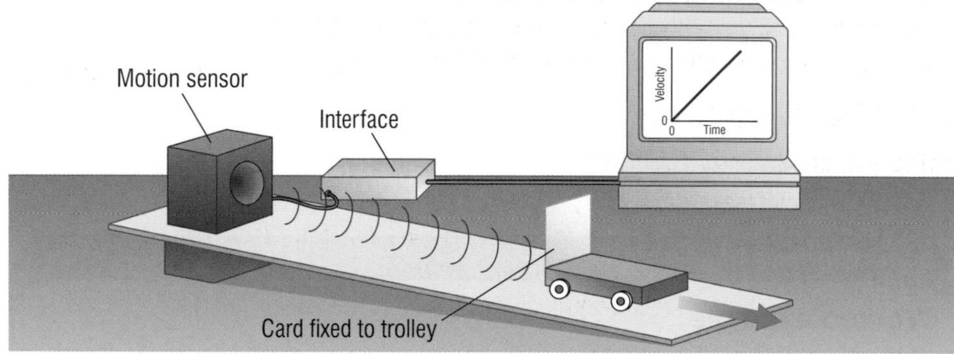

Figure 1 A velocity–time graph on a computer

Test A: If we let the trolley accelerate down the runway, its velocity increases with time. Look at the velocity–time graph from a test run in Figure 1.

- The line goes up because the velocity increases with time. So, it shows the trolley was accelerating as it ran down the runway.
- The line is straight, which tells us that the increase in velocity was the same every second. In other words, the acceleration of the trolley was constant.

Test B: If we make the runway steeper, the trolley accelerates faster. This would make the line on the graph in Figure 1 steeper than for test A. So, the acceleration in test B is greater.

The tests show that:

the gradient of the line on a velocity–time graph represents acceleration.

Practical

Investigating acceleration

Use a motion sensor and a computer to find out how the gradient of a runway affects a trolley's acceleration.

- In this investigation, name:
  - **i** the independent variable
  - **ii** the dependent variable.
- What relationship do you find between the variables?

Safety: Use foam or an empty cardboard box to stop the trolley falling off the bench. 'Mind your feet!'

links

For more information on variables and relationships between them, see 'Experimental data handling' on pages 236–40.

Braking

Braking reduces the velocity of a vehicle. Look at the graph in Figure 3. It is the velocity–time graph for a vehicle that brakes and stops at a set of traffic lights. The velocity is constant until the driver applies the brakes.

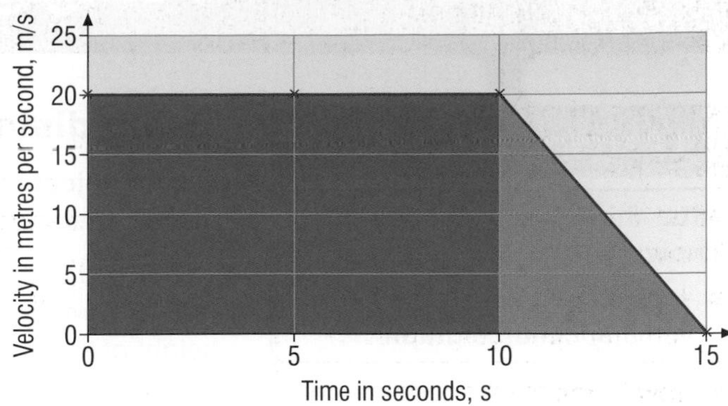

Figure 3 Braking

Using the gradient of the line:

- The section of the graph for constant velocity is horizontal. The gradient of the line is zero so the acceleration in this section is zero.
- When the brakes are applied, the vehicle decelerates and its velocity decreases to zero. The gradient of the line is negative in this section. So the acceleration is negative.

Look at Figure 3 again.

Using the area under the line:

- Before the brakes are applied, the vehicle moves at a velocity of 20 m/s for 10 s. It therefore travels 200 m in this time (= 20 m/s × 10 s). This distance is represented on the graph by the area under the line from 0 s to 10 s. This is the rectangle shaded red on the graph.
- When the vehicle decelerates in Figure 3, its velocity drops from 20 m/s to 0 m/s in 5 s. We can work out the distance travelled in this time from the area of the purple triangle in Figure 3. This area is ½ × the height × the base of the triangle. So, the vehicle must have travelled a distance of 50 m when it was decelerating.

The area under the line on a velocity–time graph represents distance travelled.

Did you know ... ?

A speed camera flashes when a vehicle travelling over the speed limit has gone past. Some speed cameras flash twice and measure the distance the car travels between flashes.

Examiner's tip

If you are drawing a straight line graph, always use a ruler.

Summary questions

1 Match each of the following descriptions to one of the lines, labelled **A**, **B**, **C** and **D**, on the velocity–time graph.
   1 Accelerated motion throughout.
   2 Zero acceleration.
   3 Accelerated motion, then decelerated motion.
   4 Deceleration.

2 Look at the graph in Question **1**.
   a Which line represents the object that travelled:
      i the furthest distance?
      ii the least distance?
   b Which object, **B** or **D**, travelled further?

3 Look again at the graph in Question **1**.
   a Show that the object that produced the data for line **A** (the horizontal line) travelled a distance of 160 m.
   b Which one of the other three lines represents the motion of an object that decelerated throughout its journey?
   c Calculate the distance travelled by this object.
   d Calculate the difference in the distances travelled by **A** and **D**.

Key points

- If a velocity–time graph is a horizontal line, the acceleration is zero.
- The gradient of the line on a velocity–time graph represents acceleration.
- The area under the line on a velocity–time graph represents distance travelled.

P1.4 Using graphs

Learning objectives

After this topic, you should know:

- how to calculate speed from a distance–time graph
- how to calculate acceleration from a velocity–time graph
- how to calculate distance from a velocity–time graph.

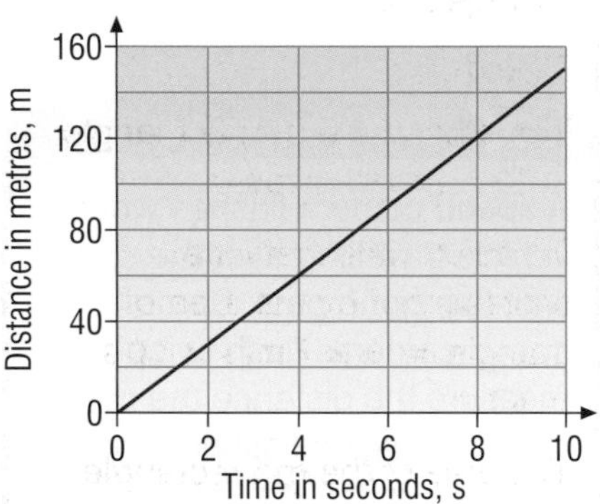

Figure 1 A distance–time graph for constant speed

Using distance–time graphs

For an object moving at constant speed, we saw at the start of this chapter that the distance–time graph is a straight line sloping upwards.

The speed of the object is represented by the gradient of the line. To find the gradient, we need to draw a triangle under the line, as shown in Figure 1. The height of the triangle represents the distance travelled and the base represents the time taken. So:

$$\text{the gradient of the line} = \frac{\text{the height of the triangle}}{\text{the base of the triangle}}$$

and this represents the object's speed.

For a moving object with a changing speed, the distance–time graph is not a straight line. The red line in Figure 2 shows an example.

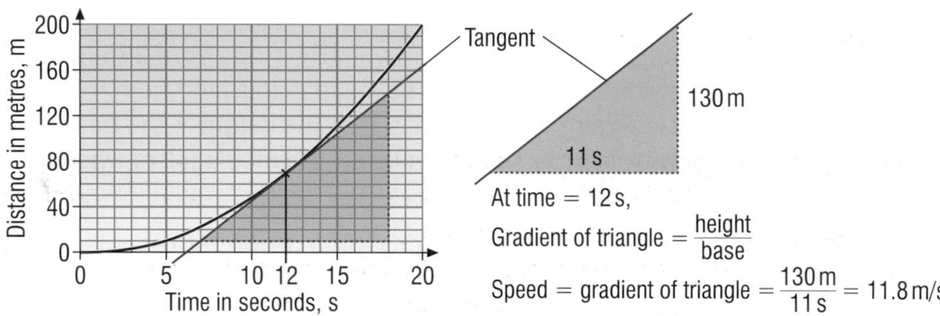

Figure 2 A distance–time graph for changing speed

In Figure 2, the gradient of the line increases gradually, so the object's speed must have increased gradually. We can find the speed at any point on the line by drawing a tangent to the line at that point, as shown in Figure 2. The **tangent** to the curve is a straight line that touches the curve at a single point without cutting through it. The gradient of the tangent is equal to the speed at that point.

Using velocity–time graphs

Look at the graph in Figure 3. It shows the velocity–time graph of an object X moving with a constant acceleration. Its velocity increases at a steady rate. So the graph shows a straight line that has a constant gradient.

To find the acceleration from the graph, remember the gradient of the line on a velocity–time graph represents the acceleration.

In Figure 3, the gradient is given by the height divided by the base of the triangle under the line.

The height of the triangle represents the change of velocity and the base of the triangle represents the time taken.

Therefore, the gradient represents the acceleration, because:

$$\text{acceleration} = \frac{\text{change of velocity}}{\text{time taken}}$$

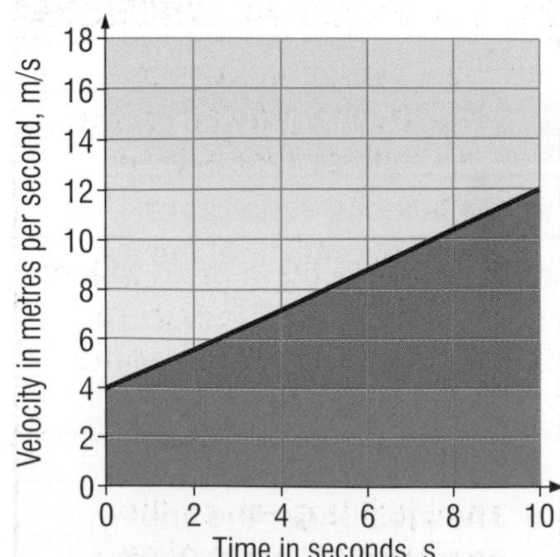

Figure 3 A velocity–time graph for constant acceleration

Maths skills

Worked example

Use the graph in Figure 3 to find the acceleration of object X.

Solution

The height of the triangle represents an increase of velocity of 8 m/s (= 12 m/s − 4 m/s).

The base of the triangle represents a time of 10 s.

$$\text{Therefore, the acceleration} = \frac{\text{change of velocity}}{\text{time taken}}$$

$$= \frac{8\,\text{m/s}}{10\,\text{s}} = \mathbf{0.8\,m/s^2}$$

To find the distance travelled from the graph, remember the area under a line on a velocity–time graph represents the distance travelled. The shape under the line in Figure 3 is a triangle on top of a rectangle. So the distance travelled is represented by the area of the triangle plus the area of the rectangle under it.

Look at the worked example to the right.

Summary questions

1 **a** Find the speed of the object in the graph in Figure 1.

b **i** What does the gradient of the line at the origin of the graph in Figure 2 tell you about the speed at time = 0?

ii What can you say about the speed in the graph of Figure 2?

2 The graph shows how the velocity of a cyclist on a straight road changes with time.

a Describe the motion of the cyclist.

b Use the graph to work out the acceleration of the cyclist and the distance travelled in:

i the first 40 seconds

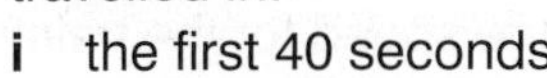

ii the next 20 seconds.

c Calculate the average speed of the cyclist over the journey.

3 In a motorcycle test, the speed from rest was recorded at intervals.

Time (seconds, s)	0	5	10	15	20	25	30
Velocity (metres per second, m/s)	0	10	20	30	40	40	40

a Plot a velocity–time graph of these results.

b What was the initial acceleration?

c How far did it move in:

i the first 20 s?

ii the next 10 s?

Examiner's tip

Make sure that you know whether you are dealing with a distance–time graph or a velocity–time graph. The gradients of the two types of graph represent different quantities.

Maths skills

Worked example

Use the graph in Figure 3 to calculate the distance moved by object X.

Solution

The area of the purple triangle = ½ × height × base.

Therefore, the distance represented by the area of triangle = ½ × 8 m/s × 10 s = 40 m

The area of the red rectangle under the triangle = height × base

Therefore, the distance represented by the area of the rectangle = 4 m/s × 10 s = 40 m

So the distance travelled by X = 40 m + 40 m = **80 m**

Key points

- The speed of an object is given by the gradient of the line on its distance–time graph.
- The acceleration of an object is given by the gradient of the line on its velocity–time graph.
- The distance travelled by an object is given by the area under the line of its velocity–time graph.

Summary questions

1 A model car travels round a circular track at constant speed.

If you were given a stopwatch, a marker and a tape measure, how would you measure the speed of the car?

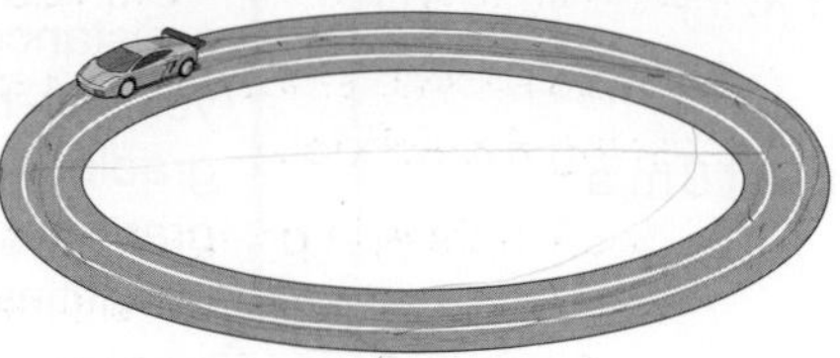

2 The figure shows the distance–time graph for a car on a motorway.

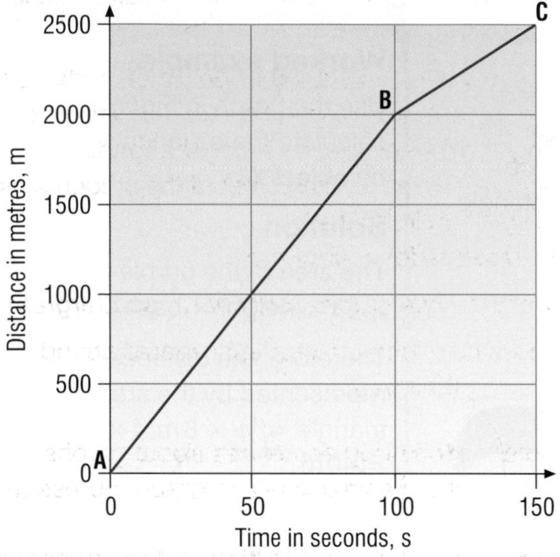

a Which part of the journey was faster: **A** to **B** or **B** to **C**?

b i Calculate the speed of the car between **A** and **B**.

ii Calculate the speed of the car between **B** and **C**.

c If the car had travelled the whole distance of 2500 m at the same speed as between **A** and **B**, how long would the journey have taken?

3 The figure shows a distance–time graph for a motorcycle approaching a speed limit sign.

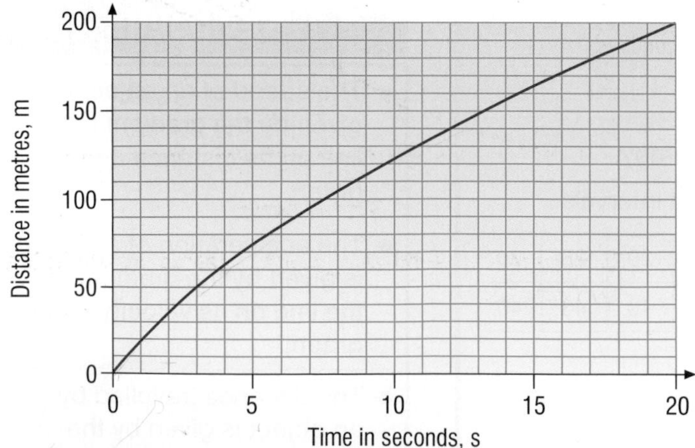

a Describe how the speed of the motorcycle changed with time.

b Use the graph to determine the speed of the motorcycle:

i initially

ii 10 seconds later.

4 a A car took 10 s to increase its velocity from 5 m/s to 30 m/s. Calculate its acceleration.

b The graph shows how the velocity of the car changed with time during the 10 seconds.

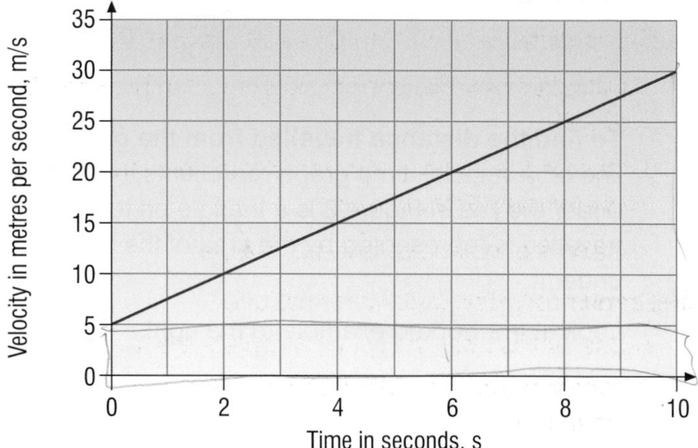

i How far did the car travel in this time?

ii What was the average speed of the car in this time?

5 The table shows how the velocity of a train changed as it travelled from one station to the next.

Time (seconds)	0	20	40	60	80	100	120	140	160
Velocity (m/s)	0	5	10	15	20	20	20	10	0

a Plot a velocity–time graph using this data.

b Calculate the acceleration in each of the three parts of the journey.

c Calculate the total distance travelled by the train.

d Show that the average speed for the train's journey was 12.5 m/s.

6 A water skier started from rest and accelerated steadily to 12 m/s in 15 seconds, then travelled at constant speed for 45 seconds before slowing down steadily and coming to a halt 90 seconds after she started.

a Draw a velocity–time graph for this journey.

b Calculate the acceleration of the water skier in the first 15 s.

c Calculate the deceleration of the water skier in the final 30 s.

d Calculate the total distance travelled by the water skier.

AQA Examination-style questions

1 A van has a fault and leaks one drop of oil every second.

The diagram shows the oil drops left on the road as the van moves from **A** to **D**.

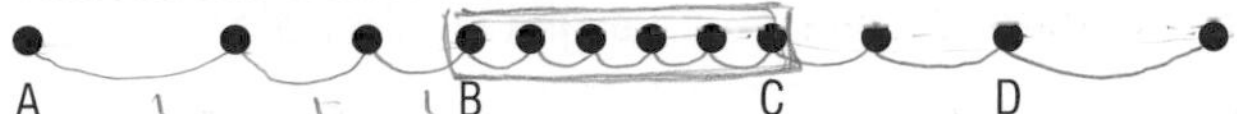

a Describe the motion of the van as it moves from:

i **A** to **B**

ii **B** to **C**

iii **C** to **D** (3)

b The distance from **B** to **C** is 100 metres.

Calculate the average speed of the van between **B** and **C**. (3)

c Later in the journey, the van slows down from a speed of 25 m/s to 5 m/s in 10 s.

Calculate the acceleration of the van. (5)

2 Graphs can give useful information.

a Use words from the list to complete the sentences.

accelerating *travelling at constant speed* *stationary*

i In a distance–time graph, a horizontal line shows that the vehicle was .... (1)

ii In a velocity–time graph, a horizontal line shows that the vehicle was .... (1)

b A car driver sees a dog on the road ahead and has to make an emergency stop.

The graph shows how the speed of the car changes with time after the driver first sees the dog.

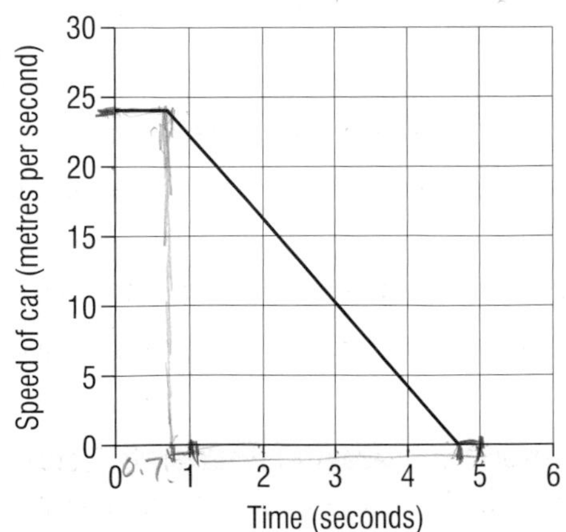

i What is the time interval between the driver seeing the dog and applying the brakes? (1)

ii How far does the car travel between the driver seeing the dog and applying the brakes? (3)

c i Calculate the deceleration of the car, in m/s^2, after the brakes are applied. (4)

ii How far does the car travel after the brakes are applied? (3)

3 A headteacher wants the local council to put a 20 mph speed limit on the road outside the school.

She asks some students to carry out a survey of vehicles passing the school.

a She wants one group of students to investigate the average speed of vehicles passing the school.

i Describe how the students would obtain the data needed. Your description should include the equipment they would use. (QWC) (6)

ii Outline how they could make the result as accurate as possible. (3)

b The headteacher wants another group of students to produce a graph showing the number of vehicles travelling at different speeds along the road.

i Which two of the following could the students use to display their results?
Give reasons for your choice. (5)

bar chart *line graph* *pie chart* *scattergram*

ii Discuss how long the students should spend collecting their data. (2)

4 a Complete the following sentences about graphs.

i The gradient of a velocity–time graph represents .... (1)

ii The gradient of a distance–time graph represents .... (1)

iii Distance is represented by the area under a .... graph. (1)

b The graphs describe the motion of two runners in a race.

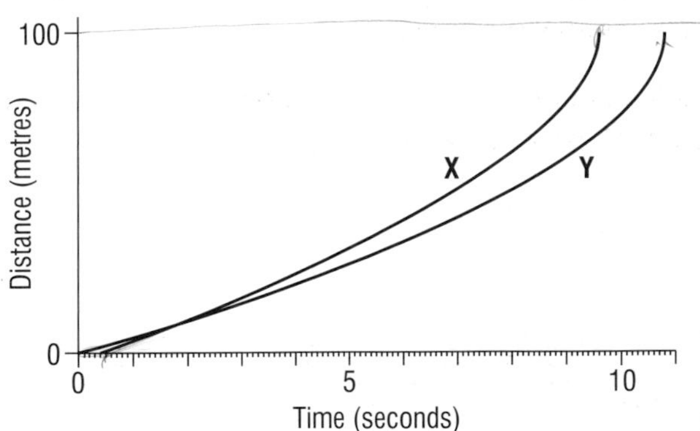

Compare and evaluate the information shown in the two graphs. (6)

P2.1 Forces between objects

Learning objectives

After this topic, you should know:

- what forces can do
- what the unit of force is
- what we can say about the forces being exerted when two objects interact.

When you apply a **force** to a tube of toothpaste, be careful not to apply too much force. The force you apply to squeeze the tube changes its shape and pushes toothpaste out of the tube. If you apply too much force, the toothpaste might come out too fast.

A force can change the shape of an object or change its state of rest or its motion.

Equal and opposite forces

Whenever two objects push or pull on each other, they exert equal and opposite forces on one another.

The unit of force is the **newton** (abbreviated as N).

- A boxer who punches an opponent with a force of 100 N experiences a reverse force of 100 N from his opponent.
- Two roller skaters pull on opposite ends of a rope. The skaters move towards each other because they pull on each other with equal and opposite forces. Two newtonmeters could be used to show this.

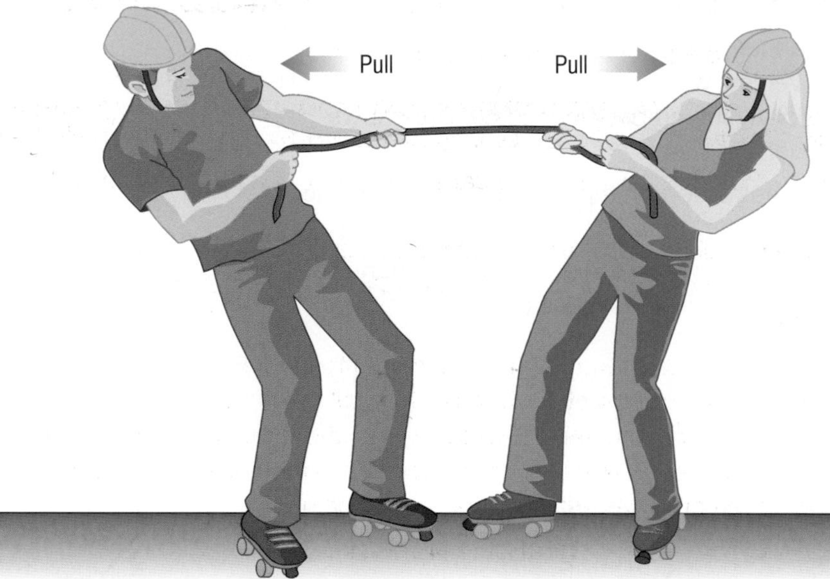

Figure 1 Equal and opposite forces

Did you know ... ?

Quicksand victims sink because they can't get enough support from the sand. The gravitational force on the victim (acting downwards) is greater than the upwards force of the sand on the victim. People caught in quicksand should not struggle but flatten themselves on the surface and crawl to a safe place.

Examiner's tip

Remember that when two objects interact, although they exert equal and opposite forces on each other, the effects of those forces will depend on the masses of the objects – larger mass, smaller effect.

Practical

Action and reaction

Test this with a friend if you can, using roller skates and two newtonmeters. Don't forget to wear protective head gear!

- What did you find out?
- Comment on the precision of your repeat readings.

Safety: You might want a friend to help support you.

In the mud

A car stuck in mud can be difficult to shift. A tractor can be very useful here. Figure 2 shows the idea. At any stage, the force of the rope on the car is equal and opposite to the force of the car on the rope.

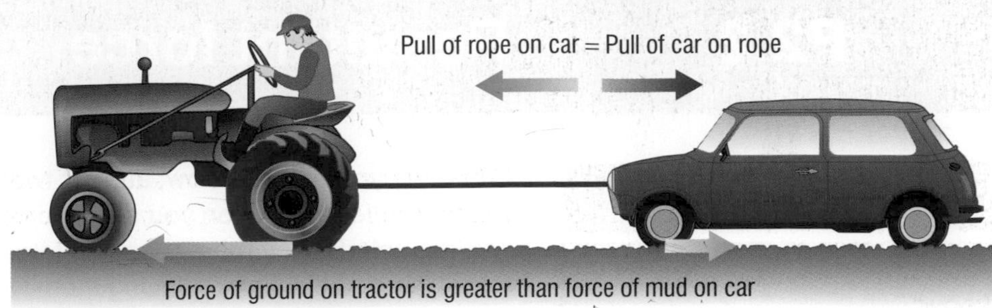
Pull of rope on car = Pull of car on rope
Force of ground on tractor is greater than force of mud on car

Figure 2 In the mud

To pull the car out of the mud, the force of the ground on the tractor needs to be greater than the force of the mud on the car. These two forces aren't necessarily equal to one another, because the objects are not the same.

Friction in action

The driving force on a car is the force that makes it move. This is sometimes called the engine force or the **motive force**. This force is caused by **friction** between the ground and the tyre of each drive wheel. Friction acts where the tyre is in contact with the ground.

When the car moves forwards:

- the force of friction of the road on the tyre is in the forward direction
- the force of friction of the tyre on the ground is in the reverse direction.

The two forces are equal and opposite to one another.

Direction of car

Force of tyre on road

Force of road on tyre

Figure 3 Driving force

Summary questions

1 a When the brakes of a moving car are applied, what is the effect of the braking force on the car?

b When you sit on a cushion, what forces act on you?

c When you kick a football, what is the effect of the force of your foot on the ball?

2 a i A hammer hits a nail with a downward force of 50 N. What is the size and direction of the force of the nail on the hammer?

ii A lorry tows a broken-down car. When the force of the lorry on the tow rope is 200 N, what is the force of the tow rope on the lorry?

b Copy and complete **i–iii** using the words below:

downwards equal opposite upwards

i The force on a ladder resting against a wall is .... and .... to the force of the wall on the ladder.

ii A book is at rest on a table. The force of the book on the table is .... The force of the table on the book is ....

iii When a ball is dropped onto the floor, the force of the floor on the ball is ....

3 When a student is standing at rest on bathroom scales, the scales read 500 N.

a What is the size and direction of the force of the student on the scales?

b What is the size and direction of the force of the scales on the student?

c What is the size and direction of the force of the floor on the scales?

Key points

- A force can change the shape of an object, or change its motion, or its state of rest.
- The unit of force is the newton (N).
- When two objects interact, they always exert equal and opposite forces on each other.

P2.2 Resultant force

Learning objectives

After this topic, you should know:

- what a resultant force is
- what happens if the resultant force on an object is:
  - zero
  - not zero
- how to calculate the resultant force when an object is acted on by two forces acting along the same line.

Wherever you are right now, at least two forces are acting on you. These are the gravitational force on you and a force supporting you. Most objects around you are acted on by more than one force. We can work out the effect of the forces on an object by replacing them with a single force, the **resultant force**. This is a single force that has the same effect as all the forces acting on the object.

Zero resultant force

When the resultant force on an object is zero, the object:

- remains stationary if it was at rest (i.e. it was in equilibrium), or
- continues to move at the same speed and in the same direction if it was already moving.

If only two forces act on the object, they must be equal to each other and act in opposite directions.

Practical

Investigating forces

Use a glider on an air track to investigate the relationship between force and acceleration.

- What relationship do you find between force and acceleration?

Alternatively:

Make and test a model hovercraft floating on a cushion of air provided by an inflated balloon.

1 **A glider on a linear air track** floats on a cushion of air. As long as the track stays level, the glider moves at constant velocity (i.e. with no change of speed or direction) along the track. That's because friction is absent. The resultant force on the glider is zero.

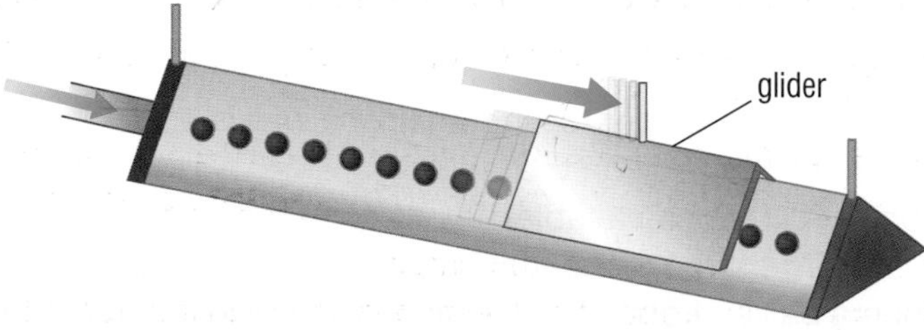

Figure 1 The linear air track

2 **When a heavy crate is pushed across a rough floor at a constant velocity**, the resultant force on the crate is zero. The push force on the crate is equal in size but acts in the opposite direction to the force of friction of the floor on the crate.

Figure 2 Overcoming friction

Non-zero resultant force

When the resultant force on an object is not zero, the movement of the object depends on the size and direction of the resultant force.

1 **When a jet plane is taking off**, the thrust force of its engines is greater than the force of air resistance on it. The resultant force on it is the difference between the thrust force and the force of air resistance on it. The resultant force is therefore non-zero. The greater the resultant force, the quicker the take-off is.

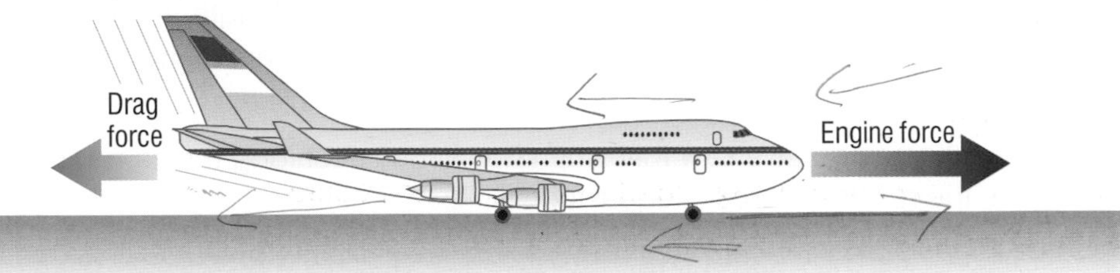

Figure 3 A passenger jet on take-off

2 **When a car driver applies the brakes**, the braking force is greater than the force from the engine. The resultant force is the difference between the braking force and the engine force. It acts in the opposite direction to the car's direction so it slows the car down.

The examples above show that if an object is acted on by two unequal forces acting in opposite directions, the resultant force is:

- equal to the difference between the two forces
- in the direction of the larger force.

Note what happens if the two forces act in the same direction. The resultant force is equal to the sum of the two forces and acts in the same direction as the two forces.

Examiner's tip

A common error is to think that when the resultant force on an object is zero it must be stationary – it may just be travelling at constant velocity.

Figure 4 Braking

Summary questions

1 a What happens to the glider in Figure 1 if the air track blower is switched off, and why?
  b When a jet plane is moving at constant velocity at a constant height, what can be said about the thrust force and the force of air resistance?

2 A jet plane lands on a runway and stops.
  a What can you say about the direction of the resultant force on the plane as it lands?
  b What can you say about the resultant force on the plane when it has stopped?

3 A car is stuck in the mud. A tractor tries to pull it out.
  a The tractor pulls the car with a force of 250 N. Explain why the car doesn't move.
  b Increasing the tractor force to 300 N pulls the car steadily out of the mud at constant velocity. What is the force of the mud on the car now?

Key points

- The resultant force is a single force that has the same effect as all the forces acting on an object.
- If the resultant force on an object is zero, the object stays at rest or at constant velocity.
- If the resultant force on an object is not zero, the velocity of the object will change.
- If two forces act on an object along the same line, the resultant force is:
  1 their sum if the forces act in the same direction
  2 their difference if the forces act in opposite directions.

P2.3 Force as a vector

Learning objectives

After this topic, you should know:

- how to represent a force accurately on a diagram
- how to find the resultant of two forces
- what the parallelogram of forces is.

Force diagrams

When an object is acted on by more than one force, we can draw a **force diagram** to work out the resultant force on the object. A force diagram shows the forces acting on the object. Each force can be represented accurately on the diagram by a **vector**, which is shown as an arrow. The length of the arrow is proportional to the size (i.e. magnitude) of the force and the arrow points in the direction of the force.

In 2.2 'Resultant force', we saw that when two forces act along the same line on an object, the resultant force is equal to:

- the sum of the two forces if the forces are in the same direction
- the difference between the two forces if the forces are in opposite directions.

Figure 1 shows a tug-of-war in which the pull force of each team is represented by a vector. A scale of 10 mm to 200 N is used. Team A pulls with a force of 1000 N and team B pulls with a force of 800 N. So the resultant force is 200 N in team A's direction.

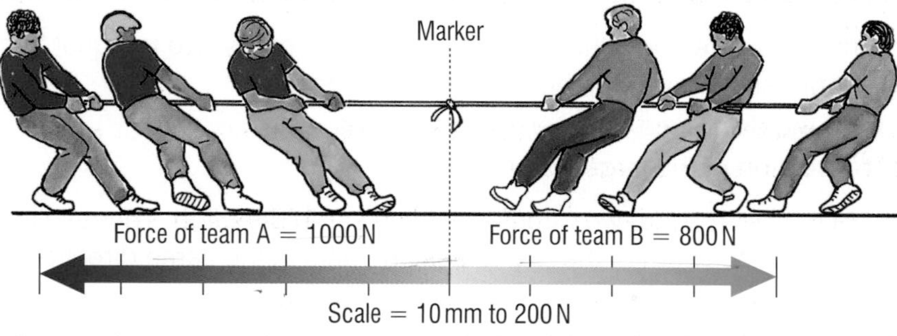

Figure 1 A tug-of-war

Figure 2 In tow

The parallelogram of forces

What if the two forces do not act along the same line, as shown in Figure 2? Here we can see a ship being towed by cables from two tugboats. The tension force in each cable pulls on the ship. The combined effect of these tension forces is to pull the vessel forwards. This is the resultant force.

Figure 3 shows how the two tension forces T_1 and T_2, represented as vectors, combine to produce the resultant force. The tension forces are drawn as adjacent sides of a parallelogram; the resultant force is the diagonal of the parallelogram from the origin of T_1 and T_2. This geometrical method is called the **parallelogram of forces**.

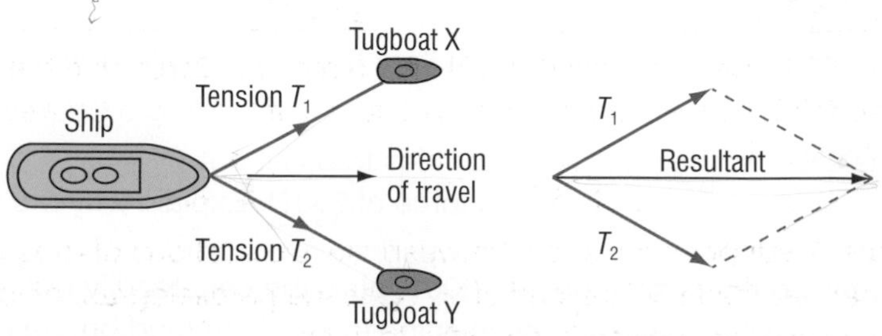

Figure 3 Combining forces

Investigating the parallelogram of forces

We can use weights and pulleys to demonstrate the parallelogram of forces, as shown in Figure 4. The tension in each string is equal to the weight it supports, either directly or over a pulley.

The point where the three strings meet is in equilibrium (i.e. at rest). The string supporting the middle weight (W_3) is vertical. Using a protractor, measure angles θ_1 and θ_2 and note the values of the three known weights. Draw a scale diagram of a parallelogram such that:

- the line down the centre of the diagram represents a vertical line
- adjacent sides of the parallelogram at angles θ_1 and θ_2 to the 'vertical' line represent the tensions in the strings supporting W_1 and W_2.

The resultant of W_1 and W_2 represented by the diagonal line should be equal and opposite in direction to the vector representing W_3.

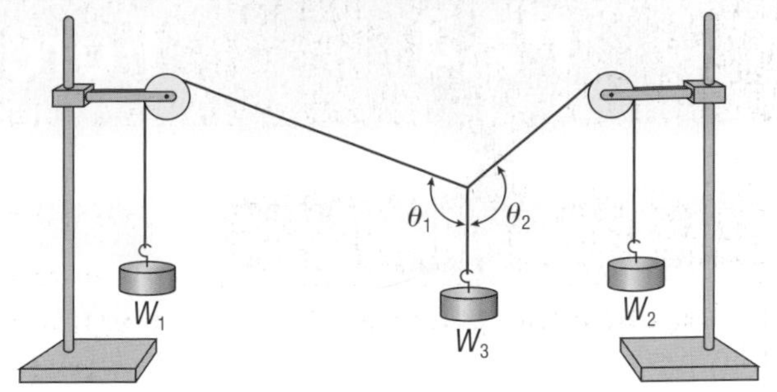

Figure 4 The parallelogram of forces

Maths skills

Worked example

A tow rope is attached to a car at two points 0.80 m apart. The two sections of rope joined to the car are of the same length and are at 30° to each other (see Figure 5). The pull on each attachment should not exceed 3000 N. Use the parallelogram of forces to determine the maximum tension in the main tow rope.

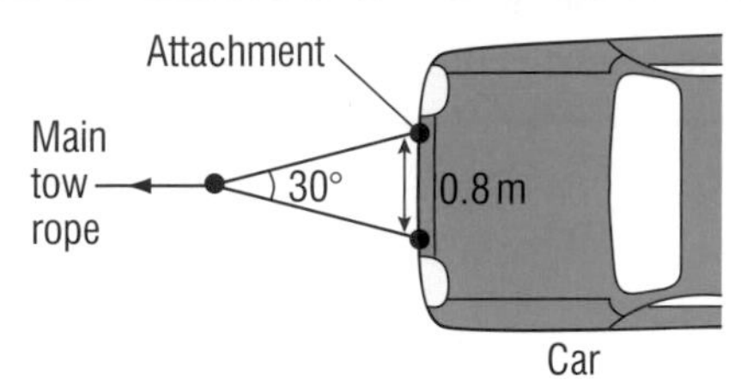

Solution

The maximum tension T in the main tow rope is the resultant of the two 3000 N forces at 30° to each other.

Drawing the parallelogram of forces as shown in Figure 5 gives:

$$T = 5800\,\text{N}$$

Figure 5

Summary questions

1 The diagrams below show several examples where two forces act on an object X. In each case, work out the magnitude and direction of the resultant force on X.

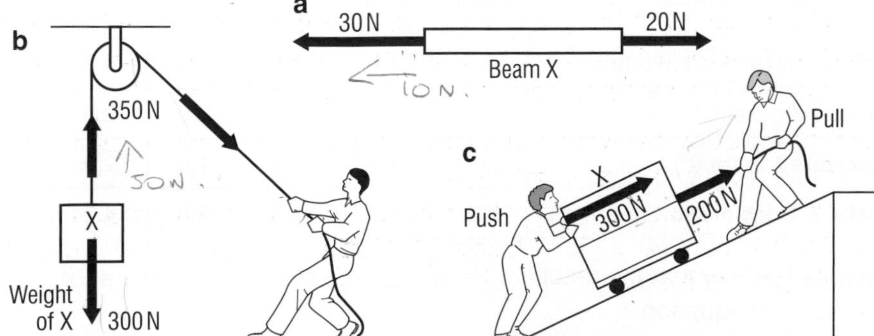

2 A force of 3.0 N and a force of 4.0 N act on a point. Determine the magnitude of the resultant of these two forces if the angle between their lines of action is:

a 90° **b** 60° **c** 45°.

3 In Figure 5, suppose the angle between the two sections of rope joined to the car had been 50° instead of 30°. Use the parallelogram of forces to find the maximum tension in the main tow rope.

Examiner's tip

Remember you cannot always use arithmetic to add and subtract forces. When the two forces act at an angle, you will have to use geometry (the parallelogram of forces).

Key points

- On a diagram, a force as a vector is shown as an arrow.
- The parallelogram of forces is used to find the resultant of two forces that do not act along the same line.

P2.4 Force and acceleration

Learning objectives

After this topic, you should know:

- how the acceleration of an object depends on the size of the resultant force
- the effect that the mass of an object has on its acceleration
- how to calculate the resultant force on an object from its acceleration and its mass.

Practical

Investigating force and acceleration

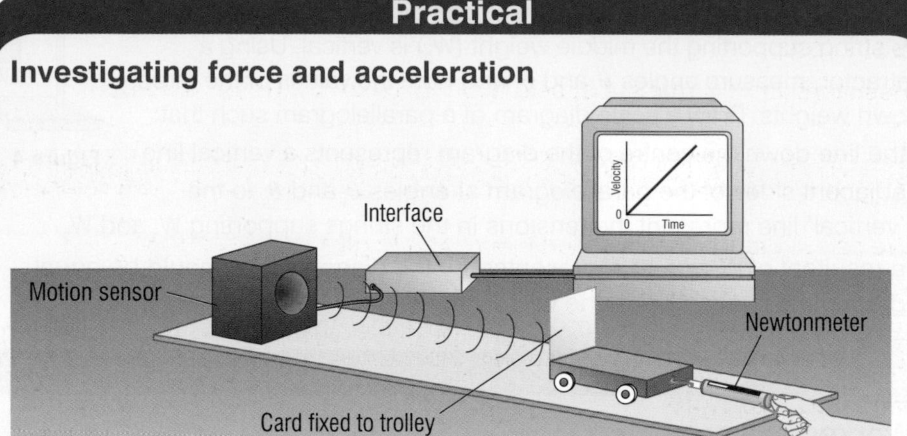

Figure 1 Investigating the link between force and motion

We can use the apparatus above to accelerate a trolley with a constant force.

Use the newtonmeter to pull the trolley along with a constant force.

You can double or treble the total moving mass by using double-deck and triple-deck trolleys.

A motion sensor and a computer can be used to record the velocity of the trolley as it accelerates.

- What are the advantages of using a data logger and computer in this investigation?

Safety: Protect bench and feet from falling trolley.

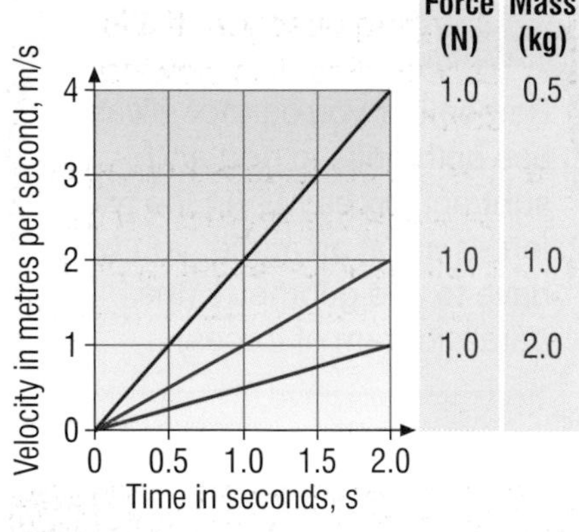

Figure 2 Velocity–time graph for different combinations of force and mass

You can display the results as a velocity–time graph on the computer screen.

Figure 2 shows velocity–time graphs for different masses. You can work out the acceleration from the gradient of the line, as explained in 1.4 'Using graphs'.

Look at some typical results in the table below:

Resultant force (newtons)	0.5	1.0	1.5	2.0	4.0	6.0
Mass (kilograms)	1.0	1.0	1.0	2.0	2.0	2.0
Acceleration (m/s²)	0.5	1.0	1.5	1.0	2.0	3.0
Mass × acceleration (kg m/s²)	0.5	1.0	1.5	2.0	4.0	6.0

The results show that the resultant force, the mass and the acceleration are linked by the equation

resultant force = **mass** × **acceleration**
(newtons, N) (kilograms) (metres/second²)

We can write the word equation above using symbols as follows:

resultant force $F = m \times a$,

where:
F = resultant force in newtons
m = mass in kilograms
a = acceleration in metres/second².

Maths skills

Worked example

Calculate the resultant force on an object of mass 6.0 kg when it has an acceleration of $3.0\,\text{m/s}^2$.

Solution

Resultant force = mass × acceleration = $6.0\,\text{kg} \times 3.0\,\text{m/s}^2 = \mathbf{18.0\,N}$

Maths skills

We can rearrange the equation $F = m \times a$ to give $a = \frac{F}{m}$ or $m = \frac{F}{a}$

Maths skills

Worked example

Calculate the acceleration of an object of mass 5.0 kg acted on by a resultant force of 40 N.

Solution

Rearranging $F = m \times a$ gives $a = \frac{F}{m} = \frac{40\,\text{N}}{5.0\,\text{kg}} = \mathbf{8.0\,m/s^2}$

Speeding up or slowing down

If the velocity of an object changes, it must be acted on by a resultant force. Its acceleration is always in the same direction as the resultant force.

- The velocity of the object increases if the resultant force is in the **same** direction as the velocity. We say its acceleration is positive because it is in the same direction as its velocity.
- The velocity of the object decreases (i.e. it decelerates) if the resultant force is **opposite** in direction to its velocity. We say its acceleration is negative because it is opposite in direction to its velocity.

Summary questions

1 a Calculate the resultant force on a sprinter of mass 80 kg who accelerates at $8\,\text{m/s}^2$.

b Calculate the acceleration of a car of mass 800 kg acted on by a resultant force of 3200 N.

2 Copy and complete the following table:

	a	b	c	d	e
Force (newtons, N)		200	840		5000
Mass (kilograms, kg)	20		70	0.40	
Acceleration (metres/second squared, m/s²)	0.80	5.0		6.0	0.20

3 A car and a trailer have a total mass of 1500 kg.

a Find the force needed to accelerate the car and the trailer at $2.0\,\text{m/s}^2$.

b The mass of the trailer is 300 kg. Find:

i the force of the tow bar on the trailer

ii the resultant force on the car.

Did you know ... ?

If you're in a car that suddenly brakes, your neck pulls on your head and slows it down. The equal and opposite force of your head on your neck can injure your neck.

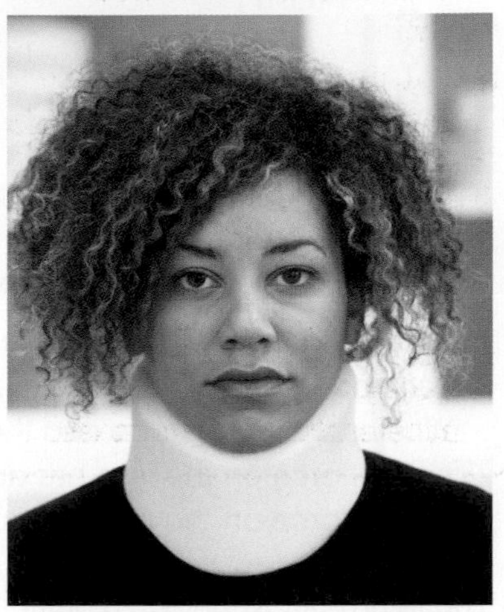

Figure 3 A 'whiplash' injury

Examiner's tip

- If an object is accelerating, it can be speeding up or changing direction. If it is decelerating, it is slowing down.
- If an object is accelerating or decelerating, there must be a resultant force acting on it.

Key points

- The bigger the resultant force on an object, the greater the object's acceleration.
- The greater the mass of an object, the smaller its acceleration for a given force.
- Resultant force (newtons, N) = mass (kilograms) × acceleration (metres/second²).

Summary questions

1 The figure below shows an iron bar suspended at rest from a spring balance that reads 1.6 N.

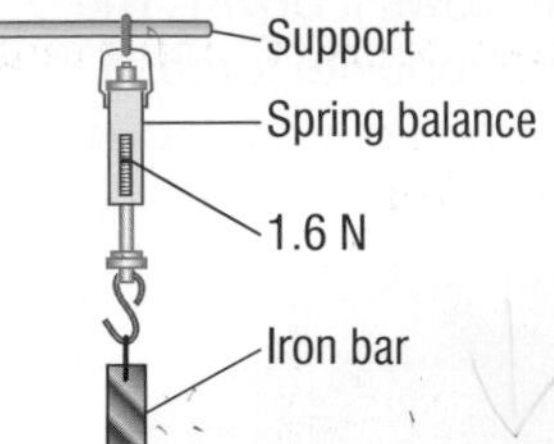

a i What is the magnitude and the direction of the force on the spring balance due to the iron bar?

ii What is the weight of the bar in newtons?

b When a magnet is held under the iron bar, the spring balance reading increases to 2.0 N.
What is the magnitude and the direction of:

i the force on the iron bar due to the magnet?

ii the force on the magnet due to the iron bar?

2 The figure below shows a stationary helium-filled balloon attached to a vertical thread. Because helium is lighter than air, an upward force, or upthrust, acts on the balloon. The lower end of the string is attached to a weight on a table.

a i What can you say about the resultant force on the balloon?

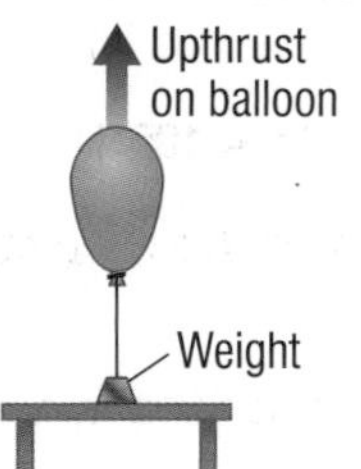

ii Which force is greater: the gravitational force on the balloon or the upthrust? Give a reason for your answer.

b Describe and explain what would happen to the balloon if the thread was cut.

3 A car on a straight road accelerates for 5 seconds, then travels at constant velocity.

Copy and complete the following sentences using words from the list below.

decreases increases stays the same

a The velocity of the car .... then ....

b The acceleration of the car .... after 5 seconds.

c The resultant force on the car is zero when its velocity ....

4 A car accelerates from rest with an initial acceleration of 1.2 m/s^2 The total mass of the car and its occupants is 800 kg.

a Assuming the resultant force is initially due to the driving force of the car engine only, calculate the initial driving force of the car.

b i If the car was used to pull a trailer of mass 70 kg, what would be its initial acceleration for the same driving force?

ii Calculate the force on the trailer at this acceleration.

5 a A tugboat is towing a ship steadily into a port. The tugboat cable exerts a horizontal force of 7200 N on the ship, which is moving at a constant velocity. A resistive force acts on the ship because of water flowing past it as it moves through the water. The resistive force acts in the opposite direction to the force of the cable.

i What is the magnitude of the **resistive** force on the ship?

ii What is the resultant force on the ship?

b Near the port, the ship stops and two tugboats are used to pull the ship towards the quay. Each tugboat exerts a force of 7200 N on the ship at an angle of 45° between their cables, as shown in the figure. Use the parallelogram of forces to find the magnitude of the resultant of the tugboat forces on the ship.

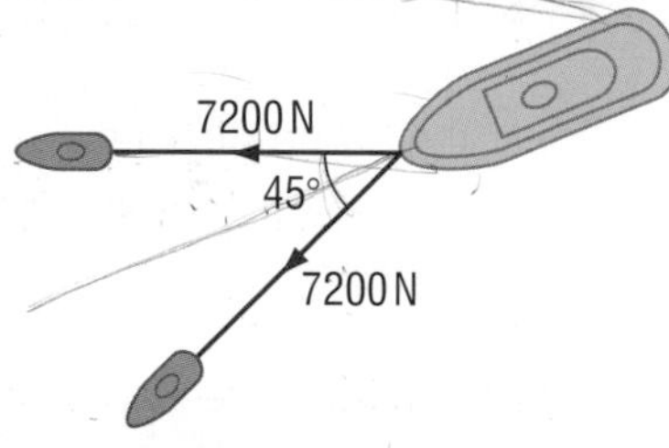

6 An aircraft in level flight is travelling at a constant velocity due east with an engine force of 9.50 kN when it experiences a horizontal crosswind acting due north with a force of 1.20 kN.

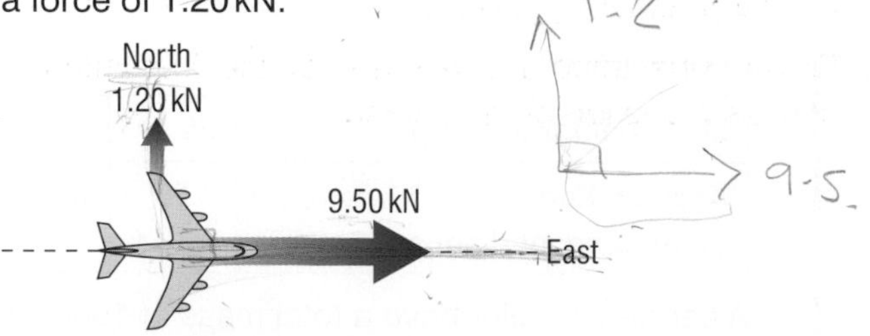

a Use the parallelogram of forces to show that the aircraft is pushed off course by about 7°.

b Calculate the magnitude of the resultant force on the aircraft.

AQA Examination-style questions

1 Some quantities are vector quantities; others are scalar quantities.

a Which three of the following are vector quantities? (3)

acceleration force mass speed velocity

b A toy train travels round a track at a steady 50 cm/s.

Discuss whether the train is accelerating. (4)

c Two tugboats tow a ship along a river.

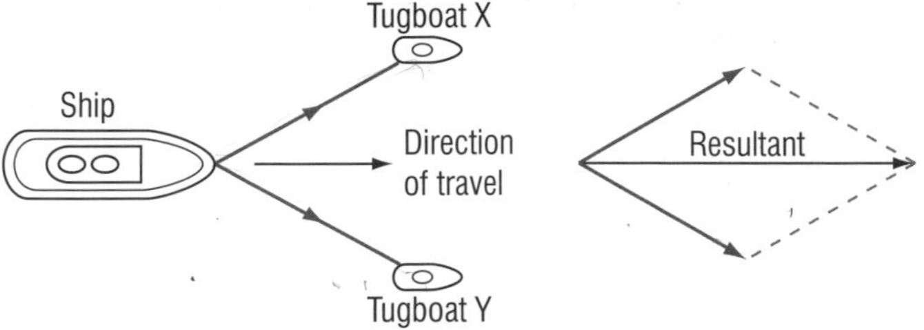

Use the parallelogram of forces to explain why it is better to use long tow ropes rather than short ones. (3)

2 The diagram shows a car of mass 1200 kg travelling along a level road.

The diagram also shows the two forces, **A** and **B**, acting on the car.

The car is travelling at constant speed.

a Force **B** is 1600 N.

What is the size of force **A**? (1)

b Force **B** is increased to 4000 N.

Calculate the acceleration of the car when force **B** is increased to 4000 N. (4)

c Explain what happens to the speed of the car if force **B** is kept at 4000 N. (QWC) (6)

d During a Formula 1 motor race, the amount of fuel in the car gradually gets less.

Explain what effect this will have on the time taken to complete one lap of the course. (4)

3 A truck, **X**, loaded with coal is travelling at a speed of 10 m/s.

It collides with an empty, stationary truck, **Y**, and exerts a force of 800 N on truck **Y**.

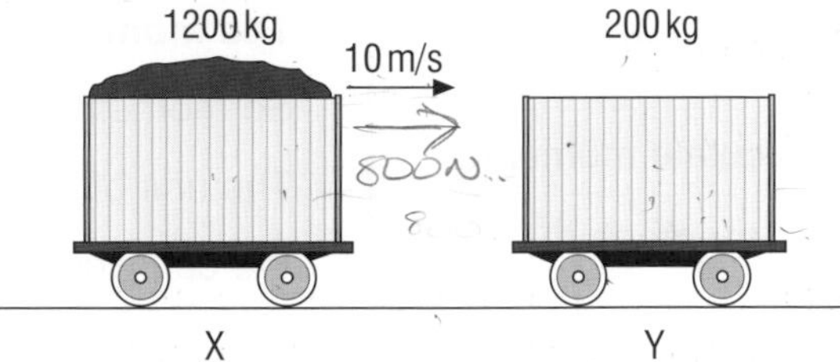

a i In which direction does the force exerted on truck **Y** act? (1)

ii In which direction does the force exerted on truck **X** act? (1)

b Explain and evaluate the effect that these two forces have on the trucks. (6)

4 Two boys pull a sledge through snow. The diagram shows the forces they exert on the sledge.

The dotted line shows the direction in which the sledge moves.

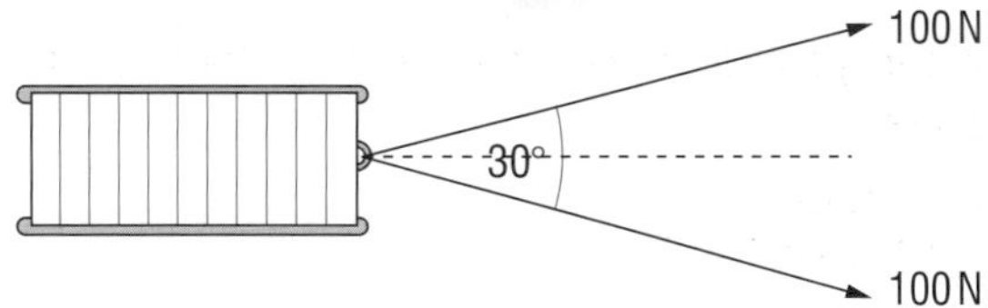

a Describe how you would determine the resultant force acting on the sledge. (6)

b One of the boys is stronger than the other and increases his force to 150 N.

Explain what he would have to do to keep the sledge moving forward in the same straight line. (2)

P3.1 Momentum

Learning objectives

After this topic, you should know:

- how to calculate momentum
- the unit of momentum
- what happens to the total momentum of two objects when they collide.

Momentum is important to anyone who plays a contact sport. In a game of rugby, a player with a lot of momentum is very difficult to stop.

The momentum of a moving object = mass × velocity.

So momentum has a size and a direction.

The unit of momentum is the kilogram metre/second (kg m/s).

We can write the word equation above using symbols: $\boldsymbol{p = m \times v}$
where:
p = momentum in kilogram metres/second, kg m/s
m = mass in kilograms, kg
v = speed in metres/second, m/s.

Figure 1 A contact sport

Examiner's tip

Make sure you know the unit of momentum – kg m/s.

Maths skills

Worked example

Calculate the momentum of a sprinter of mass 50 kg running at a velocity of 10 m/s.

Solution

Momentum = mass × velocity
= 50 kg × 10 m/s = **500 kg m/s**

Practical

Investigating collisions

When two objects collide, the momentum of each object changes. Figure 2 shows how to use a computer and a motion sensor to investigate a collision between two trolleys.

Trolley A is given a push so it collides with a stationary trolley B. The two trolleys stick together after the collision. The computer gives the velocity of A before the collision and the velocity of both trolleys afterwards.

- What does each section of the velocity–time graph show?

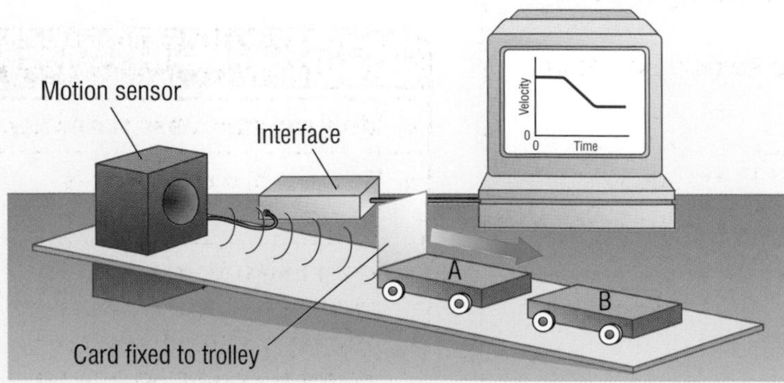

Figure 2 Investigating collisions

1 **For two trolleys of the same mass**, the velocity of trolley A is halved by the impact. The combined mass after the collision is twice the moving mass before the collision. So the momentum (= mass × velocity) after the collision is the same as before the collision.
2 **For a single trolley pushed into a double trolley**, the velocity of A is reduced to one-third. The combined mass after the collision is three times the initial mass. So in this test as well, the momentum after the collision is the same as the momentum before the collision.

In both tests, the total momentum is unchanged (i.e. is conserved) by the collision. This is an example of the **conservation of momentum**.
It applies to any system of objects as long as the system is closed, which means that no resultant force acts on it.

Safety: Use foam or an empty cardboard box to stop trolleys. Protect bench and feet from falling trolleys.

Figure 3 A 'shunt' collision

In general, the **law of conservation of momentum** states that:

In a closed system, the total momentum before an event is equal to the total momentum after the event.

We can use this law to predict what happens whenever objects collide or push each other apart in an 'explosion'. Momentum is conserved in any collision or explosion as long as no external forces act on the objects.

Maths skills

Worked example

A 0.5 kg trolley A is pushed at a velocity of 1.2 m/s into a stationary trolley B of mass 1.5 kg as shown in Figure 4. The two trolleys stick to each other after the impact.

Calculate:

a the momentum of the 0.5 kg trolley before the collision

b the velocity of the two trolleys straight after the impact.

Solution

a Momentum = mass × velocity = 0.5 kg × 1.2 m/s = **0.6 kg m/s**

b The momentum after the impact = the momentum before the impact = 0.6 kg m/s

$$(1.5\,\text{kg} + 0.5\,\text{kg}) \times \text{velocity after the impact} = 0.6\,\text{kg m/s}$$

$$\text{the velocity after the impact} = \frac{0.6\,\text{kg m/s}}{2\,\text{kg}} = \mathbf{0.3\,m/s}$$

Summary questions

1 **a** Define momentum and state its unit.

b Calculate the momentum of a 40 kg person running at 6 m/s.

c In the worked example shown by Figure 4, calculate the speed after the collision if trolley A had a mass of 1.0 kg.

2 **a** Calculate the momentum of an 80 kg rugby player running at a velocity of 5 m/s.

b An 800 kg car moves with the same momentum as the rugby player in **a**. Calculate the velocity of the car.

c Calculate the velocity of a 0.40 kg ball that has the same momentum as the rugby player in **a**.

3 A 1000 kg rail wagon moving at a velocity of 5.0 m/s on a level track collides with a stationary 1500 kg wagon. The two wagons move together after the collision.

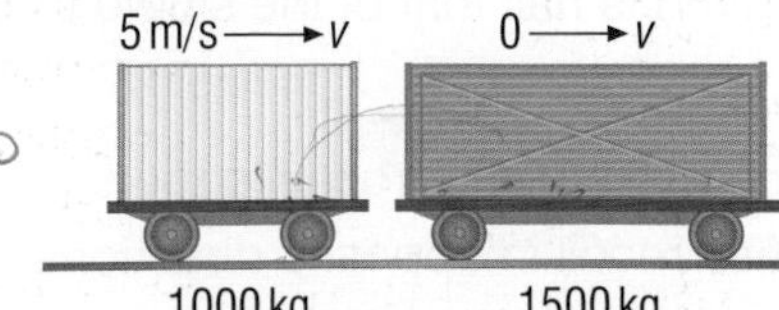

a Calculate the momentum of the 1000 kg wagon before the collision.

b Calculate the velocity of the wagons after the collision.

Did you know ... ?

If a vehicle crashes into the back of a line of cars, each car in turn is 'shunted' into the one in front. Momentum is transferred along the line of cars to the one at the front.

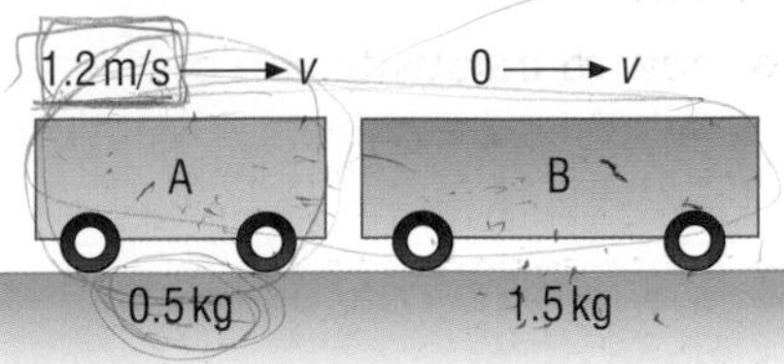

Figure 4 Worked example

Maths skills

Worked example

A 3000 kg truck moving at a velocity of 16 m/s crashes into the back of a stationary 1000 kg car. The two vehicles move together immediately after the impact. Calculate their velocity.

Solution

Let v represent the velocity of the vehicles after the impact.

momentum of the truck before the impact = 48 000 kg m/s

momentum of car before impact = 0 m/s

momentum of truck after impact = 3000 kg × v

momentum of car after impact = 1000 kg × v

$3000v + 1000v = 48\,000 + 0$

$4000v = 48\,000$; $v =$ **12 m/s**

Key points

- Momentum = mass × velocity.
- The unit of momentum is kg m/s.
- Momentum is conserved whenever objects interact, as long as the objects are in a closed system so that no external forces act on them.

P3.2 Explosions

Learning objectives

After this topic, you should know:

- how momentum can be described as having direction as well as size
- why two objects that push each other apart:
  - move away at different speeds
  - have zero total momentum.

If you are a skateboarder, you will know that the skateboard can shoot away from you when you jump off it. Its momentum is in the opposite direction to your own momentum. What can we say about the total momentum of objects when they fly apart from each other?

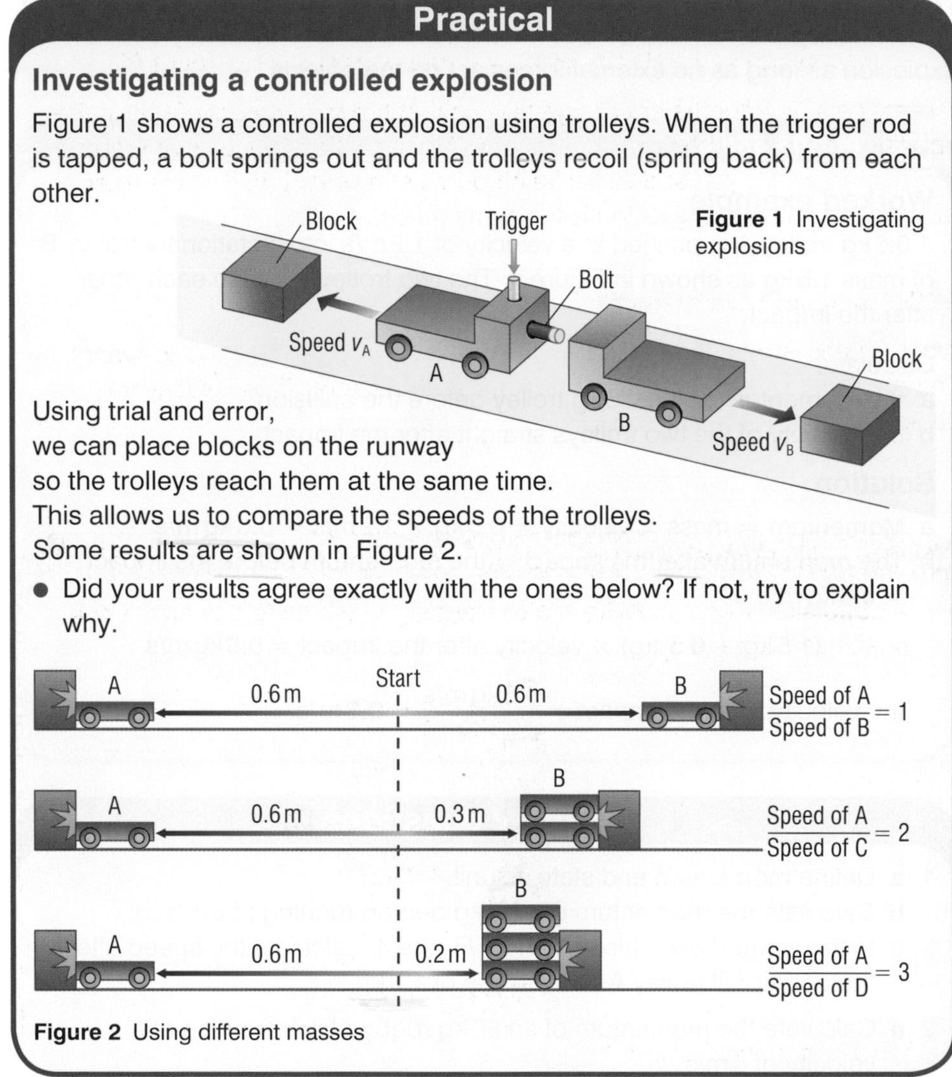

Practical

Investigating a controlled explosion

Figure 1 shows a controlled explosion using trolleys. When the trigger rod is tapped, a bolt springs out and the trolleys recoil (spring back) from each other.

Figure 1 Investigating explosions

Using trial and error, we can place blocks on the runway so the trolleys reach them at the same time. This allows us to compare the speeds of the trolleys. Some results are shown in Figure 2.

- Did your results agree exactly with the ones below? If not, try to explain why.

Figure 2 Using different masses

- Two single trolleys travel equal distances in the same time. This shows that they recoil at equal speeds.
- A double trolley only travels half the distance that a single trolley does. Its speed is half that of the single trolley.

In each test:

1 the mass of the trolley × the speed of the trolley is the same, and

2 they recoil in opposite directions.

So momentum has size and direction. The results show that the trolleys recoil with equal and opposite momentum.

Examiner's tip

Be careful in calculations – momentum is a vector quantity, so if two objects are travelling in opposite directions, one has positive momentum, and the other has negative momentum.

Conservation of momentum

In the trolley examples:

- momentum of A after the explosion = (mass of A × velocity of A)
- momentum of B after the explosion = (mass of B × velocity of B)
- total momentum before the explosion = 0 (because both trolleys were at rest).

Using conservation of momentum gives:

$$(\text{mass of A} \times \text{velocity of A}) + (\text{mass of B} \times \text{velocity of B}) = 0$$

Therefore

$$\mathbf{(mass\ of\ A \times velocity\ of\ A) = -(mass\ of\ B \times velocity\ of\ B)}$$

The minus sign after the equal sign tells us that the momentum of B is in the opposite direction to the momentum of A. The equation tells us that A and B move apart with equal and opposite amounts of momentum. So, the total momentum after the explosion is the same as before it.

Momentum in action

When a shell is fired from an artillery gun, the gun barrel recoils backwards. The recoil of the gun barrel is slowed down by a spring. This lessens the backwards motion of the gun.

Maths skills

Worked example

An artillery gun of mass 2000 kg fires a shell of mass 20 kg at a velocity of 120 m/s. Calculate the recoil velocity of the gun.

Solution

Applying the conservation of momentum gives:

mass of gun × recoil velocity of gun = – (mass of shell × velocity of shell)

If we let V represent the recoil velocity of the gun,

$$2000\,\text{kg} \times V = -(20\,\text{kg} \times 120\,\text{m/s})$$

$$V = -\frac{2400\,\text{kg m/s}}{2000\,\text{kg}} = \mathbf{-1.2\,m/s}$$

Figure 3 An artillery gun in action

Summary questions

1 A 60 kg skater and an 80 kg skater standing in the middle of an ice rink push each other away.

What can be said about:

a the force they exert on each other when they push apart?
b the momentum each skater has just after they separate?
c each of their velocities just after they separate?
d their total momentum just after they separate?

2 In Question **1**, the 60 kg skater moves away at 2.0 m/s. Calculate:

a her momentum
b the velocity of the other skater.

3 A 600 kg cannon recoils at a speed of 0.5 m/s when a 12 kg cannon ball is fired from it.

a Calculate the velocity of the cannon ball when it leaves the cannon.
b How would the recoil velocity of the cannon have been different if a 4 kg cannon ball had been used instead?

Key points

- Momentum is mass × velocity and has direction.
- When two objects push each other apart, they move:
  - with different speeds if they have unequal masses
  - with equal and opposite momentum, so their total momentum is zero.

P3.3 Impact forces

Learning objectives

After this topic, you should know:

- what affects the force of impact when two vehicles collide
- how the impact force depends on the impact time
- what we can say about the impact forces and the total momentum when two vehicles collide.

Figure 2 A crash test. Car makers test the design of a crumple zone by driving a remote control car into a brick wall

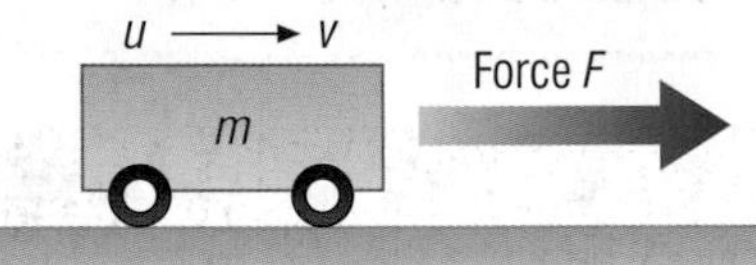

Figure 3 Impact force

Examiner's tip

Remember that the time of impact is important. Sometimes we want a force to be large – for example when hitting a ball – so the time of impact should be as short as possible. At other times, we want the force to be small – for example in a crash – so the time of impact should be as long as possible.

Crumple zones at the front end and rear end of a car are designed to lessen the force of an impact. The force changes the momentum of the car.

- In a front-end impact, the momentum of the car is reduced.
- In a rear-end impact (where a vehicle is struck from behind by another vehicle), the momentum of the car is increased.

In both cases the effect of a crumple zone is to increase the impact time and so lessen the impact force.

Practical

Investigating impacts

We can test an impact using a trolley and a brick, as shown in Figure 1. When the trolley hits the brick, the plasticine flattens on impact, making the impact time longer. This is the key factor that reduces the impact force.

Safety: Protect bench and feet from bricks and trolleys.

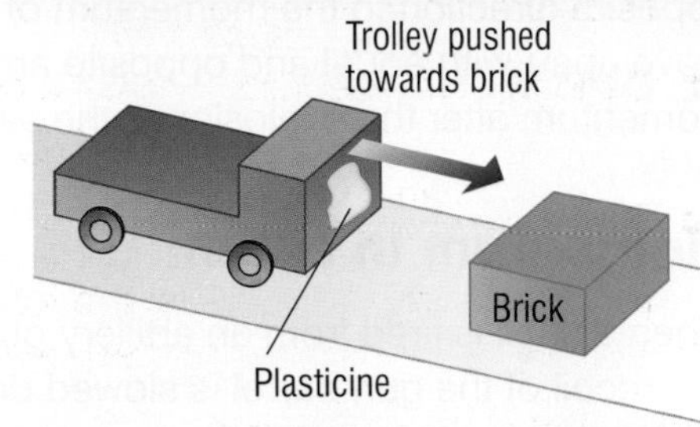

Figure 1 Investigating impacts

Impact time

Let's see why making the impact time longer reduces the impact force.

Suppose a moving trolley hits another object and stops. The impact force on the trolley acts for a certain time (the impact time) and causes it to stop. A soft pad on the front of the trolley would increase the impact time and would allow the trolley to travel further before it stops. The momentum of the trolley would be lost over a longer time and its kinetic energy would be transferred over a greater distance.

1. The kinetic energy of the trolley is transferred to the pad as work done by the impact force in squashing the pad.
2. Since work done = force × distance, the impact force is therefore reduced because the distance is increased. See 5.1 for more about energy and work.

The longer the impact time, the more the impact force is reduced.

If we know the impact time, we can calculate the impact force as follows:

- From 1.2, we know that

$$\text{acceleration} = \frac{\text{(final velocity – initial velocity)}}{\text{time taken}} = \frac{\text{change of velocity}}{\text{time taken}}$$

- From 2.4, we know that force = mass × acceleration

Therefore, because mass × change of velocity = change of momentum, then

$$\text{force} = \frac{\text{mass} \times \text{change of velocity}}{\text{time taken}} = \frac{\text{change of momentum}}{\text{time taken}}$$

For a change of momentum Δp in time t, we can write the above equation as

$$\textbf{force } F = \frac{\Delta p}{t}$$

The above method shows how much the impact force can be reduced by increasing the impact time. Car safety features such as crumple zones and side bars increase the impact time and so reduce the impact force.

Maths skills

Worked example

A bullet of mass 0.004 kg moving at a velocity of 90 m/s is stopped by a bulletproof vest in 0.0003 s.

Calculate **a** the deceleration, **b** the change of momentum, and **c** the impact force.

Solution

a Initial velocity of bullet = 90 m/s
Final velocity of bullet = 0
Change of velocity = final velocity − initial velocity = 0 − 90 m/s = −90 m/s
(the minus sign tells us that the change of velocity is a decrease)

$$\text{Deceleration} = \frac{\text{change of velocity}}{\text{impact time}} = \frac{-90\,\text{m/s}}{0.0003\,\text{s}} = \mathbf{-300\,000\,m/s^2}$$

b Change of momentum = mass × change of velocity
= 0.004 kg × (0 − 90 m/s) = **−0.36 kg m/s**

$$\textbf{c}\quad \text{Force} = \frac{\text{change of momentum}}{\text{time taken}} = \frac{-0.36\,\text{kg m/s}}{0.0003\,\text{s}} = \mathbf{-1200\,N}$$

(the minus sign tells us that the force decelerates the bullet)

Two-vehicle collisions

When two vehicles collide, they exert equal and opposite impact forces on each other at the same time. The change of momentum of one vehicle is therefore equal and opposite to the change of momentum of the other vehicle. The total momentum of the two vehicles is the same after the impact as it was before the impact, so momentum is conserved – assuming no external forces act.

For example, suppose a fast-moving truck runs into the back of a stationary car. The impact decelerates the truck and accelerates the car. Assuming that the truck's mass is greater than the mass of the car, the truck loses momentum and the car gains momentum.

Summary questions

1 **a** In a car crash, when a passenger wears a seat belt, why does it reduce the impact force on him?
b A ball of mass 0.12 kg moving at a velocity of 18 m/s is caught by a person in 0.0003 s. Calculate the impact force.

2 **a** An 800 kg car travelling at 30 m/s is stopped safely when the brakes are applied. What braking force is required to stop it in:
i 6.0 s? **ii** 30 s?
b If the vehicle in **a** had been stopped in a collision lasting less than a second, explain by referring to momentum why the force on it would have been much greater.

3 A 2000 kg van moving at a velocity of 12 m/s crashes into the back of a stationary truck of mass 10 000 kg. Immediately after the impact, the two vehicles move together.
a Show that the velocity of the van and the truck immediately after the impact was 2 m/s.
b The impact lasted for 0.3 seconds. Calculate:
i the deceleration of the van
ii the change of momentum of the van
iii the force of the impact on the van.

Did you know ... ?

Scientists at Oxford University have developed new lightweight material for bulletproof vests. The material is so strong and elastic that bullets bounce off it.

Maths skills

The equation $F = \frac{\Delta p}{t}$ tells us that force F is **inversely proportional** to time t. For example, if t is doubled, F is halved. See p241 for more about inverse proportion.

Did you know ... ?

We sometimes express the effect of an impact on an object or person as a force-to-weight ratio. We call this the **g-force**.

For example, a g-force of 2 g means that the force on an object is twice its weight. You would experience a g-force of:

- about 3 to 4 g on a fairground ride that whirls you round
- about 10 g in a low-speed car crash
- more than 50 g in a high-speed car crash that you would be lucky to survive.

Key points

- **When vehicles collide, the force of the impact depends on mass, change of velocity and the duration of the impact.**
- **The longer the impact time, the more the impact force is reduced.**
- **When two vehicles collide:**
  - **they exert equal and opposite forces on each other**
  - **their total momentum is unchanged.**

P3.4 Car safety

Learning objectives

After this topic, you should know:
- why seat belts and air bags reduce the force on people in car accidents
- how side impact bars and crumple zones work
- how to work out if a car in a crash was 'speeding'.

When you travel in a car, you want to feel safe if the car is in a crash. In this topic, we look at different car safety features that are designed to keep us safe.

Clunk click!

When seat belts were first introduced, some car users claimed they should not be forced by law to wear them. A very successful campaign was launched to convince car users to 'belt up'. It included the catchy phrase '*Clunk click every trip*'. As a result, deaths and injuries in road accidents fell significantly.

A **seat belt** stops its wearer from continuing forwards when the car suddenly stops. Someone without a seat belt would hit the windscreen in a 'short sharp' impact and suffer major injury.

- The time taken to stop someone in a car is longer if they are wearing a seat belt than if they are not. So the decelerating force is reduced by wearing a seat belt.
- The seat belt acts across the chest so it spreads the force out. Without the seat belt, the force would act on the head when it hit the windscreen.

Air bags

Most new cars are fitted with front air bags that protect the driver and the front passenger. Some new cars also have side air bags. These bags protect people in the car from an impact on the side of the car. In a car crash, an inflated air bag spreads the force of an impact across the upper part of the body. It also increases the duration of the impact time. So the effect of the force is lessened compared with a seat belt.

Figure 1 An air bag in action

Child car seats

Any baby or child in a car must be strapped in a child car seat. This law applies to children up to 12 years old or up to 1.35 metres in height. Different types of child car seat must be used for babies up to 9 months old, infants up to about 4 years old and children over 4.

- Baby seats must face backwards.
- Children under 4 years old should usually be in a child car seat fitted to a back seat.

The law was brought in to reduce deaths and serious injuries of children in cars. Before the law was passed, dozens of children were killed and hundreds were seriously injured each year in car accidents. Many such accidents happened during the school run. The driver is responsible for making sure every child in their car is seated safely in a correct type of seat.

Figure 2 A child car seat

Examiner's tip

Make sure that you can explain how seatbelts, airbags and crumple zones make cars safer.

Safety costs

Car makers need to sell cars. If their cars are too expensive, people won't buy them. Safety features add to the cost of a new car. Some safety features (e.g. seat belts) are required by law and some (e.g. side impact bars) are optional.

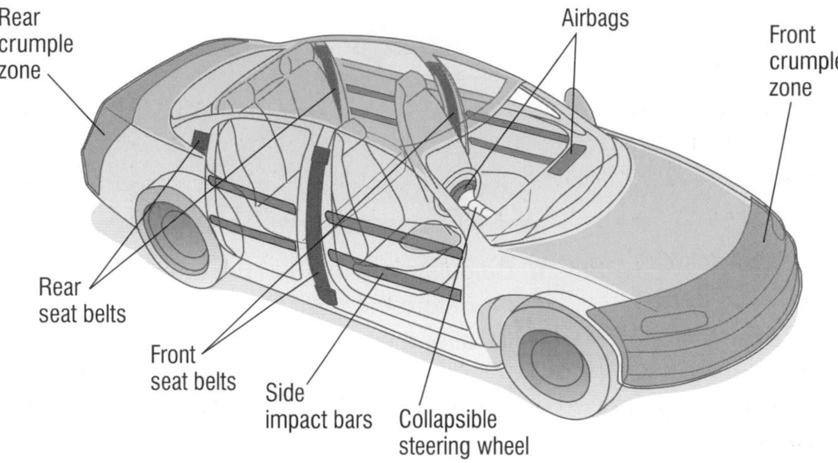

Figure 3 Car safety features

Summary questions

1 Why are rear-facing car seats for babies safer than front-facing seats?

2 Explain why an inflated air bag in front of a car user reduces the force on a user in a 'head-on' crash.

3 A car crashed into a lorry that was crossing a busy road. The speed limit on the road was 60 miles per hour (27 m/s).

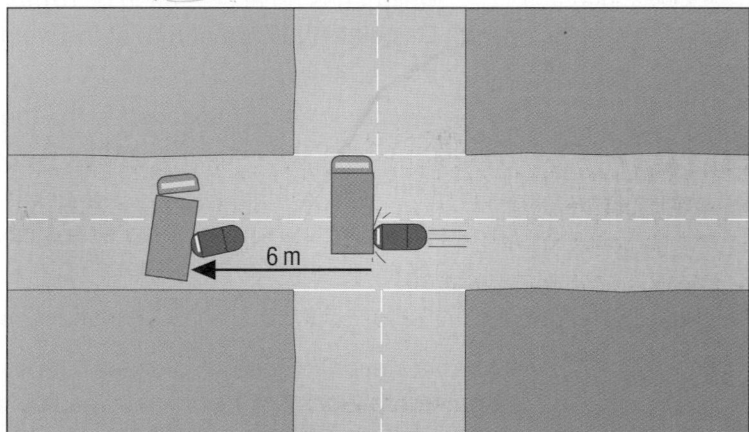

The following measurements were made by police officers at the scene of the crash:
The car and lorry ended up 6 m from the point of impact.
The car's mass was 750 kg and the lorry's mass was 2150 kg.
The speed of a vehicle for a braking distance of 6 m is 9 m/s.

a Use this speed to calculate the momentum of the car and the lorry immediately after the impact.

b Use conservation of momentum to calculate the velocity of the car immediately before the collision.

c Was the car travelling over the 60 mph speed limit before the crash?

Activity

a With the help of your friends, find out what safety features are in new cars. Find out if they are compulsory or optional. List the price (including tax) of each car.

b Use your information to say if cheaper cars have fewer safety features than more expensive cars.

Activity

Brakes are very important vehicle safety features! Flywheel brakes can transfer large amounts of energy very quickly and very efficiently, unlike ordinary friction brakes which can overheat and wear away. Electric brakes (see 5.4 'Kinetic energy') waste energy due to the heating effect of the electric current.

a State and explain the advantages of fitting flywheel brakes in addition to friction brakes in a racing car.

b Explain why flywheel brakes would be better than electric brakes for additional braking on a racing car.

Key points

- Seat belts and air bags spread the force across the chest and increase the impact time.
- Side impact bars and crumple zones 'give way' in an impact, so increasing the impact time.
- We can use the conservation of momentum to find the speed of a car before an impact.

Summary questions

1 A car of mass 1500 kg is moving at a speed of 30 m/s on a horizontal road when the driver applies the brakes and the car stops 12 seconds later.

a **i** Calculate the initial momentum of the car before the brakes are applied.

ii Calculate the braking force.

b Describe how the momentum of the car changes when the brakes are applied.

c Discuss the effect on the motion of the car if the brakes had been applied with much greater force.

2 A child of mass 14 kg is strapped into a forward-facing car seat in a car. When the car was moving at a speed of 8.2 m/s the driver suddenly brakes and stops the car.

a **i** Calculate the momentum of the child before the driver applied the brakes.

ii What was the direction of the force on the child that stopped her continuing to move forward when the brakes were applied?

b Explain why the child would have suffered an injury if she had not been strapped into the car.

3 A student of mass 50 kg standing at rest on a boat of mass 75 kg jumps off the boat onto a pier. The boat recoils and moves away at a speed of 0.5 m/s.

a Explain why the boat recoiled when the student jumped off it.

b Calculate:

i the momentum of the boat when it recoiled

ii the speed of the student when he jumped off the boat.

4 A 2000 kg truck moving at a velocity of 18.0 m/s on a level road collides with a stationary vehicle of mass 1200 kg. The velocity of the truck is reduced to 10.0 m/s as a result of the collision.

a Calculate the momentum of the truck:

i before the collision

ii after the collision.

b For the 1200 kg vehicle after the collision, calculate:

i the momentum

ii the velocity.

5 Safety footwear is designed to protect the wearer's feet if a heavy weight falls on a foot. In a test of a safety boot a 7.0 kg weight is dropped from a certain height above the boot.

a **i** The time of descent of the weight was measured electronically and found to be 0.63 s. Show that the speed of the weight just before the impact was 6.3 m/s. As explained in 9.2, assume that the falling weight has an acceleration of 10 m/s^2.

ii Calculate the momentum of the weight just before the impact.

b An electronic sensor attached to the toecap of the boot recorded that the impact lasted for 0.0022 seconds. Calculate the impact force.

c Discuss how the impact force would have differed if the same weight had been dropped from a greater height without damaging the boot.

6 When a stationary football of mass 0.44 kg was kicked, it gained a velocity of 19 m/s as a result of the impact.

a Calculate the gain of momentum of the football due to the impact.

b The impact lasted 0.0384 s. Show that the impact force was 220 N.

AQA Examination-style questions

1 Momentum is a vector quantity.

a Explain why momentum is a vector quantity. (3)

b Two lorries, **P** and **Q**, are travelling in the same direction along a motorway.

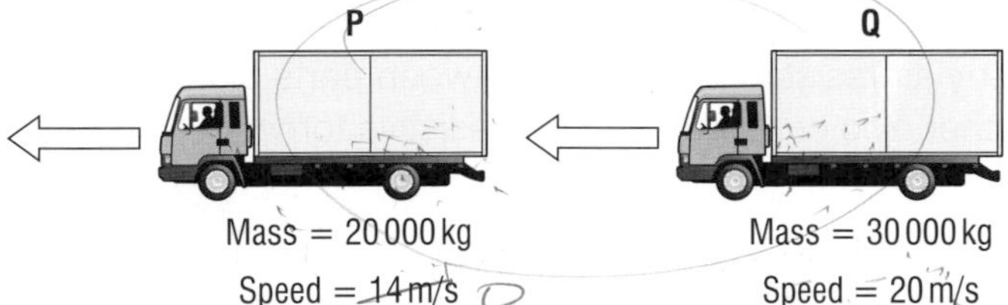

i Calculate the momentum of lorry **P**.

ii Calculate the momentum of lorry **Q**. (4)

iii Lorry **Q** collides with lorry **P** and they stick together. Calculate the speed of the lorries immediately after the collision. (4)

2 The picture shows an ice dancer and her coach.

They are standing still on the ice facing each other.

The dancer pushes her coach and they move away from each other.

a When the dancer pushes her coach, the momentum of each of them changes.

i What are the units of momentum?

Choose from the list below. (1)

kg m s   *kg m/s*   *kg m/s²*   *kg/m/s*

ii Outline the similarities and the differences between the momentum of the coach and the momentum of the dancer after the push. (3)

b The mass of the dancer is 50 kg. The mass of her coach is 90 kg.

As they move away from each other, the speed of the dancer is 1.5 m/s.

Calculate the speed of her coach. (3)

3 Modern cars have many safety features.

a Explain how seatbelts and airbags keep passengers safe. (QWC) (6)

b Discuss the importance of impact time when a player uses a cricket bat to hit a cricket ball and when a fielder catches the cricket ball. (4)

4 Most cars have crumple zones at the front and at the back of the car.

a Explain how crumple zones reduce impact forces. (4)

b A snooker player uses a cue to hit the stationary white ball. The cue hits the ball of mass 0.2 kg with a force of 60 N. The cue is in contact with the ball for 0.008 s.

Calculate the speed of the ball immediately after impact. (5)

5 In a vehicle test, the velocity of a car was recorded when it collided with a fixed concrete block. The graph shows how the velocity *v* of the car varied with time *t* during the impact.

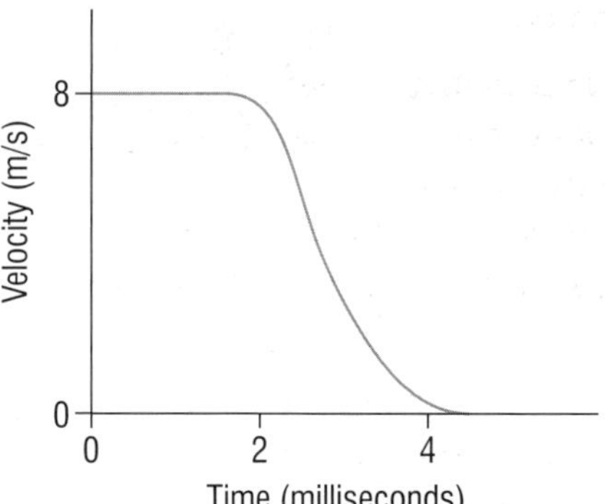

a The mass of the car was 1200 kg.

i Use the graph to determine the velocity of the car before the impact and hence determine the car's momentum before the impact. (2)

ii Estimate the impact time from the graph and hence calculate the impact force. (4)

b Explain how the graph shows that the impact force varied with time during the impact. (4)

P4.1 Forces and braking

Learning objectives

After this topic, you should know:

- the forces that oppose the driving force of a vehicle
- what the stopping distance of a vehicle depends on
- the factors that can increase the stopping distance of a vehicle.

Did you know ... ?

The mass of a BMW Mini Cooper car is just over 1000 kg.

Did you know ... ?

When the brakes of a car are applied, friction between the brake pads and the car wheels causes kinetic energy to be transferred from the vehicle by heating the brakes and the brake pads. If the brake pads wear away too much, they need to be replaced.

Practical

Reaction times

Use an electronic stopwatch to test your own reaction time. Ask a friend to start the stopwatch when you are looking at it with your finger on the stop button. The read-out from the watch will give your reaction time.

- How can you make your data as precise as possible?
- What conclusions can you draw?

Forces on the road

For any car travelling at constant velocity, the resultant force on it is zero. This is because the **driving force** of its engine is balanced by the **resistive forces**, which are mostly caused by air resistance. Friction between parts of the car that move against each other also contributes to the resistive forces.

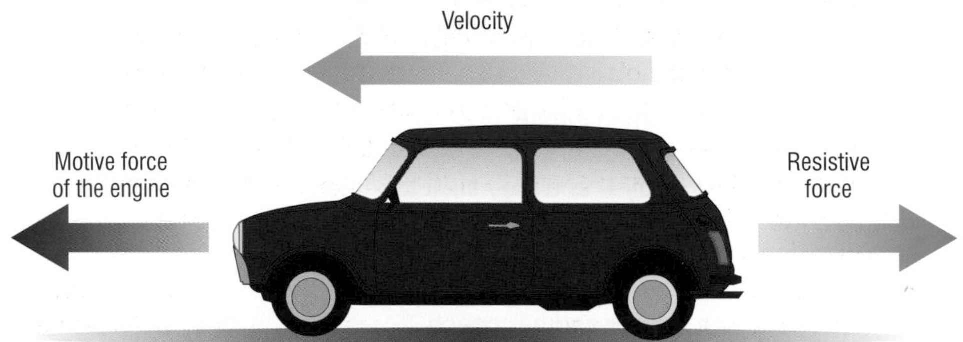

Figure 1 Constant velocity

A car driver uses the accelerator pedal (also called the gas pedal) to vary the driving force of the engine.

The **braking force needed to stop a vehicle** in a certain distance depends on:

- the speed of the vehicle when the brakes are first applied
- the mass of the vehicle.

We can see this using the equation 'resultant force = mass × acceleration', in which the braking force is the resultant force.

1 The greater the speed, the greater the deceleration needed to stop the vehicle within a certain distance. So, the braking force must be greater than it would be at lower speeds.
2 The greater the mass, the greater the braking force needed for a given deceleration.

Stopping distances

Driving tests always ask about **stopping distances**. This is the shortest distance a vehicle can safely stop in, and is in two parts:

The **thinking distance**: the distance travelled by the vehicle in the time it takes the driver to react (i.e. during the driver's reaction time).

The **braking distance**: the distance travelled by the vehicle during the time the braking force acts.

stopping distance = thinking distance + braking distance

Figure 2 shows the stopping distance for a vehicle on a dry flat road travelling at different speeds. Check for yourself that the stopping distance at 31 m/s (70 miles per hour) is 96 m.

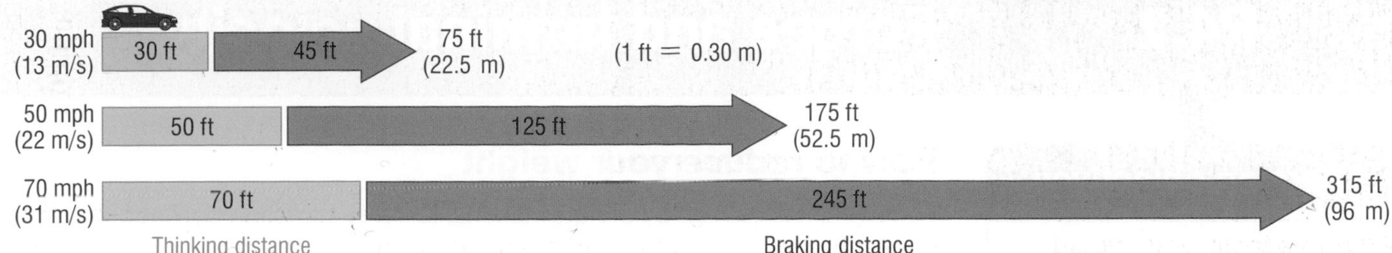

Figure 2 Stopping distances

Factors affecting stopping distances

1 **Tiredness, alcohol and drugs** all increase reaction times. Distractions such as using a mobile phone can also affect reaction time. All these factors increase the thinking distance (because thinking distance = speed × reaction time). Therefore, the stopping distance is greater.

2 **The faster a vehicle is travelling**, the further it travels before it stops. This is because the thinking distance and the braking distance both increase with increased speed.

3 **In adverse road conditions**, for example on wet or icy roads, drivers have to brake with less force to avoid skidding. Stopping distances are therefore greater in poor road conditions.

4 **Poorly maintained vehicles**, for example with worn brakes or tyres, take longer to stop because the brakes and tyres are less effective.

Figure 3 Stopping distances are further than you might think!

Summary questions

1 For each of the following factors, which distance is affected: the thinking distance or the braking distance of a vehicle?
   a The road surface.
   b The tiredness of the driver.
   c Poorly maintained brakes.

2 **a** Use the chart in Figure 2 to work out, in metres, what is the effect of the increase from 13 m/s (30 mph) to 22 m/s (50 mph) on the following:
   i the thinking distance
   ii the braking distance
   iii the stopping distance from 13 m/s (30 mph) to 22 m/s (50 mph).
   b A driver has a reaction time of 0.8 s. Calculate the change in her thinking distance if she travels at 15 m/s instead of 30 m/s.

3 **a** When the speed of a car is doubled:
   i explain why the thinking distance of the driver is doubled, assuming that the driver's reaction time is unchanged
   ii explain why the braking distance is more than doubled.
   b A student reckons that braking distance is proportional to the square of the speed. Use the chart in Figure 2 to decide whether this is a valid claim.

Maths skills

- The thinking distance is equal to the car's speed multiplied by the driver's reaction time. So it is directly proportional to the car's speed.
- The braking distance is equal to the average speed of the car during braking multiplied by the braking time. Since both of these quantities are directly proportional to the car's speed (before the brakes are applied), the braking distance is directly proportional to the square of the car's speed.

Examiner's tip

Don't mix up thinking distance and braking distance. Make sure you know which distance is affected by reaction time.

Key points

- **Friction and air resistance oppose the driving force of a vehicle.**
- **The stopping distance of a vehicle depends on the thinking distance and the braking distance.**
- **High speed, poor weather conditions and poor vehicle maintenance all increase the braking distance. Poor reaction time and high speed both increase the thinking distance.**

P4.2 Forces and terminal velocity

Learning objectives

After this topic, you should know:
- the difference between mass and weight
- about the motion of a falling object acted on only by gravity
- what terminal velocity means.

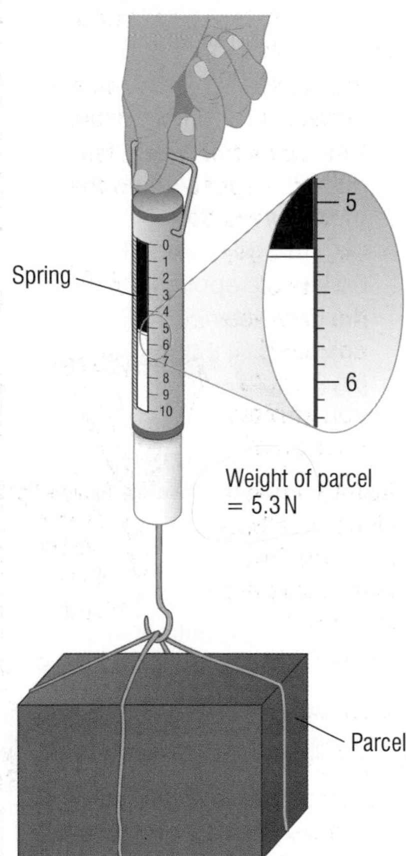

Figure 1 Using a newtonmeter to weigh an object

Maths skills

Worked example

Calculate the weight in newtons of a person of mass 55 kg.

Solution

Weight = mass × gravitational field strength = 55 kg × 10 N/kg = **550 N**

How to reduce your weight

Your weight is caused by the gravitational force of attraction between you and the Earth. This force is very slightly weaker at the equator than at the poles. So, if you want to reduce your weight, go to the equator. However, your mass will be the same no matter where you are.

- The **weight** of an object is the force of gravity on it. Weight is measured in newtons.
- The **mass** of an object is the quantity of matter in it. Mass is measured in kilograms.

We can measure the weight of an object using a newtonmeter.

The weight of an object:
- of mass 1 kg is 10 N
- of mass 5 kg is 50 N.

The gravitational force on a 1 kg object is the **gravitational field strength** at the place where the object is. The unit of gravitational field strength is the newton per kilogram (N/kg).

The value of the Earth's gravitational field strength at its surface is about 10 N/kg.

If we know the mass of an object, we can calculate the gravitational force on it (i.e. its weight) using the equation:

weight	=	**mass**	×	**gravitational field strength**
(newtons, N)		(kilograms, kg)		(newtons/kilogram, N/kg)

We can write the word equation above using symbols as:

$$\text{weight, } \boldsymbol{W = mg},$$

where:
W = weight in newtons, N
m = mass in kilograms, kg
g = gravitational field strength in newtons per kilogram, N/kg.

The forces on falling objects

If we release an object above the ground, it falls because of its weight (i.e. the gravitational force on it).

If the object falls with no other forces acting on it, the resultant force on it is its weight. It accelerates downwards at a constant acceleration of 10 m/s². This is called the acceleration due to gravity, or the acceleration of free fall. For example, if we release a 1 kg object above the ground:

- the gravitational force on it is 10 N, and
- its acceleration $\left(= \frac{\text{force}}{\text{mass}} = \frac{10\text{ N}}{1\text{ kg}}\right) = 10\text{ m/s}^2$.

Examiner's tip

When the upward force acting on an object falling in a fluid balances the downward force, the object continues at a constant speed – it doesn't stop!

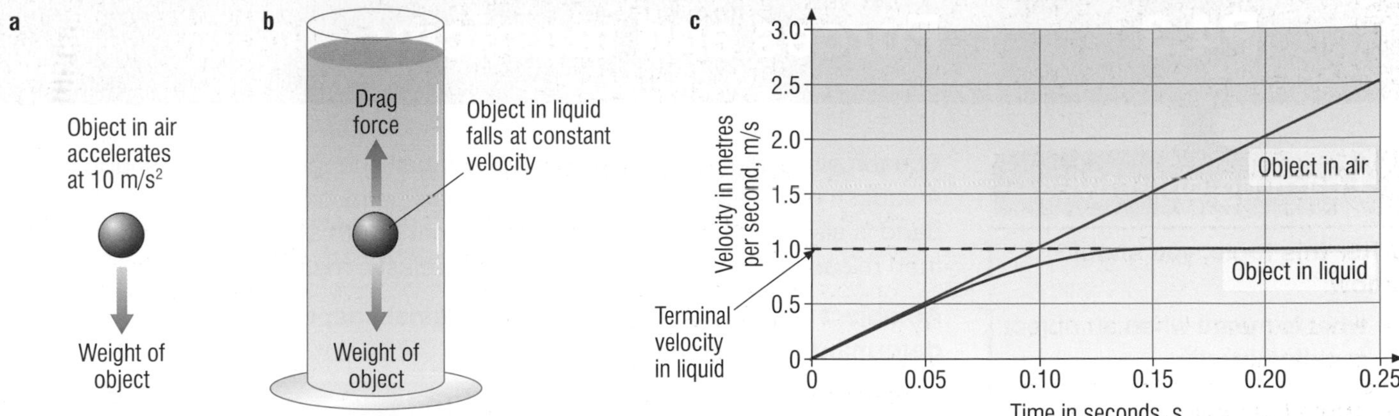

Figure 2 Falling objects. **a** Falling in air, **b** falling in a liquid, **c** velocity–time graph for **a** and **b**.

If the object falls in a fluid, the fluid drags on the object because of friction between the fluid and the surface of the moving object. This frictional force increases with speed. At any instant, the resultant force on the object is its weight minus the frictional force on it.

- The acceleration of the object decreases as it falls. This is because the frictional force increases as it speeds up. So the resultant force on it decreases and therefore its acceleration decreases.
- The object reaches a constant velocity when the frictional force on it is equal and opposite to its weight. We call this velocity its **terminal velocity**. The resultant force is then zero, so its acceleration is zero.

When an object moves through the air (i.e. the fluid is air) the frictional force is called **air resistance**. This is not shown in Figure 2a because air resistance is very small in a short descent.

Summary questions

1 When an object is released in a fluid, what can be said about:
 - **a** the resultant force on it initially?
 - **b** the weight of the object and the frictional force on it before it reaches its terminal velocity?
 - **c** its acceleration after it reaches its terminal velocity?
 - **d** the resultant force on it when it moves at its terminal velocity?

2 The gravitational field strength at the surface of the Earth is 10 N/kg. For the Moon, it is 1.6 N/kg.
 - **a** Calculate the weight of a person of mass 50 kg at the surface of the Earth.
 - **b** Calculate the weight of the same person if she was on the surface of the Moon.
 - **c** A lunar vehicle has a weight of 300 N on the Earth. Calculate its weight on the Moon.

3 A parachutist of mass 70 kg supported by a parachute of mass 20 kg reaches a constant speed.
 - **a** Explain why the parachutist reaches a constant speed.
 - **b** Calculate:
   - **i** the total weight of the parachutist and the parachute
   - **ii** the size and direction of the force of air resistance on the parachute when the parachutist falls at constant speed.

Practical

Investigating falling

Release an object with and without a parachute.

Make suitable measurements to compare the two situations.

- Why does the object fall at constant speed when the parachute is open?
- Evaluate the quality of the data you collected. How could you improve your data?

Safety: Do not climb on stools and benches. Find a safe area to release parachutes.

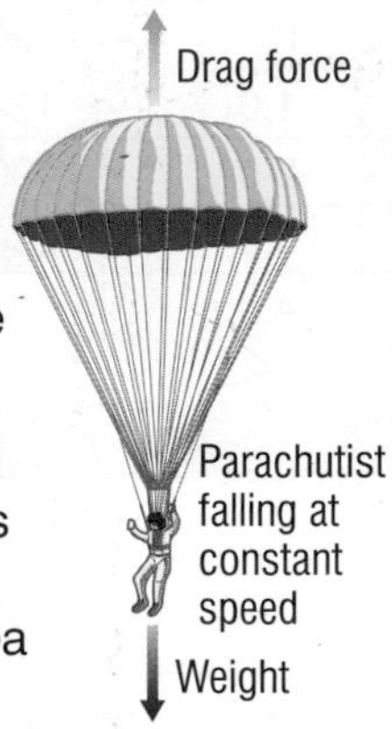

Drag force

Parachutist falling at constant speed

Weight

Figure 3 Using a parachute

Key points

- The weight of an object is the gravitational force acting on it. Its mass is the quantity of matter in the object.
- An object acted on only by gravity accelerates at about 10 m/s^2.
- The terminal velocity of an object is the velocity it eventually reaches when it is falling in a fluid. The weight of the object is then equal to the frictional force on the object.

P4.3 Forces and elasticity

Learning objectives

After this topic, you should know:

- what is meant when an object is called elastic
- how to measure the extension of an object when it is stretched
- how the extension of a spring varies with the force applied to it.

Table 1 Weight versus length measurements for a rubber strip

Weight (N)	Length (mm)	Extension (mm)
0	120	0
1.0	152	32
2.0	190	70
3.0	250	
4.0		

Did you know ...?

Rubber and other soft materials such as flowers that are frozen by being dipped in liquid nitrogen become as brittle as glass. The materials then shatter when struck with a hammer, or explode when hit with a projectile.

Figure 2 A flower dipped in nitrogen and then smashed

Squash players know that hitting a squash ball changes the ball's shape briefly. A squash ball is **elastic** because it goes back to its original shape. A rubber band is also elastic as it returns to its original length after it is stretched and then released. Rubber is an example of an elastic material.

An object is elastic if it returns to its original shape when the forces deforming it are removed.

Practical

Stretch tests

We can investigate how easily a material stretches by hanging weights from it, as shown in Figure 1.

- The strip of material to be tested is clamped at its upper end. A weight hanger is attached to the material to keep it straight.
- The length of the strip is measured using a metre ruler. This is its original length.
- The weight hung from the material is increased by adding weights one at a time. The strip stretches each time more weight is hung from it.
- The length of the strip is measured each time a weight is added. The total weight added and the total length of the strip are recorded in a table.

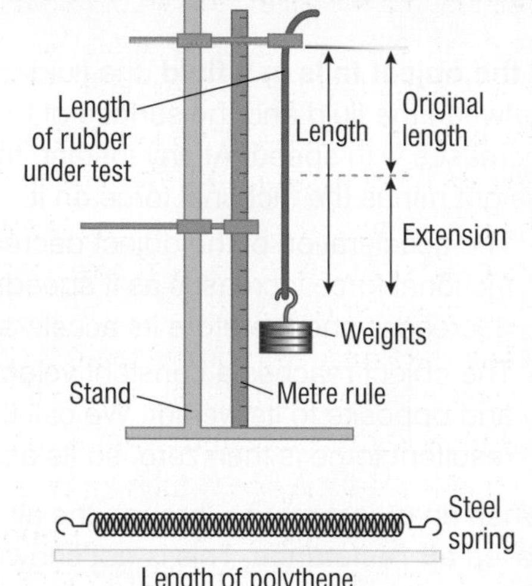

Figure 1 Investigating stretching

Safety: Take care with falling weights.

The increase of length from the original is called the **extension**. This is calculated each time a weight is added and recorded, as shown in Table 1.

The extension of the strip of material at any stage = its length at the stage – its original length

The measurements may be plotted on a graph of extension on the vertical axis against weight on the horizontal axis. Figure 3 shows the results for strips of different materials and a steel spring plotted on the same axes.

- The steel spring gives a straight line through the origin. This shows that the extension of the steel spring is **directly proportional** to the weight hung on it. For example, doubling the weight from 2.0 N to 4.0 N doubles the extension of the spring.
- The rubber band does not give a straight line. When the weight on the rubber band is doubled from 2.0 N to 4.0 N, the extension more than doubles.
- The polythene strip does not give a straight line either. As the weight is increased from zero, the polythene strip stretches very little at first, then it 'gives' and stretches easily.

Elastic energy

When an elastic object is stretched, elastic potential energy is stored in the object. This is because work is done on the object by the stretching force.

When the stretching force is removed, the elastic energy stored in the object is released. Some of this energy may be transferred into kinetic energy of the object or may make its atoms vibrate more so it becomes warmer.

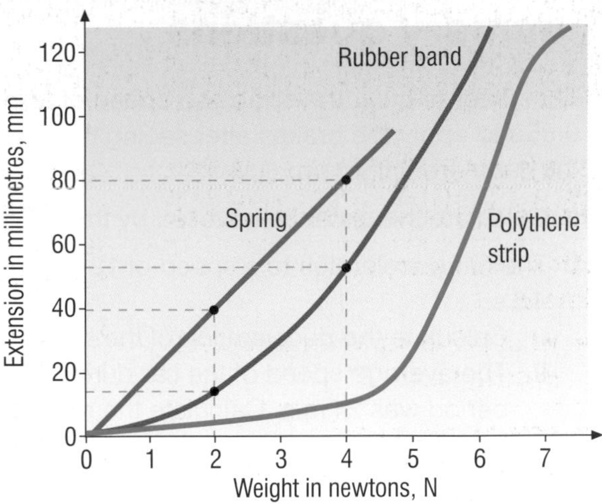

Figure 3 Extension versus weight for different materials

Hooke's law

In the tests above, the extension of a steel spring is directly proportional to the force applied to it. We can use the graph to predict what the extension would be for any given force. But if the force is too large, the spring stretches more than predicted. This is because the spring has been stretched beyond its **limit of proportionality**.

The extension of a spring is directly proportional to the force applied, as long as its limit of proportionality is not exceeded.

The above statement is known as **Hooke's law**. If the extension of any stretched object or material is directly proportional to the stretching force, we say it obeys Hooke's law.

1. The lines on the graph in Figure 3 show that rubber and polythene have a low limit of proportionality. Beyond this limit, they do not obey Hooke's law. A steel spring has a much higher limit of proportionality.
2. Hooke's law may be written as an equation:

Force applied = **spring constant** × **extension**
(in newtons, N) (in newtons per metre, N/m) (in metres, m)

The **spring constant** is equal to the force per unit extension needed to extend the spring, assuming its limit of proportionality is not reached. The stiffer a spring is, the greater its spring constant is.

Maths skills

We can write the word equation for Hooke's law using symbols as:

$$\boldsymbol{F} = \boldsymbol{k} \times \boldsymbol{e},$$

where:
F = force in newtons, N
k = the spring constant in newtons per metre, N/m
e = extension in metres, m.

Examiner's tip

Remember that you have to subtract the original length from the stretched length to find the extension.

Summary questions

1 a i State Hooke's law.
ii A spring has a spring constant of 25 N/m. How much force is needed to make the spring extend by 0.10 m?
b i What happens to a strip of polythene if it is stretched beyond its elastic limit of proportionality?
ii How does the result of stretching then releasing a rubber band differ from that of stretching a strip of polythene?

2 What is meant by:
a the limit of proportionality of a spring?
b the spring constant of a spring?
c the extension of a stretched spring?

3 a In Figure 3, when the weight is 4.0 N, what is the extension of:
i the spring?
ii the rubber band?
iii the polythene strip?
b i What is the extension of the spring when the weight is 3.0 N?
ii Calculate the spring constant of the spring.
iii What does the gradient of the line for the spring in Figure 3 represent?

Key points

- **An object is called elastic if it returns to its original shape after removing the force deforming it.**
- **The extension is the difference between the length of the spring and its original length.**
- **The extension of a spring is directly proportional to the force applied to it, as long as the limit of proportionality is not exceeded.**

Summary questions

1 The driver of a car travelling at a speed of 30 m/s takes 0.85 s to apply the brakes after seeing the brake lights of the car in front light up.

a Calculate the distance travelled by the car in this time.

b The car decelerates to a speed of 12 m/s in a time of 4.5 s.

- **i** Calculate the deceleration of the car.
- **ii** The average speed of the car during this braking period was 21 m/s. Calculate the distance travelled by the car in this time.

2 **a** Explain why the stopping distance of a car is increased if:

- **i** the road is wet instead of dry
- **ii** the driver is tired instead of alert.

b A driver travelling at 18 m/s takes 0.7 s to react when a dog walks into the road 40 m ahead. The braking distance for the car at this speed is 24 m.

- **i** Calculate the distance travelled by the car in the time it takes the driver to react.
- **ii** How far in front of the dog does the car stop?
- **iii** The total mass of the car and its contents is 1200 kg. Calculate the car's deceleration when the brakes are applied and so calculate the braking force.

3 A space vehicle of mass 200 kg rests on its four wheels on a flat area of the lunar surface. The gravitational field strength at the surface of the Moon is 1.6 N/kg.

a Calculate the weight of the space vehicle on the lunar surface.

b Calculate the force each wheel exerts on the lunar surface.

4 **a** The gravitational field strength g at the surface of the Earth is 10 N/kg. Explain why a freely falling object released near the Earth's surface has a constant acceleration of 10 m/s^2 as it falls.

b A stone dropped from the top of a water well hits the water in the well 1.7 seconds later. Calculate the speed of the object just before it hits the surface of the water.

c The figure at the top of the next column shows the velocity–time graphs for a metal object **X** dropped in air and a similar object **Y** dropped in a tank of water.

- **i** What does the graph for **X** tell you about its acceleration?
- **ii** In terms of the forces acting on **Y**, explain why it reached a constant velocity.

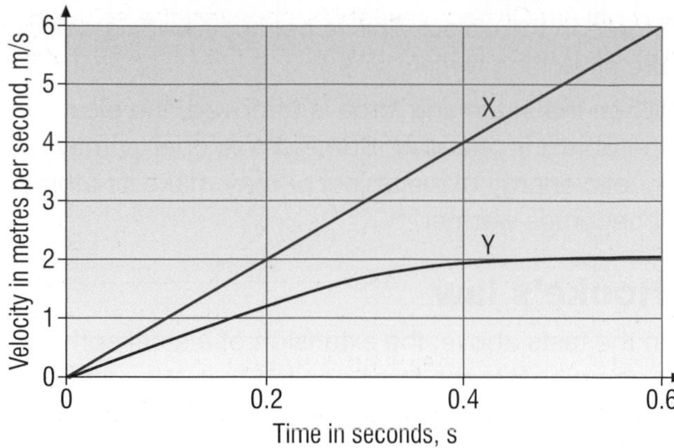

5 **a** A racing cyclist accelerates at 5.0 m/s^2 when she starts from rest. The total mass of the cyclist and her bicycle is 45 kg. Calculate:

- **i** the resultant force that produces this acceleration
- **ii** the total weight of the cyclist and the bicycle.

b Explain why she can reach a higher speed by crouching than by staying upright.

6 **a** An unstretched spring of length 0.300 m hangs vertically from a fixed point. When an object of weight 1.2 N is suspended on the end of a spring, the spring extends to a length of 0.348 m.

- **i** Calculate the extension of the spring.
- **ii** Calculate the spring constant.

b The 1.2 N weight is removed from the spring and an object **X** is suspended on the spring, causing it to extend to a length of 0.340 m. Calculate the weight of **X**.

7 In a Hooke's law test on a spring, the following results were obtained.

Weight (N)	Length (mm)	Extension (mm)
0	245	0
1.0	285	40
2.0	324	
3.0	366	
4.0	405	
5.0	446	
6.0	484	

a Copy and complete the third column of the table.

b Plot a graph of the extension on the vertical axis against the weight on the horizontal axis.

c If a weight of 7.0 N is suspended on the spring, what would be the extension of the spring?

d **i** Calculate the spring constant of the spring.

- **ii** An object suspended on the spring gives an extension of 140 mm. Calculate the weight of the object.

AQA Examination-style questions

1 The Highway Code gives tables showing the shortest stopping distances for cars travelling at different speeds.

An extract from the Highway Code is given below.

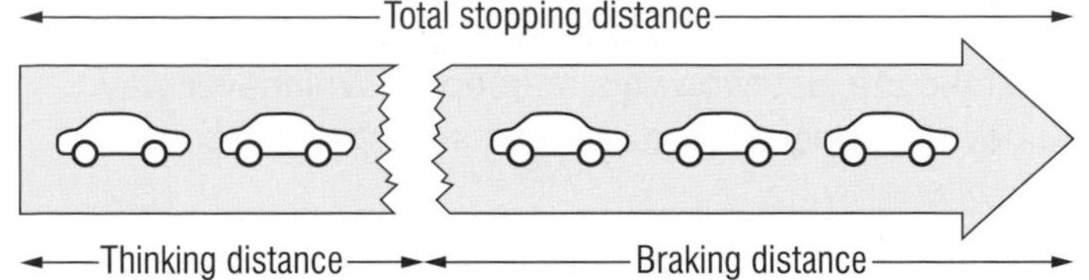

a What is meant by thinking distance? (1)

b Explain how the thinking distance is affected by:

- **i** the driver drinking alcohol (3)
- **ii** the speed of the car. (2)

c A car was travelling at 30 m/s. The driver applied the brakes to decelerate the car uniformly in 4.8 s.

Calculate:

- **i** the deceleration of the car during braking (2)
- **ii** the braking force if the mass of the car is 900 kg (2)
- **iii** the braking distance. (3)

d Discuss the factors that affect the braking distance of a car. (5)

2 A student wanted to time a steel ball-bearing falling through thick oil.

a i The student wanted to use a timer with the greatest range and the highest resolution.

Which of the timers, **A**, **B**, **C** or **D**, should he choose? (1)

Timer	A	B	C	D
	0–30 s	0–30 s	0–60 s	0–60 s
	1 s	0.1 s	0.01 s	1 s

ii When the RESET button is pressed the reading on the timer does not return to 0.

What type of error is this? Choose from the list. (1)

human error   *random error*   *zero error*

b Two forces, **X** and **Y**, act on the ball-bearing as it falls through the oil.

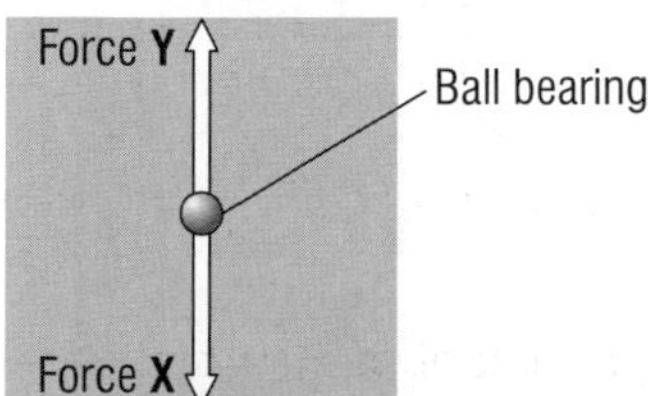

What causes:

- **i** Force **X**? (1)
- **ii** Force **Y**? (1)

c The graph shows how the speed of the ball-bearing changes as it falls through the oil.

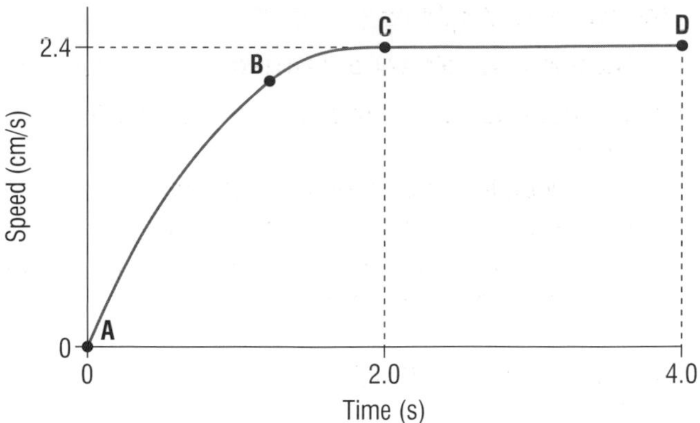

- **i** Describe and explain, in terms of forces **X** and **Y**, what happens to the speed of the ball-bearing between **A** and **B**. (4)
- **ii** Describe and explain, in terms of forces **X** and **Y**, what happens to the speed of the ball-bearing between **C** and **D**. (4)

3 a Describe, with the aid of a diagram, how you would test a spring to find out if its extension is directly proportional to the force used to stretch it. (QWC) (6)

b The table gives the results of a test carried out on another material.

The original length of the sample used in the test was 10.0 cm.

Force (in N)	New length (in cm)
1	10.5
2	11.0
3	11.5
4	12.0
5	12.5
6	13.0

- **i** By plotting a graph, how could you tell whether the extension of the material is directly proportional to the stretching force? (2)
- **ii** Without plotting a graph, use the data in the table to determine whether the extension of the material is directly proportional to the stretching force. (3)

c What is meant by saying that a material is *elastic*? (2)

P5.1 Energy and work

Learning objectives

After this topic, you should know:

- what is meant by 'work' in science
- the relationship between work and energy
- how to calculate the work done by a force
- what happens to the work done to overcome friction.

Figure 1 Working out

Working out

In a fitness centre or a gym, you have to work hard to keep fit. Lifting weights and pedalling on an exercise bike are just two ways to keep fit. Whichever way you choose to keep fit, you have to apply a force to move something. So the work you do causes **transfer** of energy.

When an object is moved by a force, we say that **work** is done on the object by the force. The force therefore transfers energy to the object. The amount of energy transferred to the object is equal to the work done on it. For example, to raise an object, you need to apply a force to it to 'overcome' the force of gravity on it. If the work you do on the object is 20 J, the energy transferred to it must be 20 J. So its gravitational potential energy increases by 20 J.

Energy transferred = work done

The work done by a force depends on the size of the force and the distance moved. We use the following equation to calculate the work done by a force when it moves an object:

work done = force applied × distance moved in the direction of the force
(joules, J) (newtons, N) (metres, m)

We can write the above word equation using symbols:

$$W = F \times d$$

where:
W = work done in joules, J
F = force in newtons, N
d = distance moved in metres in the direction of the force, m.

Maths skills

Worked example

A builder pushed a wheelbarrow a distance of 5.0 m across flat ground with a force of 50 N. How much work was done by the builder?

Solution

Work done = force applied × distance moved = 50 N × 5.0 m = **250 J**

Did you know ...?

Imagine pulling a heavy goods vehicle over 40 metres. On level ground, a pull force of about 2000 N is needed. Very few people can manage to pull with such force. Don't even try it though. The people who can do it are very, very strong and have trained specially for it.

Figure 2 Pulling a heavy goods vehicle

Practical

Doing work

Carry out a series of experiments to calculate the work done in performing the tasks below. Use a newtonmeter to measure the force applied and a metre ruler to measure the distance moved.

1 Drag a small box a measured distance across a rough surface.
2 Repeat the test above with two rubber bands wrapped around the box as shown in Figure 3.

- What is the resolution of your measuring instruments? Repeat your tests and comment on the precision of your repeat measurements. Can you be confident about the accuracy of your results?

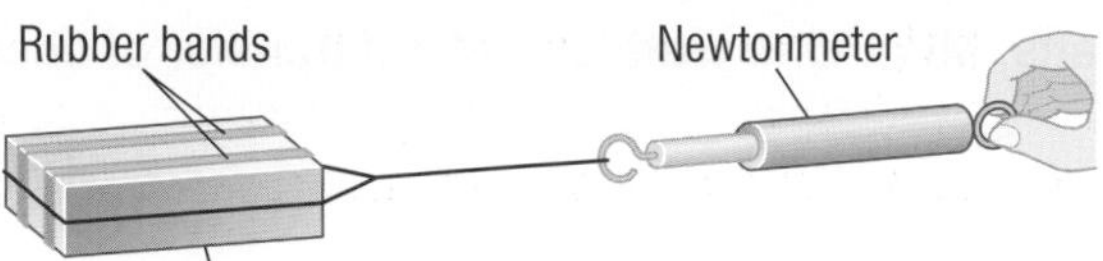

Figure 3 At work

Did you know ... ?

Meteorites are small objects from space that enter the Earth's atmosphere and fall to the ground. As they pass through the atmosphere, friction caused by air resistance acts on them and kinetic energy is transferred by heating. If a meteorite becomes hot enough, it glows and becomes visible as a 'shooting star'. Very small objects may burn up completely. The surface of a space vehicle is designed to withstand the very high temperatures caused by such friction when it re-enters the Earth's atmosphere.

Friction at work

Work done to overcome friction is mainly transferred into energy by heating.

1 If you rub your hands together vigorously, they become warm. Your muscles do work to overcome the friction between your hands. The work you do is transferred into energy that warms your hands.
2 Brake pads become hot if the brakes are applied for too long a time. Friction between the brake pads and the wheel discs opposes the motion of the wheel. The kinetic energy of the vehicle is transferred into energy that heats the brake pads and the wheel discs, as well as the surrounding air. A small proportion of the energy will be transferred to the surroundings by sound waves if the brakes 'squeal'.

Examiner's tip

Remember that energy is needed to do work. If you calculate the work done, that equals the energy transferred.

Summary questions

1 a State what happens to the energy transferred:
   i by a rower rowing a boat
   ii by an electric motor used to raise a car park barrier.
  b How much work is done when a force of 2000 N pulls a truck through a distance of 40 m in the direction of the force?

2 A car is brought to a standstill when the driver applies the brakes.
  a Explain why the brake pads become warm.
  b The car travelled a distance of 20 metres after the brakes were applied. The braking force on the car during this time was 7000 N. Calculate the work done by the braking force.

3 a Calculate the work done when:
   i a force of 20 N makes an object move 4.8 m in the direction of the force
   ii an object of weight 80 N is raised through a height of 1.2 m.
  b When a cyclist brakes, his kinetic energy is reduced from 1400 J to zero in a distance of 7.0 m. Calculate the braking force.

Key points

- **Work is done on an object when a force makes the object move.**
- **Energy transferred = work done.**
- **Work done (joules) = force (newtons) × distance moved in the direction of the force (metres).**
- **Work done to overcome friction is transferred as energy that heats the objects that rub together and heats the surroundings.**

P5.2 Power

Learning objectives

After this topic, you should know:

- what is meant by 'power' in science
- how power is measured
- the relationship between power and energy transferred.

Figure 1 Rocket power for launching into space

Did you know ... ?

The unit of power is named after James Watt, who invented the steam engine. Before this invention, horse-drawn carriages and barges were used to transport people and goods overland. When steam engines first replaced horses, each engine was rated in terms of the number of horses it could replace. The output power of a road vehicle is still sometimes expressed in 'horse power', where 1 horse power is equal to 756 watts.

Powerful machines

When you use a lift to go up, a powerful electric motor pulls you and the lift up. The work done by the lift motor transfers energy from electricity to gravitational potential energy. Sound and energy that heats the motor and its surroundings are also transferred.

- The work done per second by the motor is the output **power** of the motor.
- The more powerful the lift motor, the faster it takes you up.

We measure the power of an appliance in watts (W) or kilowatts (kW) or megawatts (millions of watts, MW). One **watt** is a rate of transfer of energy of 1 joule per second (J/s).

For example:

- a 5 W electric torch would transfer 5 J every second as light energy and heat energy to its surroundings
- a lift motor with an output power of 6000 W would transfer 6000 J to the lift as gravitational potential energy every second.

Here are typical values of power levels for some energy transfer 'mechanisms':

- A torch 1 W
- An electric light bulb 100 W
- An electric cooker 10 000 W = 10 kW (where 1 kW = 1000 watts)
- A railway engine 1 000 000 W = 1 megawatt (MW) = 1 million watts
- A Saturn V rocket 100 MW
- A very large power station 10 000 MW
- The Sun 100 000 000 000 000 000 000 MW

Energy and power

Machines are labour-saving devices that do work for us. The faster a machine can do work, the more powerful it is.

Whenever a machine does work on an object, energy is transferred to the object. The useful energy transferred is equal to the work done by the machine. This is the form of energy needed that is transferred to the object.

The output power of a machine is the rate it does work at. This is the same as the rate at which it transfers useful energy.

$$\textbf{Power } P \text{ (in watts)} = \frac{\textbf{work done} \text{ (in joules)}}{\textbf{time taken} \text{ (in seconds)}} = \frac{\textbf{useful energy transferred} \text{ (in joules)}}{\textbf{time taken} \text{ (in seconds)}}$$

If work W is done (or energy E is transferred) in time t:

$$\textbf{power } P = \frac{W}{t} = \frac{E}{t}$$

Maths skills

Worked example

A crane lifts an object of weight 4000 N through a vertical distance of 2.5 m in 5.0 s. Calculate:

a the force needed to lift the object steadily
b how much gravitational potential energy the object gains
c the output power of the crane.

Solution

a Force needed = weight of object = **4000 N**
b Work done on the object = force needed × distance moved
= 4000 N × 2.5 m = **10 000 J**
c Output power $= \frac{\text{work done}}{\text{time taken}} = \frac{10\,000\,\text{J}}{5.0\,\text{s}} =$ **2000 W**

Figure 2 A crane at work

Did you know … ?

How powerful is a weightlifter?
A 30 kg dumbbell has a weight of 300 N. Raising it by 1 m would give it 300 J of gravitational potential energy. A weightlifter could lift it in about 0.5 seconds.
The rate of transfer of energy would be 600 J/s (= 300 J ÷ 0.5 s). So, the weightlifter's output power would be about 600 W in total!

Examiner's tip

Be careful with units – power is sometimes in kilowatts.

Summary questions

1 a Which is more powerful:
  i a torch bulb or a mains-connected filament lamp?
  ii a 3 kW electric kettle or a 10 000 W electric cooker?
b There are about 2 million homes in a certain city. If a 3 kW electric kettle was switched on in 1 out of 10 homes in the city at the same time, how much power would need to be supplied to the homes?

2 An electric motor raises an object of weight 200 N by a height of 4.0 m in 5.0 s. Calculate:
a how much gravitational potential energy the object gains
b the work done by the motor on the object
c the output power of the motor.

3 The engine of a goods vehicle has an output power of 150 kW when the vehicle is travelling at a constant velocity of 30 m/s on a level road.
a Calculate:
  i the distance travelled by the vehicle in 60 seconds
  ii the useful energy transferred by the engine in this time.
b Show that the driving force of the engine is 5000 N.

Key points

- Power is the rate at which energy is transferred.
- The unit of power is the watt (W), which is equal to 1 J/s.
- Power (in watts) $= \frac{\text{energy transferred (in joules)}}{\text{time taken (in seconds)}}$

P5.3 Gravitational potential energy

Learning objectives

After this topic, you should know:

- what happens to the gravitational potential energy of an object when it moves up or down
- why an object moving up gains gravitational potential energy
- how to calculate the change of gravitational potential energy of an object when it moves up or down.

Gravitational potential energy transfers

Every time you lift an object up, you do some work. Some of your muscles transfer chemical energy from your muscles into **gravitational potential energy** of the object. Gravitational potential energy is energy stored in an object because of its position in the Earth's gravitational field.

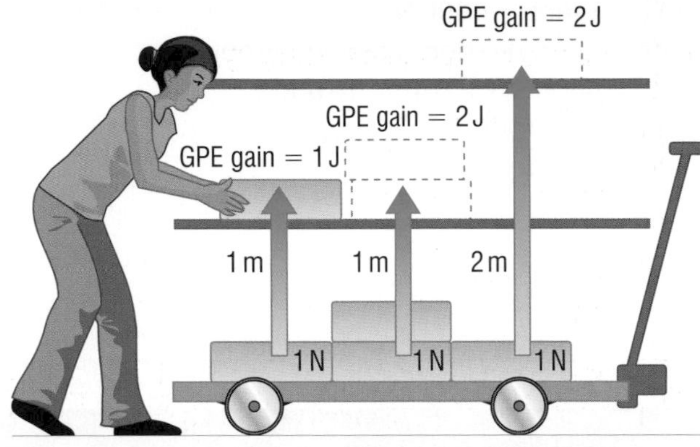

Figure 1 Using joules

The force you need to lift an object steadily is equal and opposite to the gravitational force on the object. Therefore, the upward force you need to apply to it is equal to the object's weight. For example, a force of 80 N is needed to lift a box of weight 80 N.

- **When an object is moved up**, its gravitational potential energy increases. The increase in its gravitational potential energy is equal to the work done on it by the lifting force to overcome the gravitational force on the object.
- **When an object moves down**, its gravitational potential energy decreases. The decrease in its gravitational potential energy is equal to the work done by the gravitational force acting on it.

The work done when an object moves up or down depends on:

1 how far it is moved vertically (its change of height)

2 its weight.

We know from 5.1 'Energy and work', that $W = F \times d$ (work done = force applied × distance moved in the direction of the force). We can therefore say:

the change of its gravitational potential energy (in joules) = **its weight** (in newtons) × **its change of height** (in metres)

Did you know ... ?

You use energy when you hold an object stationary in your outstretched hand. The biceps muscle of your arm is in a state of contraction. Energy must be supplied to keep the muscles contracted. No work is done on the object because it doesn't move. The energy supplied heats the muscles and is transferred by heating to the surroundings.

Gravitational potential energy and mass

Astronauts on the Moon can lift objects much more easily than they can on the Earth. This is because, at their surfaces, the gravitational field strength of the Moon is only about a sixth of the Earth's gravitational field strength.

In 4.2 'Forces and terminal velocity', we saw that the weight of an object in newtons is equal to its mass × the gravitational field strength.

Therefore, when an object is lifted or lowered, because its change of gravitational potential energy is equal to its weight × its change of height:

change of gravitational potential energy (in J) = **mass** (in kg) × **gravitational field strength** (in N/kg) × **change of height** (in metres)

Examiner's tip

Watch out for objects going up a slope. To calculate a gain in gravitational potential energy, you need the vertical height gained, not the distance up the slope.

Maths skills

Worked example

A student of weight 300 N climbs on a platform that is 1.2 m higher than the floor. Calculate the increase of her gravitational potential energy.

Solution

Increase of GPE = 300 N × 1.2 m
= **360 J**

Note: We often use the abbreviation 'GPE' or E_p for gravitational potential energy.

We can write the equation at the bottom of page 44 using symbols:

$$\boldsymbol{E_p = m \times g \times h}$$

where:

E_p = change of gravitational potential energy in joules, J
m = mass in kilograms, kg
g = gravitational field strength in newtons per kilogram, N/kg
h = change of height in metres, m.

Maths skills

Worked example

A 2.0 kg object is raised through a height of 0.4 m. Calculate the gain of gravitational potential energy of the object. The gravitational field strength of the Earth at its surface is 10 N/kg.

Solution

Gain of GPE = mass × gravitational field strength × height gain
= 2.0 kg × 10 N/kg × 0.4 m
= **8.0 J**

Summary questions

1 a Describe the energy changes of a ball when it falls and rebounds without regaining its initial height.
b When a ball of weight 1.4 N is dropped from rest from a height of 2.5 m above a flat surface, it rebounds to a height of 1.7 m above the surface.
i Calculate the total loss of energy of the ball on reaching this maximum rebound height.
ii State two causes of the energy loss.

2 A student of weight 450 N steps on a box of height 0.20 m.
a Calculate the gain of gravitational potential energy of the student.
b Calculate the work done by the student if she steps on and off the box 50 times.

3 a A weightlifter raises a steel bar of mass 25 kg through a height of 1.8 m. Calculate the change of gravitational potential energy of the bar. The gravitational field strength at the surface of the Earth is 10 N/kg.
b The weightlifter then lowers the bar by 0.3 m and then throws it so it falls to the ground. Assume that air resistance is unimportant. What is the change of its gravitational potential energy in this fall?

4 Read the 'Did you know?' box on the previous page. Explain what happens to the energy supplied to the muscles to keep them contracted.

Practical

Stepping up

Measure your mass in kilograms using floor scales.

Step on and off a sturdy box or low platform.

Measure the height of the box.

Use the equation 'change of GPE = $m \times g \times h$', where g = 10 N/kg, to calculate how much GPE you gained when you stepped on the box.

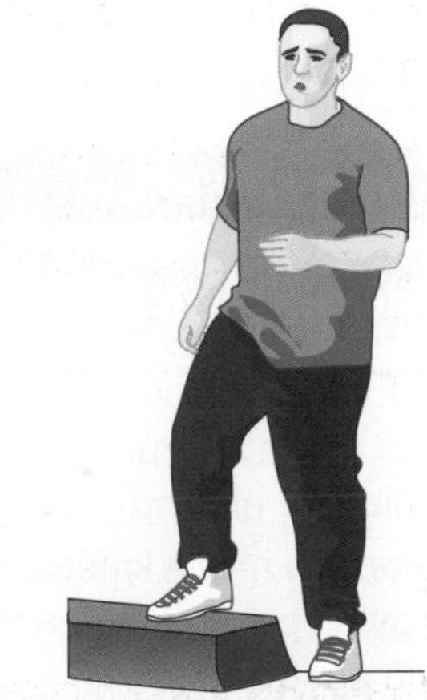

Figure 2 Stepping on and off a platform

Key points

- The gravitational potential energy of an object increases when it moves up and decreases when the object moves down.
- An object gains gravitational potential energy when it is lifted up because work is done on it to overcome the gravitational force.
- The change of gravitational potential energy of an object is equal to its mass × the gravitational field strength × its change of height.

P5.4 Kinetic energy

Learning objectives

After this topic, you should know:

- what the kinetic energy of an object depends on
- how to calculate kinetic energy
- what elastic potential energy is.

?? Did you know ... ?

Sports scientists design running shoes:

- to reduce the force of each impact when the runner's foot hits the ground
- to return as much kinetic energy as possible to each foot in each impact.

Figure 2 A sports shoe

Practical

Investigating a catapult

Use rubber bands to 'catapult' a trolley along a horizontal runway. Find out how the speed of the trolley depends on how much the catapult is pulled back before the trolley is released. For example, see if the distance needs to be doubled to double the speed. Figure 1 shows how the speed of the trolley can be measured.

Practical

Investigating kinetic energy

- The **kinetic energy** of an object is the energy it has because of its motion. Its kinetic energy depends on its mass and its speed.

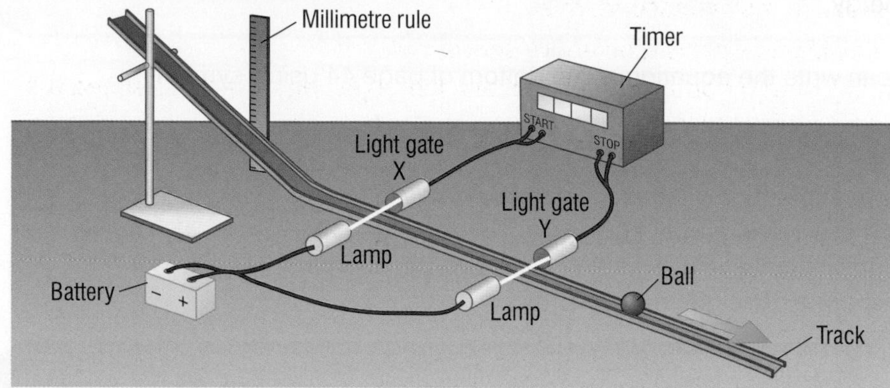

Figure 1 Investigating kinetic energy

Figure 1 shows how we can investigate how the kinetic energy of a ball depends on its speed.

1. The ball is released on a slope from a measured height above the foot of the slope. We can calculate the gravitational potential energy it loses from its mass × gravitational field strength × its drop of height. This is equal to its gain of kinetic energy.
2. The ball is timed, using light gates, over a measured distance between X and Y after the slope.

- Why do light gates improve the quality of the data you can collect in this investigation?

Some sample measurements for a ball of mass 0.5 kg are shown in the table:

Height drop to foot of slope (metres, m)	0.05	0.10	0.16	0.20
Initial kinetic energy of ball (joules, J)	0.25	0.50	0.80	1.00
Time to travel 1.0 m from X to Y (seconds, s)	0.98	0.72	0.57	0.50
Speed (metres/second, m/s)	1.02			2.00

Work out the speed in each case. The first and last values have been worked out for you. Can you see a link between speed and the height drop? The results show that the greater the height drop, the faster the speed is. So we can say that the kinetic energy of the ball increases if the speed increases.

The kinetic energy formula

The above table shows that when the height drop is increased by four times from 0.05 m to 0.20 m, the speed doubles. The height drop is directly proportional to the $(\text{speed})^2$. Since the height drop is a measure of the ball's kinetic energy, we can say that the ball's kinetic energy is directly proportional to the square of its speed.

The exact link between the kinetic energy of an object and its speed is given by the equation:

kinetic energy (joules, J) = ½ × **mass** (kilograms, kg) × **speed²** (metres/second, m/s)²

We can write this word equation using symbols:

$$E_K = \frac{1}{2} \times m \times v^2$$

where:
E_K = kinetic energy in joules, J
m = mass in kilograms, kg
v = speed in metres/second, m/s.

The kinetic energy equation above shows that:

- an object with double the mass of another object and the same speed will have double the kinetic energy
- an object travelling at double the speed of another with the same mass will have four times the kinetic energy.

Kinetic energy recovery systems (KERS) in vehicles store energy when the vehicle brakes and use it later. In 2009, some Formula 1 racing cars were fitted with a flywheel. The kinetic energy of the vehicle could be transferred to the flywheel in braking and used later to boost the vehicle's speed when overtaking. Other vehicles, including hybrid cars, use an electric generator to transfer kinetic energy into electrical energy, which is then stored in a battery.

Maths skills

Worked example

Calculate the kinetic energy of a vehicle of mass 500 kg moving at a speed of 12 m/s.

Solution

kinetic energy
$= \frac{1}{2} \times m \times v^2$
$= 0.5 \times 500\,\text{kg} \times (12\,\text{m/s})^2$
$= \mathbf{36\,000\,J}$

Examiner's tip

Don't forget to square the speed when calculating kinetic energy. Don't forget to take the square root when calculating the speed from kinetic energy.

Many calculations involve transfers between gravitational potential energy and kinetic energy – use $m \times g \times h = \frac{1}{2} \times m \times v^2$

Using elastic potential energy

When you stretch a rubber band or a bowstring, the work you do is stored in it as **elastic potential energy**. Figure 3 shows one way you can **transfer** elastic potential energy into kinetic energy.

From 4.3 'Forces and elasticity', we know that an object is **elastic** if it regains its shape after being stretched or squashed. A rubber band is an example of an elastic object.

Elastic potential energy is the energy stored in an elastic object when work is done on it to change its shape.

Figure 3 Using elastic potential energy

Summary questions

1 a Calculate the kinetic energy of:
 i a vehicle of mass 500 kg moving at a speed of 12 m/s
 ii a football of mass 0.44 kg moving at a speed of 20 m/s.
 b Calculate the velocity of a 500 kg vehicle with twice as much kinetic energy as calculated in **a i**.

2 a A catapult is used to fire an object into the air. Describe the energy transfers when the catapult is:
 i stretched
 ii released.
 b An object of weight 2.0 N fired vertically upwards from a catapult reaches a maximum height of 5.0 m. Calculate:
 i the gain of gravitational potential energy of the object
 ii the speed of the object when it left the catapult.

3 A car moving at a constant speed has 360 000 J of kinetic energy. When the driver applies the brakes, the car stops in a distance of 100 m.
 a Calculate the force that stops the vehicle.
 b The speed of the car was 30 m/s when its kinetic energy was 360 000 J. Calculate its mass.

Key points

- **The kinetic energy of a moving object depends on its mass and its speed.**
- **Kinetic energy (J) = ½ × mass (kg) × speed² (m/s)²**
- **Elastic potential energy is the energy stored in an elastic object when work is done on the object.**

Summary questions

1 A train on a straight level track is pulled at a constant speed of 23 m/s by an engine with an output power of 700 kW.

a **i** How much energy is transferred from the train to the surroundings in 300 s?

ii How far does the train travel in 300 s?

iii Show that the resistive force on the engine is approximately equal to 30 000 N.

iv Explain why the driving force of the engine is equal and opposite to the resistive force on the train.

b The train then moves on to an inclined section of the railway line where the track rises by 1 m for every kilometre of track. Explain why the output power of the engine needs to be increased to maintain the same speed of 23 m/s.

2 A student pushes a trolley of weight 150 N up a slope of length 20 m. The slope is 1.2 m high.

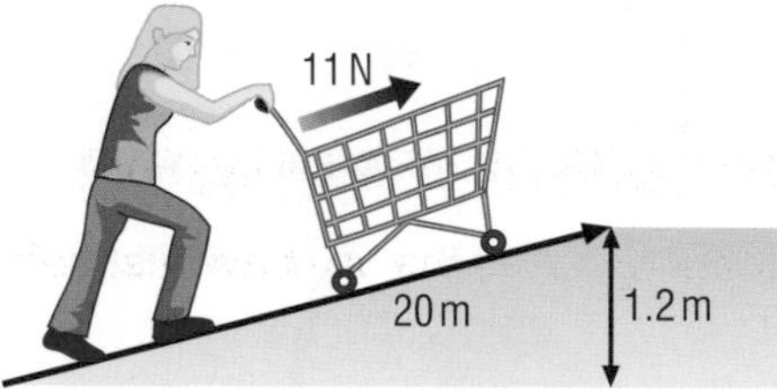

a Calculate the gravitational potential energy gained by the trolley.

b The student pushed the trolley up the slope with a force of 11 N. Show that the work done by the student was 220 J.

c If the student pushed the trolley up the slope at constant speed, explain why all the work done by the student was not transferred to the trolley as gravitational potential energy.

3 **a** A 1100 kg car is moving at 31 m/s on a dry flat road when the brakes are applied to stop it safely.

i Calculate the kinetic energy of the car before the brakes are applied.

ii The car stopped in a distance of 75 m. Calculate the braking force.

iii The braking distance for a car travelling on a dry flat road should not be less than 73.5 m. State what would happen if a much greater braking force had been applied.

b A motorist organisation wants to raise the speed limit on a motorway from 70 mph (31 m/s) to 80 mph (36 m/s). By applying physics to road safety, do you think this is a good idea? Give reasons for your answer.

4 A 2000 kg rail wagon moving at a velocity of 3.1 m/s on a level track collides with a stationary wagon of mass 1100 kg. The two wagons couple together on impact and move at the same velocity after the impact.

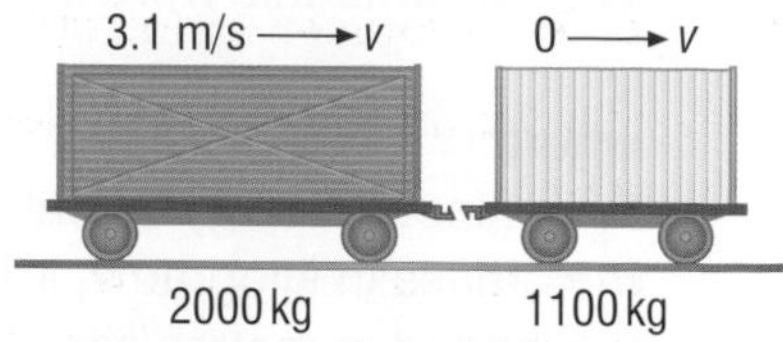

a Calculate the velocity of the wagons after the impact.

b Calculate the kinetic energy of:

i the 2000 kg wagon before the collision

ii the 2000 kg wagon after the collision

iii the 1100 kg wagon after the collision.

c **i** In the impact, spring-loaded buffers increase the duration of the impact. Explain why this reduces the force of the impact.

ii Give two reasons why the total kinetic energy after the collision is not equal to the total kinetic energy before the collision.

5 **a** A stone is fired into the air from a catapult and falls to the ground some distance away. Describe the energy transfers that take place after the catapult is released.

b A stone of mass 0.015 kg is catapulted into the air at a speed of 25 m/s. It reaches a height of 20 m before it descends and hits the ground some distance away.

i Calculate its initial kinetic energy.

ii Calculate the increase of gravitational potential energy of the stone when it reached its maximum height (g = 10 N/kg).

iii Estimate its speed when it was at its maximum height.

6 A parachutist of total mass 75 kg jumps from an aeroplane moving at a speed of 60 m/s at a height of 900 m above the ground.

a Calculate her kinetic energy when she left the aeroplane.

b Her parachute reduced her speed of descent to 5 m/s.

i Calculate her kinetic energy at this speed.

ii Calculate her loss of gravitational potential energy as a result of the descent.

c Calculate the work done by air resistance during her descent.

AQA Examination-style questions

1 Energy is measured in various units.

a Which of the following are units of energy?

joule kilojoule kilowatt newton watt (3)

b The picture shows a woman using a step machine in a gym.

The display panel shows the readings at the end of the exercise.

i Calculate the woman's weight. (2)

ii Calculate the total amount of work done in the exercise. (2)

iii Calculate the average power developed. (3)

2 The picture shows a high jumper.

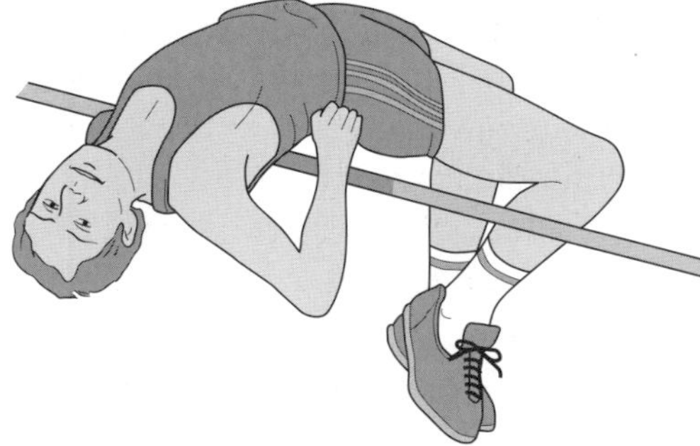

The high jumper runs along a short track before taking off in the jump.

The high jumper has a mass of 65 kg.

To jump over the bar, the high jumper must raise his mass 1.25 m.

a i Discuss the energy transfers that take place. (3)

ii Calculate the gain in the jumper's gravitational potential when he just clears the bar. (2)

b i Calculate the speed the high jumper must reach along the track in order to just clear the bar. (4)

ii Explain why the high jumper's speed will need to be more than this. (3)

3 a Two students carry out an experiment to measure their own power by running up some stairs.

Describe how the students should carry out the experiment to obtain the data needed.

Your description should include the equipment they will need. (QWC) (6)

b One of the students has a mass of 45 kg. The stairs are 400 cm high and she takes 2.5 s to climb them.

Calculate her power. (3)

4 a A ball of mass 200 g is dropped from a height of 2 m. It hits the floor and bounces back to a height of 1.5 m.

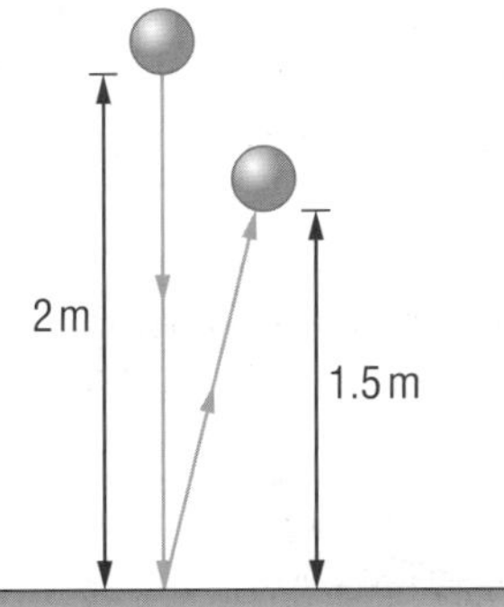

i What type of energy does the ball have just before it is released?

Choose from the list.

gravitational potential kinetic strain potential thermal (1)

ii What percentage of its energy does the ball lose when it hits the floor? (3)

iii Explain what happens to the 'lost' energy and why it is difficult to re-use. (3)

b i Calculate the kinetic energy of the ball just before it hits the floor. (3)

ii Calculate the speed of the ball just before it hits the floor. (4)

iii Explain why the ball accelerates when it hits the floor, even though its speed is less when it leaves the floor. (4)

P6.1 Centre of mass

Learning objectives

After this topic, you should know:

- what the centre of mass of an object is
- about the centre of mass of an object that is suspended from a fixed point
- how to find the centre of mass of a symmetrical object.

Did you know ... ?

Tightrope walkers carry a long pole to keep balanced. They use the pole to keep their centre of mass (and pole) directly above the rope. A slight body movement one way is counterbalanced by shifting the pole slightly the other way.

The design of racing cars has changed a lot since the first models. But one thing that has not changed is the need to keep the car near the ground. The weight of the car must be as low as possible. Otherwise the car would overturn when cornering at high speeds.

Figure 1 Racing cars from the 1920s to modern day

We can think of the weight of an object as if it acts at a single point. This point is called the **centre of mass** (or the centre of gravity) of the object.

The centre of mass of an object is the point at which its mass may be thought to be concentrated.

Practical

Suspended equilibrium

If you suspend an object and then release it, it will sooner or later come to rest with its centre of mass directly below the point of suspension, as shown in Figure 2a. The object is then in equilibrium, which means it is at rest. Its weight does not exert a turning effect on the object because its centre of mass is directly below the point of suspension.

If the object is turned from this position and then released, it will swing back to its equilibrium position. This is because its weight has a turning effect that returns the object to equilibrium, as shown in Figure 2b. We say the object is *freely suspended* if it returns to its equilibrium position.

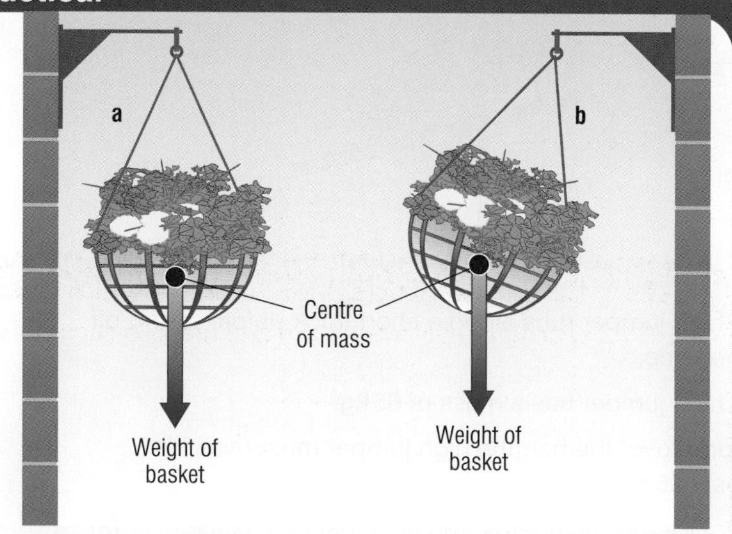

Figure 2 Suspension **a** In equilibrium **b** Non-equilibrium

The centre of mass of a symmetrical object

For a symmetrical object, its centre of mass is along the axis of symmetry. You can see this in Figure 3.

If the object has more than one axis of symmetry, its centre of mass is where the axes of symmetry meet.

- A rectangle has two axes of symmetry, as shown Figure 3a. The centre of mass is where the axes meet.
- The equilateral triangle in Figure 3b has three axes of symmetry, each bisecting one of the angles of the triangle. The three axes meet at the same point. This is where the centre of mass of the triangle is.

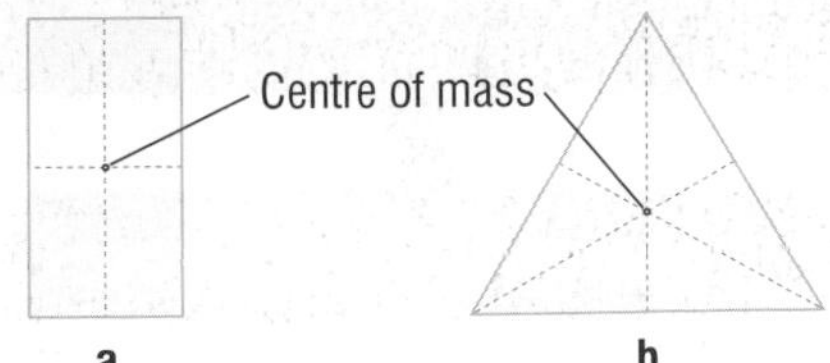

Figure 3 Symmetrical objects

Practical

A centre of mass test

Figure 4 shows how to find the centre of mass of an irregular-shaped flat card. The card is at rest, freely suspended from a rod.

Its centre of mass is directly below the rod. A 'plumbline' can be used to draw a vertical line on the card from the rod downwards.

The procedure is repeated with the card suspended from a second point to give another similar line. The centre of mass of the card is where the two lines meet.

Try drawing a third line to see if all three cross at the same point.

- What can you say about the accuracy of your experiment?

Test your results to see if you can balance the card at this point on the end of a pencil.

- Now find the centre of mass of a semicircular card of radius 100 mm.

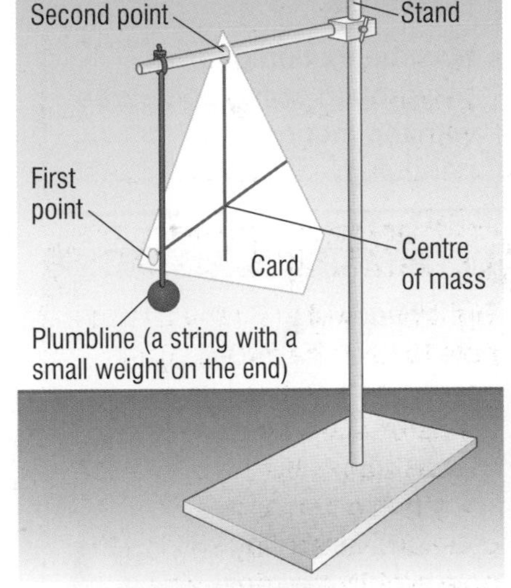

Figure 4 Finding the centre of mass of a card

Examiner's tip

Make sure you can describe all the steps in the practical to find the centre of mass of a thin sheet of material.

Summary questions

1 Sketch each of the objects shown and mark its centre of mass.

a

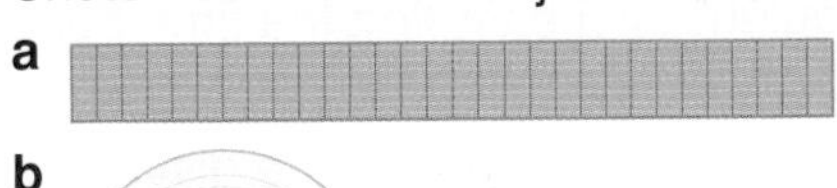

b

c

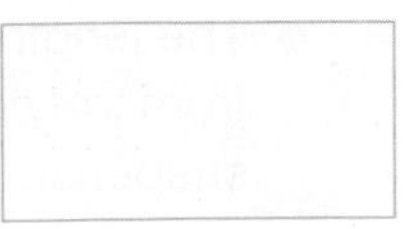

2 Explain why a child on a swing comes to rest directly below the top of the swing.

3 Describe how you would find the centre of mass of a flat semicircular card.

Key points

- **The centre of mass of an object is the point where its mass may be thought to be concentrated.**
- **When an object is freely suspended, it comes to rest with its centre of mass directly beneath the point of suspension.**
- **The centre of mass of a symmetrical object is along the axis of symmetry.**

P6.2 The pendulum

Learning objectives

After this topic, you should know:

- what affects the time period of a pendulum
- how to measure the time period of a pendulum accurately
- how the motion of a playground swing compares with the motion of a pendulum.

Figure 1 On a playground swing

When you sit on a playground swing moving backwards and forwards, you move fastest when the swing's seat is nearest the ground. This position is also the **equilibrium position** of the swing. This is its position when it eventually stops moving altogether. The motion of a swing is an example of **oscillating motion**. This is the motion of any object that moves to and fro along the same line.

The motion of a pendulum

Figure 2 shows a snapshot of a pendulum in motion. This type of pendulum is called a **simple pendulum**. It moves like a playground swing along the line between the bob's highest positions at A and B on each side. There is very little air resistance on it or friction at the point of suspension, so it takes a long time to stop swinging.

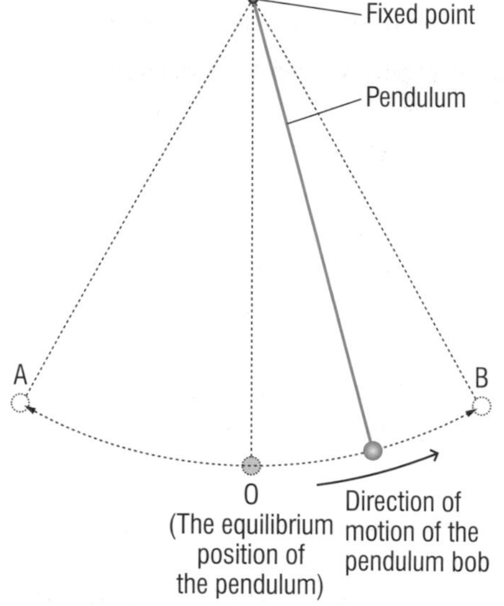

Figure 2 The pendulum

The **amplitude of an oscillating object** is the distance it moves from its equilibrium position O to its highest position A or B on either side.

Its **time period** is the time taken for one complete cycle of its motion. In other words, it is:

- the time it takes to swing across and back from its highest position on one side, for example from A to B and back to A, or
- the time between successive passes in the same direction through its equilibrium position O.

Practical

Investigating the time period of a pendulum

Task 1 To measure the time period, use a stopwatch to time 20 complete cycles of the pendulum's motion. Repeat this twice more and find the average of the three timings. Divide this timing by 20 to obtain the time period.

Each cycle takes the pendulum from when it passes through 'equilibrium' to the next time it passes through 'equilibrium' moving in the same direction. You could use a 'marker' to help see exactly when it passes through equilibrium.

Task 2 Find out if the time period depends on the amplitude of the oscillations by measuring the time period for different amplitudes.

- Use a millimetre ruler to measure the amplitude.
- Record your measurements and plot a suitable graph.

Task 3 Find out if the time period depends on the length of the pendulum by measuring the time period for different lengths.

- The length of a simple pendulum is the distance from the centre of mass of the bob to the point of suspension on the string. Use a metre ruler marked in millimetres to measure the length of the pendulum.
- Record your measurements and plot a suitable graph.

Your results from the last investigation should show that the time period of a pendulum depends on its length. Further investigations will show that the time period of a pendulum increases as its length increases.

The frequency of the oscillations is the number of complete cycles of oscillation per second.

The unit of frequency is the hertz (Hz) where 1 hertz is 1 cycle per second.

Note that the greater the frequency of the oscillations, the shorter the time period is. This is because:

$$\textbf{the time period} \text{ (in seconds, s)} = \frac{1}{\textbf{frequency of the oscillations} \text{ (in hertz, Hz)}}$$

Practical

Testing a model swing

1 Make a model swing with a plasticine person fixed to the seat. Measure the time period of small oscillations.

2 Repeat the test with a 'person' with a higher centre of mass on the seat. Use the same lump of plasticine so the mass of the person is unchanged.

3 Record your results.

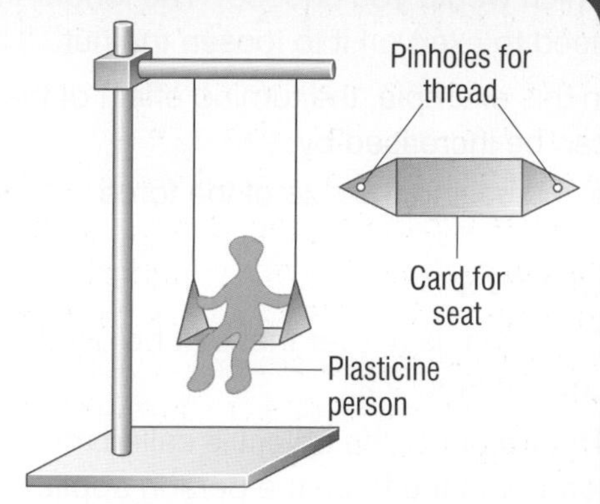

Figure 3 Testing a model swing

What conclusions can you draw from your results?

The fairground swingboat

A fairground swingboat can seat several people. They can make the boat oscillate by rocking backwards and forwards in their seats or by pulling on ropes hanging from the supporting frame above the boat. As with a swing, the centre of mass of the boat and its occupants is higher than the centre of mass of the empty boat. So the oscillations of the empty boat have a longer time period than when people are in it.

Summary questions

1 **a** State the effect on the time period of a pendulum after:
  i decreasing its length
  ii replacing the bob with a bob of smaller mass without changing the length of the pendulum.
 b When a simple pendulum is released from rest, it undergoes 20 oscillations in 28 s. Calculate:
  i the time period of the pendulum
  ii the frequency of the oscillations.

2 Three timings were taken for 20 oscillations of a simple pendulum, as follows: 37.95 s, 37.73 s, 38.12 s.
 a Calculate the mean value of these timings.
 b Calculate the frequency of the oscillations.

3 **a** State one similarity and one difference between the motion of a playground swing carrying a child and the motion of a simple pendulum of the same length as the swing.
 b Explain why the time period of the swing is less than the time period of the pendulum.

Maths skills

We can write the word equation for the time period of a pendulum using symbols, as follows:

$$T = \frac{1}{f}$$

where:

T = time period in seconds, s

f = frequency in hertz, Hz.

Note: Rearranging $T = \frac{1}{f}$ to make f the subject gives:

$$f = \frac{1}{T}$$

Worked example

A pendulum undergoes 20 complete cycles of oscillation in 4.0 seconds.

Calculate **a** the frequency of the oscillations, **b** the time period.

Solution

a For 20 complete cycles in 4 seconds, there must be 5 cycles each second ($20 \div 4 = 5$). The frequency is therefore **5 Hz**.

b $T = \frac{1}{f}$ so the time period is $\frac{1}{5}$ = **0.2 seconds**.

Key points

- **The time period of a simple pendulum depends only on its length.**
- **To measure the time period of a pendulum, we can measure the average time for 20 oscillations and divide the timing by 20.**
- **Friction at the top of a playground swing and air resistance will stop it oscillating if it is not pushed repeatedly.**

P6.3 Moments at work

Learning objectives

After this topic, you should know:

- what the moment of a force measures
- how to calculate the moment of a force
- how the moment of a force can be increased.

Figure 1 A turning effect

To undo a very tight wheel-nut on a bicycle, you need a spanner. The force you apply to the spanner has a turning effect on the nut. You couldn't undo a tight nut with your fingers but you can with the spanner. The spanner exerts a much larger turning effect on the nut than the force you apply to the spanner.

If you had a choice between a long-handled spanner and a short-handled one, which would you choose? The longer the spanner handle, the less force you need to exert on it to loosen the nut.

In this example, the turning effect of the force, called the **moment** of the force, can be increased by:

- increasing the size of the force
- using a spanner with a longer handle.

Levers

A crowbar is a lever that can be used to raise one edge of a heavy object. Look at Figure 2.

The weight of the object is called the **load**, and the force the person applies to the crowbar is called the **effort**. The point about which the crowbar turns is called the **pivot** or the **fulcrum**. Using the crowbar, the effort needed to lift the same object is only a small fraction of its weight. The lever used in this way is an example of a **force multiplier** because the effort moves a much bigger load.

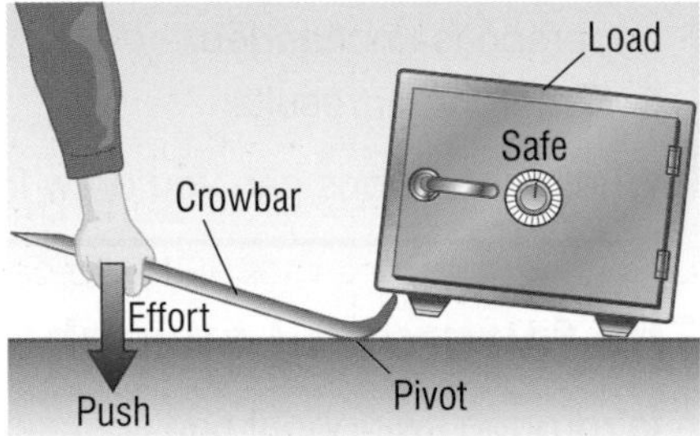

Figure 2 Using a crowbar

The line along which a force acts is called its **line of action**.

Did you know ... ?

A patient fitted with a replacement hip joint has to be very careful at first. A slight movement can cause a turning effect that pulls the hip joint apart.

Practical

Investigating the turning effect of a force

The diagram in Figure 3 shows one way to investigate the turning effect of a force. The weight *W* is moved along the metre ruler.

- How do you think the reading on the newtonmeter compares with the weight?

You should find that the newtonmeter reading (i.e. the force needed to support the ruler) increases if the weight is increased.

- How does this reading change as the weight is moved away from the pivot?

You should find that the newtonmeter reading increases as the weight is moved away from the pivot.

Safety: Protect feet and bench top from falling weights.

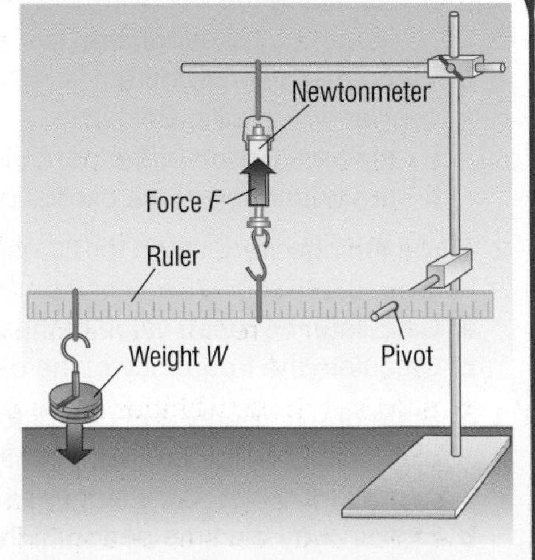

Figure 3 Investigating turning forces

We work out the moment of a force using this equation:

moment (newton metres, N m) = **force** (newtons, N) × **perpendicular distance from the line of action of the force to the pivot** (metres, m)

Maths skills

The word equation can be written using symbols, as follows:

$$\text{moment } M = F \times d$$

where:
M = moment in newton metres, N m
F = force in newtons, N
d = perpendicular distance from the line of action of the force to the pivot, in metres, m.

Look at Figure 4. The claw hammer is being used to remove a nail from a wooden beam.

- The applied force F on the claw hammer tries to turn it clockwise about the pivot.
- The moment of force F about the pivot is $F \times d$, where d is the perpendicular distance from the pivot to the line of action of the force.
- The effect of the moment is to cause a much larger force to be exerted on the nail.

Summary questions

1 **a** A force acts on an object and makes it turn about a fixed point. State the effect on the moment of the force if:
   i the force is increased without changing its line of action
   ii the force is doubled and the perpendicular distance from its line of action to the pivot is halved
   iii the force is halved and the perpendicular distance from its line of action to the pivot is halved.
 b A force of 72 N is exerted on a claw hammer of length 0.25 m, as shown in Figure 4. Calculate the moment of the force.

2 In Figure 1, a force is applied to a spanner to undo a nut. State whether the moment of the force is:
 a clockwise or anticlockwise
 b increased or decreased by:
   i increasing the force
   ii exerting the force nearer the nut.

3 Explain each of the following statements:
 a it is easier to remove a nail with a claw hammer if the hammer has a long handle
 b a door with rusty hinges is more difficult to open than a door of the same size with lubricated hinges.

4 A spanner of length 0.25 m is used to turn a nut as in Figure 1. Calculate the force that needs to be applied to the end of the spanner if the moment it exerts is to be 18 N m.

Maths skills

Worked example

A force of 50 N is exerted on a claw hammer of length 0.30 m, as shown in Figure 4. Calculate the moment of the force.

Solution

Moment = 50 N × 0.30 m = **15 N m**

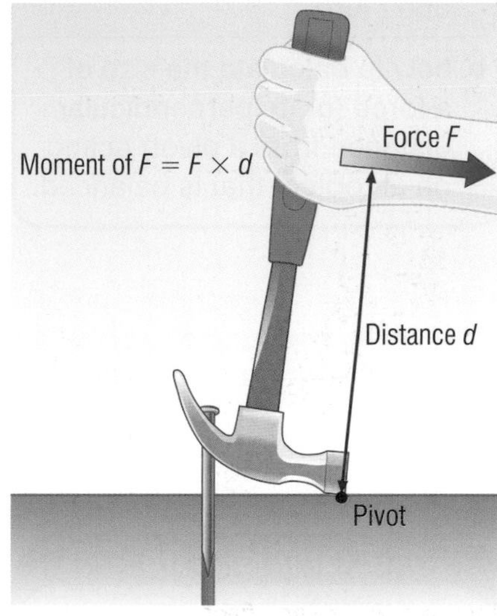

Figure 4 Using a claw hammer

Examiner's tip

Remember when calculating moments, it is the perpendicular distance from the pivot that is needed.

Be careful with units: you need to be consistent – Nm or Ncm.

Key points

- **The moment of a force is a measure of the turning effect of the force on an object.**
- **The moment of a force M about a pivot = $F \times d$, where d is the perpendicular distance from the line of action of the force, F, to the pivot.**
- **To increase the moment of a force, increase F or increase d.**

P6.4 Moments in balance

Learning objectives

After this topic, you should know:

- how to use our knowledge of forces and moments to explain why objects at rest don't turn
- how to calculate the size of a force (or its perpendicular distance from a pivot) acting on an object that is balanced.

A seesaw is an example in which clockwise and anticlockwise moments might balance each other out. The girl in Figure 1 sits near the pivot to balance her younger brother at the far end of the seesaw. Her brother is not as heavy as his big sister. She sits nearer the pivot than he does. That means her anticlockwise moment about the pivot balances his clockwise moment.

A model seesaw

Look at the model seesaw in Figure 2. The ruler is balanced horizontally by adjusting the position of the two weights. When it is balanced:

- the anticlockwise moment due to W_1 about the pivot = W_1d_1, and
- the clockwise moment due to W_2 about the pivot = W_2d_2

The anticlockwise moment due to W_1 = the clockwise moment due to W_2 and therefore:

$$\mathbf{W_1d_1 = W_2d_2}$$

Figure 1 The seesaw

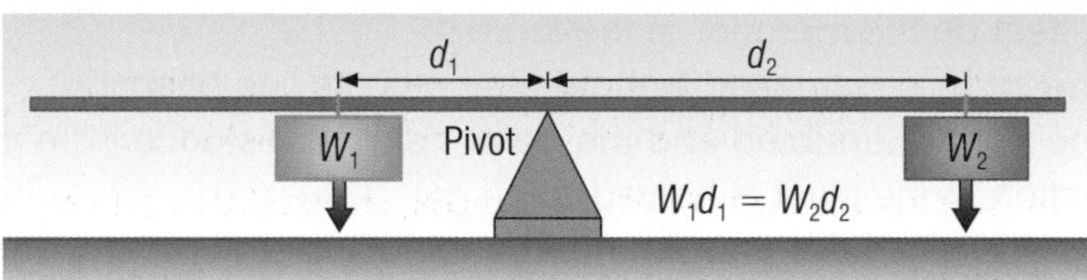

Figure 2 The principle of moments

The seesaw is an example of the **principle of moments**. This states that, for an object that is not turning:

the sum of all the clockwise moments about any point = the sum of all the anticlockwise moments about that point

Examiner's tip

Make sure the units in your calculations are consistent.

Practical

Measuring an unknown weight

You can use the arrangement in Figure 2 to find an unknown weight, W_1, if we know the other weight, W_2, and we measure the distances d_1 and d_2. Then you can calculate the unknown weight using the equation $W_1d_1 = W_2d_2$

Safety: Take care with falling weights.

Maths skills

Worked example

Calculate W_1 in Figure 2, if W_2 = 4.0 N, d_1 = 0.25 m and d_2 = 0.20 m.

Solution

Rearranging $W_1d_1 = W_2d_2$ gives

$$W_1 = \frac{W_2d_2}{d_1} = 4.0\,\text{N} \times \frac{0.20}{0.25\,\text{m}} = \mathbf{3.2\,N}$$

Practical

Measuring the weight of a beam

Figure 3 shows how we can measure the weight of a beam by balancing it off-centre using a known weight. The weight of the beam acts at its centre of mass, which is at distance d_0 from the pivot.

- The moment of the beam about the pivot = W_0d_0 clockwise, where W_0 is the weight of the beam.
- The moment of W_1 about the pivot = W_1d_1 anticlockwise, where d_1 is the perpendicular distance from the pivot to the line of action of W_1.

Applying the principle of moments gives $W_1d_1 = W_0d_0$.

So we can calculate W_0 if we know W_1 and distances d_1 and d_0.

Safety: Take care with falling weights.

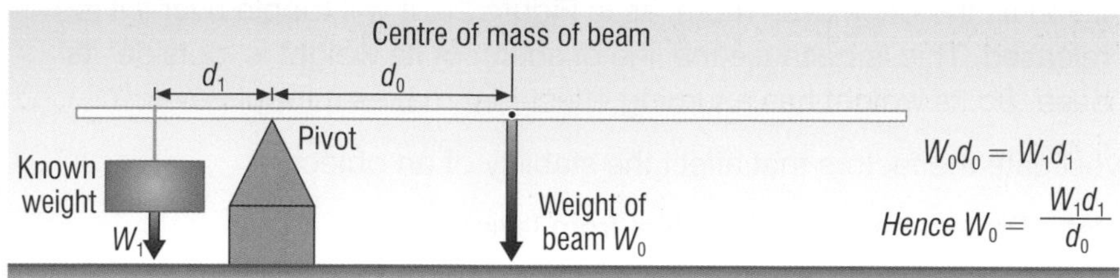

Figure 3 Finding the weight of a beam

Examiner's tip

In calculations, be systematic: write down the clockwise moments; then the anticlockwise moments; and then equate them.

If you have to move a heavy load, think beforehand about how to make the job easier. Figure 4 shows a wheelbarrow and a trolley being used to move a load. The load (weight W_0) is lifted and moved using a much smaller effort (force F_1).

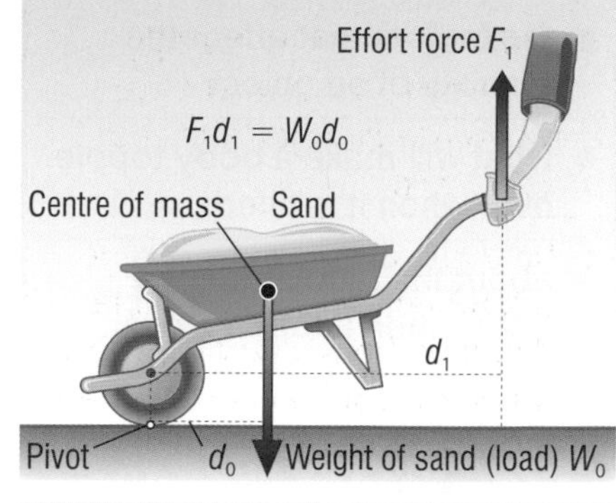

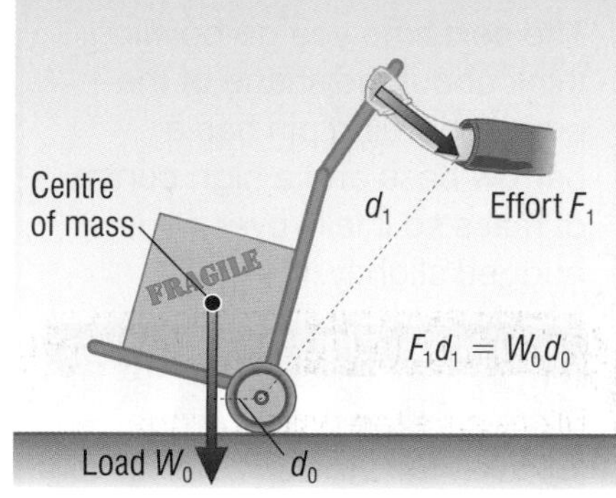

Figure 4 Using moments

Summary questions

1 a i In Figure 2, calculate W_1 if $W_2 = 6.0\,\text{N}$, $d_1 = 0.30\,\text{m}$ and $d_2 = 0.15\,\text{m}$.
   ii In Figure 3, calculate the weight of the beam above if $W_1 = 2.0\,\text{N}$, $d_1 = 0.15\,\text{m}$ and $d_0 = 0.25\,\text{m}$.
  b In Figure 4 explain why the effort is smaller than the load.

2 Dawn sits on a seesaw 2.50 m from the pivot. Jasmin balances the seesaw by sitting 2.00 m on the other side of the pivot.
  a Who is lighter, Dawn or Jasmin?
  b Jasmin weighs 425 N. What is Dawn's weight?
  c John now sits on the seesaw on the same side as Dawn at a distance of 0.50 m from the pivot. Jasmin stays in the same position as before. John's weight is 450 N. How far and in which direction should Dawn move to rebalance the seesaw?

3 For the balanced beam in the figure, work out its weight, W.

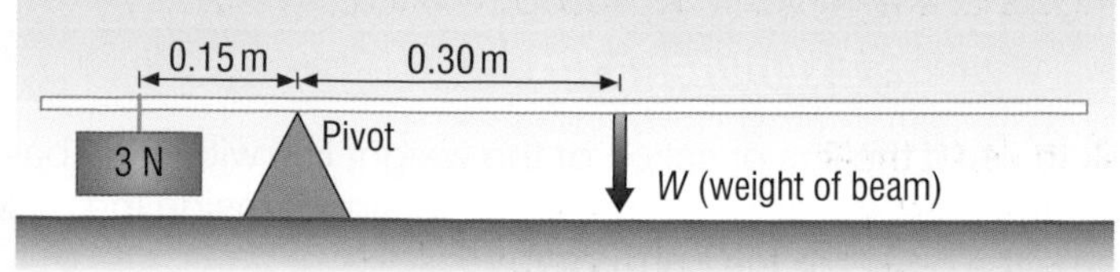

Key points

- If an object at rest doesn't turn, the sum of the anticlockwise moments about any point = the sum of the clockwise moments about that point.
- To calculate the force needed to stop an object turning we use the equation above. We need to know all the forces that don't act through the pivot and their perpendicular distances from the line of action to the pivot.

P6.5 Stability

Learning objectives

After this topic, you should know:

- the factors that affect the stability of an object
- what will make a body topple over when it is tilted
- about the moments on a body when it topples over.

Did you know ... ?

The next time you go bowling, think about the shape of the pins. A bowling pin has a narrow base and a high centre of mass so it falls over if it is nudged slightly.

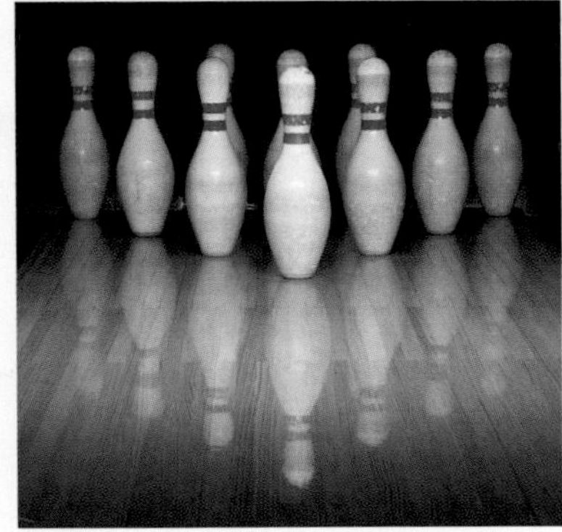

Figure 1 At the bowling alley

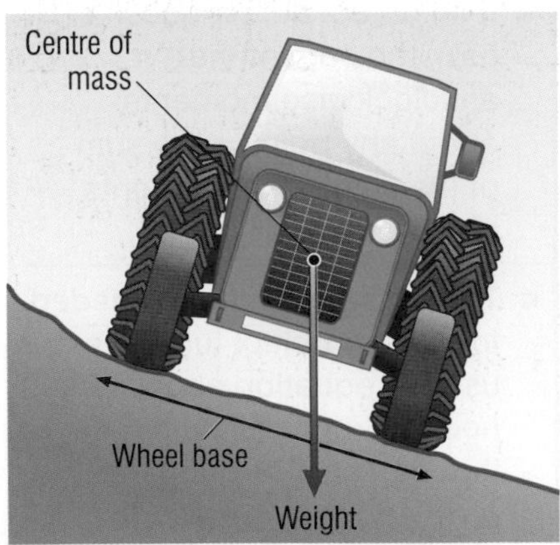

Figure 3 Forces on a tilting tractor

Practical

Tilting and toppling tests

How far can you tilt something before it topples over? Figure 2 shows how you can test your ideas using a tall box or a brick on its end.

- If you tilt the brick slightly, as in Figure 2a, and release it, the turning effect of its weight returns it to its upright position.
- If you tilt the brick more, you can just about balance it on one edge, as in Figure 2b. Its centre of mass is then directly above the edge on which it balances. Its weight has no turning effect in this position.
- If you tilt the brick even more, as in Figure 2c, it will topple over if it is released. This is because the line of action of its weight is 'outside' its base. So its weight has a turning effect that makes it topple over.

Investigate the factors that affect the stability of an object.

Safety: Protect bench top and feet from falling bricks.

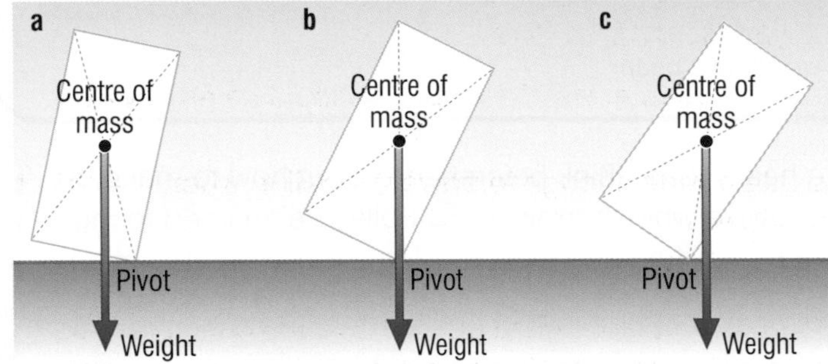

Figure 2 Tilting and toppling **a** tilted **b** at balance **c** toppled over

Stability and safety

Look around you and see how many objects could topple over. Bottles, table lamps and floor-standing bookcases are just a few objects that can easily topple over. Lots of objects are designed for stability so they can't topple over easily.

1 Tractor safety

Look at the tractor on a hillside in Figure 3. It doesn't topple over because the line of action of its weight acts within its wheelbase.

If it is tilted more, it will topple over when the line of action of its weight acts outside its wheelbase. This is because the moment about the lower wheel of the weight is clockwise.

The moment of the support force from the ground on the upper wheel is clockwise. So the resultant moment about the lower wheel makes it topple over.

Examiner's tip

In diagrams, look to see if the line of action of the weight lies within the base (stable) or outside the base (unstable). If the line of action is inside the base, the moment returns the object to the horizontal.

2 Bus tests

Look at the double-decker bus in Figure 4. It is being tested on a platform to see how much it can tilt without toppling. Such tests are important to make sure buses are safe to travel on, especially when they go round bends and on hilly roads. The explanation of why it topples over when the platform is tilted too much is the same as for the tractor.

Figure 4 A toppling test

3 High chairs

A high chair for a young infant needs to have a wide base. When the child is sitting in it, the centre of mass is above the seat. If the base were narrow and the child was strapped in, the chair would topple over when the child leant sideways too much. That's why a highchair should have a wide base (see Figure 5).

The chair topples over if the child's weight acts outside the chair base on one side. The high chair will turn about the position where the chair legs on that side are in contact with the floor.

Toppling happens if the moment of the child's weight about this position is greater than the moment of the chair's weight.

Figure 5 A high chair needs a wide base

How to stop an object toppling over

To prevent toppling, the centre of mass of the object should be as low as possible and:

- either the base should be wide enough to prevent toppling when the object is tilted or knocked sideways
- or the base should be bolted or clamped down.

Suppose an object is not clamped or bolted down. If the line of action of its weight lies outside its base, the object will topple over. This is because there is a **resultant moment** on the object. In other words, the object topples over because the sum of the clockwise moments about any point is **not** equal to the sum of the anticlockwise moments about that point.

Summary questions

1 a i Would a double-decker bus be more stable or less stable if everyone on it sat upstairs?

ii Why are stabiliser wheels fitted to bicycles designed for young children?

b Think of an object that needs to be redesigned because it is knocked over too easily. Sketch the object and explain how it could be redesigned to make it more stable.

2 A well-designed baby chair has a wide base and a low seat.

a If the base of a baby chair was too narrow, why would the chair be unsafe?

b Why is a baby chair with a low seat safer than one with a high seat?

3 a Explain why a tall plastic bottle is less stable when it is empty than when it is half-full of water, using the idea of moments.

b Explain why a traffic cone is difficult to knock over.

Key points

- **The stability of an object is increased by making its base as wide as possible and its centre of mass as low as possible.**
- **An object will tend to topple over if the line of action of its weight is outside its base.**
- **An object topples over if the resultant moment about its point of turning is not zero.**

P6.6 Circular motion

Learning objectives

After this topic, you should know:

- **why an object moving on a circular path at constant speed is accelerating**
- **what is meant by centripetal force and centripetal acceleration**
- **what affects the centripetal force on an object in circular motion.**

Figure 1 A hammer thrower

Practical

Testing circular motion

An object whirled round on the end of a string moves in a circle, as shown in Figure 2. The pull force on the object from the string changes the object's direction of motion.

What factors affect the centripetal force?

Safety: Spin objects responsibly and carefully.

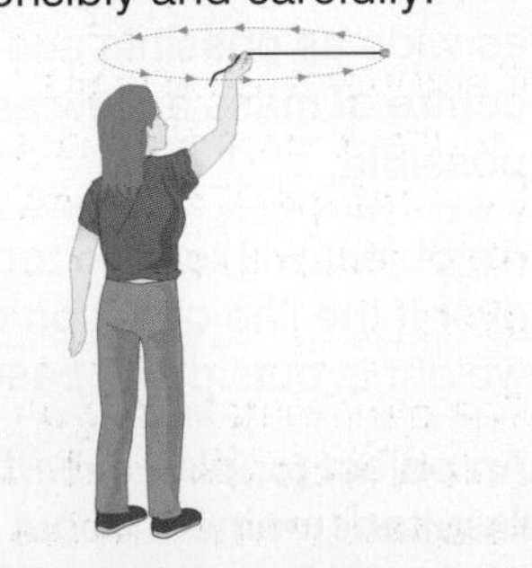

Figure 2 Whirling an object round

Fairground rides whirl you round in circles and make your head spin. But you don't need to go to a fairground to see objects moving in circles:

- a vehicle on a roundabout or moving round a corner travels on a circular path
- a satellite moving across the sky moves on a circular orbit round the Earth
- an athlete throwing the hammer spins round in a circle before releasing it.

For an object moving in a circle at constant speed, at any instant:

- the object's velocity is directed along a tangent to the circle
- its velocity changes direction as it moves round
- the change of velocity is towards the centre of the circle.

The object therefore accelerates continuously towards the centre of the circle. The acceleration changes the direction of motion of the object, not its speed.

Because the acceleration always acts towards the centre of the circle, we call it a **centripetal acceleration**.

So the resultant force on the object acts towards the centre of the circle.

Centripetal force

Any object moving in a circle must be acted on by a resultant force that acts towards the centre of the circle. We call the resultant force a **centripetal force** because it *always* acts towards the centre of the circle.

- The centripetal force on a vehicle moving round a roundabout is due to friction between the tyres and the road.
- A person in a capsule on the London Eye moves round at a constant speed. The centripetal force on the person acts towards the centre of the 'wheel'. This force is the resultant force of the person's weight and the support force from the floor.
- A fairground 'gravity wheel' starts off spinning horizontally. When it is spinning fast enough, the wheel is turned until it is spinning vertically. The riders are strapped to the inside of the wheel. **When a rider is at or near the top of the wheel**, the rider experiences a downward push from the wheel to keep him or her moving round the circle. The centripetal force is due to the weight of the rider and the downward push from the wheel on the rider.

a

b

Figure 3 **a** The London Eye **b** A fairground gravity wheel

Centripetal force factors

How is centripetal force affected by the speed of the object and the radius of the circle?

You could find out using a radio-controlled model car.

- If it goes too fast, the car will skid off in a straight line. The centripetal force needed increases if the speed is increased.
- If the circle is too small, the car will skid off. So the centripetal force needed increases if the radius of the circle is decreased.

How is the centripetal force affected by the mass of the object?

If you whirl a rubber bung round on the end of a thread, you can feel the force on it. If you tie another rubber bung on, you will find the force (for the same speed and radius) has increased. This shows that the greater the mass of the object, the greater the centripetal force is.

Figure 4 Centripetal force factors

Examiner's tip

Centripetal force is not a force in its own right. It is the name we give to the resultant force acting on an object moving round a circle.

Did you know ... ?

A spin drier contains a drum that rotates very fast. When the drum spins, the cylindrical sides of the drum keep the wet clothing inside the drum.

- The force of the drum on the clothing provides the necessary centripetal force to keep the wet clothing moving in a circle.
- Water from the wet clothing leaves the spinning drum through tiny holes in the sides of the drum.

Summary questions

1 The figure shows an object moving clockwise in a circle at constant speed.
Copy and complete **a** and **b** below using directions A, B, C or D, as shown in the figure.

A
D B
C
Object

a When the object is at the position shown, its velocity is in direction .... and the force on it is in direction ....

b When the object has moved round by 90° from the position shown in the diagram, its velocity is in direction .... and the force on it is in direction ....

2 In each of the following situations, a single force acts as the centripetal force. Match each situation with the force, **a** to **d**, that causes the circular motion.

electrostatic force   friction   gravity   pull (tension)

a A car travelling round a bend.
b A stone being whirled round on the end of a string.
c A planet moving round the Sun.
d An electron orbiting the nucleus of an atom.

3 **a** A student testing a model car measured its speed and found it could go round a bend at that speed without skidding off, as long as its speed was no more than 2.2 m/s. What would happen to the model car if the test were repeated:

i at a higher speed on the same bend? Give a reason for your answer.
ii at the same speed on a bend that was more curved? Give a reason for your answer.

b Explain why a high-speed railway track is sloped or banked where there is a curve.

Key points

- The velocity of an object moving in a circle at constant speed is continually changing because the object's direction is continually changing.
- Centripetal acceleration is the acceleration of an object moving round a circle towards the centre of the circle.
- Centripetal force is the resultant force that causes the centripetal acceleration of an object moving round a circle.
- The centripetal force on an object depends on its mass, its speed and the radius of the circle.

P6.7 Hydraulics

Learning objectives

After this topic, you should know:

- what is meant by pressure
- about the pressure in a liquid
- how a hydraulic system works
- how a hydraulic system can be used as a force multiplier.

Figure 1 Caterpillar tracks

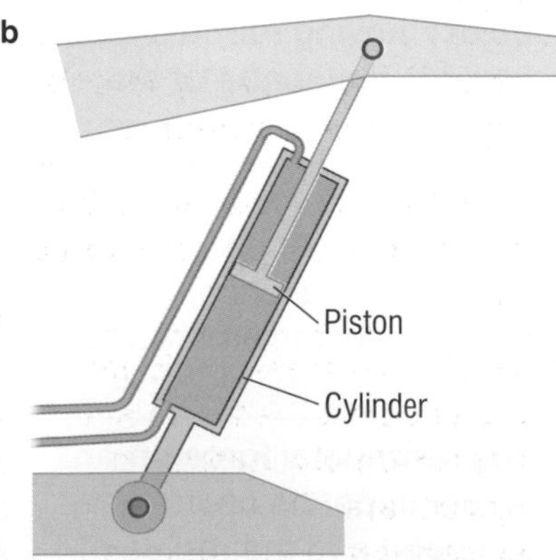

Figure 3 a A mechanical digger
b A hydraulic system

Caterpillar tracks fitted to vehicles are essential on sandy, muddy or snow-covered ground. The reason is that the contact area of the tracks on the ground is much greater than it would be if the vehicle had wheels instead. The tracks therefore reduce the pressure of the vehicle on the ground. That is because its weight is spread over a much greater contact area.

About pressure

Pressure is defined as force per unit area. The unit of **pressure** is the **pascal (Pa)**, which is equal to one **newton per square metre (N/m²)**.

For a force *F* acting evenly on a surface of area *A* at right angles to the surface, the pressure *p* on the surface is given by the equation:

$$\textbf{pressure} = \frac{\textbf{force}}{\textbf{area}}$$

Pressure in a liquid

The pressure in a liquid acts equally in all directions. Figure 2 shows how we can demonstrate this. There are several holes around the bottle at the same depth below the water level in the bottle. The jets from these holes hit the bench at the same distance from the bottle so they are at the same pressure.

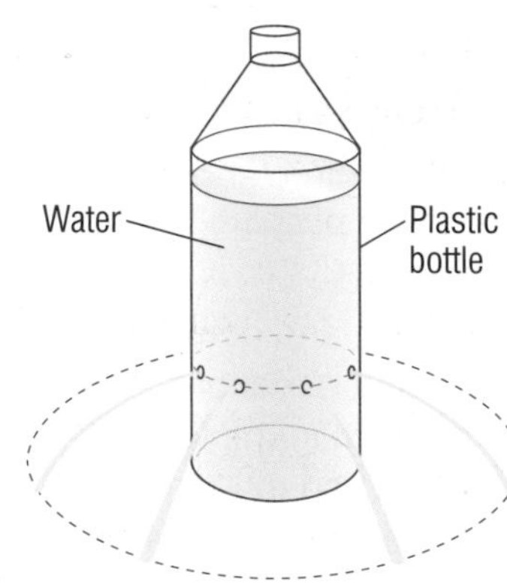

Figure 2 Pressure in a liquid at rest

Hydraulic machines

Mechanical diggers are used to remove large quantities of earth. An example is when soil has to be removed from above an underground pipe to reach the pipe. The 'grab' of the digger is operated by a **hydraulic pressure** system. The hydraulic system of a machine is its 'muscle power'.

Look at the hydraulic system shown in Figure 3b. Oil is pumped into the upper or lower part of the cylinder to make the piston move in or out of the cylinder.

Liquids are virtually incompressible. This means that its volume does not change when it is under pressure. This is why **a force exerted on one part of a liquid is transmitted to other parts of the liquid**. In other words, the pressure in a hydraulic system is transmitted through the oil.

A hydraulic car jack can be used to lift a car. When the handle is pressed down, oil is forced out of a narrow cylinder and into a wider cylinder. The pressure of the oil forces the piston in the wider cylinder outwards. As a result, the piston forces the pivoted lever to raise the car.

The force of a hydraulic system is much greater than the force applied to it. In Figure 4, the force F_1 applied to the system is called the **effort**. The force F_2 exerted by the system is called the **load**. As explained opposite, the load is moved by a much smaller effort.

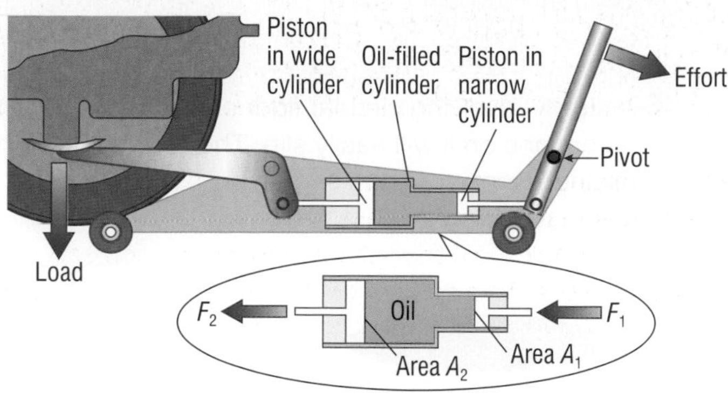

Figure 4
A hydraulic car jack

- The force F_1 acts on the piston in the narrow cylinder. This creates a pressure $p = \frac{F_1}{A_1}$ in the oil, where A_1 is the piston cross-sectional area.
- This pressure in the oil acts on the wide cylinder.
- The force F_2 on the wider piston $= p \times A_2$ where A_2 is the piston cross-sectional area.

  Therefore $F_2 = \frac{F_1}{A_1} \times A_2$

The force F_2 is therefore much greater than F_1 because area A_2 is much greater than area A_1. In other words, the hydraulic system is a **force multiplier**.

Examiner's tip

Remember that the same pressure ($p = F \div A$) is transmitted equally in all directions through a fluid. In a hydraulic system, you can amplify a force by using a narrow piston to create pressure on a wide piston.

Summary questions

1 Explain each of the following:

a When you do a handstand, the pressure on your hands is greater than the pressure on your feet when you stand upright.

b A sharp knife cuts more easily than a blunt knife.

2 a Write down as many machines as you can think of that are operated hydraulically.

b Figure 3a shows the arm of a mechanical digger.It is controlled by three hydraulic pistons called 'rams', labelled X, Y and Z.

i Explain why the arm is raised when compressed air is released into ram X so it extends.

ii State and explain what happens to the 'bucket' on the end of the arm when rams Y and Z are both extended.

3 The hydraulic lift shown in the figure is used to raise a vehicle so its underside can be inspected.

a The lift has 4 pistons, each of area 0.01 m², to lift the platform. The pressure in the system must not be greater than 5.0×10^5 Pa. The platform weight is 2000 N. Calculate the maximum load that can be lifted on the platform.

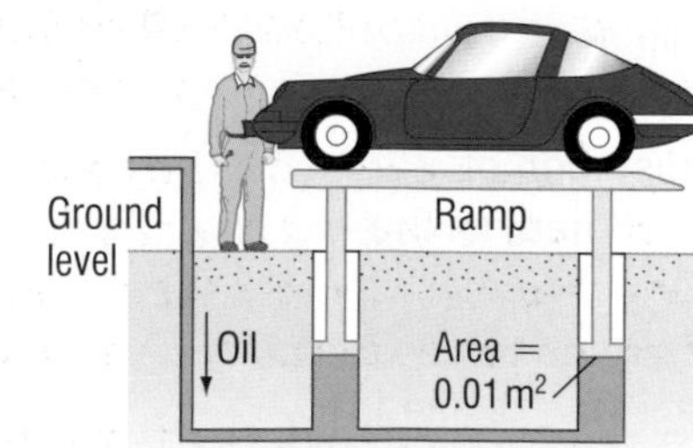

b When a vehicle is on the ramp, the pressure in the hydraulic system is 3.0×10^5 kPa. Calculate the weight of the vehicle.

Maths skills

We can write the equation for pressure using symbols as:

$$p = \frac{F}{A}$$

where:
p = pressure in pascals, Pa
F = force in newtons, N
A = cross-sectional area in square metres, m².

Note: Rearranging this equation gives

$$F = p \times A \text{ or } A = \frac{F}{p}$$

Maths skills

Worked example

A caterpillar vehicle of weight 12 000 N is fitted with tracks that have an area of 3.0 m² in contact with the ground. Calculate the pressure of the vehicle on the ground.

Solution

$$\text{Pressure} = \frac{\text{force}}{\text{cross-sectional area}} = \frac{12\,000\,\text{N}}{3.0\,\text{m}^2} = \mathbf{4000\,Pa}$$

Key points

- **Pressure is force divided by the area that the force acts on. The unit of pressure is the pascal (Pa), which is equal to 1 N/m².**
- **The pressure in a liquid acts equally in all directions.**
- **A hydraulic system uses the pressure in a liquid to exert a force.**
- **When the cross-sectional areas on the load side and effort side of a hydraulic system are different, the system can be used as a force multiplier.**

Summary questions

1 The bottle opener in the figure is being used to force the cap off a bottle.

a Explain why the force of the bottle opener on the cap is much larger than the force applied to the bottle opener by the person opening the bottle.

b In the figure, a force of 25 N had to be applied to force the cap off the bottle. By measuring the appropriate distances in the figure, estimate the force exerted by the bottle opener on the cap. Explain your working.

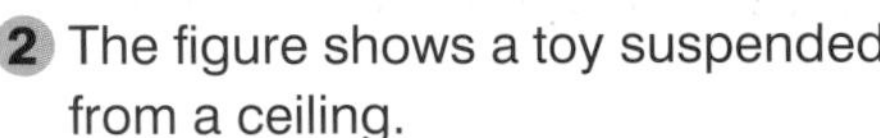

2 The figure shows a toy suspended from a ceiling.

a How would the stability of the toy be affected if the Sun were removed from it?

b The star on the toy has a weight of 0.04 N and is a distance of 0.30 m from the point **P** where the thread is attached to the toy. The crescent moon attached to the toy is at a distance of 0.20 m from **P**. Calculate the weight of the crescent.

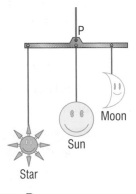

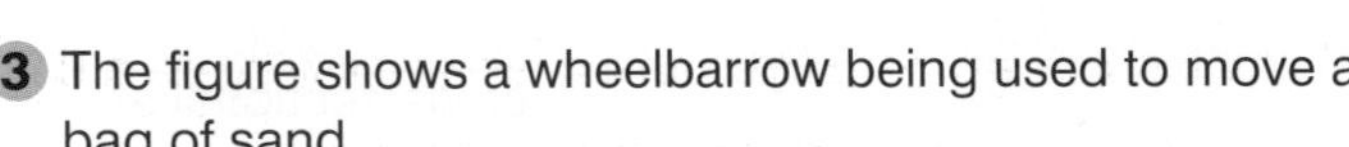

3 The figure shows a wheelbarrow being used to move a bag of sand.

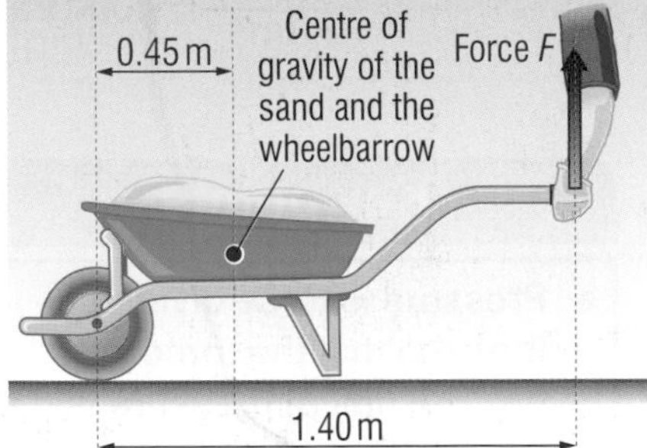

a Explain why the vertical force F needed to lift the wheelbarrow's legs off the ground is much less than the combined weight of the sand and the wheelbarrow.

b A vertical force of 48 N was needed to lift the wheelbarrow's legs off the ground. The force was applied to the handles at a horizontal distance of 1.40 m from the wheel axle. The centre of mass of the bag of sand and the wheelbarrow was a horizontal distance of 0.45 m from the wheel axle.

- **i** Calculate the combined weight of the bag of sand and the wheelbarrow.
- **ii** The weight of the wheelbarrow was 65 N. Calculate the weight of the sand.

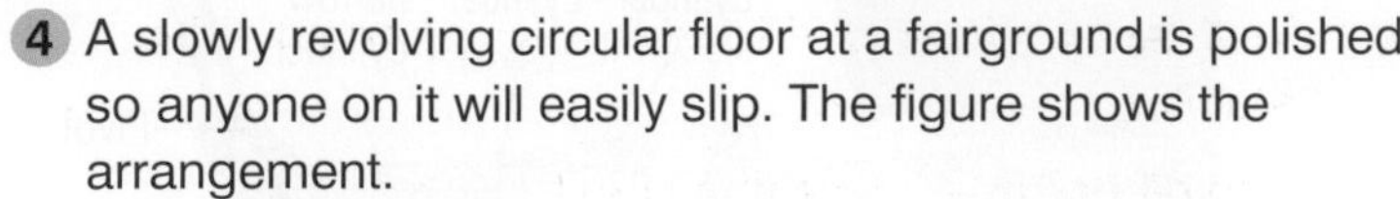

4 A slowly revolving circular floor at a fairground is polished, so anyone on it will easily slip. The figure shows the arrangement.

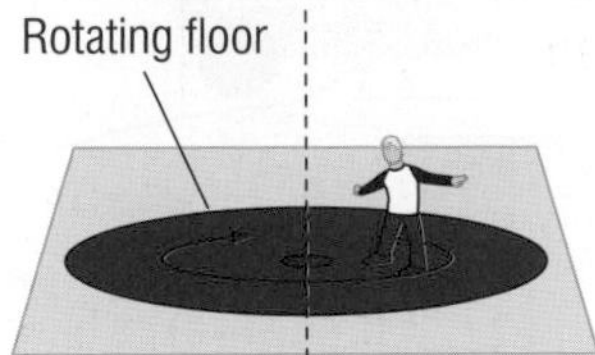

Explain why anyone standing on the revolving floor near its edge would find it difficult to stay on the floor as it revolves.

5 When the foot brake of a vehicle is applied, a force is applied to the piston in the master cylinder of the brake system, as shown in the figure.

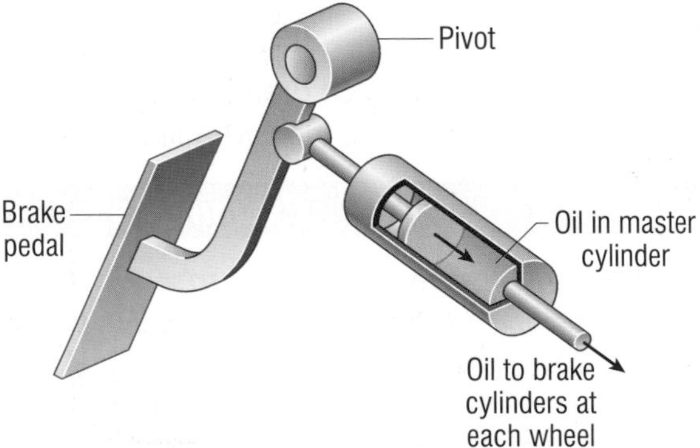

a Use the principle of moments to estimate the force that needs to be applied to the brake pedal in order to exert a force of 20 N on the piston in the cylinder.

b
- **i** The cylinder has a cross-sectional area of 0.0006 m^2. Calculate the pressure in the brake system when a force of 20 N is applied to the piston in the cylinder.
- **ii** The master cylinder is connected by pipes to a brake cylinder at each wheel. Each brake cylinder is much wider than the master cylinder. Explain why the force of the brake cylinder on each wheel is much greater than 20 N.

6 **a** What is meant by the time period of a pendulum?

b The data below shows the time taken for 10 cycles of a pendulum that consists of a metal bob on a thread.

30.5 s, 29.8 s, 30.6 s

- **i** Use this information to calculate the time period of the pendulum.
- **ii** If the length of the pendulum is shortened, state how its time period and its frequency would change.

c Describe how you would carry out an investigation to find out if the time period depends on the amplitude of the oscillations.

AQA Examination-style questions

1 a The centre of mass of an object is important to its stability.

The diagram shows a thin sheet of metal with two holes drilled in it.

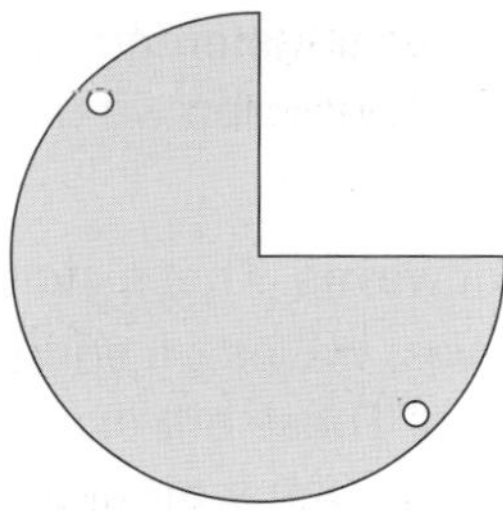

Describe how you would carry out an experiment to find the centre of mass of the sheet of metal. (QWC) (6)

b The diagrams show a table lamp. The lamp is at the end of an arm that can be rotated about the pivot.

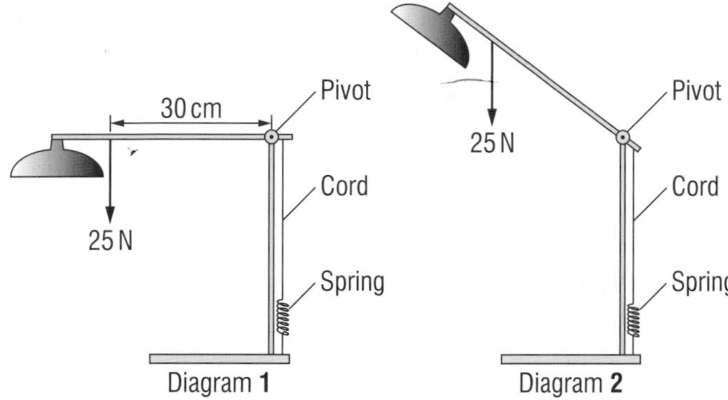

A cord is fixed near the right-hand end of the arm. The cord passes vertically downwards to a stretched spring. The centre of mass of the lamp and arm is 30 cm from the pivot. The weight of the lamp and arm is 2.5 N.

i From Diagram **1**, calculate the moment of the weight about the pivot. (2)

ii The arm is now raised, as in Diagram **2**. Explain what has happened to the tension in the spring. (4)

2 a The following article appeared in a newspaper.

Four-wheel-drive vehicle fails tilt test

A four-wheel-drive vehicle rolled over yesterday when travelling at 40 mph during stability tests carried out by the government. A motoring organisation had complained that the narrow-track, short-wheel-base vehicles are prone to rolling over. The government tests emphasised how passengers raise the centre of mass of the vehicle.

i Name **two** factors mentioned in the article that affect the stability of the vehicle. (2)

ii Why should stability tests be carried out by the government and not by the manufacturers? (1)

b The diagram shows a tilted vehicle.

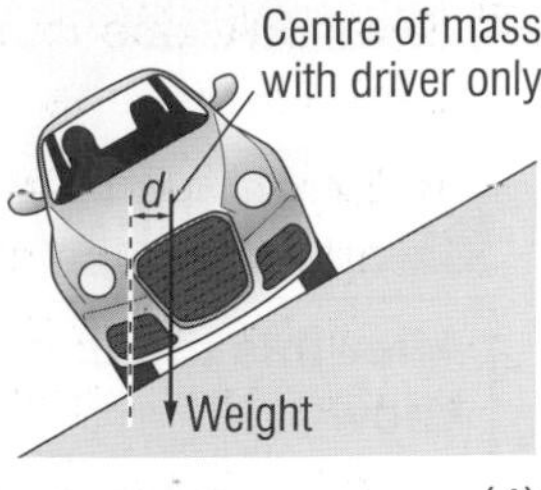

i The distance 'd' in the diagram, is 50 cm. The mass of the vehicle is 1200 kg. Calculate the moment of the weight about the point of contact with the road. (4)

ii Explain why the vehicle is stable. (3)

iii Explain how passengers make the vehicle less stable. (3)

3 A resultant force is needed to make an object travel in a circular path.

a What is the name of the resultant force? (1)

Choose a name from the list.

centrifugal centreline centripetal centrepoint

b What provides the resultant force for the following:

an electron orbiting a nucleus?
a planet orbiting the Earth? (2)

c In which direction does the resultant force act? (1)

d On what **three** factors does the size of the resultant force depend? (3)

4 The diagram shows a hydraulic braking system on a bike.

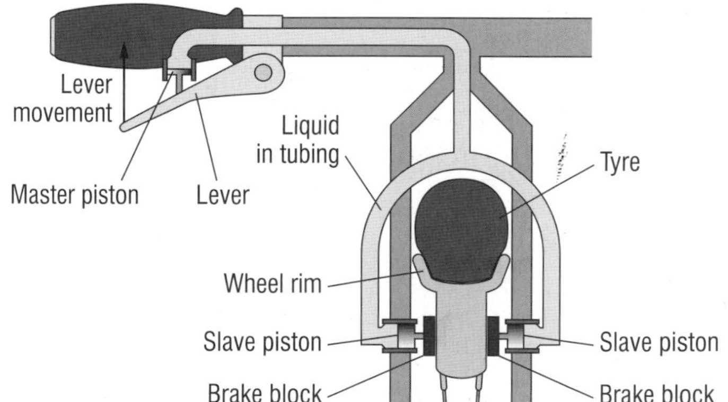

When the brake lever is pulled, the brake blocks push against the wheel rim.

a Why is a liquid used in the tubing? (2)

b There are two brake blocks, one on each side of the rim.

Explain how the system ensures that the same force is applied to each brake block. (2)

c The pressure exerted by the brake blocks on the rim is 250 N/cm^2. The area of a brake block is 2 cm^2. Calculate the total force on the wheel rim. (3)

d Explain how this hydraulic system is a force multiplier. (3)

P7.1 The nature of waves

Learning objectives

After this topic, you should know:

- what waves can be used for
- what transverse waves are
- what longitudinal waves are
- which types of waves are transverse and which are longitudinal.

Figure 1 Waves in water are examples of mechanical waves

Waves transfer energy without transferring matter. We can also use waves to transfer information, for example when we use a mobile phone or listen to the radio.

There are different types of waves. These include:

- sound waves, water waves, waves on springs and ropes and seismic waves produced by earthquakes. These are examples of **mechanical waves**, which are vibrations that travel through a **medium** (a substance).
- light waves, radio waves and microwaves. These are examples of **electromagnetic waves**, which can all travel through a vacuum at the same speed of 300 000 kilometres per second. No medium is needed.

Practical

Observing mechanical waves

- Figure 2 shows how we can make waves on a rope by moving one end up and down.

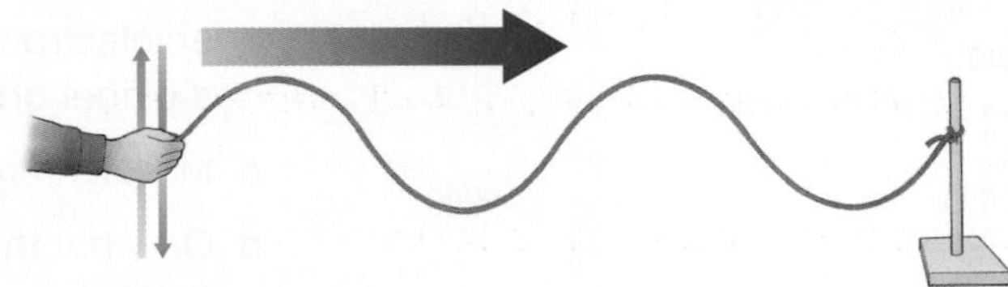

Figure 2 Transverse waves

Tie a ribbon to the middle of the rope. Move one end of the rope up and down. You will see that the waves move along the rope but the ribbon doesn't move along the rope – it just moves up and down. This type of wave is known as a **transverse wave**. We say that the ribbon **vibrates** or **oscillates**. This means it moves repeatedly between two positions. When the ribbon is at the top of a wave, we say it is at the **peak** (or crest) of the wave.

Repeat the test with the slinky. You should observe the same effects if you move one end of the slinky up and down.

However, if you push and pull the end of the slinky as shown in Figure 3, you will see a different type of wave, known as a **longitudinal wave**. Notice that there are areas of **compression** (coils squashed together) and areas of **rarefaction** (coils spread further apart) moving along the slinky.

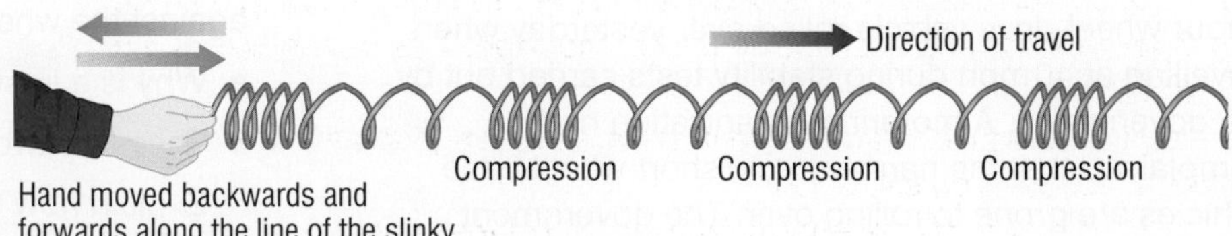

Figure 3 Making longitudinal waves on a slinky

- How does the ribbon move when you send **longitudinal** waves along the slinky?

Safety: Handle the slinky spring carefully.

links

For more information on electromagnetic waves, see 8.1 'The electromagnetic spectrum'.

Transverse waves

Imagine we send waves along a rope which has a white spot painted on it. The spot would be seen to move up and down without moving along the rope. In other words, the spot would oscillate **perpendicular** (at right angles) to the direction in which the waves are moving. The waves on a rope are called **transverse waves** because the vibrations (called oscillations) are up and down or from side to side. All electromagnetic waves are transverse waves.

The oscillations of a transverse wave are perpendicular to the direction in which the waves transfer energy.

Longitudinal waves

The slinky spring in Figure 3 is useful to demonstrate how sound waves travel. When one end of the slinky is pushed in and out repeatedly, vibrations travel along the spring. These oscillations are parallel to the direction in which the waves transfer energy, along the spring. Waves that travel in this way are called **longitudinal waves**.

Sound waves are longitudinal waves. When an object vibrates in air, it makes the air around it vibrate as it pushes and pulls on the air. The oscillations (**compressions** and **rarefactions**) that travel through the air are sound waves. The oscillations are along the direction in which the wave travels.

The oscillations of a longitudinal wave are parallel to the direction in which the waves are travelling.

Therefore, mechanical waves can be transverse or longitudinal.

links

For more information on sound, see 7.4 'Diffraction' and 9.1 'Sound'.

Examiner's tip

- Make sure that you understand the difference between transverse waves and longitudinal waves.
- Remember that electromagnetic waves are transverse and sound waves are longitudinal.

Did you know ... ?

When we pluck a guitar string, it oscillates because we send transverse waves along the string. The oscillating string sends sound waves into the surrounding air. The sound waves are longitudinal.

Summary questions

1 a What is the difference between a longitudinal wave and a transverse wave?

b State **one** example of:

i a transverse wave

ii a longitudinal wave.

c When a sound wave passes through air, what happens to the air particles at a compression?

2 A long rope with a knot tied in the middle lies straight along a smooth floor. A student picks up one end of the rope. This sends waves along the rope.

a Are the waves on the rope transverse or longitudinal waves?

b What can you say about:

i the direction of energy transfer along the rope?

ii the movement of the knot?

3 a Describe how to use a slinky spring to demonstrate to a friend the difference between longitudinal waves and transverse waves.

b A blue slinky spring has one of its coils painted red. Describe the motion of the red coil when longitudinal waves travel along the slinky.

Key points

- **We use waves to transfer energy and to transfer information.**
- **Transverse waves oscillate perpendicular to the direction of energy transfer of the waves. All electromagnetic waves are transverse waves.**
- **Longitudinal waves oscillate parallel to the direction of energy transfer of the waves. Sound waves are longitudinal waves.**
- **Mechanical waves, which need a medium (a substance) to travel through, may be transverse or longitudinal waves.**

P7.2 Measuring waves

Learning objectives

After this topic, you should know:

- what is meant by the amplitude, frequency and wavelength of a wave
- the relationship between the speed, wavelength and frequency of a wave
- how to use the wave speed equation in calculations.

Examiner's tip

A common error is to think that the amplitude is the distance from the top of the crest to the bottom of the trough (but that is twice the amplitude).

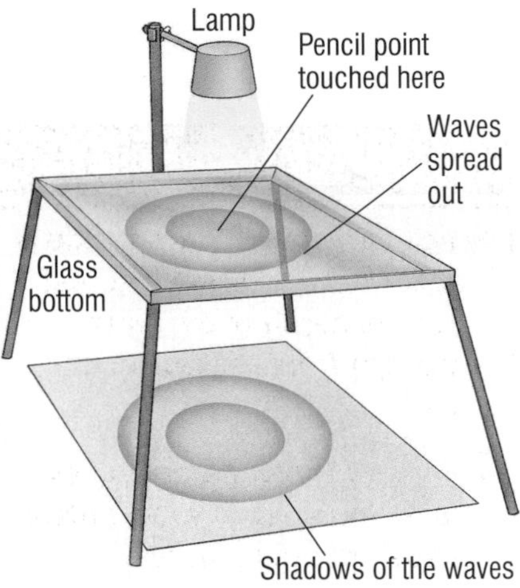

Figure 2 The ripple tank

Maths skills

We can write the wave speed equation as $v = f \times \lambda$
where
v = speed
f = frequency
λ = wavelength.
Note: The Greek letter λ is pronounced 'lambda'.

We need to measure waves if we want to find out how much energy or information they carry. Figure 1 shows a snapshot of waves on a rope. The **crests**, or peaks, are at the top of the wave. The **troughs** are at the bottom. They are equally spaced.

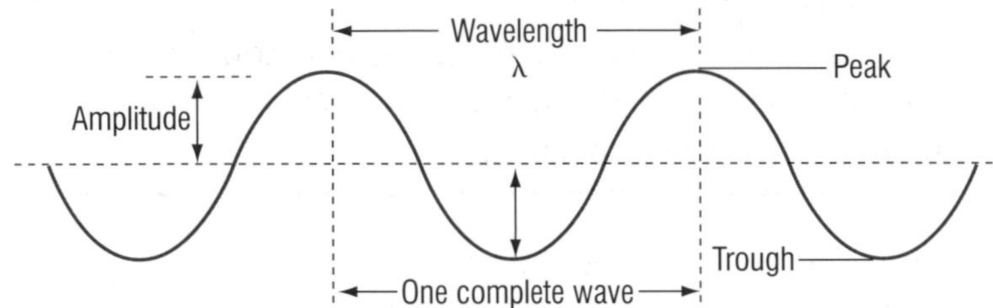

Figure 1 Waves on a rope

- The **amplitude** of the waves is the height of the wave crest (or the depth of the wave trough) from the middle, which is the position of the rope at rest.
- **The bigger the amplitude of the waves, the more energy the waves carry.**
- The **wavelength** of the waves is the distance from one wave crest to the next crest.

Frequency

If we made a video of the waves on the rope, we would see the waves moving steadily across the screen. The number of wavecrests passing a fixed point every second is the **frequency** of the waves.

The unit of frequency is the **hertz** (Hz). One wave crest passing each second is a frequency of 1 Hz.

Wave speed

Figure 2 shows a ripple tank, which is used to study water waves in controlled conditions. We can make straight waves by moving a ruler up and down on the water surface in a ripple tank. Straight waves are called **plane** waves. The waves all move at the same speed and stay the same distance apart.

The **speed** of the waves is the distance travelled by a wave crest (or a wave trough) every second.

For example, sound waves in air travel at a speed of 340 m/s. In 5 seconds, sound waves travel a distance of 340 m/s × 5 s = **1700 m**.

For waves of constant frequency, the speed of the waves depends on the frequency and the wavelength as follows:

wave speed	= **frequency**	× **wavelength**
(metres/second, m/s)	(hertz, Hz)	(metres, m)

Examiner's tip

- Be careful with powers of ten when using $v = f \times \lambda$
- Frequencies can have high positive powers of ten – e.g. light waves can have a frequency of 5×10^{14} Hz.
- Wavelengths can have high negative powers of ten – e.g. X-rays can have a wavelength of 1×10^{-12} m.

Practical

Making straight (plane) waves

To measure the speed of the waves:

Use a stopwatch to measure the time it takes for a wave to travel from the ruler to the side of the ripple tank.

Measure the distance the waves travel in this time.

Use the equation 'speed = distance ÷ time' to calculate the speed of the waves.

Observe the effect on the waves of moving the ruler up and down faster. More waves are produced every second and they are closer together.

- Find out if the speed of the waves has changed.

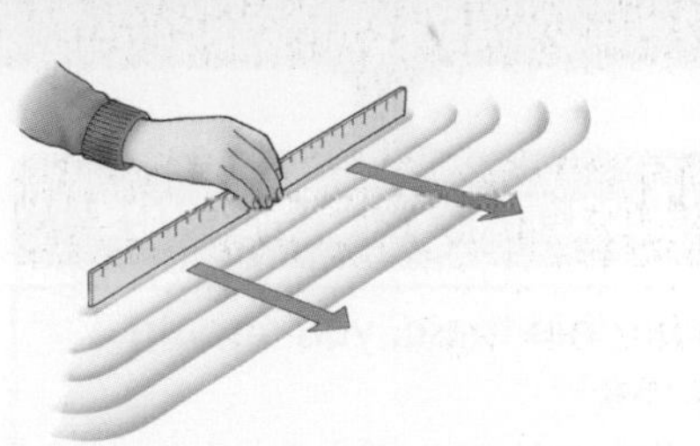

Figure 3 Making water waves

To understand what the wave speed equation means, look at Figure 4. The surfer is riding on the crest of some unusually fast waves.

Suppose the frequency of the waves is 3 Hz and the wavelength of the waves is 4.0 m.

- At this frequency, 3 wave crests pass a fixed point once every second (because the frequency is 3 Hz).
- The surfer therefore moves forward a distance of 3 wavelengths every second, which is 3 × 4.0 m = 12 m.

The speed of the surfer is therefore **12 m/s**.

This speed is equal to the frequency × the wavelength of the waves: $v = f \times \lambda$.

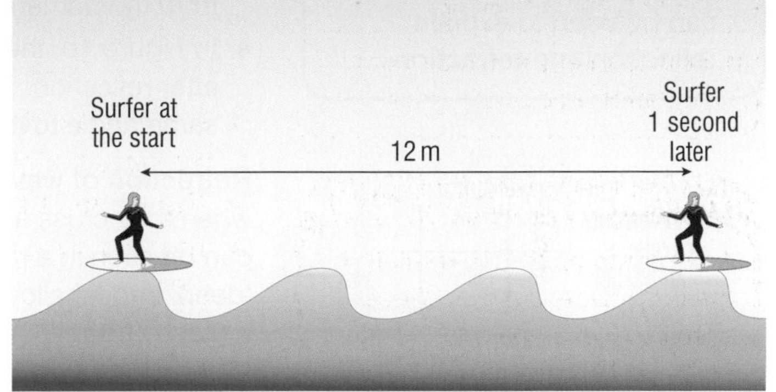

Figure 4 Surfing

Summary questions

1 **a** Use a millimetre ruler to measure the amplitude and the wavelength of the waves in Figure 1.

b What is meant by the frequency of a wave?

2 The figure shows a snapshot of a wave travelling from left to right along a rope.

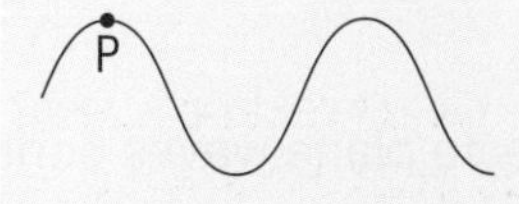

a Copy the figure and mark on your diagram:

i one wavelength

ii the amplitude of the waves.

b Describe the motion of point P on the rope when the wave crest at P moves along by a distance of one wavelength.

3 **a** A speedboat on a lake sends waves travelling across a lake at a frequency of 2.0 Hz and a wavelength of 3.0 m. Calculate the speed of the waves.

b If the waves had been produced at a frequency of 1.0 Hz and travelled at the speed calculated in **a**:

i what would be their wavelength?

ii calculate the distance travelled by a wave crest in 60 seconds.

Key points

- For any wave, its amplitude is the height of the wave crest (or the depth of the wave trough) from the position at rest.
- For any wave, its frequency is the number of wave crests passing a point in one second.
- For any wave, its wavelength is the distance from one wave crest to the next wave crest. This is the same as the distance from one wave trough to the next wave trough.
- Wave speed = frequency × wavelength:

$$v = f \times \lambda$$

P7.3 Reflection and refraction

Learning objectives

After this topic, you should know:

- the patterns of reflection and refraction of plane waves in a ripple tank
- what causes refraction
- how the behaviour of waves can be used to explain reflection and refraction.

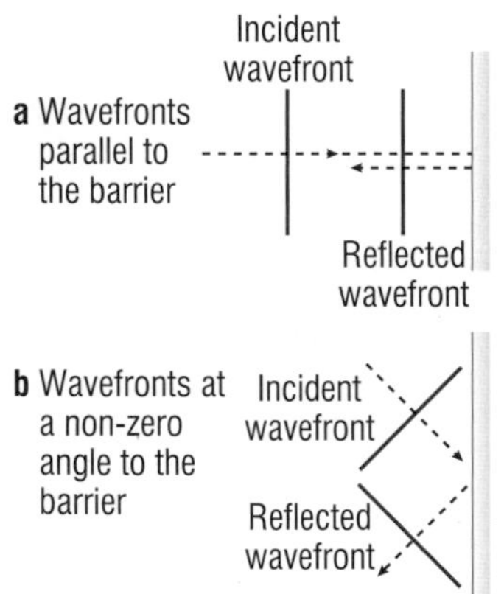

Figure 1 Reflection of plane waves

Practical

A reflection test

Use a ruler to create and direct plane waves at a straight barrier, as shown in Figure 1. Find out if the reflected waves are always at the same angle to the barrier as the incident waves. You could align a second ruler with the reflected waves and measure the angle of each ruler to the barrier. Repeat the test for different angles.

Investigating waves using a ripple tank

Reflection of plane waves can be investigated using the ripple tank shown in Figure 2 on page 68. Plane (i.e. straight) waves, produced by repeatedly dipping a ruler in water, are directed at a metal barrier in the water. These waves are referred to as the incident waves to distinguish them from the reflected waves. The incident waves are reflected by the barrier.

Figures 1a and b each show a wavefront before and after hitting the barrier.

- In Figure 1a, the incident wavefront is parallel to the barrier as it approaches the barrier. It is still parallel to the barrier after reflection as it travels away from the barrier.
- In Figure 1b, the incident wavefront is not parallel to the barrier before or after reflection. The reflected wavefront moves away from the barrier at the same angle to the barrier as the incident wavefront.

Refraction of waves is the change of the direction in which they are travelling when they cross a boundary between one medium and another medium. This can be seen in a ripple tank when water waves cross a boundary between 'deep' and 'shallow' water. An area of shallow water can be created by placing a glass or transparent plastic plate flat in the water. The water above the plate is shallower than the water outside the plate area. Plane waves are directed at a non-zero angle to a boundary. The wavefronts change direction as they cross the boundary, as shown in Figure 2.

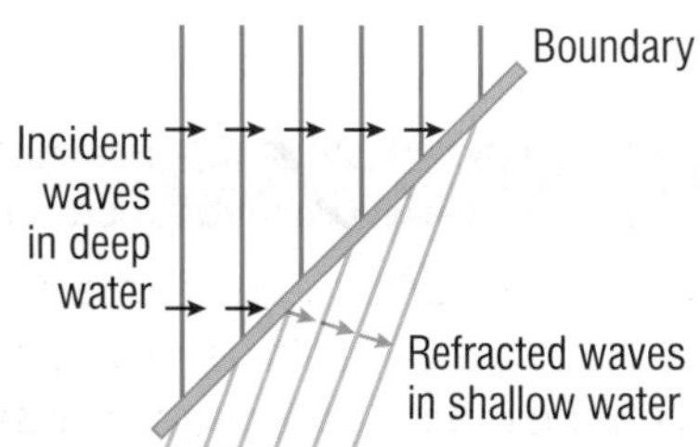

Figure 2 Refraction

Practical

Refraction tests

Use a vibrating beam to create plane waves continuously in a ripple tank containing a transparent plastic plate.

Arrange the plate so the waves cross a boundary between the deep and shallow water. The water over the plate needs to be very shallow.

- **At a non-zero angle to a boundary.** The waves change direction when they cross the boundary. Find out if plane waves change direction towards or away from the boundary when they cross from deep to shallow water.
- **Parallel to a boundary.** The waves cross the boundary without changing direction. However, their speed changes.

Find out if the waves travel slower or faster when they cross the boundary. As we shall see later in this topic, this change of speed explains why the waves are refracted when they cross a boundary at a non-zero angle.

Explaining reflection and refraction

To explain how a wavefront moves forward, imagine that each tiny section creates a wavelet that travels forward, as shown in Figure 3. The wavelets move forward together to recreate the wavefront that created them.

Refraction: When plane waves cross a boundary at a non-zero angle to the boundary they slow down, and each wavefront changes its direction. When the wavelets reach the boundary they line up with the previous wavelets that have crossed the boundary. These wavelets form a refracted wavefront.

In Figure 3, the wavefronts move more slowly after they have crossed the boundary. They are not as far from the boundary as they would have been if their speed had not changed. So the refracted wavefronts are at a smaller angle to the boundary than the incident wavefronts.

Reflection: When plane waves reflect from a flat barrier, the reflected waves are at the same angle to the barrier as the incident waves. When each point on the wavefront reaches the barrier, it creates a wavelet moving away from the barrier. This wavelet lines up with the previous 'reflected' wavelets to form a reflected wavefront moving away from the barrier. All parts of a wavefront move at the same speed. This means that the reflected wavefront is at the same angle to the barrier as the incident wavefront.

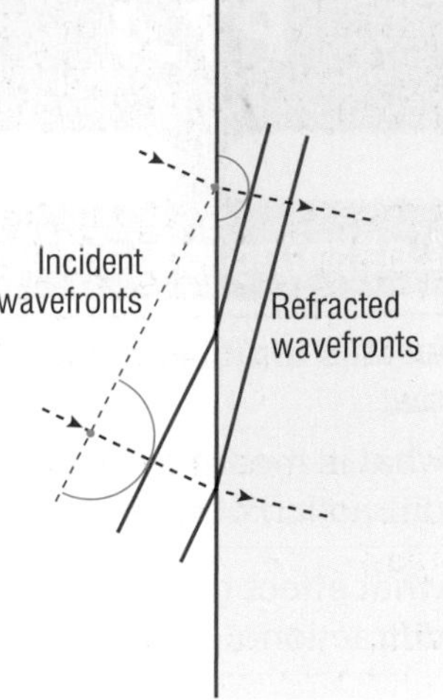

Figure 3 Explaining refraction

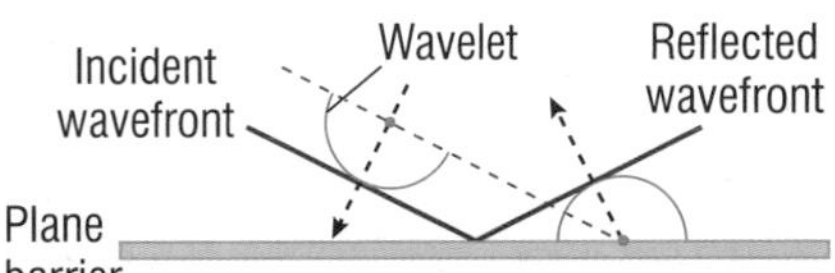

Figure 4 Explaining reflection

Summary questions

1 a When plane waves reflect from a straight barrier, what can be said about the angle of each reflected wavefront to the barrier and the angle of each incident wavefront to the barrier?

b When waves speed up on crossing a boundary, what can be said about the angle of each refracted wavefront to the boundary and the angle of each incident wavefront to the boundary?

2 Copy the figure, which shows plane waves passing from deep to shallow water where they move slower than in the deep water. Draw some refracted wavefronts, indicating their direction.

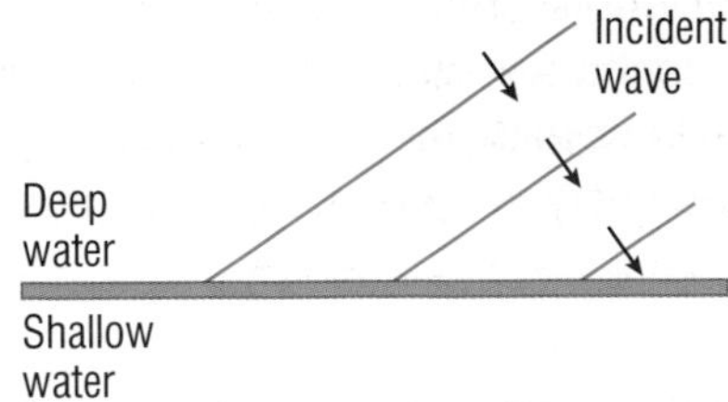

3 Sea waves rolling up a sandy beach are not reflected.

a Why are the sides of a ripple tank sloped?

b What would happen if the sides of a ripple tank were vertical instead of sloped?

Key points

- Plane waves reflected from a straight barrier reflect at the same angle to the barrier as the incident waves.
- Refraction is the change in direction of waves caused by a change in their speed when they cross a boundary between one medium and another.

P7.4 Diffraction

Learning objectives

After this topic, you should know:

- what is meant by the diffraction of waves
- what effect gap width has on diffraction
- what effect diffraction has on TV and radio reception in hilly areas.

Did you know ... ?

Sea waves entering a harbour through a narrow entrance spread out after passing through the entrance. Look out for this diffraction effect the next time you visit a harbour.

Figure 2 Image of two colliding galaxies taken by the Hubble Space Telescope

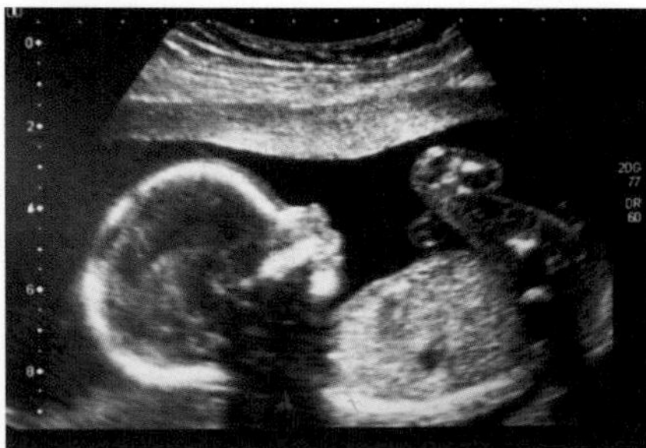

Figure 3 An ultrasound scan of a baby in the womb

links

To learn more about ultrasound, see 9.3 'Ultrasound'.

Diffraction is the spreading of waves when they pass through a gap or move past an obstacle. The waves that pass through the gap or past the edges of the obstacle can spread out. Figure 1 shows waves in a ripple tank spreading out after they pass through two gaps. The effect is most noticeable if the wavelength of the waves is similar to the width of the gap. You can see from Figure 1 that:

- the narrower the gap, the more the waves spread out
- the wider the gap, the less the waves spread out.

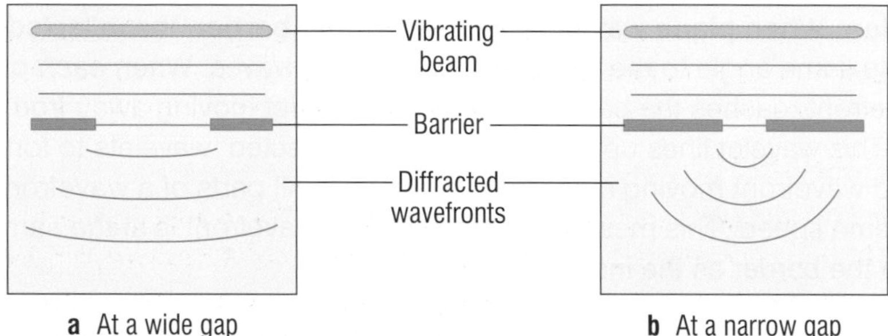

Figure 1 Diffraction of waves by a gap: **a** A wide gap **b** A narrow gap

Practical

Investigating diffraction

Use a ripple tank as in Figure 1 to direct plane waves continuously at a gap between two metal barriers. Notice that the waves spread out after they pass through the gap. In other words, they are diffracted by the gap.

Change the gap spacing and observe the effect on the diffraction of the waves that pass through the gap. You should find that the diffraction of the waves increases as the gap is made narrower, as shown in Figure 1.

Diffraction details

Diffraction of light is important in any optical instrument. The Hubble Space Telescope in its orbit above the Earth has provided amazing images of objects far away in space. Its focusing mirror has a diameter of 2.4 m. When light passes through the Hubble Space Telescope only a small amount of diffraction occurs, because the telescope is so wide. So its images are very clear and detailed. This allows astronomers to see separate images of objects that are far too close to be seen as separate objects using a narrower telescope.

Diffraction of ultrasound waves is an important factor in the design of an ultrasound scanner. Ultrasound waves are sound waves at frequencies above the range that can be heard by the human ear. An ultrasound scan can be taken of a baby in the womb. The ultrasound waves spread out from a hand-held transmitter and then reflect from the tissue boundaries inside the womb. If the transmitter is too narrow, the waves spread out too much and the image is not very clear.

Demonstration

Tests using microwaves

A microwave transmitter and a detector can be used to demonstrate diffraction of microwaves. The transmitter produces microwaves of wavelength 3.0 cm.

1 Place a metal plate between the transmitter and the detector across the path of the microwaves. Microwaves can still be detected behind the metal plate. This is because some microwaves diffract round the edge of the plate.

- Why do the microwaves not go through the metal plates?

2 Place two metal plates separated by a gap across the path of the microwaves, as shown in Figure 4. The microwaves pass through the gap but not through the plates. When the detector is moved along an arc centred on the gap, it detects microwaves that have spread out from the gap.

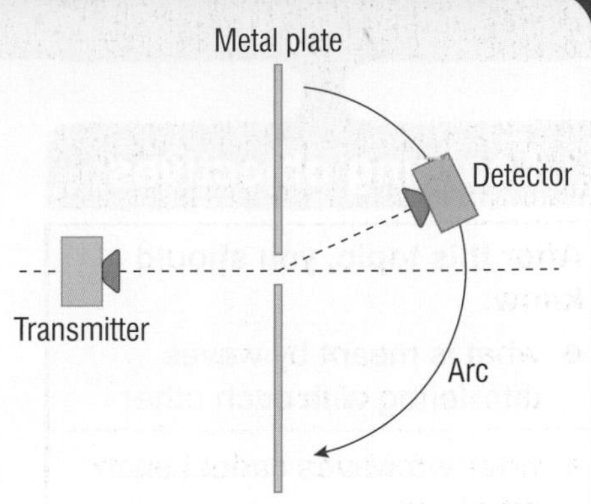

Figure 4 Using microwaves (top view)

When the gap is made wider, the microwaves passing through the gap spread out less. The detector needs to be nearer the centre of the arc to detect the microwaves.

Signal problems

People in hilly areas often have poor TV reception. The signal from a TV transmitter mast is carried by radio waves. If there are hills between a TV receiver and the transmitter mast, the signal may not reach the receiver. The radio waves passing the top of a hill are diffracted by the hill but they do not spread enough behind the hill.

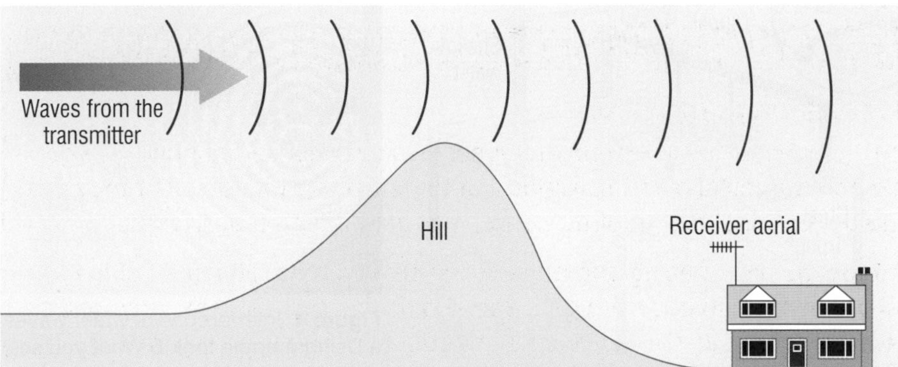

Figure 5 Poor reception

Examiner's tip

- Remember that diffraction can be through a hole OR round an obstacle.
- The smaller the hole, the greater the diffraction.
- Diffraction is most noticeable when the hole is the same size as the wavelength of the wave.

Summary questions

1 Waves spread out when they pass through a gap.
   a What can be said about the wavelength of the waves before and after passing through the gap?
   b What happens to the waves if the gap is made:
      i narrower?   ii wider?

2 a State what is meant by diffraction.
   b A transmitter mast transmits TV signals.
      i Explain why the TV reception can be poor in hilly areas.
      ii The transmitter also transmits electromagnetic waves of a much longer wavelength that carry the signal from a radio station. Explain why this signal can be detected at some locations where the TV signal cannot be detected.

3 A small portable radio inside a room can be heard all along a corridor that runs past the room when its door is open. Explain why it can be heard by someone in the corridor who is not near the door.

Key points

- **Diffraction is the spreading out of waves when they pass through a gap or around the edge of an obstacle.**
- **The narrower a gap, the greater the diffraction.**
- **If radio waves do not diffract enough when they go over hills, radio and TV reception will be poor.**

P7.5 Interference

Learning objectives

After this topic, you should know:

- what is meant by waves interfering with each other
- how two waves cancel each other out
- how two waves reinforce each other.

Television programmes can sometimes be disturbed by poor reception if a low-flying aircraft passes nearby. TV signals are carried by radio waves. Radio waves reflected from the aircraft arrive at the TV aerial at the same time as radio waves direct from the TV transmitter. The two sets of waves might cancel out or reinforce each other at different places. This effect is called **interference**.

Figure 1 shows two waves travelling along a rope towards each other. One wave is a **crest** and the other is a **trough**. They meet and pass through each other. When they meet, they **cancel** each other out at that instant.

Figures 2 and 3 show what happens when a crest meets a crest or when a trough meets a trough. The waves reinforce each other to make a larger crest in Figure 2 or a larger trough in Figure 3.

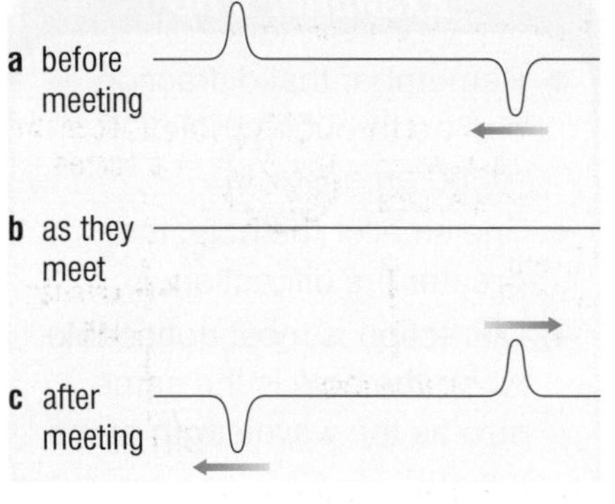

Figure 1 A crest meets a trough

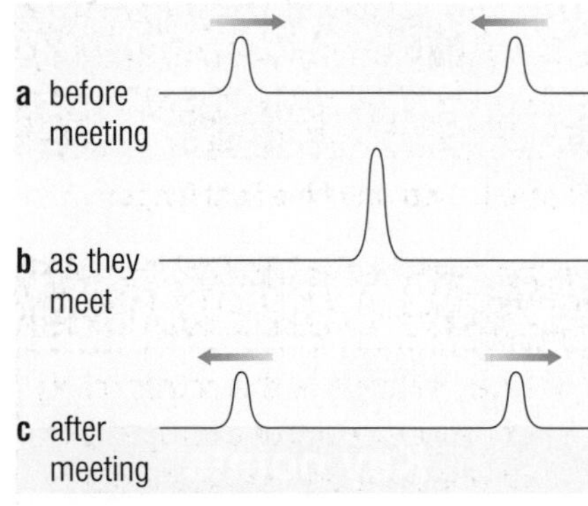

Figure 2 A crest meets a crest

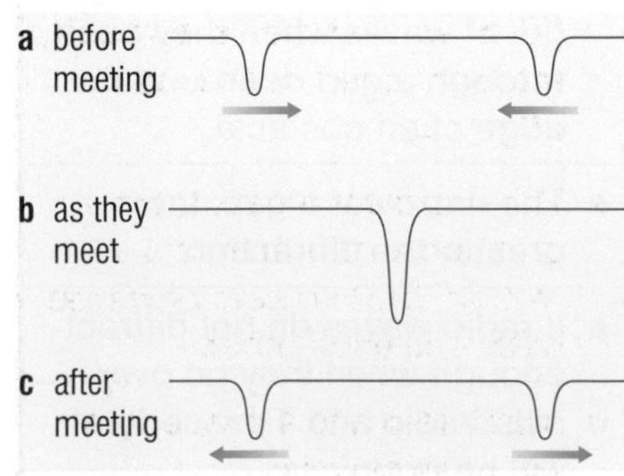

Figure 3 A trough meets a trough

Observing the interference of water waves

All types of wave can be made to interfere. We can do this by creating two sets of waves. Figure 4 shows what happens in a ripple tank where two sets of water waves overlap.

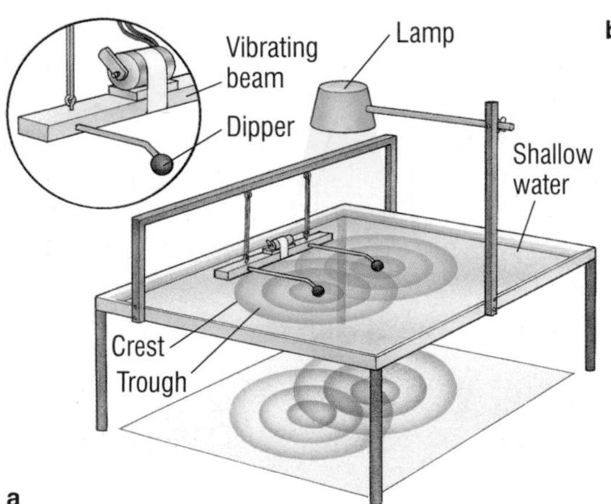

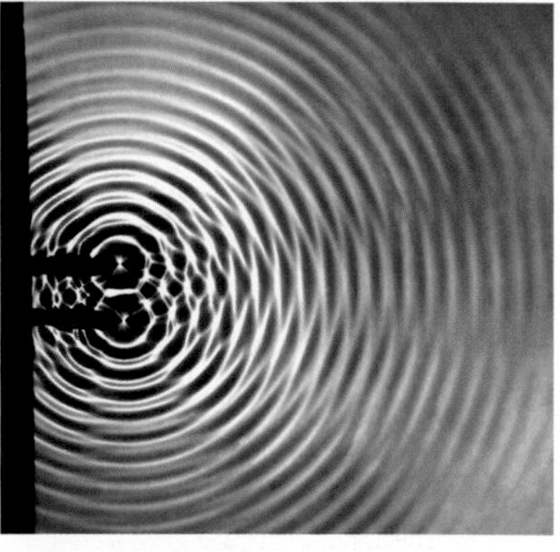

Figure 4 Interference of water waves **a** Using a ripple tank **b** What you see

Each identical set of waves is created by making a dipper vibrate on the water surface. Each dipper creates crests and troughs as expanding circles on the water surface. Adjacent crests and troughs from the same dipper are always half a wavelength apart.

Interference occurs where the two identical sets of waves overlap.

- Cancellation occurs where crests from one dipper cancel troughs from the other dipper. Gaps in the waves are seen where this happens.
- Reinforcement occurs where crests from each dipper meet or where troughs meet. This happens between the gaps.

Notice that if the dippers are moved closer together, the gaps move further apart.

Examiner's tip

- When waves overlap crest to crest OR trough to trough, constructive interference/reinforcement takes place.
- When waves overlap crest to trough, destructive interference/cancellation takes place.

Using microwaves to demonstrate interference

Figure 5 shows how an interference pattern is produced using microwaves. The microwaves from the transmitter are diffracted as a result of passing through the slits. Interference occurs where the diffracted waves overlap.

By moving a detector connected to a voltmeter, the points of cancellation and reinforcement can be located from the detector signal. In Figure 5, the detector is at a point where a trough from slit A meets a crest from slit B. The waves cancel each other out at this point, so no signal is detected here.

In general, at any point **P**:

- if the difference in the distances to each slit is a whole number of wavelengths + *an extra half wavelength*, the waves always **cancel** each other out. This is because a crest from one slit arrives at **P** at the same time as a trough from the other slit. Figure 6 shows this.
- if the difference in the distances to each slit is a whole number of wavelengths, the waves always **reinforce** each other. This is because:
  - a crest from one slit arrives at **P** at the same time as a crest from the other slit
  - a trough from one slit arrives at **P** at the same time as a trough from the other slit.

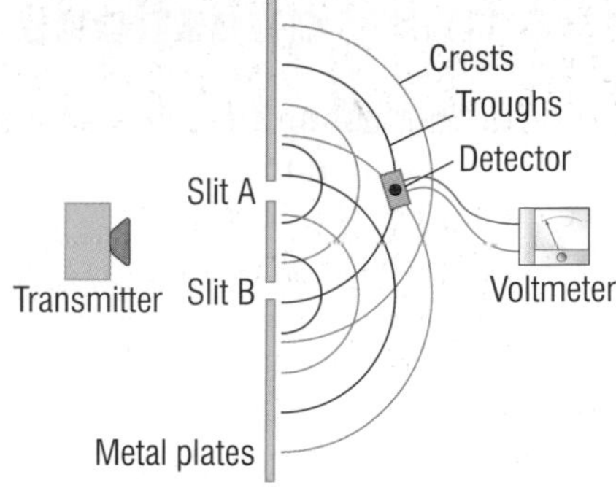

Figure 5 Using microwaves to investigate interference

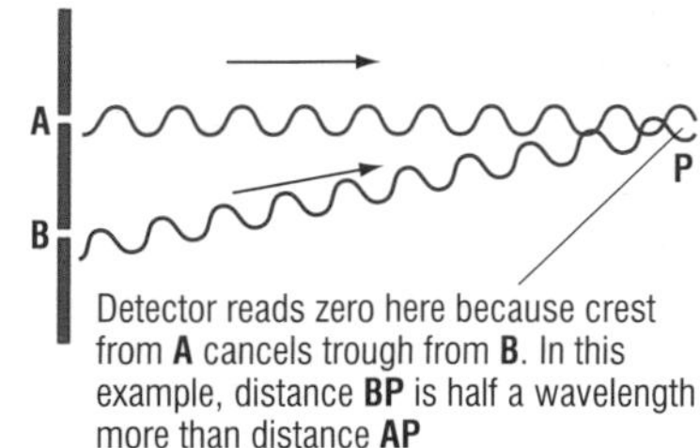

A
B
P
Detector reads zero here because crest from **A** cancels trough from **B**. In this example, distance **BP** is half a wavelength more than distance **AP**

Figure 6 Interference rules

Practical

Investigating interference using light

Interference of light from a filament lamp can be seen by using double slits in the path of light from a narrow source, as shown in Figure 7. Light from the single slit passes through each of the double slits. Where the light from the double slits overlaps, interference occurs and alternate bright and dark fringes parallel to the slits are seen. This shows that light consists of waves.

- Dark fringes are seen where the crests from one of the double slits meet the troughs from the other double slit.
- Bright fringes are seen where crests and crests meet or where troughs and troughs meet.
- The outer bright fringes are tinged with the colours of the spectrum. This is because the light from a filament lamp contains all the colours of the spectrum.
- **If a coloured filter is placed in the path of the light from the lamp**, all the other colours of the spectrum are stopped by the filter. So the colour of the bright fringes will be the same as that of the filter. Figure 8 shows the result of using a red filter and a blue filter separately. Notice that the spacing of the red fringes is greater than that of the blue fringes. This is because red light has a longer wavelength than blue light so the red fringes are further apart than the blue fringes.

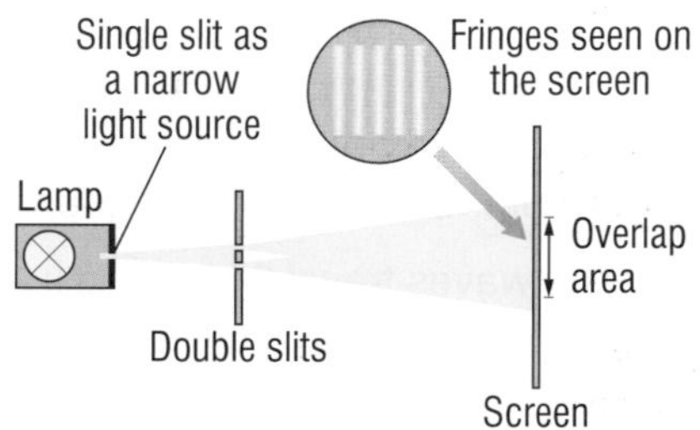

Figure 7 Interference of light

Figure 8 Red and blue light fringes

Summary questions

1 When a metal tea tray is moved near the aerial of a portable television, the television reception is affected. Why do you think this happens?

2 In Figure 5, the detector is moved to a point that is an equal distance away from each of the slits. Explain why the detector signal strength is a maximum at this position.

3 In the double slits experiment, how would the pattern of light fringes change if:

a the double slits had been replaced by double slits closer together?

b a green filter had been used instead of a red filter?

Key points

- **Interference is the reinforcing or cancelling out of any type of wave when two identical sets of waves overlap.**
- **When a crest meets a trough, the two waves cancel each other out.**
- **When a crest meets a crest, or when a trough meets a trough, the two sets of waves reinforce each other.**
- **Interference is a property of all types of wave.**

Summary questions

1 **a** The figure shows transverse waves on a string. Copy the diagram and label distances on it to show what is meant by:

i the wavelength

ii the amplitude of the waves.

b Explain the difference between a transverse wave and a longitudinal wave.

c Give **one** example of:

i a transverse wave

ii a longitudinal wave.

2 A speedboat on a lake creates waves that make a buoy bob up and down as shown in the figure.

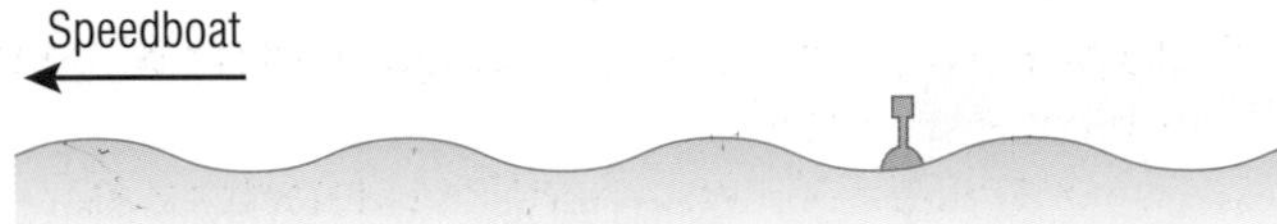

a The buoy bobs up and down three times in one minute. Calculate the frequency of the waves.

b The waves travel 24 metres in one minute. Calculate the speed of the waves in metres per second.

c Calculate the wavelength of the waves.

3 **a** When a wave is refracted at a boundary where its speed is reduced, state what change, if any, happens to:

i its wavelength

ii its frequency.

b When a wave is reflected, what change, if any, happens to:

i its wavelength?

ii its frequency?

iii its speed?

4 **a** Copy and complete the diagram in the left-hand figure to show the reflection of a straight wavefront at a straight reflector.

b Copy and complete the diagram in the right-hand figure to show the refraction of a straight wavefront at a straight boundary as the wavefront moves from deep to shallow water.

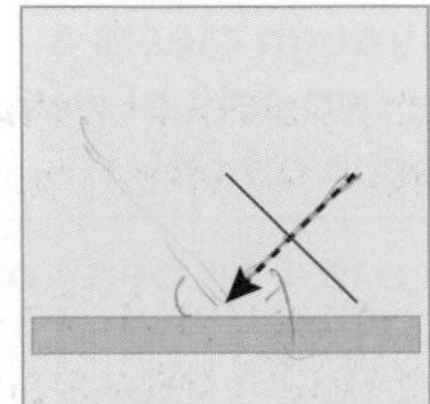

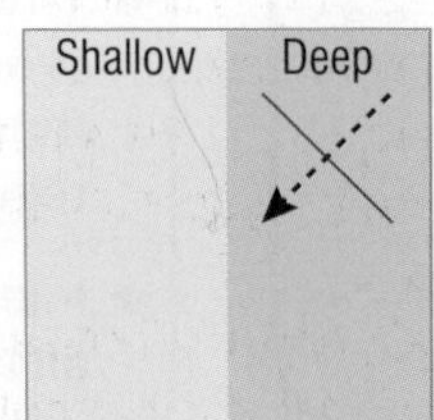

5 **a** Calculate the frequency in air of electromagnetic waves of wavelength 3.0 m. The speed of electromagnetic waves in a vacuum is 300 000 km/s.

b The signal from a radio station is carried by radio waves of wavelength 3.0 m. Explain why the signal may be difficult to receive in hilly locations.

6 The diagram shows straight waves directed at a gap in a barrier.

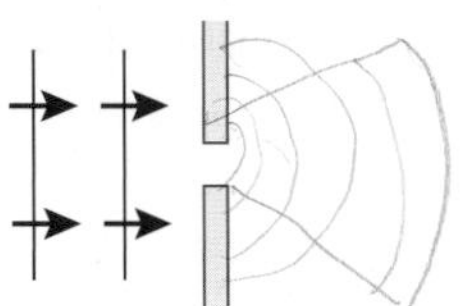

a Copy the diagram and draw **two** waves showing their shape and spacing after they have passed through the gap in the barrier.

b **i** What is the name for the change in the shape of the waves?

ii How would the shape of the waves differ if the gap had been wider?

7 The figure shows waves in a ripple tank before and after passing through two narrow gaps **A** and **B**. Wave crests are shown as solid lines, and wave troughs are shown as dashed lines.

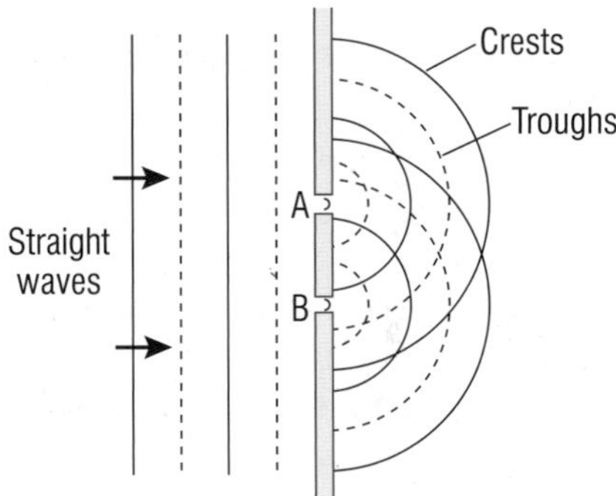

a Use the words below to complete the sentences **i** to **v**:

cancellation *diffraction* *interference* *reinforcement*

i .... occurs as the waves pass through the gaps.

ii .... occurs where the waves overlap.

iii .... occurs where crests and troughs meet.

iv .... occurs where crests and crests meet.

v .... occurs where troughs and troughs meet.

b State **one** difference in the pattern of overlapping waves if:

i the gaps had been further apart

ii the wavelength of the waves had been longer.

AQA Examination-style questions

1 The diagrams, **A**, **B**, **C** and **D**, show four processes that can happen to waves.

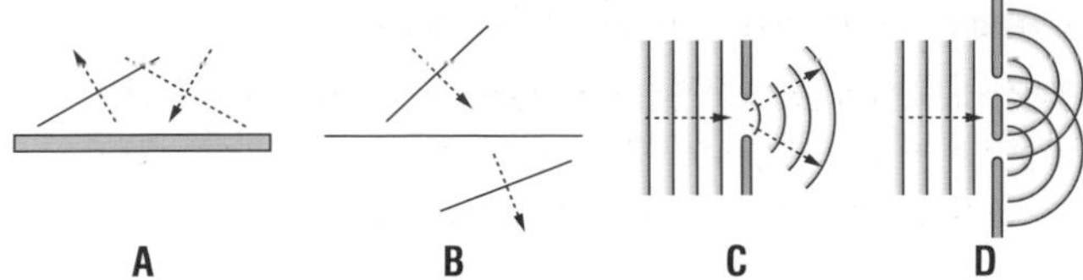

a Which diagram, **A**, **B**, **C** or **D**, shows:

i diffraction?

ii interference?

iii reflection?

iv refraction? (4)

b A man was driving his car on a long straight motorway. He was listening to the car radio.

The music became louder and softer at regular intervals. There are two radio transmitters, one at either end of the motorway.

i Explain why the music became louder and softer when he was listening to the car radio. (5)

ii Explain why he would not hear the music becoming louder and softer when he was listening to a CD in the car. (2)

2 The diagrams, **X** and **Y**, show two types of waves travelling along a slinky spring.

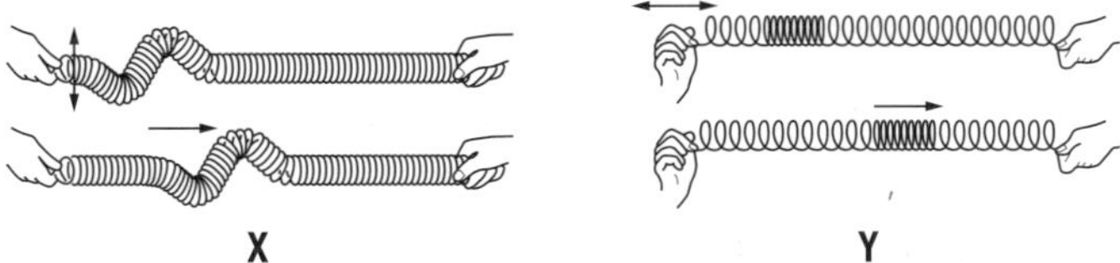

a **i** What type of wave is shown in diagram **X**? (1)

ii What type of wave is shown in diagram **Y**? (1)

iii Describe the oscillations of the slinky spring that cause the wave shown in diagram **X**. (1)

iv Describe the oscillations of the slinky spring that cause the wave shown in diagram **Y**. (1)

b Light, sound and radio waves can all transfer information.

What are the similarities and differences in the way that light, sound and radio waves travel? (QWC) (6)

3 **a** A student showed three waves, **P**, **Q** and **R**, on an oscilloscope screen.

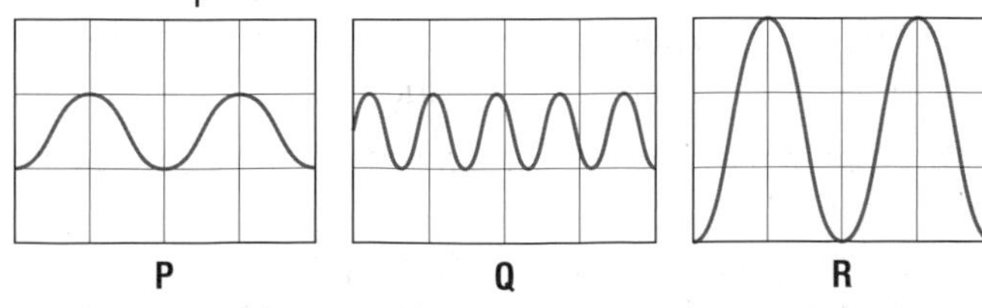

Which wave, **P**, **Q** and **R**,

i has the largest amplitude? (1)

ii has the highest frequency? (1)

b The behaviour of waves is often demonstrated by teachers using microwaves with a wavelength of 3 cm. Microwaves have a wave speed of 3×10^8 m/s. Calculate the frequency of these microwaves. (4)

c A teacher demonstrated the interference of microwaves using the apparatus shown below.

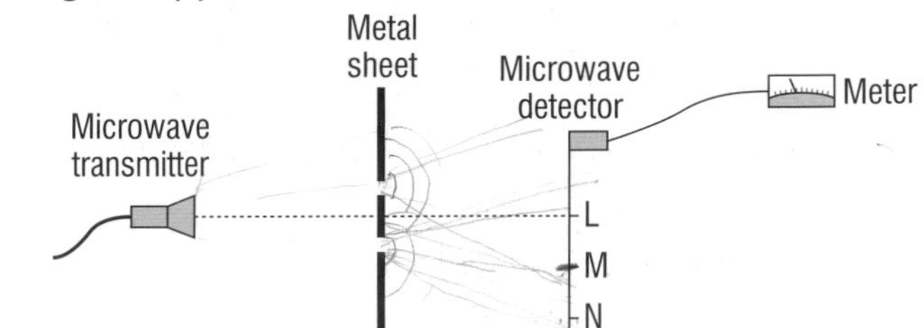

The meter read zero when the detector was at **M** but had a high reading when the detector was at **N**.

i Explain why the meter read zero when the detector was at **M**. (3)

ii Explain why the meter had a high reading when the detector was at **N**. (2)

iii What would the meter read if the detector was placed at **L**?

Choose an answer from the list.

higher than N ***lower than N*** ***zero*** (1)

4 Waves can spread through gaps.

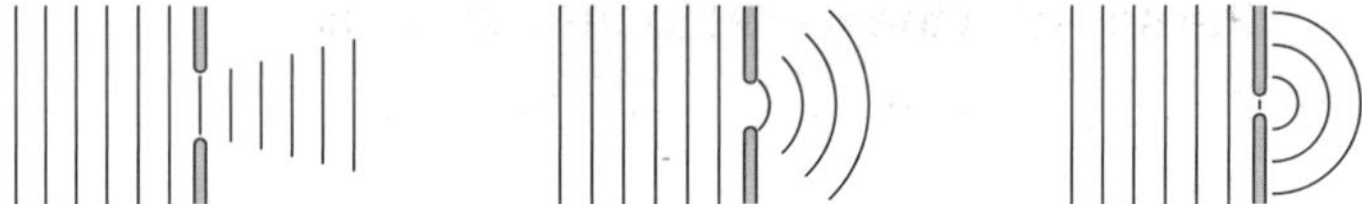

a Looking at the diagrams above, what conclusion can be reached about how waves spread through gaps? (2)

b The front door of a house is open at night. The lights are on in the house and shine down the front path. The television is also on. A woman stands in the garden to the side of the front path. She is in shadow.

Explain why she can hear the television even though the light from the house does not reach her. (3)

c A communication mast transmits both radio and television programmes.

The carrier wave for Radio 4 has a frequency of 200 kHz.

The carrier wave for BBC 1 television has a frequency of 600 MHz.

One householder can receive Radio 4 but cannot receive BBC 1 television.

There is a large hill between the householder and the communication mast.

i How does the wavelength of the Radio 4 carrier wave compare with that of BBC 1 television carrier wave? (2)

ii Explain how the householder can receive Radio 4. (2)

iii Explain why he cannot receive BBC 1 television. (2)

P8.1 The electromagnetic spectrum

Learning objectives

After this topic, you should know:

- the parts of the electromagnetic spectrum
- how to calculate the frequency or wavelength of electromagnetic waves.

We all use waves from different parts of the **electromagnetic spectrum**. Figure 1 shows the spectrum and some of its uses. Electromagnetic waves are electric and magnetic disturbances that transfer energy from one place to another.

Electromagnetic waves do not transfer matter. The energy they transfer depends on the **wavelength** of the waves. This is why waves of different wavelengths have different effects. Figure 1 shows some of the uses of each part of the electromagnetic spectrum.

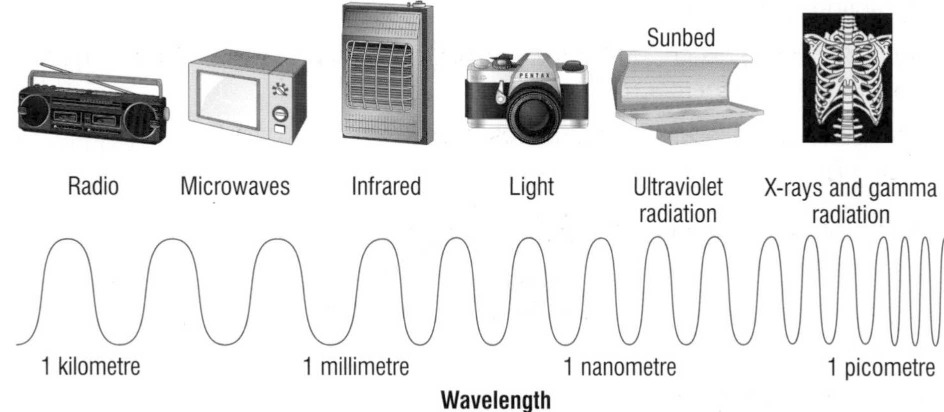

Figure 1 The spectrum is continuous. The frequencies and wavelengths at the boundaries are approximate as the different parts of the spectrum are not precisely defined.

Examiner's tip

The spectrum of visible light covers just a very tiny part of the electromagnetic spectrum. The wavelength decreases from radio waves to gamma rays.

Waves from different parts of the electromagnetic spectrum have different wavelengths.

- Long-wave radio waves have wavelengths as long as 10 km (10^4 m).
- X-rays and gamma rays have wavelengths as short as a millionth of a millionth of a millimetre (= 0.000 000 000 001 mm or 10^{-15} m).

The speed of electromagnetic waves

All electromagnetic waves travel at a speed of 300 million m/s through space or in a vacuum. This is the distance the waves travel each second.

We can link the speed of the waves to their frequency and wavelength using the **wave speed** equation:

$$v = f \times \lambda$$

where:
v = wave speed in metres per second, m/s
f = frequency in hertz, Hz
λ = wavelength in metres, m.

links

For more information on the wave speed equation, look back at 7.2 'Measuring waves'.

Maths skills

We can work out the wavelength if we know the frequency and the wave speed. To do this, we rearrange the wave speed equation into:

$$\lambda = \frac{v}{f}$$

We can work out the frequency if we know the wavelength and the wave speed. To do this, we rearrange the equation into:

$$f = \frac{v}{\lambda}$$

where:
v = speed in metres per second, m/s
f = frequency in hertz, Hz
λ = wavelength in metres, m.

Worked example

A mobile phone gives out electromagnetic waves of frequency 900 million Hz. Calculate the wavelength of these waves.

The speed of electromagnetic waves in air = 300 million m/s.

Solution

$$\text{wavelength } \lambda \text{ (in metres)} = \frac{\text{wave speed } v \text{ (in m/s)}}{\text{frequency } f \text{ (in Hz)}}$$

$$= \frac{300\,000\,000\,\text{m/s}}{900\,000\,000\,\text{Hz}} = \mathbf{0.33\,m}$$

Examiner's tip

Remember that the wavelength decreases from radio waves to gamma rays.

Energy and frequency

The wave speed equation shows us that the shorter the wavelength of the waves, the higher their frequency. The energy of the waves increases as the frequency increases. Therefore, the energy and frequency of the waves increases from radio waves to gamma rays as the wavelength decreases.

Summary questions

1 **a** Which is greater: the wavelength of radio waves or the wavelength of visible light waves?
b What can we say about the speed in a vacuum of different electromagnetic waves?
c Which is greater: the frequency of X-rays or the frequency of infrared radiation?
d Where in the electromagnetic spectrum would you find waves of wavelength 10 millimetres?

2 Fill in the missing parts of the electromagnetic spectrum in the list below.

radio ------ **infrared** **visible light** ------ **X-rays** ------

3 Electromagnetic waves travel through space at a speed of 300 million metres per second. Calculate:
a the wavelength of radio waves of frequency 600 million Hz
b the frequency of microwaves of wavelength 0.30 m.

4 A distant star explodes and emits visible light and gamma rays simultaneously.
a Which of these two types of wave has greater frequency?
b Explain why the gamma rays and the visible light waves reach the Earth at the same time.

Key points

- **The electromagnetic spectrum (in order of decreasing wavelength and increasing frequency and energy) is made up of:**
  - **radio waves**
  - **microwaves**
  - **infrared radiation**
  - **visible light**
  - **ultraviolet radiation**
  - **X-rays and gamma radiation.**
- **The wave speed equation is used to calculate the frequency or wavelength of electromagnetic waves.**

P8.2 Light, infrared, microwaves and radio waves

Learning objectives

After this topic, you should know:

- **the nature of white light**
- **what we use infrared radiation, microwaves and radio waves for**
- **why these types of electromagnetic radiation are hazardous.**

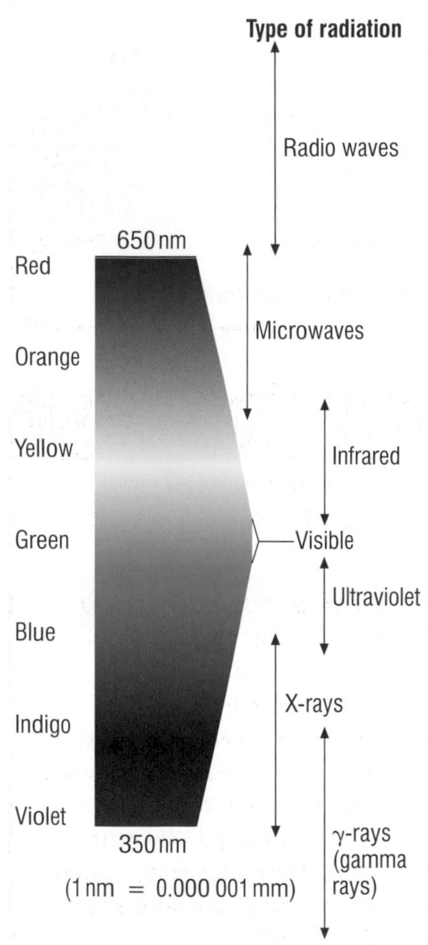

Figure 1 The electromagnetic spectrum with an expanded view of the visible range

links

For more information on infrared radiation, look at 14.4 'Infrared radiation'.

Light and colour

Light from ordinary lamps and from the Sun is called **white light**. This is because it has all the colours of the visible spectrum in it. The wavelength increases across the spectrum as you go from violet to red.

You see the colours of the spectrum when you look at a rainbow. You can also see them if you use a glass prism to split a beam of white light.

Photographers need to know how shades and colours of light affect the photographs they take.

1. In a film camera, the light is focused by the camera lens on to a light-sensitive film. The film then needs to be developed to see the image of the objects that were photographed.
2. In a digital camera, the light is focused by the lens on to a sensor. This consists of thousands of tiny light-sensitive cells called pixels. Each pixel gives a dot of the image. The image can be seen on a small screen at the back of the camera. When a photograph is taken, the image is stored electronically on a memory card.

Infrared radiation

All objects emit infrared radiation.

- The hotter an object is, the more infrared radiation it emits.
- Infrared radiation is absorbed by the skin. It can damage or kill skin cells because it heats up the cells.

Infrared devices

- **Optical fibres** in communications systems use infrared radiation instead of visible light. This is because infrared radiation is absorbed less than visible light in the glass fibres.
- **Remote control handsets** for TV and video equipment transmit signals carried by infrared radiation. When you press a button on the handset, it sends out a sequence of infrared pulses.
- **Infrared scanners** are used in medicine to detect 'hot spots' on the body surface. These hot areas can mean the underlying tissue is unhealthy.
- You can use **infrared cameras** to see people and animals in darkness.

Microwaves

Microwaves lie between radio waves and infrared radiation in the electromagnetic spectrum. They are called **microwaves** because they are shorter in wavelength than radio waves.

We use microwaves for communications, e.g. **satellite TV**, because they can pass through the atmosphere and reach satellites above the Earth. We also use them to beam signals from one place to another because microwaves don't spread out as much as radio waves. Microwaves (as well as radio waves) are used to carry **mobile phone** signals.

Radio waves

Radio wave frequencies range from about 300 000 Hz to 3000 million Hz (where microwave frequencies start). Radio waves are longer in wavelength and lower in frequency than microwaves.

As we will see in 8.3 'Communications', we use radio waves to carry **radio**, **TV** and **mobile phone** signals.

We can also use radio waves instead of cables to connect a computer to other devices such as a printer or a 'mouse'. For example, Bluetooth-enabled devices can communicate with each other over a range of about 10 metres. No cables are needed – just a Bluetooth radio in each device and the necessary software. Such wireless connections work at frequencies of about 2400 million Hz, and they operate at low power.

Bluetooth was set up by the electronics manufacturers. They realised the need to agree on the radio frequencies to be used for common software.

Microwaves and radio waves can be hazardous because they penetrate our bodies and can heat the internal parts of our bodies.

Practical

Testing infrared radiation

Can infrared radiation pass through paper? Use a remote control handset to find out.

Examiner's tip

The spectrum of visible light covers just a very small part of the electromagnetic spectrum.

links

Is mobile phone radiation dangerous? See 8.3 'Communications'.

Demonstration

Demonstrating microwaves

Look at the demonstration.

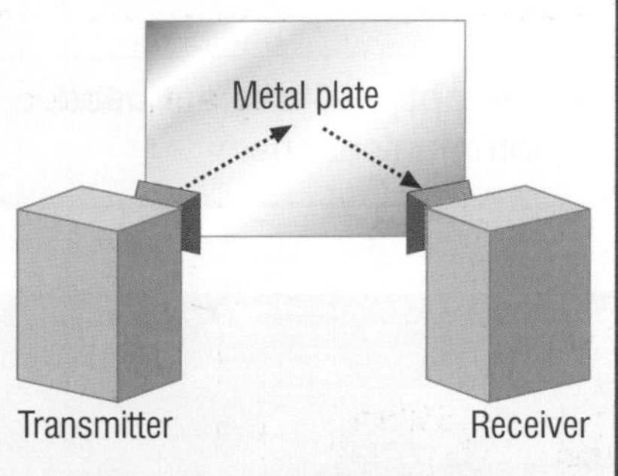

- What does this show?

Summary questions

1 a When you watch a TV programme, what type of electromagnetic wave is:
   i detected by the aerial?
   ii emitted by the screen?
 b What type of electromagnetic wave is used:
   i to carry signals to and from a satellite?
   ii to send signals to a printer from a computer without using a cable?

2 Mobile phones use electromagnetic waves in a wavelength range that includes short-wave radio waves and microwaves.
 a What would be the effect on mobile phone users if remote control handsets operated in this range as well?
 b Why do our emergency services use radio waves in a wavelength range that no else is allowed to use?

3 a The four devices listed below each emit a different type of electromagnetic radiation. State the type of radiation each one emits.
   i A TV transmitter mast.
   ii A TV satellite.
   iii A TV remote handset.
   iv A TV receiver.
 b The speed of electromagnetic waves in air is 300 000 km/s. Calculate the wavelength in air of electromagnetic waves of frequency 2400 MHz.

Key points

- **White light contains all the colours of the visible spectrum.**
- **Infrared radiation is used for carrying signals from remote handsets and inside optical fibres. We use microwaves to carry satellite TV programmes and mobile phone calls. Radio waves are used for radio and TV broadcasting, radio communications and mobile phone calls.**
- **Different types of electromagnetic radiation are hazardous in different ways. Microwaves and radio waves can heat the internal parts of our bodies. Infrared radiation can cause skin burns.**

P8.3 Communications

Learning objectives

After this topic, you should know:

- why we use radio waves of different frequencies for different purposes
- which waves we use for satellite TV
- how to assess whether or not mobile phones are safe to use
- how optical fibres are used in communications.

Figure 1 Sending microwave signals to a satellite

Figure 2 A mobile phone mast

Radio communications

Radio waves are emitted from an aerial when we apply an alternating voltage to the aerial. The frequency of the radio waves produced is the same as the frequency of the alternating voltage.

When the radio waves pass across a receiver aerial, they cause a tiny alternating voltage in the aerial. The frequency of the alternating voltage is the same as the frequency of the radio waves received. The aerial is connected to a loudspeaker. The alternating voltage from the aerial is used to make the loudspeaker send out sound waves.

The radio and microwave spectrum is divided into **bands** of different wavelength ranges. This is because the shorter the wavelength of the waves:

- the more information they can carry
- the shorter their range (due to increasing absorption by the atmosphere)
- the less they spread out (because they diffract less).

Radio wavelengths

Microwaves and radio waves of different wavelengths are used for different communications purposes. Examples are given below.

- **Microwaves** are used for satellite phone and TV links and satellite TV broadcasting. This is because microwaves can travel between satellites in space and the ground. Also, they spread out less than radio waves do, so the signal doesn't weaken as much.
- **Radio waves of wavelengths less than about 1 metre** are used for TV broadcasting from TV masts because they can carry more information than longer radio waves.
- **Radio waves of wavelengths from about 1 metre up to about 100 m** are used by local radio stations (and for the emergency services) because their range is limited to the area round the transmitter.
- **Radio waves of wavelengths greater than 100 m** are used by national and international radio stations because they have a much longer range than shorter-wavelength radio waves.

Mobile phone radiation

A mobile phone sends a radio signal from your phone. The signal is picked up by a local mobile phone mast and is sent through the phone network to the other phone. The 'return' signal goes through the phone network back to the mobile phone mast near you and then on to you. The signals to and from your local mast are carried by radio waves of different frequencies.

The radio waves to and from a mobile phone have a wavelength of about 30 cm. Radio waves at this wavelength are not quite in the microwave range, but they do have a similar heating effect to microwaves. So they are usually referred to as microwaves.

Examiner's tip

Remember that in communications, electromagnetic waves carry the information.

Optical fibre communications

Optical fibres are very thin glass fibres. We use them to transmit signals carried by light or infrared radiation. The light rays can't escape from the fibre. When they reach the surface of the fibre, they are reflected back into the fibre, as shown in Figure 3.

In comparison with radio waves and microwaves:

- optical fibres can carry much more information – this is because light has a much smaller wavelength than radio waves so can carry more pulses of waves
- optical fibres are more secure because the signals stay in the fibre.

Is mobile phone radiation dangerous?

The radiation is much weaker than the microwave radiation in an oven. However, when you use a mobile phone, it is very close to your brain. Some scientists think the radiation might affect the brain. As children have thinner skulls than adults, their brains might be more affected by mobile phone radiation. A UK government report published in May 2000 recommended that the use of mobile phones by children should be limited.

Activity

Mobile phone hazards

Here are some findings by different groups of scientists:

- The short-term memory of volunteers using a mobile phone was found to be unaffected by whether the phone was on or off.
- The brains of rats exposed to microwaves were found to respond less to electrical impulses than the brains of unexposed rats.
- Mice exposed to microwaves by some scientists developed more cancers than unexposed mice. Other scientists were unable to confirm this effect.

A survey of mobile phone users in Norway and Sweden found they experienced headaches and fatigue. No control group of people who did not use a mobile phone was surveyed.

What conclusions do you make from the evidence above?

Suggest how researchers could improve the validity of any conclusions we can make.

Summary questions

1 a What types of electromagnetic wave are used to carry:
   i mobile phone signals?
   ii signals along a thin transparent fibre?
  b i Why should signals to and from a mobile phone be at different frequencies?
   ii Why are signals in an optical fibre more secure than radio signals?

2 a Why could children be more affected by mobile phone radiation than adults?
  b Why can light waves carry more information than radio waves?

3 a Explain why microwaves are used for satellite TV and radio waves for terrestrial TV.
  b Why can microwave signals be sent a long distance between two transmitter dishes provided that the two transmitter masts are within sight of each other?

links

For more information on optical fibres, see 10.4 'Total internal reflection'.

Did you know ... ?

Satellite TV signals are carried by microwaves. We can detect the signals on the ground because they pass straight through a layer of ionised gas in the upper atmosphere. This layer reflects lower-frequency radio waves.

Demonstration

Demonstrating an optical fibre

Observe light shone into an optical fibre. You should see the reflection of light inside an optical fibre. This is known as total internal reflection.

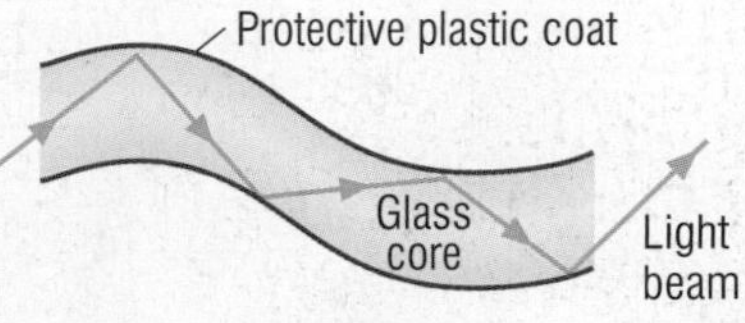

Figure 3 Optical fibres

Key points

- Radio waves of different frequencies are used for different purposes because the wavelength (and therefore the frequency) of waves affects:
  - how far they can travel
  - how much they spread
  - how much information they can carry.
- Microwaves are used for satellite TV signals.
- Further research is needed to evaluate whether or not mobile phones are safe to use.
- Optical fibres are very thin transparent fibres that are used to transmit signals by light and infrared radiation.

P8.4 Ultraviolet rays, X-rays and gamma rays

Learning objectives

After this topic, you should know:

- the differences between ultraviolet and visible light
- what we use X-rays and gamma rays for
- why ultraviolet rays, X-rays and gamma rays are dangerous.

Figure 1 Using an ultraviolet lamp to detect biological stains

Examiner's tip

Make sure that you know the dangers, as well as the uses, of electromagnetic waves.

Did you know ... ?

The ozone layer in the atmosphere absorbs some of the Sun's ultraviolet radiation. Unfortunately, gases such as CFCs from old refrigerators react with the ozone layer and make it thinner. Many countries now have strict regulations about how to dispose of unwanted refrigerators.

Ultraviolet radiation

Ultraviolet (often written as 'UV') radiation lies between violet light and X-rays in the electromagnetic spectrum. It makes some chemicals emit light. Posters and ink that glow in ultraviolet light contain these chemicals. Security marker pens containing this kind of ink are used to mark valuable objects. The chemicals absorb ultraviolet rays and then emit visible light as a result.

Ultraviolet radiation is harmful to human eyes and can cause blindness. UV wavelengths are smaller than visible light wavelengths. UV rays carry more energy than light rays. Too much UV radiation causes sunburn and can cause skin cancer.

- If you stay outdoors in summer, use skin creams to block UV radiation and prevent it reaching your skin.
- If you use a sunbed to get a suntan, don't exceed the recommended time. You should also wear special 'goggles' to protect your eyes.

Demonstration

Ultraviolet radiation

Watch your teacher place different-coloured clothes under an ultraviolet lamp. The lamp must point downwards so you can't look directly at the glow from it. Observe what happens.

- What do white clothes look like under a UV lamp?

X-rays and gamma rays

X-rays and gamma rays both travel straight into substances and may pass through them if the substances are not too dense and not too thick. A thick plate made of lead will stop them.

X-rays and gamma rays have similar properties because they both:

- are at the short-wavelength end of the electromagnetic spectrum
- carry much more energy per second than longer-wavelength electromagnetic waves.

They differ from each other because:

- X-rays are produced when electrons or other particles moving at high speeds are stopped; X-ray tubes are used to produce X-rays
- gamma rays are produced by radioactive substances when unstable nuclei release energy (you will learn about radioactive substances in Chapter 19)
- gamma rays can have shorter wavelengths than X-rays and can therefore penetrate substances more than X-rays can.

As we will see in 8.5 'X-rays in medicine', X-rays are used in hospitals to make X-ray pictures of broken limbs. The X-rays are stopped by bone but travel though the surrounding soft tissues. So the bone shows up as a 'shadow' on an X-ray picture. A crack in a bone would show up as a break in the shadow. X-rays are also used to detect internal cracks in metal objects. These kinds of application are usually possible because the more dense a substance is, the more X-rays it absorbs from an X-ray beam passing through it.

Using gamma radiation

High-energy gamma radiation has several important uses:

- **Killing harmful bacteria in food**
  About 20% of the world's food is lost through spoilage. One of the major causes is bacteria. The bacteria produce waste products that cause food poisoning. Exposing food to gamma radiation kills 99% of disease-carrying organisms, including *Salmonella* (found in poultry) and *Clostridium* (which causes botulism).
- **Sterilising surgical instruments**
  Exposing surgical instruments in sealed plastic wrappers to gamma radiation kills any bacteria on the instruments. This helps to stop infection spreading in hospitals.
- **Killing cancer cells**
  Doctors and medical physicists use gamma-ray therapy to destroy cancerous tumours. A narrow beam of gamma radiation from a radioactive source (cobalt-60) is directed at the tumour. The beam is aimed at it from different directions so as to kill the tumour but not the surrounding tissue. The cobalt-60 source is in a thick lead container. When it is not in use, it is rotated away from the exit channel (see Figure 2).

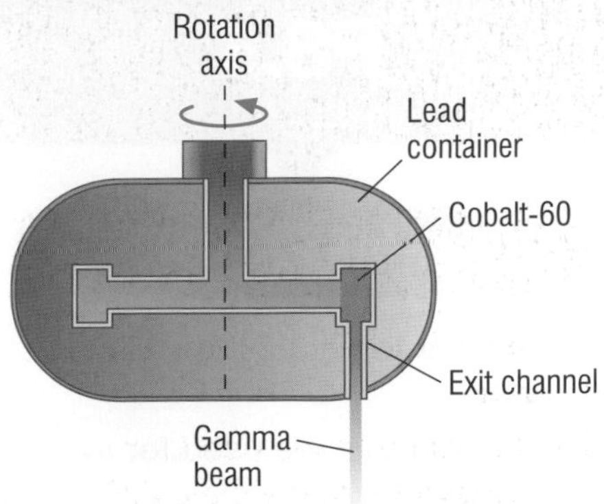

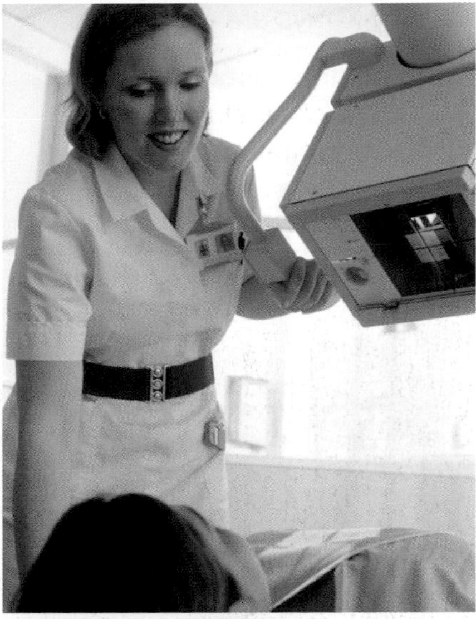

Figure 2 Gamma treatment

Safety matters

X-rays and gamma rays passing through substances can knock electrons out of atoms in the substance. The atoms become charged because they lose electrons. This process is called **ionisation**. Charged atoms are called **ions**.

If ionisation happens to a living cell, it can damage or kill the cell. For this reason, exposure to too much X-radiation or gamma radiation is dangerous and can cause cancer. High doses kill living cells, and low doses cause cell mutation and cancerous growth.

People who use equipment or substances that produce any form of ionising radiation (e.g. X-radiation or gamma radiation) must wear a film badge. If the badge shows that it is over-exposed to ionising radiation, its wearer is not allowed to continue working with the equipment for a period of time.

Figure 3 A film badge tells you how much ionising radiation the wearer has received. Who might wear these?

Summary questions

1 a Why does a crack inside a metal object show up on an X-ray image?
  b Will gamma radiation pass through thin plastic wrappers?
  c Why does a film badge used for monitoring radiation need to have a plastic case, not a metal case?

2 a Why is ultraviolet radiation harmful?
  b i How does the Earth's ozone layer help to protect us from ultraviolet radiation from the Sun?
    ii Why do people outdoors in summer need suncream?

3 a Which types of electromagnetic radiation can penetrate thin metal sheets?
  b Which metal can be used most effectively to absorb X-rays and gamma rays?
  c Which types of electromagnetic radiation:
    i ionise substances they pass through?
    ii damage the human eye?

Key points

- Ultraviolet radiation has a shorter wavelength than visible light and harms the skin and the eyes.
- X-rays are used in hospitals to make X-ray images.
- Gamma rays are used to kill harmful bacteria in food, to sterilise surgical equipment and to kill cancer cells.
- X-rays and gamma rays damage living tissue when they pass through it.

P8.5 X-rays in medicine

Learning objectives

After this topic, you should know:

- what X-rays are used for in hospitals
- why X-rays are dangerous
- about the absorption of X-rays when they pass through the body
- what a CT scan is.

Have you ever broken one of your bones? If you have, you will have gone to your local hospital for an X-ray photograph. X-rays are electromagnetic waves at the short-wavelength end of the electromagnetic spectrum. They are produced in an X-ray tube when fast-moving electrons hit a target. Their wavelengths are about the same as the diameter of an atom.

To make a **radiograph** or X-ray photograph, X-rays from an X-ray tube are directed at the patient. A lightproof cassette containing a photographic film or a **flat-panel detector** is placed on the other side of the patient.

- When the X-ray tube is switched on, X-rays from the tube pass through the part of the patient's body under investigation.
- X-rays pass through soft tissue, but they are absorbed by bones, teeth and metal objects that are not too thin. The parts of the film or the detector that the X-rays reach become darker than the other parts. So the bones appear lighter than the surrounding tissue which appears dark. The radiograph shows a 'negative image' of the bones. A hole or a cavity in a tooth shows up as a dark area in the bright image of the tooth.
- An organ that consists of soft tissue can be filled with a substance called a **contrast medium** which absorbs X-rays easily. This enables the internal surfaces in the organ to be seen on the radiograph. For example, to obtain a radiograph of the stomach, the patient is given a barium meal before the X-ray machine is used. The barium compound is a good absorber of X-rays.
- Lead 'absorber' plates between the tube and the patient stop X-rays reaching other parts of the body. Lead is used because it is a good absorber of X-rays. The X-rays reaching the patient pass through a gap between the plates.
- A flat-panel detector is a small screen that contains a **CCD (charge-coupled device)**. The sensors in the CCD are covered by a layer of a substance that converts X-rays to light. The light rays then create electronic signals in the sensors that are sent to a computer, which displays a digital X-ray image.

a

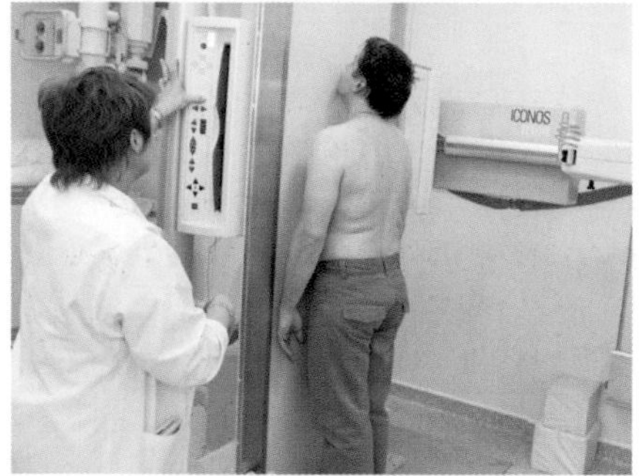

b

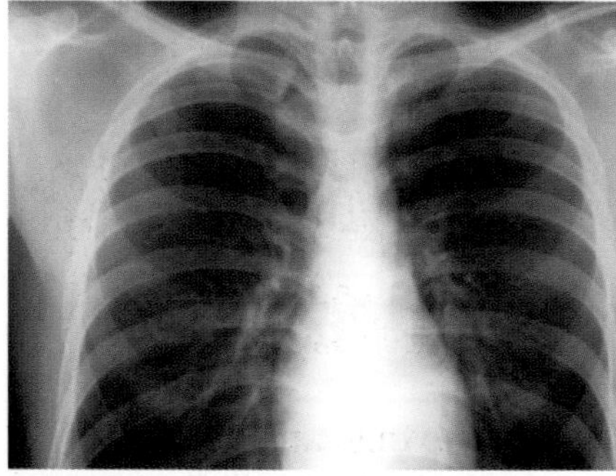

Figure 1 **a** Taking a chest X-ray
b A chest X-ray

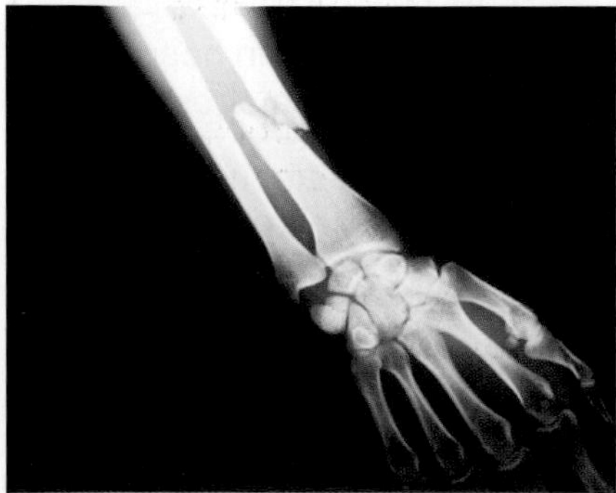

Figure 2 Spot the break

Safety matters

X-radiation, as well as gamma radiation, is dangerous because it ionises substances it passes through. High doses kill living cells. Low doses can cause cell mutation and cancerous growth. There is no evidence of a safe limit below which living cells would not be damaged.

Workers who use equipment or substances that produce X-radiation (or alpha, beta or gamma radiation) must wear a film badge (see 8.4 'Ultraviolet rays, X-rays and gamma rays').

X-ray therapy

Doctors use X-ray therapy to destroy cancerous tumours in the body. Thick plates between the X-ray tube and the body stop X-rays from reaching healthy body tissues. A gap between the plates allows X-rays through to reach the tumour. X-rays for therapy are shorter in wavelength than X-rays used for imaging.

The CT scanner

A computerised tomography scanner (**CT scanner**) produces a digital image of any cross-section through the body. It can also be used to construct a three-dimensional (3-D) image of an organ.

Figure 3 shows an end-view of a CT scanner. The patient lies stationary on a bed that is in a ring of detectors.

- The X-ray tube automatically moves round the inside of the ring in small steps.
- At each position, X-rays from the tube pass through the patient and reach the detector ring.
- Electronic signals from the detector are recorded by a computer until the tube has moved round the ring.
- The computer displays a digital image of the scanned area.

Each detector receives X-rays that have travelled through different types of tissue. The detector signal depends on:

- the different types of tissue along the X-ray path
- how far the X-rays pass through each type of tissue.

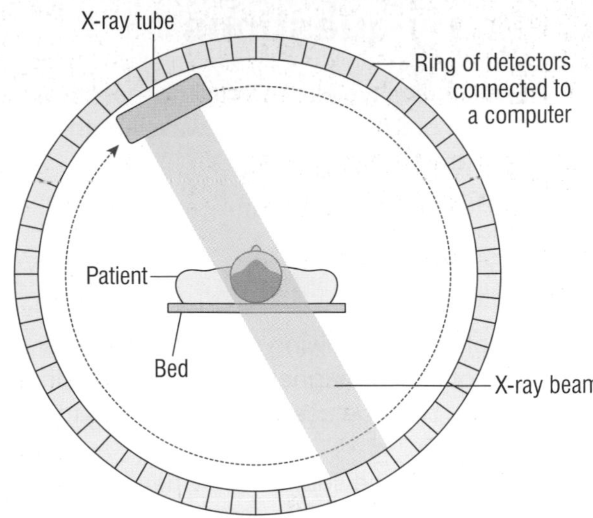

Figure 3 The CT scanner – it can distinguish between different types of soft tissue, as well as bone

Table 1 Comparison of a CT scanner with an ordinary X-ray machine

	CT scanner	Ordinary X-ray machine
Image distinguishes between bone and soft tissue	Yes	Yes
Image distinguishes between different types of soft tissue	Yes	No
Three-dimensional image	Yes	No
Radiation dose	CT scanner gives a much higher dose than an ordinary X-ray machine	
Cost	CT equipment cost is much greater than an ordinary X-ray machine	

Examiner's tip

Make sure that you know the advantages and disadvantages of CT scanners.

Summary questions

1 a What is a contrast medium used for when an X-ray photograph of the stomach is taken?
  b What can X-ray therapy be used for?

2 When an X-ray photograph is taken, why is it necessary:
  a to place the patient between the X-ray tube and the film cassette?
  b to have the film in a lightproof cassette?
  c to shield the parts of the patient not under investigation from X-rays? Explain what would happen to healthy cells.

3 a What type of electromagnetic radiation is used in a CT scanner?
  b State one advantage and one disadvantage of a CT scanner in comparison with an ordinary X-ray machine.

Key points

- **X-rays are used in hospitals:**
  - **to make images and CT scans**
  - **to destroy tumours at or near the body surface.**
- **X-rays can damage living tissue when they pass through it.**
- **X-rays are absorbed more by bones and teeth than by soft tissues.**
- **CT scans distinguish between different types of soft tissue as well as between bone (or teeth) and soft tissue.**

Summary questions

1 **a** Place the five types of electromagnetic wave listed below in order of increasing wavelength.

A Infrared waves
B Microwaves
C Radio waves
D Gamma rays
E Ultraviolet rays.

b Complete the following sentences using one of the types of electromagnetic radiation listed in **a**:

i .... can be used to send signals to and from a satellite.

ii .... ionise substances when they pass through them.

iii .... are used to carry signals in thin transparent fibres.

2 **a** The radio waves from a local radio station have a wavelength of 2.9 metres in air. The speed of electromagnetic waves in air is 300 000 km/s.

i Write down the equation that links frequency, wavelength and wave speed.

ii Calculate the frequency of the radio waves.

b A certain local radio station transmitter has a range of 30 km. State and explain the effect on the range if the power supplied to the transmitter is reduced.

3 Mobile phones send and receive signals using electromagnetic waves near or in the microwave part of the electromagnetic spectrum. New mobile phones are tested for radiation safety and given an SAR value before being sold. The SAR is a measure of the energy per second absorbed by the head while the phone is in use. For use in the UK, SAR values must be less than 2.0 W/kg. SAR values for two different mobile phones are given below.

Phone **A** 0.2 W/kg
Phone **B** 1.0 W/kg

a What is the main reason that mobile phones are tested for radiation safety?

b Which phone, **A** or **B**, is safer? Give a reason for your answer.

c The UK government recommends caution in the use of mobile phones, particularly by children and young people, until scientists and doctors find out more. Explain why children and young people may be more at risk than adults.

4 The figure shows an X-ray source which is used to direct X-rays at a broken leg. A photographic film in a lightproof wrapper is placed under the leg. When the film is developed, an image of the broken bone is observed.

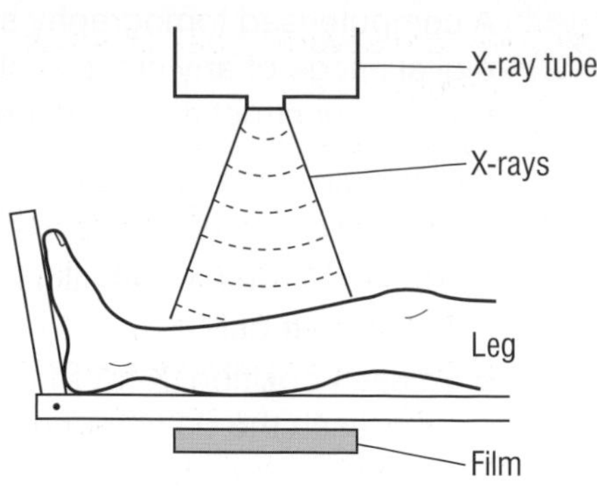

a **i** Explain why an image of the bone is seen on the film.

ii Why is it possible to see the fracture on the image?

b When an X-ray photograph of the stomach is taken, the patient is given food containing barium before the photograph is taken.

i Why is it necessary for the patient to be given this food before the photograph is taken?

ii The exposure time for a stomach X-ray must be shorter than the X-ray time for a limb. Why?

iii Low-energy X-rays from the X-ray tube can be absorbed by placing a metal plate between the patient and the X-ray tube. Such X-rays would otherwise be absorbed by the body. What is the benefit of removing such low-energy X-rays in this way?

c An ultrasound scanner is used to observe an unborn baby. Why is ultrasound instead of X-rays used to observe an unborn baby?

5 **a** Explain what is meant by ionisation.

b Name the **two** types of electromagnetic radiation that can ionise substances.

c Give **two** reasons why ionising radiation is harmful.

6 **a** Describe and explain how invisible ink works. In your explanation, state the type of radiation that is absorbed and the type of radiation that is emitted.

b Explain why a beam of infrared radiation cannot be used to carry signals to a detector that is more than a few metres from a transmitter.

c Explain why a local radio channel can broadcast only to a limited area, whereas a satellite TV channel can broadcast to a much larger area.

AQA Examination-style questions

1 There are several types of waves in the electromagnetic spectrum.

Some are listed below.

infrared light radio waves ultraviolet X-rays

a Which of the waves in the list:

i has the highest frequency?

ii has the longest wavelength?

iii carries the most energy?

iv causes skin cancer? (4)

b A newspaper headline states:

AIRPORT BODY SCANNERS MAY POSE HEALTH RISK

The X-ray scanners were introduced in 2009 to detect hidden weapons and explosives.

i What properties of X-rays make them suitable for use in body scanners? (4)

ii Explain why X-rays may pose health risks. (4)

2 Electromagnetic waves have many uses.

a Match each electromagnetic wave in the left-hand column to its use in the right-hand column. (4)

Electromagnetic wave		Use
Gamma		Carrying TV programmes
Infrared		In a TV remote control
Radio		Prolonging the shelf-life of fruit
Ultraviolet		Security marking of TV sets

b Microwaves are used to send signals to and from satellites.

i What property of microwaves makes them suitable for sending signals to satellites? (1)

ii Some people are worried about the dangers of very young children using mobile phones.

Discuss the reasons for their concerns. (QWC) (6)

3 Hospitals use different types of scanner.

a i What are the advantages of a CT scan over a normal X-ray scan? (2)

ii What are the disadvantages of a CT scan when compared with a normal X-ray scan? (2)

b Why do hospitals not use X-ray scans on pregnant women? (2)

c The charts below give information about exposure to radiation.

The average annual exposure to radiation is given in millisieverts (mSv).

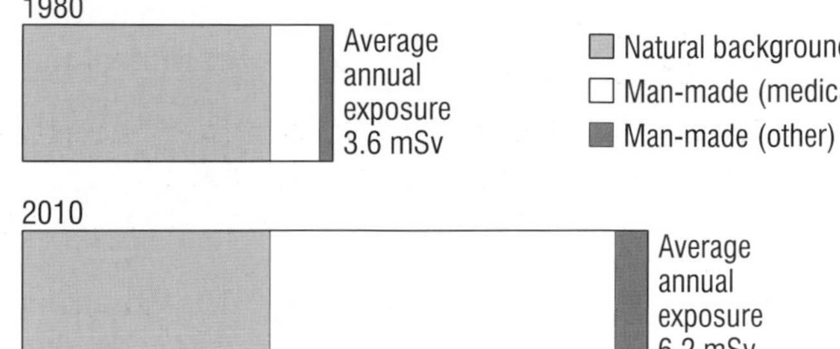

Outline the changes in average annual exposure to radiation that occurred between 1980 and 2010.

Suggest reasons for the changes. (6)

4 Electromagnetic waves are used for communication.

a Which types of electromagnetic waves can be transmitted by optical fibres? (2)

b Radio waves have a large range of wavelengths.

The table gives information about some radio waves.

Wavelength	less than 1 m	1 to 100 m	greater than 100 m
Information	can carry a lot of information	have a limited range	are reflected by a layer of the atmosphere

Suggest a wavelength of radio wave suitable for carrying:

i international radio.

ii local radio.

iii national TV. (3)

c 'Bluetooth' is a short-range radio communication system which can link mobile phones to laptop computers.

A typical 'Bluetooth' frequency is 2.4×10^3 MHz.

Electromagnetic waves travel at a speed of 3×10^8 m/s.

Calculate the wavelength of these 'Bluetooth' waves. (3)

P9.1 Sound

Learning objectives

After this topic, you should know:

- the range of frequencies that can be detected by the human ear
- what sound waves are
- what echoes are.

Figure 1 Making sound waves

Investigating sound waves

Sound waves are easy to produce. Your vocal cords vibrate and produce sound waves every time you speak. Any object vibrating in air makes the layers of air near the object vibrate, which makes the layers of air next to them vibrate. The vibrating object pushes and pulls repeatedly on the air. This sends out the vibrations of the air in waves of compressions and rarefactions. When the waves reach your ears, they make your eardrums vibrate in and out so you hear sound as a result.

The vibrations travelling through the air are sound waves. The waves are longitudinal because the air particles vibrate (or oscillate) along the direction in which the waves transfer energy. Energy transfer by sound waves is sometimes called acoustic energy.

Practical

Investigating sound waves

You can use a loudspeaker to produce sound waves by passing alternating current through it. Figure 2 shows how to do this using a signal generator. This is an alternating current supply unit with a variable frequency dial.

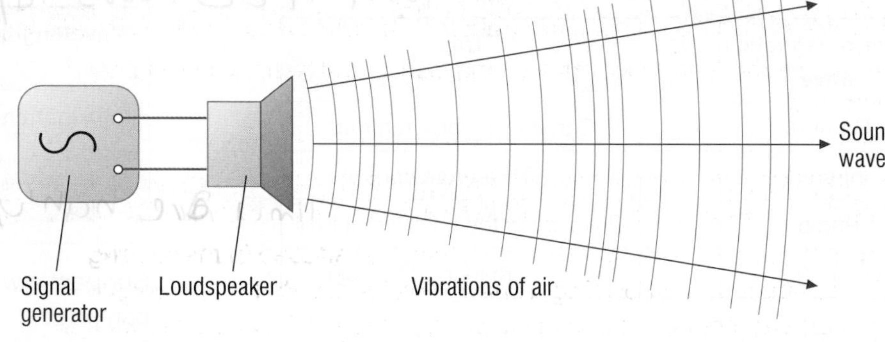

Figure 2 Using a loudspeaker

- If you observe the loudspeaker closely, you can see it vibrating. It produces sound waves as it pushes the surrounding air backwards and forwards.
- If you alter the frequency dial of the signal generator, you can change the frequency of the sound waves.

Find out the lowest and the highest frequency you can hear. Young people can usually hear sound frequencies from about 20 Hz to about 20 000 Hz. Older people, in general, can't hear frequencies at the higher end of this range.

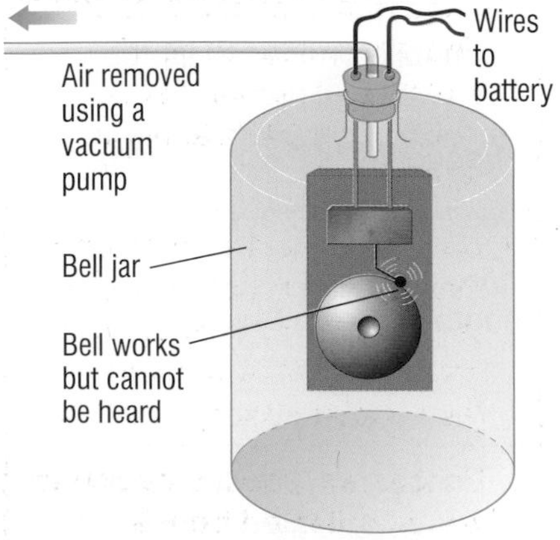

Sound waves cannot travel through a vacuum. You can test this by listening to an electric bell in a bell jar, see Figure 3. As the air is pumped out of the bell jar, the ringing sound fades away.

Air removed using a vacuum pump
Wires to battery
Bell jar
Bell works but cannot be heard

Figure 3 A sound test – sound waves can't travel through a vacuum

Reflection of sound

Have you ever created an echo? An **echo** is an example of reflection of sound. Echoes can be heard in a large hall or gallery that has bare, smooth walls.

- If the walls are covered in soft fabric, the fabric will absorb sound instead of reflecting it. No echoes will be heard.
- If the wall surface is uneven (not smooth), echoes will not be heard because the reflected sound is 'broken up' and scattered.

Refraction of sound

Sound travels through air at a speed of about 340 m/s. The warmer the air, the faster the speed of sound. Refraction takes place at the boundaries between layers of air at different temperatures. At night you can hear sound a long way from its source because sound waves refract back to the ground instead of travelling away from the ground. In the daytime, sound refracts upwards, not downwards, because the air near the ground is warmer than air higher up.

Diffraction of sound

Sound waves are diffracted when they pass through a suitable-sized opening such as a doorway. As waves pass through the opening, they are diffracted and so they spread out. This is partly why you can hear around corners. The width of the opening needs to be of the same order of magnitude as the wavelength of the sound waves for diffraction to be big enough to be measurable. Sound waves of much smaller wavelengths would pass straight through with little diffraction.

Examiner's tip

Remember that sound waves are longitudinal and need a medium to compress.

Did you know ... ?

When you blow a round whistle, you force a small ball inside the whistle to go round and round inside. Each time it goes round, its movement draws air in then pushes it out. Sound waves are produced as a result.

Figure 4 Refraction of sound

Summary questions

1 a The sound from a vehicle engine can be reduced in the seating compartment by placing a suitable material between the engine compartment and the seating compartment. What type of material would be most suitable for this purpose?

b Traffic noise from an urban motorway can be reduced by planting tall bushes near the motorway and installing concrete fence panels behind the bushes. Explain why each of these measures reduces traffic noise for people in the area.

2 a What is the highest frequency of sound the human ear can hear?

b Why does a round whistle produce sound at a constant frequency when you blow steadily into it?

3 a A boat is at sea in a mist. The captain wants to know if the boat is near any cliffs so he sounds the horn and listens for an echo.

i Why would hearing an echo tell him he is near the cliffs?

ii The captain hears an echo 5.0 s after sounding the horn. Show that the distance from the ship to the cliff is 850 m. The speed of sound in air = 340 m/s.

b Explain why someone in a large cavern can sometimes hear more than one echo of a sound.

Key points

- The frequency range of the normal human ear is from about 20 Hz to about 20 000 Hz.
- Sound waves are vibrations that travel through a medium (a substance). They cannot travel through a vacuum (as in outer space).
- Echoes are caused by sound waves reflected from a smooth, hard surface.

P9.2 Musical sounds

Learning objectives

After this topic, you should know:

- what determines the pitch of a musical note
- what happens to the loudness of a note as the amplitude increases
- how sound waves are created by musical instruments.

Figure 1 Making music

What type of music do you like? Whatever your taste in music is, when you listen to it you usually hear sounds produced by specially designed instruments. Even your voice is produced by a biological organ that has the job of producing sound.

- Musical notes are easy to listen to because they are rhythmic. The sound waves change smoothly and the wave pattern repeats itself regularly.
- Noise consists of sound waves that vary in frequency without any pattern.

Practical

Investigating different sounds

Use a microphone connected to an oscilloscope to display the waveforms of different sounds.

Figure 2 Investigating different sound waves

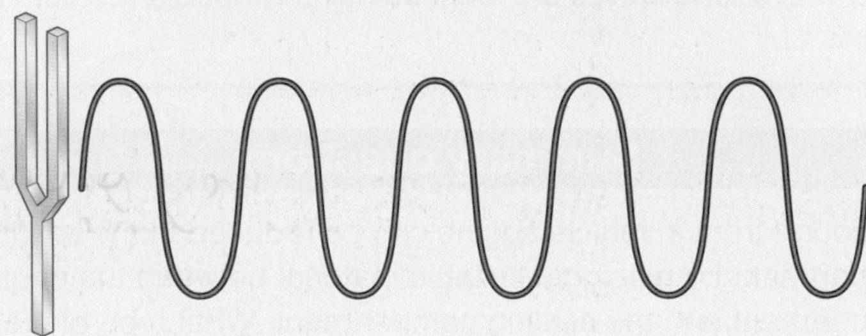

Figure 3 Tuning-fork waves

1 Test a tuning fork to see the waveform of a sound of constant frequency.
2 Compare the pure waveform of a tuning fork with the sound you produce when you talk or sing or whistle. You may be able to produce a pure waveform when you whistle or sing but not when you talk.
3 Use a signal generator connected to a loudspeaker to produce sound waves. The waveform on the oscilloscope screen should be a pure waveform.

Your investigations should show you that:

- **increasing the loudness** of a sound increases the **amplitude** of the waves. So the waves on the screen become taller.
- **increasing the frequency of a sound** (the number of waves per second) increases its **pitch**. This makes more waves appear on the screen.

Figure 4 shows the waveforms for different sounds from the loudspeaker.

Examiner's tip

Frequency controls the pitch of a note – how high it is; amplitude controls how loud the note sounds.

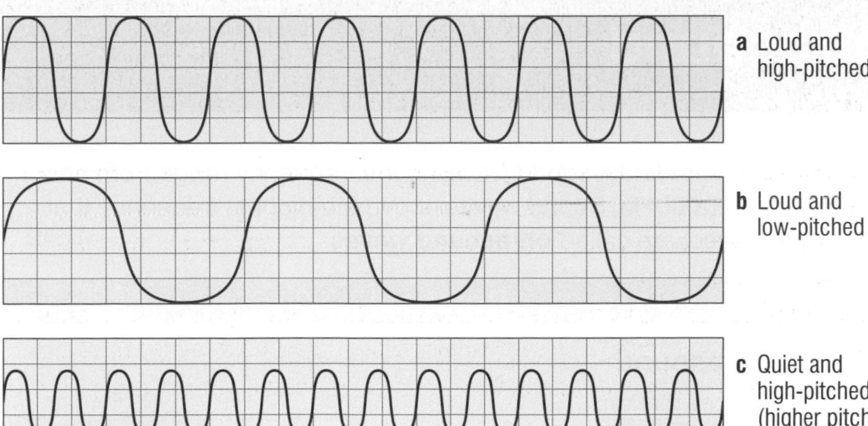

Figure 4 Investigating sounds

Musical instruments

When you play a musical instrument, you create sound waves by making the instrument and the air inside it vibrate. Each new cycle of vibrations makes the vibrations stronger at certain frequencies. We say the instrument **resonates** at these frequencies. Because the instrument and the air inside it vibrate strongly at these frequencies when it is played, we hear recognisable notes of sound from the instrument.

- A wind instrument such as a flute is designed so that the air inside resonates when it is played. You can make the air in an empty bottle resonate by blowing across the top gently.
- A string instrument such as a guitar produces sound when the strings vibrate. The vibrating strings make the surfaces of the instrument vibrate and produce sound waves in the air. In an acoustic guitar, the air inside the hollow body of the guitar (the sound box) vibrates too.
- A percussion instrument such as a drum vibrates and produces sound when it is struck.

Summary questions

1 a A tuning fork creates a note of sound when it is struck briefly. How does the waveform of the sound from a tuning fork change as the sound becomes quieter?
  b When a key of a piano is pressed, a 'hammer' briefly strikes a stretched wire in the piano and a note of sound is produced. Describe and explain how the note changes after the key has been pressed.

2 A microphone and an oscilloscope are used to investigate sound from a loudspeaker connected to a signal generator. What change would you expect to see on the oscilloscope screen if the sound is:
  a made louder at the same frequency?
  b made lower in frequency at the same loudness?

3 a How does the note produced by a guitar string change if the string is:
  i shortened? ii tightened?
  iii loosened?
  b Compare the sound produced by a violin with the sound produced by a drum.
  c Explain why the sound from a vibrating tuning fork is much louder if the base of the tuning fork is held on a table.

Examiner's tip

Be sure you know the meaning of the words **frequency** and **amplitude**.

Practical

Musical instruments

Investigate the waveform produced by a musical instrument, such as a flute.

You should find its waveform changes smoothly, like the one in Figure 5 – but only if you can play it correctly. The waveform is a mixture of frequencies instead of a single frequency waveform like Figure 3.

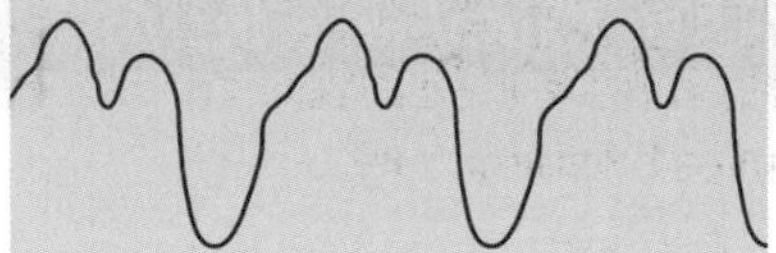

Figure 5 Flute wave pattern

Key points

- The pitch of a note increases if the frequency of the sound waves increases.
- The loudness of a note increases if the amplitude of the sound waves increases.
- Vibrations created in a musical instrument when it is played produce sound waves.

P9.3 Ultrasound

Learning objectives

After this topic, you should know:

- **the nature of ultrasound waves**
- **how ultrasound waves are used in medicine**
- **why ultrasound waves can be used to scan the human body**
- **why an ultrasound scan is safer than taking an X-ray photograph.**

The human ear can detect sound waves in the frequency range from about 20 Hz to about 20 000 Hz. Sound waves above the highest frequency that humans can detect are called **ultrasound waves**.

Practical

Testing ultrasound

High-frequency signal generator
Loudspeaker
Oscilloscope
Microphone

Figure 1 Testing ultrasounds

Use a loudspeaker connected to a signal generator to produce ultrasound waves. Connect a microphone to an oscilloscope to detect the waves and display them. You can use the apparatus to:

- measure the frequency of the ultrasound waves
- test different materials to see if they absorb ultrasound waves
- show that ultrasound waves can be partly reflected.

links

To learn more about what an oscilloscope is used for, look at 17.1 'Alternating current'.

Examiner's tip

Ultrasound is often reflected – it goes there and back, so be careful, in calculations, about distance.

Ultrasound scanners

Ultrasound waves are used for prenatal scans of a baby in the womb. They are also used to 'see' organs in the body such as a kidney or damaged ligaments and muscles. An ultrasound scanner consists of an electronic device called a **transducer** placed on the body surface, a control system and a display screen. The transducer produces and detects pulses of ultrasound waves.

Each pulse from the transducer:

- is partially reflected from the different tissue boundaries in its path
- returns to the transducer as a sequence of reflected pulses from the boundaries, arriving back at different times.

The transducer is moved across the surface of part of the body. The pulses are then detected by the transducer. They are used to build up an image on a screen of the internal tissue boundaries in the body.

The advantages of using ultrasound waves instead of X-rays for medical scanning are that ultrasound waves (unlike X-rays) are:

- non-ionising and therefore harmless when used for scanning
- reflected at boundaries between different types of tissue (different media), so they can be used to scan organs and other soft tissues in the body.

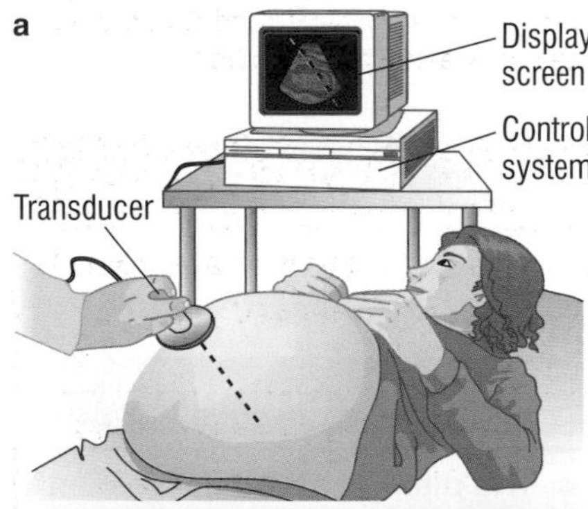

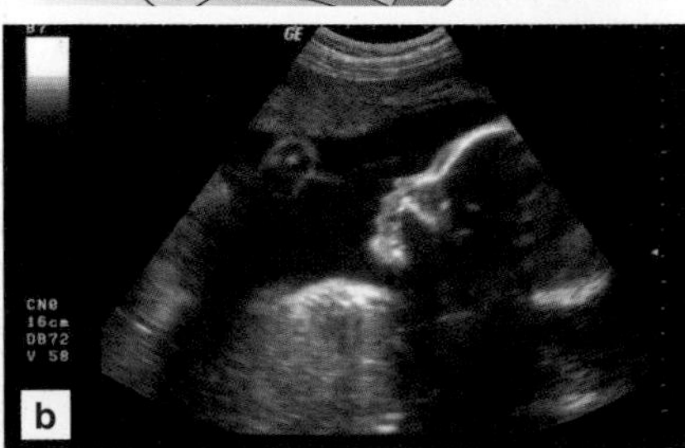

Figure 2 **a** An ultrasound scanner system **b** An ultrasound image of a baby in the womb

Distance measurements

Sight can sometimes be restored to a blind person by replacing the eye lens with an artificial lens. Before this is done, the eye surgeon needs to know how long the eyeball is. This is to make sure the new lens gives clear vision. Figure 3 shows how ultrasound is used to measure the length of the eyeball. This type of scan is called an A-scan.

A transducer at the front of the eye sends ultrasound pulses into the eye. The reflected pulses are detected by the transducer and displayed on an oscilloscope screen or on a computer monitor, as shown in Figure 3.

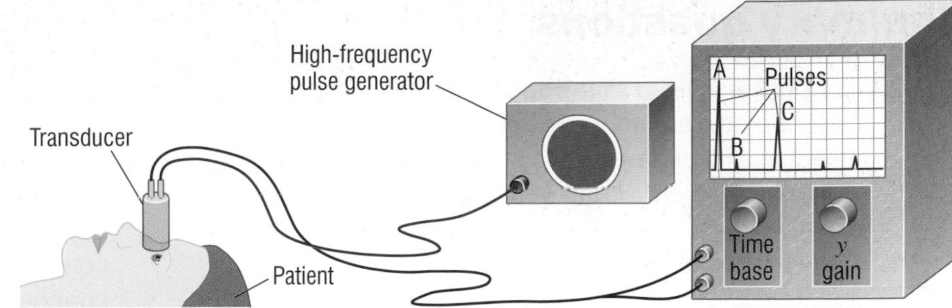

Figure 3 Pulse A is due to partial reflection at the front surface of the eye. Pulse B is due to partial reflection at the surfaces of the eye lens. Pulse C is due to reflection at the back of the eye. Some further pulses are present due to partial reflection beyond the back of the eye.

We can use the oscilloscope to measure the 'transit time' of each pulse. This is the time taken by the pulse to travel from the transmitter at the surface to and from the boundary that reflected it. To calculate distance travelled:

the distance travelled by the pulse = **speed of ultrasound waves in body tissue** × **its transit time**

Since the pulse travels from the surface to the boundary then back to the surface, the depth of the boundary below the surface is therefore half the distance travelled by each pulse to and from the boundary. So:

the depth of the boundary below the surface = ½ × **speed of the ultrasound waves** × **transit time**

Maths skills

The distance equation in symbols:

$$s = v \times t$$

where:
s is the distance in metres, m
v is the wave speed in metres per second, m/s
t is the time taken in seconds, s.

Ultrasound therapy

Kidney stones can be very painful. Powerful ultrasound waves can be used to break a kidney stone into tiny bits. The fragments are small enough to leave the kidney naturally. The transmitter is used in an A-scan system so that the waves are aimed exactly at the kidney stone.

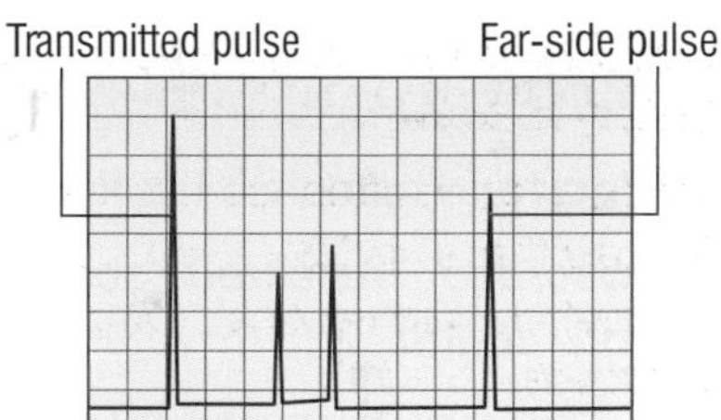

Figure 4 The screen of an oscilloscope connected to an ultrasound detector on the surface of a patient's body

Summary questions

1 **a** Why are ultrasound waves partly reflected by body organs?
b Why is an ultrasound scanner better than an X-ray scanner for scanning a body organ?
c The wavelength of ultrasound waves used for scanning needs to be much smaller than the transducer width, otherwise the waves would spread out too much because of diffraction. How would too much diffraction affect the reflected pulses?

2 Look at the screen in Figure 4. It shows the reflected pulses that are detected for each transmitted pulse.
a How many internal boundaries are present according to this display?
b The oscilloscope beam takes 32 millionths of a second to travel across each grid square on the screen.
i How long does each pulse take to travel from the body surface to the nearest internal boundary?
ii The speed of ultrasound in the body is 1500 m/s. What is the distance from the body surface to the nearest tissue boundary?

3 **a** In an A-scan of a 'model' eye, the distance from the front to the back of the eye was known to be 48 mm. If Figure 3 represented the oscilloscope display for the model eye, what would be the distance from the eye lens to the front of the model eye?
b Estimate the accuracy of the distance you calculated in **a**.

Key points

- **Ultrasound waves are sound waves of frequency above 20 000 Hz.**
- **Ultrasound waves are used in medicine for ultrasound scanning and for destroying kidney stones.**
- **Ultrasound waves are partly reflected at a boundary between two different types of body tissue.**
- **An ultrasound scan is non-ionising, so it is safer than an X-ray.**

Summary questions

1 **a** A loudspeaker is used to produce sound waves.

i Describe how sound waves are created when an object in air vibrates.

ii In terms of the amplitude of the sound waves, explain why the sound is fainter further away from the loudspeaker.

b A microphone is connected to an oscilloscope. The figure shows the display on the screen of the oscilloscope when the microphone detects sound waves from a loudspeaker which is connected to a signal generator.

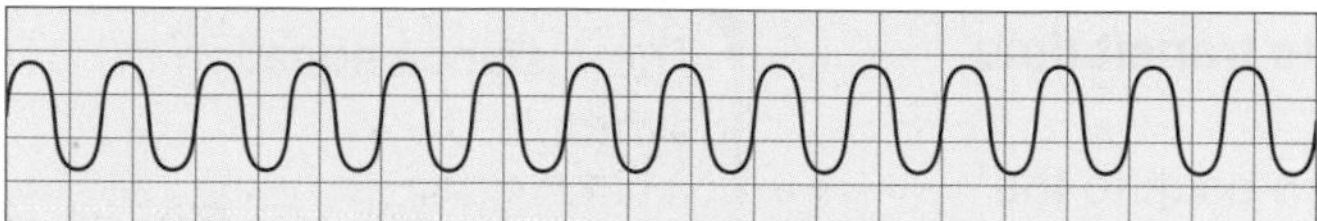

Describe how the waveform displayed on the oscilloscope screen changes if the sound from the loudspeaker is:

i made louder

ii reduced in pitch.

c Describe how you would use the arrangement to measure the upper limit of frequency of a person's hearing.

2 **a** Copy and complete **i** to **iii** using the words below.

absorbed reflected scattered smooth soft rough

i An echo is caused by sound waves that are .... from a .... wall.

ii When sound waves are directed at a .... surface, they are broken up and ....

iii When sound waves are directed at a wall covered with a .... material, they are .... and not reflected.

b The warmer air is, the faster sound waves travel through it. Explain why outdoor sounds at night can be heard a long distance from their source.

3 **a** What is the highest frequency the human ear can hear?

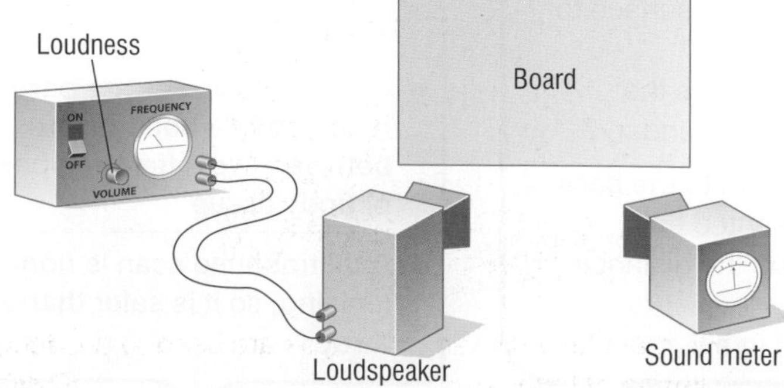

b A sound meter is used to measure the loudness of the sound reflected from an object. Describe how you would use the meter and the arrangement shown in the figure to test if more sound is reflected from a board than from a cushion in place of the board. The control knob and a frequency dial can be used to change the loudness and the frequency of the sound from the loudspeaker. List the variables that you would need to keep constant in your test.

4 A person is standing a certain distance from a flat side wall of a tall building. She claps her hands and hears an echo.

a Explain the cause of the echo.

b She hears the sound 0.30 s after clapping her hands. Calculate how far she is from the nearest point of the wall. The speed of sound in air = 340 m/s.

5 In a test to measure the depth of the sea bed, ultrasound pulses took 0.40 s to travel from the surface to the sea bed and back. Given that the speed of sound in sea water is 1350 m/s, calculate the depth of the sea bed below the surface.

6 **a** Calculate the wavelength in air of ultrasound waves of frequency 40 kHz. The speed of sound in air = 340 m/s.

b Bats navigate by detecting the echoes of ultrasound pulses they emit. Describe how such echoes enable bats to avoid flying into obstacles.

7 Ultrasound waves used for medical scanners have a frequency of 2000 kHz.

a Use the equation 'speed = frequency × wavelength' to calculate the wavelength of these ultrasound waves in human tissue. (The speed of ultrasound in human tissue is 1500 m/s.)

b Ultrasound waves of this frequency in human tissue are not absorbed much and they do not spread out.

i Why is it important in a medical scanner that they are not absorbed?

ii Why is it important in a medical scanner that they do not spread out?

c State and explain which is better, ultrasound or X-rays, for producing images of babies in the womb.

AQA Examination-style questions

1 **a** A teacher wants to display sound as a waveform so that the students can both hear and 'see' the sound.

i What four pieces of equipment will she need? (4)

ii The diagram shows two waveforms, **A** and **B**, that she displays.

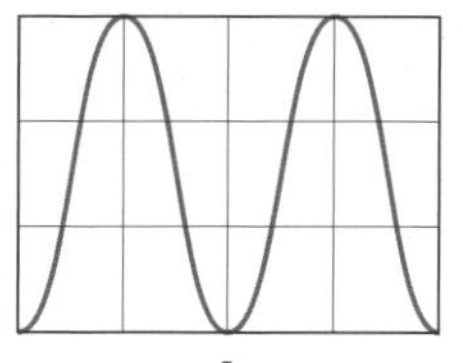

A

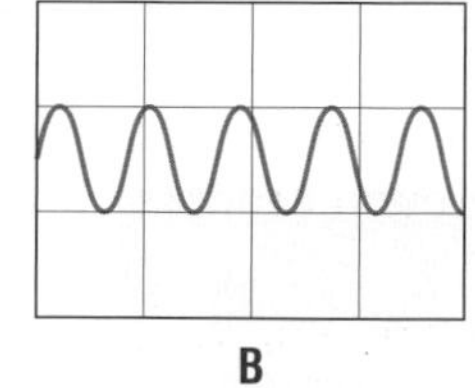

B

Describe how **A** sounds different from **B**. (2)

b The teacher takes the class outside to measure the speed of sound. All the students stand as far away from a wall of the sports hall as possible. The teacher bangs two sticks together. She asks them to listen to the sound reflected from the wall.

i What name is given to the reflected sound? (1)

ii Describe how the students would take the measurements needed and how they would calculate the speed of sound. (5)

iii What should they do to minimise random errors in their measurements? (2)

2 **a** Both light and sound travel as waves.

Choose words from the list to complete the following sentences.

can cannot faster longitudinal slower transverse

i Sound waves are .... waves and light waves are .... waves.

ii In air, sound waves travel .... than light waves.

iii Sound waves .... travel through a vacuum, but light waves .... (3)

b The diagram shows a sound wave.

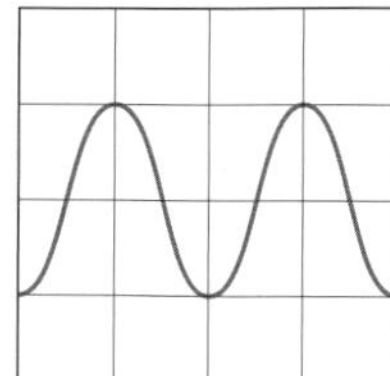

Scale: X – each square equals 0.001 s
Y – each square equals 1 cm

i What is the amplitude of the wave? (1)

ii Calculate the frequency of the wave. (2)

iii The speed of sound in air is 340 m/s. Calculate the wavelength of the sound wave. (2)

iv Discuss whether this sound wave would be diffracted by an open doorway. (3)

3 **a** Sound and ultrasound waves travel through water at 1400 m/s

i Describe how sound waves travel through water. (3)

ii Why can a sound wave not travel through a vacuum? (1)

iii A sound wave has a frequency of 2000 Hz. Calculate the wavelength of the wave in water. (2)

b Echo sounders use ultrasound waves to detect underwater objects such as submarines.

The diagram shows how an echo sounder works.

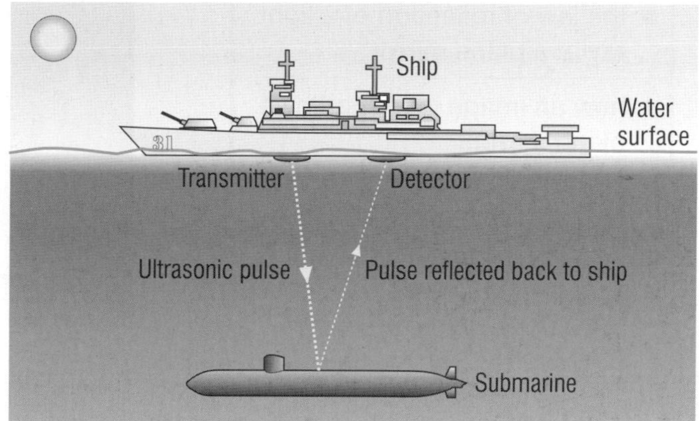

i What are ultrasound waves? (2)

ii An ultrasound pulse returns to the detector 0.1 s after leaving the transmitter. Calculate the distance of the submarine from the ship. (3)

iii State **one** other use of ultrasound waves. (1)

4 **a** Dentists often use ultrasound waves to clean plaque from teeth.

Which of the following frequencies is an ultrasound frequency? (1)

3 Hz 30 Hz 300 Hz 3000 Hz 30 000 Hz

b The diagram shows an ultrasound scan being carried out on a pregnant woman.

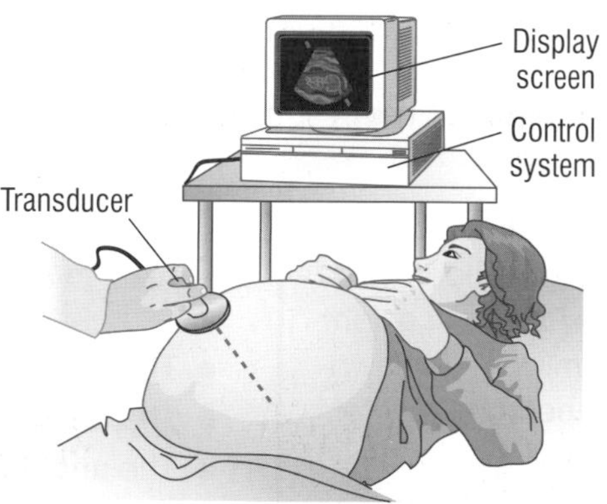

Explain how ultrasound waves are used to produce an image of the foetus. (QWC) (6)

P10.1 Reflection of light

Learning objectives

After this topic, you should know:

- what the normal is in a diagram showing light rays
- what the angle of incidence is
- the law of reflection of a light ray at a plane mirror
- how an image is formed by a plane mirror.

If you visit a Hall of Mirrors at a funfair, you will see some strange images of yourself. A tall, thin image or a short, broad image of yourself means you are looking into a mirror that is curved. If you want to see an ordinary image of yourself, look in a **plane mirror**. Such a mirror is perfectly flat. You see an exact **mirror image** of yourself.

Figure 1 A good image

Light consists of waves. In 7.3 'Reflection and refraction', we used a ripple tank to investigate the reflection of waves. The investigations showed that when plane (straight) waves reflect from a flat reflector, the reflected waves are at the same angle to the reflector as the incident waves.

The law of reflection

We use light rays to show us the direction that light waves are moving in. Figure 2 shows how we can investigate the reflection of a light ray from a ray box using a plane mirror.

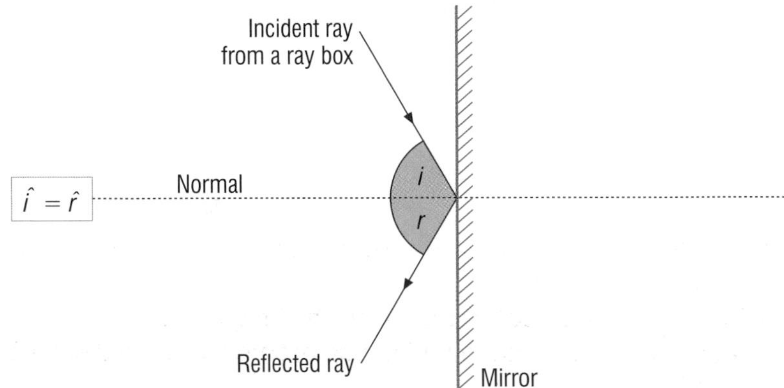

Figure 2 The law of reflection

- The perpendicular line to the mirror is called the **normal**.
- The **angle of incidence** is the angle between the incident ray and the normal.
- The **angle of reflection** is the angle between the reflected ray and the normal.

Measurements show that **for any light ray reflected by a plane mirror**:

the angle of incidence = the angle of reflection

Examiner's tip

Remember that angles of reflection and angles of incidence are measured between the ray and the normal.

Practical

A reflection test

Test the law of reflection by using a ray box to direct a light ray at a plane mirror as shown in Figure 2. Repeat the test for different angles of incidence.

Safety: If mirrors are glass, take care with sharp edges.

Image formation by a plane mirror

Figure 3 shows how an image is formed by a plane mirror. This ray diagram shows the path of two light rays from a point object that reflect off the mirror. The image and the object in Figure 3 are at equal distances from the mirror.

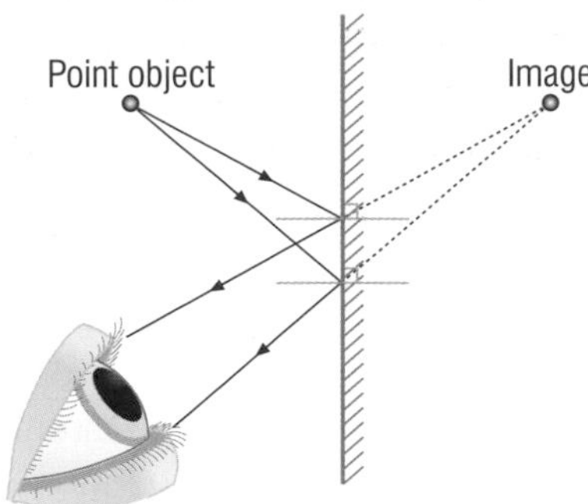

Figure 3 Image formation by a plane mirror

Real and virtual images

The image formed by a plane mirror is virtual, upright (the same way up as the object) and laterally inverted (back to front but not upside down). A **virtual image** can't be projected onto a screen like the movie images that you see at a cinema. An image on a screen is described as a **real image** because it is formed by focusing light rays onto the screen.

Summary questions

1 a In Figure 2 if the angle of reflection of a light ray from a plane mirror is 20°, what is:
 i the angle of incidence?
 ii the angle between the incident ray and the reflected ray?
b If the mirror is turned so the angle of incidence is increased to 21°, what is the angle between the incident ray and the reflected ray?

2 A point object O is placed in front of a plane mirror, as shown.

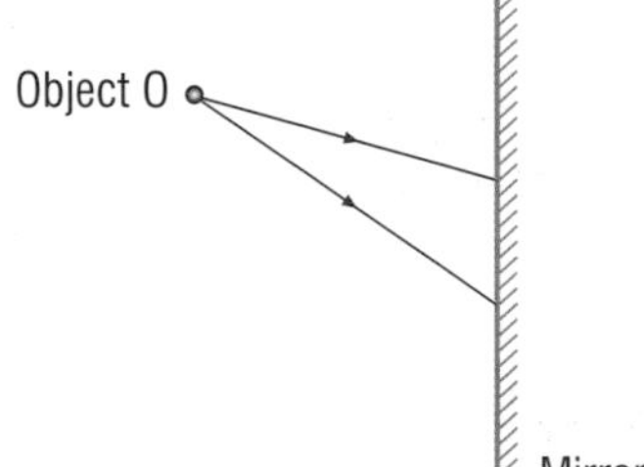

a Complete the path of the two rays shown from O after they have reflected off the mirror.
b i Use the reflected rays to locate the image of O.
 ii Show that the image and the object are the same distance from the mirror.

3 Two plane mirrors are placed perpendicular to each other.
a Draw a ray diagram to show the path of a light ray at an angle of incidence of 60° that reflects off both mirrors.
b i Measure the angle A between the final reflected ray and the incident ray.
 ii Show that angle A is always equal to 180° whatever the angle of incidence is.

Did you know ...?

Ambulances and police cars often carry a 'mirror image' sign at the front. This is so a driver in a vehicle in front looking at their rear-view mirror can read the sign as it gets 'laterally inverted' (back to front but not upside down).

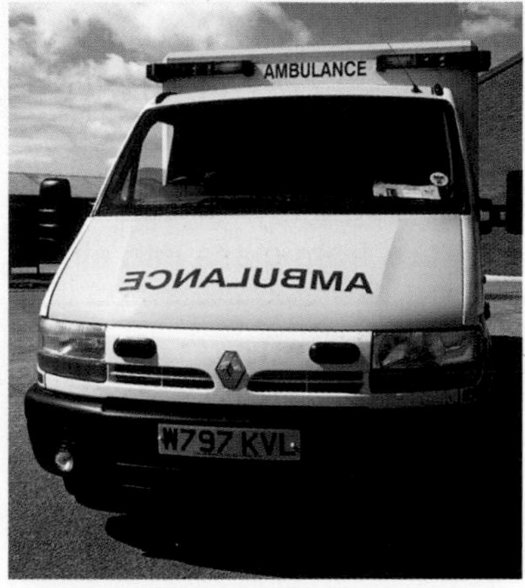

Figure 4 A mirror sign on an ambulance

Key points

- The normal at a point on a mirror is a line drawn perpendicular to the mirror.
- For a light ray reflected by a plane mirror:
  - The angle of incidence is the angle between the incident ray and the normal
  - The angle of reflection is the angle between the reflected ray and the normal.
- The law of reflection states that: the angle of incidence = the angle of reflection.

P10.2 Refraction of light

Learning objectives

After this topic, you should know:

- where refraction of light can occur
- how a light ray refracts when it goes from air into glass
- how a light ray refracts when it goes from glass into air.

When you have your eyes tested, the optician might test different lenses in front of each of your eyes. Each lens changes the direction of light passing through it. This change of direction is known as **refraction**.

Refraction is a property of all forms of waves, including light and sound. In 7.3 'Reflection and refraction', we investigated the refraction of water waves in a ripple tank. Water waves travel more slowly in shallow water than in deep water. Refraction occurs when the waves cross a boundary between the deep and the shallow water at a non-zero angle to the boundary. The change of speed at the **boundary**, or **interface**, causes them to change direction.

- Light waves are refracted as shown in Figure 1 when they travel across a boundary between air and a transparent medium or between two transparent media. This is because the speed of light changes at such a boundary.

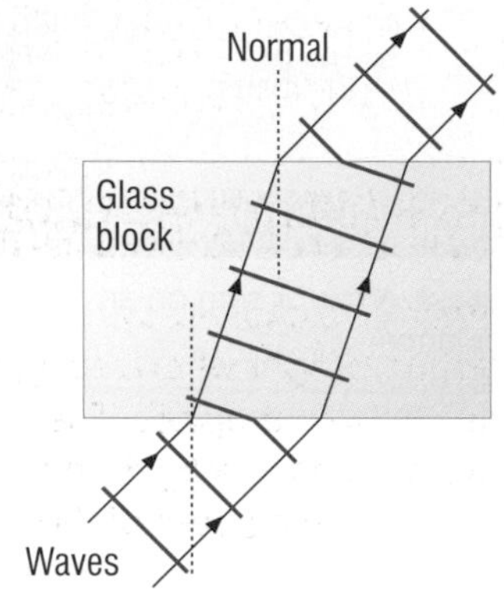

Figure 1 Refraction of waves

Figure 1 shows light waves (in blue) entering then leaving a glass block. The direction in which the light waves are moving is represented by light rays (in red). The change of direction of each ray relative to the normal at each boundary is:

- towards the normal when light travels from air into glass
- away from the normal when light travels from glass to air.

Both changes occur because light travels more slowly in glass than in air. Because light travels more slowly in glass than in air, we say glass is 'optically more dense' than air. In general:

- when light enters a more dense medium, it is refracted towards the normal
- when light enters a less dense medium, it is refracted away from the normal.

Practical

Investigating refraction of light

Figure 2 shows how you can use a ray box and a rectangular glass block to investigate the refraction of a light ray when it enters glass. The ray changes direction at the boundary between air and glass (unless it is along the normal).

At the point where the light ray enters the glass, compare the angle of refraction (the angle between the refracted ray and the normal) with the angle of incidence.

You should find that the angle of refraction at the point of entry is always less than the angle of incidence.

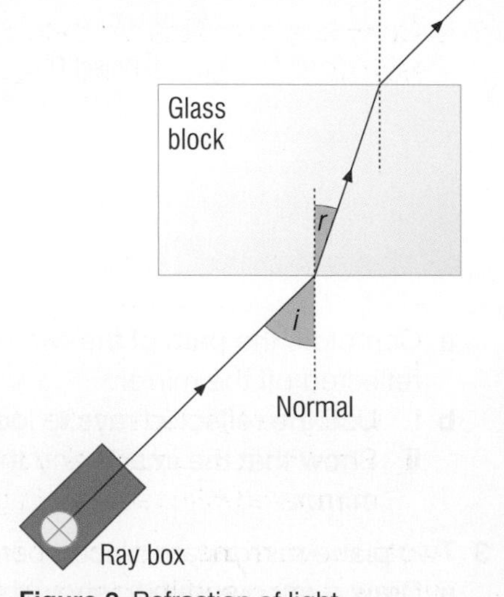

Figure 2 Refraction of light

Safety: Make sure the glass block doesn't have any sharp edges.

Examiner's tip

- Remember that angles of incidence, reflection and refraction are always measured between the ray and the normal.
- Make sure you know that light bends towards the normal when entering a denser medium, and away from the normal when entering a less dense medium.

Refraction rules

Your investigation should show that a light ray:

- changes direction towards the normal when it travels from air into glass. The angle of refraction (*r*) is smaller than the angle of incidence (*i*).
- changes direction away from the normal when it travels from glass into air. The angle of refraction (*r*) is greater than the angle of incidence (*i*).

Refraction by a prism

Figure 3 shows what happens when a narrow beam of white light passes through a triangular glass prism. The ray comes out of the prism in a different direction to the incident ray and is split into the colours of the spectrum.

White light contains all the colours of the spectrum. Each colour of light is refracted slightly differently. So the prism splits the light into colours. The splitting of white light into the colours of the spectrum is called **dispersion**.

Figure 3 The incident beam of white light enters the prism at its right hand side

Summary questions

1 When a light ray travels from air into glass, its speed changes at the boundary.
  a State whether there is an increase or a decrease in the speed of the light waves when they cross the boundary.
  b If the angle of incidence is zero, what is the angle of refraction?
  c If the angle of incidence is non-zero, state whether the angle of refraction is greater than or smaller than the angle of incidence.

2 a Copy and complete the path of the light ray through each glass object below:

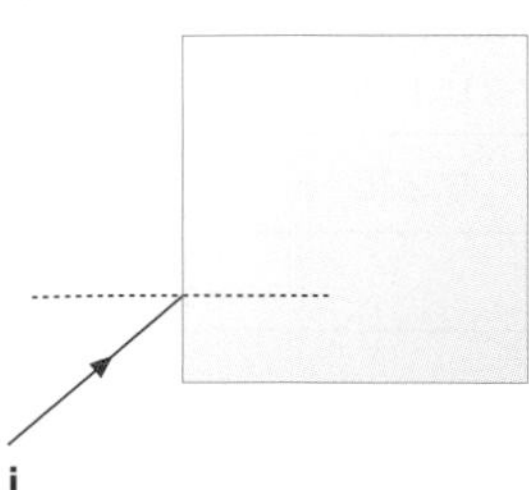

i

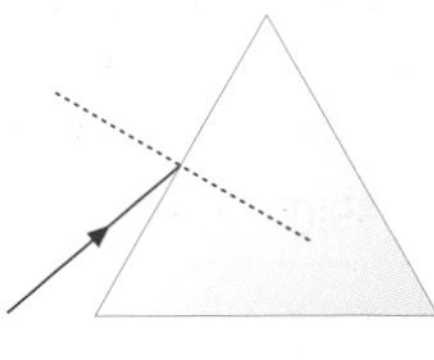

ii

  b i In Figure 3, which colour, blue or red, is refracted most?
    ii What does Figure 3 tell you about the speed of blue light in glass compared with red light in glass?

3 A light ray from the bottom of a swimming pool refracts at the water surface. Its angle of incidence is 40 degrees and its angle of refraction is 75 degrees.
  a Draw a diagram to show the path of this light ray from the bottom of the swimming pool into the air above the pool.
  b Use your diagram to explain why the swimming pool appears shallower than it really is when viewed from above.

Did you know ... ?

A swimming pool always appears shallower than it really is. The next time you jump into water, make sure you know how deep it is. Light from the bottom refracts at the surface. This makes the water appear shallower than it is.

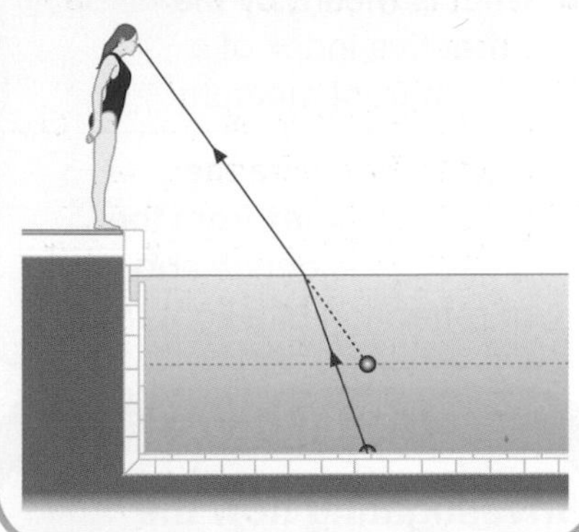

Did you know ... ?

A **rainbow** is caused by refraction of light when sunlight shines on rain droplets. The droplets refract sunlight and split it into the colours of the spectrum.

Key points

- Refraction is the change of direction of waves when they travel across a boundary from one medium to another.
- When a light ray refracts as it travels from air into glass, the angle of refraction is less than the angle of incidence.
- When a light ray refracts as it travels from glass into air, the angle of refraction is more than the angle of incidence.

P10.3 Refractive index

Learning objectives

After this topic, you should know:

- what is meant by the refractive index of a transparent medium
- how to calculate the refractive index from the angle of incidence and angle of refraction of a light ray.

Practical

Investigating how the angle of refraction varies with the angle of incidence

We can use a semicircular transparent glass block as shown in Figure 2.

- Measure the angle of refraction, *r*, for different angles of incidence, *i*.
- Record all your measurements in a table.

Safety: Make sure glass block does not have any sharp edges.

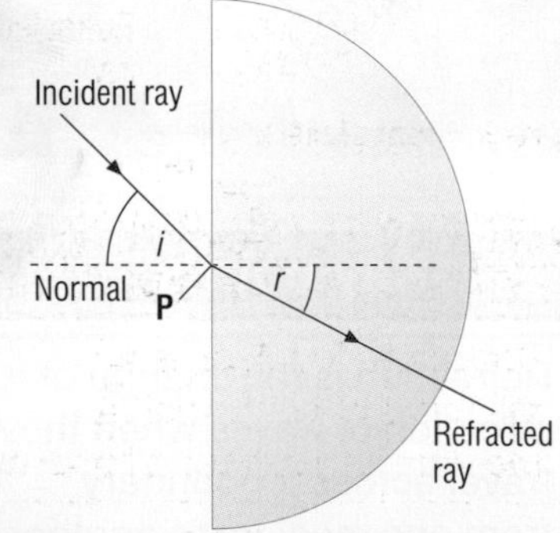

Figure 2 Using a semicircular block

Examiner's tip

- Remember that angles *i* and *r* are measured between the ray and the normal.
- When calculating the refractive index, remember it is the sine of the angle, not the angle itself, that is needed.

When a light ray travels from air into a transparent medium, the angle of refraction depends on the medium as well as on the angle of incidence. For example, for the same angle of incidence, glass refracts a light ray more than water does. Figure 1 shows the refraction of a light ray travelling from air into water. If glass had been used instead, the light ray would have been refracted much more.

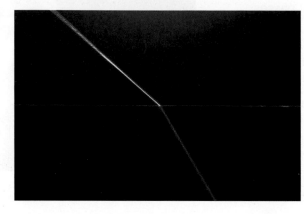

Figure 1 A laser beam entering water

For a light ray travelling into glass from air as in Figure 2, your results should show that:

1 the angle of refraction is always less than the angle of incidence

2 the greater the angle of incidence, *i*, the greater the angle of refraction, *r*.

Snell's law

Some typical results are shown below in Table 1.

Table 1

i (degrees)	*r* (degrees)	sin *i*	sin *r*	$\frac{\sin i}{\sin r}$
10.0	6.5	0.174	0.113	1.54
20.0	13.0	0.342	0.225	1.52
30.0	19.0			

The measurements can be used to show that sin *i* ÷ sin *r* always has the same value for the same medium that the block is made of, regardless of the angle of incidence. This relationship was discovered in 1618 and is known as **Snell's law** after its discoverer.

It can be shown that $\frac{\sin i}{\sin r}$ is equal to the ratio $\frac{\text{speed of light in vacuum (air)}}{\text{speed of light in the medium}}$

This ratio is defined as the **refractive index** of the medium. The symbol ***n*** is used for the refractive index.

$$\textbf{refractive index, } n = \frac{\textbf{speed of light in vacuum (air)}}{\textbf{speed of light in the medium}}$$

Calculate the mean value of sin *i* ÷ sin *r* for your own measurements. This is the refractive index of the block that you used in your investigations.

Maths skills

Using a calculator

To find the value of the sine of a given angle in degrees or the angle in degrees for a given sine value, make sure your calculator is in degree mode. Key the angle in degrees into your calculator, then press the button marked 'sin' (or on some calculators press 'sin' first). The calculator will then display the sine of the angle.

To find the angle for a given sine value, key the sine value into your calculator and press the button marked 'inv sin' (or '$\sin^{-1}$' on some calculators).

The law of refraction

For a light ray travelling from air into a transparent medium, the ratio of sin $i \div \sin r$ is always the same for the same medium.

This ratio is the refractive index of the medium. In other words:

$$\textbf{the refractive index of the medium, } n = \frac{\sin i}{\sin r}$$

where i is the angle of incidence and r is the angle of refraction.

Rearranging the above equation to make sin i the subject gives us $\sin i = n \sin r$

Rearranging the above equation to make sin r the subject gives us $\sin r = \frac{\sin i}{n}$

When a light ray travels from a transparent medium into air at a non-zero angle of incidence:

- the light ray is refracted **away** from the normal, as shown at point P in Figure 3
- the larger the angle of incidence, the larger the angle of refraction.

If the light ray in Figure 3 were reversed, the direction arrows would be reversed but the path would be the same. We can adapt the law of refraction to cover both situations by writing it as:

the sine of the angle in air = n × the sine of the angle in glass

Maths skills

Worked example

A light ray travels from glass into air across a straight boundary, as shown at P in Figure 3. The angle of incidence of the light ray in the glass is 32.0°. The refractive index of the glass is 1.55. Calculate the angle of refraction of the light ray in the air.

Solution

Let r be the angle of refraction in air.

The sine of the angle in air = n × the sine of the angle in glass.

Hence, $\sin r = 1.55 \times \sin 32.0° = 0.821$

Therefore, r = **55.2°**

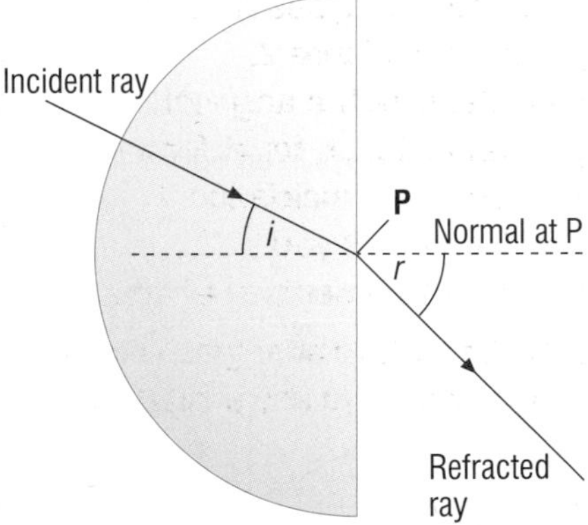

Figure 3 From glass to air

Summary questions

1 In Table 1, the angle of refraction is 19.0° for an angle of incidence of 30°.
  a Use this data to calculate the refractive index of the block.
  b Use your result in **a** and the data in the table to calculate a mean value for the refractive index.

2 In an experiment like that shown in Figure 2 to measure the refractive index of a glass block, when i = 40°, r = 26°:
  a calculate the refractive index
  b give **two** possible reasons why the value of refractive index in **a** differs so much from the values obtained in **1b**.

3 The refractive index of water is 1.33.
  a A light ray enters a flat water surface at an angle of incidence of 35.0°. Calculate the angle of refraction of the light ray.
  b A light ray travels from water into air. The angle of incidence of the light ray in the water is 45.0°. Calculate the angle of refraction of the light ray in the air.
  c In Figure 3, when angle i is equal to 35.0°, angle r is equal to 60.5°. Calculate the refractive index of the glass.

Key points

- Refractive index, n, is a measure of how much a medium can refract a light ray.
- $n = \frac{\text{speed of light in vacuum (air)}}{\text{speed of light in the medium}}$
- Angle of incidence, i, and angle of refraction, r, are related to refractive index n by the law of refraction: $n = \frac{\sin i}{\sin r}$

P10.4 Total internal reflection

Learning objectives

After this topic, you should know:

- what is meant by the critical angle of a medium
- how the critical angle is related to the refractive index of the medium
- what is meant by total internal reflection
- what doctors use an endoscope for.

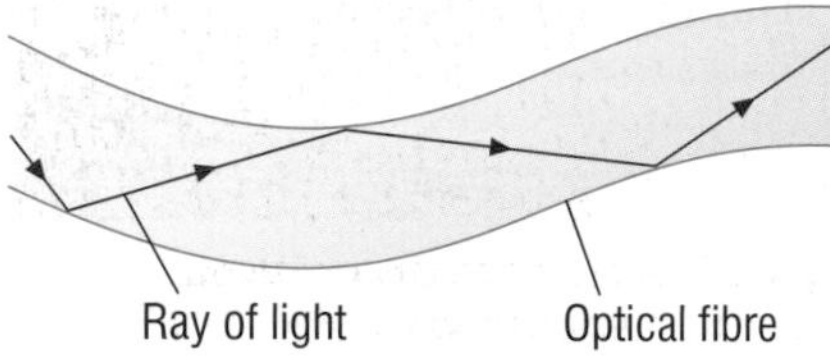

Figure 1 Light rays in an optical fibre

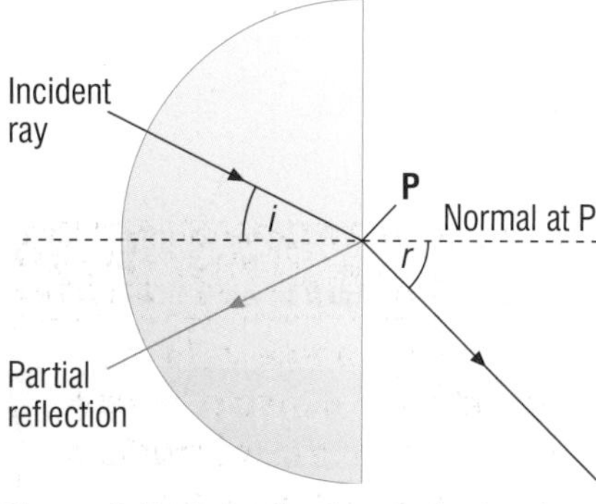

Figure 2 Partial reflection and refraction

Optical fibres are very thin glass fibres that are designed to transmit light or infrared radiation. We use them in medicine to see inside the body, without cutting the body open, by using an endoscope. In telecommunications they are used to send signals securely. The light rays can't escape from the fibre. Each light ray entering a fibre at one end leaves the fibre at the other end even if the fibre bends round. This is because a light ray in the fibre is **totally internally reflected** each time it reaches the fibre's boundary (Figure 1).

Investigating total internal reflection

In 10.3 'Refractive index', we saw that a light ray travelling from glass into air at a non-zero angle of incidence is refracted away from the normal. A partially reflected ray is also seen, as shown in Figure 2. The angle of reflection of this ray in the glass is the same as the angle of incidence.

- If the angle of incidence in the glass is gradually increased, the angle of refraction increases until the refracted ray emerges along the boundary, as shown in Figure 3. The angle of incidence at this position is referred to as the **critical angle**, labelled *c* in Figure 3.
- If the angle of incidence is increased beyond the critical angle, the light ray is **totally internally reflected** at P, as shown in Figure 4. When **total internal reflection** occurs, the angle of reflection *r* at P is equal to the angle of incidence *i*.

Critical angle and refractive index

If the light ray in Figure 2 was reversed, the direction arrows would be reversed but the path would be the same. We can adapt the law of refraction for this situation by writing it as:

the sine of the angle in air = *n* × the sine of the angle in glass

We can apply this equation to the critical ray in Figure 3. The angle in air is 90° and the angle in glass is *c*:

$$\sin 90° = n \times \sin c$$

Because $\sin 90° = 1$, the equation above becomes $1 = n \times \sin c$. Rearranging this equation gives:

$$n = \frac{1}{\sin c} \quad \text{or} \quad \sin c = \frac{1}{n}$$

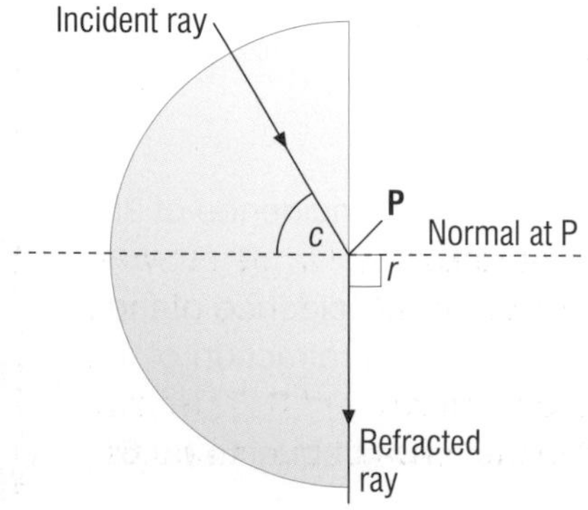

Figure 3 At the critical angle

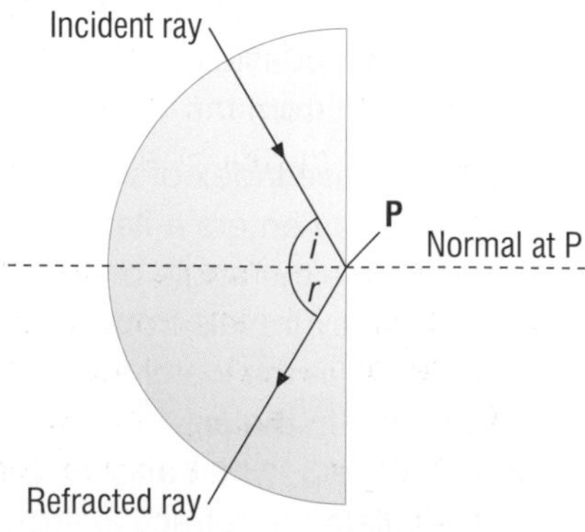

Figure 4 Total internal reflection

Examiner's tip

Remember that total internal reflection only occurs when light is trying to enter a less dense medium.

The endoscope

The **endoscope** is used by a surgeon to see inside a body cavity, such as the stomach, without cutting the body open. The endoscope is inserted into the stomach via the patient's throat.

The endoscope contains two bundles of optical fibres alongside each other. One of the bundles is used to shine light into the cavity and the other to see the internal surfaces of the cavity. A tiny lens over the second bundle is used to form an image on the ends of the fibres in the bundle. The image can then be seen directly or by using a digital camera at the other end of the fibre bundle.

For example, the endoscope can be used to observe a stomach ulcer or a bone fragment in the knee joint. The surgeon can then use keyhole surgery to remove them.

Laser light may be used as a source of energy in an endoscope to carry out some surgical procedures. It can cut away or burn away and destroy diseased tissue. It can also seal off (cauterise) leaking blood vessels. This is possible with laser light because the energy can be focused on to a very small area of a surface.

In addition, the colour of laser light can be matched to the type of tissue. By choosing an appropriate laser source, it ensures the most effective absorption. Eye surgery on the retina can be carried out by applying the laser light through the pupil of the eye for a very short time.

Safety note: Never look into or along a laser beam, even after reflection. It will damage the retina and may cause permanent blindness. Special safety goggles should always be worn in the presence of a laser beam.

Maths skills

Worked example

Calculate the critical angle for glass of refractive index 1.59.

Solution

$$\sin c = \frac{1}{n} = \frac{1}{1.59} = 0.629$$

Therefore c = **39.0°**

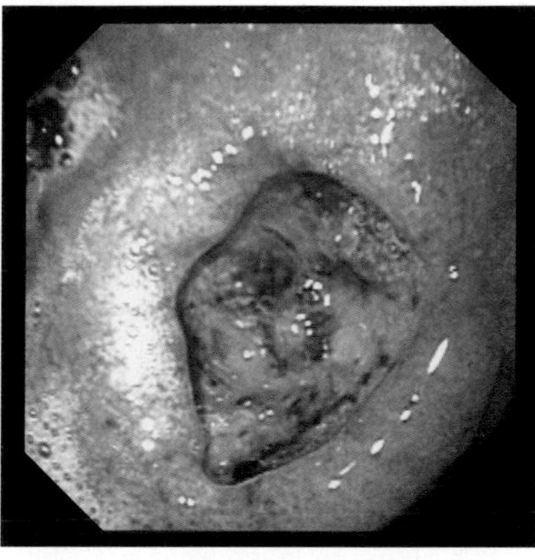

Figure 5 A stomach ulcer viewed through an endoscope

Summary questions

1 a When a light ray travelling in a refractive medium reaches a boundary with a less refractive medium, what is the condition under which total internal reflection can occur?

b What is the angle between the normal and the refracted ray when the angle of incidence is equal to the critical angle?

c The critical angle for a certain type of glass is 43.0°. Calculate the refractive index of this glass.

2 a The figure shows a light ray in an optical fibre. The angle of incidence of the light ray at P is greater than the critical angle of the optical fibre. Copy the diagram and complete the path of the light ray inside the optical fibre.

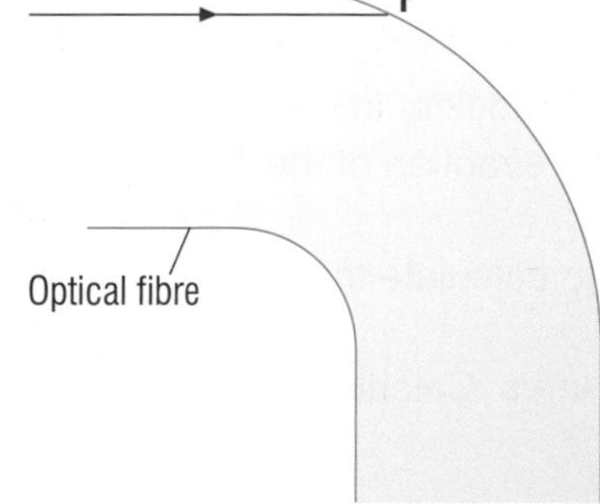

b State **two** advantages of using an endoscope instead of X-rays to observe fragments of bone in a knee joint.

3 a The refractive index of water is 1.33. Calculate the critical angle of water.

b i The critical angle for a certain type of glass is 42.0°. Calculate the refractive index of the glass.

ii The critical angle in **i** was measured to a precision of 0.5°. Show that this gives an uncertainty of 0.02 in the value of the refractive index.

Key points

- The critical angle, **c**, is the angle of incidence of a light ray in a transparent medium that produces refraction along the boundary.
- Refractive index = $\frac{1}{\sin c}$
- Total internal reflection occurs when the angle of incidence of a light ray in a transparent medium is greater than the critical angle.
- An endoscope uses total internal reflection to see inside the body directly.

Summary questions

1 a The figure shows an incomplete ray diagram of image formation by a plane mirror.

i What can you say about the angles x and y in the diagram?

ii Copy and complete the ray diagram to locate the image.

iii What can you say about the distance from the image to the mirror compared with the distance from the object to the mirror?

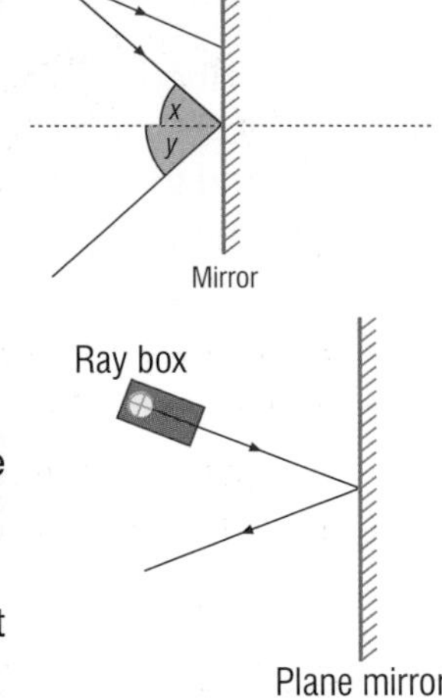

b Describe an experiment to test the law of reflection using the ray box and plane.

2 a The figure shows a light ray directed into a rectangular glass block.

i Sketch the path of the light ray through the block.

ii Explain why the light ray that emerges from the block is exactly parallel to the incident light ray.

b The figure shows a ray of red light directed into a triangular glass prism.

i Copy the drawing and complete the path of the red light ray through the prism.

ii The red light ray is replaced by a white light ray, and the light coming out from the prism is observed on a white screen. Describe and explain what is observed on the screen.

3 a A light ray is directed into a transparent block at an angle of incidence of 25°. The angle of refraction of the light ray is 16°.

i Use the equation $n = \sin i \div \sin r$ to calculate the refractive index of the glass.

ii The speed of light in air is 300 000 km/s. Calculate the speed of light in the glass.

b A light ray is directed from air into a glass block of refractive index 1.5. Use the equation in **a i** to calculate:

i the angle of refraction when the angle of incidence is 30°

ii the angle of incidence when the angle of refraction is 41°.

4 a The figure shows a light ray directed at a semicircular glass block. Copy the diagram and draw the path of the light ray through the glass block into the air.

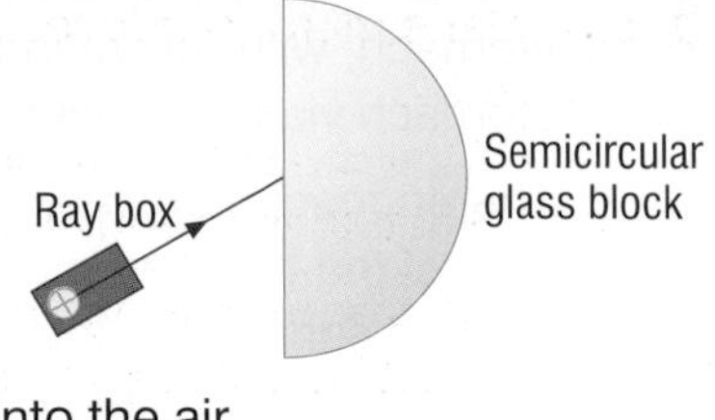

b Describe how you would measure the refractive index of a rectangular glass block using the arrangement shown in the figure and any other necessary items of equipment.

5 a i Explain what is meant by total internal reflection.

ii What is the condition for the angle of incidence of a light ray in a transparent medium for it to be totally internally reflected at a boundary with air?

iii Use the equation $n = 1 \div \sin c$ to calculate the refractive index of a transparent medium for which the critical angle is 40°.

b An endoscope is used to see inside the body. The figure shows a light ray entering the end of the transparent core of an endoscope.

i The core of the endoscope is surrounded by air. The refractive index of the core is 1.52. Use the equation $n = 1 \div \sin c$ to calculate the critical angle of a boundary between the core and air.

ii The angle of incidence of the light ray in the figure when it reaches the core boundary at **X** is 70°. Copy and complete the figure to show the path of the light ray along the optical fibre.

iii Explain why an endoscope needs to have two bundles of optical fibres.

6 a The figure shows a light ray entering a glass block of refractive index 1.59 at an angle of incidence of 40° at point **P**. Use the equation $n = \sin i \div \sin r$ to show by calculation that the angle of refraction at **P** is 24°.

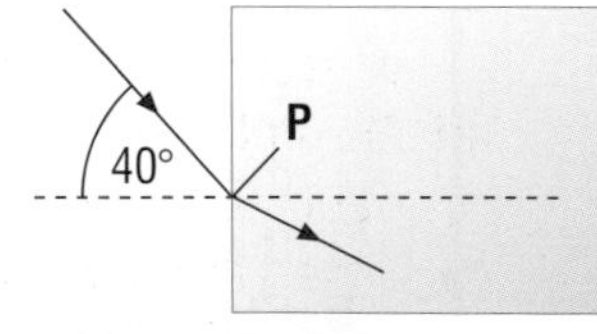

b i Use the equation $n = 1 \div \sin c$ to calculate the critical angle of the glass.

ii Copy the diagram and continue the path of the ray in the glass until it reaches a point **Q** at the bottom of the block. Explain why the angle of incidence at **Q** is 66°.

iii Explain why the light ray does not enter the air at **Q**.

AQA Examination-style questions

1 **a** A plane mirror produces a virtual image that is laterally inverted.

  i What is a *virtual* image? (2)

  ii What does *laterally inverted* mean? (1)

b A man stands in a lift. The walls of the lift have plane mirrors fixed to them.

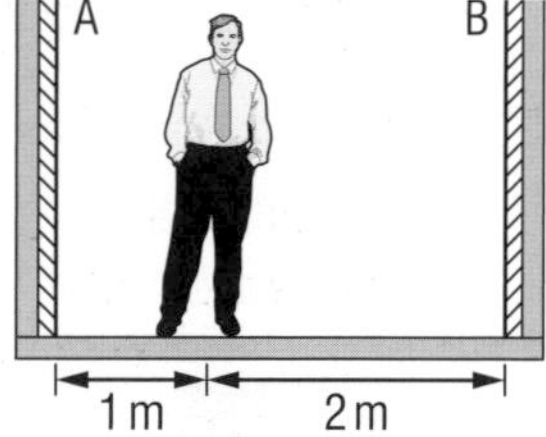

The man looks into mirror **A** and sees lots of images of himself, one behind the other.

When he looks into mirror **B**, he again sees lots of images of himself, one behind the other.

  i Calculate the distance between the nearest image that he sees in mirror **A** and the nearest image that he sees in mirror **B**. (3)

  ii Explain why he sees lots of images when he looks into mirror **A**. (2)

2 Light waves change direction when they travel from air into another transparent medium. The diagram shows a wavefront XY in air moving towards water.

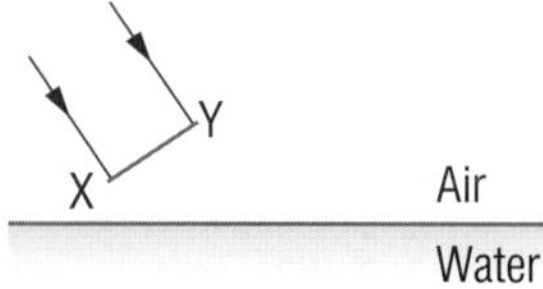

a **i** Explain how light waves change direction when they travel from air into water. (3)

  ii Under what conditions do light waves not change direction when they travel from air into water? (1)

b Some students use the apparatus below to determine the refractive index of glass.

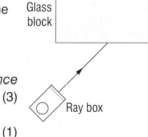

  i Copy and complete the diagram to show what is meant by *angle of incidence and angle of refraction*. (3)

  ii What would they use to measure the angles? (1)

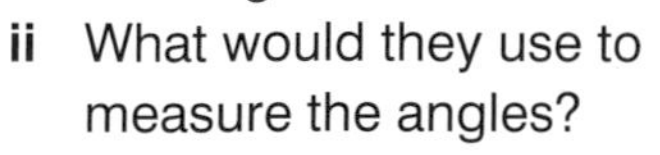

  iii Describe what they need to do to obtain an accurate value for the refractive index of glass. (3)

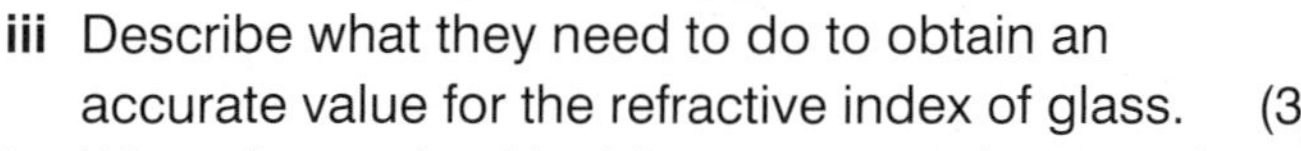

  iv When the angle of incidence was 35 degrees, the angle of refraction was 22 degrees. Calculate the critical angle of glass. (4)

3 Below is part of an advert.

Brighten your darkest room with our light pipe

Use one of our light pipes to catch sunlight and send it into the darkest corner of your house.

The pipes contain hi-tech optical fibres that can make light go round corners.

a The diagram shows how light passes through an optical fibre.

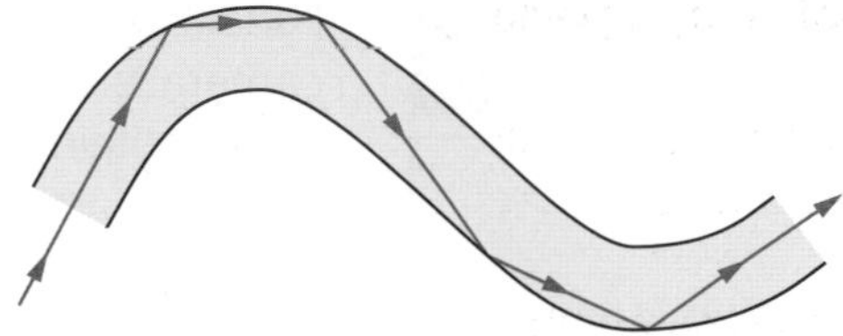

  i What is the process shown in the diagram? (2)

  ii Give two other uses for optical fibres. (2)

b A student investigated the process shown above. The diagrams give three stages of the investigation.

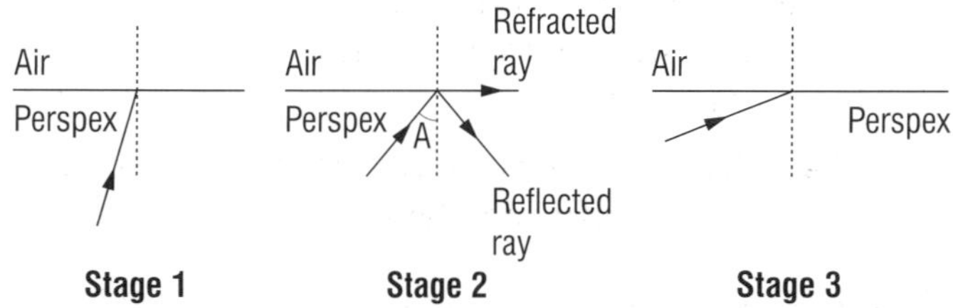

  i What is the name of the dotted line in the diagrams? (1)

  ii Copy and complete the **Stage 1** diagram to show what happened to the ray of light after it hit the boundary between the Perspex and the air. (2)

  iii Name angle **A** in the **Stage 2** diagram. (1)

  iv Copy and complete the **Stage 3** diagram to show what happened to the ray of light after it hit the boundary between the Perspex and the air. (1)

4 A ray of red light is incident on one face of a glass prism.

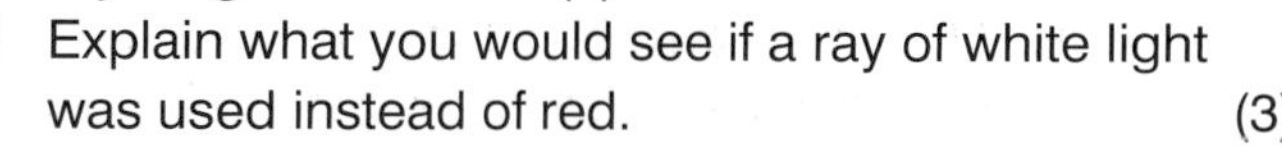

a **i** Copy and complete the ray diagram. (2)

  ii Explain what you would see if a ray of white light was used instead of red. (3)

b Light can be totally internally reflected. What are the conditions necessary for total internal reflection to occur? (2)

c Doctors sometimes use endoscopes to see inside patients' stomachs. The diagram shows an endoscope.

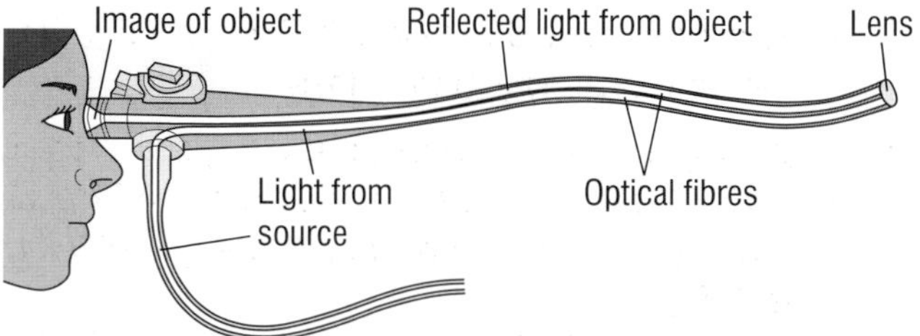

Explain how this endoscope works and discuss the advantages of this method of investigation over other methods of investigation of a stomach. (QWC) (6)

P11.1 Lenses

Learning objectives

After this topic, you should know:

- what a converging (convex) lens is
- what a diverging (concave) lens is
- what a real image is and what a virtual image is
- what is meant by magnification.

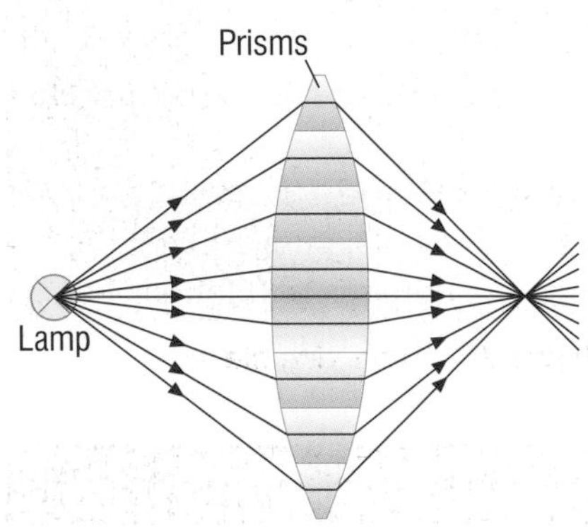

Figure 2 How a lens works

Examiner's tip

Remember that a diverging lens makes light rays from a point object spread out (diverge) more.

Lenses are used in optical devices such as the camera. Although a digital camera is very different from the first cameras made over 160 years ago, they both contain a lens that is used to form an image.

Types of lenses

A lens works by changing the direction of light passing through it. Figure 1 shows the effect of a lens on the light rays from a ray box. The curved shape of the lens surfaces refracts the rays so they meet at a point.

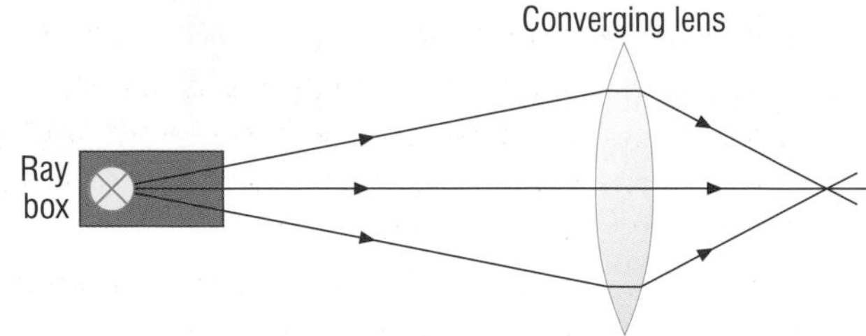

Figure 1 Investigating lenses

Each section of the lens acts like a tiny prism, refracting light as it goes in and again as it comes out. Because each section refracts light differently, the overall effect is to make the light rays converge, as shown in Figure 2.

Different lens shapes can be tested using this arrangement.

- A **converging (convex) lens** makes parallel rays converge to a focus. The point where parallel rays are focused to is the **principal focus** (or focal point) of the lens. See Figure 3. We use a converging lens as a **magnifying glass** and in a camera to form a clear image of a distant object.
- A **diverging (concave) lens** makes parallel rays diverge (spread out). The point where the rays appear to come from is the principal focus of the lens. See Figure 4. We use diverging lenses to correct short sight.
- In both cases, the distance from the centre of the lens to the principal focus is the **focal length** of the lens. Notice that the principal focus is usually shown in ray diagrams on each side of the lens.

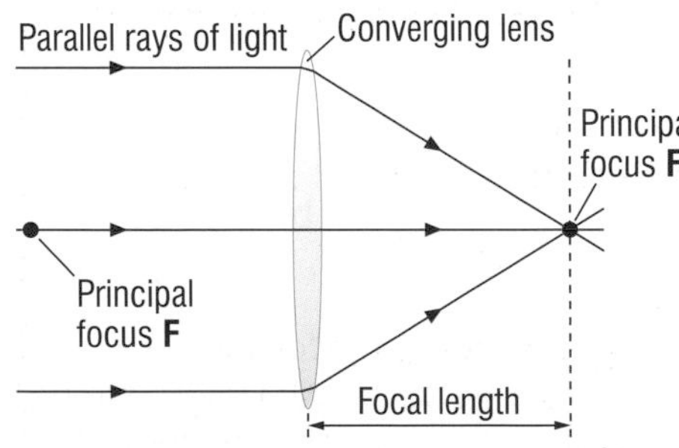

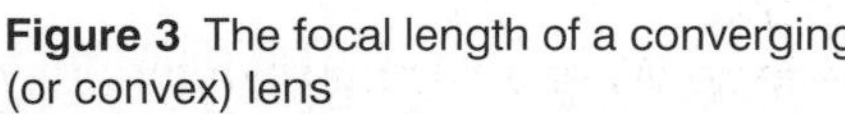

Figure 3 The focal length of a converging (or convex) lens

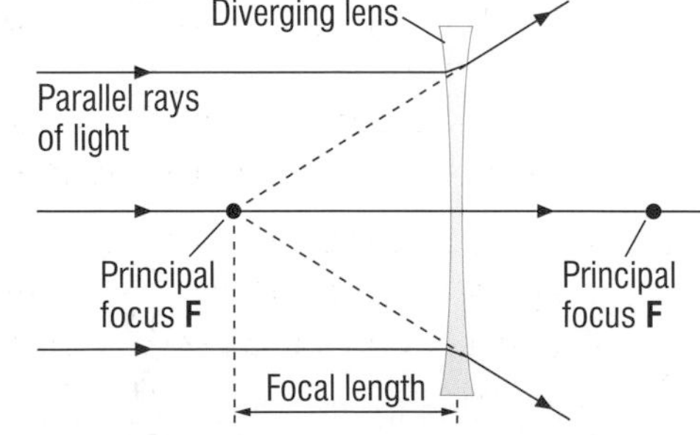

Figure 4 The focal length of a diverging (or concave) lens

Practical

Investigating the converging lens

Use the arrangement in Figure 5 to investigate the image formed by a converging lens.

Safety: Make sure glass lenses are not sharp.

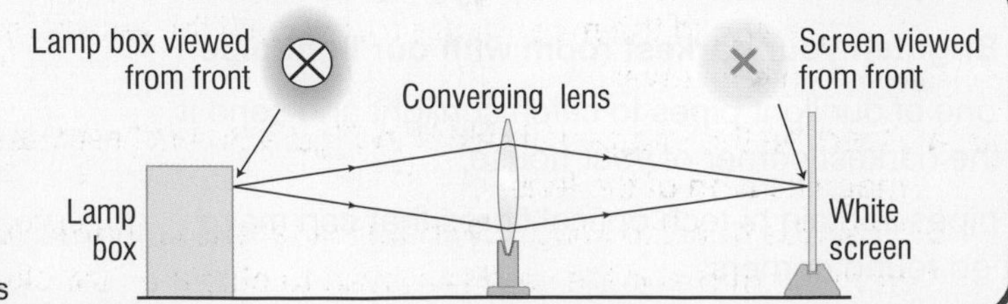

Figure 5 Investigating images

The converging lens

1 *With the object at different distances beyond the principal focus of the lens*, adjust the position of the screen until you see a clear image of the object on it. This is called a **real image** because it is formed on the screen where the light rays meet.

- When the object is a long distance away, the image is formed at the principal focus of the lens. This is because the rays from any point on the object are effectively parallel to each other when they reach the lens.
- If the object is moved nearer the lens towards its principal focus, the screen must be moved further from the lens to see a clear image. The nearer the object is to the lens, the larger the image is.

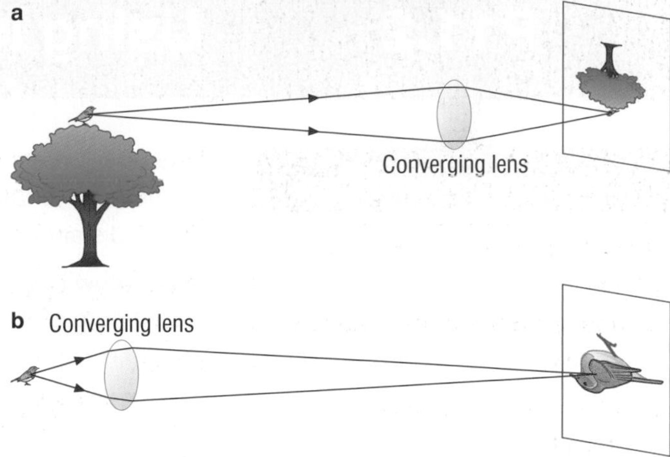

Figure 6 **a** The image of a distant object, **b** an enlarged image

2 *With the object nearer to the lens than the principal focus*, a magnified image is formed. The image is called a **virtual image** because it's formed where the rays appear to come from. But you can see the image only when you look into the lens from the side opposite to the object. The lens acts as a magnifying glass in this situation.

Figure 7 A magnifying glass

Magnification

The **magnification** produced by a lens = $\dfrac{\textbf{image height}}{\textbf{object height}}$

If the image is larger than the object, as in Figure 6b and Figure 7, the magnification is greater than 1.

If the image is smaller than the object, as in Figure 6a, the magnification is less than 1.

Summary questions

1 a What is the difference between a real image and a virtual image?
  b State whether a real image or a virtual image is formed when:
    i a converging lens is used to form an image of a distant object on a screen
    ii a converging lens is used as a magnifying glass
    iii a diverging lens is used to form an image of a distant object.

2 a A postage stamp is inspected using a converging lens as a magnifying glass. Describe the image.
  b A converging lens is used to form a magnified image of a slide on a screen.
    i Describe the image formed by the lens.
    ii The screen is moved away from the lens. What adjustment must be made to the position of the slide to focus its image on the screen again?
  c i Estimate the magnification of the flower in Figure 7.
    ii How would the magnification change if the lens is moved away from the flower?

3 a Describe the image of the bird in Figure 6b and estimate the magnification of the lens.
  b Describe how the image changes if the lens is moved further away from the bird and the card is moved to obtain a new clear image.

Key points

- A converging (convex) lens focuses parallel rays to a point called the principal focus.
- A diverging (concave) lens makes parallel rays spread out as if they had come from a point called the principal focus.
- A real image is formed by a converging lens if the object is further away than the principal focus.
- A virtual image is formed by a diverging lens.
- A virtual image is formed by a converging lens if the object is nearer to the lens than the principal focus.
- Magnification = $\dfrac{\text{image height}}{\text{object height}}$

P11.2 Using lenses

Learning objectives

After this topic, you should know:

- how to find the position and nature of an image formed by a lens
- what type of image is formed by a converging lens when the object is between the lens and its principal focus
- what type of lens is used in a camera and in a magnifying glass
- what type of image is formed in a camera and in a magnifying glass, and by a diverging (concave) lens.

The position and nature of the image formed by a lens depends on:

- the focal length, *f*, of the lens
- the distance from the object to the lens.

If we know the focal length and the object distance, we can find the position and nature of the image by drawing a ray diagram.

Formation of a real image by a converging lens

To form a real image using a converging (convex) lens, the object must be beyond the principal focus, F, of the lens. See Figure 1. The image is formed on the other side of the lens to the object.

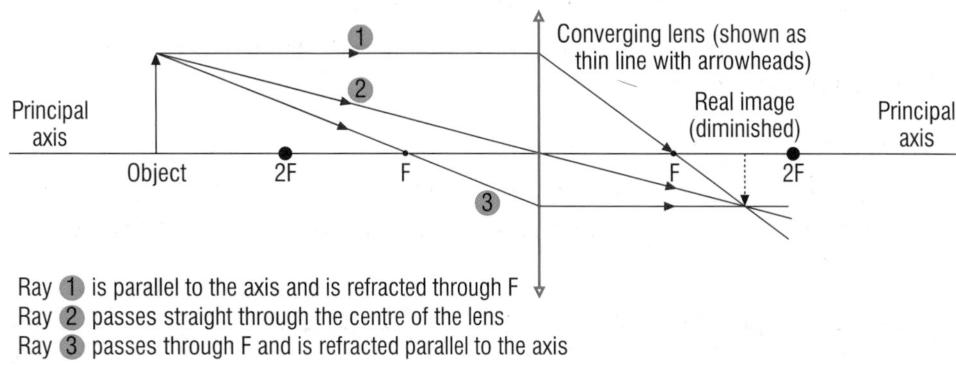

Figure 1 Formation of a real image by a converging lens

The diagram shows that we can use three key 'construction' rays from a single point of the object to locate the image.

- The **principal axis** of the lens is the straight line that passes along the normal at the centre of each lens surface. Notice we draw the lens as a straight line with 'outward' arrows to show it is a converging lens.
- The image is real, inverted and smaller than the object.

Notice how light acts along the different ray paths:

- ***ray 1*** is refracted through F, the principal focus of the lens, because it is parallel to the principal axis of the lens before it passes through the lens
- ***ray 2*** passes through the centre of the lens (its pole) without change of direction; this is because the lens surfaces at the principal axis are parallel to each other
- ***ray 3*** passes through F, the principal focus of the lens, before the lens, so it is refracted by the lens parallel to the principal axis.

The image is smaller than the object because the object distance is greater than twice the focal length (*f*) of the lens. This is how a **camera** is used.

Examiner's tip

- Always use a ruler when drawing ray diagrams – and don't forget the arrows to show the direction of the rays.
- Make sure your ray diagrams are neat and that you put arrows on the rays. You need to be able to draw a scale diagram to find the focal length of a lens for a particular magnification. See Summary question 3.

The camera

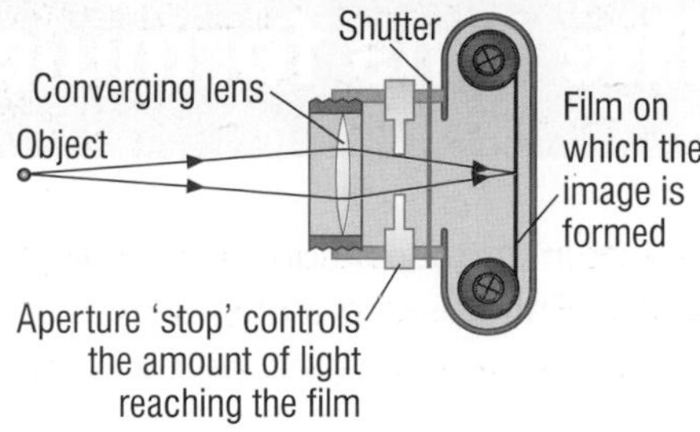

Figure 2 The camera

In a camera, a converging lens is used to produce a real image of an object on a film (or on an array of 'pixels' for a digital camera). The position of the lens is adjusted to focus the image on the film.

- For a distant object, the distance from the lens to the film must be equal to the focal length of the lens.
- The nearer an object is to the lens, the greater the distance from the lens to the film.

Formation of a virtual image by a converging lens

The object must be between the lens and its principal focus, as shown in Figure 3. The image is formed on the same side of the lens as the object.

The image is virtual, upright and larger than the object.

The image can be seen only by looking at it through the lens. This is how a **magnifying glass** works.

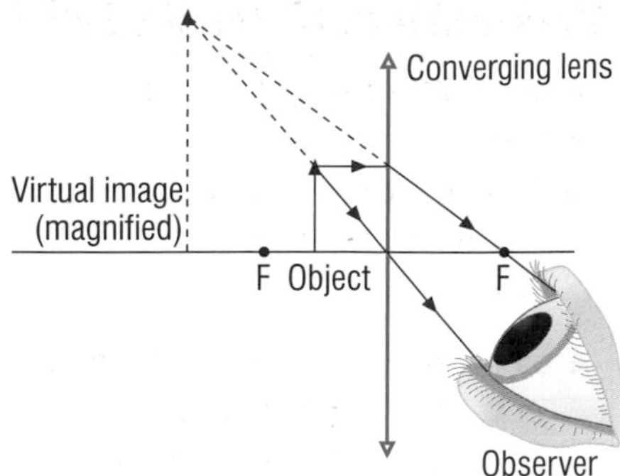

Figure 3 Formation of a virtual image by a converging lens

Formation of a virtual image by a diverging lens

The image formed by a diverging (concave) lens is always virtual, upright and smaller than the object. Figure 4 shows why. A diverging lens is shown as a line with 'inward' arrows.

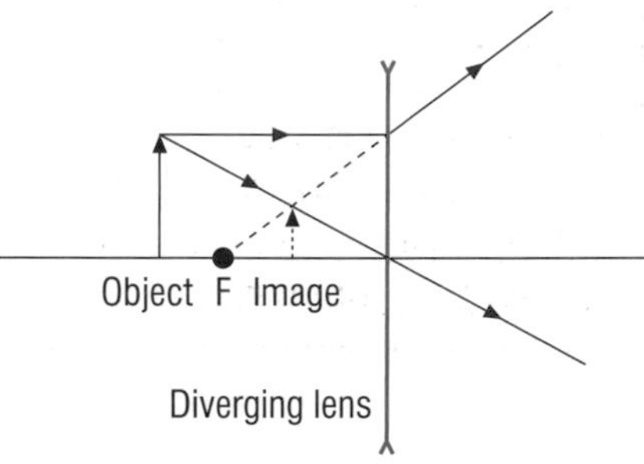

Figure 4 Image formation by a diverging lens

Summary questions

1 a Copy and complete the ray diagram in the figure to show how a converging lens forms an image of an object that is smaller than the object, as in a camera.

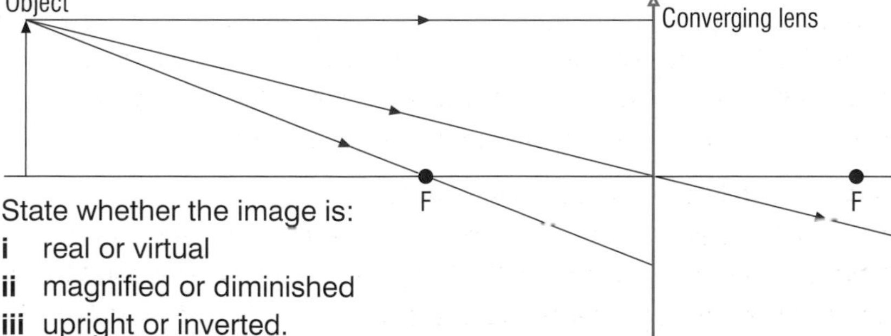

b State whether the image is:
  i real or virtual
  ii magnified or diminished
  iii upright or inverted.

2 a Draw a ray diagram to show how a converging lens is used as a magnifying glass.
  b State whether the image is:
  i real or virtual
  ii magnified or diminished
  iii upright or inverted.
  c Why is a diverging lens no use as a magnifying glass?

3 A converging lens produces a magnification of ×2 when it is used to form a real image that is at a distance of 8.0 cm from the object.
  a Draw a scale ray diagram to show the formation of this image.
  b Use your diagram to find the focal length of the lens.
  c Describe how the position and height of the image would change if the object is moved gradually towards the focal point of the lens.

Key points

- A ray diagram can be drawn to find the position and nature of an image formed by a lens.
- When an object is placed between a converging lens and its principal focus F, the image formed is virtual, upright, magnified and on the same side of the lens as the object.
- A camera contains a converging lens that is used to form a real image of an object.
- A magnifying glass is a converging lens that is used to form a virtual image of an object.

P11.3 The lens formula

Learning objectives

After this topic, you should know:

- how to use the lens formula
- the difference between real and virtual images in the lens formula
- the difference between converging and diverging lenses in the lens formula

Maths skills

The **reciprocal** of a number is 1 ÷ the number. Your calculator should have a button to calculate the reciprocal of any number. This is usually marked as $1/x$ or x^{-1}.

Worked example

A converging lens in a camera is required to form a real image 0.027 m from the lens when an object is 0.250 m from the lens. Calculate the focal length of the lens.

Solution

To work out focal length f, use the lens formula

$$1/u + 1/v = 1/f$$

where, $u = +\ 0.250$ m and $v = +\ 0.027$ m

$$\text{Hence, } \frac{1}{f} = \frac{1}{+0.250} + \frac{1}{0.027}$$
$$= 4.00 + 37.0$$
$$= +\ 41.0\,\text{m}^{-1}$$

$$\text{giving, } f = +\frac{1}{41.0} = \mathbf{+\ 0.024\,m}$$

Examiner's tip

When you have calculated $1/f$, don't forget to use the reciprocal button again to calculate f.

Note: You don't need to know the proof of the lens formula

Optical instruments such as cameras, binoculars and film projectors all contain lenses. The designers of such instruments have to find out what the focal length f of each lens should be in each type of instrument. To do this, they need to know for each lens the distance from the object to the lens and the distance from the lens to the image, and then they use the lens formula below:

$$\frac{1}{u} + \frac{1}{v} = \frac{1}{f}$$

where:

u = the distance from the object to the lens

v = the distance from the lens to the image

To use the formula, real objects and images are given positive values of u and v, and virtual objects and images are given negative values for u and v. This rule is called the '**real is positive**' sign convention.

Also:

- for a converging (convex) lens, the focal length is given a positive value
- for a diverging (concave) lens, the focal length is given a negative value.

Virtual image calculations

1 **The magnifying glass** is a converging lens placed close to the object. As we discovered in 11.2, the viewer looking into the lens sees a virtual image of the object. The object must lie between the lens and its focal point. In other words, the object distance u must be less than the focal length f of the lens.

Practical

Testing the lens formula

Use a convex lens to form a real image of an object on a screen as shown in Figure 1. Observe that the image on the screen is always inverted compared with the object.

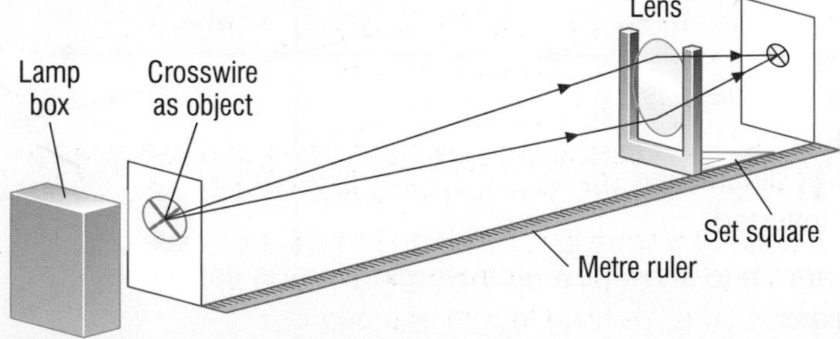

Figure 1 Testing a convex lens

For different object distances, adjust the distance from the screen to the lens to obtain a real image on the screen.

For each object distance, use a metre ruler and a set square as shown in Figure 1 to measure the image distance and the object distance. Always measure these distances to the centre of the lens.

Use each pair of measurements of u and v in the lens formula to calculate the focal length f of the lens. Calculate the mean value of f.

Safety: Make sure lenses are not sharp.

Maths skills

Worked example

A small object is placed at a distance of 0.040 m from a converging lens of focal length 0.098 m. Calculate the distance from the lens to the image.

Solution

To work out the image distance v, use the lens formula $1/u + 1/v = 1/f$, where $u = +0.040$ m and $f = +0.098$ m.

Hence $\frac{1}{0.040} + \frac{1}{v} = \frac{1}{0.098}$

$\frac{1}{v} = \frac{1}{0.098} - \frac{1}{0.040} = 10.2 - 25.0 = -14.8\,\text{m}^{-1}$

giving $v = \frac{1}{-14.8} = \mathbf{-0.068\,m}$

The minus sign tells us the image is virtual. The image is therefore formed 0.068 m from the lens on the same side as the object.

2 **A diverging lens always gives a virtual image** when it is used to view an object, no matter how far the lens is from the object. The ray diagram in Figure 4 of 11.2 shows how the image is formed. Note that the image is always smaller than the object.

Maths skills

Worked example

A small object is placed at a distance of 0.400 m from a diverging lens of focal length 0.025 m. Calculate the distance from the lens to the image.

Solution

To work out the image distance v, use the lens formula $1/u + 1/v = 1/f$, where $u = +0.400$ m and $f = -0.025$ m. Remember that the focal length of the lens is negative because the lens is a diverging lens.

Hence $\frac{1}{0.400} + \frac{1}{v} = \frac{1}{-0.025}$

$\frac{1}{v} = \frac{1}{-0.025} - \frac{1}{0.400} = -40.0 - 2.5 = -42.5\,\text{m}^{-1}$

giving $v = \frac{1}{-42.5} = \mathbf{-0.0235\,m}$

The minus sign tells us the image is virtual. The image is therefore formed 0.0235 m from the lens on the same side as the object.

Summary questions

1 a An object placed 0.310 m from a converging lens gives a real image at distance of 0.760 m from the lens on the other side of the lens. Use the lens formula to calculate the focal length of the lens.

b A converging lens of focal length 0.020 m is used to form an image of an object that is placed 0.051 m from the lens.

i Use the lens formula to calculate the image distance.

ii State whether the image is real or virtual.

2 A converging lens of focal length 0.081 m is used as a magnifying glass to observe a small object at a distance of 0.058 m from the lens. Use the lens formula to calculate the image distance.

3 A diverging lens of focal length 0.050 m is used to form an image of an object that is placed 0.025 m from the lens.

a Use the lens formula to calculate the image distance.

b State whether the image is real or virtual.

Maths skills

Worked example

A slide transparency is placed 0.170 m from a lens of focal length 0.150 mm used to project an image of the slide onto a screen. Calculate the image distance.

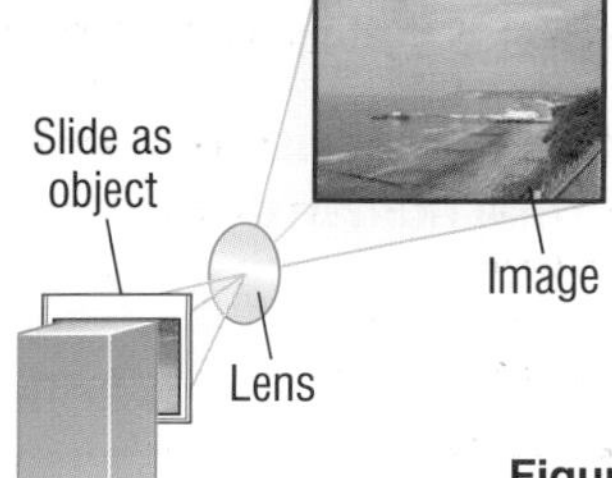

Figure 2

Solution

To work out the image distance v, use the lens formula

$$1/u + 1/v = 1/f$$

where, $u = +0.170$ m and $f = +0.150$ m.

Hence $\frac{1}{0.170} + \frac{1}{v} = \frac{1}{0.150}$

$\frac{1}{v} = \frac{1}{0.150} - \frac{1}{0.170}$

$= 6.667 - 5.882 = 0.784\,\text{m}^{-1}$

giving $v = \frac{1}{0.784} = \mathbf{1.275\,m}$

A real image is therefore formed 1.275 m from the lens on the opposite side to the object.

Examiner's tip

Be careful when using the lens formula in a calculation. Whatever you are calculating – u, v or f – you have to turn it upside down at the end (hit the reciprocal ($1/x$) button on your calculator).

Key points

- The lens formula is $\frac{1}{u} + \frac{1}{v} = \frac{1}{f}$.
- Real images have positive values. Virtual images have negative values.
- Converging lens are given positive values. Diverging lens are given negative values.

P11.4 The eye

Learning objectives

After this topic, you should know:

- how the eye forms an image
- the range of vision of a normal human eye
- how the eye and the camera compare as optical devices.

Did you know ...?

The conjuctiva membrane is a thin transparent membrane over the front of the eye. A watery fluid from your tear glands under the eyelids spreads across this membrane every time you blink. The fluid contains lyosyme – a chemical that destroys bacteria.

Did you know ...?

The blind spot is a region where the retina is not sensitive to light (no light-sensitive cells are present).

Inside the eye

Figure 1 shows the inside of a human eye. Light enters the eye through a tough transparent layer called the **cornea**. This protects the eye and helps to focus light onto the **retina**. The retina is a layer of light-sensitive cells at the back of the inside of the eye.

The amount of light entering the eye is controlled by the **iris**, which adjusts the size of the **pupil** – the circular opening at the centre of the iris. The **eye lens** is a converging lens that focuses light to give a sharp image on the retina. Although the image on the retina is inverted, the brain interprets it so you can see it the right way up.

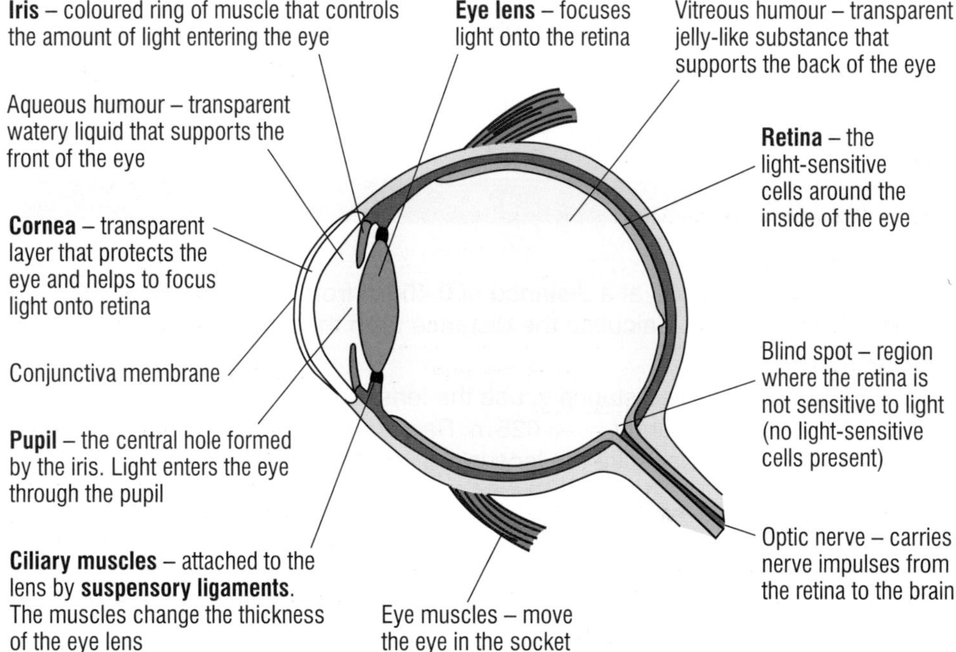

Figure 1 The human eye

How does the eye focus on objects at different distances? If you look up from this book and gaze out of a window, your eye lens automatically becomes thinner to keep what you see in focus. The **ciliary muscle** alters the thickness of the eye lens. It is attached to the edge of the lens by means of the **suspensory ligaments**. The fibres of the ciliary muscle are parallel to the circular edge of the eye lens. When the muscle contracts, the fibres shorten and squeeze the eye lens, making the lens thicker.

The normal human eye has a **range of vision** from 25 cm to infinity. This means it can see clearly any object that is 25 cm or more from the eye. In other words, the normal eye has a **near point** of 25 cm and a **far point** at infinity.

To see a nearby object clearly, the eye lens has to be thicker than if the object is far away. Figure 2a and b show this.

Comparison of the eye and the camera

How do the eye and the camera compare as optical instruments? They are similar in that they both contain a converging lens which forms a real image. Look at Table 1 to see how they compare in other ways.

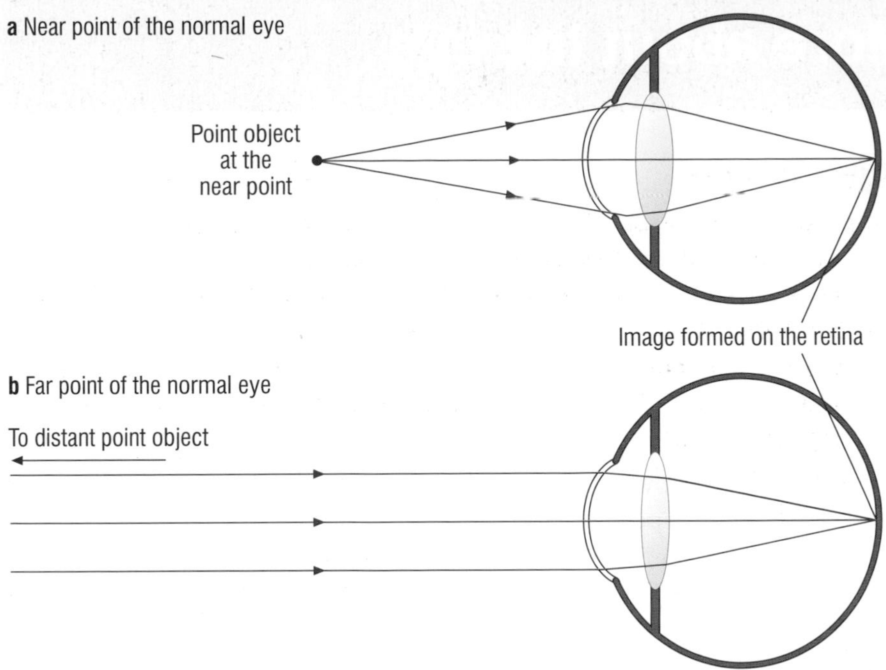

Figure 2 The normal eye

Examiner's tip

Make sure that you can correctly label a diagram of the eye and that you know the function of each part of the eye.

Table 1 Comparison of the optics of the eye and a camera

	The eye	The camera
Type of lens	Variable-focus converging lens	Fixed-focus converging lens
Focusing adjustment	Ciliary muscle alters the lens thickness	Adjustment of lens position
Image	Real, inverted, magnification less than 1	
Image detection	Light-sensitive cells on the retina	Photographic film (or CCD sensors in a digital camera)
Brightness control	Iris controls the width of the eye pupil	Adjustment of aperture 'stop'

Summary questions

1 a State the function of the following parts of the eye:
- **i** ciliary muscles
- **ii** eye lens
- **iii** pupil
- **iv** suspensory ligaments
- **v** cornea
- **vi** iris
- **vii** retina.

b Why does the pupil of the eye appear much wider in darkness than in daylight?

2 A person with normal eyesight who is reading a book looks up to observe a distant object.

a Describe what happens to the shape of each eye lens in this change.

b What change takes place in the power of each eye lens?

3 a Describe the change that takes place in the eye when it adjusts to very bright light.

b What change is made in a camera when it is adjusted to very bright light?

Key points

- Light is focused onto the retina by the cornea and the eye lens, whose shape is changed by the ciliary muscle.
- The normal human eye has a range of vision from 25 cm to infinity.
- An image is brought to focus:
  - on the film in a camera by changing the distance between the film and lens
  - on the retina in an eye by changing the shape of the eye lens.

P11.5 More about the eye

Learning objectives

After this topic, you should know:

- what short sight is and how to correct it
- what long sight is and how to correct it
- why the refractive index of glass is important in making spectacle lenses
- what is meant by lens power.

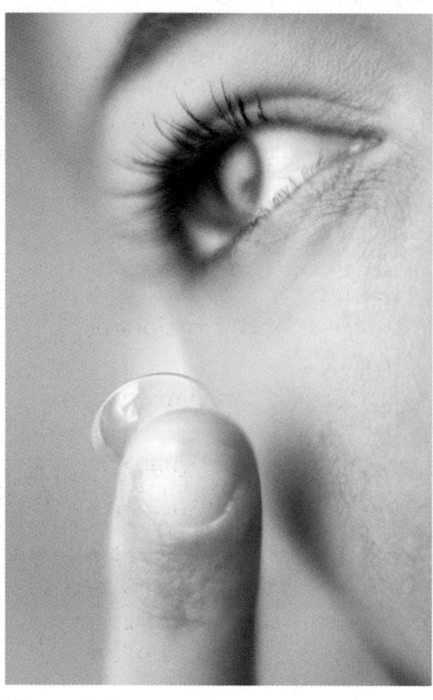

Figure 2 A contact lens

Sight defects

Short sight occurs when an eye cannot focus on distant objects. The **uncorrected** image is formed in front of the retina, as shown in Figure 1. This is because the eyeball is too long or the eye lens is too powerful. The ciliary muscle cannot make the eye lens thin enough to focus the image of a faraway object on the retina of the eye. The eye can focus nearby objects, so the defect is called 'short sight'.

Short sight is corrected by placing a diverging lens of a suitable focal length in front of the eye as shown in Figure 1. The diverging lens counteracts some of the 'excess' focusing power of the eye lens.

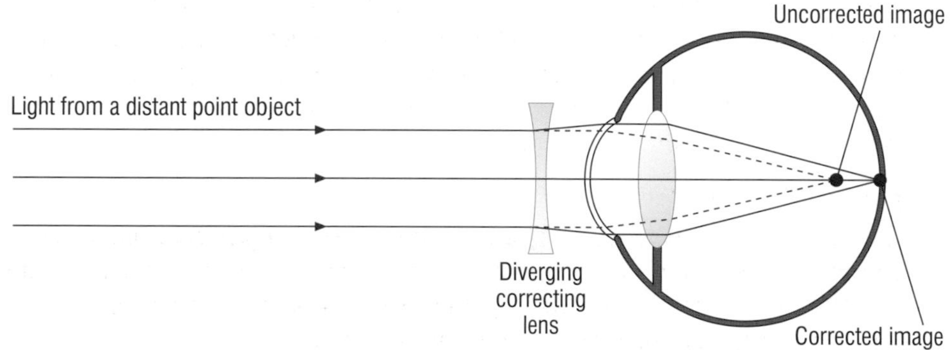

Figure 1 Short sight and its correction

Long sight occurs when an eye cannot focus on nearby objects. The uncorrected image is formed behind the retina, as shown in Figure 3. The eyeball is too short or the eye lens is too weak. The eye lens cannot be made thick enough to focus an image on the retina. The eye can focus distant objects, so the defect is called 'long sight'.

Long sight is corrected by placing a converging lens of a suitable focal length in front of the eye, as shown in Figure 3. The correcting lens makes the rays from the object diverge less. The eye lens can then focus the rays onto the retina. The correcting lens adds to the focusing power of the eye lens.

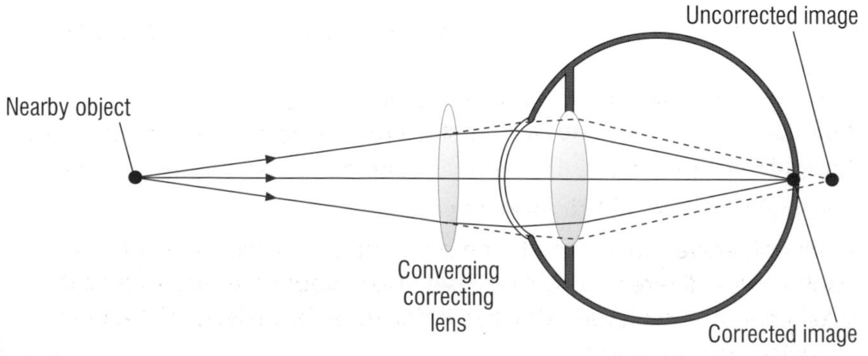

Figure 3 Long sight and its correction

Examiner's tip

Make sure that you know: the difference between short sight and long sight; what causes the defect; and how the defect can be corrected.

Lens power

The **power of a lens** is defined as $\frac{1}{\textbf{focal length in metres}}$

The unit of power is the **dioptre** (D) or m^{-1}. The type of lens is indicated by:

- a positive value for the power of a converging lens (e.g. +5.0 D for a converging lens of focal length 0.20 m)
- a negative value for a diverging lens (e.g. –4.0 D for a diverging lens of focal length 0.25 m).

Lens makers at work

The eye lens is a remarkable optical device, as it has a variable focal length that depends on its thickness. Lens makers working for opticians need to make contact lenses and spectacle lenses exactly the right shape to obtain the exact focal length for each lens.

The focal length of a lens depends on the refractive index of the lens material and the curvature of the two lens surfaces.

- The larger the refractive index or the greater the curvature of the lens surfaces, the greater the power of the lens (and the shorter its focal length).
- For a lens of a given focal length, the greater the refractive index of the lens material, the flatter and thinner the lens can be manufactured. This is because the lens surfaces would be less curved.

Laser treatment

A laser produces a narrow concentrated beam of light. High-power lasers can be used to burn through metal. Low-power lasers are also dangerous because laser light entering the eye will damage the retina. Special protective eye goggles should always be worn when lasers are in use.

Lasers are used in medicine for cutting tissue and for sealing blood vessels (called cauterising). They are also used to correct sight defects. For example, short sight can be corrected by using a special laser called an 'excimer' to make part of the cornea slightly thinner. This has the same effect as a diverging correcting lens because it cancels out some of the 'excess' focusing power of the eye lens.

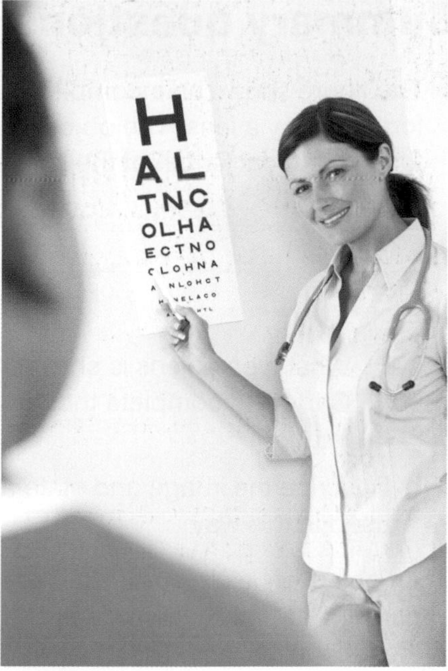

Figure 4 An eye test

Maths skills

We can write this word equation in symbols as:

$$\text{lens power } \boldsymbol{P} = \frac{1}{f}$$

where:
P = lens power in dioptres, D, or m^{-1}
f = focal length in metres, m.

Summary questions

1 Using his left eye, a student can only see the writing on a board at the front of the class if he sits near the board.
  a What sight defect is he suffering from in this eye?
  b What type of lens should be used to correct this defect?

2 An optician prescribes a lens of power +2.0 dioptres to correct a sight defect.
  a What type of lens is it, and what is its focal length?
  b State what the sight defect is and give **one** possible cause of the defect.
  c Explain why the sight defect could **not** be corrected by making the cornea flatter using laser treatment.

3 a A lens of a given focal length can be made using two materials that each have a different refractive index. How would the lens differ if it was made of the higher refractive index material instead of the lower refractive index material?
  b What is the power in dioptres of:
    i a converging lens of focal length 0.50 m?
    ii a diverging lens of focal length 0.40?

Key points

- **A short-sighted eye is an eye that can see only nearby objects clearly. We use a diverging (concave) lens to correct it.**
- **A long-sighted eye is an eye that can see only distant objects clearly. We use a converging (convex) lens to correct it.**
- **The higher the refractive index of the lens material, the flatter and thinner the lens can be.**
- **The power of a lens in dioptres = 1 ÷ its focal length in metres**

Summary questions

1 The figure shows an incomplete ray diagram of image formation by a lens. The object distance from the lens is 2.5 × the focal length of the lens.

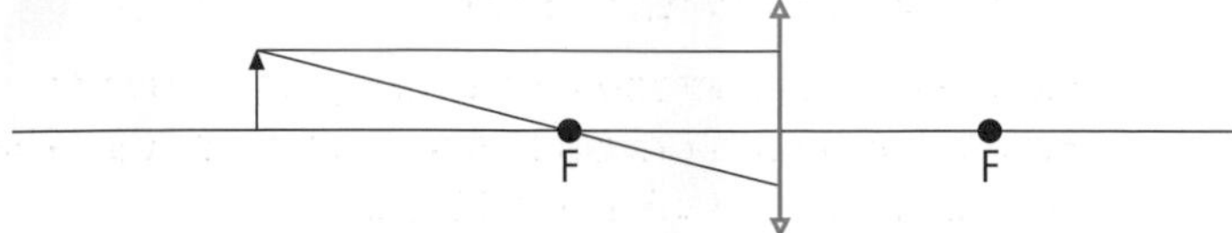

a **i** What type of lens is shown in this diagram?
ii Copy and complete the ray diagram and label the image.

b Describe the image and state an application of the lens used in this way.

2 An object of height 40 mm is placed perpendicular to the principal axis of a convex lens at a distance of 80 mm from the pole of the lens. The focal length of the lens is 50 mm.

a Draw a scale ray diagram to find the distance from the lens to the image.

b State whether the image is:
i real or virtual
ii upright or inverted.

c Determine the magnification produced by the lens.

d The object is moved to a distance of 60 mm from the lens. Use the lens formula $1/u + 1/v = 1/f$ to determine the new image distance.

3 An object is placed perpendicular to the principal axis of a diverging lens.

a Draw a scale ray diagram to show where the image of the object is formed.

b State whether the image is:
i real or virtual
ii upright or inverted.

c The object is moved to a distance of 80 mm from the pole of the lens. The focal length of the lens is 160 mm. Calculate the distance from the image to the lens.

4 **a** Copy and complete the ray diagram in the figure to show how a converging lens is used as a magnifying glass.

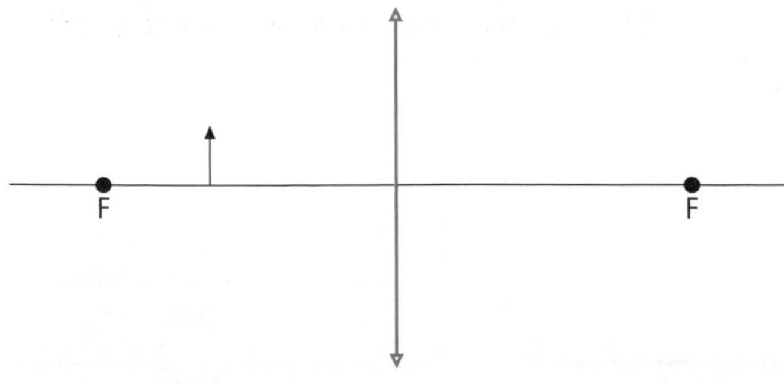

b An object is placed at a distance of 0.10 m from the pole of a +8.0 D converging lens as shown in the figure.
i Calculate the focal length of the lens.
ii Calculate the distance from the image to the lens.

c State whether the image in **b** is:
i real or virtual
ii upright or inverted.

5 **a** **i** Explain what is meant by short sight.
ii A short-sighted eye views a distant object. Copy and complete the figure to show the path of two light rays that enter the eye from a point on a distant object.

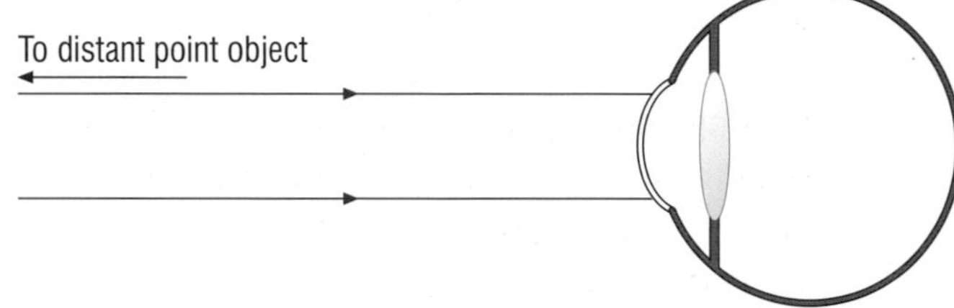

b **i** State the type of lens that is used to correct short sight.
ii A lens of focal length 0.80 m is needed to correct a short-sighted eye. Calculate the power of this lens in dioptres.

c Short sight may be corrected by eye surgeons using a laser.
i Which part of the eye is treated in this operation, and what is done to it with the laser?
ii Give **one** reason why laser light is dangerous.

6 The figure shows a long-sighted eye when it is viewing a nearby object.

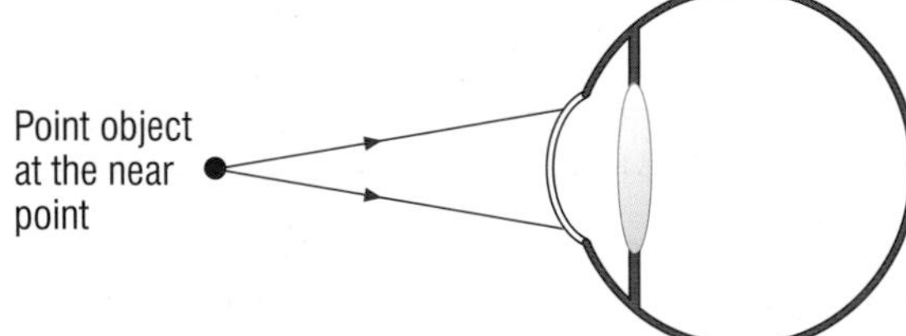

a **i** Copy and complete the figure to show the path of two light rays that enter the eye from a point on a distant object.
ii Explain why the eye is unable to see the nearby object clearly.

b **i** State the type of lens that is used to correct long sight.
ii To correct a long-sighted eye, an optician recommends that a lens with a focal length of 2.0 m be used. What is the optical power of this lens?

AQA Examination-style questions

1 The focal length of a lens determines how powerful it is.

a Draw diagrams to show what is meant by the focal length of:

i a convex lens (3)

ii a concave lens. (3)

b An object, **AB**, is placed 5 cm from a convex lens of focal length 10 cm.

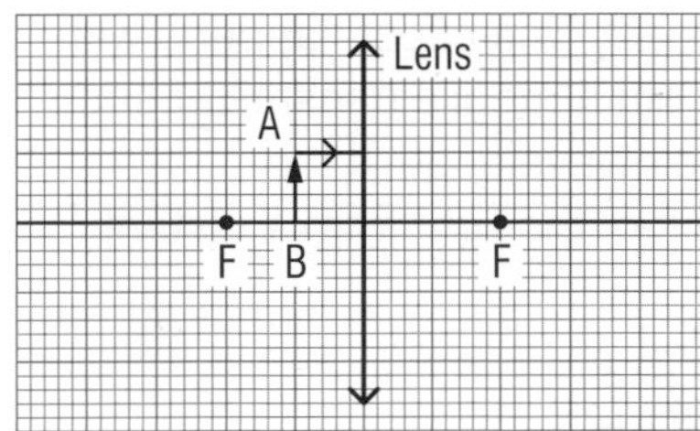

i Copy and complete the ray diagram, which is drawn to scale, to show how the convex lens forms an image of the object.
Draw and label the image. (4)

ii Calculate the magnification. (2)

iii State **three** differences between the image and the object.

c A convex lens is used in both the camera and the eye.

i Give **two** other similarities between the camera and the eye. (2)

ii Describe how the camera and the eye use different methods to produce sharp images of objects at different distances. (4)

iii Give **two** other differences between the camera and the eye. (2)

2 Devices containing lenses form different types of image.

a Match each device in the left-hand column to the correct image in the right-hand column. (3)

Device		Nature of image
Camera		real; magnified; inverted
Magnifying glass		virtual; magnified; upright
Projector		real; diminished; inverted

b Some students used the following apparatus to determine the focal length of a converging lens.

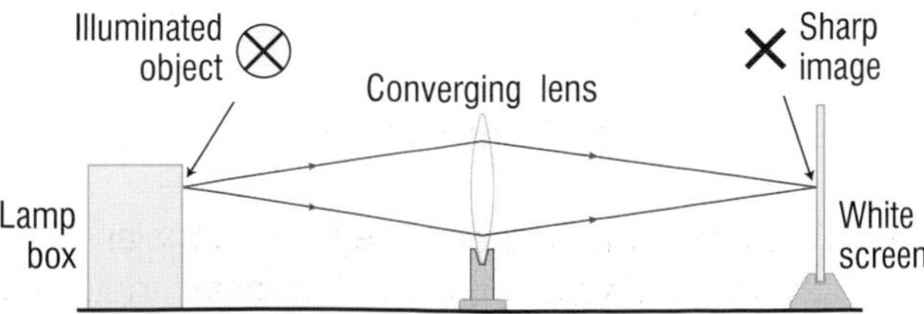

They placed the object 40.0 cm from the lens. Then they moved the screen away from the lens until they saw a sharp image on the screen. They measured the image distance. It was 13.1 cm.

Next they put the screen further away and moved it towards the screen until they saw a sharp image. This time the image distance was 13.5 cm.

i What was the resolution of the ruler they were using? (1)

ii Use their results to calculate the focal length of the lens. (4)

iii They repeated the experiment using six different object distances.
How should they use their results to obtain a more accurate value for the focal length? (2)

iv When they made the object distance 5 cm, they could not get a sharp image on the screen.
Explain why. (3)

3 The diagram shows a cross section of an eye.

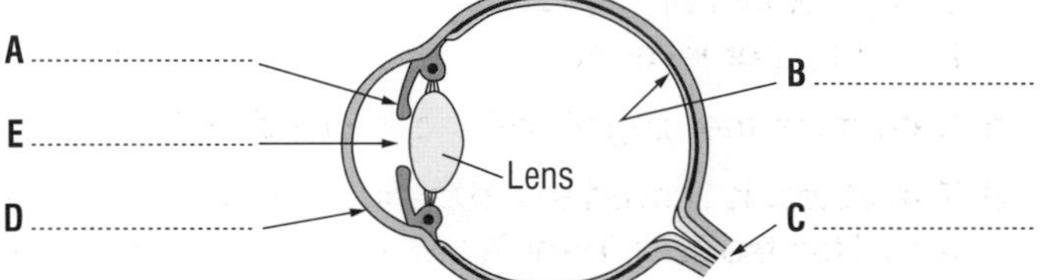

a Label the parts marked **A**, **B**, **C**, **D** and **E**. (5)

b Describe and explain how the eye adapts to different light conditions and to objects at different distances. (QWC) (6)

c The diagram shows an eye with a defect.

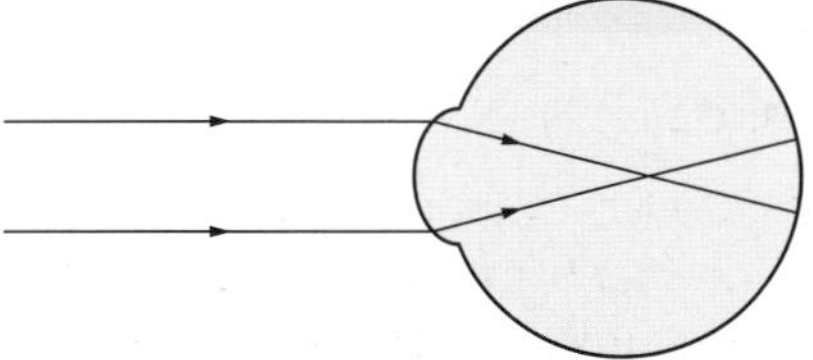

i What is this eye defect? (1)

ii What type of lens is used to correct the defect? (1)

iii The power of the lens used to correct the defect is −2.5 D.
Calculate the focal length, in cm, of the lens. (3)

P12.1 The expanding universe

Learning objectives

After this topic, you should know:

- what is meant by the red-shift of a light source
- how red-shift depends on speed
- how we know that the distant galaxies are moving away from us
- why we think the universe is expanding.

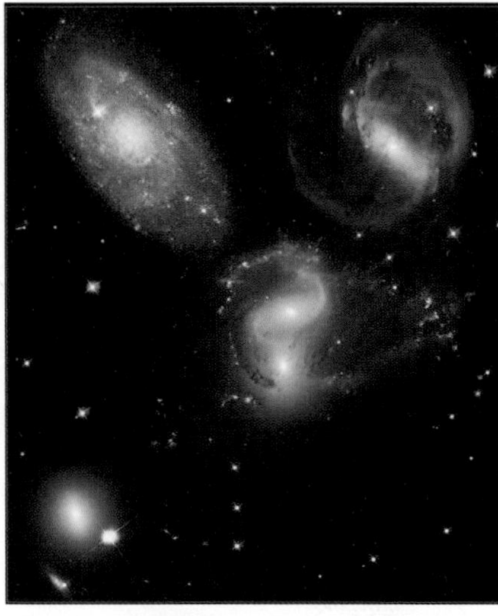

Figure 1 Galaxies

The Doppler effect

The **Doppler effect** is the change in the observed wavelength (and frequency) of waves because of the motion of the source of the waves. Christian Doppler discovered the effect in 1842 using sound waves. He demonstrated it by using an open railway carriage filled with trumpeters. The spectators had to listen to the change in pitch of the trumpets as they sped past. The effect happens with any type of wave. For example, the microwaves from a mobile transmitter such as a police 'radar speed-detector gun' change their wavelength if the transmitter moves. Another example is the red-shift of the light from a distant galaxy moving away from us.

Red-shift

We live on the third rock out from a middle-aged star on the outskirts of a big galaxy we call the Milky Way. The galaxy contains about 100 000 million stars. Its size is about 100 000 light years across. This means that light takes 100 000 years to travel across it. But it's just one of billions of galaxies in the universe. The furthest galaxies are about 13 000 million light years away!

We can find out lots of things about stars and galaxies by studying the light from them. We can use a prism to split the light into a spectrum. The wavelength of light increases across the spectrum from blue to red. We can tell from its spectrum if a star or galaxy is moving towards us or away from us. This is because:

- the light waves are stretched out if the star or galaxy is moving away from us. The wavelength of the waves is increased. We call this a **red-shift** because the spectrum of light is shifted towards the red part of the spectrum.
- the light waves are squashed together if the star or galaxy is moving towards us. The wavelength of the waves is reduced. We call this a **blue-shift** because the spectrum of light is shifted towards the blue part of the spectrum.

The dark spectral lines shown in Figure 2 are caused by absorption of light by certain atoms such as hydrogen that make up a star or galaxy. The position of these lines tells us if there is a shift and if so, whether it is a red-shift or a blue-shift.

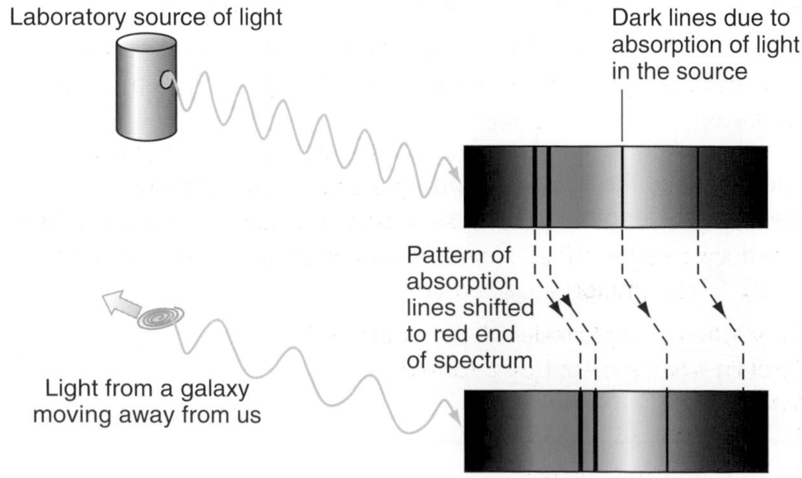

Figure 2 Red-shift

The bigger the shift, the more the waves are squashed together or stretched out. So the faster the star or galaxy must be moving towards or away from us. In other words:

the faster a star or galaxy is moving (relative to us), the bigger the shift is.

Expanding universe

In 1929, Edwin Hubble discovered that:

1 the light from distant galaxies was red-shifted

2 the further a galaxy is from us, the bigger its red-shift is.

He concluded that:

- the distant galaxies are moving away from us (i.e. receding)
- the greater the distance a galaxy is from us, the greater the speed is at which it is moving away from us (its speed of recession).

Why should the distant galaxies be moving away from us? We have no special place in the universe, so all the distant galaxies must be moving away from each other. In other words, **the whole universe is expanding**.

Examiner's tip

Make sure you know the evidence for the expanding universe.

Did you know ... ?

You can hear the Doppler effect when an ambulance with its siren on goes speeding past.

- As it gets closer to you, the sound waves it sends out are squashed up so their frequency is higher (and the wavelength is shorter) than if the siren was stationary. So you hear a higher pitch.
- As it travels away from you, the sound waves it sends out are stretched out so their frequency is lower (and the wavelength is longer) than if the siren was stationary. So you hear a lower pitch.

This effect helps you determine where the ambulance is, so you don't hinder its progress.

Summary questions

1 a State whether each of the following is approaching the Earth or receding from the Earth:

i a distant galaxy

ii a galaxy that shows a blue-shift in its light.

b The Sun is in the Milky Way galaxy. Astronomers think that the Andromeda Galaxy will eventually collide with the Milky Way galaxy. What evidence do astronomers have to support this prediction?

2 a Put these objects in order of increasing size:

Andromeda galaxy Earth Sun universe

b Quasars are astronomical objects much smaller than galaxies, and they have red-shifts of the same order of magnitude as the distant galaxies.

i What part of the above statement makes you conclude that quasars are much further away than nearby galaxies?

ii Quasars can be as bright as a distant galaxy even though they are much smaller. What does this tell you about the power of the radiation emitted by a quasar?

3 Galaxy X has a larger red-shift than galaxy Y.

a Explain what is meant by a red-shift.

b Which galaxy, X or Y, is:

i nearer to us?

ii moving away faster?

Key points

- **The red-shift of a distant galaxy is the shift to longer wavelengths (and lower frequencies) of the light from it because the galaxy is moving away from us. This change is called the Doppler effect.**
- **The faster a distant galaxy is moving away from us, the greater its red-shift is.**
- **All the distant galaxies show a red-shift. The further away a distant galaxy is from us, the greater its red-shift is.**
- **The distant galaxies are all moving away from us because the universe is expanding.**

P12.2 The Big Bang

Learning objectives

After this topic, you should know:

- what the Big Bang theory of the universe is
- why the universe is expanding
- what cosmic microwave background radiation is
- what evidence there is that the universe was created in a Big Bang.

Figure 1 The Big Bang

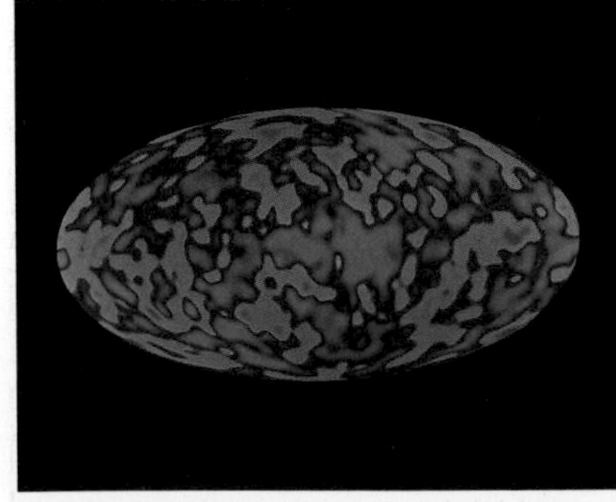

Figure 2 A microwave image of the universe from the Cosmic Background Explorer satellite

The universe is expanding, but what is making it expand? The **Big Bang theory** was put forward to explain the expansion. This states that:

- the universe is expanding after exploding suddenly in a Big Bang from a very small initial point
- space, time and matter were created in the Big Bang.

Many scientists disagreed with the Big Bang theory. They put forward an alternative theory, the Steady State theory. The scientists said that the galaxies are being pushed apart. They thought that this is caused by matter entering the universe through 'white holes' (the opposite of black holes).

Which theory is weirder – everything starting from a Big Bang or matter leaking into the universe from outside? Until 1965, most people supported the Steady State theory.

Evidence for the Big Bang

Scientists had two conflicting theories about the evolution of the universe: it was in a Steady State or it began at some point in the past with a Big Bang. Both theories could explain why the galaxies are moving apart, so scientists needed to find some way of selecting which theory was correct. They worked out that if the universe began in a Big Bang then high-energy electromagnetic radiation should have been produced very soon after the universe began. This radiation would have 'stretched' as the universe expanded and become lower-energy radiation. Experiments were devised to look for this trace energy as extra evidence for the Big Bang model.

It was in 1965 that scientists first detected microwaves coming from every direction in space. The existence of this **cosmic microwave background radiation** (CMBR) can be explained only by the Big Bang theory.

The cosmic microwave background radiation is not as perfectly evenly spread as scientists thought it should be. Their model of the early universe needs to be developed further by gathering evidence and producing theories to explain this 'unevenness' in the early universe.

Cosmic microwave background radiation

- It was created as high-energy gamma radiation just after the Big Bang.
- It has been travelling through space since then.
- As the universe has expanded, it stretched out to longer and longer wavelengths and is now microwave radiation.
- It has been mapped out using microwave detectors on the ground and on satellites.

Did you know ... ?

You can use an analogue TV or radio to detect background microwave radiation very easily – just disconnect your TV aerial or move your radio tuner until you hear a hiss. The radiation causes lots of fuzzy spots on the TV screen and the hiss on the radio.

The future of the universe

Will the universe expand for ever? Or will the force of gravity between the distant galaxies stop them from moving away from each other? The answer to this question depends on their total mass and how much space they take up – in other words, the density of the universe.

- If the density of the universe is less than a certain amount, it will expand for ever. The stars will die out and so will everything else as the universe heads for a Big Yawn!
- If the density of the universe is more than a certain amount, it will stop expanding and go into reverse. Everything will head for a Big Crunch!

Recent observations by astronomers suggest that the distant galaxies are accelerating away from each other. These observations have been checked and confirmed by other astronomers. So astronomers have concluded that the expansion of the universe is accelerating. It could be we're in for a Big Ride followed by a Big Yawn.

The discovery that the distant galaxies are accelerating is puzzling astronomers. Scientists think some unknown source of energy, called 'dark energy', must be causing this accelerating motion. The only known force on the distant galaxies, the force of gravity, can't be used to explain 'dark energy' because it is an attractive force and so acts against their outward motion away from each other.

Examiner's tip

When answering questions about the Big Bang theory, you need to say more than 'the universe started with a big bang'.

links

To learn more about what happened just after the Big Bang, see 20.4 'The early universe'.

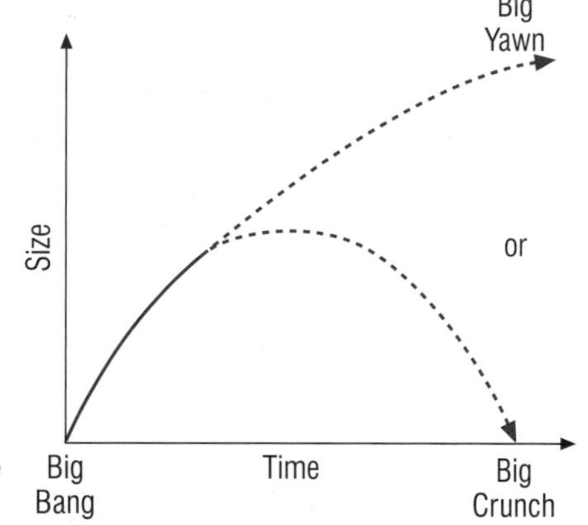

Figure 3 The future of the universe?

Summary questions

1 a What is the Big Bang theory of the universe?
  b Why did many astronomers not support the Big Bang theory when it was first proposed?
  c What was the significance of the discovery of cosmic microwave background radiation?

2 Put the following events A–D in the correct time sequence:
  A The distant galaxies were created.
  B Cosmic microwave background radiation was first detected.
  C The Big Bang happened.
  D The expansion of the universe began.

3 a Why do astronomers think that the expansion of the universe is accelerating?
  b What would have been the effect on the expansion of the universe if its density had been greater than a certain value?

Key points

- The universe started with the Big Bang, a massive explosion from a very small point.
- The universe has been expanding ever since the Big Bang.
- Cosmic microwave background radiation (CMBR) is electromagnetic radiation created just after the Big Bang.
- CMBR can be explained only by the Big Bang theory.

Summary questions

1 Complete the following sentences:

a Light from a distant .... is shifted to the red part of the spectrum. This is because it has been stretched to longer ....

b The distant galaxies are moving .... from each other because the .... is expanding.

c The .... of light from a galaxy that is moving towards us is .... than it would be if the galaxy was not moving.

2 **a** Complete the following sentences:

i The universe was created in a massive explosion called ....

ii The expansion of the universe is making the distant galaxies move ....

iii The universe was created about thirteen .... years ago.

b **i** What is cosmic microwave background radiation (CMBR)?

ii What did the discovery of CMBR prove?

3 Light from a distant galaxy has a change of wavelength because of the motion of the galaxy.

a **i** Is this change of wavelength an increase or a decrease?

ii Why is this effect called a red-shift?

iii What does the change of wavelength tell us about the motion of the galaxy?

b Light from a particular nearby galaxy is found to have undergone a blue-shift because of the motion of the galaxy. What does this tell us about the motion of this galaxy?

c **i** Edwin Hubble discovered that the further a distant galaxy is from us, the greater the red-shift of the light from it. What does this tell us about the universe?

ii What crucial observational evidence led scientists to accept the Big Bang theory of the universe?

4 **a** Galaxy **A** is further from us than galaxy **B**.

i Which galaxy, **A** or **B**, produces light with a greater red-shift?

ii Galaxy **C** gives a bigger red-shift than galaxy **A**. What can we say about the distance to galaxy **C** compared with galaxy **A**?

b All the distant galaxies are moving away from each other.

i What does this tell us about the universe?

ii What does it tell us about our place in the universe?

5 The diagram shows two galaxies **X** and **Y**, which have the same diameter.

a **i** Which galaxy, **X** or **Y**, is further from Earth? Give a reason for your answer.

ii Which galaxy, **X** or **Y**, produces the larger red-shift?

b A third galaxy **Z** seen from Earth appears to be the same size as **X** but it has a larger red-shift than **X**. What can you deduce from these observations about **Z** compared with **X**?

6 In a demonstration of the expansion of a one-dimensional universe, 11 students representing galaxies stand along a straight line spaced 1 metre apart. The students are told to increase their spacing by 0.5 metres every 10 seconds.

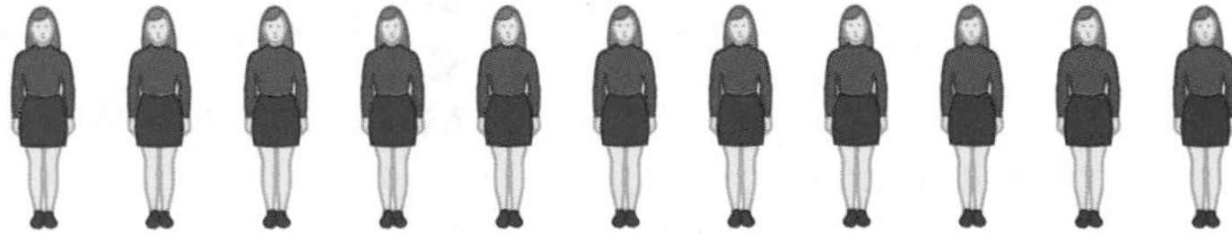

What is the average speed of separation of two students who are:

a next to each other?

b at opposite ends of the line?

AQA Examination-style questions

1 The diagram shows a police car travelling at a steady speed towards a man standing at the side of the road. The siren on the police car is sounding.

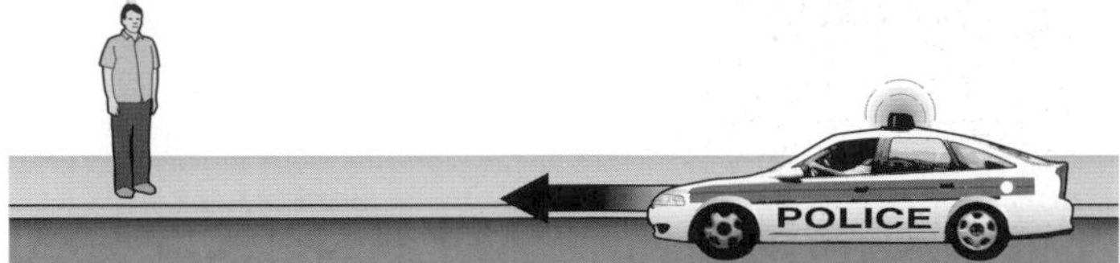

a As the police car passes the man, he notices that the sound changes.

- **i** What changes in the sound would the man notice as the police car approached him and then moved away from him? (3)
- **ii** A driver in a car behind the police car does not notice any change in the sound. Explain why. (3)

b Explain why the man in the diagram hears changes in the sound of the siren. (QWC) (6)

2 Astronomers have observed distant galaxies and discovered that the light from these distant galaxies shows a red-shift.

a
- **i** What is meant by red-shift?
- **ii** What causes light to undergo a red-shift?
- **iii** The table below gives values of the red-shift for different galaxies.

Name of galaxy	Red-shift in nm
M60	18.8
M99	32.1
NGC 2366	1.3
NGC 2976	0.04

Which galaxy is furthest from the Earth? (1)

b The Big Bang theory is one theory about how the universe began.

- **i** What is the Big Bang theory? (3)
- **ii** Explain how the discovery of red-shift led to the Big Bang theory. (4)

3 The visible part of the electromagnetic spectrum from galaxies includes dark lines. These lines are at specific wavelengths. The diagrams show the positions of the dark lines in the spectrum from the Sun and in the spectra from four distant galaxies, **A**, **B**, **C** and **D**. Each box covers the same wavelength range.

Increasing wavelength

Spectrum of light from the Sun

Spectrum of light from Galaxy **A**

Spectrum of light from Galaxy **C**

Spectrum of light from Galaxy **B**

Spectrum of light from Galaxy **D**

Increasing wavelength   Increasing wavelength

a
- **i** What is the name of the phenomenon shown in the spectrum from galaxy **B**? (1)

  Choose from the list.

  blue-shift   green-shift   red-shift   yellow-shift
- **ii** Which of the galaxies, **A**, **B**, **C** or **D**, is the furthest from Earth? (1)
- **iii** Which galaxy, **A**, **B**, **C** or **D**, is moving towards the observer? (1)
- **iv** What change has occurred to the speed and frequency of light from galaxy **A**? (2)

b Edwin Hubble investigated the relationship between the speed of a galaxy moving away from Earth and its distance from Earth.

Graph **P** shows his results.

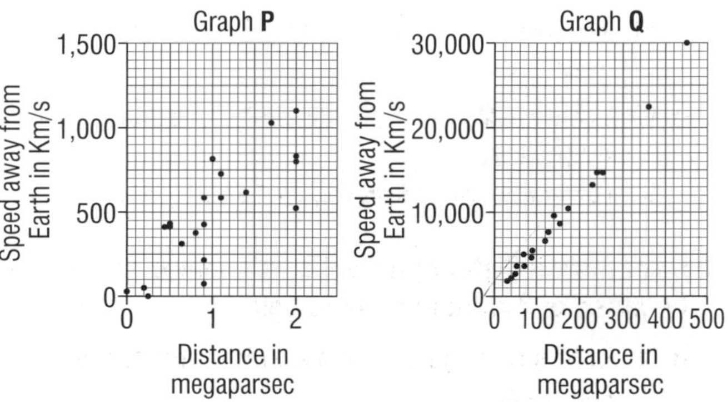

(A megaparsec is a very large unit of distance used by astronomers)

Other astronomers have confirmed Hubble's results.

Their results are shown in graph **Q**.

Outline the differences in the data obtained by Hubble and the data obtained by the other astronomers. (4)

c The gradient of the line of best fit on graphs **P** and **Q** is called the Hubble constant.

Astronomers have used the Hubble constant to calculate the age of the universe.

- **i** Calculate the Hubble constant from graph **Q**. (3)
- **ii** Graph **P** gives a value for the Hubble constant of approximately 500 km/s per megaparsec. Why is graph **Q** likely to give a more accurate estimate of the age of the universe than graph **P**? (3)

P13.1 States of matter

Learning objectives

After this topic, you should know:

- the different properties of solids, liquids and gases
- the arrangement of particles in a solid, a liquid and a gas
- the difference in energy of particles in a solid, a liquid and a gas.

Figure 1 Spot the three states of matter

Everything around us is made of matter and exists in one of three states – solid, liquid or gas. The table below summarises the main differences between the three **states of matter**.

	Flow	Shape	Volume	Density
Solid	no	fixed	fixed	much higher than a gas
Liquid	yes	fits container shape	fixed	much higher than a gas
Gas	yes	fills container	can be changed	low compared with a solid or liquid

Change of state

A substance can change from one state to another, as shown in Figure 2. We can make these changes by heating or cooling the substance.

For example:

- when water in a kettle boils, the water turns to steam. Steam, also called water vapour, is water in its gaseous state
- when solid carbon dioxide or 'dry ice' warms up, the solid turns into gas directly
- when steam touches a cold surface, the steam condenses and turns to water.

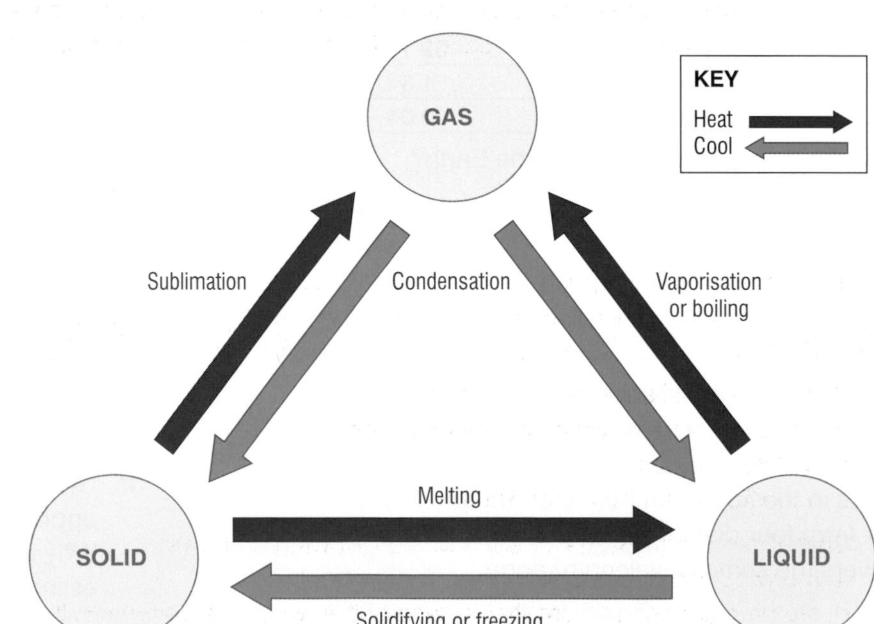

Figure 2 Change of state

Did you know ...?

Density is a measure of how much matter is in a certain volume. Lead is 11 times more dense than water so the mass of a volume of 1 cm^3 of lead is 11 times greater than the mass of 1 cm^3 of water.

Examiner's tip

Make sure you know how particles are arranged in solids, liquids and gases.

Practical

Changing state

Heat some water in a beaker using a Bunsen burner, as shown in Figure 3. Notice that:

- steam or 'vapour' leaves the water surface before the water boils
- when the water boils, bubbles of vapour form inside the water and rise to the surface to release steam.

Switch the Bunsen burner off and hold a cold beaker or cold metal object above the boiling water. Observe condensation of steam from the boiling water on the cold object.

Safety: Take care with boiling water and wear eye protection.

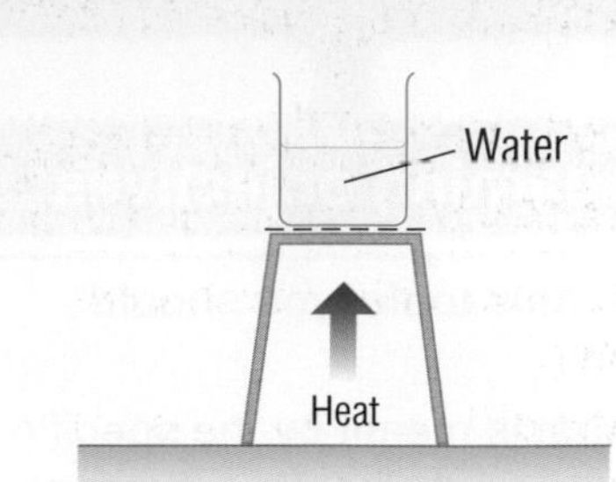

Figure 3 Changing state

The kinetic theory of matter

Solids, liquids and gases are made of particles. Figure 4 shows the arrangement of the particles in a solid, a liquid and a gas. When the temperature of the substance is increased, the particles move faster.

- The particles in a solid are held next to each other in fixed positions. They vibrate about their fixed positions, so the solid keeps its own shape.
- The particles in a liquid are in contact with each other. They move about at random. So a liquid doesn't have its own shape and it can flow.
- The particles in a gas move about at random much faster. They are, on average, much further apart from each other than the particles in a liquid. So, the density of a gas is much less than that of a solid or liquid.
- The particles in solids, liquids and gases have different amounts of energy. For a given amount of a substance, its particles have more energy in the gas state than in the liquid state, and more energy in the liquid state than in the solid state.

a

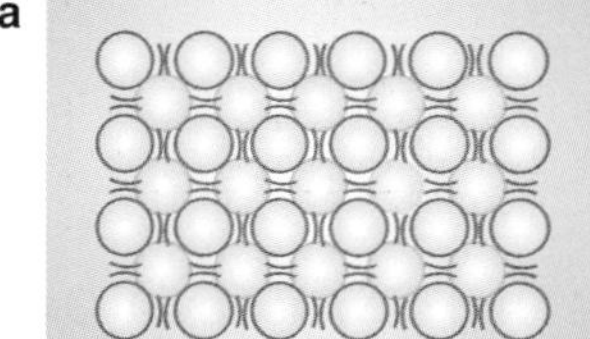

b

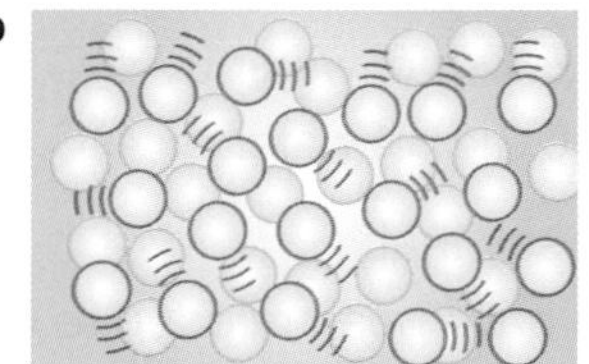

c

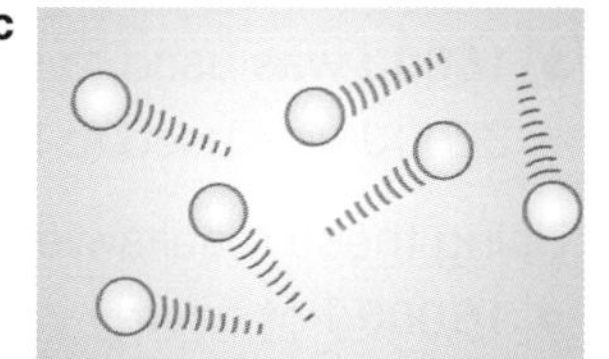

Figure 4 The arrangement of particles in **a** a solid, **b** a liquid and **c** a gas

Did you know ... ?

Random means unpredictable. Lottery numbers are chosen at random.

Summary questions

1 What change of state occurs when:
   a wet clothing on a washing line dries out?
   b hailstones form?
   c snowflakes turn to liquid water?

2 State the scientific word for each of the following changes:
   a the windows in a bus full of people 'mist up'
   b steam is produced from the surface of the water in a pan when the water is heated before it boils
   c ice cubes taken from a freezer thaw out
   d water put into a freezer gradually turns to ice.

3 Describe the changes that take place in the movement and arrangement of the particles in:
   a an ice cube when the ice melts
   b water vapour when it condenses on a cold surface.

Key points

- **Flow, shape, volume and density are the characteristics used to describe each state of matter.**
- **The particles in a solid are held next to each other in fixed positions. They are the least energetic of the states of matter.**
- **The particles in a liquid move about at random and are in contact with each other. They are more energetic than particles in a solid.**
- **The particles in a gas move about randomly and are much further apart than particles in a solid or liquid. They are the most energetic of the states of matter.**

P13.2 Specific heat capacity

Learning objectives

After this topic, you should know:

- what is meant by the specific heat capacity of a substance
- how the mass of a substance affects how quickly its temperature changes when it is heated
- how to measure the specific heat capacity of a substance.

A car in strong sunlight can become very hot. A concrete block of equal **mass** would not become as hot. Metal heats up more easily than concrete. Investigations show that when a substance is heated, its temperature rise depends on:

- the amount of energy supplied to it
- the mass of the substance
- what the substance is.

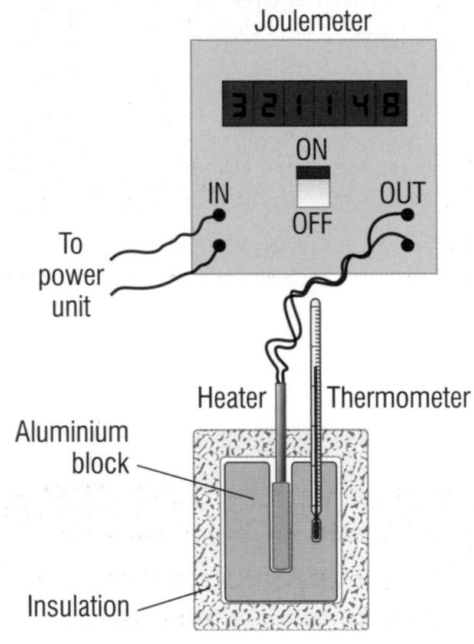

Figure 1 Heating an aluminium block

Practical

Investigating heating

Figure 1 shows how we can use a low-voltage electric heater to heat an aluminium block.

Energy is measured in units called joules (J) or kilowatt-hours (kWh).

Use the energy meter (or joulemeter) to measure the energy supplied to the block. Use the thermometer to measure its temperature rise.

Replace the block with an equal mass of water in a suitable container. Measure the temperature rise of the water when the same amount of energy is supplied to it by the heater.

Your results should show that aluminium heats up more than water.

Safety: Take care with hot objects.

The following results were obtained using two different amounts of water. They show that:

- 1600 J was used to heat 0.1 kg of water by 4 °C
- 3200 J was used to heat 0.2 kg of water by 4 °C.

Using these results we can say that:

- 16 000 J of energy would have been needed to heat 1.0 kg of water by 4 °C
- 4000 J of energy is needed to heat 1.0 kg of water by 1 °C.

More accurate measurements would give 4200 J per kg °C for water. This is its **specific heat capacity**.

The specific heat capacity of a substance is the energy needed or energy transferred to 1 kg of the substance to raise its temperature by 1 °C.

The unit of specific heat capacity is the joule per kilogram degree Celsius (J/(kg °C)).

For a known change of temperature of a known mass of a substance:

$$E = m \times c \times \theta$$

where:
E is the energy transferred in joules, J; m is the mass in kilograms, kg; c is the specific heat capacity, J/(kg °C); θ is the temperature change in degrees Celsius, °C

To find the specific heat capacity we need to rearrange the above equation:

$$c = \frac{E}{m \times \theta}$$

Did you know ... ?

Coastal towns are usually cooler in summer and warmer in winter than towns far inland. This is because water has a very high specific heat capacity. Energy from the Sun (or lack of energy) affects the temperature of the sea much less than it affects the land.

Practical

Measuring the specific heat capacity of a metal

Use the arrangement shown in Figure 1 to heat a metal block of known mass.

Here are some measurements using an aluminium block of mass 1.0 kg.

Starting temperature = 14 °C
Final temperature = 22 °C
Energy supplied = 7200 J

To find the specific heat capacity of aluminium, the measurements above give:

E = energy transferred = energy supplied = 7200 J
θ = temperature change = 22 °C − 14 °C = 8 °C

Inserting these values into the rearranged equation gives:

$$c = \frac{E}{m \times \theta} = \frac{7200\,\text{J}}{1.0\,\text{kg} \times 8\,°\text{C}} = 900\ \text{J/kg °C}$$

Note: An ammeter, a voltmeter and a stopwatch can be used instead of the joulemeter to measure the electrical energy supplied to the block. The circuit for this is shown in Figure 2. The ammeter is used to measure the heater current, and the voltmeter is used to measure the heater voltage.

As we will see in 17.6, the electrical energy supplied E = heater potential difference $V \times$ heater current $I \times$ heating time t.

Safety: Take care with hot objects.

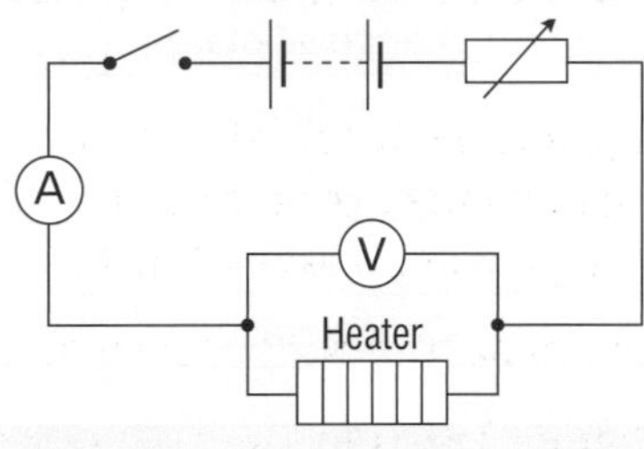

Figure 2 Circuit diagram

Storage heaters

A storage heater uses electricity at night (off-peak) to heat special bricks or concrete blocks in the heater. Energy transfer from the bricks keeps the room warm. The bricks have a high specific heat capacity so they store lots of energy. They warm up slowly when the heater element is on and cool down slowly when it is off.

Electricity used at off-peak times is sometimes charged for at a cheaper rate, so storage heaters are designed to be cost effective.

Figure 3 A storage heater

The table below shows the values for some other substances.

Substance	water	oil	aluminium	iron	copper	lead	concrete
Specific heat capacity (joules per kg degree Celsius)	4200	2100	900	390	490	130	850

Examiner's tip

Remember the factors that affect the temperature rise of something when it is heated.

Summary questions

1 A small bucket of water and a large bucket of water are left in strong sunlight. Which one warms up faster? Give a reason for your answer.

2 Use the information in the table above to answer this question.
 a Explain why a mass of lead heats up more quickly than an equal mass of aluminium.
 b Calculate the energy needed:
  i to raise the temperature of 0.20 kg of aluminium from 15 °C to 40 °C
  ii to raise the temperature of 0.40 kg of water from 15 °C to 40 °C
  iii to raise the temperature of 0.40 kg of water in an aluminium container of mass 0.20 kg from 15 °C to 40 °C.
 c A copper water tank of mass 20 kg contains 150 kg of water at 15 °C. Calculate the energy needed to heat the water and the tank to 55 °C.

3 State **two** ways in which a storage heater differs from a radiant heater.

Key points

- **The specific heat capacity of a substance is the amount of energy needed to change the temperature of 1 kg of the substance by 1 °C.**
- **The greater the mass of an object, the more slowly its temperature increases when it is heated.**
- $E = m \times c \times \theta$

P13.3 Change of state

Learning objectives

After this topic, you should know:

- what is meant by the melting point and the boiling point of a substance
- what is needed to melt a solid or to boil a liquid
- how to explain the difference between boiling and evaporation.

Melting points and boiling points

When pure ice is heated and melts, its temperature stays at 0 °C until all the ice has melted. When water is heated and boils at atmospheric pressure, its temperature stays at 100 °C.

For any pure substance undergoing a change of state, its temperature stays the same. As shown in Table 1, depending on the change of state, we call this temperature the **melting point** or the **boiling point** of the substance. The temperature at which a liquid changes to a solid is called its freezing point and is the same temperature as the melting point of the solid.

The melting point of a solid and the boiling point of a liquid are affected by impurities in the substance. For example, the melting point of water is lowered if salt is added to the water. This is why salt is added to grit used for gritting roads in freezing weather, so that roads have to be colder before they get icy.

Table 1

Change of state	Initial and final state	Temperature
Melting	solid to liquid	melting point
Freezing (also called solidification)	liquid to solid	
Boiling	liquid to vapour	boiling point
Condensation	vapour to liquid	

Practical

Measuring the melting point of a substance

The substance in its solid state is placed in a suitable test tube in a beaker of water, as shown in Figure 1a. The water is heated, and the temperature of the substance is measured when it melts. If its temperature is measured every minute, the measurements can be plotted on a graph, as shown in Figure 1b. The melting point is the temperature of the flat section of the graph because this is when the temperature stays the same as the substance melts.

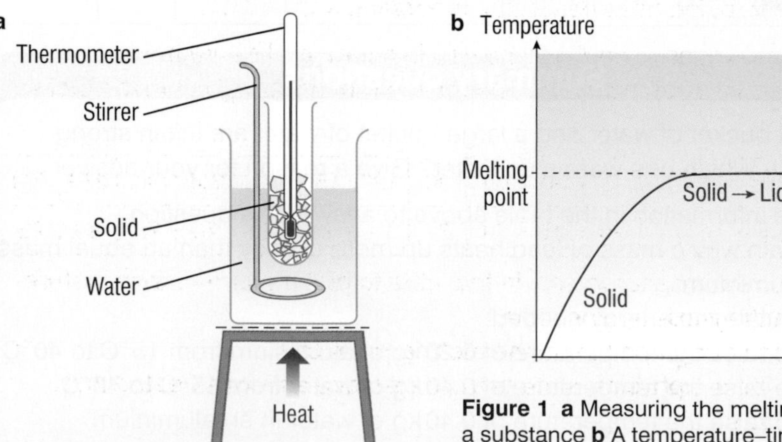

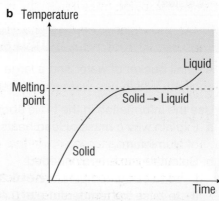

Figure 1 **a** Measuring the melting point of a substance **b** A temperature–time graph

The same arrangement without the beaker of water can be used to find the boiling point of a liquid.

Safety: Wear eye protection.

Examiner's tip

Don't forget that when a pure substance is changing state, its temperature does not change.

Energy and change of state

Suppose a beaker of ice below 0 °C is heated steadily so that the ice melts and then the water boils. Figure 2 shows how the temperature changes with time. The temperature:

1 increases until it reaches 0 °C when the ice starts to melt at 0 °C, then
2 stays constant at 0 °C until all the ice has melted, then
3 increases from 0 °C to 100 °C until the water in the beaker starts to boil at 100 °C, then
4 stays constant at 100 °C as the water turns to steam.

The energy supplied to a substance when it changes its state is called **latent heat**. 'Latent' means 'hidden'. The energy supplied to melt or boil it is 'hidden' by the substance because its temperature does not change at the melting point or the boiling point.

Most pure substances produce a temperature–time graph with similar features to Figure 2. Note that:

- **fusion** is often used to describe melting because different solids can be joined, or 'fused', together when they melt
- **evaporation** from a liquid occurs at its surface when the liquid is below its boiling point. At its boiling point, a liquid boils because bubbles of vapour form inside the liquid and rise to the surface to release the gas.

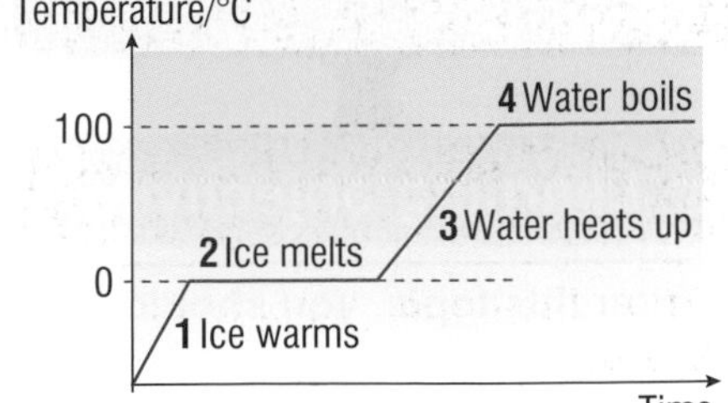

Figure 2 Melting and boiling of water

Figure 3 Boiling water at high altitude

Examiner's tip

Evaporation takes place at any temperature; boiling occurs only at the boiling point.

Did you know ... ?

At high altitude, a liquid boils at a lower temperature than at sea level. This is because the boiling point of a liquid depends on pressure, and atmospheric pressure is lower at high altitude than it is at sea level.

Summary questions

1 State three differences between evaporation and boiling.

2 A pure solid substance X was heated in a tube and its temperature was measured every 30 seconds. The measurements are given in the table below.

time in seconds	0	30	60	90	120	150	180	210	240	270	300
temperature in °C	20	35	49	61	71	79	79	79	79	86	92

a **i** Use the measurements in the table to plot a graph of temperature on the *y*-axis against time.
ii Use your graph to find the melting point of X.
b Describe the physical state of the substance as it was heated from 60 °C to 90 °C.

3 Salt water has a lower freezing point than pure water. In icy conditions in winter, gritting lorries are used to scatter a mixture of salt and grit on roads. Explain the purpose of each of the two components of the mixture.

Key points

- For a pure substance:
  - its melting point is the temperature at which it melts (which is the same temperature at which it solidifies)
  - its boiling point is the temperature at which it boils (which is the same temperature at which it condenses).
- Energy is needed to melt a solid or to boil a liquid.
- Boiling occurs throughout a liquid at its boiling point. Evaporation occurs from the surface of a liquid when its temperature is below its boiling point.

P13.4 Specific latent heat

Learning objectives

After this topic, you should know:

- what is meant by latent heat of fusion and of vaporisation
- what is meant by ***specific*** latent heat of fusion and of vaporisation
- how to use the equation $E = m \times L$ in latent heat calculations.

Examiner's tip

Be careful with units when doing calculations, especially joules and kilojoules.

Latent heat of fusion

When a solid substance is heated:

- **below its melting point**, its temperature increases until the melting point is reached. Before it reaches this point, the energy supplied to the solid increases the kinetic energy of its particles. As a result, the particles vibrate more and more and the temperature rises.
- **at its melting point**, it melts and turns to liquid. Its temperature stays constant until all of it has melted. The energy supplied is called **latent heat of fusion**. It is the energy used by the particles to break free from each other.

If the substance in its liquid state is cooled, it will solidify at the same temperature as its melting point. When this happens, the particles bond together into a rigid structure. Latent heat is released as the substance solidifies.

The **specific latent heat of fusion, L_F**, of a substance is the energy needed to melt 1 kg of the substance at its melting point (i.e. without changing its temperature).

The unit of specific latent heat of fusion is the **joule per kilogram (J/kg)**.

If energy E is supplied to a solid at its melting point and mass m of the substance melts without change in temperature:

$$\textbf{Specific latent heat of fusion, } L_F = \frac{E}{m}$$

Note that rearranging this equation gives $\mathbf{E = m \times L_F}$

Practical

Measuring the specific latent heat of ice

In this experiment, a low-voltage heater is used to melt crushed ice in a funnel. The melted ice is collected using a beaker under the funnel, as shown in Figure 1. A joulemeter is used as shown to measure the energy supplied to the heater.

To take account of energy transfer from the surroundings, the mass of ice melted in a certain time must be measured with the heater turned off, then with it turned on. The difference in the two measurements gives the mass of ice melted because of the heater only.

1 With the heater off, water from the funnel is collected in the beaker for a measured time (e.g. 10 minutes). The mass of the beaker and water, m_1, is then measured. The beaker is then emptied for the next stage.

2 With the heater on, the procedure is repeated for exactly the same time. The joulemeter readings before and after the heater is switched on are recorded. After the heater is switched off, the mass of the beaker and the water, m_2, is measured once more.

To calculate the specific latent heat of fusion of ice, note that:

- the mass of ice melted because of the heater, $m = m_2 - m_1$
- the energy supplied E to the heater = the difference between the joulemeter readings
- the specific latent heat of fusion of ice, $L_F = \frac{E}{m} = \frac{E}{m_2 - m_1}$

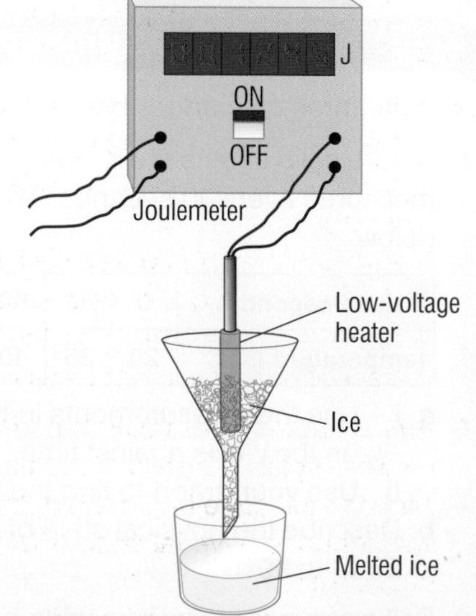

Figure 1 Measuring the specific latent heat of ice

Instead of using a joulemeter, the energy supplied to the heater can also be measured using the circuit and information in 13.2, Figure 2.

Safety: Take care with hot immersion heater and wear eye protection.

Latent heat of vaporisation

When a liquid is heated:

- **above its freezing point**, its temperature increases until the boiling point is reached. Before it reaches this point, the energy supplied to the liquid increases the kinetic energy of its particles. As a result, the particles move about faster and faster and the temperature rises.
- **at its boiling point**, it turns to vapour. Its temperature stays constant until all of it has boiled. The energy supplied is called **latent heat of vaporisation**. It is the energy used by the particles to break away from the liquid.

If the substance in its gaseous state is cooled, it will condense at the same temperature as its boiling point. When this happens, the particles bond and get much closer together. Latent heat is released as the substance condenses into a liquid.

The **specific latent heat of vaporisation, L_v**, of a substance is the energy needed to change 1 kg of the substance at its boiling point from liquid to vapour.

The unit of specific latent heat of vaporisation is the **joule per kilogram (J/kg)**.

If energy E is supplied to a liquid at its boiling point and mass m of the substance boils away without change in temperature:

$$\textbf{Specific latent heat of vaporisation, } L_v = \frac{E}{m}$$

Note that rearranging this equation gives $E = m \times L_v$

Summary questions

1 In the experiment shown in Figure 1, 0.024 kg of water was collected in the beaker in 300 seconds with the heater turned off. The beaker was then emptied and placed under the funnel again. With the heater on for exactly 300 s, the joulemeter reading increased from zero to 15 000 J and 0.068 kg of water was collected in the beaker.
  a Calculate the mass of ice melted because of the heater being on.
  b Calculate the specific latent heat of fusion of water.

2 a In the experiment shown in Figure 2, the balance reading decreased from 0.144 kg to 0.152 kg in the time taken to supply 18 400 J of energy to the boiling water. Calculate the specific latent heat of vaporisation of water.
  b After the heater in **a** was switched off, the temperature of the water in the beaker gradually decreased. What does this observation tell you about the experiment and the value calculated for the specific latent heat of vaporisation of water?

3 An ice cube of mass 0.008 kg at 0 °C was placed in water at 15 °C in an insulated plastic beaker. The mass of water in the beaker was 0.120 kg. After the ice cube had melted, the water was stirred and its temperature was found to have fallen to 9 °C. The specific heat capacity of water is 4200 J/kg °C.
  a Calculate the energy transferred from the water.
  b Show that when the melted ice warmed from 0 °C to 9 °C, it gained 300 J of energy.
  c Hence calculate the specific latent heat of fusion of water.

Practical

Measuring the specific latent heat of vaporisation of water

In this experiment, the arrangement shown in Figure 2 can be used. The low-voltage heater is switched on to bring the water to its boiling point. When the water is boiling, the joulemeter reading and the top pan balance reading are measured and then remeasured after a measured time (e.g. 5 minutes).

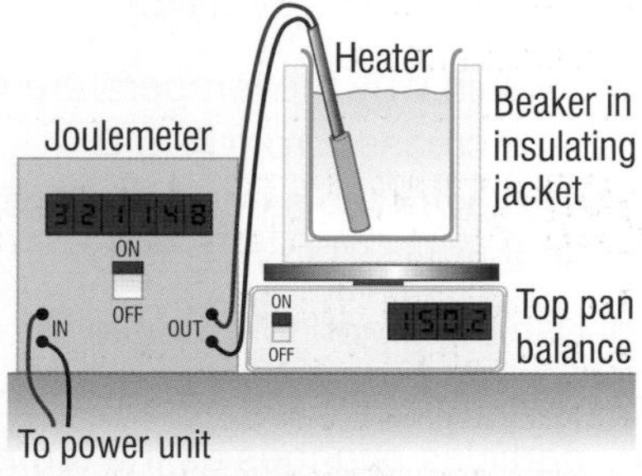

Figure 2 Measuring the specific latent heat of vaporisation of water

The energy supplied, E, during this time = the difference between the joulemeter readings.

The mass of water boiled away in this time, m = the difference between the readings of the top pan balance.

The equation $L_v = \frac{E}{m}$ is used to calculate the specific latent heat of vaporisation of water.

Safety: As opposite.

Key points

- **Latent heat is the energy needed or released when a substance changes its state without changing its temperature.**
- **Specific latent heat of fusion (or of vaporisation) is the energy needed to melt (or to boil) 1 kg of a substance with no change in temperature.**

Summary questions

1 A test tube containing a solid substance is heated in a beaker of water. The temperature–time graph shows how the temperature of the substance changed with time as it was heated.

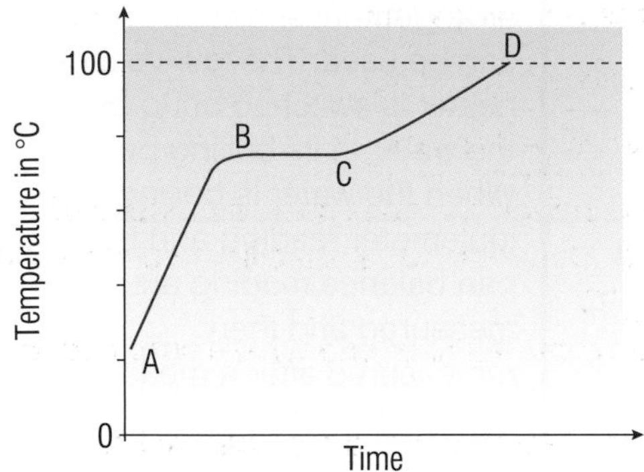

a Explain why the temperature of the substance:

i increased from **A** to **B**

ii stayed the same from **B** to **C**

iii increased from **C** to **D**?

b Use the graph to estimate the melting point of the solid.

c Describe how the arrangement and motion of the particles changes as the temperature increases from **A** to **D**.

2 Geothermal energy is obtained from hot rocks underground by pumping water through the rock.

a i When 400 kg of water is pumped through the rocks at a certain location, the temperature of the water is increased from 20 °C to 80 °C. Calculate the energy transferred to the water. The specific heat capacity of water is 4200 J/kg °C.

ii If the water is pumped through the rocks in a time of 50 seconds, calculate the rate of transfer of energy to the water.

b The temperature of the underground rocks stays constant because the rocks gain energy by heating from the Earth's core. If water had been pumped through the rocks at a much slower rate, discuss the effect this would have had on the temperature of the water flowing out of the rocks.

3 The figure shows a large heater used to heat a big hall. Hot water is pumped through pipes which pass through the heater. Fins attached to the pipes transfer energy by heating to air, which is blown by fans through the heater.

a Water enters the heater at 77 °C and leaves it at a temperature of 15 °C. The water flows through the heater at a rate of 0.050 kg per second. Calculate the energy transferred from the water to the heater each second. The specific heat capacity of water is 4200 J/kg °C.

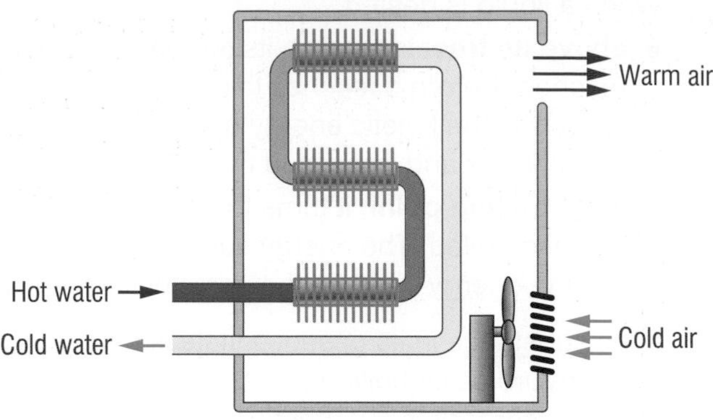

b At a certain fan speed, air enters the heater at 12 °C and leaves it at a temperature of 26 °C. State and explain how the temperature of the air leaving the heater would change if the fan speed is turned up to increase the rate of flow of air through the heater.

4 A plastic beaker containing 0.10 kg of water at 18 °C was placed in a refrigerator for 450 seconds. After this time, the temperature of the water was found to be 3 °C. The specific heat capacity of water is 4200 J/kg °C.

a Calculate the energy transferred from the water.

b Calculate the rate of transfer of energy from the water.

5 A 3.0 kW electric kettle is fitted with a safety cut-out designed to switch it off as soon as the water boils. Unfortunately, the cut-out does not operate correctly and allows the water to boil for 30 seconds longer than it is supposed to.

a How much electrical energy is supplied to the kettle in this time?

b The specific latent heat of vaporisation of water is 2.3 MJ/kg. Estimate the mass of water boiled away in this time.

6 When the brakes of a vehicle are applied, the vehicle decelerates and comes to rest from a velocity of 30 m/s.

a The mass of the vehicle is 1200 kg. Show that the loss of kinetic energy of the vehicle is 0.54 MJ.

b The brakes become hot as a result of the energy transferred to them by the braking force. The brakes contain a total of 16 kg of metal of specific heat capacity 560 J/kg °C. Estimate the increase of temperature of the metal in the brakes.

AQA Examination-style questions

1 **a** A student put some crushed ice in a beaker and measured the temperature. She then put the beaker on a tripod and gauze and gently heated it with a Bunsen burner. She measured the temperature every minute.

The graph shows how the temperature changed with time.

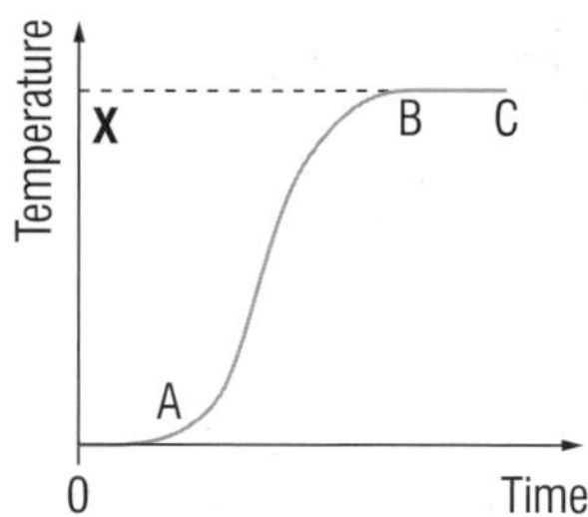

i Name the temperature marked **X** on the graph. (1)

ii The crushed ice does not absorb all the energy supplied by the Bunsen burner.
What happens to the energy that is not absorbed by the crushed ice? (3)

iii Use the graph to help you explain what happens to the energy that is absorbed. (QWC) (6)

iv Another student carried out a similar experiment. She used a temperature sensor and a data logger instead of a thermometer and a clock.
Give **two** advantages of her method. (2)

2 **a** A leaflet about saving energy states:

Only boil the water you need

Explain how doing this saves energy. (2)

b A dishwasher heats 8 kg of water. The normal setting of the dishwasher uses water at 65°C.

The specific heat capacity of water is 4200 J/kg °C. Calculate how much energy, in kJ, is saved by using the economy setting of water at 45°C. (3)

3 The diagram shows a storage heater.

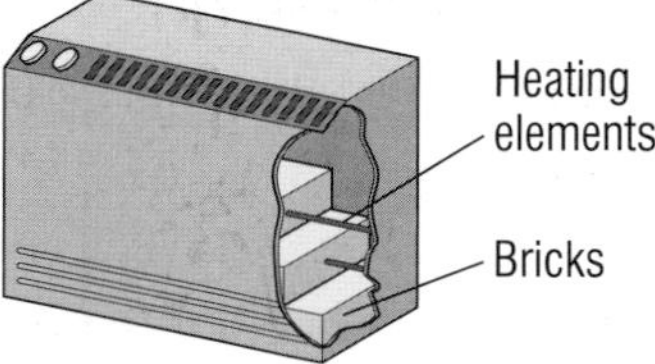

The bricks are heated up during the night when electrical energy is cheaper. During the day, the bricks release energy into the room.

a **i** The bricks may be made from different materials.

Choose **two** properties that the bricks should have if they are to store as much energy as possible. (1)

large mass per unit volume
small mass per unit volume
large specific heat capacity
small specific heat capacity

ii The storage heater contains concrete bricks of mass 12 kg. Concrete has a specific heat capacity of 900 J/kg °C.
During the night 540 kJ of energy are supplied to the bricks.
Calculate the temperature rise of the bricks. (3)

iii Actually the temperature rise will be different from the calculated value.
Explain how the temperature rise will be different. (3)

b The diagram shows an oil-filled heater.

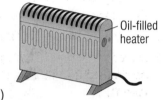

Oil-filled heater

i Give **one** advantage of the oil-filled heater over the storage heater. (1)

ii Give **one** advantage of the storage heater over the oil-filled heater. (1)

4 **a** The diagram shows one method of determining the specific latent heat of steam.

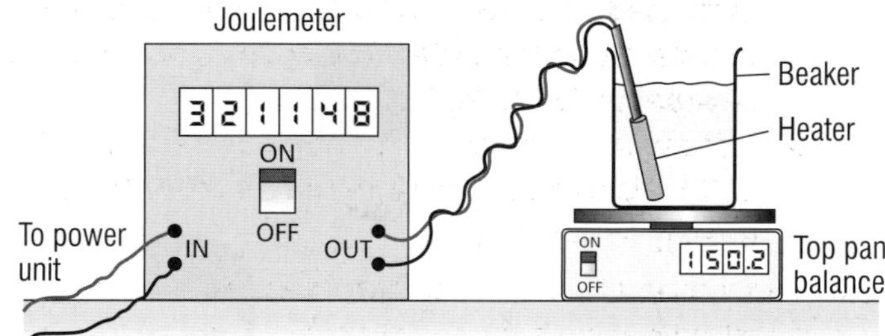

Some students switch on the heater to boil the water. When the water is boiling they take the reading on the top pan balance and set the joulemeter to zero. After heating for a further ten minutes, they take the joulemeter reading and the new reading on the top pan balance.

Their results are shown below.

1st balance reading	184 g
2nd balance reading	168 g
Joulemeter reading	36 800 J

i Use the students' results to calculate the specific latent heat of steam. (4)

ii Suggest how the method could be improved. (1)

P14.1 Conduction

Learning objectives

After this topic, you should know:

- which materials make the best conductors
- which materials make the best insulators
- why metals are good conductors
- why non-metals are poor conductors.

Figure 1 At a barbecue – the steel cooking utensils have wooden or plastic handles

When you have a barbecue, you need to know which materials are good **conductors** and which ones are good **insulators**. If you can't remember, you're likely to burn your fingers!

Testing rods of different materials as conductors

The rods need to be the same width and length for a fair test. Each rod is coated with a thin layer of wax near one end. The uncoated ends are then heated together.

Look at Figure 2. The wax melts fastest on the rod that conducts best.

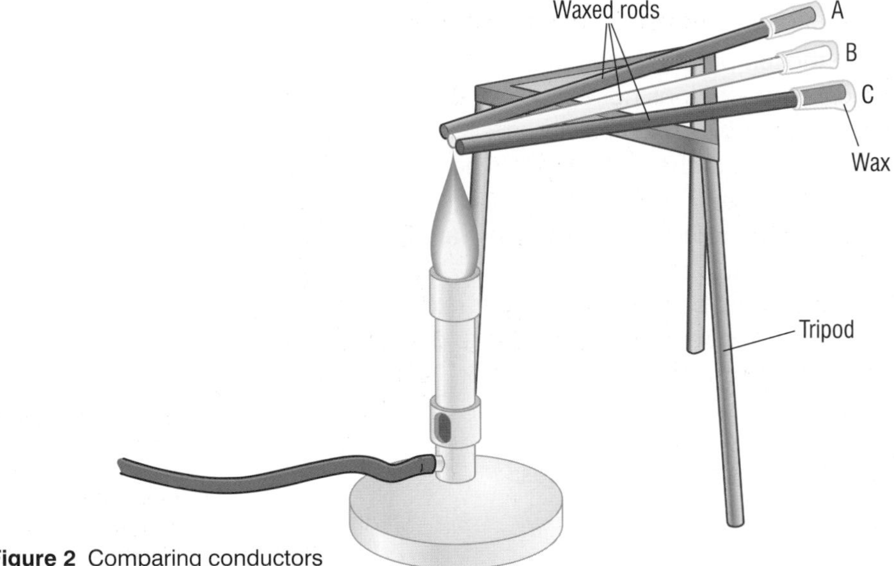

Figure 2 Comparing conductors

- Metals conduct energy better than non-metals.
- Copper is a better conductor than steel.
- Wood conducts better than glass.

Practical

Testing sheets of materials as insulators

Use different materials to insulate identical cans (or beakers) of hot water. The volume of water and its temperature at the start should be the same.

Use a thermometer to measure the water temperature after a fixed time. The results should tell you which insulator was best.

Safety: Take care if using very hot water.

The table below gives the results of comparing two different materials using the method explained in the practical.

Material	Starting temperature (°C)	Temperature after 300 s (°C)
paper	40	32
felt	40	36

Conduction in metals

Metals contain lots of **free electrons**. These electrons move about at random inside the metal and hold the positive metal ions (charged atoms) in their fixed positions. The free electrons collide with each other and with the positive ions.

When a metal rod is heated at one end, the free electrons at the hot end gain kinetic energy and move faster.

- These electrons **diffuse** (i.e. spread out) and collide with other free electrons and ions in the cooler parts of the metal.
- As a result, they transfer kinetic energy to these electrons and ions.

So energy is transferred from the hot end of the rod to the colder end.

In a non-metallic solid, all the electrons are held in the atoms. Energy transfer only takes place because the atoms vibrate and shake each other. This is much less effective than energy transfer by free electrons. This is why metals are much better conductors than non-metals.

Examiner's tip

Make sure you know the part played by free electrons in the process of conduction.

Figure 3 Insulating a loft. The air trapped between fibres make fibreglass a good insulator.

Did you know ... ?

Materials such as wool and fibreglass are good insulators. This is because they contain air trapped between the fibres. Trapped air is a good insulator. We use materials such as fibreglass for insulating lofts and hot water pipes.

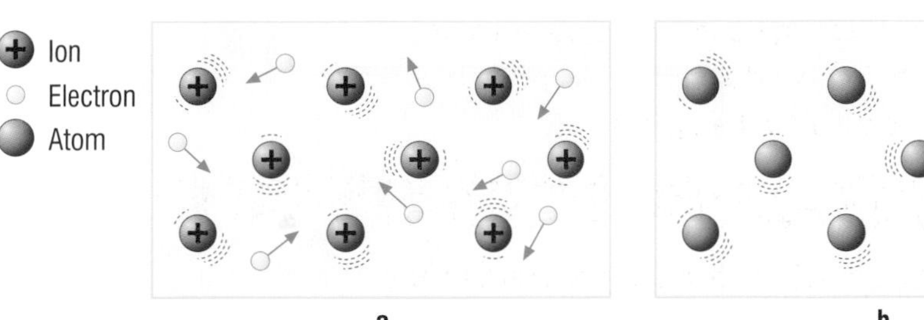

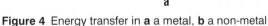

Figure 4 Energy transfer in **a** a metal, **b** a non-metal

Summary questions

1. **a** Why do steel pans have handles made of plastic or wood?
   b Which material, felt or paper, is the better insulator? Give a reason for your answer.
2. **a** Choose a material you would use to line a pair of winter boots. Explain your choice of material.
   b How could you carry out a test on three different lining materials?
3. **a** Explain why metals are good conductors of energy.
   b Describe how non-metals conduct energy.

Key points

- Metals are the best conductors of energy.
- Materials such as wool and fibreglass are the best insulators.
- Conduction of energy in a metal is caused mainly by free electrons transferring energy inside the metal.
- Non-metals are poor conductors because they do not contain free electrons.

P14.2 Convection

Learning objectives

After this topic, you should know:
- what convection is
- where convection can occur
- why convection occurs.

Did you know ... ?

The Gulf Stream is a stream of warm water that flows across the Atlantic Ocean from the Gulf of Mexico to the British Isles. If it ever turned away from us, our winters would be much colder!

Figure 1 A natural glider – some birds use convection to soar high above the ground

Glider aircraft and birds use convection to stay in the air. **Convection** streams can keep them high above the ground for hours.

Convection happens whenever we heat **fluids**. A fluid is a gas or a liquid. Look at the diagram in Figure 2. It shows a simple demonstration of convection.

- The hot gases from the burning candle go straight up the chimney above the candle.
- Cold air is drawn down the other chimney to replace the air leaving the box.

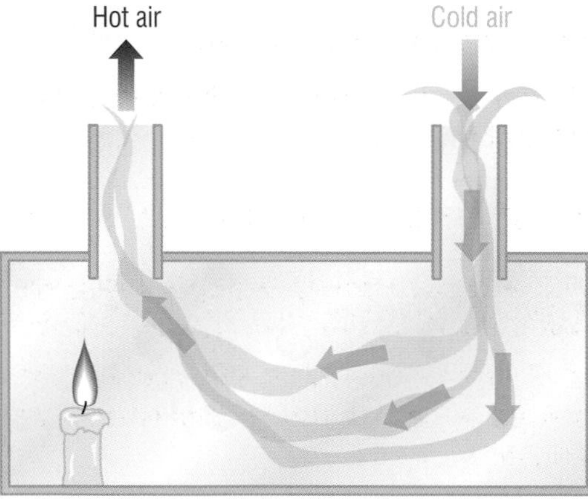

Figure 2 Convection

Using convection

Hot water at home

Many homes have a hot water tank. Hot water from the boiler rises and flows into the tank where it rises to the top. Figure 3 shows the system. When you use a hot water tap at home, you draw off hot water from the top of the tank.

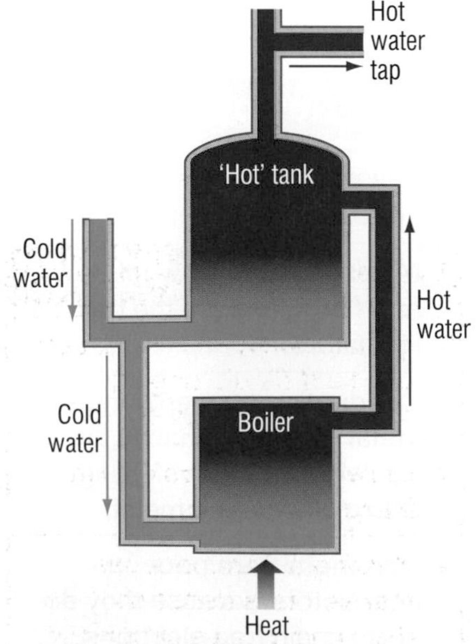

Figure 3 Hot water at home

Sea breezes

Sea breezes keep you cool at the seaside. On a sunny day, the ground heats up faster than the sea. So the air above the ground warms up and rises. Cooler air from the sea flows in as a 'sea breeze' to take the place of the rising warm air (see Figure 4).

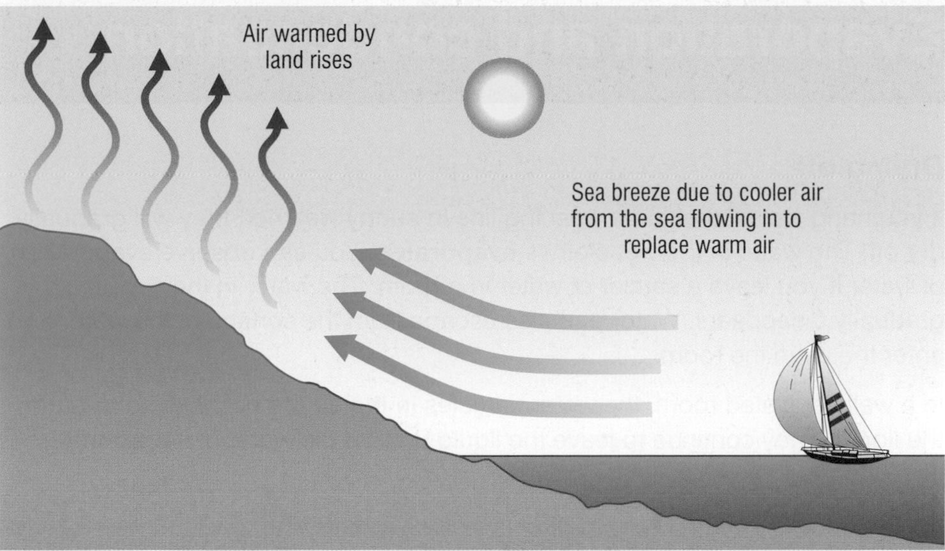

Figure 4 Sea breezes

How convection works

Convection takes place:

- only in fluids (liquids and gases)
- because of circulation (convection) within the fluid.

The convection occurs because fluids rise where they are heated (because heating makes them less dense). Then they stop rising where they cool down (because cooling makes them more dense). Convection streams transfer energy from the hotter parts to the cooler parts.

So why do fluids rise when heated?

Most fluids expand when heated. This is because the particles move about more and they move apart, taking up more space. Therefore the **density** decreases because the same mass of fluid now occupies a bigger volume. So heating part of a fluid makes that part less dense and therefore it rises.

Examiner's tip

Remember that it is **not** heat energy that rises – it is the hot fluid that moves around. Make sure that you can explain why a hot fluid rises.

Summary questions

1 A pan of water is heated on a gas cooker. Describe how energy is transferred by heating from the gas flame under the pan to all of the water in the pan.

2 The figure shows a convector heater. It has an electric heating element inside and a metal grille on top.

Hot air

- **a** What does the heater do to the air inside the heater?
- **b** Why is there a metal grille on top of the heater?
- **c** Where does air flow into the heater?

3 a Describe how you could demonstrate convection in water using a strongly coloured crystal or a suitable dye. Explain in detail what you would see.

b A wall-mounted radiator in a room is often fitted under a window. Give one advantage and one disadvantage of fitting such a radiator under a window rather than away from the window.

Key points

- **Convection is the circulation of a fluid (liquid or gas) caused by heating it.**
- **Convection occurs only in liquids and gases.**
- **Heating a liquid or a gas makes it less dense so it rises and causes circulation.**

P14.3 Evaporation and condensation

Learning objectives

After this topic, you should know:

- what evaporation is
- what condensation is
- how evaporation causes cooling
- what affects the rate of evaporation from a liquid
- what affects the rate of condensation on a surface.

Drying off

If you hang wet clothes on a washing line in sunny weather, they will gradually dry off. The water in the wet clothes **evaporates**. You can observe evaporation of water if you leave a saucer of water in a room. The water in the saucer gradually disappears. Water particles escape from the surface of the water and enter the air in the room.

In a well-ventilated room, the water particles in the air are not likely to re-enter the liquid. They continue to leave the liquid until all the water has evaporated.

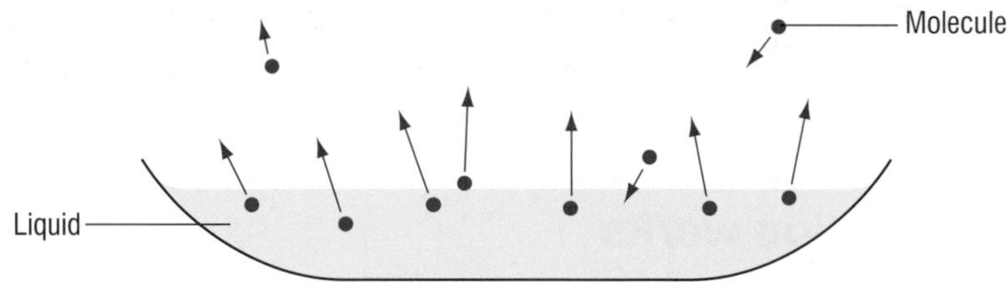

Figure 1 Water particles escaping from a liquid

Figure 2 Condensation

Condensation

In a steamy bathroom, a mirror is often covered by a film of water. There are lots of water particles in the air. Some of them hit the mirror, lose energy and stay there as the liquid. We say water vapour in the air **condenses** on the mirror.

Cooling by evaporation

If you have an injection, the doctor or nurse might 'numb' your skin by dabbing it with a liquid that easily evaporates. As the liquid evaporates, your skin becomes too cold to feel any pain.

Examiner's tip

Make sure that you can use the kinetic theory to explain why a liquid cools when it evaporates.

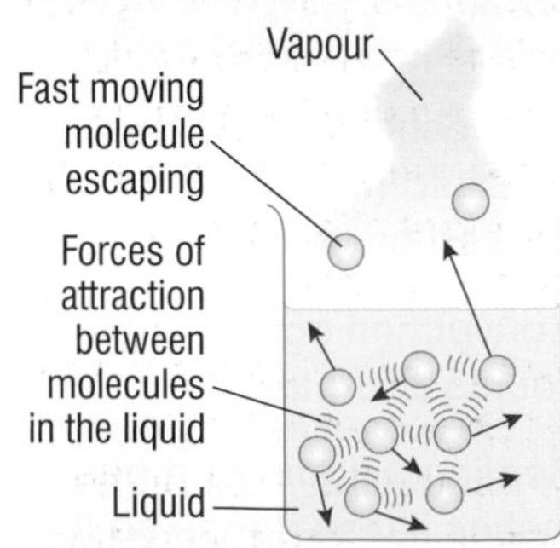

Figure 3 Explanation of cooling by evaporation

Demonstration

Cooling by evaporation

Watch your teacher carry out this experiment in a fume cupboard.

Why is ether used in this experiment?

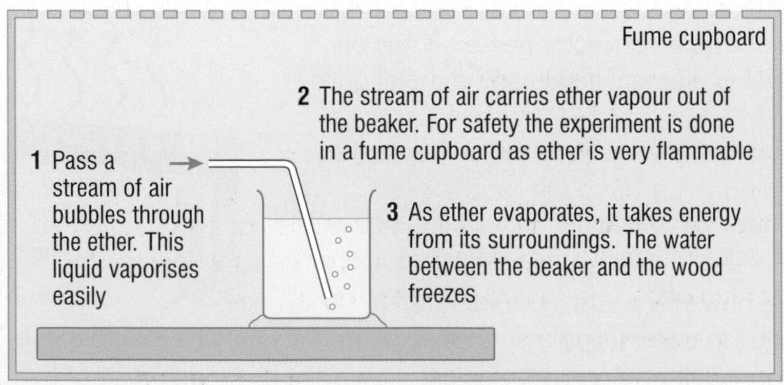

Fume cupboard
1 Pass a stream of air bubbles through the ether. This liquid vaporises easily
2 The stream of air carries ether vapour out of the beaker. For safety the experiment is done in a fume cupboard as ether is very flammable
3 As ether evaporates, it takes energy from its surroundings. The water between the beaker and the wood freezes

Figure 4 A demonstration of cooling by evaporation

Safety: There should be no naked flames in the laboratory.

We can use the kinetic theory of matter, as shown in Figure 3, to explain why evaporation causes this cooling effect.

- Relatively weak attractive forces exist between the particles in the liquid.
- The faster particles, which have more kinetic energy, break away from the attraction of the other particles at the surface and escape from the liquid.
- After they leave, the liquid is cooler because the average kinetic energy of the particles left in the liquid has decreased.

Factors affecting the rate of evaporation

Clothes dry faster on a washing line:

- if each item of wet clothing is spread out when it is hung on the line. This increases the area of the wet clothing that's in contact with dry air.
- if the washing line is in sunlight. Wet clothes dry faster the warmer they are.
- if there is a breeze to take away the particles that escape from the water in the wet clothes.

The example above shows that the rate of evaporation from a liquid is increased by:

- increasing the surface area of the liquid
- increasing the temperature of the liquid
- creating a draught of air across the liquid's surface.

Factors affecting the rate of condensation

In a steamy kitchen, water can often be seen trickling down a window pane. The glass pane is a cold surface, so water vapour condenses on it. The air in the room is moist, or 'humid'. The bigger the area of the window pane, or the colder it is, the greater the rate of condensation. This example shows that the rate of condensation of a vapour on a surface is increased by:

- increasing the surface area
- reducing the surface temperature.

Summary questions

1 Describe in terms of particles what happens in each of the following situations:
  a water droplets form on a cold surface
  b a liquid cools because of evaporation.

2 a In terms of particles, explain why the windows on a bus become misty when there are lots of people on the bus.
  b A refrigerator usually has a drip tray to collect any water that runs to the bottom of the inside of the refrigerator. Explain why opening the refrigerator too often might cause the drip tray to fill.

3 Explain the following statements.
  a Wet clothes on a washing line dry faster on a hot day than on a cold day.
  b A person wearing wet clothes on a cold windy day is likely to feel much colder than someone wearing dry clothes.

Did you know ... ?

Air conditioning

An **air-conditioning unit** in a room transfers energy from inside the room to the outside. The unit contains a 'coolant' liquid that easily evaporates. The coolant is pumped round a sealed circuit of pipes that go through the unit and the outside.

- The liquid coolant evaporates in the pipes in the room and cools the room.
- The evaporated coolant condenses in the pipes outside and transfers energy to the surroundings.

Figure 5 An air-conditioning unit

Key points

- Evaporation is when a liquid turns into a gas.
- Condensation is when a gas turns into a liquid.
- The cooling of a liquid by evaporation is caused by faster-moving particles escaping from the liquid.
- Evaporation can be increased by increasing the surface area of the liquid, by increasing the liquid's temperature or by creating a draught of air across the liquid's surface.
- Condensation on a surface can be increased by increasing the area of the surface or by reducing the temperature of the surface.

P14.4 Infrared radiation

Learning objectives

After this topic, you should know:

- what infrared radiation is
- what gives out infrared radiation
- how infrared radiation depends on the temperature of an object.

Figure 1 Keeping watch in darkness

Examiner's tip

Remember that all bodies emit **and** absorb infrared radiation.

Did you know ... ?

A **passive infrared (PIR) detector** in a burglar alarm circuit will 'trigger' the alarm if someone moves in front of the detector. The detector contains sensors that detect infrared radiation from different directions.

links

For more information on electromagnetic waves, look back to 8.1 'The electromagnetic spectrum'.

Seeing in the dark

We can use special cameras to 'see' animals and people in the dark. These cameras detect **infrared radiation**. Every object gives out (**emits**) infrared radiation.

The higher the temperature of an object, the more infrared radiation it emits in a given time.

Look at the photo in Figure 1. The rhinos are hotter than the ground.

Practical

Detecting infrared radiation

You can use a thermometer with a blackened bulb to detect infrared radiation. Figure 2 shows how to do this.

- The glass prism splits a narrow beam of white light into the colours of the spectrum.
- The thermometer reading rises when it is placed just beyond the red part of the spectrum. Some of the infrared radiation in the beam goes there. Our eyes cannot detect it but the thermometer can.
- **Infrared radiation** is beyond the red part of the visible spectrum.

What would happen to the thermometer reading if the thermometer were moved away from the screen?

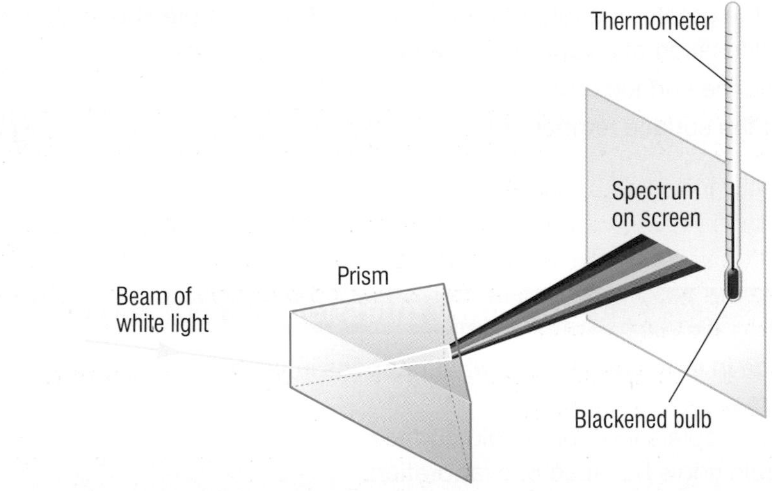

Figure 2 Detecting infrared radiation

The electromagnetic spectrum

Radio waves, **microwaves**, **infrared radiation** and **visible light** are parts of the electromagnetic spectrum. So too are ultraviolet rays and X-rays. Electromagnetic waves are electric and magnetic waves that travel through space.

Energy from the Sun

The Sun emits all types of electromagnetic radiation. Fortunately for us, the Earth's atmosphere blocks most of the radiation that would harm us, but it doesn't block infrared radiation from the Sun.

Figure 3 shows a solar furnace. This uses a giant reflector that focuses sunlight.

The temperature at the focus can reach thousands of degrees. That's almost as hot as the surface of the Sun, which is 5500 °C.

Figure 3 A solar furnace in the Eastern Pyrenees, France

The greenhouse effect

The Earth's atmosphere acts like a greenhouse made of glass. In a greenhouse:

- short-wavelength infrared radiation (and light) from the Sun can pass through the glass to warm the objects inside the greenhouse
- infrared radiation from these warm objects is trapped inside by the glass because the objects emit infrared radiation of longer wavelengths that can't pass through the glass.

So the greenhouse stays warm.

Gases in the atmosphere, such as water vapour, methane and carbon dioxide, trap infrared radiation from the Earth. This makes the Earth warmer than it would be if it had no atmosphere.

But the Earth is becoming too warm. If the polar ice caps melt, it will cause sea levels to rise. Reducing our use of fossil fuels will help to reduce the production of 'greenhouse gases'.

Practical

A huddle test

Design an investigation to model the effect of penguins huddling together. You could use beakers of hot water to represent the penguins.

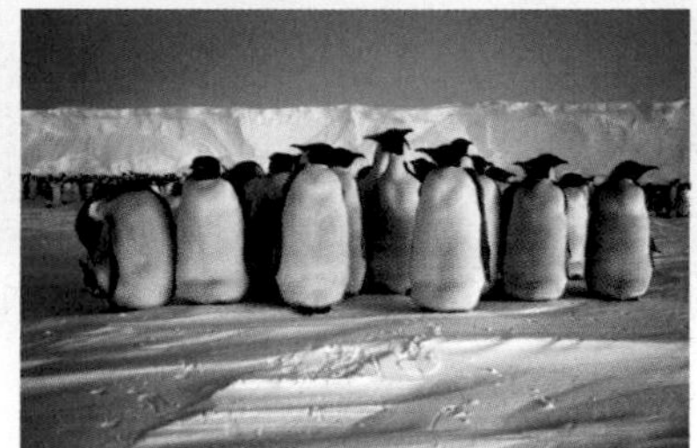

Figure 4 Penguins keeping warm

Safety: Take care with hot water.

Summary questions

1 a What is infrared radiation?

b An infrared camera on a satellite shows that more infrared radiation is emitted at night from a city than from the surrounding rural area. What does this tell you about the city compared with the rural area? Give a reason for your answer.

2 a Copy and complete the table to show if the object emits infrared radiation or light or both.

Object	Infrared	Light
A hot iron		
A light bulb		
A TV screen		
The Sun		

b How can you tell if an electric iron is hot without touching it?

3 a Explain why penguins huddle together to keep warm.

b What can you deduce from Figure 2 about the wavelength of the infrared radiation that passes through the prism?

Key points

- **Infrared radiation is energy transfer by electromagnetic waves.**
- **All objects emit infrared radiation.**
- **The hotter an object is, the more infrared radiation it emits in a given time.**

P14.5 Surfaces and radiation

Learning objectives

After this topic, you should know:

- which surfaces are the best emitters of infrared radiation
- which surfaces are the best absorbers of infrared radiation
- which surfaces are the best reflectors of infrared radiation.

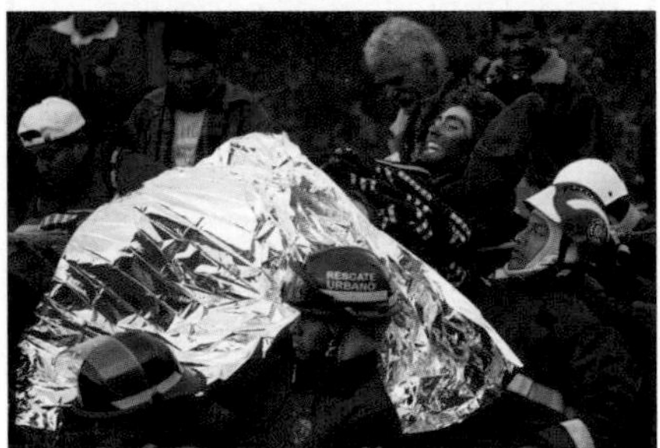

Figure 1 An emergency blanket in use

Which surfaces are the best emitters of radiation?

Rescue teams use light, shiny blankets to keep accident survivors warm (see Figure 1). A light, shiny outer surface emits much less radiation than a dark, matt (non-glossy) surface.

Practical

Testing radiation from different surfaces

To compare the radiation from two different surfaces, you can measure how fast two cans of hot water cool. The surface of one can is light and shiny, and the other has a dark, matt surface (see Figure 2).

At the start, the volume and temperature of the water in each can must be the same.

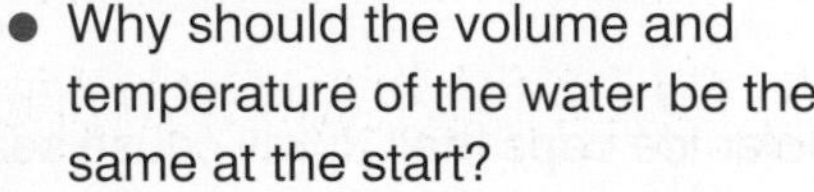

- Why should the volume and temperature of the water be the same at the start?
- Which can will cool faster?

Safety: Take care with hot water.

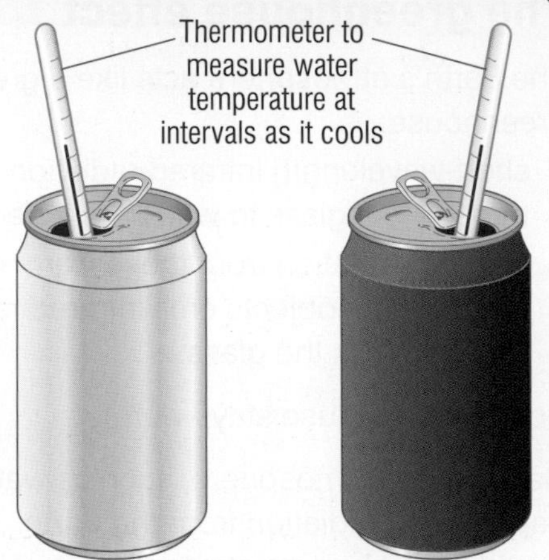

Figure 2 Testing different surfaces

Your tests should show that:

- **Dark, matt surfaces are better at emitting infrared radiation than light, shiny surfaces.**

Which surfaces are the best absorbers and reflectors of radiation?

When you use a photocopier, infrared radiation from a lamp dries the ink on the paper. Otherwise, the copies would be smudged. Black ink absorbs more infrared radiation than white paper. Just as all objects emit infrared radiation, all objects absorb it.

A light, shiny surface absorbs less radiation than a dark, matt surface. A matt surface has lots of cavities, as shown in Figure 3:

- the radiation reflected from the matt surface hits the surface again
- the radiation reflected from the shiny surface travels away from the surface.

So, the shiny surface absorbs less and reflects more radiation than a matt surface.

In general:

- **Light, shiny surfaces absorb less infrared radiation than dark, matt surfaces.**
- **Light, shiny surfaces reflect more infrared radiation than dark, matt surfaces.**

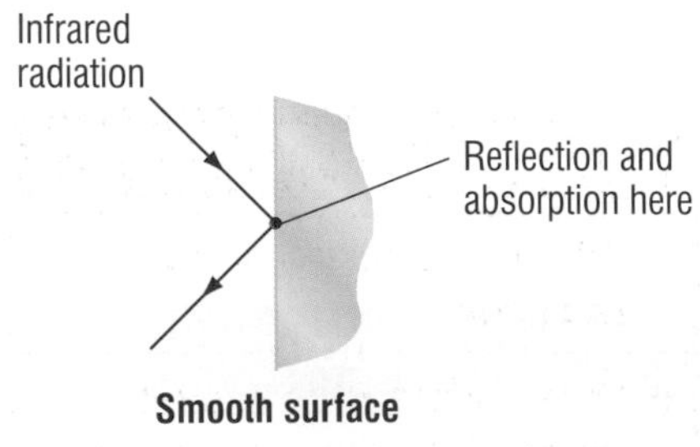

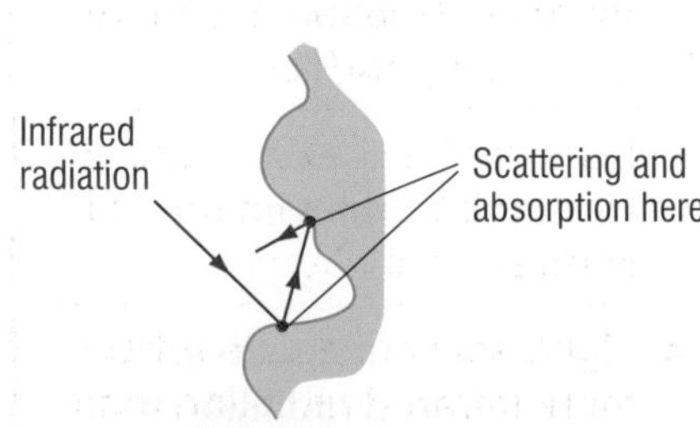

Figure 3 Absorbing infrared radiation

Practical

Absorption tests

Figure 4 shows how we can compare absorption by two different surfaces.

- The front surfaces of the two metal plates are at the same distance from the heater.
- The back of each plate has a coin stuck on with wax. The coin drops off the plate when the wax melts.
- The coin at the back of the matt black surface drops off first. The matt black surface absorbs more radiation than the light, shiny surface.

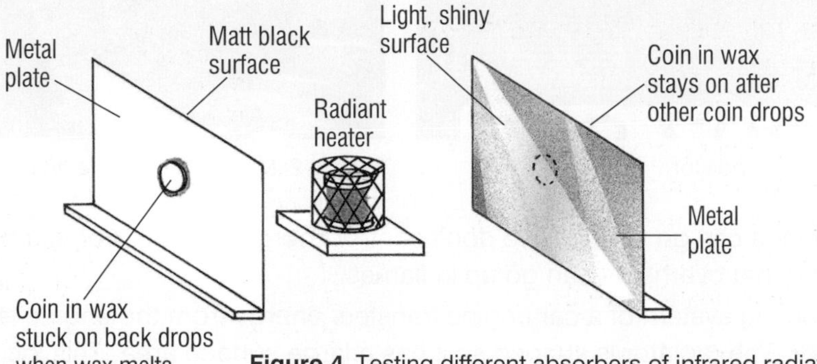

Figure 4 Testing different absorbers of infrared radiation

Safety: Take care with hot water.

Examiner's tip

Don't mix up absorption and emission – in an explanation, make sure you know which of the two processes is occurring.

Did you know ... ?

Scientists are developing blacker and blacker materials. These new materials have very tiny pits in the surface to absorb almost all the light that hits them. They can be used to coat the insides of telescopes so that there are no reflections.

Summary questions

1 **a** Why does ice on a road melt faster in sunshine if sand is sprinkled on it?
b Why are solar heating panels painted matt black?

2 **a** A black car and a metallic silver car that are otherwise identical are parked next to each other on a sunny day. Why does the temperature inside the black car rise more quickly than the temperature inside the silver car?
b Which of the two cars in **a** would cool down more quickly at night in winter?

3 A metal cube filled with hot water was used to compare the infrared radiation emitted from its four vertical faces, A, B, C and D. An infrared sensor was placed opposite each face at the same distance. The sensors were connected to a computer. The results of the test are shown in the graph opposite.

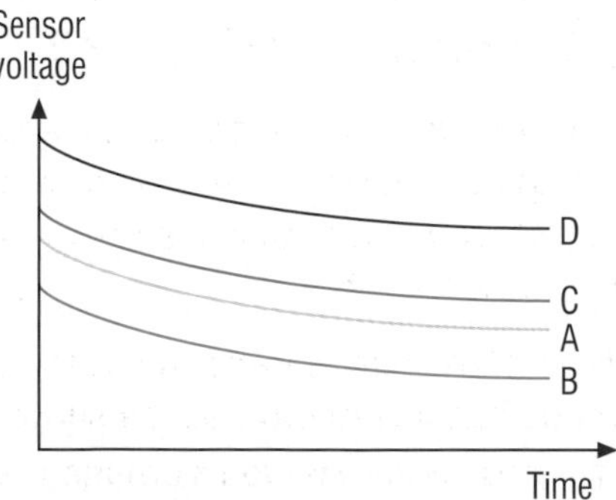

a Why was it important for the distance from each sensor to the face to be the same?
b One face was light and shiny, one was light and matt, one was dark and shiny, and one was dark and matt. Which face, A, B, C or D, emits the:
i least radiation?
ii most radiation?
c What are the advantages of using data-recording equipment to collect the data in this investigation?

Key points

- All objects absorb infrared radiation.
- Dark, matt surfaces emit more infrared radiation than light, shiny surfaces.
- Dark, matt surfaces absorb more infrared radiation than light, shiny surfaces.
- Light, shiny surfaces reflect more infrared radiation than dark, matt surfaces.

P14.6 Energy transfer by design

Learning objectives

After this topic, you should know:

- what design factors affect the rate at which a hot object transfers energy
- how we can control the rate of energy transfer to or from an object.

Figure 1 A car radiator

Figure 2 Motorcycle engine fins

Lots of things can go wrong if we don't control energy transfer. For example, a car engine that overheats can go up in flames.

- The cooling system of a car engine transfers energy from the engine to a radiator. The radiator is shaped so it has a large surface area. This increases the rate of energy transfer through convection in the air and through radiation.
- A motorcycle engine is shaped with **fins** on its outside surface. The fins increase the surface area of the engine in contact with air so the engine transfers energy to its surroundings faster than if it had no fins.

Most cars also have a cooling fan that switches on when the engine is too hot. This increases the flow of air over the surface of the radiator.

Did you know ... ?

Some electronic components get warm when they are working, but if they become too hot they stop working. Such components are often fixed to a metal plate to keep them cool. The metal plate increases the effective surface area of the component. We call the metal plate a **heat sink**.

Figure 3 A heat sink in a computer

The vacuum flask

If you are outdoors in cold weather, a hot drink from a vacuum flask keeps you warm. In the summer the same vacuum flask keeps your drinks cold.

In Figure 4, the liquid you drink is in the double-walled glass container.

- The vacuum between the two walls of the container cuts out energy transfer by conduction and convection between the walls.
- Glass is a poor conductor so there is little energy transfer by conduction through the glass.
- The glass surfaces are silvery to reduce radiation from the outer wall.
- The spring supporting the double-walled container is made of plastic, which is a good insulator.
- The plastic cap stops cooling by evaporation as it stops vapour loss from the flask. In addition, energy transfer by conduction is cut down because the cap is made from plastic.

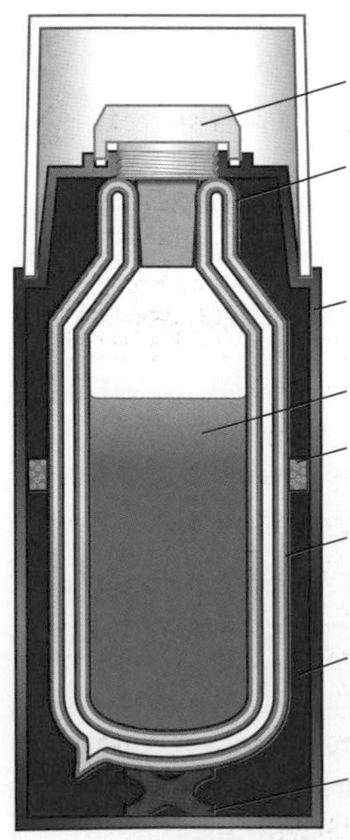

Figure 4 A vacuum flask

So why does the liquid in the flask eventually cool down?

The above features decrease but do not totally stop the transfer of energy from the liquid. Energy transfer occurs at a very low rate because of radiation from the silvery glass surface and conduction through the cap, spring and glass walls. The liquid transfers energy slowly to its surroundings so it eventually cools.

Factors affecting the rate of energy transfer

The bigger the **temperature difference** between an object and its surroundings, the faster the rate at which energy is transferred. In addition, the above examples show that the rate at which an object transfers energy depends on its design. The design factors that are important are:

- the nature of the surface that is in contact with the object
- the object's volume and surface area.

Also important are:

- the object's mass
- the material the object is made from.

This is because they affect how quickly its temperature changes (and therefore the rate of transfer of energy to or from it) when it loses or gains energy.

links

For more information on factors affecting energy transfer, look back to 13.2 'Specific heat capacity'.

Practical

Investigating the rate of energy transfer

You can plan an investigation using different beakers and hot water to find out what affects the rate of cooling.

- Write a question that you could investigate.
- Identify the independent, dependent and control variables in your investigation.

Safety: Take care with hot water.

Summary questions

1 Hot water is pumped through a radiator like the one in the photo below. Describe how energy is transferred from the hot water to the surrounding air.

2 An electronic component in a computer is attached to a heat sink.
  a **i** Explain why the heat sink is necessary.
  ii Why is a metal plate used as the heat sink?
  b Plan a test to show that double glazing is more effective at preventing energy transfer than single glazing.

3 **a** Explain, in detail, how the design of a vacuum flask reduces the rate of energy transfer.
  b A freezer is defrosted. Explain why a bowl of warm water placed in the freezer speeds up the defrosting process.

Did you know ... ?

Foxy survivors

A desert fox has much larger ears than an arctic fox. Blood flowing through the ears transfers energy from inside the body to the surface of the ears. Big ears have a much larger surface area than little ears so they transfer energy to the surroundings more quickly than little ears.

A desert fox has big ears so it keeps cool by transferring energy quickly to its surroundings.

An arctic fox has little ears so it transfers energy more slowly to its surroundings. This helps keep it warm.

a

b

Figure 5 Fox ears **a** A desert fox **b** An arctic fox

Key points

- The rate of energy transferred to or from an object depends on:
  - the shape, size and type of material of the object
  - the nature of the surface that the object is in contact with
  - the temperature difference between the object and its surroundings.

P14.7 Expansion by heating

Learning objectives

After this topic, you should know:

- how solids, liquids and gases expand when heated
- some applications and hazards of expansion by heating.

Comparing the expansion by heating of liquids and gases

Most substances expand when heated. If air did not expand when heated, a hot-air balloon would never fill up and take off. A burner under the balloon causes the balloon to fill with hot air, which then lifts the balloon. The expansion of a substance due to increasing its temperature is called **expansion by heating**.

Figure 1 Filling a hot-air balloon

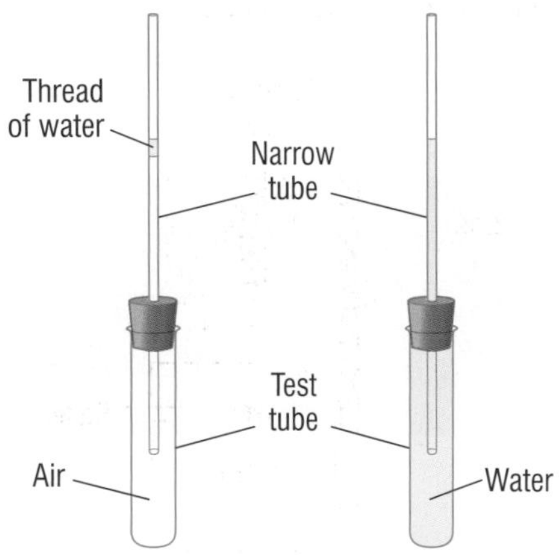

Figure 2 Comparing the expansion by heating of air and water

Gases expand much more than solids or liquids. Usually, the volume of a solid increases by no more than about 0.01% for a temperature increase of 1 °C. Most liquids expand slightly more. Gases at constant pressure expand about 30 times more than liquids and solids do.

Figure 2 shows how we can compare the expansion by heating of air with that of water. The air in the air-filled test tube is trapped by a 'thread' of water in the narrow tube which is open at both ends. In each case, expansion of the air or water in the test tube causes the level of the water in the narrow tube to move towards the top end of the narrow tube. To ensure both test tubes are heated exactly the same, both test tubes could be placed next to each other in strong sunlight (or in the same beaker of warm water). The results show that air expands much more than water for the same temperature rise. The same result applies to a comparison between any gas and any liquid.

Examiner's tip

Make sure you know some examples where expansion by heating is a nuisance and some examples where expansion by heating is useful.

A **radiator thermostat** in a car makes use of the expansion of oil when it becomes warm. Figure 3 shows how it works. The valve stays closed until it has been warmed up by energy from the engine. The metal tube is forced out of the oil chamber as the oil becomes hotter and expands. The movement of the metal tube opens the valve, allowing the hot water to flow to the radiator.

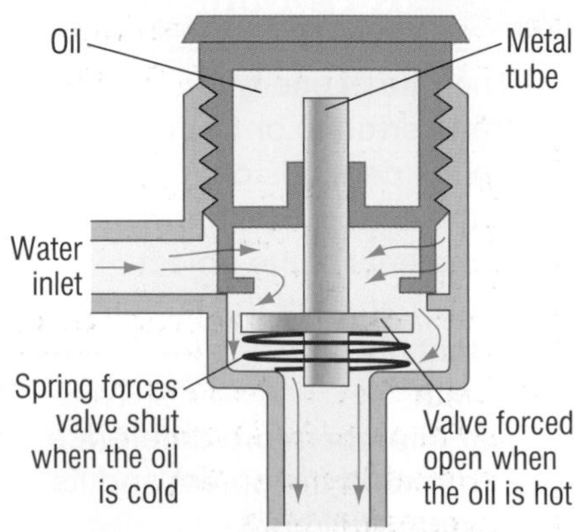

Figure 3 A radiator thermostat

A **liquid in glass thermometer** makes use of the expansion of a liquid such as alcohol or mercury. When the thermometer bulb becomes warm, the liquid in the bulb expands into the long narrow tube joined to the bulb. The temperature reading is given by the position on the thermometer scale of the end of the thread of liquid in the tube.

Expansion of solids by heating

A jar with a tight-fitting lid is sometimes difficult to open. Warming the lid in warm water may help to open the jar. The increase of temperature of the lid causes it to expand just enough to unscrew the lid. As with liquids, the expansion of a solid by heating is much less than that of a gas. Even so, the expansion of a solid by heating has some interesting applications and consequences.

Expansion gaps are needed in buildings, bridges and railway tracks to allow for expansion by heating. Outdoor temperatures can change by as much as 50 °C between summer and winter. A 100 m concrete bridge span would expand by about 5 cm if its temperature increased by 50 °C. Without expansion gaps, the bridge would buckle. The gaps are usually filled with soft material such as rubber to prevent rubble falling in.

Steel tyres are fitted on train wheels by heating the tyre so it expands when fitting it on the wheel. As the tyre cools, it contracts so it fits very tightly on the wheel.

Bimetallic strips are used as thermostats in devices fitted with safety cut-out switches or valves. A bimetallic switch consists of a strip of two different metals such as brass and steel bonded together. When the temperature of the strip rises, one metal expands more than the other (e.g. brass expands more than steel) so the strip bends. This can be used to switch on or off an electrical device. Figure 5 shows a bimetallic strip in a fire alarm. When heated, the strip bends towards the contact screw, and when it touches it, the circuit is completed and the bell rings.

In a heater thermostat, when the strip becomes hot, it bends away from the contact screw and loses contact with it. As a result, the heater is switched off.

Figure 4 Expansion gaps

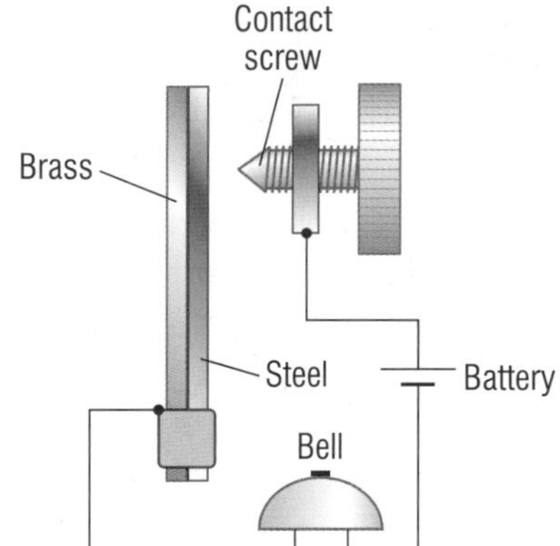

Figure 5 A bimetallic strip in an alarm circuit

Summary questions

1 The figure below shows a thermostat in a gas oven. When the oven overheats, the brass tube expands more than the Invar rod. Explain why this change reduces the flow of gas through the valve.

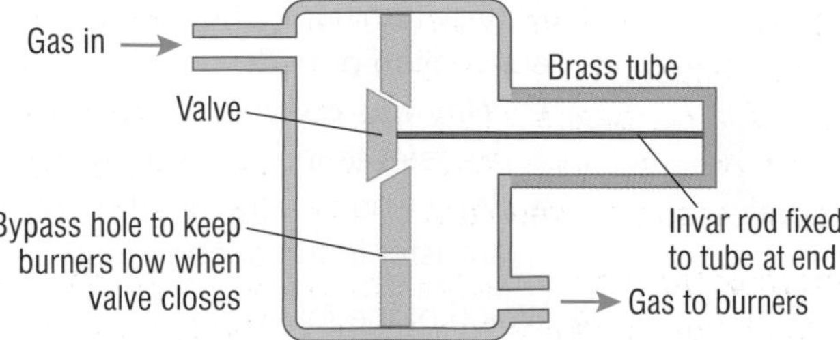

2 Explain why expansion gaps are:
  a needed between concrete sections in buildings
  b usually filled with soft material such as rubber.

3 a Explain why a bimetallic strip bends when it is heated.
  b A bimetallic thermostat is used to switch off the electricity supply to a heater if the heater overheats. With the aid of a diagram, describe such a thermostat and explain how it works.

Key points

- Gases expand on heating much more than solids and liquids.
- Applications of expansion by heating include glass thermometers and thermostats containing liquid.
- Expansion by heating must be allowed for in buildings and bridges by using expansion gaps.

Summary questions

1 **a** **i** Why could seasonal variations in temperature cause a flat roof surface to develop cracks?

ii What type of surface is better for a flat roof: matt or smooth, dark or shiny? Explain your answer.

b A solar heating panel is used to heat water. Some panels have a transparent cover and a matt black base. Others have a matt black cover and a shiny base.

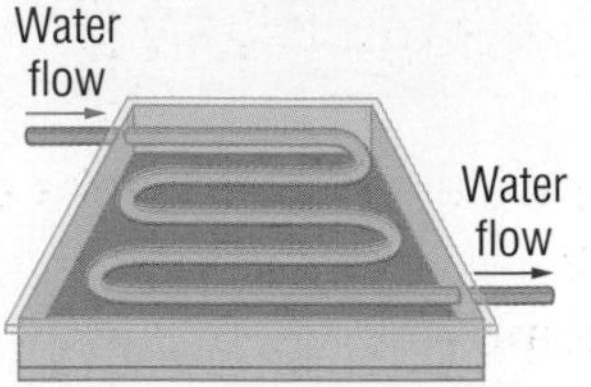

Panel X with a transparent cover and a matt black base

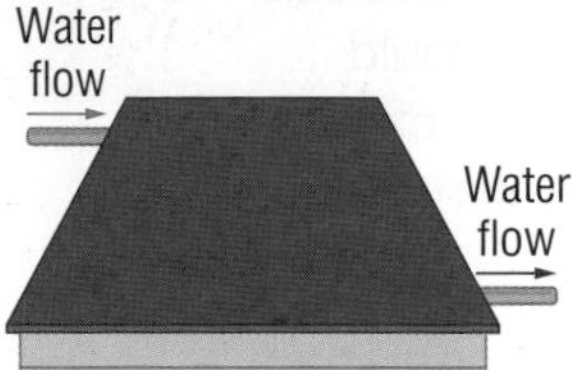

Panel Y with a matt black cover and a shiny base

Which of these two designs, Panel X or Panel Y, do you think is better? Give reasons for your answer.

2 A heat sink is a metal plate or clip fixed to an electronic component to stop it overheating.

a When the component becomes hot, how does energy transfer from:

i where it is in contact with the plate to the rest of the plate?

ii the plate to the surroundings?

b What is the purpose of the metal fins on the plate?

c Heat sinks are made from metals such as copper or aluminium. Copper is approximately 3 times more dense than aluminium and its specific heat capacity is about twice as large. Discuss how these physical properties are relevant to the choice of whether or not to use copper or aluminium for a heat sink in a computer.

3 **a** The figure shows a central heating radiator fixed to a wall and consisting of two parallel panels separated by an air gap.

i Describe how energy transfer by heating to the surroundings from hot water takes place when the hot water passes through the radiator pipes.

ii Explain the advantage of having two panels with an air gap between the panels.

b An electric storage heater contains bricks that become hot when the heater is switched on and cool down slowly when the heater is switched off. Explain in terms of conduction, convection and radiation how the bricks store energy and release it to the surroundings.

4 **a** Explain why woolly clothing is very effective at keeping people warm in winter.

b Wearing a hat in winter is a very effective way of keeping your head warm. Describe how a hat helps to reduce energy loss from your head.

c Keeping your ears warm is important too. Explain why energy transfer from your ears to the surroundings can be significant in winter.

5 Marathon runners at the end of a race are often supplied with a shiny emergency blanket. These silvery blankets are very light in weight because they are made from plastic film with a reflective metallic coating inside.

a At the end of a race, the runners can't stop sweating. Explain why this continued sweating might cause them to become cold if an emergency blanket is not worn.

b **i** What form of energy transfer is reduced by the reflective coating inside the emergency blanket?

ii Explain why an emergency blanket helps to stop the runners becoming cold.

6 A glass tube containing water with a small ice cube floating at the top was heated at its lower end. The time taken for the ice cube to melt was measured. The test was repeated with a similar ice cube weighted down at the bottom of the tube of water. The water in this tube was heated near the top of the tube. The time taken for the ice cube to melt was much longer than in the first test.

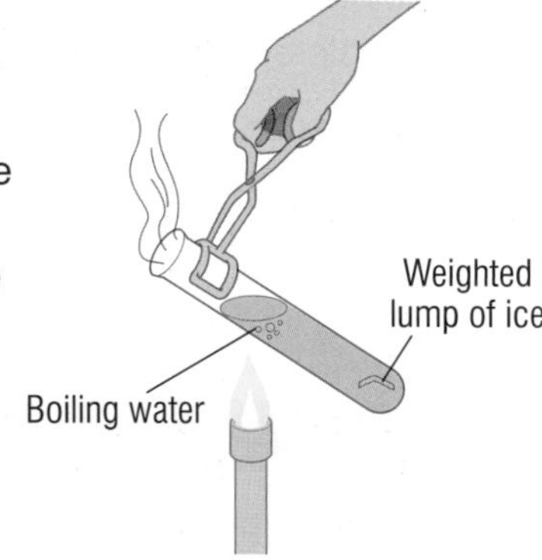

a Energy transfer in the tube is caused by conduction, convection or both.

i Why was convection the main cause of energy transfer to the ice cube in the first test?

ii Why was conduction the only cause of energy transfer in the second test?

b Which of the following conclusions about these tests is true?

1 Energy transfer caused by conduction does not take place in water.

2 Energy transfer in water is mainly caused by convection.

3 Energy transfer in water is mainly caused by conduction.

AQA Examination-style questions

1 **a** The diagram shows apparatus used to find out which of four materials is the best conductor of heat.

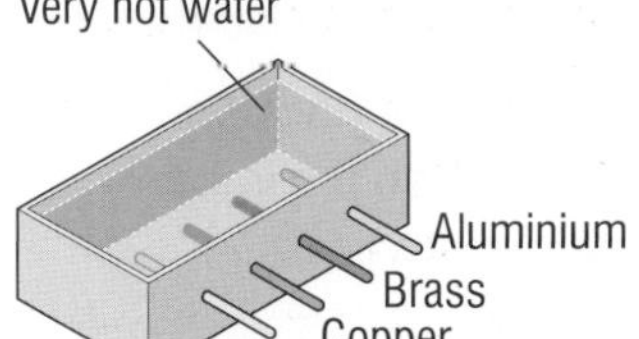

i Which two variables in the table should be controlled? (2)

colour of rods
diameter of rods
length of rods
material of rods

ii Describe how the experiment can tell you which of the four materials is the best conductor of heat. (2)

b Water in a house is often heated by an electric immersion heater.

The diagram shows a metal tank containing water and a heating element.

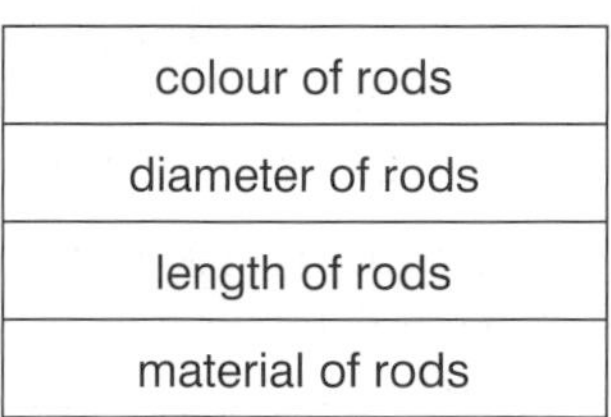

When the heating element is switched on, the water near the element becomes hot.

i Explain the process that transfers energy through the whole tank of water. (QWC) (6)

ii Energy is lost to the surroundings by transfer through the metal wall of the tank.
Explain the process that transfers energy through the metal wall of the tank. (5)

c Metal pipes expand when they are heated. This can cause problems in a central heating system.

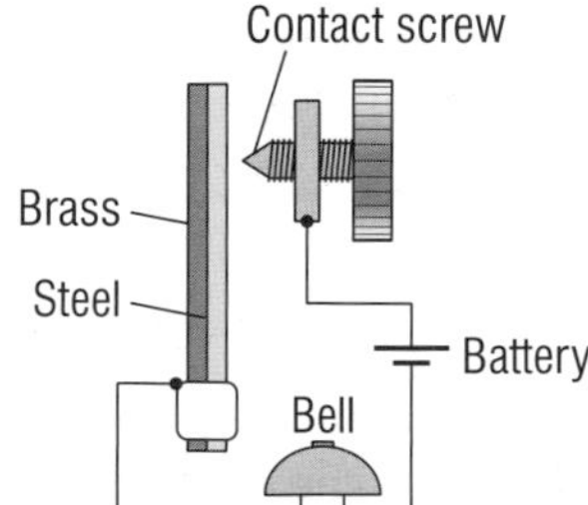

i Give another example of where expansion by heating can be a problem, and state how the problem can be overcome. (2)

ii Expansion by heating can also be useful.
The diagram shows a bimetallic strip in a fire alarm.

Explain how the fire alarm works. (6)

2 The diagram shows an outdoor swimming pool. Water is heated in pipes in a solar panel. The heated water is pumped into the pool.

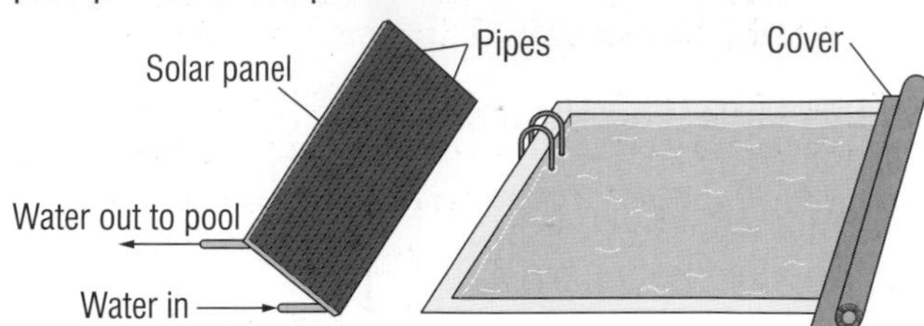

The pipes in the solar panel are painted black. The panel underneath the pipes is shiny.

Use words from the list to complete **a** and **b** below.

absorbers emitters insulators reflectors

a The pipes are painted black because black surfaces are good .... of heat radiation. (1)

b The panel underneath the pipes is shiny because shiny surfaces are good .... of heat radiation. (1)

c What other feature of the solar panels can ensure that they absorb as much energy from the Sun as possible? (1)

3 Hot water in a mug cools by transferring energy to its surroundings.

a **i** Which of the following factors affect the rate at which hot water transfers energy to its surroundings? (4)

Choose **four** of the factors.

nature of the surface of the mug
specific latent heat of ice
specific latent heat of steam
surface area of the mug
temperature of the water
temperature of surroundings

ii State **two** other factors that control the rate at which the hot water's temperature falls. (2)

b A man spilled some petrol on his hand whilst refuelling his car. He noticed that the petrol soon disappeared from his hand, and he also noticed that his hand felt cold.

Explain why. (4)

c The diagram shows a washing basket of wet clothes.

Wet clothes
Basket

The wet clothes dry quicker when they are hung on a washing line outside on a sunny day.

i Explain why. (3)

ii Describe how the particles of water on the wet clothes differ in behaviour from the particles leaving the wet clothes that are hanging on the washing line. (3)

P15.1 Conservation of energy

Learning objectives

After this topic, you should know:
- what is meant by 'conservation of energy'
- why conservation of energy is a very important idea.

Figure 1 Energy transfers on a roller coaster

At the funfair

Funfairs are very exciting places because lots of energy transfers happen quickly. A roller coaster gains gravitational potential energy when it climbs. This energy is then transferred as the roller coaster races downwards.

As it descends:

its gravitational potential energy → kinetic energy + sound + energy transfer by heating due to air resistance and friction

The energy transferred by heating is 'wasted' energy, which you will learn more about in 15.2 'Useful energy'.

Practical

Investigating energy changes

Pendulum swinging

When energy changes happen, does the total amount of energy stay the same? We can investigate this question with a simple pendulum.

Figure 2 shows a pendulum bob swinging from side to side.

As it moves towards the middle, its gravitational potential energy is transferred to kinetic energy.

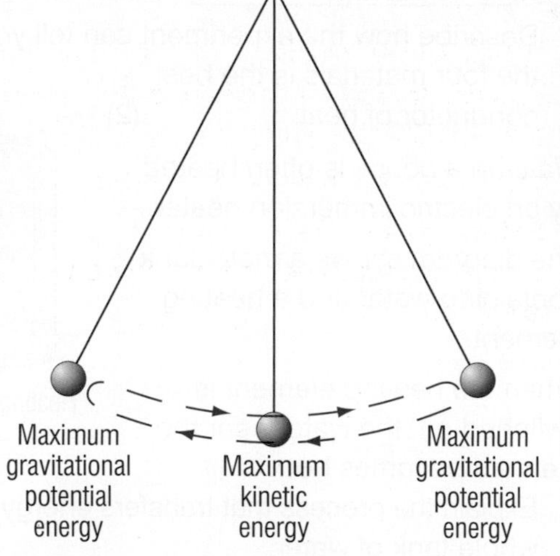

Figure 2 A pendulum in motion

As it moves away from the middle, its kinetic energy transfers back to gravitational potential energy. If the air resistance on the bob is very small, you should find that the bob reaches the same height on each side.

- What does this tell you about the energy of the bob when it goes from one side at maximum height to the other side at maximum height?
- Why is it difficult to mark the exact height the pendulum bob rises to? How could you make your judgement of height more accurate?

Conservation of energy

Scientists have done lots of tests to find out if the total energy after a transfer is the same as the energy before the transfer. All the tests so far show it is the same.

This important result is known as the **conservation of energy**.

It tells us that **energy cannot be created or destroyed**.

Energy can be stored in various ways. For example:
- elastic energy is stored in a rubber band by stretching it
- gravitational potential energy is stored in an object when it's lifted.

Examiner's tip

Never use the terms 'movement energy' or 'motion energy' in an exam; you will only gain marks by using 'kinetic energy'.

Bungee jumping

What energy transfers happen to a bungee jumper after jumping off the platform?

- When the rope is slack, some of the gravitational potential energy of the bungee jumper is transferred to kinetic energy as the jumper falls.
- Once the slack in the rope has been used up, the rope slows the bungee jumper's fall. Most of the gravitational potential energy and kinetic energy of the jumper is transferred into elastic potential energy of the rope. This elastic energy is stored in the rope.
- After reaching the bottom, the rope pulls the jumper back up. As the jumper rises, most of the elastic energy of the rope is transferred back to gravitational potential energy and kinetic energy of the jumper.

The bungee jumper doesn't return to the same height as at the start. This is because some of the initial gravitational potential energy has been transferred to its surroundings by heating as the rope stretched then shortened again.

Figure 3 Bungee jumping

Practical

Bungee jumping

You can try out the ideas about bungee jumping using the experiment shown in Figure 4.

Safety: Make sure the stand is secure. Protect feet and bench from falling objects.

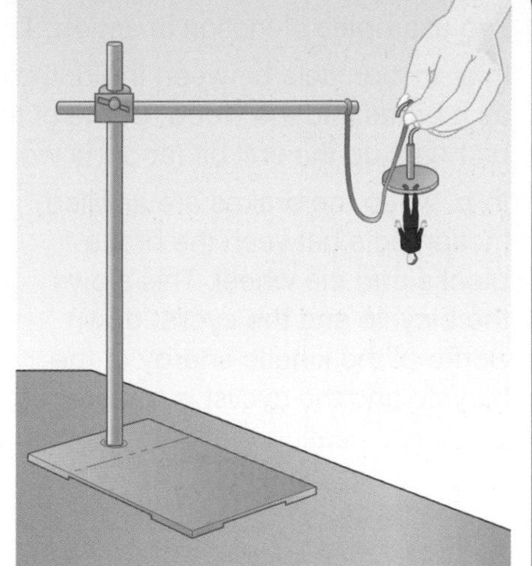

Figure 4 Testing a bungee jump

Summary questions

1. When a roller coaster gets to the bottom of a descent, what energy transfers happen if:
   - **a** the brakes are applied to stop it?
   - **b** it goes up and over a second 'hill'?
2. **a** A ball dropped onto a trampoline returns to almost the same height after it bounces. Describe the energy transfer of the ball from the point of release to the top of its bounce.
   - **b** What can you say about the energy of the ball at the point of release compared with at the top of its bounce?
   - **c** Describe how would you use the test in **a** above to see which of three trampolines is the bounciest.
3. One exciting fairground ride acts like a giant catapult. The capsule, in which you are strapped, is fired high into the sky by the rubber bands of the catapult. Explain the energy transfers taking place in the ride.

Key points

- Energy cannot be created or destroyed.
- Conservation of energy applies to all energy changes.
- Energy can be stored in various ways.

P15.2 Useful energy

Learning objectives

After this topic, you should know:

- what 'useful' energy is
- what is meant by 'wasted' energy
- what eventually happens to wasted energy
- whether energy is still as useful after it is used.

Figure 1 Using energy

Energy for a purpose

Where would we be without **machines**? We use washing machines at home. We use machines in factories to make the goods we buy. We use them in the gym to keep fit and we use them to get us from place to place.

A machine transfers energy for a purpose. Friction between the moving parts of a machine causes the parts to warm up. So, not all of the energy supplied to a machine is usefully transferred. Some energy is wasted.

- **Useful energy** is energy transferred to where it is wanted, in the form that is wanted.
- **Wasted energy** is the energy that is not usefully transferred.

Practical

Investigating friction

Friction in machines always causes energy to be wasted. Figure 2 shows two examples of friction in action. Try one of them out.

In **a**, friction acts between the drill bit and the wood. The bit becomes hot as it bores into the wood. Some of the electrical energy supplied to the bit heats up the drill bit (and the wood).

In **b**, when the brakes are applied, friction acts between the brake blocks and the wheel. This slows the bicycle and the cyclist down. Some of the kinetic energy of the bicycle and the cyclist is transferred to energy heating the brake blocks (and the bicycle wheel).

a

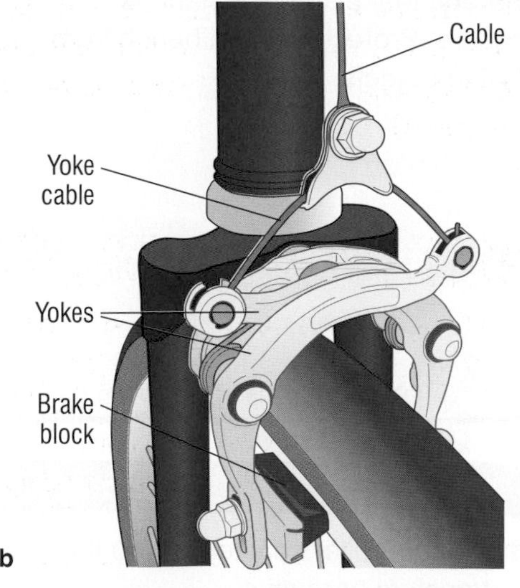

b

Figure 2 Friction in action
a Using a drill **b** Braking on a bicycle

Safety: Use a battery drill. Do not touch the drill bit or wheel until they have stopped.

Did you know ... ?

Lots of energy is transferred in a car crash. The faster the car travels the more kinetic energy it has and the more it has to transfer before stopping. In a crash, kinetic energy is quickly transferred to elastic strain energy, distorting the car's shape, and energy is transferred by heating the metal. There is usually quite a lot of sound energy too!

Examiner's tip

Try to decide what you want from an appliance: e.g. a lamp – light.

Disc brakes at work

The next time you are in a car slowing down at traffic lights, think about what is making the car stop. Figure 3 shows how the disc brakes of a car work. When the brakes are applied, the pads are pushed on to the disc in each wheel. Friction between the pads and each disc slows the wheel down. Some of the kinetic energy of the car is transferred to energy heating the disc pads and the discs. In Formula One racing cars you can sometimes see the discs glow red hot.

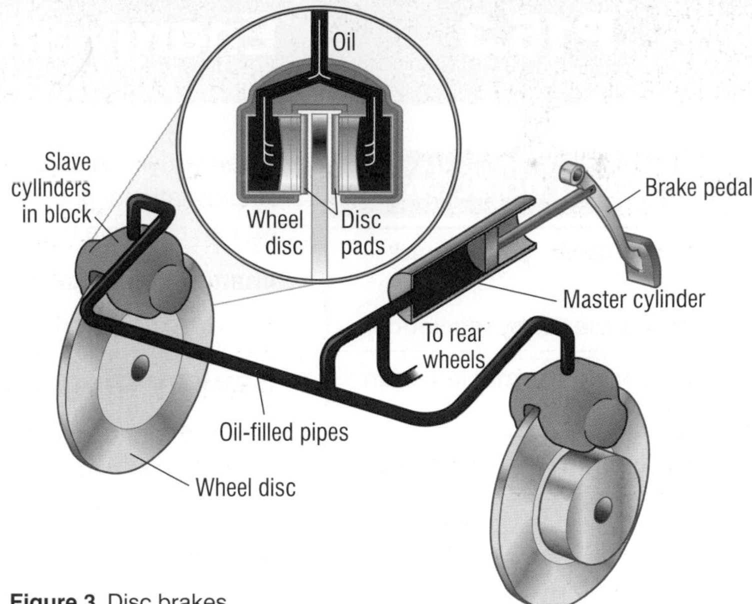

Figure 3 Disc brakes

Spreading out

- **Wasted energy is dissipated (spreads out) to the surroundings.**
  For example, the gears of a car get hot because of friction when the car is running. So energy transfers from the gear box to the surrounding air.
- **Useful energy eventually transfers to the surroundings too.**
  For example, the useful energy supplied to the wheels of a car is transferred by heating to the tyres. This energy is then transferred to the road and the surrounding air.
- **Energy becomes less useful the more it spreads out.**
  For example, the hot water from the cooling system of a CHP (combined heat and power) power station gets used to heat nearby buildings. The energy supplied to heat the buildings will eventually be transferred to the surroundings.

Summary questions

1 Copy and complete the table below.

Energy transfer by	Useful energy output	Wasted energy output
a An electric fan heater	warms the air and surrounding objects	
b A television		
c An electric kettle		
d Headphones		

2 What would happen, in terms of energy transfer, to:
a a gear box that was insulated so it could not transfer energy by heating to the surroundings?
b the running shoes of a jogger if the shoes are well insulated?
c a blunt electric drill if you use it to drill into hard wood?
d the metal wheel discs of the disc brakes of a car when the brakes are applied?

3 **a** Describe the energy transfers of a pendulum as it swings from one side to the middle, then to the opposite side.
b Explain why a swinging pendulum eventually stops.

Key points

- **Useful energy is energy in the place we want it and in the form we need it.**
- **Wasted energy is the energy that is not useful energy.**
- **Wasted energy is eventually transferred to the surroundings, which become warmer.**
- **As energy spreads out (dissipates), it gets less and less useful.**

P15.3 Energy and efficiency

Learning objectives

After this topic, you should know:

- what is meant by efficiency
- how efficient a machine can be
- how to show the energy flow in a system as a diagram.

When you lift an object, the useful energy from your muscles goes to the object as gravitational potential energy. As we saw in 5.3 'Gravitational potential energy', we can calculate the gain in gravitational potential energy using the formula:

change in gravitational potential energy = weight of object × gain in height
(in joules) (in newtons) (in metres)

Sankey diagrams

Figure 1 represents the energy flow through a system. It shows how we can represent any energy transfer where energy is wasted. This type of diagram is called a **Sankey diagram**.

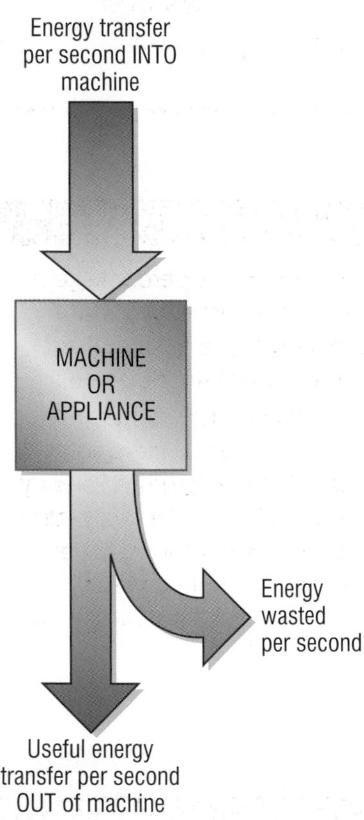

Figure 1 A Sankey diagram. The width of each arrow may be used to show how much energy transfer it represents.

Because energy cannot be created or destroyed:

input energy (energy supplied) = useful energy delivered + energy wasted

For any device that transfers energy:

$$\textbf{efficiency} = \frac{\textbf{useful energy transferred out of the device}}{\textbf{total energy supplied into the device}}\ (\times 100\%)$$

Note: Because power is energy transferred per second, we can also calculate efficiency in terms of power using the equation:

$$\textbf{efficiency} = \frac{\textbf{useful power out}}{\textbf{total power in}}\ (\times 100\%)$$

Maths skills

Efficiency can be written as a number (which is never more than 1) or as a percentage (which is never more than 100%).

For example, a light bulb with an efficiency of 0.15 would radiate 15 J of energy as light for every 100 J of electrical energy we supply to it.

- Its efficiency (as a number) $= \frac{15}{100} = 0.15$
- Its percentage efficiency $= 0.15 \times 100\% = 15\%$

Maths skills

Worked example

An electric motor is used to raise an object. The object gains 60 J of gravitational potential energy when the motor is supplied with 200 J of electrical energy. Calculate the percentage efficiency of the motor.

Solution

Total energy supplied to the device = 200 J
Useful energy transferred by the device = 60 J
Percentage efficiency of the motor

$$= \frac{\text{useful energy transferred out of the motor}}{\text{total energy supplied into the motor}} \times 100\%$$

$$= \frac{60\,\text{J}}{200\,\text{J}} \times 100\% = 0.30 \times 100\% = \mathbf{30\%}$$

Examiner's tip

Remember that in a calculation, if you obtain an answer for efficiency of over 100% or greater than 1, you have made a mistake!

Efficiency limits

No machine can be more than 100% efficient, because we can never get more energy from a machine than we put into it.

Practical

Investigating efficiency

Figure 2 shows how you can use an electric winch to raise a weight. You can use the joulemeter to measure the electrical energy supplied.

- If you double the weight for the same increase in height, do you need to supply twice as much electrical energy to do this task?

The gravitational potential energy gained by the weight
= weight in newtons × height increase in metres.

- Use this equation and the joulemeter measurements to work out the percentage efficiency of the winch.

Safety: Protect the floor and your feet. Stop the winch before the masses wrap round the pulley.

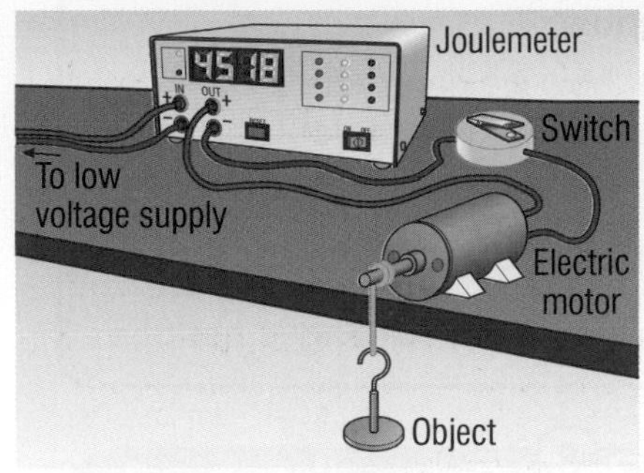

Figure 2 An electric winch

Improving efficiency

	Why machines waste energy	How to reduce the problem
1	Friction between the moving parts causes heating.	Lubricate the moving parts to reduce friction.
2	The resistance of a wire causes the wire to get hot when a current passes through it.	In circuits, use wires with as little electrical resistance as possible.
3	Air resistance causes energy transfer by heating to the surroundings.	Streamline the shapes of moving objects to reduce air resistance.
4	Sound created by machinery causes energy transfer to the surroundings.	Cut out noise (e.g. tighten loose parts to reduce vibration).

Examiner's tip

The greater the percentage of the energy that is usefully transferred in a device, the more efficient the device is. Efficiency and percentage efficiency are numbers without units. The maximum efficiency is 1 or 100%, so if a calculation produces a number greater than this it must be wrong.

Summary questions

1 A certain light bulb has an efficiency of 15%.
  a How much energy is wasted for every 100 J of electrical energy supplied?
  b What happens to the wasted energy?
  c Complete a Sankey diagram for the light bulb showing the useful and wasted energies.

2 An electric motor is used to raise a weight. When you supply 60 J of electrical energy to the motor, the weight gains 24 J of gravitational potential energy. Work out:
  a the energy wasted by the motor
  b the efficiency of the motor.

3 A machine is 25% efficient. If the total energy supplied to the machine is 3200 J:
  a how much useful energy can be transferred?
  b what is the output power of the machine if the energy is supplied in 16 seconds?

Key points

- **The efficiency of a device = useful energy transferred out of the device ÷ total energy supplied into the device (×100%).**
- **Devices can be made more efficient, but never more than 100% efficient.**
- **Sankey diagrams are used to show energy flow in a system.**

P15.4 Heating and insulating buildings

Learning objectives

After this topic, you should know:

- how we can reduce the rate of energy transfer from our homes
- what U-values measure
- why solar heating is not free.

Reducing the rate of energy transfers at home

Home heating bills can be expensive. Figure 1 shows how we can reduce the rate of **energy transfer** from our homes and reduce our home heating bills.

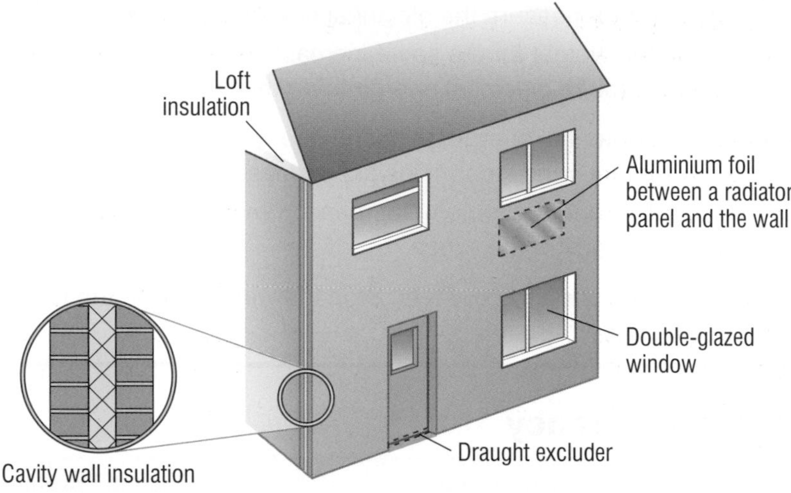

Figure 1 Saving money

- **Loft insulation** such as fibreglass reduces the rate of energy transfer through the roof. Fibreglass is a good insulator. The air between the fibres also helps to reduce the rate of energy transfer by conduction.
- **Cavity wall insulation** reduces energy loss through the outer walls of the house. The 'cavity' of an outer wall is the space between the two layers of brick that make up the wall. The insulation is pumped into the cavity. It is a better insulator than the air it replaces. It traps the air in small pockets, reducing convection.
- **Aluminium foil** between a radiator panel and the wall reflects radiation away from the wall.
- **Double-glazed windows** have two glass panes with dry air or a vacuum between the panes. Dry air is a good insulator so it reduces the rate of energy transfer by conduction. A vacuum cuts out energy transfer by convection as well.

Did you know ...?

A duvet is a bed cover filled with 'down' or soft feathers or some other suitable insulator such as wool. Because the filling material traps air, a duvet on a bed cuts down the transfer of energy from the sleeper. The 'tog' rating of a duvet tells us how effective it is as an insulator. The higher its tog rating is, the more effective it is as an insulator.

U-values

We can compare different insulating materials if we know their **U-values**. This is the energy per second that passes through one square metre of material when the temperature difference across it is 1°C.

The lower the U-value, the more effective the material is as an insulator.

For example, replacing a single-glazed window with a double-glazed window that has a U-value four times smaller would make the energy loss through the window four times smaller.

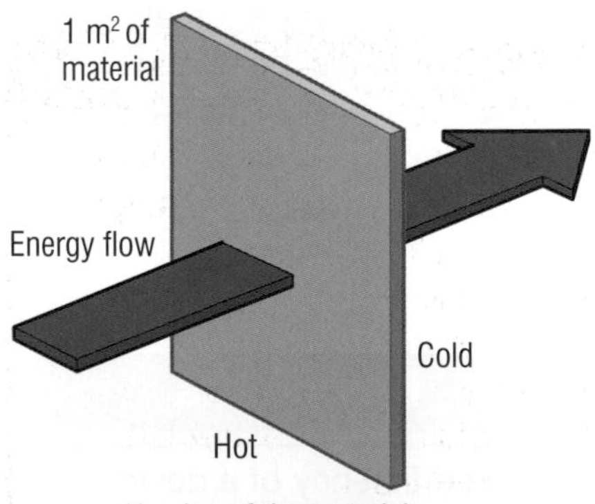

U-value of the material = energy/s passing per m^2 for 1 °C temperature difference

Figure 2 U-values

Examiner's tip

Remember that U-values tell you how good an insulator a material is: low U-value = good insulator.

Solar heating panels

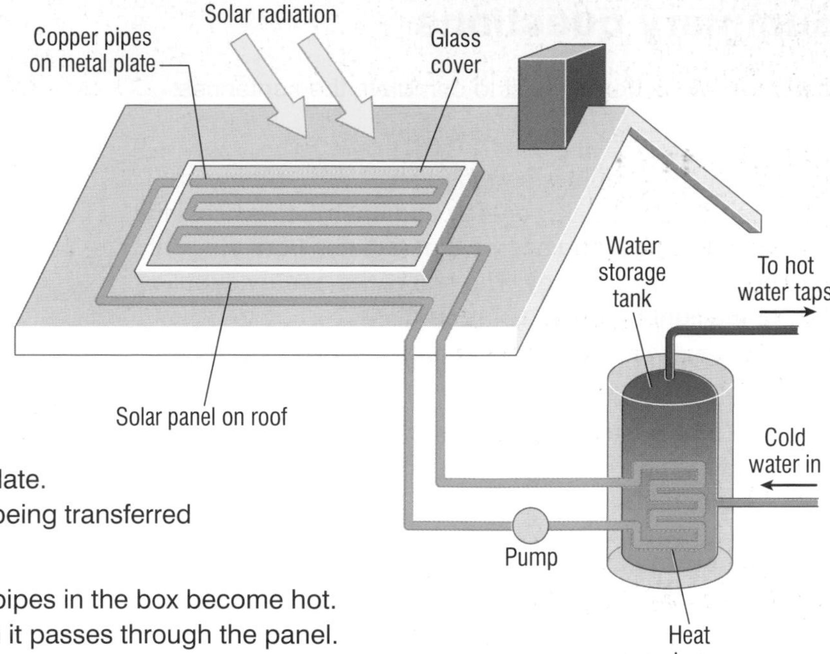

Figure 3 A solar heating panel

Heating water at home using electricity or gas can be expensive. A **solar heating panel** uses solar energy to heat water. The panel is usually fitted on a roof that faces south, making the most of the Sun's energy. Figure 3 shows the design of one type of solar heating panel.

The panel is a flat box containing liquid-filled copper pipes on a matt black metal plate. The pipes are connected to a heat exchanger in a water storage tank in the house.

A transparent cover on the top of the panel allows solar radiation through to heat the metal plate. Insulating material under the plate stops energy being transferred through the back of the panel.

On a sunny day, the metal plate and the copper pipes in the box become hot. Liquid pumped through the pipes is heated when it passes through the panel. The liquid may be water or a solution containing antifreeze. The hot liquid passes through the heat exchanger and transfers energy to the water in the storage tank.

Payback time

Solar heating panels save money because no fuel is needed to heat the water. But they are expensive to buy and to install.

Suppose you pay £2000 to buy and install a solar panel and you save £100 each year on your fuel bills. After 20 years you would have saved £2000. In other words, the **payback time** for the solar panel is 20 years. This is the time taken to recover the up-front costs from the savings on fuel bills.

Summary questions

1 **a** Why is cavity wall insulation better than air in the cavity between the walls of a house?
  b Why does fixing aluminium foil to the wall behind a radiator reduce energy loss through the wall?

2 Some double-glazed windows have a plastic frame and a vacuum between the panes.
  a Why is a plastic frame better than a metal frame?
  b Why is a vacuum between the panes better than air?
  c Two manufacturers advertise double-glazed windows of the same size with different U-values at the same price. Explain which one you would choose.

3 A manufacturer of loft insulation claimed that each roll of loft insulation would save £10 per year on fuel bills. A householder bought 6 rolls of the loft insulation at £15 per roll and paid £90 to have the insulation fitted in her loft.
  a How much did it cost to buy and install the loft insulation?
  b What would be the saving each year on fuel bills?
  c Calculate the payback time.

Key points

- **Energy loss from our homes can be reduced by fitting:**
  - **loft insulation**
  - **cavity wall insulation**
  - **double glazing**
  - **draught proofing**
  - **aluminium foil behind radiators.**
- **U-values tell us how effective different materials are as insulators. The lower the U-value, the better the material is as an insulator.**
- **Solar heating panels use the Sun's energy to heat water, but their payback time is high because they are expensive to buy and install.**

Summary questions

1 **a** Use words from the list to complete the sentences:

useful wasted light electrical

When a light bulb is switched on, ... energy is changed into .... energy and energy that heats the surroundings. The energy that radiates from the light bulb is .... energy. The rest of the energy supplied to the light bulb is .... energy.

b The output power of a machine is 270 W when the input power is 1500 W.

i What is the percentage efficiency of the machine?

ii How much energy is wasted by the machine in 300 seconds?

2 An electric motor raised a load of 800 N through a height of 1.5 m when it was supplied with 10 000 J of electrical energy.

a i Calculate the gravitational potential energy gained by the load.

ii Calculate the percentage efficiency of the motor.

b How much energy is wasted?

c Copy and complete the Sankey diagram below for the motor.

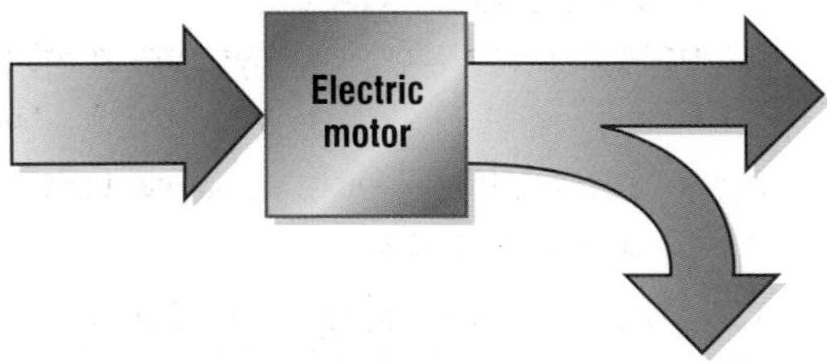

3 **a** A low-energy light bulb has an efficiency of 80%. Using an energy meter, a student found the light bulb used 1200 J of electrical energy in 100 s.

i How much useful energy did the light bulb transfer in this time?

ii How much energy was wasted by the light bulb?

iii Draw a Sankey diagram for the light bulb.

b A filament light bulb that gives the same light intensity as the low-energy light bulb has an efficiency of 16%. Calculate the energy wasted by this filament light bulb in 100 s.

4 A pile driver is designed to push a vertical girder into the ground by repeatedly raising a heavy metal block and then releasing it so it drops it onto the top end of the girder.

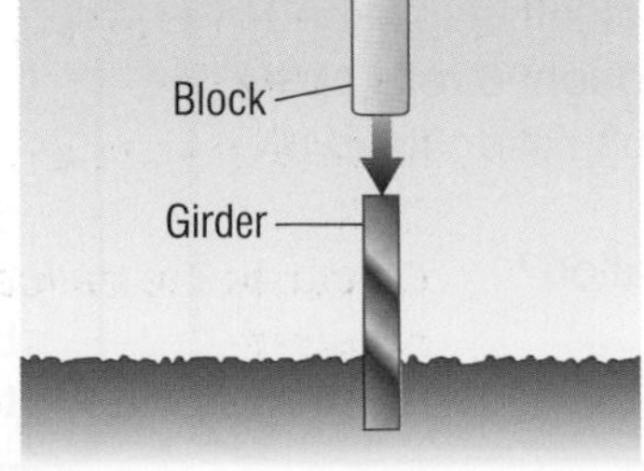

a Describe the energy transfers that occur after the block is released.

b The metal block of a pile driver has a mass of 600 kg. It is raised through a height of 1.5 m in 5.0 seconds then released.

i Calculate its gain in gravitational potential energy when it is raised.

ii Estimate the output power of the motor that raised the block.

5 On a building site, an electric winch and a pulley were used to lift bricks from the ground.

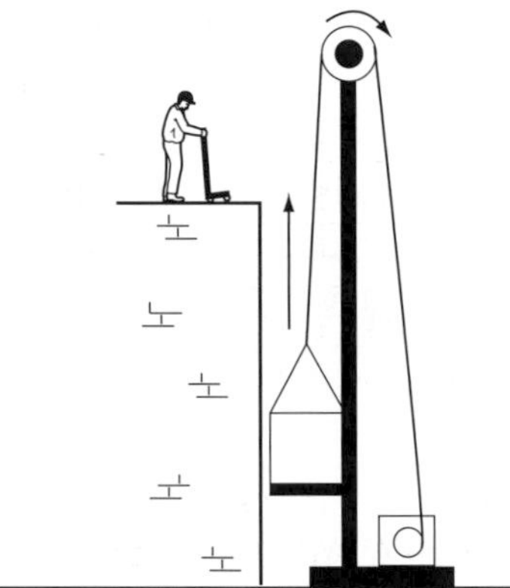

The winch raised a load of 500 N through a height of 3.0 m in 25 s. During this time, the average power supplied to the winch was 600 W.

a i How much useful energy was transferred by the motor?

ii Calculate the energy wasted.

iii Calculate the percentage efficiency of the system.

b i How could the efficiency of the winch be improved?

ii Explain why the efficiency of a winch can never be as much as 100%.

6 A detached building has a total window area of 10 m^2 and a total external wall area of 70 m^2.

The U-value of the windows is 3.2 $W/m^2\,°C$. The U-value of the walls is 0.5 $W/m^2\,°C$.

a Explain what is meant by U-value.

b Explain why more energy is lost from the building through the windows than through the walls.

c The building is heated by electrical heaters. A building surveyor estimates that by fitting cavity wall insulation the cost of heating the building could be reduced by 15% and the payback time would be 5 years.

i Describe what cavity wall insulation is, and explain why it reduces energy transfer through the walls.

ii Explain what is meant by payback time.

AQA Examination-style questions

1 The diagrams show four appliances, **A**, **B**, **C** and **D**, that transfer electrical energy.

A Toaster

B Fan

C Lamp

D Radio

a Match the appliances, **A**, **B**, **C** and **D**, with the numbers **1–4** in the table. (4)

Appliance	Useful energy transfer	Wasted energy transfer
1	to sound	by heating
2	to kinetic	to sound and by heating
3	to light	by heating
4	by heating	to light

b A table-tennis player drops a ball on to the table and catches it. The ball does not bounce back to the starting height.

Discuss the energy transfers that occur and explain why the ball does not bounce back to its original height. (QWC) (6)

2 The diagram shows an electronic road sign.

Wind turbine
Solar cells
Screen

a Choose words from the list to complete the sentences below.

electrical light kinetic
sound strain potential energy

i The useful energy output from the screen is ....

ii The useful energy output from the solar cells is ....

iii The energy input to the wind turbine is .... (3)

b What is meant by the *Principle of Conservation of Energy*? (1)

c The Sankey diagram shows energy transfers in a petrol engine.

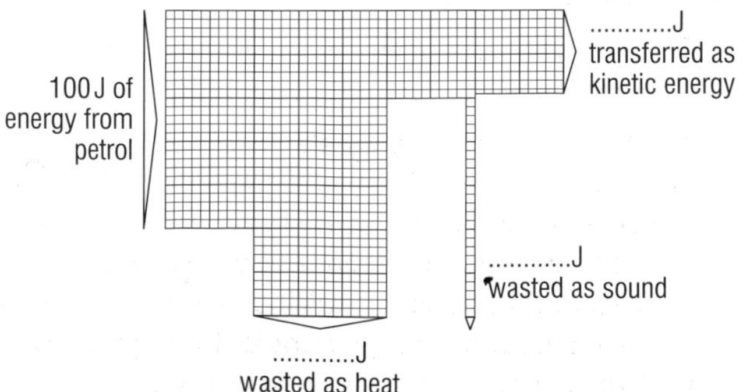

i How much energy is usefully transferred as kinetic energy? (1)

ii How much energy is wasted as sound? (1)

iii How much energy is wasted by heating the surroundings? (1)

iv Calculate the efficiency of the petrol engine. (1)

3 The diagram shows how energy is lost from a house.

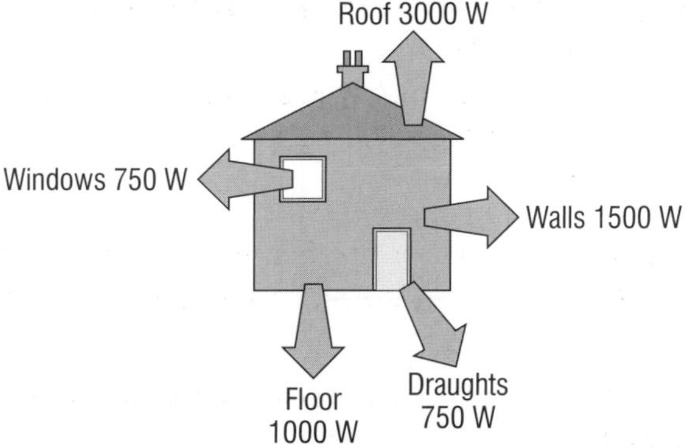

a i By which process does energy leave the house through the floor? (1)

ii What percentage of energy is lost through the roof? (2)

iii The house has a heating system.
Explain what power the heating system must have to maintain the house at a steady temperature. (2)

b The house owner uses the Internet to investigate ways of reducing the energy losses.

He prints off a table summarising his findings.

Method of insulation	Cost to install in £	% reduction in energy loss after installation
Cavity wall insulation	600	50
Double glazing	4000	33
Floor insulation	300	25
Loft insulation	200	33

i Which type of insulation saves most energy? (1)

ii Which type of insulation saves most energy for each pound (£) spent? (1)

iii The house owner decides to insulate the walls, floor and loft only.
In the first year, the saving on the heating bill is £400.
Calculate the payback time if heating costs stay constant. (2)

P16.1 Electrical charges

Learning objectives

After this topic, you should know:
- what happens when insulating materials are rubbed together
- what is transferred when objects become charged
- what happens when charges are brought together.

Have you ever stuck a balloon on a ceiling? All you need to do is to rub the balloon on your clothing before you touch it on the ceiling. The rubbing action charges the balloon with **static electricity**. In other words, the balloon becomes electrically charged. The charge on the balloon attracts it to the ceiling.

Practical

The Van de Graaff generator

A Van de Graaff generator can make your hair stand on end. The dome charges up when the generator is switched on. Massive sparks are produced if the charge on the dome builds up too much.

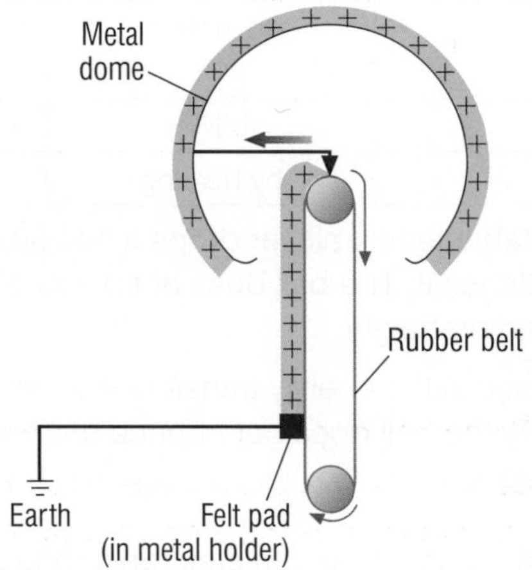

Figure 1 The Van de Graaff generator

The Van de Graaff generator charges up because:
- the belt rubs against a felt pad and becomes charged
- the belt carries the charge onto an insulated metal dome
- sparks are produced when the dome can no longer hold any more charge.

- Why should you keep away from a Van de Graaff generator?

Safety: Do not take part in this experiment if you have a heart condition. All electronic equipment should be switched off and kept well away from the generator.

Did you know ... ?

Take off a woolly jumper and listen out! You can hear it crackle as tiny sparks from static electricity are created. If the room is dark, you can even see the sparks.
You can get charged up just by sitting in a plastic chair. If this happens, you may feel a slight shock from static electricity when you stand up.

Examiner's tip

Objects become electrically charged by gaining electrons (so becoming more negative) or losing electrons (so becoming more positive).

Inside the atom

The **protons** and **neutrons** make up the nucleus of the atom. Electrons move about in the space round the nucleus.

- A proton has a positive charge.
- An electron has an equal negative charge.
- A neutron is uncharged.

An uncharged atom has equal numbers of electrons and protons. Only electrons can be transferred to or from an atom. A charged atom is called an **ion**.

1 Adding electrons to an uncharged atom makes it negative (because the atom then has more electrons than protons).
2 Removing electrons from an uncharged atom makes it positive (because the atom has fewer electrons than protons).

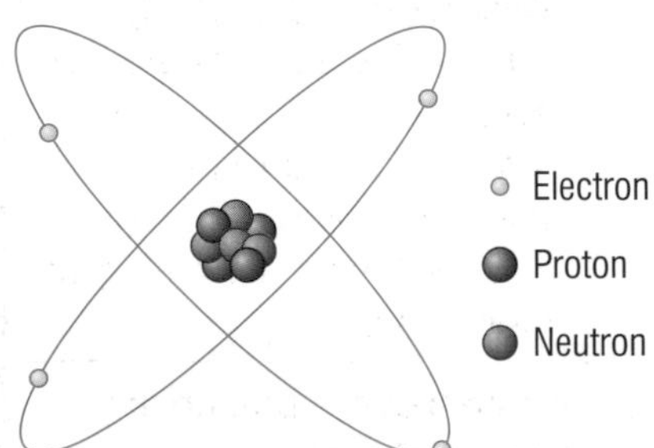

Figure 2 Inside an atom

Charging by friction

Some insulators become charged by rubbing them with a dry cloth.

- Rubbing a polythene rod with a dry cloth transfers electrons to the surface atoms of the rod from the cloth. So the polythene rod becomes negatively charged.
- Rubbing a perspex rod with a dry cloth transfers electrons from the surface atoms of the rod on to the cloth. So the perspex rod becomes positively charged.

Atoms become positive as a result of losing electrons

Electrons gained by rod

Polythene rod

Dry cloth

Atoms become positive as a result of losing electrons

Electrons gained by cloth

Perspex rod

Dry cloth

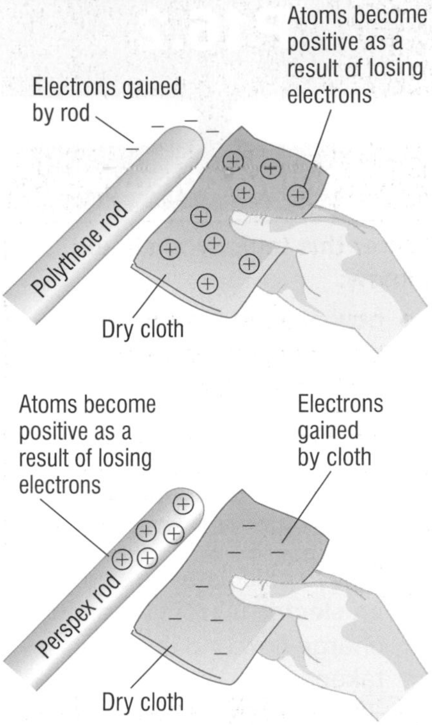

Figure 3 Charging by friction

Practical

The force between two charged objects

Two charged objects exert a force on each other. Figure 4 shows how you can investigate this force.

- What happens?

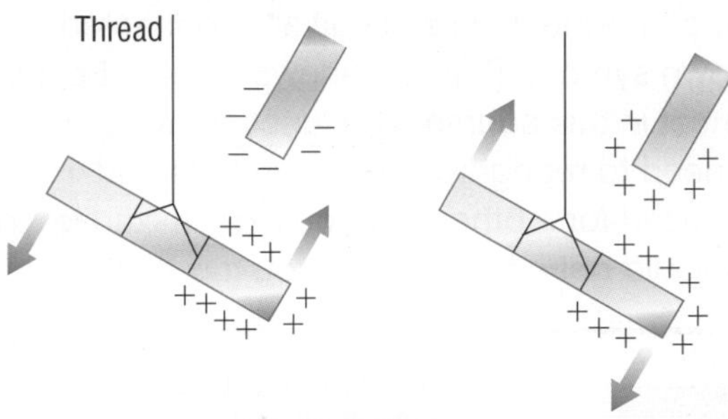

Figure 4 The law of force for charges

Your results in the experiment above should show that:

- two objects with the same type of charge (i.e. like charges) repel each other
- two objects with different types of charge (i.e. unlike charges) attract each other.

Like charges repel. Unlike charges attract.

Summary questions

1 a In terms of electrons, explain why:
   i a polythene rod becomes negatively charged when rubbed with a dry cloth
   ii a perspex rod becomes positively charged when rubbed with a dry cloth.
  b Glass is charged positively when it is rubbed with a cloth. Does glass gain or lose electrons when it is charged?

2 When rubbed with a dry cloth, perspex becomes positively charged. Polythene and ebonite become negatively charged. State whether or not attraction or repulsion takes place when:
  a a perspex rod is held near a polythene rod
  b a perspex rod is held near an ebonite rod
  c a polythene rod is held near an ebonite rod.

3 a After two rods X and Y made of different insulating materials are charged, they are found to repel each other. What does this tell you about the charge on the two rods?
  b Given a rod R that is known to charge positively, how would you determine the type of charge on X and on Y?

Key points

- **Certain insulating materials become charged when rubbed together.**
- **Electrons are transferred when objects become charged:**
  - **Insulating materials that become positively charged when rubbed lose electrons.**
  - **Insulating materials that become negatively charged when rubbed gain electrons.**
- **Like charges repel; unlike charges attract.**

P16.2 Electric circuits

Learning objectives

After this topic, you should know:

- how electric circuits are shown as diagrams
- the difference between a battery and a cell
- what determines the size of an electric current
- how to calculate the size of an electric current from the charge flow and the time taken.

An electric torch can be very useful in a power cut at night. But it needs to be checked to make sure it works. Figure 1 shows what is inside a torch. The circuit shows how the torch bulb is connected to the switch and the two cells.

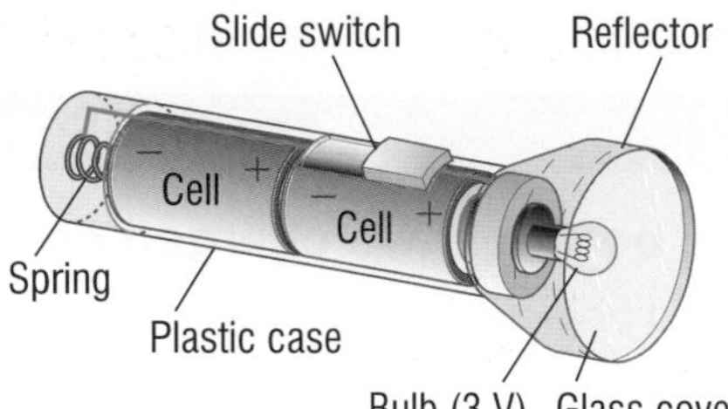

Figure 1 An electric torch

A circuit diagram shows us how the components in a circuit are connected together. Each component has its own symbol. Figure 2 shows the symbols for some of the components you will meet in this course. The function of each component is also described. You need to recognise these symbols and remember what each component is used for – otherwise you'll get mixed up in your exams. More importantly, you could get a big shock if you mix them up!

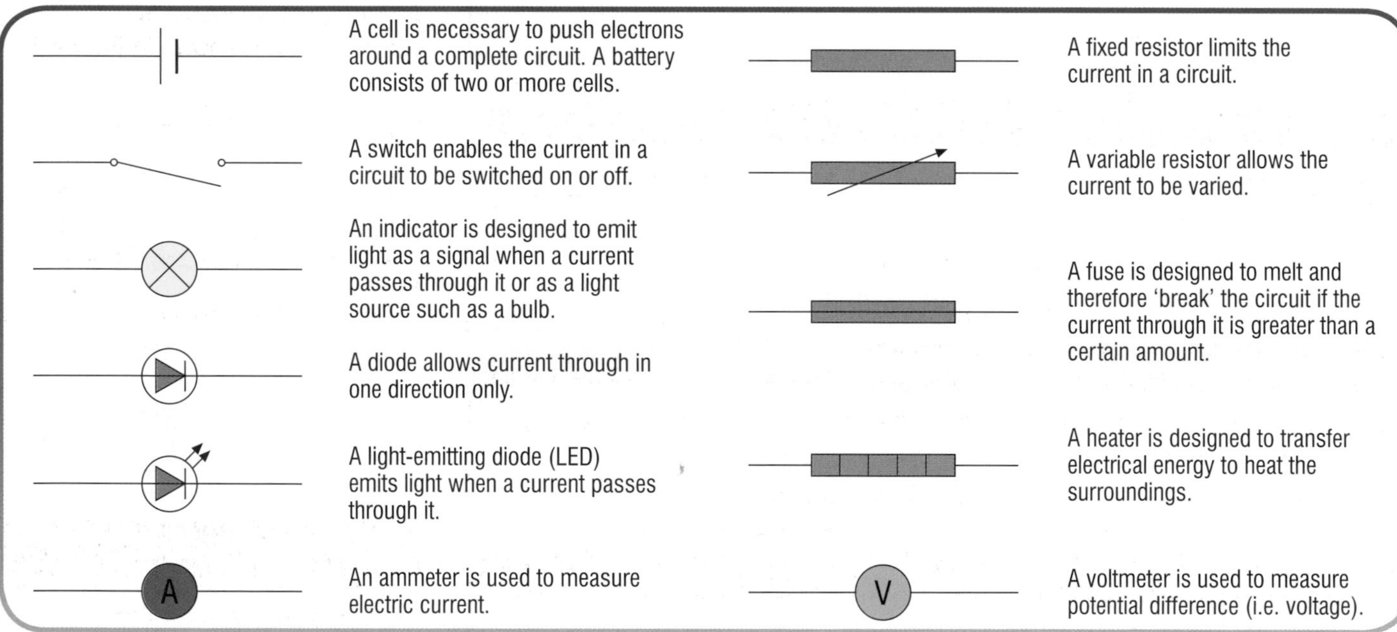

A cell is necessary to push electrons around a complete circuit. A battery consists of two or more cells.
A switch enables the current in a circuit to be switched on or off.
An indicator is designed to emit light as a signal when a current passes through it or as a light source such as a bulb.
A diode allows current through in one direction only.
A light-emitting diode (LED) emits light when a current passes through it.
A
An ammeter is used to measure electric current.
A fixed resistor limits the current in a circuit.
A variable resistor allows the current to be varied.
A fuse is designed to melt and therefore 'break' the circuit if the current through it is greater than a certain amount.
A heater is designed to transfer electrical energy to heat the surroundings.
V
A voltmeter is used to measure potential difference (i.e. voltage).

Figure 2 Components and symbols

Electric current

An electric current is a flow of charge. When an electric torch is on, millions of **electrons** pass through the torch bulb and through the cell every second. Each electron carries a negative charge. Metals contain lots of electrons that move about freely between the positively charged metal ions. These electrons stop the ions moving away from each other. The electrons pass through the bulb because its filament is made of a metal. The electrons transfer energy from the cell to the torch bulb.

The size of an electric current is the rate of flow of electric charge. This is the flow of charge per second. The greater the number of electrons that pass through a component, the bigger the current passing through it.

Examiner's tip

Direction matters

We mark the direction of the current in a circuit from + to – round the circuit. This convention was agreed long before electrons were discovered.

Electric charge is measured in **coulombs (C)**. Electric current is measured in **amperes (A)**, sometimes abbreviated as 'amps'.

An electric current of 1 ampere is a rate of flow of charge of 1 coulomb per second. If a certain amount of charge flows steadily through a wire or a component in a certain time:

$$\textbf{current}\text{ (amperes)} = \frac{\textbf{charge flow}\text{ (coulombs)}}{\textbf{time taken}\text{ (seconds)}}$$

We can write the equation above using symbols as:

$$I = \frac{Q}{t}$$

where:
I = current in amperes, A
Q = charge in coulombs, C
t = time taken in seconds, s.

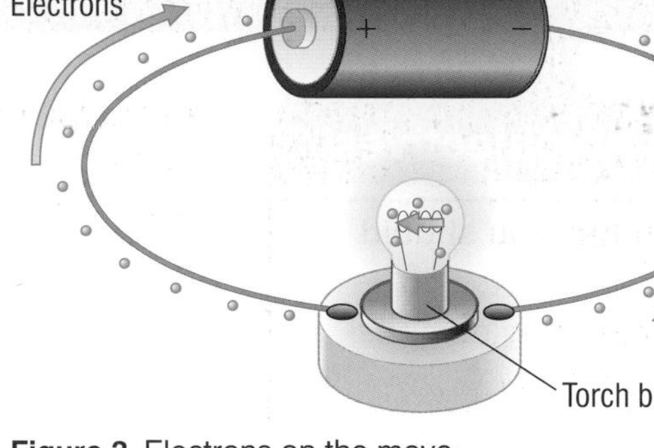

Figure 3 Electrons on the move

Maths skills

Worked example

A charge of 8.0 C passes through a bulb in 4.0 seconds. Calculate the current through the bulb.

Solution

$$I = \frac{Q}{t} = \frac{8.0\,\text{C}}{4.0\,\text{s}} = \mathbf{2.0\,A}$$

Did you know ... ?

You would damage a portable radio if you put the batteries in the wrong way round, unless a diode is in series with the battery. The diode allows current through only when it is connected as shown in Figure 4.

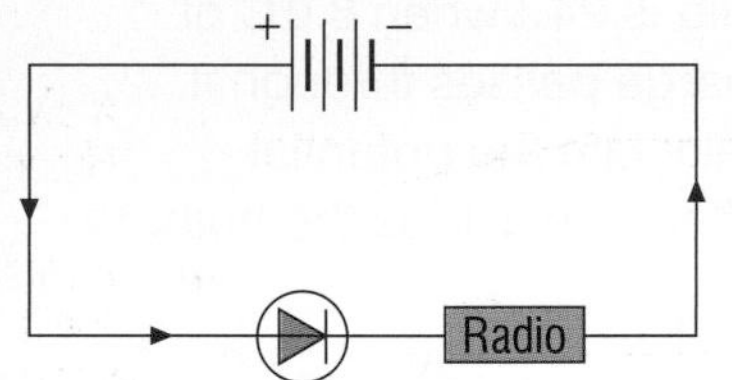

Figure 4 Using a diode

Practical

Circuit tests

Connect a variable resistor in series with the torch bulb and a cell, as shown in Figure 5.

Adjust the slider of the variable resistor. This alters the amount of current flowing through the bulb and therefore affects its brightness.

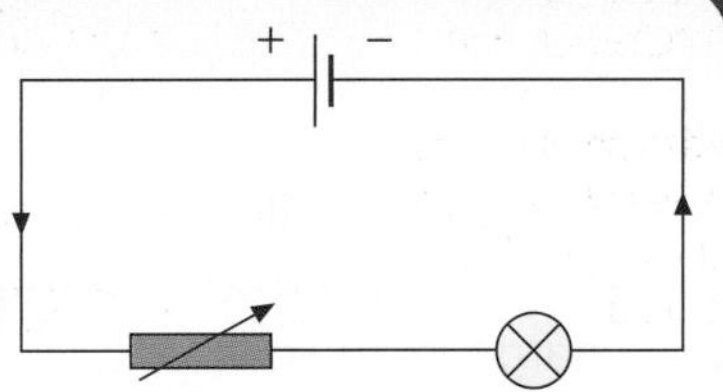

Figure 5 Using a variable resistor

- In Figure 5, the torch bulb goes dim when the slider is moved one way. What happens if the slider is moved back again?
- What happens if you include a diode in the circuit?

Summary questions

1 Name the numbered components in the circuit diagram in the figure opposite.

2 a Redraw the circuit diagram in Question **1** with a diode in place of the switch so it allows current through.
b What further component would you need in this circuit to change the current in it?
c When the switch is closed in the figure for Question **1**, a current of 0.25 A passes through the lamp. Calculate the charge that passes through the lamp in 60 seconds.

3 a What is a light-emitting diode?
b What is a variable resistor used for?

Key points

- Every component has its own agreed symbol. A circuit diagram shows how components are connected together.
- A battery consists of two or more cells connected together.
- The size of an electric current is the rate of flow of charge.
- Electric current = $\frac{\text{charge flow}}{\text{time taken}}$

P16.3 Potential difference and resistance

Learning objectives

After this topic, you should know:

- what is meant by potential difference
- what resistance is and what its unit is
- what Ohm's law is
- what happens when you reverse the current in a resistor.

Maths skills

Worked example

The energy transferred to a bulb is 24 J when 8.0 C of charge passes through it. Calculate the potential difference across the bulb.

Solution

$V = \frac{E}{Q} = \frac{24\,\text{J}}{8.0\,\text{C}} = \mathbf{3.0\,V}$

Maths skills

Rearranging the equation

$R = \frac{V}{I}$ gives $V = I \times R$ or $I = \frac{V}{R}$

The last equation shows that for a fixed potential difference across a component, the greater the resistance, the smaller the current.

The equation tells us that the current I is **inversely proportional** to the resistance R. For example, if R was ten times greater, I would be ten times smaller. See p241 for more about inverse proportionality.

Potential difference

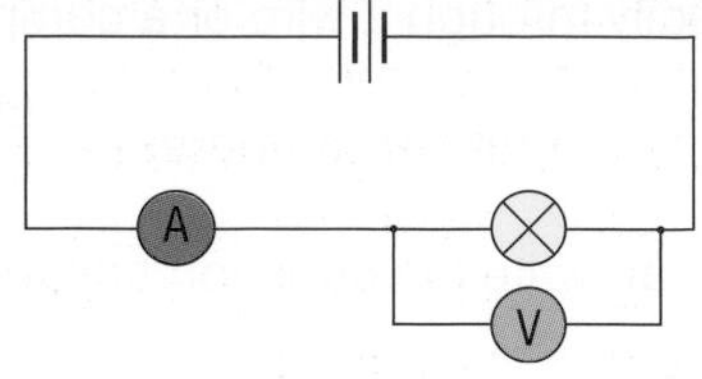

Figure 1 Using an ammeter and a voltmeter

Look at the circuit in Figure 1. The battery forces electrons to pass through the ammeter and the bulb.

- The ammeter measures the current through the torch bulb. It is connected in **series** with the bulb so the current through them is the same. The ammeter reading gives the current in amperes (or milliamperes (mA) for small currents, where 1 mA = 0.001 A).
- The voltmeter measures the **potential difference** (pd or **voltage**) across the torch bulb. This is the energy transferred to the bulb or the work done on it by each coulomb of charge that passes through it. The unit of potential difference is the **volt (V)**.
- The voltmeter is connected in **parallel** with the torch bulb so it measures the potential difference across it. The voltmeter reading gives the potential difference in volts (V).

When charge flows steadily through a component:

$$\textbf{potential difference across the component}\text{ (volts)} = \frac{\textbf{energy transferred}\text{ (joules)}}{\textbf{charge}\text{ (coulombs)}}$$

We can write the equation above using symbols as:

$$V = \frac{E}{Q}$$

where:
V = the potential difference in volts, V
E = energy transferred in joules, J
Q = charge in coulombs, C.

Resistance

Electrons passing through a torch bulb have to push their way through lots of vibrating ions in the metal filament. The ions resist the passage of electrons through the torch bulb.

We define the **resistance** of an electrical component as:

$$\textbf{resistance}\text{ (ohms)} = \frac{\textbf{potential difference}\text{ (volts)}}{\textbf{current}\text{ (amperes)}}$$

The unit of resistance is the **ohm**. The symbol for the ohm is the Greek capital letter Ω (omega). Note that a resistor in a circuit limits the current. For a given potential difference, the larger the resistance of a resistor, the smaller the current is.

We can write the definition above as:

$$R = \frac{V}{I}$$

where:
R = resistance in ohms, Ω
V = potential difference in volts, V
I = current in amperes, A.

Examiner's tip

Make sure that you can re-arrange the equation $V = I \times R$.

Practical

Investigating the resistance of a wire

Does the resistance of a wire change when the current through it is changed? Figure 2 shows how we can use a variable resistor to change the current through a wire. Make your own measurements and use them to plot a current–potential difference graph like the one in Figure 2.

- Discuss how your measurements compare with the ones from the table below used to plot the graph in Figure 2.
- Calculate the resistance of the wire you tested.

Current (A)	0	0.05	0.10	0.15	0.20	0.25
Potential difference (V)	0	0.50	1.00	1.50	2.00	2.50

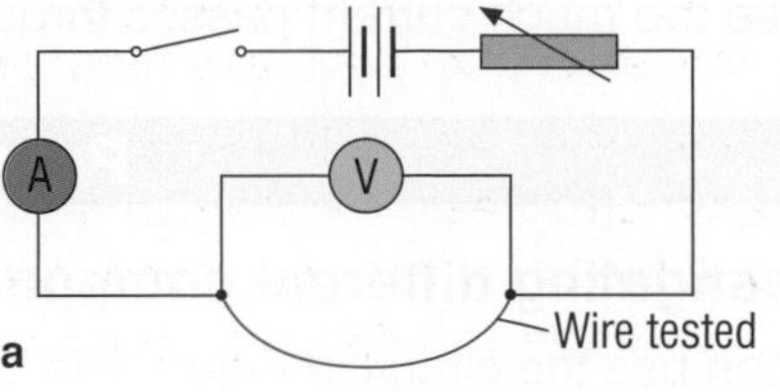

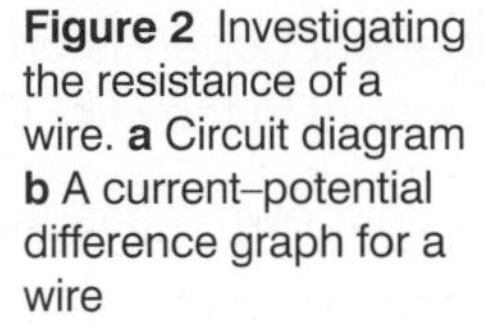

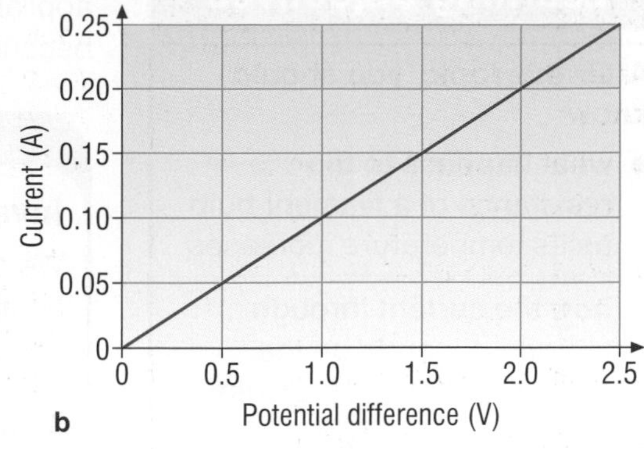

Figure 2 Investigating the resistance of a wire. **a** Circuit diagram **b** A current–potential difference graph for a wire

Current–potential difference graphs

The graph in Figure 2 is a straight line through the origin. This means that the current is directly proportional to the potential difference. In other words, the resistance (= potential difference ÷ current) is constant. This was first discovered for a wire at constant temperature by Georg Ohm and is known as **Ohm's law**:

The current through a resistor at constant temperature is directly proportional to the potential difference across the resistor.

We say a wire is an **ohmic conductor** because its resistance is constant. As shown in Figure 3, reversing the potential difference makes no difference to the shape of the line. The resistance is the same whichever direction the current is in.

Note: The gradient of the line depends on the resistance of the resistor. The greater the resistance of the resistor, the less steep the line.

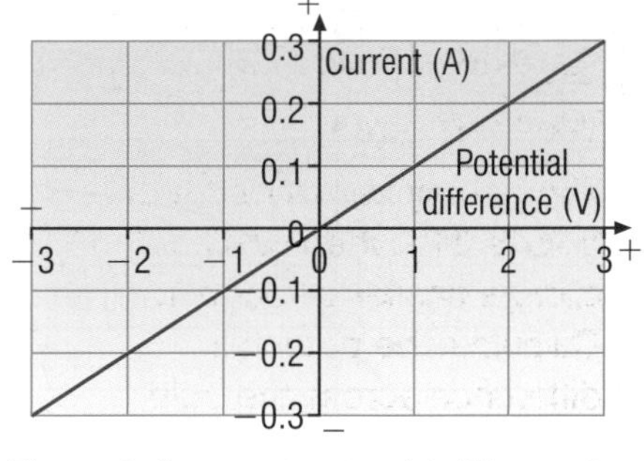

Figure 3 A current–potential difference graph for a resistor

Summary questions

1 **a** The current through a wire is 0.5 A when the potential difference across it is 4.0 V. Calculate the resistance of the wire.
b Calculate the resistance of the wire that gave the results in the graph in Figure 2.

2 Calculate the missing value in each line of the table, using the equation $V = I \times R$ or a rearrangement of it.

Resistor	Current (A)	Potential difference (V)	Resistance (Ω)
W	2.0	12.0	
X	4.0		20
Y		6.0	3.0

3 A torch bulb lights normally when the current through it is 0.060 A and the potential difference across it is 3.0 V.
a Calculate the resistance of the torch bulb when it lights normally.
b When the torch bulb lights normally, calculate:
i the charge passing through the torch bulb in 300 s
ii the energy delivered to the torch bulb in this time.

Key points

- The potential difference across a component (volts) $= \dfrac{\text{energy transferred (joules)}}{\text{charge (coulombs)}}$
- Resistance (ohms) $= \dfrac{\text{potential difference (volts)}}{\text{current (amperes)}}$
- Ohm's law states that the current through a resistor at constant temperature is directly proportional to the potential difference across the resistor.
- Reversing the current through a component reverses the potential difference across it.

P16.4 More current–potential difference graphs

Learning objectives

After this topic, you should know:

- what happens to the resistance of a filament bulb as its temperature increases
- how the current through a diode depends on the potential difference across it
- what happens to the resistance of a thermistor as its temperature increases and of an LDR as the light level increases.

Have you ever switched a light bulb on only to hear it 'pop' and fail? Electrical appliances can fail at very inconvenient times. Most electrical failures are because too much current passes through a component in the appliance.

Practical

Investigating different components

We can use the circuit in Figure 2 in 16.3 to find out if the resistance of a component depends on the current. We can also see if reversing the component in the circuit has any effect.

Make your own measurements using a resistor, a filament bulb and a diode.

Plot your measurements on a current–potential difference graph. Plot the 'reverse' measurements on the negative section of each axis.

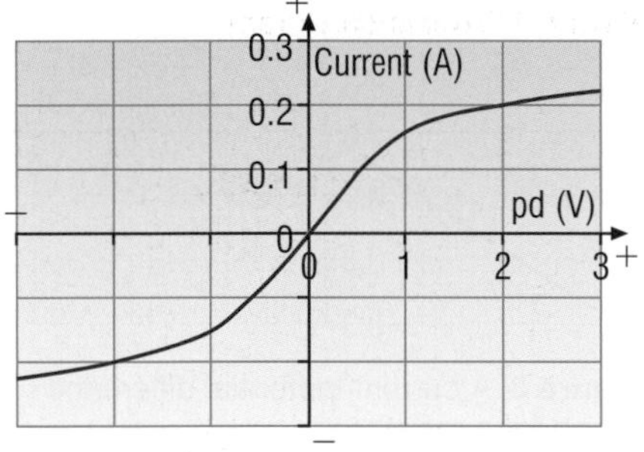

Figure 1 A current–potential difference graph for a filament bulb

Using current–potential difference graphs

A filament bulb

Figure 1 shows the graph for a torch bulb (i.e. a low-voltage filament bulb).

- The line **curves** away from the current axis. So, the current is *not* directly proportional to the potential difference. The filament bulb is a non-ohmic conductor.
- **The resistance (= potential difference ÷ current) increases as the current increases.** So, the resistance of a filament bulb increases as the filament temperature increases. This is because the ions in the metal filament vibrate more as the temperature increases. So they resist the passage of the electrons through the filament more. The resistance of any metal increases as its temperature increases.
- Reversing the potential difference makes no difference to the shape of the curve. The resistance is the same for the same current, regardless of its direction.

Examiner's tip

Try to learn the current–potential difference graphs for a resistor, a filament lamp and a diode.

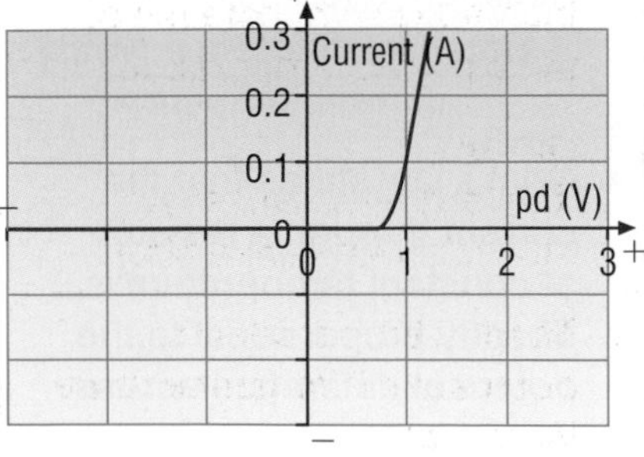

Figure 2 A current–potential difference graph for a **diode**

The diode

Look at Figure 2, a graph for a diode.

- In the 'forward' direction, the line curves towards the current axis. So the current is not directly proportional to the potential difference. A **diode** is a non-ohmic conductor.
- In the reverse direction, the current is virtually zero. So the diode's resistance in the reverse direction is much higher than in the forward direction.

Note that a **light-emitting diode (LED)** emits light when a current passes through it in the forward direction.

Practical

Thermistors and light-dependent resistors

We use thermistors and light-dependent resistors in sensor circuits. A **thermistor** is a temperature-dependent resistor. The resistance of a **light-dependent resistor (LDR)** depends on how much light is on it. For example:

- an LDR is used in a sensor circuit that switches an electric light on and off
- a thermistor may be used in a thermostat used to control temperature.

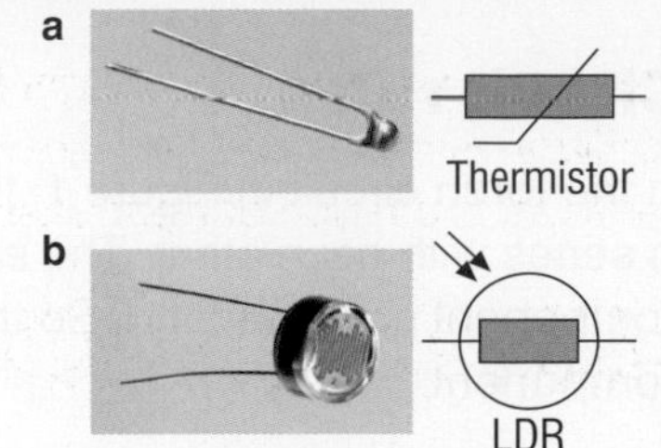

Figure 3 **a** A thermistor and its circuit symbol **b** An LDR and its circuit symbol

Test a thermistor and then an LDR in series with a battery and an ammeter.

- What did you find out about each component tested?

Did you know ... ?

When a filament light bulb fails, it usually happens when you switch it on. Because resistance is low when the bulb is off, a large current passes through it when you switch it on. If the current is too large, it burns the filament out.

Current–potential difference graphs for a thermistor and an LDR

For a thermistor, Figure 4 shows the current–potential difference graph at two different temperatures.

- At constant temperature, the line is straight so its resistance is constant.
- If the temperature is increased, its resistance decreases.

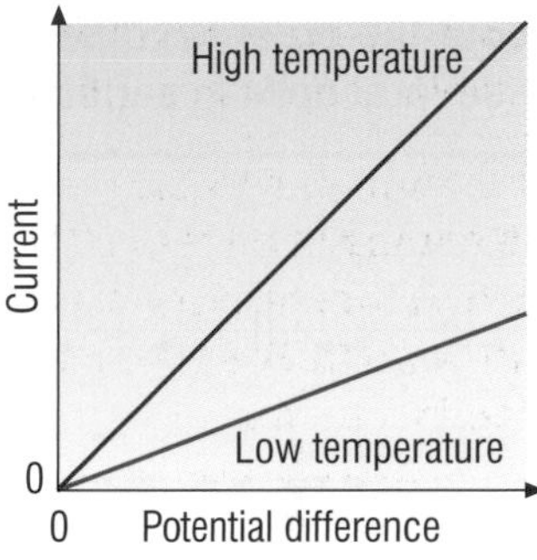

Figure 4 **Thermistor** graph

For a light-dependent resistor, Figure 5 shows the current–potential difference graph in bright light and in dim light.

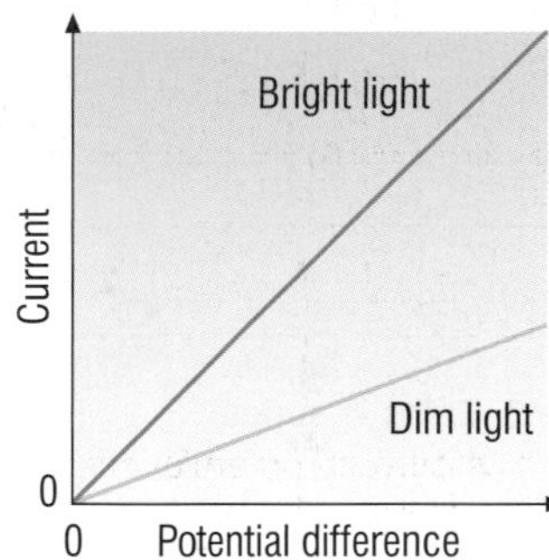

Figure 5 **LDR** graph

Summary questions

1 **a** Identify the type of component that has a resistance that:

i decreases as its temperature increases

ii depends on which way round it is connected in a circuit

iii increases as the current through it increases.

b Calculate the resistance of the filament bulb that gave the graph in Figure 1 at:

i 0.1 A **ii** 0.2 A.

2 A thermistor is connected in series with an ammeter and a 3.0 V battery, as shown in the figure opposite.

a At 15 °C, the current through the thermistor is 0.2 A and the potential difference across it is 3.0 V. Calculate its resistance at this temperature.

b State and explain what happens to the ammeter reading if the thermistor's temperature is increased.

3 **a** The thermistor in the figure for Question **2** is replaced by a light-dependent resistor (LDR). State and explain what happens to the ammeter reading when the LDR is covered.

b For the diode that gave the graph in Figure 2, describe how:

i the current

ii the resistance

changes when the potential difference is increased steadily from zero.

Key points

- **Filament bulb: resistance increases with increase of the filament temperature.**
- **Diode: 'forward' resistance low; 'reverse' resistance high.**
- **Thermistor: resistance decreases if its temperature increases.**
- **LDR: resistance decreases if the light intensity on it increases.**

P16.5 Series circuits

Learning objectives

After this topic, you should know:

- about the current, potential difference and resistance for each component in a series circuit
- about the potential difference of several cells in series.

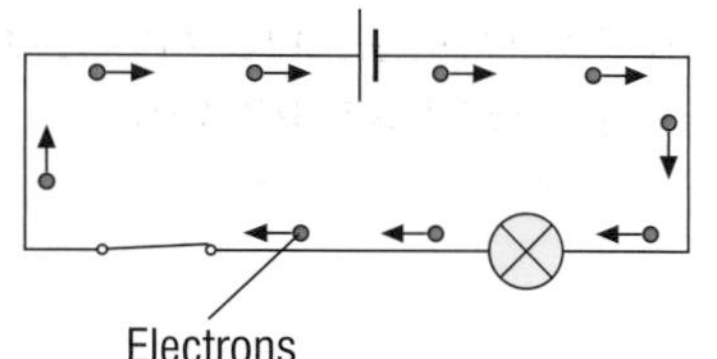

Figure 1 A torch bulb circuit

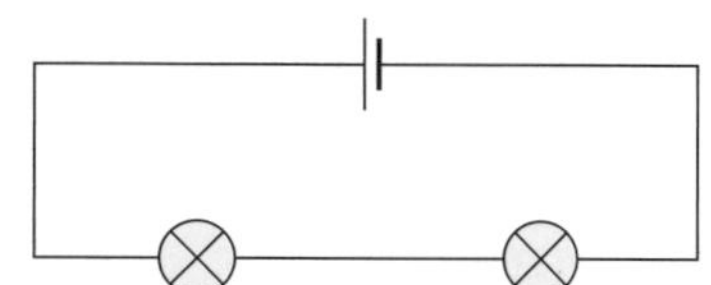

Figure 2 Bulbs in series

Table 1

Filament bulb	Voltmeter V_1 (volts)	Voltmeter V_2 (volts)
normal	1.5	0.0
dim	0.9	0.6
very dim	0.5	1.0

Circuit rules

In the torch circuit in Figure 1, the bulb, the cell and the switch are connected in series with each other. The same number of electrons passes through each component every second. So the same current passes through every component.

In a series circuit, the same current passes through each component.

In Figure 2, each electron from the cell passes through two bulbs. The electrons are pushed through each bulb by the cell. The **potential difference** (or **voltage**) of the cell is a measure of the energy transferred from the cell by each electron that passes through it. Since each electron in the circuit in Figure 2 goes through both bulbs, the potential difference of the cell is shared between the bulbs. This rule applies to any series circuit.

In a series circuit, the total potential difference of the voltage supply is shared between the components.

Cells in series

What happens if we use two or more cells in series in a circuit? As long as we connect the cells so they act in the same direction, each electron gets a push from each cell. So an electron would get the same push from a battery of three 1.5 V cells in series as it would from a single 4.5 V cell.

In other words, **as long as the cells act in the same direction**:

The total potential difference of cells in series is the sum of the potential difference of each cell.

Practical

Investigating potential differences in a series circuit

Figure 3 shows how to test the potential difference rule for a series circuit. The circuit consists of a filament bulb in series with a variable resistor and a cell. We can use the variable resistor to see how the voltmeter readings change when we change the current. Make your own measurements.

How do they compare with the data in Table 1?

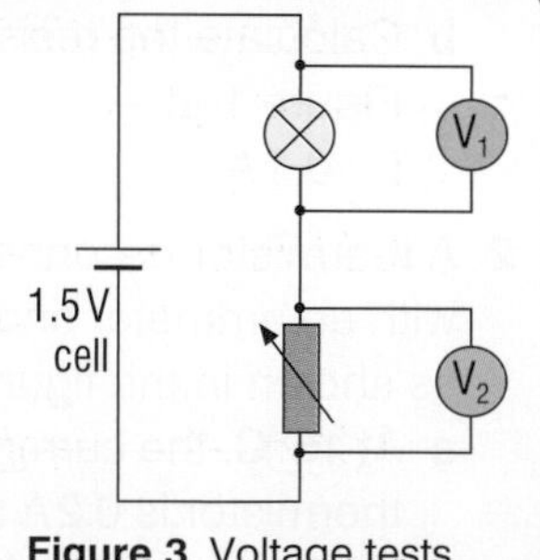

Figure 3 Voltage tests

The measurements in the table show that the voltmeter readings for each setting add up to 1.5 V. This is the potential difference of the cell. The share of the cell's potential difference across each component depends on the setting of the variable resistor.

The resistance rule for components in series

In Figure 3, suppose the current through the bulb is 0.1 A when the bulb is dim.

Using data from Table 1:

- the resistance of the bulb would then be 9Ω (= 0.9V ÷ 0.1 A),
- the resistance of the variable resistor at this setting would be 6Ω (= 0.6V ÷ 0.1 A).

If we replaced these two components by a single resistor, what should its resistance be for the same current of 0.1 A? We can calculate this because we know the potential difference across it would be 1.5V (from the cell). So the resistance would need to be 15Ω (= 1.5V ÷ 0.1 A). This is the sum of the resistance of the two components. The rule applies to any series circuit.

The total resistance of components in series is equal to the sum of the resistance of each component.

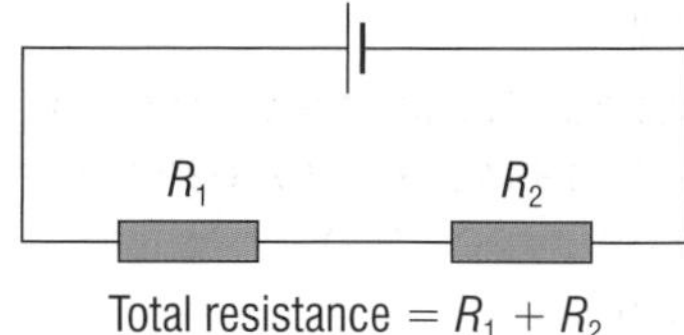

Figure 4 Resistors in series

Examiner's tip

Remember that in a series circuit the same current passes through each component.

Summary questions

1 **a** In Figure 2, if the potential difference of the cell is 1.2V and the potential difference across one bulb is 0.8V, what is the potential difference across the other bulb?

b In Figure 3, the bulb lights normally when the resistance of the variable resistor is 5.0Ω and the potential difference across the variable resistor is 1.0V. Calculate the current through the bulb and the potential difference across it.

2 A 1.5V cell is connected to a 3.0Ω resistor and 2.0Ω resistor in series with each other.

a Draw the circuit diagram for this arrangement.

b Calculate:

i the total resistance of the two resistors

ii the current through the resistors.

3 For the circuit in the figure below, each cell has a potential difference of 1.5V.

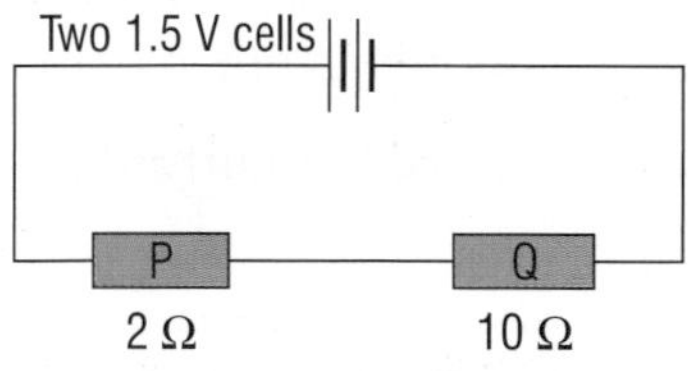

a Calculate:

i the total resistance of the two resistors

ii the total potential difference of the two cells.

b Show that the current through the battery is 0.25A.

c Calculate the potential difference across each resistor.

d If a 3Ω resistor *R* is connected in series between the two resistors, calculate:

i their total resistance

ii the current through the resistors

iii the potential difference across each resistor.

Key points

- For components in series:
  - the current is the same in each component
  - the total potential difference is shared between the components
  - adding their resistances gives the total resistance.
- For cells in series, acting in the same direction, the total potential difference is the sum of their individual potential differences.

P16.6 Parallel circuits

Learning objectives

After this topic, you should know:

- about the currents and potential differences for components in a parallel circuit
- the relationship between resistance and current for a component
- how to calculate the current through a resistor in a parallel circuit.

Did you know ... ?

A bypass is a parallel route. A heart bypass is another route for the flow of blood. A road bypass is a road that passes a town centre instead of going through it. For components in parallel, charge flows separately through each component. The total flow of charge is the sum of the flow through each component.

Examiner's tip

Remember that when components are connected in parallel there is the same potential difference across each component.

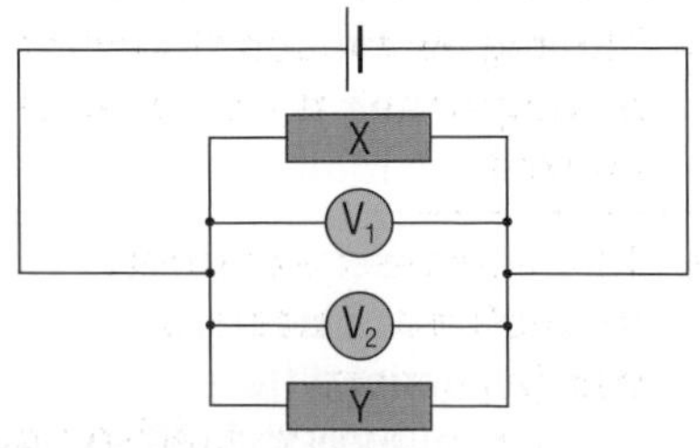

Figure 2 Components in parallel

Practical

Investigating parallel circuits

Figure 1 shows how you can investigate the current through two bulbs in parallel with each other. You can use ammeters in series with the bulbs and the cell to measure the current through each component.

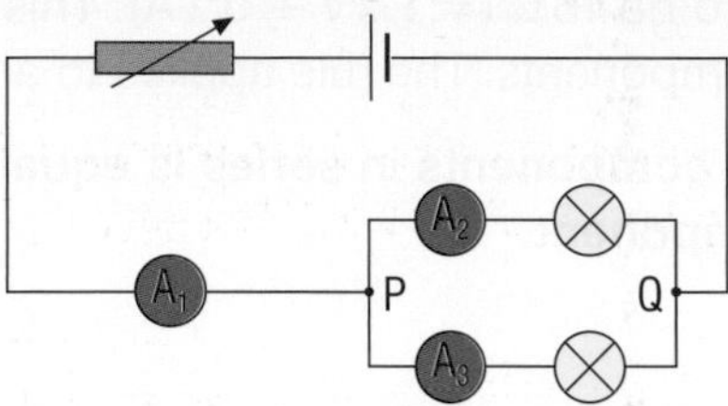

Figure 1 At a junction

Set up your own circuit and collect your data.

- How do your measurements compare with the ones for different settings of the variable resistor shown in Table 1?
- Discuss whether your own measurements show the same pattern.

Look at the sample data below.

Table 1

Ammeter A_1 (A)	Ammeter A_2 (A)	Ammeter A_3 (A)
0.50	0.30	0.20
0.30	0.20	0.10
0.18	0.12	0.06

In each case, the reading of ammeter A_1 is equal to the sum of the readings of ammeters A_2 and A_3.

This shows that the current through the cell is equal to sum of the currents through the two bulbs. This rule applies wherever components are in parallel.

The total current through the whole circuit is the sum of the currents through the separate components.

Potential difference in a parallel circuit

Figure 2 shows two resistors X and Y in parallel with each other. A voltmeter is connected across each resistor. The voltmeter across resistor X shows the same reading as the voltmeter across resistor Y. This is because each electron from the cell either passes through X or through Y. So it delivers the same amount of energy from the cell, whichever resistor it goes through. In other words:

For components in parallel, the potential difference across each component is the same.

Calculations on parallel circuits

Components in parallel have the same potential difference across them. The current through each component depends on the resistance of the component.

- The bigger the resistance of the component, the smaller the current through it. The resistor that has the largest resistance passes the smallest current.
- We can calculate the current using the equation:

$$\text{current (amperes)} = \frac{\text{potential difference (volts)}}{\text{resistance (ohms)}}$$

Maths skills

Worked example

The circuit diagram in Figure 3 shows three resistors $R_1 = 1\,\Omega$, $R_2 = 2\,\Omega$ and $R_3 = 6\,\Omega$ connected in parallel to a 6 V battery.

Calculate:

a the current through each resistor

b the current through the battery.

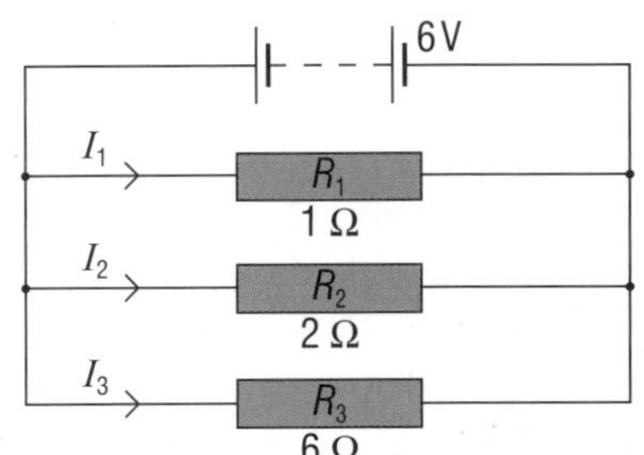

Figure 3

Solution

a $I_1 = \frac{V_1}{R_1} = \frac{6}{1} = \mathbf{6\,A}$

$I_2 = \frac{V_2}{R_2} = \frac{6}{2} = \mathbf{3\,A}$

$I_3 = \frac{V_3}{R_3} = \frac{6}{6} = \mathbf{1\,A}$

b The total current from the battery $= I_1 + I_2 + I_3 = 6\,A + 3\,A + 1\,A = \mathbf{10\,A}$

Summary questions

1 **a** In Table 1, if ammeter A_1 reads 0.40 A and A_2 reads 0.1 A, what would A_3 read?

b A 3 Ω resistor and a 6 Ω resistor are connected in parallel in a circuit. Which resistor passes the most current?

c In the circuit shown in Figure 3, what would be the resistance of a single resistor that could replace the three parallel resistors across the 6 V battery and allow the same current to pass through the battery?

2 A 1.5 V cell is connected across a 3 Ω resistor in parallel with a 6 Ω resistor.

a Draw the circuit diagram for this circuit.

b Show that the current through:

i the 3 Ω resistor is 0.50 A **ii** the 6 Ω resistor is 0.25 A.

c Calculate the current passing through the cell.

3 **a** The circuit diagram shows three resistors $R_1 = 2\,\Omega$, $R_2 = 3\,\Omega$ and $R_3 = 6\,\Omega$ connected to each other in parallel and to a 6 V battery. Calculate:

i the current through each resistor

ii the current through the battery.

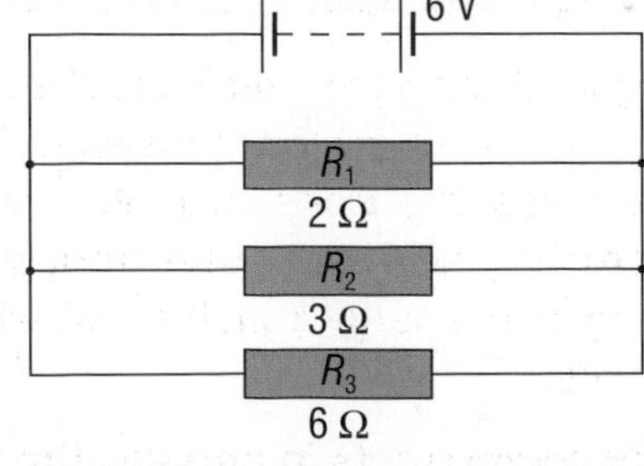

b If the 6 Ω resistor in the figure was replaced by a 4 Ω resistor, calculate the battery current now.

Key points

- For components in parallel:
  - the total current is the sum of the currents through the separate components
  - the potential difference across each component is the same.
- The bigger the resistance of a component, the smaller its current.
- To calculate the current through a resistor in a parallel circuit:

  $\text{current} = \frac{\text{potential difference}}{\text{resistance}}$

Summary questions

1 State and explain how the resistance of a filament bulb changes when the current through the filament is increased.

2 Match each component in the list to each statement **a** to **d** that describes it.

diode filament bulb resistor thermistor

- **a** Its resistance increases if the current through it increases.
- **b** The current through it is proportional to the potential difference across it.
- **c** Its resistance decreases if its temperature is increased.
- **d** Its resistance depends on which way round it is connected in a circuit.

3 **a** Sketch a circuit diagram to show two resistors **P** and **Q** connected in series to a battery of two cells in series with each other.

b In the circuit in part **a**, resistor **P** has a resistance of 4 Ω, resistor **Q** has a resistance of 2 Ω and each cell has a potential difference of 1.5 V. Calculate:

- **i** the total potential difference of the two cells
- **ii** the total resistance of the two resistors
- **iii** the current in the circuit
- **iv** the potential difference across each resistor.

4 **a** Sketch a circuit diagram to show two resistors **R** and **S** in parallel with each other connected to a single cell.

b In the circuit in part **a**, resistor **R** has a resistance of 2 Ω, resistor **S** has a resistance of 4 Ω and the cell has a potential difference of 2 V. Calculate:

- **i** the current through resistor **R**
- **ii** the current through resistor **S**
- **iii** the current through the cell in the circuit.

5 Copy and complete **a** and **b** using the phrases below. Each option can be used once, twice or not at all.

different from greater than equal to less than

- **a** For two components **X** and **Y** in series with each other and a battery, the potential difference across **X** is usually .... the potential difference across **Y** and the current is .... the battery current.
- **b** For two components **X** and **Y** in parallel connected to a battery, the potential difference across **X** is .... the potential difference across **Y** and the current through each is .... the battery current.

6 The figure shows a light-dependent resistor (LDR) in series with a 200 Ω resistor, a 3.0 V battery and an ammeter.

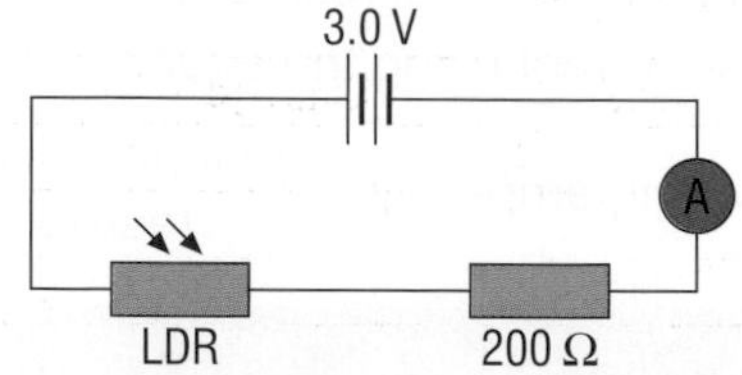

a With the LDR in daylight, the ammeter reads 0.010 A.

- **i** Calculate the potential difference across the 200 Ω resistor when the current through it is 0.010 A.
- **ii** Show that the potential difference across the LDR is 1.0 V when the ammeter reads 0.010 A.
- **iii** Calculate the resistance of the LDR in daylight.

b **i** If the LDR is then covered, explain whether the ammeter reading increases or decreases or stays the same.

- **ii** Explain how the resistance of the LDR can be calculated from the current I, the battery potential difference V and the resistance R of the LDR.

7 In the figure to Question **6**, the LDR is replaced by a 100 Ω resistor and a voltmeter connected in parallel with this resistor.

a Draw the circuit diagram for this circuit.

b Calculate:

- **i** the total resistance of the two resistors in the circuit.
- **ii** the current through the ammeter
- **iii** the voltmeter reading
- **iv** the potential difference across each resistor.

8 The figure shows a light-emitting diode (LED) in series with a resistor and a 3.0 V battery.

3.0 V

LED

1000 Ω

a The LED in the circuit emits light. The potential difference across it when it emits light is 0.6 V.

- **i** Explain why the potential difference across the 1000 Ω resistor is 2.4 V.
- **ii** Calculate the current in the circuit.

b The current through the LED must not exceed 15 mA or else it will be damaged. If the resistor in the figure is replaced by a different resistor **R**, what should be the minimum resistance of **R**?

c If the LED in the circuit is reversed, what would be the current in the circuit? Give a reason for your answer.

AQA Examination-style questions

1 **a** Some of the particles in an atom are charged.

Use words from the list to complete the table. (2)

negative positive uncharged

Particle	Charge
electron	i)
neutron	ii)
proton	iii)

b A plastic ruler is rubbed with a duster. The ruler becomes negatively charged.

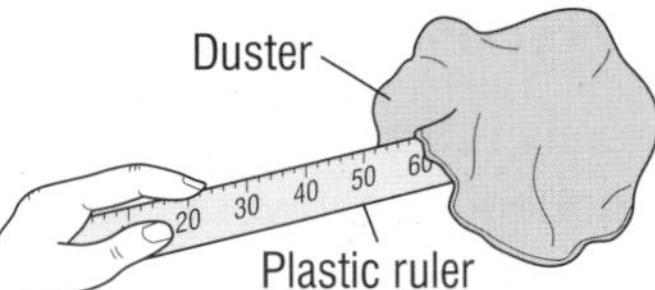

Explain what happens to the ruler and to the duster. (4)

c The diagram shows how electrical charges are used when spraying paint onto car doors.

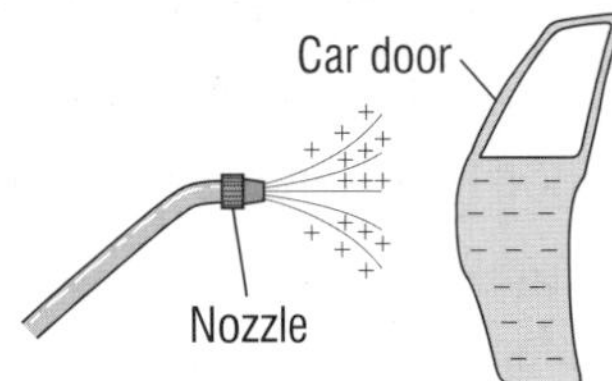

As the paint drops leave the nozzle, they become positively charged. The car door is given a negative charge.

Explain how the paint drops become electrically charged and how electrical charges improve the paint spraying process. (QWC) (6)

2 Circuit diagrams help people when they are setting up apparatus for an experiment.

a **i** Draw a circuit diagram to help someone who wants to determine the resistance of a short length of resistance wire. The circuit should have a switch and a variable resistor. (4)

ii Explain why the circuit should have a switch. (3)

iii Explain why the circuit should have a variable resistor. (2)

b The circuit diagram shows one way of connecting two **identical** heating coils, **A** and **B**, in an electric cooker hob.

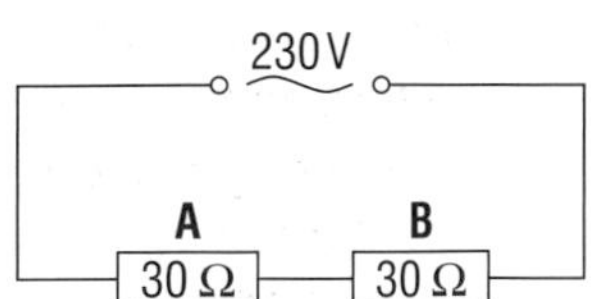

i Calculate the total resistance of the heating coils. (1)

ii Calculate the potential difference across heating coil **A**. (1)

c The circuit diagram shows another way of connecting two **identical** heating coils, **C** and **D**, in an electric cooker hob.

The current flowing through heating coil **C** is 7.7 A

i What is the potential difference across heating coil **C**? (1)

ii Calculating the resistance of heating coil **C**? (1)

iii Calculate the total current flowing in this circuit. (1)

230 V

C

D

30 Ω

4 Thermistors can be used as temperature sensors.

a The graph shows how the resistance of a thermistor changes with temperature.

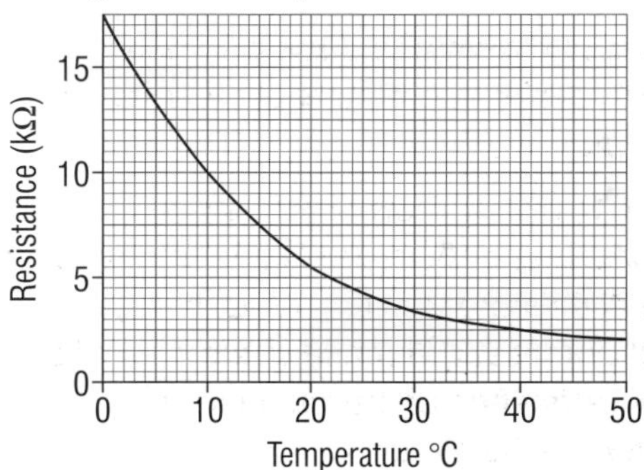

Use the graph to find the resistance of the thermistor at 33°C. (1)

b The thermistor is connected in the circuit below.

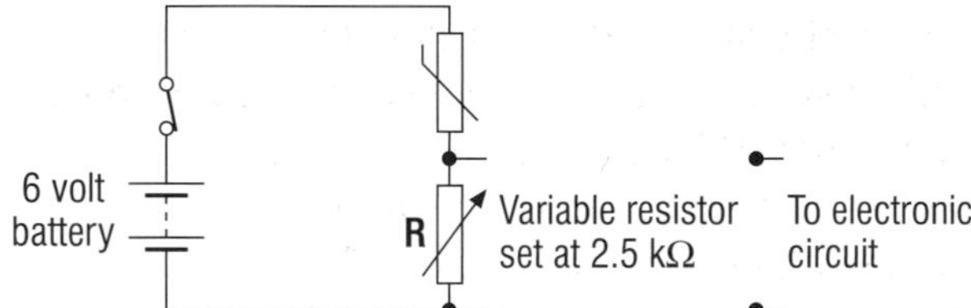

Calculate the current through the circuit, in mA, when the temperature of the thermistor is 33°C. (3)

c An electronic circuit is connected across resistor **R** as shown in the circuit diagram.

The potential difference across resistor **R** is used to power the electronic circuit.

Calculate the potential difference across resistor **R** when the temperature is:

i 33°C (2)

ii 0°C (3)

iii Explain how this circuit could be used. (4)

P17.1 Alternating current

Learning objectives

After this topic, you should know:

- what direct current is and what alternating current is
- what is meant by the live wire and the neutral wire of a mains circuit
- how a diode can be used to convert alternating current to direct current
- how to use an oscilloscope to measure the frequency and peak potential difference of an alternating current.

The battery in a torch makes the current go round the circuit in one direction only. We say the current in the circuit is a **direct current** (dc) because it is in one direction only.

When you switch a light on at home, you use **alternating current** (ac) because mains electricity is an ac supply. An alternating current repeatedly reverses its direction. It flows one way then the opposite way in successive cycles. Its **frequency** is the number of cycles it passes through each second.

In the UK, the mains frequency is 50 cycles per second (or 50 Hz). A light bulb works just as well at this frequency as it would with a direct current.

Mains circuits

Every mains circuit has a **live wire** and a **neutral wire**. The current through a mains appliance alternates. That's because the mains supply provides an alternating potential difference between the two wires.

The neutral wire is **earthed** at the local substation. The potential difference between the live wire and 'earth' is usually referred to as the 'potential' or voltage of the live wire. The live wire is dangerous because its voltage repeatedly changes from + to – and back every cycle. It reaches over 300 V in each direction, as shown in Figure 1.

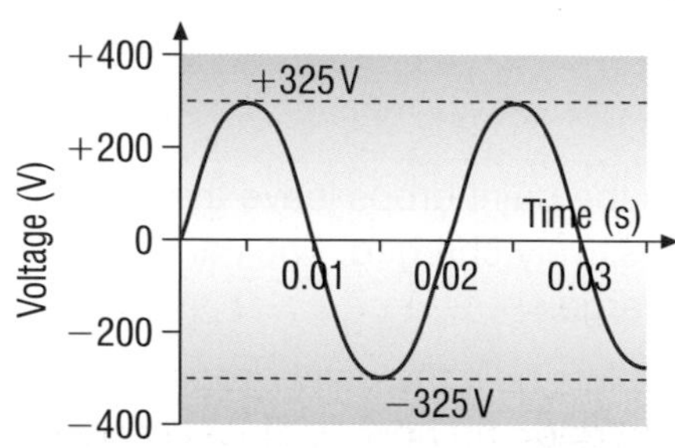

Figure 1 Mains voltage against time

Examiner's tip

Make sure that you can interpret oscilloscope traces from an ac supply.

Practical

The oscilloscope

We use an **oscilloscope** to show how an alternating potential difference changes with time.

1 Connect a signal generator to an oscilloscope, as shown in Figure 2.

- The trace on the oscilloscope screen shows electrical waves. They are caused by the potential difference increasing and decreasing continuously. Adjusting the 'Y-gain' control changes how tall the waves are. Adjusting the 'time base' control changes how many waves fit across the screen.
- The highest potential difference is reached at each peak. The **peak potential difference** (**peak voltage**) is the difference in volts between the peak and the middle level of the waves. Increasing the potential difference of the ac supply makes the waves on the screen taller.
- Increasing the frequency of the ac supply increases the number of cycles you see on the screen. So the waves on the screen get squashed together.
  - How would the trace change if the potential difference of the ac supply were reduced?

2 Connect a battery to the oscilloscope. You should see a flat line at a constant potential difference.

- What difference is made by reversing the battery?

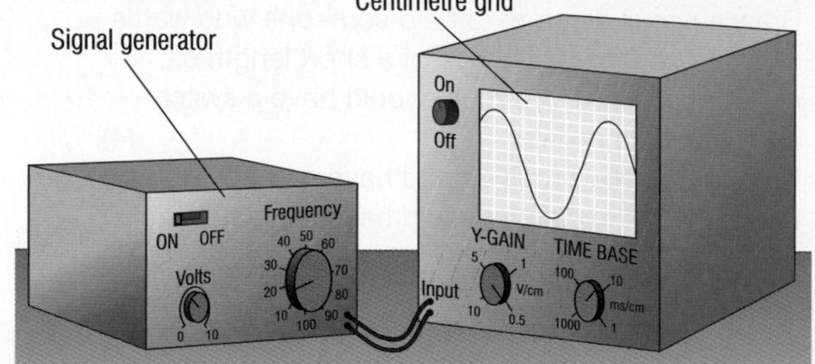

Figure 2 Using an oscilloscope

Measuring an alternating potential difference

We can use an oscilloscope to measure the peak potential difference and the frequency of a low-voltage ac supply. For example, in Figure 2:

- the peak voltage is 2.1 V if the peaks are 8.4 cm above the troughs. Each peak is 4.2 cm above the middle, which is at zero potential difference. The 'Y-gain' control at 0.5 V/cm tells us that each centimetre of height is caused by a potential difference of 0.5 V. So the peak potential difference is 2.1 V (= 0.5 V/cm × 4.2 cm).
- the frequency is 12.5 Hz if each cycle on the screen is 8 cm across. The 'time base' control at 10 milliseconds per centimetre (ms/cm) tells us that each centimetre across the screen is a time interval of 10 ms. So the time taken for one cycle is 80 ms (= 10 ms/cm × 8 cm). The frequency is therefore 12.5 Hz (= 1/80 ms or 1/0.08 s).

Note: The frequency of ac supply $= \dfrac{1}{\text{the time taken for one cycle}}$

More about mains circuits

Look at Figure 1 again. It shows how the potential of the live wire varies with time.

- The live wire alternates between +325 V and –325 V. In terms of electrical power, this is equivalent to a direct voltage of 230 V. So we say the voltage of the mains is 230 V.
- Each cycle in Figure 1 takes 0.02 seconds. The frequency of the mains supply (the number of cycles per second) is therefore 50 Hz $\left(= \dfrac{1}{0.02\ \text{seconds}}\right)$

Summary questions

1 Choose the correct potential difference from the list for each appliance **a** to **d**.

1.5 V 12 V 230 V 325 V

a a car battery
b the mains voltage
c a torch cell
d the maximum potential of the live wire.

2 In Figure 2, how would the trace on the screen change if the frequency of the ac supply was:
a increased
b reduced?

3 In Figure 2, what is the frequency if one cycle measures 4 cm across the screen for the same time base setting?

4 **a** How does an alternating current differ from a direct current?
b The figure shows a diode and a resistor in series with each other connected to an ac supply. Explain why the current in the circuit is a direct current, not an alternating current.

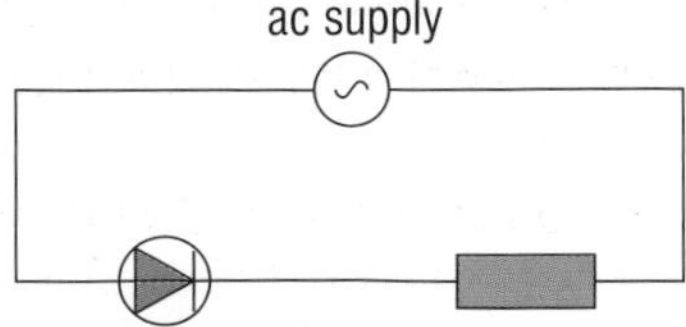

c **i** Sketch a graph to show how the current varies with time.
ii How would your graph differ if a resistor of greater resistance had been used?

Half-wave rectification

Alternating current can be converted to direct current using a diode as shown in Figure 3. The diode allows current to pass round the circuit only when the potential difference across it is in its 'forward' direction. This happens every other half-cycle of the alternating potential difference. We say the diode 'rectifies' the alternating current to direct current. You can see the 'half-wave' variation of the potential difference across the resistor in Figure 3.

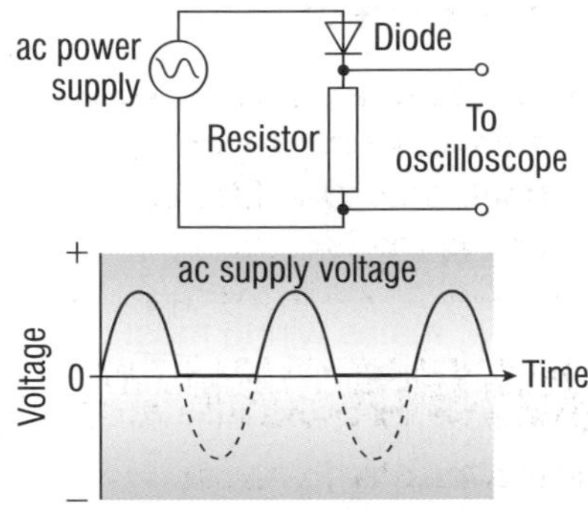

Figure 3 Half-wave rectification

Key points

- Direct current (dc) is in one direction only. Alternating current (ac) repeatedly reverses its direction.
- A mains circuit has a live wire that is alternately positive and negative every cycle and a neutral wire at zero volts.
- A diode can be used for half-wave rectification of ac.
- The peak potential difference of an ac supply is the maximum voltage measured from zero volts.
- To measure the frequency of an ac supply, we measure the time period of the waves then use the formula:

  frequency = 1 ÷ time taken for 1 cycle

P17.2 Cables and plugs

Learning objectives

After this topic, you should know:

- what the casing of a mains plug or socket is made from and why
- what is in a mains cable
- the colour of the live, neutral and earth wires
- why a 3-pin plug includes an earth pin.

Did you know ... ?

Mains electricity is dangerous. By law, mains wiring must be done by properly qualified electricians.

When you plug a heater with a metal case into a wall socket, the metal case is automatically connected to 'earth' through a wire referred to as the 'earth' wire. This stops the metal case becoming 'live' if the live wire breaks and touches the case. If the case did become live and you touched it, you would be electrocuted.

Plastic materials are good insulators. An appliance with a plastic case is doubly insulated and therefore has no earth wire connection. These appliances carry the double insulation symbol: ⧈

Plugs, sockets and cables

The outer casings of plugs, sockets and cables of all mains circuits and appliances are made of hard-wearing electrical insulators. That's because plugs, sockets and cables contain live wires. Most mains appliances are connected via a wall socket to the mains using a cable and a **three-pin plug**.

Sockets are made of stiff plastic materials with the wires inside. Figure 1 shows part of a wall socket circuit. It has an earth wire as well as a live wire and a neutral wire.

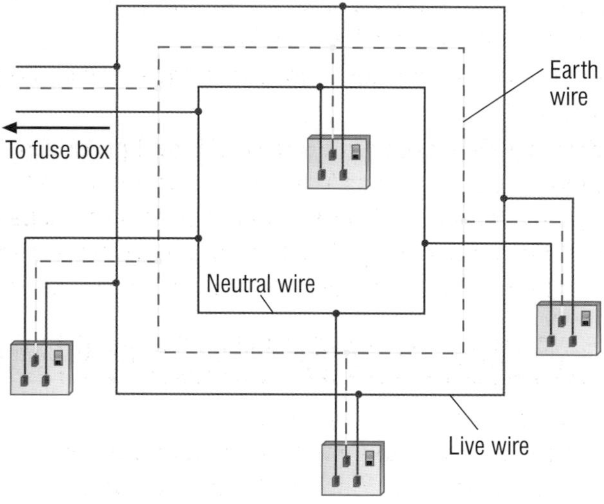

Figure 1 A wall socket circuit

- The earth wire of this circuit is connected to the ground at your home.
- The longest pin of a three-pin plug is designed to make contact with the earth wire of a wall socket circuit. So, when you plug an appliance with a metal case to a wall socket, the case is automatically earthed.

Plugs have cases made of stiff plastic materials. The live pin, the neutral pin and the earth pin stick out through the plug case. Figure 2 shows inside a **three-pin plug**.

- The pins are made of brass because brass is a good conductor and doesn't rust or oxidise. Copper isn't as hard as brass even though it conducts better.
- The case material is an electrical insulator. The inside of the case is shaped so the wires and the pins cannot touch each other when the plug is sealed.
- The plug contains a fuse between the live pin and the live wire. If too much current passes through the wire in the fuse, it melts and cuts the live wire off.

Examiner's tip

Make sure you know what's inside a three-pin plug and what colour each wire is.

- The brown wire is connected to the live pin.
- The blue wire is connected to the neutral pin.
- The green and yellow wire (of a three-core cable) is connected to the earth pin. A two-core cable doesn't have an earth wire.

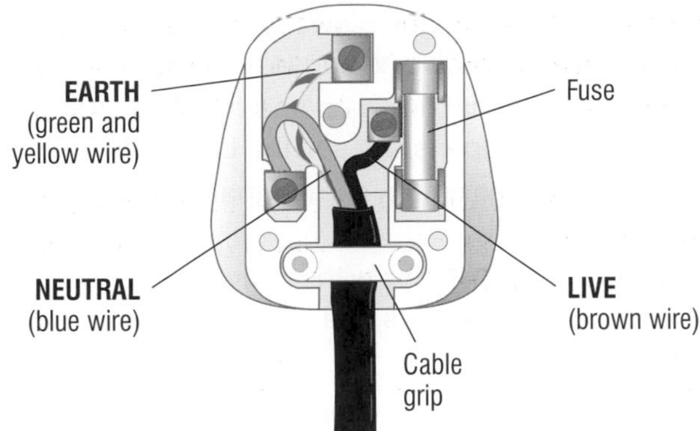

Figure 2 Inside a three-pin plug

Cables used for mains appliances (and for mains circuits) are made up of two or three insulated copper wires surrounded by an outer layer of rubber or flexible plastic material.

- Copper is used for the wires because it is a good electrical conductor and it bends easily.
- Plastic is a good electrical insulator and therefore prevents anyone touching the cable from receiving an electric shock.
- Two-core cables are used for appliances that have plastic cases (e.g. hairdryers, radios).
- Cables of different thicknesses are used for different purposes. For example, the cables joining the wall sockets in a house must be much thicker than the cables joining the light fittings. This is because more current passes along wall socket cables than along lighting circuits so the wires in them must be much thicker. This stops the heating effect of the current making the wires too hot.

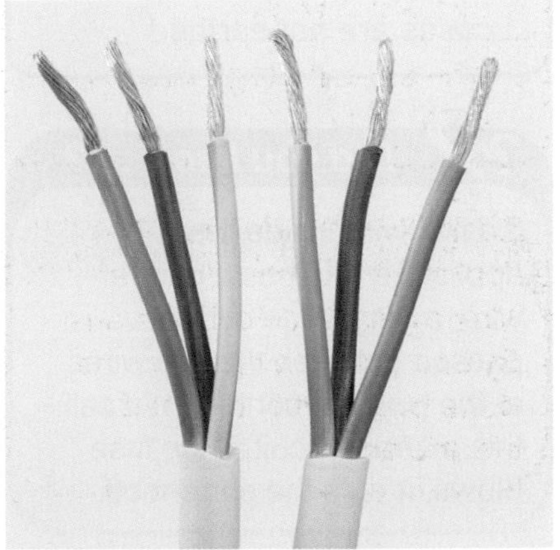

Figure 3 Mains cables

Summary questions

1 a i Which wire in a mains plug is blue?
   ii What is the colour of the earth wire in a mains cable?
  b i Why are sockets wired in parallel with each other?
   ii Why is brass, an alloy of copper and zinc, better than copper for the pins of a three-pin plug?
   iii Why are cables that are worn away or damaged dangerous?

2 a Match the list of parts 1 to 4 in a three-pin plug with the list of materials A to D.

1 cable insulation	A brass
2 case	B copper
3 pin	C rubber
4 wire	D stiff plastic

  b Explain your choice of material for each part in **a**.

3 a Why is each of the three wires in a three-core mains cable insulated?
  b How is the metal case of an electrical appliance connected to earth?
  c Why do the cables joining the wall sockets in a house need to be thicker than the cables joining the light fittings?

Key points

- **Sockets and plug cases are made of stiff plastic materials that enclose the electrical connections. Plastic is used because it is a good electrical insulator.**
- **Mains cable is made up of two or three insulated copper wires surrounded by an outer layer of flexible plastic material.**
- **In a three-pin plug or a three-core cable, the live wire is brown, the neutral wire is blue, and the earth wire is green and yellow.**
- **The earth wire is connected to the longest pin in a plug and is used to earth the metal case of a mains appliance.**

P17.3 Fuses

Learning objectives

After this topic, you should know:

- what we use a fuse for
- why a fuse is always on the 'live' side of an appliance
- what a circuit breaker is
- why appliances with plastic cases are not earthed.

Did you know ... ?

If a live wire inside the appliance touches a neutral wire, a very large current passes between the two wires at the point of contact. We call this a short circuit. If the fuse blows, it cuts the current off.

Examiner's tip

The earth wire protects the user, and the fuse protects the appliance and the wires of the circuit.

If you need to buy a fuse for a mains appliance, make sure you know the fuse rating. Otherwise, the new fuse might 'blow' as soon as it's used. Worse still, it might let too much current through and cause a fire.

- A **fuse** contains a thin wire that heats up and melts if too much current passes through it. If this happens, we say the fuse 'blows'.
- The rating of a fuse is the maximum current that can pass through it without melting the fuse wire.
- The fuse should always be in series with the live wire between the live wire and the appliance. If the fuse blows, the appliance is then cut off from the live wire.

A fuse in a mains plug must always have the correct current rating for the appliance. If the current rating is too large, the fuse will not blow when it should. The heating effect of the current could set the appliance or its connecting cable on fire. As long as the correct fuse is fitted, the connecting cable must be thick enough (so its resistance is small enough) to make the heating effect of the current in the cable insignificant. The higher the current rating of the fuse, the thicker the cable needs to be.

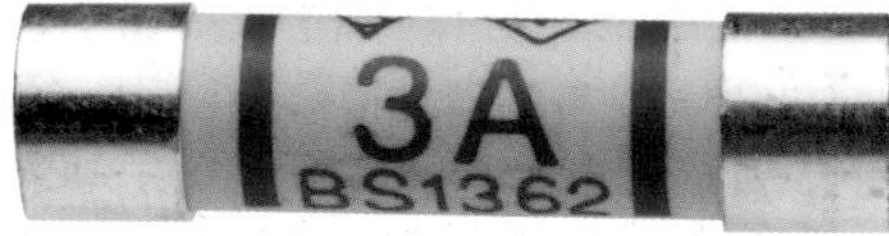

Figure 1 A cartridge fuse

The importance of earthing

Figure 2 shows why an electric heater is made safer by earthing its metal frame.

In Figure 2a, the heater works normally and its frame is earthed. The frame is safe to touch.

In Figure 2b, the earth wire is broken. The frame would become live if the live wire touched it.

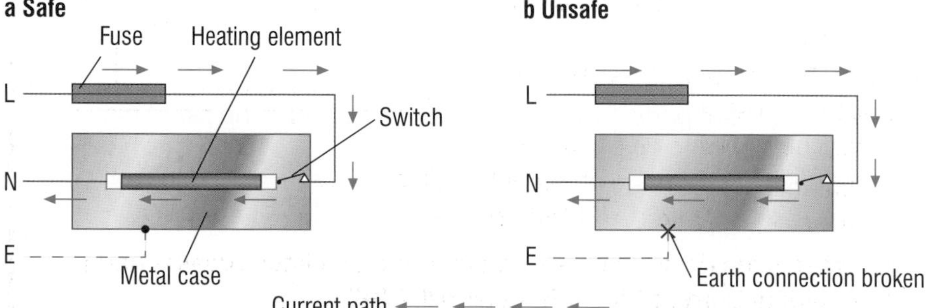

Figure 2 a and **b** Earthing an electric heater

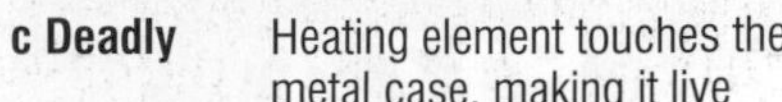

In Figure 2c, the heater element has touched the unearthed frame, so the frame is live. Anyone touching it would be electrocuted. The fuse provides no protection to the user, because a current of just 20 mA can be lethal.

In Figure 2d, the earth wire has been repaired but the heater element still touches the frame. The current is greater than in **a** or **b** because it only passes through part of the heater element. Because the frame is earthed, anyone touching it would not be electrocuted. But Figure 2d is still dangerous. This is because, although the current might not be enough to blow the fuse, it might cause the wires of the appliance to overheat.

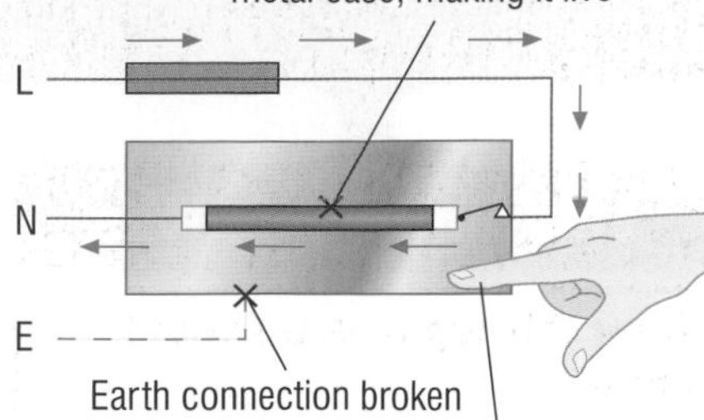
c Deadly
Heating element touches the metal case, making it live
L
N
E
Earth connection broken
Victim touches the metal case, and because the earth wire is broken, conducts current to earth

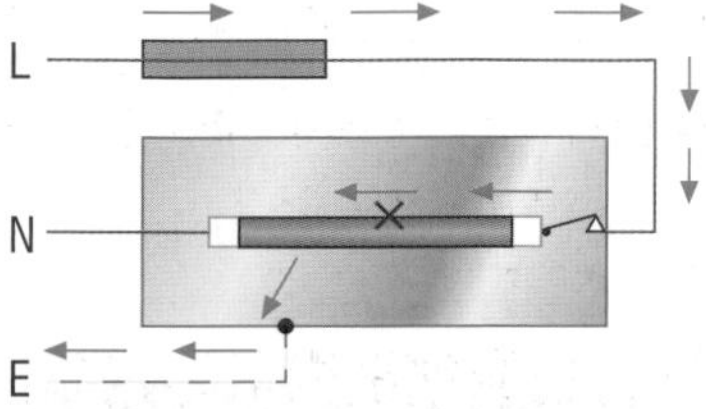
d Still dangerous as it may overheat
L
N
E

Figure 2 **c** and **d**

Circuit breakers

A **circuit breaker** is an electromagnet in series with a switch that opens (switches off or 'trips') when too much current passes through it. This can happen if there is a fault in an appliance that's in series with the circuit breaker. If the current is too large, the magnetic field of the electromagnet is strong enough to pull the switch contacts apart so that the current becomes zero. Once the switch is open, it stays open. It can then be reset after the fault that made it trip has been put right. See 18.2 'Electromagnets' for more about the circuit breaker.

Circuit breakers are often used instead of fuses. They work faster than fuses and can be reset more quickly.

The **Residual Current Circuit Breaker (RCCB)** works even faster than the ordinary circuit breaker described above. An RCCB cuts off the current in the live wire when it is different from the current in the neutral wire. The RCCB can be used where there is no earth connection. The RCCB is also more sensitive than either a fuse or an ordinary circuit breaker.

Figure 3 A circuit breaker

Summary questions

1 **a** What is the purpose of a fuse in a mains circuit?
  b Why is the fuse of an appliance always on the live side?
  c What advantages does a circuit breaker have compared with a fuse?

2 The figure opposite shows the circuit of an electric heater that has been wired incorrectly.
  a Does the heater work when the switch is closed?
  b When the switch is open, why is it dangerous to touch the element?
  c Redraw the circuit correctly wired.

L
N
E
Switch

3 **a** **i** What is the difference between an ordinary circuit breaker and a Residual Current Circuit Breaker (RCCB)?
  ii If a fault in an appliance causes the current in the neutral wire and the live wire to differ, why would an RCCB always cut the appliance off whereas an ordinary circuit breaker might not?
  b What are the advantages of an RCCB mains socket compared with an ordinary mains socket with a fuse in it?

Key points

- A fuse contains a thin wire that heats up, melts, and cuts off the current (breaks the circuit) if the current is larger than the rating of the fuse.
- A fuse is always fitted in series with the live wire. This cuts the appliance off from the live wire if the fuse blows.
- A circuit breaker is an electromagnetic switch that opens (i.e. 'trips') and breaks the circuit if too much current passes through it.
- A mains appliance with a plastic case does not need to be earthed because plastic is an insulator and cannot become live.

P17.4 Electrical power and potential difference

Learning objectives

After this topic, you should know:

- the relationship between power and energy
- how to calculate electrical power and its unit
- how to calculate, from power and potential difference, the correct current for a fuse.

When you use an electrical appliance, it transfers electrical energy into other forms of energy. The **power** of the appliance, in watts, is the energy it transfers, in joules per second. We can show this as the following equation:

$$\textbf{Power}\text{ (watts, W)} = \frac{\textbf{energy transferred}\text{ (joules, J)}}{\textbf{time}\text{ (seconds, s)}}$$

We can write the equation for the power of an appliance as:

$$P = \frac{E}{t}$$

where:

P = power in watts, W
E = energy transferred in joules, J
t = time taken in seconds, s.

Maths skills

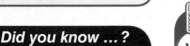

Worked example

A light bulb transfers 30 000 J of electrical energy when it is on for 300 s. Calculate its power.

Solution

$$\text{Power} = \frac{\text{energy transferred}}{\text{time}} = \frac{30\,000\,\text{J}}{300\,\text{s}} = \mathbf{100\,W}$$

Calculating power

Millions of electrons pass through the circuit of an artificial heart every second. Each electron transfers a small amount of energy to the heart from the battery. So the total energy transferred to it each second is large enough to enable the appliance to work.

For any electrical appliance:

- the current through it is the charge that flows through it each second
- the potential difference across it is the energy transferred to the appliance by each coulomb of charge that passes through it
- the power supplied to it is the energy transferred to it each second. This is the electrical energy it transfers every second.

Therefore:

The energy transfer to the appliance each second = the charge flow per second × the energy transfer per unit charge.

In other words:

power supplied (watts, W) = **current** (amperes, A) × **potential difference** (volts, V)

The equation can be written as:

$$P = I \times V$$

where:

P = electrical power in watts, W
I = current in amperes, A
V = potential difference in volts, V.

Did you know ...?

A surgeon fitting an artificial heart in a patient needs to make sure the battery will last a long time. Even so, the battery may have to be replaced every few years.

Figure 1 An artificial heart

Examiner's tip

Be careful with units. Sometimes the power is given in kilowatts, but in the equation $P = V \times I$ you need to use watts.

For example, the power supplied to:

- a 4A, 12V electric motor is 48W (= 4A × 12V)
- a 0.1A, 3V torch lamp is 0.3W (= 0.1A × 3.0V).

Rearranging the equation $P = I \times V$ gives:

potential difference, $V = \frac{P}{I}$ or

current, $I = \frac{P}{V}$

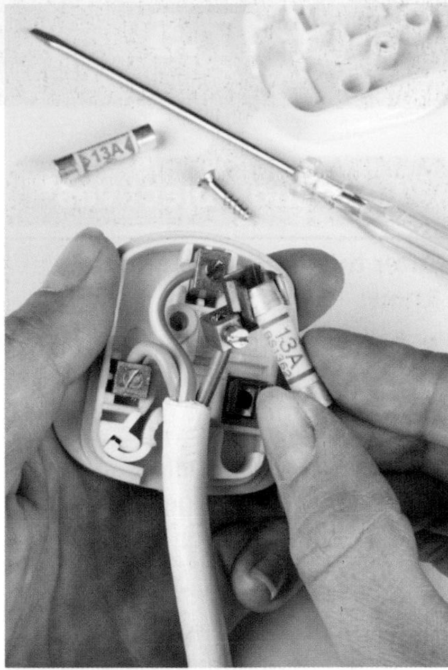

Figure 2 Changing a fuse

Choosing a fuse

Domestic appliances are often fitted with a 3A, 5A or 13A fuse. If you don't know which one to use for an appliance, you can work it out. You use the power rating of the appliance and its potential difference (voltage). The next time you change a fuse, do a quick calculation to make sure its rating is correct for the appliance (see the worked example below).

Maths skills

Worked example

a Calculate the normal current through a 500W, 230V heater.
b Which fuse, 3A, 5A or 13A, would you use for the appliance?

Solution

a Current $= \frac{500\,\text{W}}{230\,\text{V}} = \mathbf{2.2\,A}$

b You would use a **3A fuse**.

Examiner's tip

You should be able to calculate the electric current that flows through an appliance and decide on the correct fuse to use.

Summary questions

1 a The human heart transfers about 30000J of energy in about 8 hours. Calculate an estimate of the power of the human heart.
b Calculate the power supplied to a 5A, 230V electric heater.
c Why would a 13A fuse be unsuitable for a 230V, 100W table lamp?

2 a Calculate the power supplied to each of the following devices in normal use:
i a 12V, 3A light bulb
ii a 230V, 2A heater.
b Which type of fuse, 3A, 5A or 13A, would you select for:
i a 24W, 12V heater?
ii a 230V, 800W microwave oven?

3 a Why would a 3A fuse be unsuitable for a 230V, 800W microwave oven?
b The heating element of a 12V heater has a resistance of 4.0Ω. When the heating element is connected to a 12V power supply, calculate:
i the current through it
ii the electrical power supplied to it.
c A 6.0kW electric oven is connected to a fuse box by a cable of resistance 0.25Ω. When the cooker is switched on at full power, a current of 26A passes through it.
i Calculate the potential difference between the two ends of the cable and the power wasted in it because of the heating effect of the current.
ii What percentage of the power supplied to the cable is wasted?

Key points

- The power supplied to a device is the energy transferred to it each second.
- $P = \frac{E}{t}$
- Electrical power supplied (watts) = current (amperes) × potential difference (volts)
- Correct rating (in amperes) for a fuse: $= \frac{\text{electrical power (watts)}}{\text{potential difference (volts)}}$

P17.5 Electrical energy and charge

Learning objectives

After this topic, you should know:

- how to calculate the flow of electric charge from the current and time
- what energy transfers take place when charge flows through a resistor
- how the energy transferred by a flow of charge is related to potential difference
- about the electrical energy supplied by the battery in a circuit and the electrical energy transferred to the components.

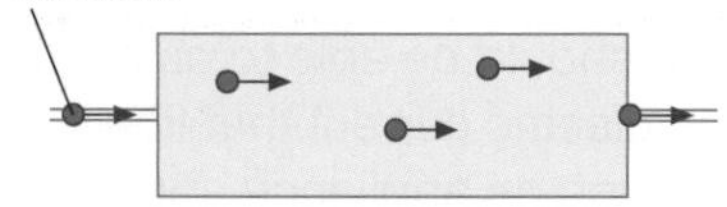

Figure 1 Charge and current

Maths skills

Worked example

Calculate the charge flow when the current is 8 A for 80 s.

Solution

Charge flow = current × time
= 8 A × 80 s
= **640 C**

links

For more information on the calculating the energy supplied to an electrical device, look at 13.2 'Specific heat capacity'.

Calculating charge

When an electrical appliance is on, electrons are forced through the appliance by the potential difference of the power supply unit. The potential difference causes a flow of charge through the appliance carried by electrons.

As explained in 16.2 'Electric circuits', the electric current is the rate of flow of charge through the appliance. The unit of charge, the **coulomb (C)**, is the amount of charge flowing through a wire or a component in 1 second when the current is 1 A.

The charge passing along a wire or through a component in a certain time depends on the current and the time.

We can calculate the charge using the equation:

charge = **current** × **time**
(coulombs) (amperes) (seconds)

The equation can be written as:

$$Q = I \times t$$

where:
Q = charge in coulombs, C
I = current in amperes, A
t = time in seconds, s.

Energy and potential difference

When a resistor is connected to a battery, electrons are made to pass through the resistor by the battery. Each electron repeatedly collides with the vibrating metal ions of the resistor, transferring energy to them. The ions of the resistor therefore gain kinetic energy and vibrate even more. The resistor becomes hotter.

When charge flows through a resistor, energy is transferred to the resistor, so the resistor becomes hotter.

The energy transferred in a certain time in a resistor depends on:

- the amount of charge that passes through it
- the potential difference across the resistor.

Because energy = power × time = potential difference × current × time, we can calculate the energy transferred using the equation:

energy transferred = **potential difference** × **charge**
(joules, J) (volts, V) (coulombs, C)

The equation can be written as:

$$E = V \times Q$$

where:
E = energy transferred in joules, J
V = potential difference in volts, V
Q = charge in coulombs, C.

Note: Substituting $Q = I \times t$ into $E = V \times Q$ gives $E = V \times I \times t$. This equation can be used to calculate the energy supplied to an electrical device in a certain time if we know the current and potential difference.

Energy transfer in a circuit

The circuit in Figure 2 shows a 12 V battery in series with a torch bulb and a variable resistor. When the voltmeter reads 10 V, the potential difference across the variable resistor is 2 V.

Each coulomb of charge:

- leaves the battery with 12 J of energy (because energy from the battery = charge × battery potential difference)
- transfers 10 J of energy to the torch bulb (because energy transfer to bulb = charge × potential difference across bulb)
- transfers 2 J of energy to the variable resistor.

The energy transferred to the bulb makes the bulb hot and emit light. The energy transferred to the variable resistor makes the resistor warm, so energy is therefore transferred to the surroundings by both the bulb and the resistor.

So, the energy from the battery is equal to the sum of the energy transferred to the bulb and to the variable resistor.

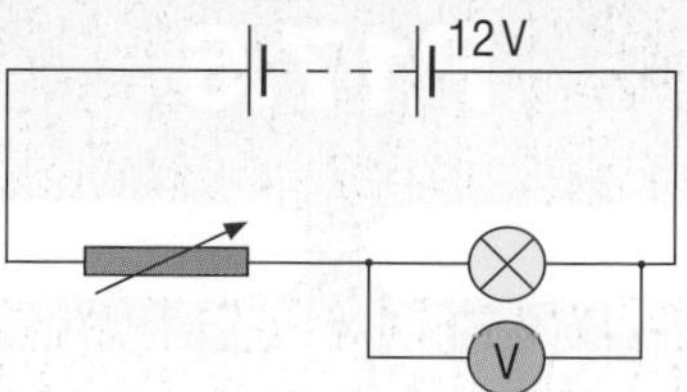

Figure 2 Energy transfer in a circuit

Maths skills

Worked example

Calculate the energy transferred in a component when the charge passing through it is 30 C and the potential difference is 20 V.

Solution

Energy transferred = 20 V × 30 C
= **600 J**

Examiner's tip

Make sure you know and can use the relationship between charge, current and time.

Summary questions

1 a Calculate the charge flowing in 50 s when the current is 3 A.
  b Calculate the energy transferred when the charge flow is 30 C and the potential difference is 4 V.
  c Calculate the energy transferred in 60 s when a current of 0.5 A passes through a 12 Ω resistor.

2 a Calculate the charge flow for:
    i a current of 4 A for 20 s
    ii a current of 0.2 A for 60 minutes.
  b Calculate the energy transfer:
    i for a charge flow of 20 C when the potential difference is 6.0 V
    ii for a current of 3 A that passes through a resistor for 20 s, when the potential difference is 5 V.
  c In Figure 2, an ammeter is connected in the circuit in series with the battery. The variable resistor is then adjusted until the ammeter reading is 2.5 A. The voltmeter reading is then 8.0 V.
    i Calculate the charge that passes through the battery in 60 s.
    ii Calculate the energy transferred to or from each coulomb of charge when it passes through each component including the battery.
    iii Show that the energy transferred from the battery in 60 s is equal to sum of the energy transferred to the lamp and to the variable resistor in this time.

3 In the figure opposite, a 4.0 Ω resistor and an 8.0 Ω resistor in series with each other are connected to a 6.0 V battery.
Calculate:
  a the resistance of the two resistors in series
  b the current through the resistors
  c the charge flow through each resistor in 60 seconds
  d the potential difference across each resistor
  e the energy transferred to each resistor in 60 seconds
  f the energy supplied by the battery in 60 seconds.

6.0 V
4.0 Ω 8.0 Ω

Key points

- Charge (coulombs) = current (amperes) × time (seconds).
- When an electrical charge flows through a resistor, energy transferred to the resistor makes it hot.
- Energy transferred (joules) = potential difference (volts) × charge flow (coulombs).
- When charge flows round a circuit for a certain time, the electrical energy supplied by the battery is equal to the electrical energy transferred to all the components in the circuit.

P17.6 Using electrical energy

Learning objectives

After this topic, you should know:

- what a kilowatt-hour is
- how to work out the energy used by a mains appliance
- how to work out the cost of mains electricity.

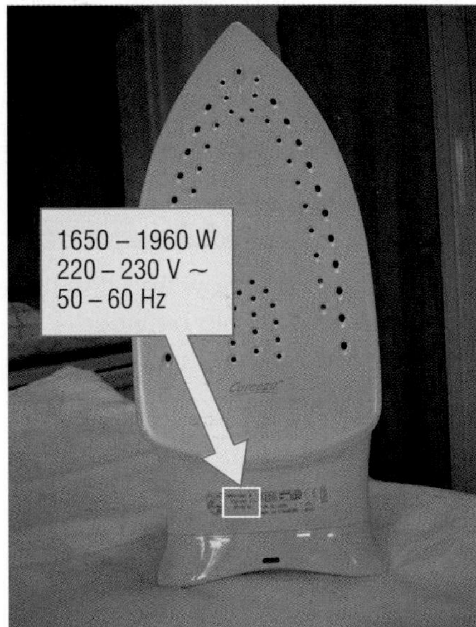

Figure 1 Mains power

When you use an electric heater, how much electrical energy is transferred from the mains? You can work this out if you know its power and how long you use it for.

For any appliance, the energy supplied to it depends on:

- how long it is switched on
- the power supplied to it.

A 1 kilowatt heater uses the same amount of electrical energy in 1 hour as a 2 kilowatt heater would use in half an hour. For ease, we say that:

the energy supplied to a 1 kW appliance in 1 hour is 1 **kilowatt-hour** (kWh).

We use the kilowatt-hour as the unit of energy supplied by mains electricity. You can use this equation to work out the energy, in kilowatt-hours, transferred by a mains appliance in a certain time:

$$\boldsymbol{E = P \times t}$$

where:
E = energy transferred from the mains in kilowatt-hours, kWh
P = power in kilowatts, kW
t = time taken for the energy to be transferred in hours, h.

Maths skills

Worked example

You have used this equation before in 5.2 'Power' to calculate the power of an appliance. It is the same equation, just rearranged and with different units.

$$E = P \times t$$

Divide both sides by t: $\frac{E}{t} = P$

This is the same as: $P = \frac{E}{t}$

For example:

- a 1 kW heater switched on for 1 hour uses 1 kWh of electrical energy (= 1 kW × 1 hour)
- a 1 kW heater switched on for 10 hours uses 10 kWh of electrical energy (= 10 kW × 1 hour)
- a 0.5 kW or 500 W heater switched on for 6 hours uses 3 kWh of electrical energy (= 0.5 kW × 6 hours).

If we want to calculate the energy transferred in joules, we can use the same equation:

$$\boldsymbol{E = P \times t}$$

where:
E = energy transferred from the mains in *joules*, J
P =power in *watts*, W
t = time taken for the energy to be transferred in *seconds*, s.

Did you know ... ?

One kilowatt-hour is the amount of electrical energy supplied to a 1 kilowatt appliance in 1 hour.

So **1 kilowatt-hour** = 1000 joules per second × 60 × 60 seconds
= 3 600 000 J
= **3.6 million joules**.

Note: In your exam, you will not need to convert between kilowatt-hours and joules.

Examiner's tip

Remember that a kilowatt-hour is a unit of energy and is used when calculating the cost of electrical energy. It is actually 3.6 million joules BUT you do not need to know that!

Paying for electrical energy

The **electricity meter** in your home measures how much electrical energy your family uses. It records the total energy supplied, no matter how many appliances you all use. It gives us a reading of the number of kilowatt-hours (kWh) of energy supplied by the mains.

In most houses, somebody reads the meter every three months. Look at the electricity bill in Figure 3.

The difference between the two readings is the number of kilowatt-hours supplied since the last bill.

We use the kilowatt-hour to work out the cost of electricity. For example, a cost of 12.79p per kWh means that each kilowatt-hour of electrical energy costs 12.79p. Therefore:

total cost = number of kWh used × cost per kWh

Figure 2 An electricity meter

NELEB

L. Jones
26 Homewood Road
Otwood M51 9YZ

Meter readings present	Meter readings previous	units	pence per unit	amount	VAT %
31534	30092	1442	12.79	184.43	Zero
Standing charge					27.30
TOTAL NOW DUE					211.73
PERIOD ENDED					31.03.12

Figure 3 Checking your bill

Summary questions

1 a How many kWh of energy are used by a 100 W lamp in 24 hours?
  b How many joules of energy are used by a 5 W torch lamp in 50 minutes (3000 seconds)?
  c An electricity bill showed that 1270 kWh of electricity was used. Work out the cost of this amount of electricity at 14p per kWh.

2 a Work out the number of kWh transferred in each case below.
    i A 3 kilowatt electric kettle is used six times for 5 minutes each time.
    ii A 1000 watt microwave oven is used for 30 minutes.
    iii A 100 watt electric light is used for 8 hours.
  b Calculate the total cost of the electricity used in part **a** if the cost of electricity is 12p per kWh.

3 a An electric heater is left on for 3 hours. During this time it uses 12 kWh of electrical energy.
    i What is the power of the heater?
    ii How many joules are supplied?
  b The mains power supply of a computer provides a current of 1.7 A at 230 V.
    i Calculate the power supplied to the computer.
    ii In one month, the computer is used for 130 hours. How many kilowatt-hours of electrical energy is supplied to the computer in this time?
    iii Calculate the cost of this electrical energy if the unit cost of electricity is 12p per kWh.

Key points

- **The kilowatt-hour is the energy supplied to a 1 kW appliance in 1 hour.**
- $E = P \times t$
- **Total cost of energy used = number of kWh used × cost per kWh**

P17.7 Electrical issues

Learning objectives

After this topic, you should know:

- why electrical faults are dangerous
- how to prevent electrical faults
- when choosing an electrical appliance, what factors in addition to cost to consider
- how different forms of lighting compare in terms of cost and energy efficiency.

An electrical fault is dangerous. It could give someone a nasty shock or even electrocute them, resulting in death. Also, a fault can cause a fire. This happens when too much current passes through a wire or an appliance and heats it up.

Fault prevention

Electrical faults can happen if sockets, plugs, cables or appliances are damaged. Users need to check for loose fittings, cracked plugs and sockets and worn cables. Any of these damaged items need to be repaired or replaced by a qualified electrician.

- If a fuse blows or a circuit breaker trips when a mains appliance is in use, switch the appliance off. Then don't use it until it has been checked by a qualified electrician.
- If an appliance (or its cable or plug or socket) overheats and/or you get a distinctive burning smell from it, switch it off. Again, don't use it until it has been checked.

Too many appliances connected to a socket may cause the socket to overheat. If this happens, switch the appliances and the socket off and disconnect the appliances from the socket.

Smoke alarms and infrared sensors connected to an alarm system are activated if a fire breaks out. An electrical fault could cause an appliance or a cable to become hot and could set fire to curtains or other material in a room. Smoke alarms and sensors should be checked regularly to make sure they work properly.

An electrician selecting a cable for an appliance needs to use:

- a two-core cable if the appliance is 'double-insulated' and no Earth wire is needed
- a three-core cable if an Earth wire is needed because the appliance has a metal case
- a cable with conductors of suitable thickness so the heating effect of the current in the cable is insignificant.

Examiner's tip

You could be asked to compare different types of lamp, so remember that low-power lamps may mean that the lamps are very efficient – they give the same amount of light energy for a lower input of electrical energy.

New bulbs for old

When choosing an electrical appliance, most people compare several different appliances. The cost of the appliance is just one factor that may need to be considered. Other factors might include the power of the appliance and its efficiency.

A filament bulb is very inefficient. The energy from the hot bulb gradually makes the plastic parts of the bulb socket brittle and they crack. If you want to replace a bulb, a visit to an electrical shop can present you with a bewildering range of bulbs.

Low-energy bulbs are much more efficient as they don't become hot like filament bulbs do. Different types of low-energy bulb are now available:

- **Low-energy compact fluorescent lamp bulbs (CFLs)** are now used for room lighting instead of filament bulbs.
- **Low-energy light-emitting diodes (LEDs)** used for spotlights are usually called high-power LEDs. They operate at low voltage and low power. They are much more efficient than filament bulbs or halogen bulbs and they last much longer.

Did you know ...?

What kills you – current or voltage? Mains electricity is dangerous. A current of no more than about 0.03 A through your body would give you a severe shock and might even kill you. Your body has a resistance of about 1000 Ω including contact resistance at the skin. If your hands get wet, your resistance is lowered.

Table 1 gives more information about these different bulbs:

Table 1

Type	Power	Efficiency	Lifetime in hours	Cost of bulb	Typical use
Filament bulb	100 W	20%	1000	50p	room lighting
Halogen bulb	100 W	25%	2500	£2.00	spotlight
Low-energy compact fluorescent bulb (CFL)	25 W	80%	15 000	£2.50	room lighting
Low-energy light-emitting diode (LED)	2 W	90%	30 000	£7.00	spotlight

Summary questions

1 An 'RCCB' socket should be used for mains appliances such as lawnmowers where there is a possible hazard when the appliance is used. Such a socket contains a residual current circuit breaker instead of a fuse. This type of circuit breaker switches the current off if the live current and the neutral current differ by more than 30 mA. This can happen, for example, if the blades of a lawnmower cut into the cable. Create a table to show a possible 'electrical' hazard for each of these appliances: lawnmower, electric drill, electric saw, hairdryer, vacuum cleaner. The first entry has been done for you.

Appliance	Hazard
Lawnmower	The blades might cut the cable.

2 a i If a mains appliance causes a fuse to melt, why is it a mistake to replace the fuse straight away?

ii Should the cable of an electric iron be a two-core or a three-core cable?

b A householder wants to replace a 100 W room light with a row of low-energy LEDs with the same light output. Use the information in Table 1 to answer the following questions.

i How many times would the filament bulb need to be replaced in the lifetime of an LED?

ii How many LEDs would be needed to give the same light output as a 100 W filament bulb?

iii The householder reckons the cost of the electricity for each LED at 10p per kWh over its lifetime of 30 000 hours would be £6. Show that the cost of the electricity for a 100 W bulb over this time would be £300.

iv Use your answers above to calculate how much the householder would save by replacing the filament bulb with LEDs.

3 An electrician needs to fit a mains cable and a mains plug to connect a 230 V, 1100 W microwave oven to a mains socket.

a Calculate the current that passes through the appliance when it is switched on at full power.

b The appliance has a metal case. Explain why a three-core cable rather than a two-core cable is necessary.

c i Which type of fuse, 3 A, 5 A or 13 A, should be fitted in the mains plug?

ii Why is it dangerous to use a fuse with a higher current rating?

Did you know … ?

All new appliances such as washing machines and freezers sold in the EU are labelled clearly with an efficiency rating. The rating is from A (very efficient) to G (lowest efficiency). Light bulbs are also labelled in this way on the packaging.

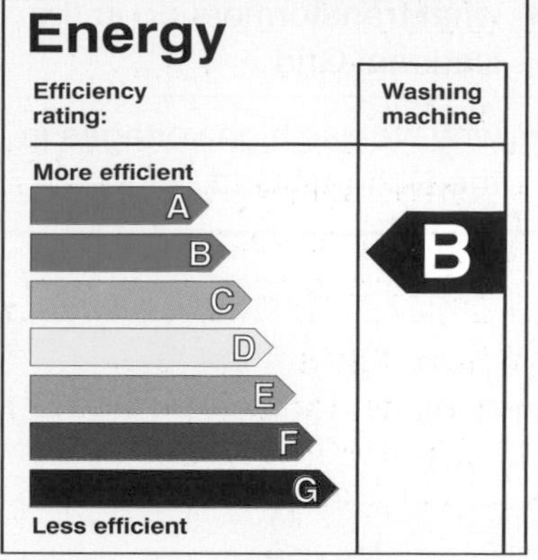

Figure 2 Efficiency measures

Key points

- Electrical faults are dangerous because they can cause electric shocks and fires.
- Never touch a mains appliance (or plug or socket) with wet hands. Never touch a bare wire or a terminal at a potential of more than 30 V.
- Check cables, plugs and sockets for damage regularly. Check smoke alarms and infrared sensors regularly.
- When choosing an electrical appliance, the power and efficiency rating of the appliance need to be considered.
- Filament bulbs and halogen bulbs are much less efficient than low-energy bulbs such as CFLs.

P17.8 The National Grid

Learning objectives

After this topic, you should know:

- what the National Grid is
- what transformers do in the National Grid
- why we use high voltages in the National Grid.

Your electricity supply at home reaches you through the **National Grid**. This is a network of cables that distributes electricity from power stations to homes and other buildings. The network also contains **transformers**. Step-up transformers are used at power stations. Step-down transformers are used at substations near homes.

The National Grid's voltage is 132 000 V or more. This is because for a given power, increasing the voltage:

reduces the current needed and therefore decreases the power loss, making the system more efficient.

Power stations produce electricity at a voltage of 25 000 V.

- We use **step-up transformers** to 'step' this voltage up to the grid voltage.
- We use **step-down transformers** at local substations to 'step' the grid voltage down to 230 V for use in homes and offices.

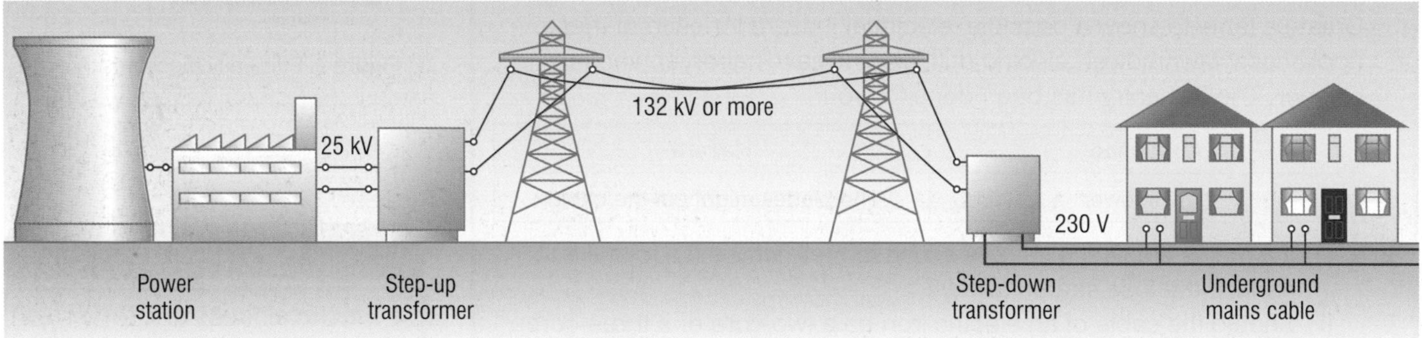

Figure 1 The National Grid

Figure 2 Electricity pylons carry the high-voltage cables of the National Grid

Demonstration

Modelling the National Grid

Watch a demonstration of the effect of a transformer using this apparatus.

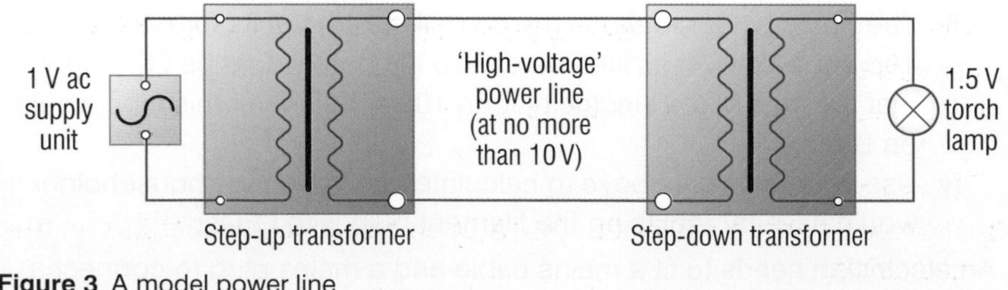

Figure 3 A model power line

Examiner's tip

Remember that step-up transformers are used at power stations and step-down transformers are used at substations near homes.

Did you know ...?

The National Grid was set up in 1926. The UK government decided electricity would be supplied to homes at 240 V. This was lowered to 230 V in 1994.

Power and the grid voltage

The electrical power supplied to any appliance depends on the appliance's current and its voltage. To supply a certain amount of power, we can lower the current if we raise the voltage. This is what a step-up transformer does in the grid system.

A step-up transformer raises the voltage, so less current is needed to transfer the same amount of power. A lower current passes through the grid cables. So, energy losses due to the heating effect of the current are reduced to almost zero. But we need to lower the voltage at the end of the grid cables before we can use mains electricity at home.

Underground or overhead?

Lots of people object to electricity pylons. They say they spoil the landscape or they affect their health. Electric currents produce electric and magnetic fields that might affect people.

So why don't we bury all cables underground?

Underground cables would be much more expensive, much more difficult to repair, and difficult to bury where they cross canals, rivers and roads.

What's more, overhead cables are high above the ground. Underground cables could affect people more because the cables wouldn't be very deep.

Summary questions

1 a What type of transformer, step-up or step-down, is connected between:
   - i a power station and the grid system?
   - ii the mains supply to a house and the grid system?

   b What difference would it make if power stations were connected directly to the grid system without using transformers?

2 a Why is electrical energy transferred through the National Grid at a much higher voltage than the voltage generated in a power station?

   b Why are transformers needed to connect local substations to the National Grid?

3 A step-up transformer connects a power station to the cables of the National Grid.

   a What does the transformer do to:
   - i the voltage?
   - ii the current?

   b The transformer supplies 25 000 kW of electrical power at 132 kV to the grid cables.
   - i Calculate the current supplied by the transformer.
   - ii The current supplied by the transformer passes through a coil in the transformer that has a resistance of 0.28 Ω. Calculate the power wasted in this coil.

   c Why are step-down transformers used between the end of the grid cables and the mains cables that supply mains electricity to our homes?

Examiner's tip

You need to remember that:
- step-up transformers raise the voltage and lower the current
- step-down transformers lower the voltage and raise the current.

Did you know ... ?

The insulators used on electricity pylons need to be very effective or else the electricity would short-circuit to the ground. In winter, ice on the cables can cause them to snap. Teams of electrical engineers are always on standby to deal with sudden emergencies.

Figure 4 Engineers at work on the grid

Key points

- **The National Grid is a network of cables and transformers that distributes electricity to our homes from distant power stations and renewable energy generators.**
- **Step-up transformers are used to raise power station voltages to the grid voltage. Step-down transformers are used to lower the grid voltage for use in our homes.**
- **A high grid voltage reduces the current needed, therefore reducing energy loss and making the system more efficient.**

Summary questions

1 a In a mains circuit, which wire:
  i is earthed at the local substation?
  ii alternates in potential?

b An oscilloscope is used to display the potential difference of an alternating voltage supply unit. State and explain how the trace would change if:
  i the potential difference is increased
  ii the frequency is increased.

2 a Explain why a mains appliance with a metal case is unsafe if the case is not earthed.

b State the colour of each wire in a mains circuit.

3 a Copy and complete the following sentences:
  i Wall sockets are connected in .... with each other.
  ii A fuse in a mains plug is in .... with the appliance and cuts off the .... wire if too much current passes through the appliance.

b i What is the main difference between a fuse and a circuit breaker?
  ii Give two reasons why a circuit breaker is safer than a fuse.

4 a i Calculate the current in a 230 V, 2.5 kW electric kettle.
  ii Which fuse, 3 A, 5 A or 13 A, would you fit in the kettle plug?
  iii If the kettle is used on average six times a day for 5 minutes each time, calculate the energy in kWh it uses in 28 days.

b A student uses a 4.0 A, 230 V microwave oven for 10 minutes every day and a 2500 W electric kettle three times a day for 4 minutes each time.
  i Which appliance uses more energy in one day?
  ii Calculate the total cost of using these appliances for 7 days if the unit cost of electricity is 14p per kW.

5 A 5 Ω resistor is in series with a bulb, a switch and a 12 V battery.

a Draw the circuit diagram.

b When the switch is closed for 60 seconds, a direct current of 0.6 A passes through the resistor. Calculate:
  i the energy supplied by the battery
  ii the energy transferred to the resistor
  iii the energy transferred to the bulb.

c The bulb is replaced by a 25 Ω resistor.
  i Calculate the total resistance of the two resistors.
  ii Calculate the battery current.
  iii Calculate the power supplied by the battery and the power delivered to each resistor.

6 A 12 V, 36 W bulb is connected to a 12 V supply.

a Calculate:
  i the current through the bulb
  ii the charge flow through the bulb in 200 s.

b i Show that 7200 J of electrical energy is delivered to the bulb in 200 s.
  ii Calculate the energy delivered to the bulb by each coulomb of charge that passes through it.

c A second 12 V, 36 W bulb is connected to the power supply in parallel with the first bulb.
  i Calculate the current through each bulb and through the battery.
  ii Show that the energy delivered per second to the two bulbs is equal to the energy supplied per second by the battery.

7 An electrician has the job of connecting a 6.6 kW electric oven to the 230 V mains supply in a house.

a Calculate the current needed to supply 6.6 kW of electrical power at 230 V.

b The table below shows the maximum current that can pass safely through five different mains cables. For each cable the cross-sectional area of each conductor is given in square millimetres (mm^2).

	Cross-sectional area of conductor (mm^2)	Maximum safe current (A)
A	1.0	14
B	1.5	18
C	2.5	28
D	4.0	36
E	6.0	46

  i To connect the oven to the mains supply, which cable should the electrician choose? Give a reason for your answer.
  ii State and explain what would happen if she chose a cable with thinner conductors.

8 a i What are transformers used for in the National Grid?
  ii What type of transformer is connected between the generators in the power station and the cables of the grid system?

b i What can you say about the voltage of the cables in the grid system compared with the voltages at the power station generator and at the mains cables into your home?
  ii What can you say about the current through the grid cables compared with the current from the power station generator?
  iii What is the reason for making the grid voltage different from the generator voltage?

AQA Examination-style questions

1 A hair dryer has a label on it.

Electrical supply	230V	50Hz
Maximum power	1200W	

a What can you deduce from the label? (5)

b The diagrams show the readings on a domestic electricity meter in February and May.

Electricity costs 15p per kilowatt-hour.

i Calculate the cost of the electricity used between the two meter readings. (3)

ii A 2000 W electric fire is used for 3 hours. Calculate the cost of using the electric fire for 3 hours. (3)

c A 60 W lamp is connected to the 230 V mains supply.

i Calculate the current flowing through the lamp. (2)

ii Calculate the amount of electrical charge that flows through the lamp in 30 hours. (3)

2 a The diagram shows a mains plug. There are several faults.

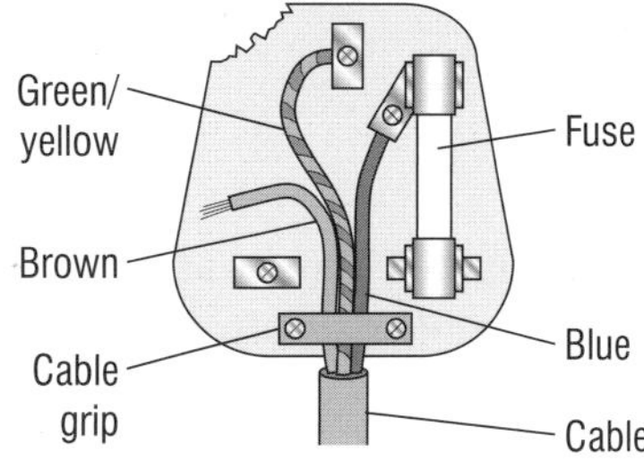

Describe the faults that make this plug dangerous to use. (3)

b If your hands are wet it is dangerous to plug in an electrical appliance.

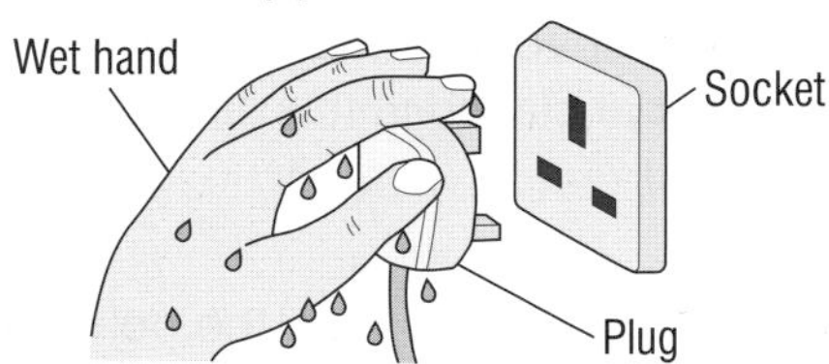

Why is this dangerous? (2)

c The diagrams show an electric kettle and an electric hair dryer.

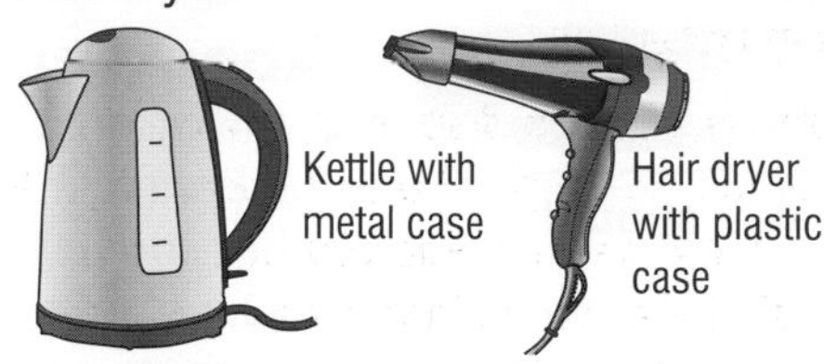

The kettle is earthed, but the hair dryer is not earthed. Explain why it is not necessary to earth the hair dryer and how earthing the kettle protects the user.

(QWC) (6)

3 The diagrams give information about four types of electric lamp.

Each lamp produces the same amount of light energy in the same time.

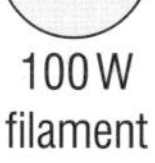

100 W filament lamp

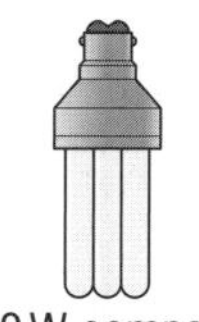

20 W compact fluorescent lamp (CFL)

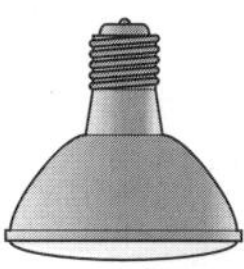

10 W LED spotlight

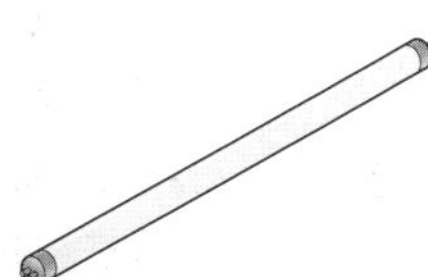

15 W fluorescent tube

a Which lamp is most efficient? (1)

b Which lamp would become hottest when it is working? (1)

c Which lamp would be the cheapest to run for 1000 hours? (1)

4 A power supply is connected to a cathode ray oscilloscope.

The trace on the oscilloscope screen is shown below.

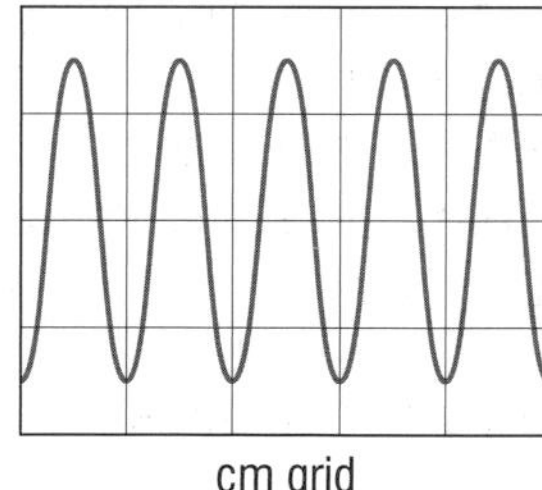

cm grid

The oscilloscope settings are:

X-axis 0.02 s per cm

Y-axis 2 V per cm

What is the:

a frequency of the supply? (3)

b peak potential difference? (2)

P18.1 Magnetic fields

Learning objectives

After this topic, you should know:

- the force rule for two magnetic poles near each other
- the pattern of magnetic field lines round a bar magnet
- what a uniform magnetic field is.

Figure 1 Using a plotting compass

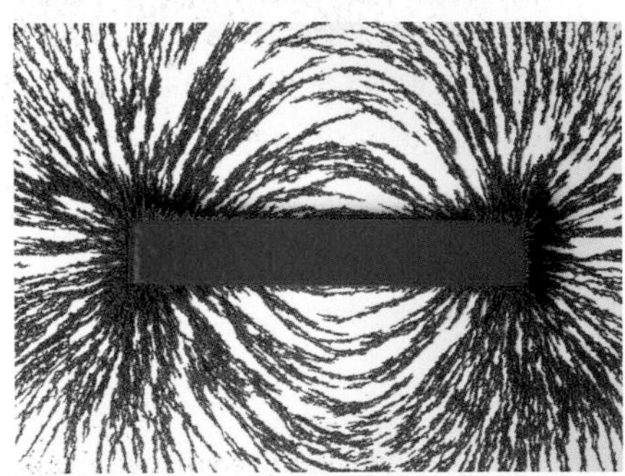

a

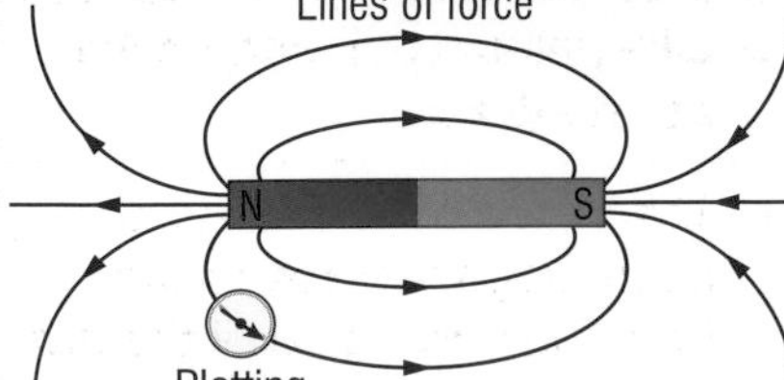

b

Figure 3 The magnetic field of a bar magnet **a** Using iron filings **b** A plotting compass

About magnets

A magnetic compass is a tiny magnetic needle pivoted at its centre. Because of the Earth's magnetic field, one end of the compass always points north and the other south. The end of the plotting compass that points north is the 'north-seeking' pole (usually called the magnet's **north pole** (N)), and the other end is the 'south-seeking' pole (the magnet's **south pole** (S)).

Practical

Investigating bar magnets

1 Suspend a bar magnet as shown in Figure 2 to check which end is its N-pole and which is its S-pole. Make sure the bar magnet is suspended horizontally and no other magnets are nearby. If the ends are unmarked, label the N-pole 'N' and the S-pole 'S'.

2 Hold the N-pole of a second bar magnet near the suspended bar magnet. You should find it attracts the S-pole of the suspended bar magnet and repels the N-pole.

3 Repeat the above test by holding the S-pole of the second bar magnet near the suspended bar magnet. This time, you should find it attracts the N-pole of the suspended bar magnet and repels its S-pole.

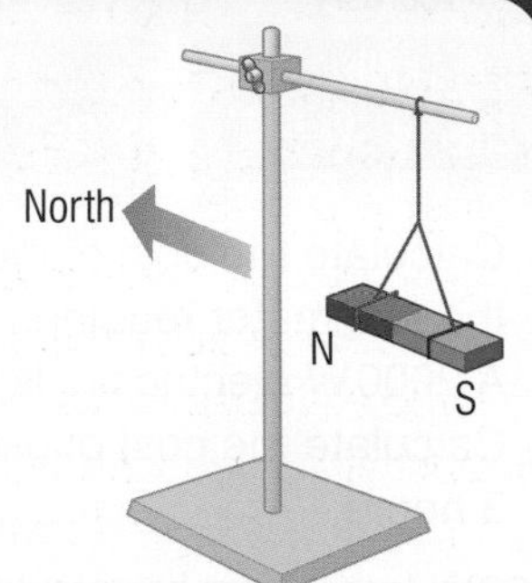

Figure 2 Checking the poles of a bar magnet

The tests above show the general rule that:

like poles repel; unlike poles attract.

Magnetic materials

Any iron or steel object can be magnetised (or demagnetised if it's already magnetised). Steel is called a ferrous material because it contains iron. Any ferrous material can be magnetised or demagnetised. Only a few non-ferrous materials can be magnetised and demagnetised. Cobalt and nickel are two examples. Oxides of these metals are used to make ceramic magnets and to coat magnetic tapes and discs.

Magnetic fields

If a sheet of paper is placed over a bar magnet and iron filings are sprinkled onto the paper, the filings form a pattern of lines. The space round the magnet is called a **magnetic field**. Any other magnetic material placed in this space experiences a force caused by the first magnet.

In Figure 3:

- the iron filings form lines as shown in Figure 3a that end at or near the poles of the magnet. These lines are lines of force also called **magnetic field lines**.
- a plotting compass placed in the magnetic field would align itself along a line of force, pointing in a direction away from the N-pole of the magnet and towards the magnet's S-pole, as shown in Figure 3b. For this reason, the direction of a line of force is always from the north pole of the magnet to the south pole.

The further the plotting compass is from the magnet, the less effect the magnet has on the plotting compass. This is because the greater the distance from the magnet, the weaker the magnetic field.

Practical

Plotting a magnetic field

Mark a dot near the north pole of the bar magnet. Place the tail of the compass needle above the dot and mark a second dot at the tip of the needle. Move the compass so the tail of the needle is above the second dot and mark a new dot at the tip. Figure 4 shows the idea. Repeat the procedure until the compass reaches the S-pole of the magnet. Draw a line through the dots and mark direction from the N-pole to the S-pole. Repeat the procedure for further lines.

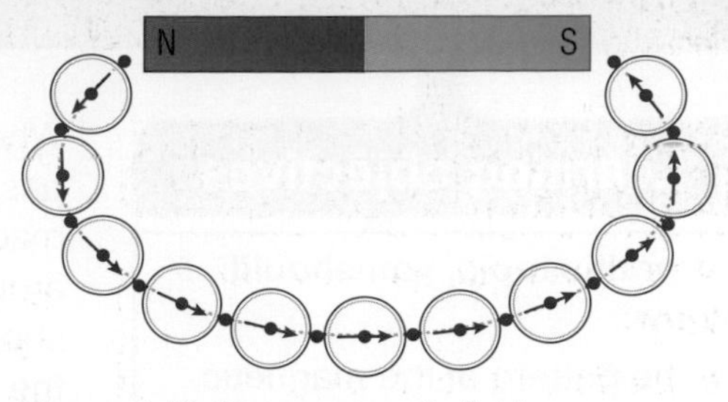

Figure 4 Plotting a magnetic field

More magnetic field patterns

Figure 5 shows two bar magnets placed end-to-end.

a **With unlike poles facing each other**, as in Figure 5a, the field lines are from the N-pole of one magnet to the S-pole of the other magnet. The field between the poles is **uniform** because the lines are parallel or almost parallel to each other here. A plotting compass moved directly from the N-pole across to the S-pole will always point to the S-pole.

b **With like poles facing each other**, as in Figure 5b, the field lines between the magnets bend away from the midpoint. A plotting compass moved directly from the one pole across to the other pole will suddenly reverse its direction as it crosses the midpoint.

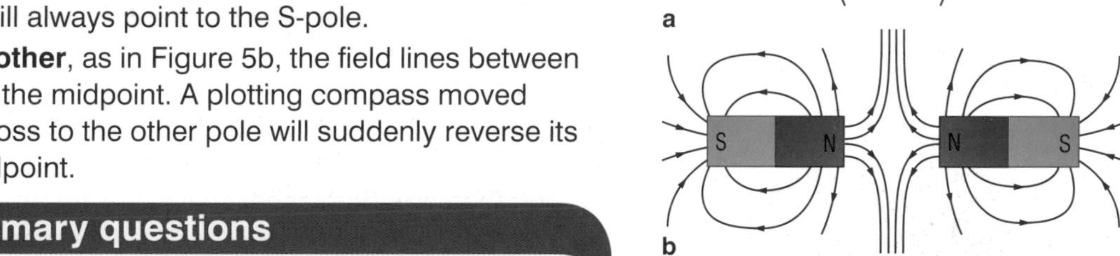

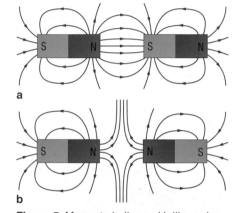

Figure 5 Magnets in line. **a** Unlike poles facing each other. **b** Like poles facing each other.

Summary questions

1 A bar magnet XY is freely suspended in a horizontal position so that end X points north and end Y points south.

a State the magnetic polarity of:

i end X **ii** end Y.

b End P of a second bar magnet PQ placed near end X of bar magnet XY repels end X and attracts end Y. State the magnetic polarity of end P and explain this observation.

2 The tip of an iron nail is held in turn near each end of a plotting compass needle. State whether the tip of the nail is a N-pole, a S-pole or is unmagnetised in each of the following possible observations:

a the N-pole of the compass needle is repelled by the tip of the nail and the S-pole is attracted by it

b the N-pole of the compass needle is attracted by the tip of the nail and the S-pole is repelled by it

c the N-pole of the plotting compass is attracted by the tip of the nail and the S-pole is also attracted by it.

3 **a** Sketch the pattern of the magnetic field lines around a bar magnet. On your diagram, label the north and south pole of the bar magnet and indicate the direction of the field lines.

b The figure shows a bar magnet XY and a plotting compass near end Y of the bar magnet. The needle of the plotting compass points towards end Y of the bar magnet.

X Y

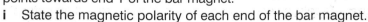

i State the magnetic polarity of each end of the bar magnet.

ii If the bar magnet was rotated gradually about its centre through 180°, describe and explain the effect on the direction of the plotting compass needle.

Examiner's tip

Remember that like magnetic poles repel and unlike poles attract.

Key points

- **Like poles repel, and unlike poles attract.**
- **The magnetic field lines of a bar magnet curve round from the north pole of the bar magnet to the south pole.**
- **In a uniform field the lines of a magnetic field are parallel to each other.**

P18.2 Electromagnets

Learning objectives

After this topic, you should know:

- the pattern of the magnetic field around a wire carrying a current
- how the strength and direction of this field varies with position
- how an electromagnet works
- some applications of electromagnets.

When an electric current passes along a wire, a magnetic field is set up around the wire. Figure 1 shows how the pattern of the magnetic field around a long straight wire can be seen using iron filings or a plotting compass. The lines of force caused by a straight current-carrying wire are a series of circles, which are centred on the wire. The field is strongest near the wire. The direction of the field is reversed if the direction of the current is reversed. We can use the corkscrew rule shown in Figure 1 to remember the direction of the magnetic field for each direction of the current.

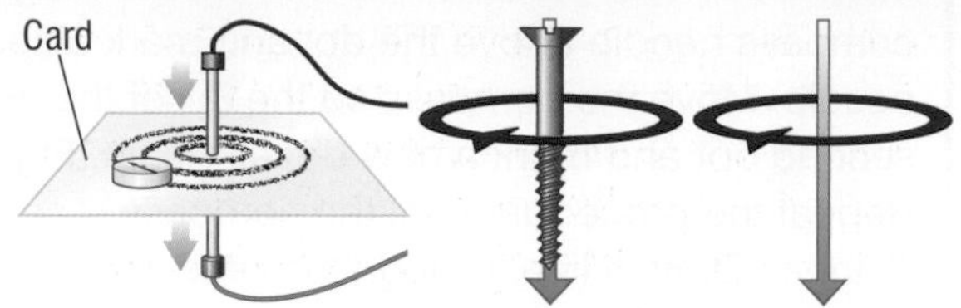

Figure 1 The magnetic field near a long straight wire

Plotting the magnetic field near a current-carrying wire

Set up the arrangement as shown in Figure 2. To eliminate magnetism caused by nearby iron objects, use a wooden stand (or any non-ferrous object) to support the cardboard sheet so it is horizontal. Use the plotting compass to plot magnetic field lines near the wire as explained in 18.1. You should find that the field lines are concentric circles (in the plane of the card) centred on and perpendicular to the wire.

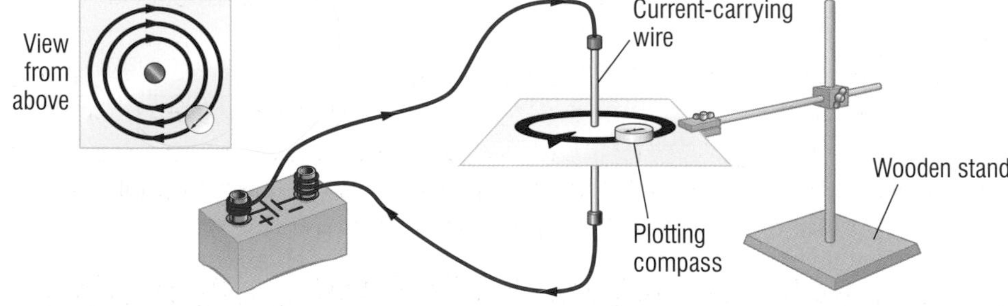

Figure 2 Plotting magnetic field lines

Use the arrangement shown in Figure 2 to observe the effect of:

1 **reversing the current**: You should find that the direction of the plotting compass reverses. This shows that the magnetic field lines reverse direction when the direction of the current is reversed.

2 **moving the plotting compass away from the wire**: You should find it points more towards 'magnetic north'. This is because the magnetic field caused by the wire decreases in strength further from the wire so the Earth's magnetic field has more effect.

Electromagnets

An **electromagnet** consists of insulated wire wrapped round an iron bar (the core). When a current is passed along a wire, a magnetic field is created around the wire. As a result, the magnetic field of the wire magnetises the iron bar. When the current is switched off, the iron bar loses most of its magnetism. Iron easily loses its magnetism when the current is switched off.

Examiner's tip

Remember the current direction is from + to – round the circuit. See page 164 if necessary.

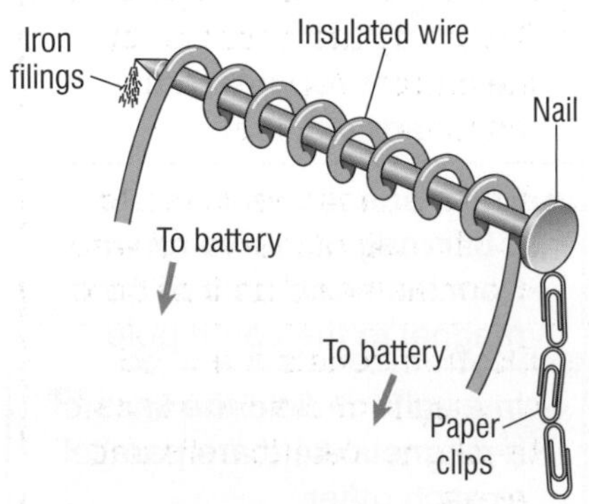

Figure 3 A simple electromagnet

We use electromagnets in many devices.
Four such devices are described below.

1 The scrapyard crane
Scrap vehicles are lifted in a scrap yard using powerful electromagnets attached to cranes. The steel frame of a vehicle sticks to the electromagnet when current passes through the coil of the electromagnet. When the current is switched off, the frame drops off the electromagnet.

Figure 4 Using an electromagnet

2 The circuit breaker
This is a switch in series with an electromagnet. The switch is normally held closed by a spring. When too much current passes through the electromagnet, the switch is pulled open by the electromagnet. The switch stays open when it has been opened until it is reset manually.

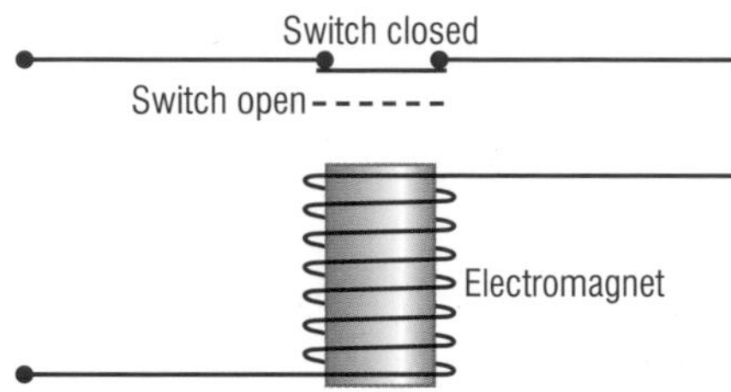

Figure 5 A circuit breaker

3 The electric bell
When the bell is connected to the battery, the iron armature is pulled on to the electromagnet. This opens the make-and-break switch, and the electromagnet is switched off. As a result, the armature springs back and the make-and-break switch closes again so the whole cycle repeats itself.

4 The relay
A relay is used to switch an electrical machine such as a motor on or off. Figure 7 shows its construction. When current passes through the electromagnet, the armature is pulled onto the electromagnet. As a result, the armature turns about the pivot and closes the switch gap. In this way, a small current (through the electromagnet) is used to switch on a much larger current.

Summary questions

1 a Sketch the pattern of the magnetic field lines near a vertical wire carrying current upwards.
  b Explain why iron, and not steel, is used for the core of an electromagnet.

2 List the statements **A**–**E** below in correct order to explain how the circuit breaker in Figure 5 works. Statement **E** is third in the correct order.
  A The current is cut off.
  B The iron core of the electromagnet is magnetised.
  C Too much current passes through the coil.
  D The circuit breaker switch is opened.
  E The switch is attracted to the core of the electromagnet.

3 The construction of a buzzer is like that of the electric bell, except that the buzzer does not have a striker or a bell.
  a Explain why the armature of the buzzer vibrates when the buzzer is connected to a battery.
  b Why does the buzzer vibrate at a higher frequency than the electric bell?

Examiner's tip

Remember the factors that affect the strength of an electromagnet.

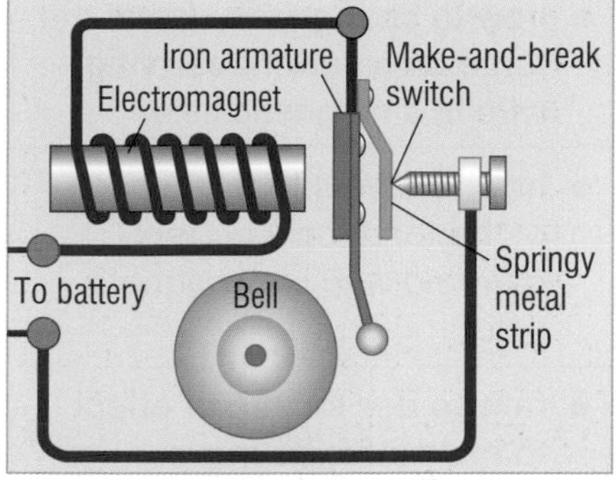

Figure 6 An electric bell

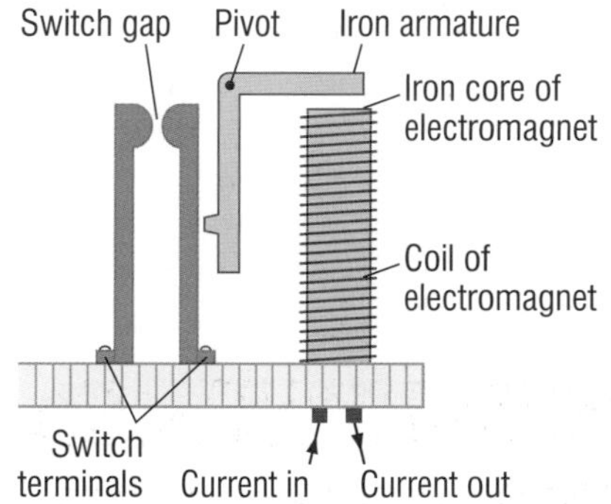

Figure 7 The construction of a relay

Key points

- The magnetic field lines around a wire are circles centred on the wire in a plane perpendicular to the wire.
- Increasing the current makes the magnetic field stronger.
- Reversing the direction of the current reverses the magnetic field lines.
- An electromagnet is made up of a coil of insulated wire wrapped round an iron core.
- Electromagnets are used in scrapyard cranes, circuit breakers, electric bells and relays.

P18.3 The motor effect

Learning objectives

After this topic, you should know:

- how to change the size of the force on a current-carrying wire in a magnetic field
- how to reverse the direction of the force on a current-carrying wire in a magnetic field
- how to use the motor effect to make objects move.

We use electric motors lots of times every day. Using a hairdryer, an electric shaver, a refrigerator pump and a computer hard drive are just a few examples. All these electrical appliances contain an electric motor. The electric motor works because a force can act on a wire in a magnetic field when we pass a current through the wire. This is called the **motor effect**.

Practical

Investigating the motor effect

Figure 1 shows how you can investigate the motor effect. You should find that a force acts on the wire unless the wire is parallel to the magnetic field lines.

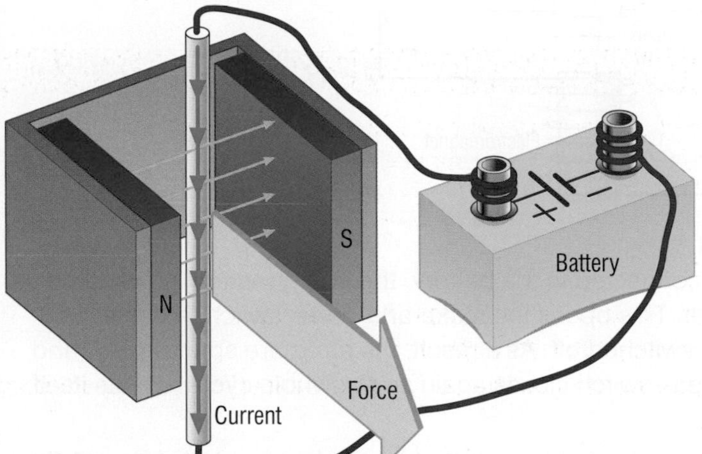

Figure 1 Investigating the motor effect

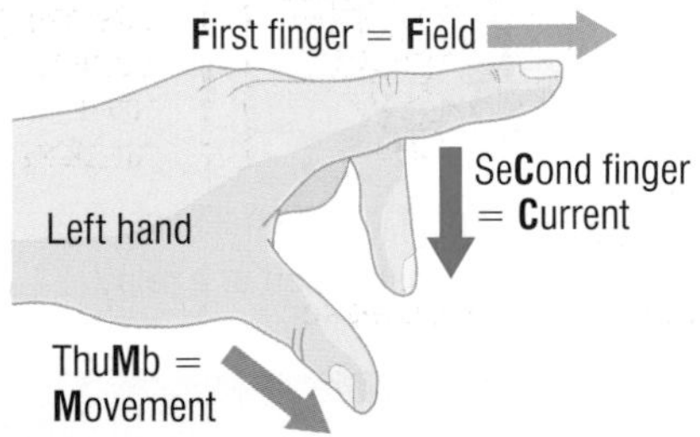

Figure 2 Fleming's left-hand rule. Hold the fingers at right angles to each other. You can use this rule to work out the direction of the force (i.e. movement) on the wire.

Force factors

Your investigations should show that:

- The size of the force can be increased by:
  - increasing the current
  - using a stronger magnet.
- The size of the force depends on the angle between the wire and the magnetic field lines. The force is:
  - greatest when the wire is perpendicular to the magnetic field
  - zero when the wire is parallel to the magnetic field lines.
- The direction of the force is always at right angles to the wire and the field lines. Also, the direction of the force is reversed if the direction of the current or the magnetic field is reversed. Figure 2 shows **Fleming's left-hand rule**, which tells us how these directions are related to each other.

Examiner's tip

Make sure you can use Fleming's left-hand rule to decide the direction of the force on a current-carrying conductor.

The electric motor

An electric motor is designed to use the motor effect. We can control the speed of an electric motor by changing the current. Also, we can reverse the direction the motor turns in by reversing the current.

The simple motor shown in Figure 3 consists of a rectangular coil of insulated wire (the armature coil) that is forced to rotate. The coil is connected via two metal or graphite 'brushes' to the battery. The brushes press onto a metal **'split-ring' commutator** fixed to the coil.

When a current is passed through the coil, the coil spins because:

- a force acts on each side of the coil due to the motor effect
- the force on one side is in the opposite direction to the force on the other side.

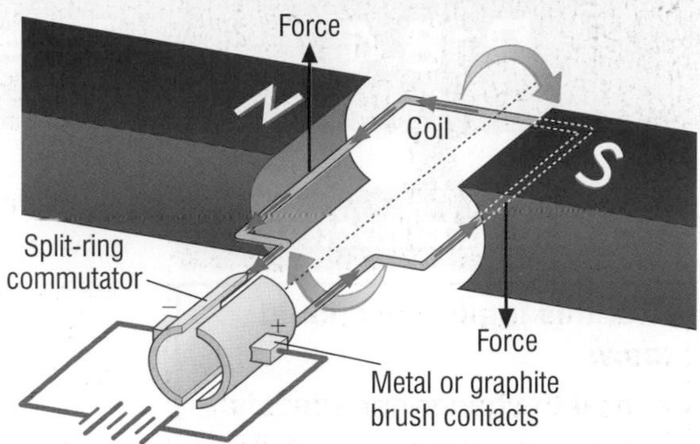

Figure 3 The electric motor

Practical

Make and test a simple electric motor like the one in Figure 3.

The split-ring commutator reverses the current round the coil every half-turn of the coil. Because the sides swap over each half-turn, the coil is pushed in the same direction every half-turn.

Did you know ... ?

Graphite is a form of carbon that conducts electricity and is very slippery. It causes very little friction when in contact with the rotating commutator.

The loudspeaker

A loudspeaker is designed to make a diaphragm attached to a coil vibrate when alternating current passes through the coil.

- When a current passes through the coil, a force caused by the motor effect makes the coil move.
- Each time the current changes its direction, the force reverses its direction. So the coil is repeatedly forced backwards and forwards. This motion makes the diaphragm vibrate so that sound waves are created.

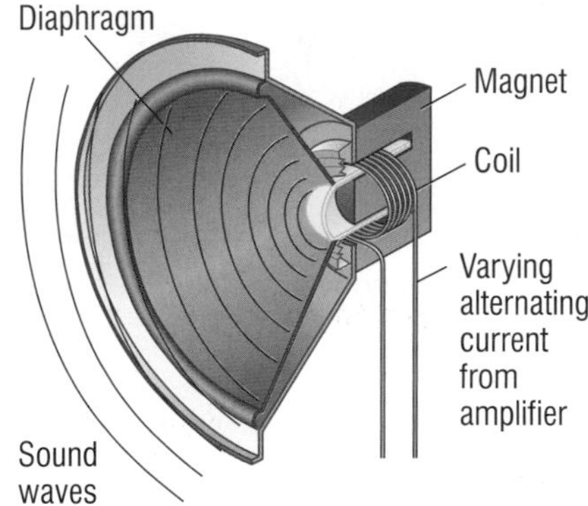

Figure 4 A loudspeaker

Summary questions

1 **a** Explain why the coil of a simple electric motor rotates continuously when the motor is connected to a battery.
  b Why does a loudspeaker not produce sound when direct current is passed through it?

2 **a** Explain why a simple electric motor connected to a battery reverses if the battery connections are reversed.
  b Discuss whether or not an electric motor would run faster if the coil was wound on:
    i a plastic block
    ii an iron block, instead of a wooden block.

3 **a** A force is exerted on a straight wire when a current is passed through it and it is at right angles to the lines of a magnetic field. Describe how the force changes if the wire is turned through 90° until it is parallel to the field lines.
  b A loudspeaker contains a small coil in a magnetic field. The coil is attached to a diaphragm. Explain why the loudspeaker produces sound waves when an alternating current passes through the coil.

Key points

- **In the motor effect, the force is:**
  - **increased if the current or the strength of the magnetic field is increased**
  - **at right angles to the direction of the magnetic field and to the wire**
  - **reversed if the direction of the current or the magnetic field is reversed**
  - **zero if the wire is parallel to the magnetic field.**
- **An electric motor has a coil that turns when a current is passed through it.**

P18.4 The generator effect

Learning objectives

After this topic, you should know:

- what the generator effect is
- how a potential difference can be induced in a wire
- what affects the size of the induced potential difference.

Figure 1 A standby generator

A hospital has its own electricity generator always 'on standby' in case of a power-cut. Patients' lives would be put at risk if the mains electricity supply failed and there was no standby generator.

A generator contains coils of wire that spin in a magnetic field. A potential difference, or voltage, is created, or **induced**, across the ends of the wire when it 'cuts' across the magnetic field lines. We call this process **electromagnetic induction**. If the wire is part of a complete circuit, the induced potential difference makes an electric current pass round the circuit.

Practical

Investigating a simple generator

Connect some insulated wire to an ammeter as shown in Figure 2. Move the wire between the poles of a U-shaped magnet and observe the ammeter. You should discover the ammeter pointer deflects as a current is generated when the wire cuts across the magnetic field. This is because a potential difference is induced in the wire when it cuts across the lines of the magnetic field. This effect is called the **generator effect**.

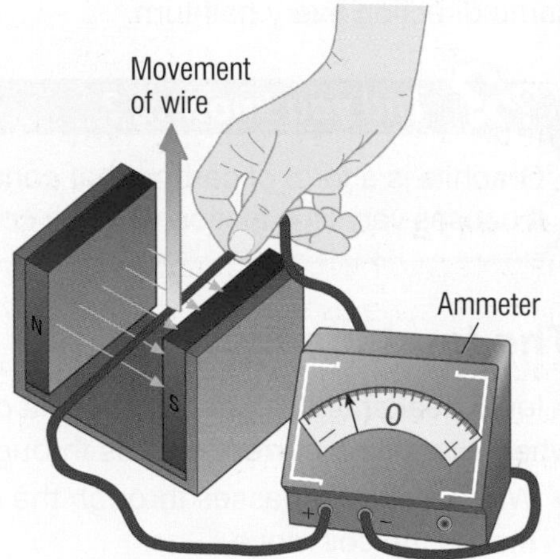

Figure 2 The generator effect

Carry out tests to see what difference is made by:

1 holding the wire stationary in the magnetic field
2 moving the magnet instead of the wire
3 moving the wire faster across the magnetic field
4 reversing the direction of motion of the wire.

Examiner's tip

Remember that there must be a **changing** magnetic field for a potential difference to be induced.

In the tests above, you should find that:

- no current is generated when the wire is stationary
- a current is generated when the magnet instead of the wire is moved
- a larger current is generated when the wire moves faster
- the current is reversed when the direction of motion is reversed.

A generator test

Look at Figure 3. It shows a coil of insulated wire connected to a centre-reading ammeter. When one end of a bar magnet is pushed into the coil, the ammeter pointer deflects.

This is because:

- the movement of the bar magnet causes an induced potential difference in the coil
- the induced potential difference causes a current, because the coil is part of a complete circuit.

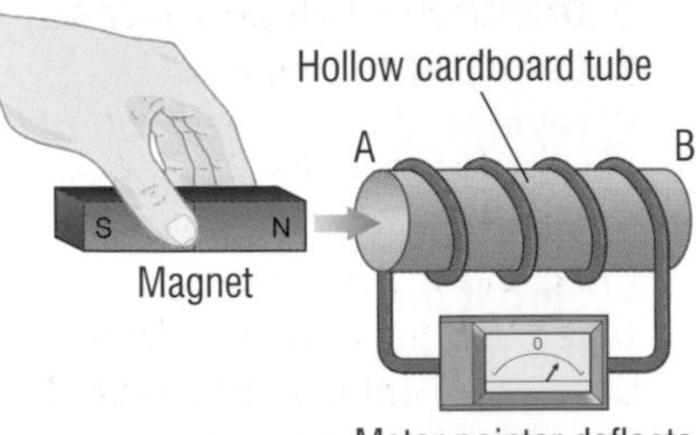

Figure 3 Testing the generator effect

In Figure 3, if the bar magnet is then withdrawn from the coil, the ammeter pointer deflects in the opposite direction. This is because the induced potential difference acts in the opposite direction, so the induced current is in the opposite direction. The direction of the induced current also depends on which way round the polarity of the magnet is. For example, in Figure 3, the north pole of the bar magnet is shown entering end A of the coil.

The table shows the results of testing each direction of motion of the magnet, with the magnet each way round. The table gives the direction of current as seen by someone viewing end A of the coil.

Magnetic pole entering or leaving the coil	Pushed in or pulled out	Direction of current	Induced polarity of Y	Magnet and coil
north pole	in	anticlockwise	north pole	repel
north pole	out	clockwise	south pole	attract
south pole	in	clockwise	south pole	repel
south pole	out	anticlockwise	north pole	attract

The induced current passing through the wires creates a magnetic field in and around the coil, but only when the magnet is moving. This induced magnetic field always opposes the movement of the magnet. So, work has to be done by the person moving the magnet. The electrical energy generated is the result of the work done by the person moving the magnet.

Note: We can use the solenoid rule shown in Figure 4 to work out from the direction of the current whether end A of the coil is like the north or like the south pole of a bar magnet.

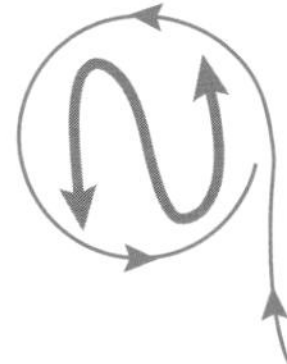
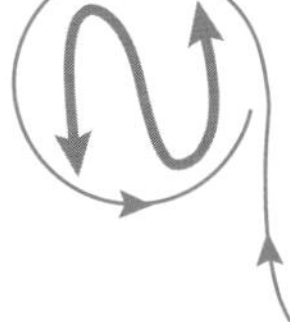

Figure 4 The solenoid rule

Practical

A magnetic puzzle

Wind two separate coils X and Y on a cardboard tube as shown in Figure 5. Connect coil X in series with a battery and a switch. Connect coil Y in a separate circuit to an ammeter.

1 Close the switch and observe that the ammeter pointer deflects briefly. This happens because a magnetic field is created in and around coil X when the switch is closed. The effect on Y because of this magnetic field is the same as pushing a magnet into it, so a potential difference is induced in coil Y.

2 Repeat test **1** with an iron bar in the tube. You should find that the deflection of the ammeter pointer is much bigger.

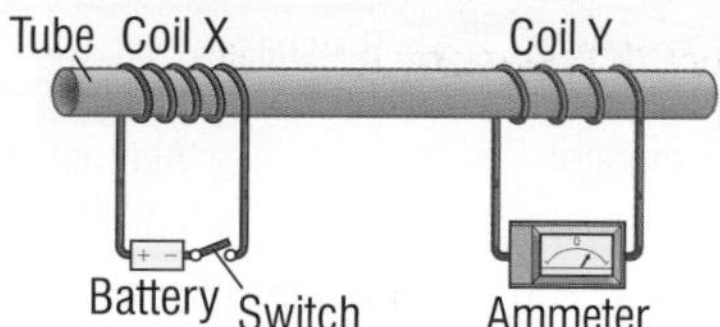

Figure 5 A magnetic puzzle

Summary questions

1 a When a wire is moved between the poles of a U-shaped magnet as shown in Figure 2, explain why a current passes through the ammeter.

b State and explain what would be observed when the wire is moved between the poles more slowly in the opposite direction.

2 A coil of wire is connected to a centre-reading ammeter. A bar magnet is inserted into the coil, making the ammeter pointer flick briefly.
What would you observe if:

a the magnet was then held at rest in the coil?

b the coil had more turns of wire wrapped round the tube?

c the magnet was withdrawn rapidly from the coil?

3 Look at Figure 5.

a Explain why the ammeter pointer deflects when the switch is closed.

b Explain why the pointer does not deflect when there is a constant current in coil X.

Key points

- The generator effect is the effect of inducing a potential difference using a magnetic field.
- When a wire cuts the lines of a magnetic field, a potential difference is induced across the ends of the wire.
- The faster a wire cuts across the lines of a magnetic field, the greater the induced potential difference. When direct current electromagnet is used, it needs to be switched on or off to induce a potential difference.

P18.5 The alternating current generator

Learning objectives

After this topic, you should know:

- how a simple alternating current generator is constructed and operated
- how the induced potential difference of an ac generator varies with time
- how a simple direct current generator is constructed and operated.

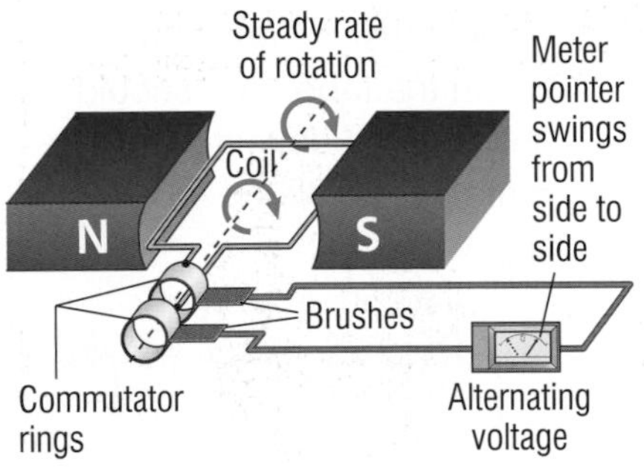

Figure 1 The construction of a simple ac generator

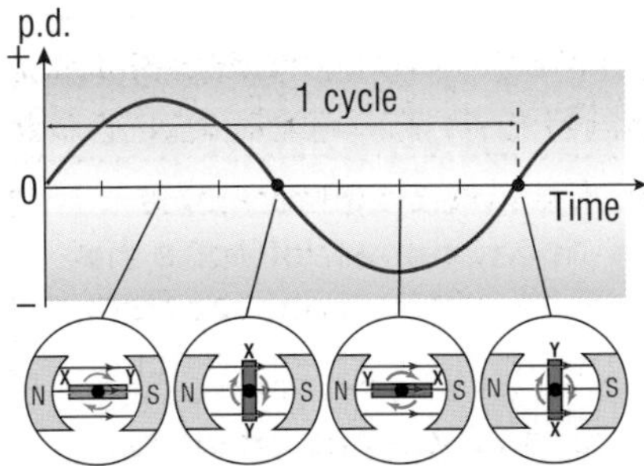

Figure 2 Alternating voltage

The simple alternating current generator

A simple ac generator consists of a rectangular coil that is forced to spin in a uniform magnetic field, as shown in Figure 1. The coil is connected to a centre-reading meter via metal 'brushes' that press on two metal slip rings. The slip rings and brushes provide a continuous connection between the coil and the meter.

When the coil turns steadily in one direction, the meter pointer deflects first one way then the opposite way, then back again. This carries on as long as the coil keeps turning in the same direction. The current in the circuit repeatedly changes its direction through the meter because the induced potential difference in the coil repeatedly changes its direction. We say that the induced potential difference and the current alternate because they repeatedly change direction.

The induced potential difference varies as the coil rotates, as shown in Figure 2. In one complete rotation of the coil (or 'one full cycle'), the induced potential difference increases from zero to a maximum value, then decreases to zero, reverses and increases to a negative maximum and then becomes zero again. We call both the positive and the negative maximum values the **peak value**.

- **The size of the induced potential difference is greatest** when the plane of the coil is parallel to the direction of the magnetic field. At this position, the sides of the coil parallel to the axis of rotation (labelled X and Y in Figure 2) cut directly across the magnetic field lines. So the induced potential difference is at its peak value.
- **The size of the induced potential difference is zero** when the plane of the coil is perpendicular to the magnetic field lines. At this position, the sides of the coil move parallel to the field lines and do not cut through them. So, the induced potential difference is zero.

The faster the coil rotates:

- **the greater the frequency (i.e. the number of cycles per second) of the alternating current.** This is because each full cycle of the alternating potential difference takes the same time as one full rotation of the coil.
- **the larger the peak value of the alternating current.** This is because the sides of the coil move faster and therefore cut the field lines at a faster rate, so the peak value of the induced potential difference is greater.

The peak value can also be increased by using a magnet with a stronger magnetic field and by using a coil with a larger area and with more turns of wire on it.

As we saw in 17.1 'Alternating current', an alternating voltage can be displayed on an oscilloscope screen. If the induced potential difference from an ac generator is displayed on an oscilloscope and the generator is rotated faster, the screen display will show more waves on the screen (because the frequency of the induced potential difference will be greater) and the waves will be taller (because the peak value of the induced potential difference will be greater).

Examiner's tip

Make sure you can explain how a generator works.

links

For more information on displaying alternating voltages on an oscilloscope, look at 17.1 'Alternating current'.

The simple direct current (dc) generator

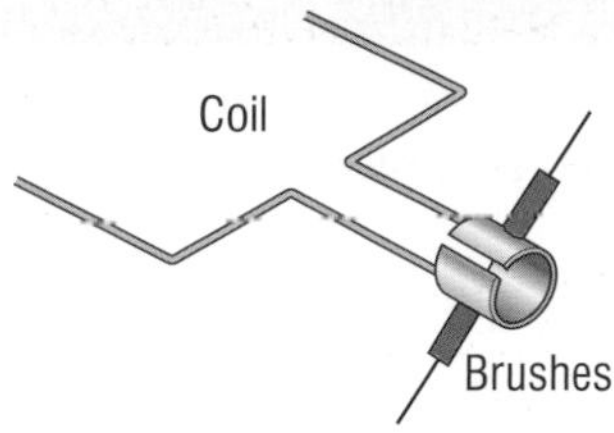

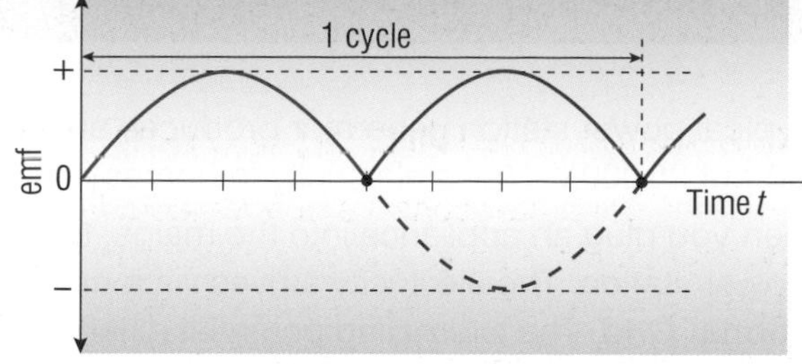

Figure 3 The dc generator

A dc generator is the same as an ac generator except that the dc generator has a split-ring commutator, as shown in Figure 3, instead of two separate slip rings. As the coil spins, the split-ring commutator reconnects the coil the opposite way round in the circuit every half-turn. This happens each time the coil is perpendicular to the magnetic field lines. As a result, the induced potential difference does not reverse its direction as it does in the ac generator. The induced potential difference varies from zero to a maximum value twice each cycle, and never changes polarity.

The cycle dynamo

Figure 5 shows the inside of a cycle dynamo. When the magnet spins, an alternating potential difference is induced in the coil. This happens because the magnetic field lines cut across the wires of the coil. The induced potential difference makes a current pass round the circuit when the lamp is on. Because the induced potential difference alternates, the current alternates too. The faster the magnet spins, the brighter the light from the lamp. This is because the induced potential difference is greater and so a bigger current passes through the lamp.

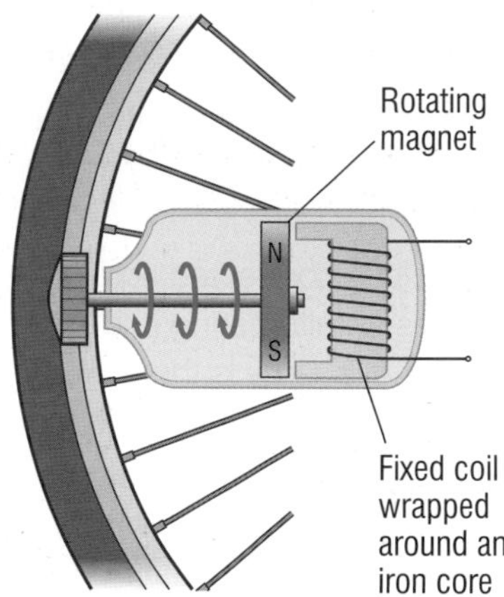

Figure 5 The dynamo

Summary questions

1 An alternating current generator has a coil that spins between the poles of a U-shaped magnet.
  a Explain why an alternating voltage is induced in the coil.
  b Describe how the alternating voltage would differ if the coil is made to spin faster.

2 Figure 2 shows how the alternating voltage produced by an ac generator changes with time.
  a How would the graph differ if the coil was rotated more slowly?
  b Give reasons for your answer to **a**.

3 a State the function of the split-ring commutator in a simple dc generator.
  b Draw a graph to show how potential difference varies with time for a simple dc generator.

Did you know ... ?

Electromagnetic induction was discovered by Michael Faraday. This discovery led to the invention of generators, transformers and many more electrical machines. Faraday was born in 1791, and on leaving school he started an apprenticeship binding books. He was so fascinated by Sir Humphry Davy's books on science that he wrote to him at the Royal Institution in London to ask for a job. Davy must have been very impressed by Faraday's enthusiasm, because he took him on and trained him in science. Many years later, Faraday followed in Davy's footsteps and became the Director of the Royal Institution.

Figure 4 Michael Faraday

Key points

- A simple ac generator is made up of a coil that spins in a uniform magnetic field.
- The waveform, seen using an oscilloscope, of the ac generator's induced potential difference is at:
  - its peak value when the sides of the coil cut directly across the magnetic field lines
  - its zero value when the sides of the coil move parallel to the field lines.
- A simple dc generator has a split-ring commutator instead of two slip rings.

P18.6 Transformers

Learning objectives

After this topic, you should know:

- why transformers work only with ac
- what the core of a transformer is made from
- how switch mode transformers differ from ordinary transformers.

A typical power station generator produces an alternating potential difference of about 25 000 V. Mains electricity in homes is 230 V.

When you plug an appliance into the mains, the electricity to run it comes from a power station. The electricity arrives via a network of cables called the **National Grid**. The alternating potential difference of the cables (the grid voltage) is typically 132 000 V. A **transformer** is used to change the size of the alternating potential difference.

How a transformer works

A transformer has two coils of insulated wire, both wound round the same soft iron core, as shown in Figure 1. This core is easily magnetised and demagnetised. The primary coil is connected to an alternating current supply. When alternating current passes through the primary coil, an alternating potential difference is induced in the secondary coil.

This happens because:

- alternating current passing through the primary coil produces an alternating magnetic field
- the lines of the alternating magnetic field pass through the secondary coil
- the magnetic field is changing.

This creates an alternating potential difference between the terminals of the secondary coil. We say that an alternating potential difference is induced in the secondary coil.

If a bulb is connected across the secondary coil, the induced potential difference causes an alternating current in the secondary circuit, so the bulb lights up. Electrical energy is therefore transferred from the primary coil to the secondary coil. This happens even though they are **not** electrically connected in the same circuit.

- A **step-up transformer** makes the potential difference across the secondary coil greater than the potential difference across the primary coil. Its secondary coil has more turns than its primary coil.
- A **step-down transformer** makes the potential difference across the secondary coil less than the potential difference across the primary coil. Its secondary coil has fewer turns than its primary coil.

For example, we use a step-down transformer in a low-voltage supply to step the mains potential difference down from 230 V.

links

For more information on the National Grid, look back at 17.8 'The National Grid'.

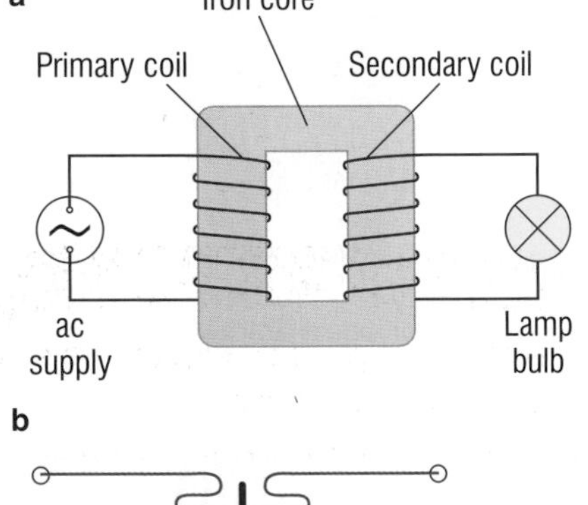

Figure 1 Transformer action **a** in a circuit **b** circuit symbol

Practical

Make a model transformer

Wrap a coil of insulated wire round the iron core of a model transformer as the primary coil. Connect the coil to a 1 V ac supply. Then connect a second length of insulated wire to a 1.5 V torch bulb. When you wrap enough turns of the second wire round the iron core, the bulb should light up.

- Test if cores made from different materials affect the transformer.

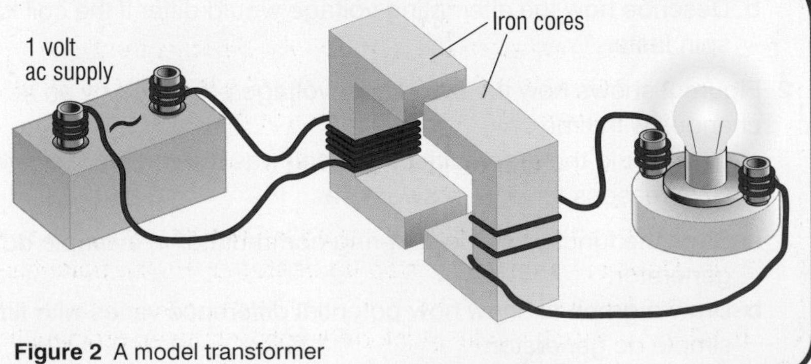

Figure 2 A model transformer

Practical transformers

Transformers only work with alternating current. With a direct current, there is no changing magnetic field, so the secondary potential difference is zero.

In the type of transformer described before, the core of the transformer 'guides' the field lines in a loop through the coils. But the field must be changing to induce a potential difference in the secondary coil.

Figure 3 shows a practical transformer. The primary and secondary coils are both wound round the same part of the core.

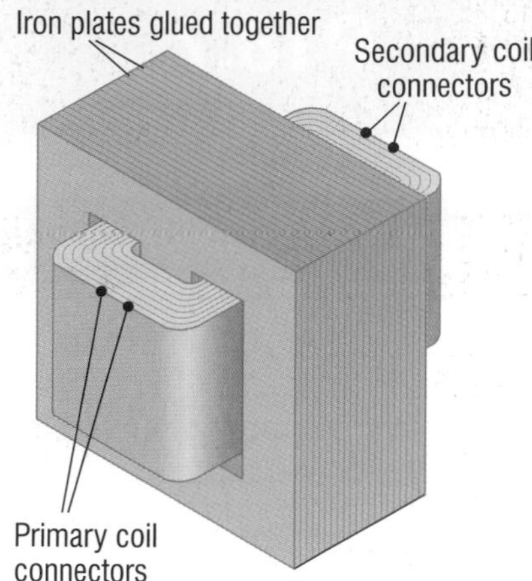

Figure 3 A practical transformer

Switch mode transformers

A **switch mode transformer** works in a different way to the traditional transformer described above. It operates at frequencies between 50 000 Hz (50 kHz) and 200 000 Hz (200 kHz). Its main features listed below make it very suitable for use in mobile-phone chargers.

- It is lighter and smaller than a traditional transformer that works at 50 Hz.
- It uses very little power when no electrical device is connected across its output terminals (i.e. no load is applied) to it.

A mobile-phone charger has three main circuits. Figure 4 shows what each circuit does.

A switch mode transformer has a ferrite core. This is much lighter than an iron core and, unlike an iron core, can work at high frequency. The circuits convert the mains potential difference (at 230 V and 50 Hz in Europe) to a much lower direct potential difference.

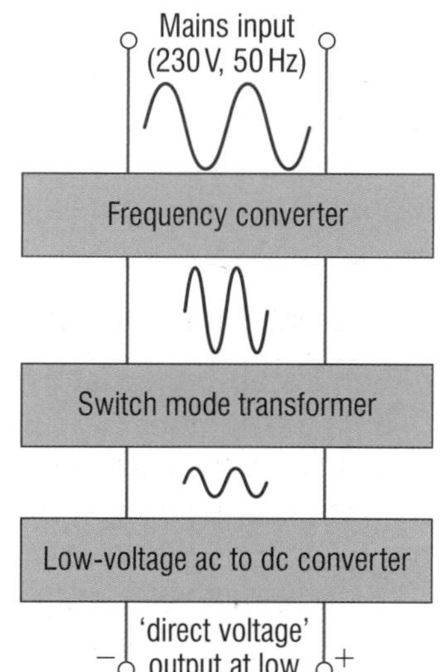

Figure 4 Block diagram of a mobile-phone charger

Examiner's tip

Make sure you can explain how a transformer works.

Summary questions

1 a Explain how a transformer works.
  b A step-down transformer contains a 200-turn coil and a 4000-turn coil wound on the same iron core.
    i Which coil is the primary coil?
    ii Permanent magnets are made from steel, not iron. Explain why the transformer would not work if the core was made of steel instead of iron.

2 a Why does a transformer not work with direct current?
  b Why is it important that the coil wires of a transformer are insulated?
  c Why is the core of a transformer made of iron?

3 a A laptop computer can operate with a 14 V battery or with a mains transformer.
    i What is the benefit of having a dual power supply?
    ii Does the transformer step up or step down the potential difference applied to it?
  b Why is a switch mode transformer lighter than an ordinary transformer?

Key points

- A transformer works only on ac because a changing magnetic field is necessary to induce ac in the secondary coil.
- A transformer has an iron core unless it is a switch mode transformer, which has a ferrite core.
- A switch mode transformer is lighter and smaller than an ordinary transformer. It operates at high frequency.

P18.7 Transformers in action

Learning objectives

After this topic, you should know:

- why transformers are used in the National Grid
- how the ratio of the primary potential difference to the secondary potential difference depends on the number of turns on each coil
- the difference between a step-up and a step-down transformer
- what we can say about a transformer that is 100% efficient.

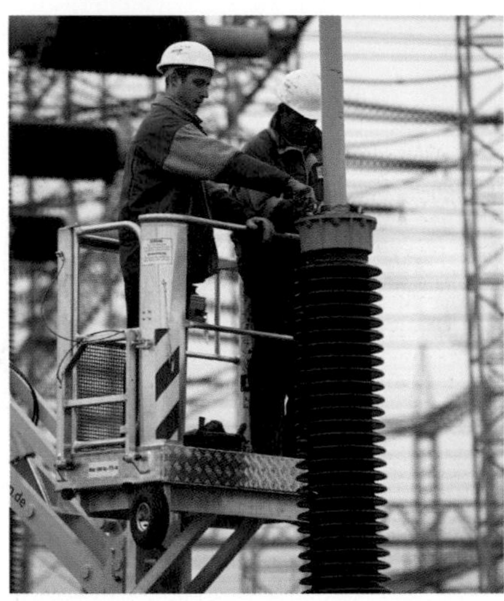

Figure 1 A power transformer under inspection

When we use mains appliances, the electricity is supplied to us through the National Grid from power stations. Figure 2 shows how the grid system is used to supply industry as well as homes.

The higher the grid potential difference, the greater is the efficiency of transferring electrical power through the grid.

This is why transformers are used to step up the potential difference from a power station to the grid potential difference and to step the grid potential difference down to the mains voltage. The grid potential difference is at least 132 000 V. So what difference would it make if the grid potential difference were much lower? Much more current would be needed to deliver the same amount of power. The grid cables would therefore heat up more and waste more energy.

The transformer equation

The secondary potential difference of a transformer depends on the primary potential difference and the number of turns on each coil.

We can use the following equation to calculate any one of these factors if we know the other factors.

$$\frac{\text{potential difference across primary, } V_P}{\text{potential difference across secondary, } V_S} = \frac{\text{number of turns on primary, } n_p}{\text{number of turns on secondary, } n_S}$$

- **For a step-up transformer**, the number of secondary turns, n_S, is greater than the number of primary turns, n_p. Therefore V_S is greater than V_P.
- **For a step-down transformer**, the number of secondary turns, n_S, is less than the number of primary turns, n_p. Therefore V_S is less than V_P.

Maths skills

Worked example

A transformer is used to step a potential difference of 230 V down to 10 V. The secondary coil has 60 turns. Calculate the number of turns of the primary coil.

Solution

$V_P = 230\text{ V}$, $V_S = 10\text{ V}$, $n_S = 60$ turns

Using $\frac{V_P}{V_S} = \frac{n_P}{n_S}$ gives $\frac{230}{10} = \frac{n_P}{60}$

Therefore $n_P = \frac{230 \times 60}{10}$

$= \mathbf{1380\ turns}$

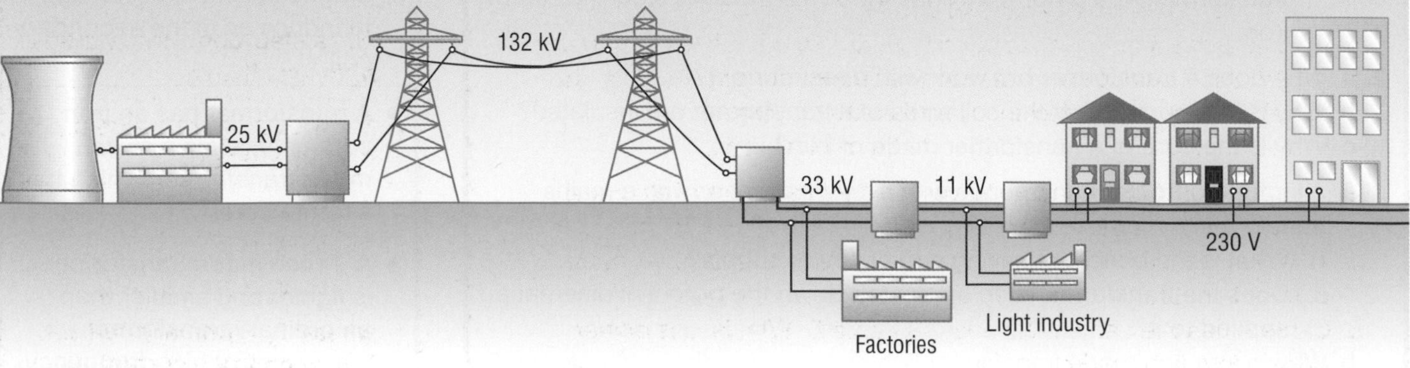

Figure 2 The grid system

Transformer efficiency

Transformers are almost 100% efficient. When a device is connected to the secondary coil (see Figure 3), almost all the electrical power supplied to the transformer is delivered to the device. If we know how much electrical power a device needs to work normally (i.e. the transformer output power), this tells us how much electrical power needs to be supplied to the transformer (i.e. the transformer input power).

- power supplied to the transformer (i.e. input power) = primary current, I_P × primary potential difference, V_P
- power delivered by the transformer (i.e. output power) = secondary current, I_S × secondary potential difference, V_S

Therefore, if we can assume 100% efficiency:

$$\text{primary potential difference} \times \text{primary current} = \text{secondary potential difference} \times \text{secondary current}$$

$$V_P \times I_P = V_S \times I_S$$

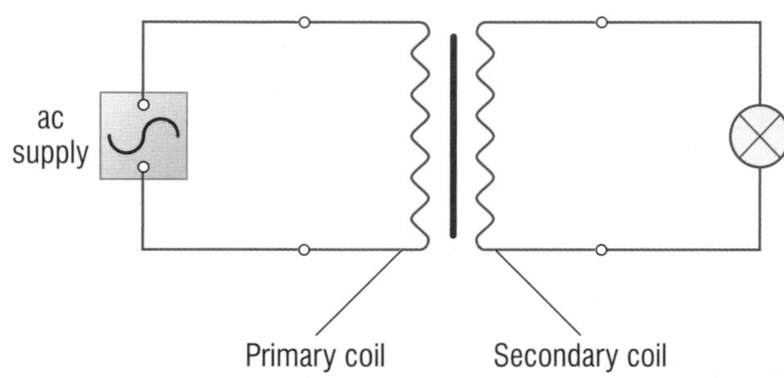

Figure 3 Transformer efficiency

Examiner's tip

Make sure you can describe how transformers are used in the National Grid.

Summary questions

1 **a** A transformer with 60 turns in the secondary coil is used to step a potential difference of 120 V down to 6 V. Calculate the number of turns on the primary coil.

b A step-up transformer is required to step an alternating potential difference of 20 V to 230 V. If a coil with 100 turns is used as the primary coil, how many turns should the secondary coil have?

c A 230 V, 60 W bulb lights normally when it is connected to the secondary coil of a transformer and a 10 V ac supply is connected to the primary coil. Assume the transformer is 100% efficient. Calculate:

i the primary current **ii** the bulb current.

2 A transformer with a secondary coil of 100 turns is to be used to step a potential difference down from 240 V to 12 V.

a Calculate the number of turns on the primary coil of this transformer.

b A 12 V, 36 W bulb is connected to the secondary coil. Assume the transformer is 100% efficient. Calculate the current in:

i the bulb **ii** the primary coil.

3 Two separate cables A and B deliver the same amount of electrical power to two factories. A is at a higher potential difference than B.

a What can we say about the current in cable A compared with the current in cable B?

b Cable A has the same resistance as cable B. Why is less power wasted in A than in B?

Key points

- Transformers are used to step potential differences up or down.
- The transformer equation is:

$$\frac{\text{primary potential difference, } V_P}{\text{secondary potential difference, } V_S} = \frac{n_P}{n_S}$$

where: n_P = number of primary turns; n_S = number of secondary turns

- For a step-down transformer, n_S is less than n_P.
- For a step-up transformer, n_S is greater than n_P.
- For a 100% efficient transformer:

$$V_P \times I_P = V_S \times I_S$$

where: I_P = primary current; I_S = secondary current

Summary questions

1 **a** Two identical bar magnets are placed end-to-end on a sheet of paper on a table with a gap between them with unlike poles facing each other.

i Draw the arrangement and the pattern of the magnetic field lines in the gap.

ii A plotting compass is placed in the gap at equal distance from the two magnets at a short distance from the midpoint of the gap. On your drawing, show the plotting compass in this position and show the direction in which it points.

b Copy and complete **i** and **ii** using the words below. Each word can be used more than once.

field force lines current

i A vertical wire is placed in a horizontal magnetic field. When a .... is passed through the wire, a .... acts on the wire.

ii A force acts on a wire in a magnetic field when a .... passes along the wire and the wire is not parallel to the .... of the ....

2 **a** The figure opposite shows the construction of a relay. Explain why the switch closes when a current passes through the coil of the electromagnet.

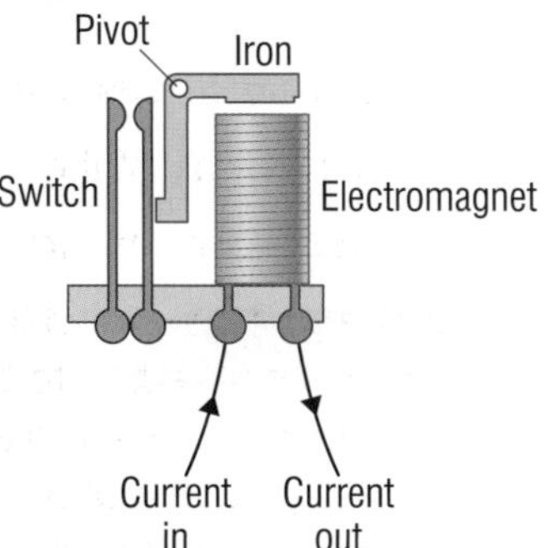

b The diagram below shows the relay coil in a circuit that is used to switch on the starter motor of a car. Explain why the motor starts when the ignition switch is closed.

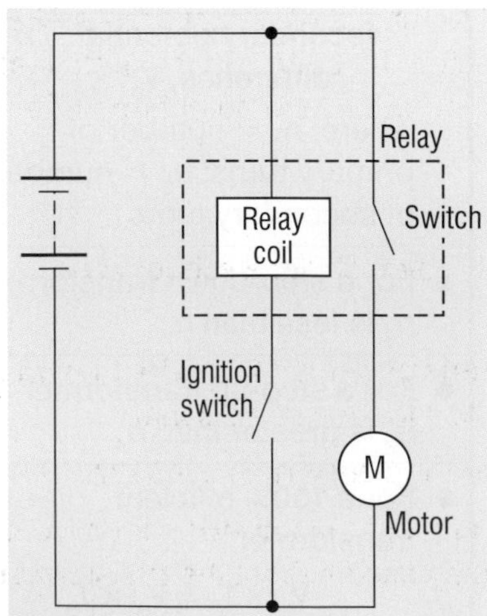

3 This figure shows a rectangular coil of wire in a magnetic field viewed from above. When a direct current passes clockwise round the coil, a downward force acts on side **X** of the coil.

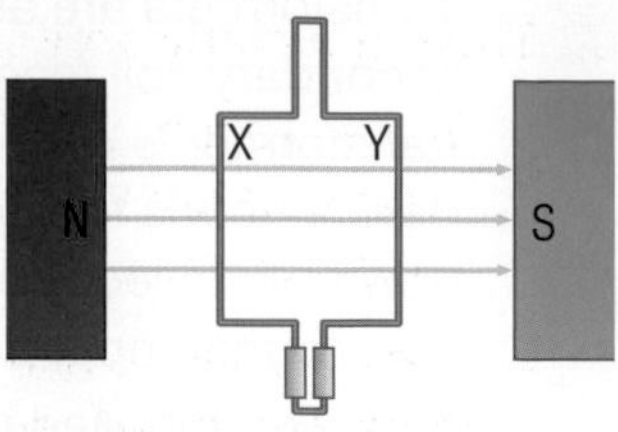

a What is the direction of the force on side **Y** of the coil?

b What can you say about the force on each side of the coil parallel to the magnetic field lines?

c What is the effect of the forces on the coil?

4 **a** **i** The arrangement shown in the figure for Question **3** could be used to generate a direct current if the coil is made to spin and the split-ring commutator is connected to a lamp. Draw a graph to show how the current would vary with time if the coil is turned steadily.

ii How you would modify the arrangement shown in the figure for Question **3** to generate an alternating current?

b Explain why a transformer does not work on direct current.

5 **a** Cables at a potential difference of 100 000 V are used to transfer 1 000 000 W of electrical power in a part of a grid system.

i Calculate the current in the cable.

ii If the potential difference had been 10 000 V, how much current would be needed to transfer the same amount of power?

b Explain why power is transmitted through the National Grid at a high potential difference rather than a low potential difference.

6 A transformer has 50 turns in its primary coil and 500 turns in its secondary coil. It is to be used to light a 120 V, 60 W bulb connected to the secondary coil. Assume the transformer is 100% efficient.

a Calculate the primary potential difference.

b Calculate the current in the bulb.

c Calculate the current in the primary coil.

7 A transformer has 3000 turns on its primary coil. An alternating potential difference of 240 V is to be connected to the primary coil, and a 12 V bulb is to be connected to the secondary coil.

a Calculate the number of turns the secondary coil should have.

b What would be the current through the primary coil if the current through the lamp is to be 3.0 A? Assume the transformer is 100% efficient.

AQA Examination-style questions

1 There are many appliances that transfer energy.

a Some students set up the apparatus shown below to investigate the motor effect.

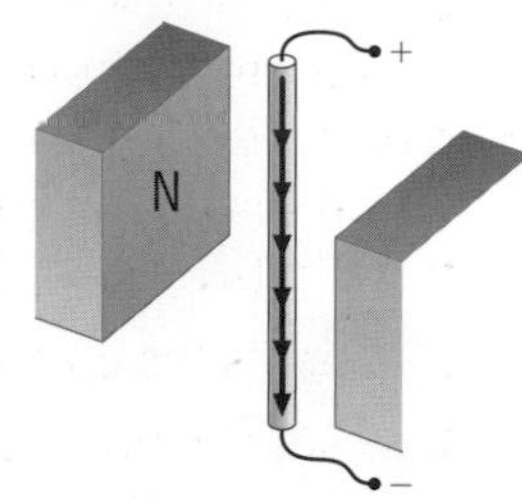

They wanted to see how the force depended on the current flowing through the strip of metal foil.

i To make the test fair, which variable in the list should they keep constant? (1)

current
size of the force
strength of magnetic field

ii The students changed the apparatus so that they could measure the force acting on the strip of metal foil. Their results are shown in the table.

current in A	0.0	0.1	0.2	0.3	0.4
force in N	0.0	0.03	0.06	0.09	0.12

Explain what you can conclude from the data in the table. (2)

b The diagrams show two positions of a rectangular coil of wire in a magnetic field.

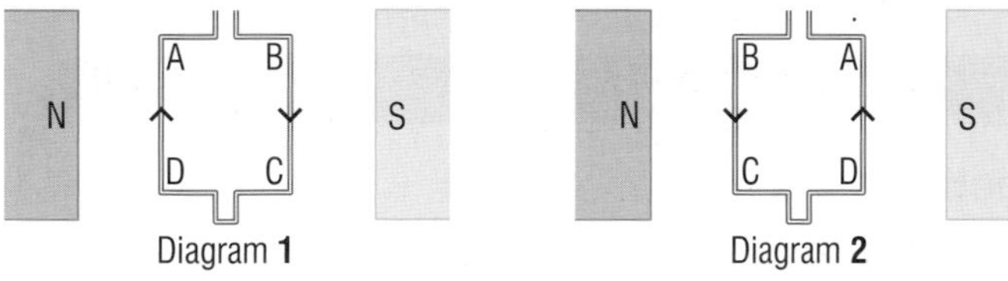

i Describe and explain what happens to the coil in diagram **1**. (4)

ii Describe and explain what happens to the coil in diagram **2**. (2)

iii To keep the coil spinning round, what has to be done to the current every half-cycle? (1)

2 a The diagram shows a simple generator.

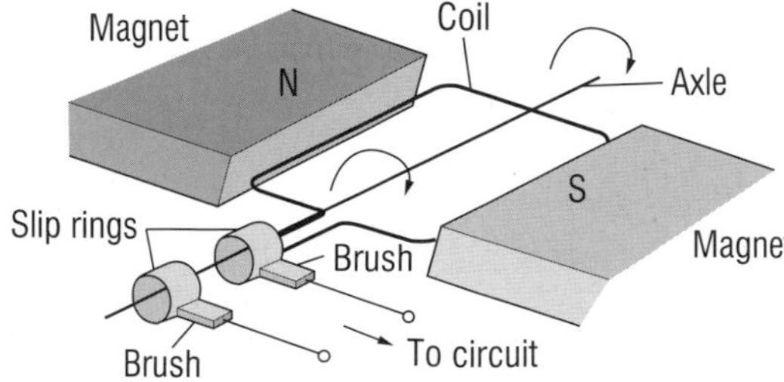

Explain how this generator produces a current in the circuit. (QWC) (6)

b The graph shows how the current from the generator varies with time.

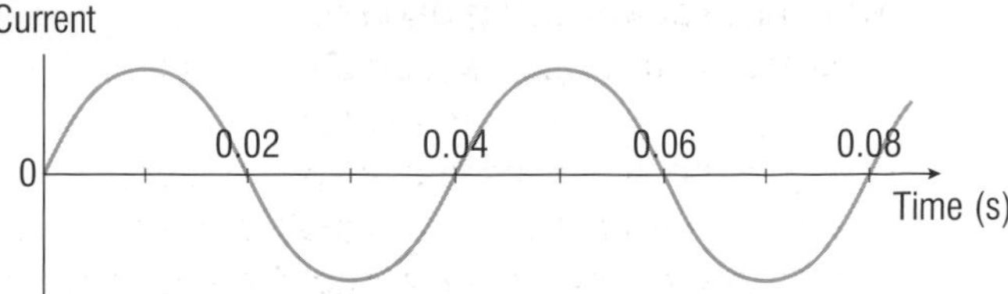

i Electric currents are either alternating or direct. Explain how the graph shows that the current from the generator is an alternating current. (2)

ii Calculate the frequency of the current. (3)

3 The diagram shows a shaver socket in a bathroom and the transformer inside it.

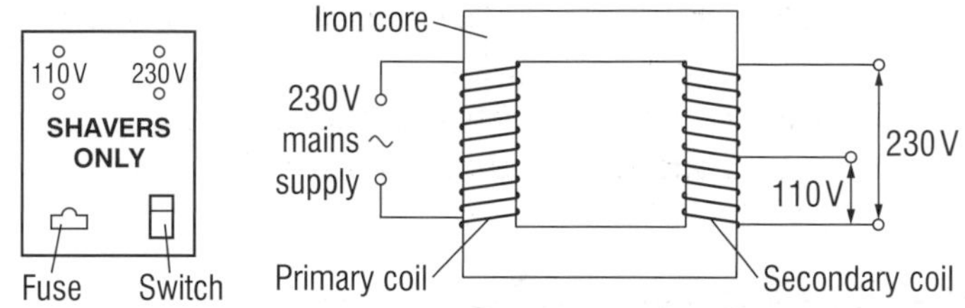

a What material is used for the core of a transformer?

Choose **one** of the materials in the list. (1)

brass copper iron steel tungsten

b The primary coil of the transformer has 5000 turns. The coil is connected to the 230 V mains supply.

i How many turns are needed on the secondary coil to give an output of 230 V? (1)

ii Calculate the number of turns needed on the secondary coil to give an output of 110 V. (3)

iii Explain how the transformer supplies an alternating current to the shaver. (5)

c A student wanted to run a 2.4 V motor from a 12 V car battery. He connected the battery to the input leads of a transformer. He found that the output from the transformer was zero.

Explain why. (2)

d Power lines supply electricity to a school via a transformer.

The input to the transformer is 415 V. The transformer changes this to 230 V for use in the school.

The power input to the transformer is 48 kW.

Calculate the current that the transformer delivers to the school. (You may assume that the transformer is 100% efficient.) (3)

P19.1 Atoms and radiation

Learning objectives

After this topic, you should know:

- what a radioactive substance is
- the types of radiation given out from a radioactive substance
- when a radioactive source gives out radiation (radioactive decay)
- the origins of background radiation.

Figure 2 Marie Curie 1867–1934

Did you know ... ?

Becquerel and the Curies were awarded the Nobel Prize for the discovery of radioactivity. When Pierre died in a road accident, Marie went on with their work. She was awarded a second Nobel Prize in 1911 for the discovery of polonium and radium. She died in 1934 from leukaemia, a disease of the blood cells. It was probably caused by the radiation from the radioactive materials she worked with.

A key discovery

Figure 1 Becquerel's key

If your photos showed a mysterious image, what would you think? In 1896, a French physicist, **Henri Becquerel**, discovered the image of a key on a film he developed. He remembered the film had been in a drawer under a key. On top of that there had been a packet of uranium salts. The uranium salts must have sent out some form of radiation that passed through paper (the film wrapper) but not through metal (the key).

Becquerel asked a young research worker, **Marie Curie**, to investigate. She found that the salts gave out radiation all the time. It happened no matter what was done to them. She used the word **radioactivity** to describe this strange new property of uranium.

She and her husband, Pierre, did more research into this new branch of science. They discovered new radioactive elements. They named one of the elements **polonium**, after Marie's native country, Poland.

Practical

Investigating radioactivity

We can use a **Geiger counter** to detect radioactivity. Look at Figure 3. The counter clicks each time a particle of radiation from a radioactive substance enters the Geiger tube.

Safety: Avoid touching and inhaling radioactive material.

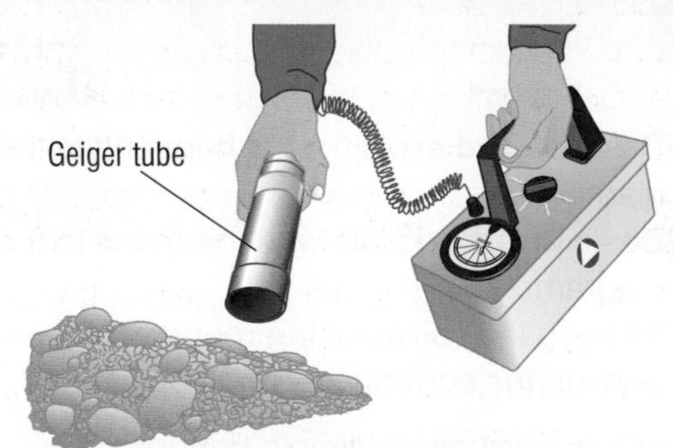

Figure 3 Using a Geiger counter

Inside the atom

What stops the radiation? Ernest Rutherford carried out tests to answer this question about a century ago. He put different materials between the radioactive substance and a detector.

He discovered two types of radiation:

- One type (**alpha radiation**, symbol α) was stopped by paper.
- The other type (**beta radiation**, symbol β) went through the paper.

Scientists later discovered a third type, **gamma radiation** (symbol γ), even more penetrating than beta radiation.

Rutherford carried out further investigations and discovered that alpha radiation is made up of positively charged particles. He realised that these particles could be used to probe the atom. His research students included Hans Geiger, who invented what was later called the Geiger counter. They carried out investigations in which a narrow beam of alpha particles was directed at a thin metal foil. Rutherford was astonished that some of the alpha particles rebounded from the foil. He proved that this happens because every atom has at its centre a positively charged nucleus containing most of the mass of the atom. He went on to propose that the nucleus contains two types of particle – protons and neutrons.

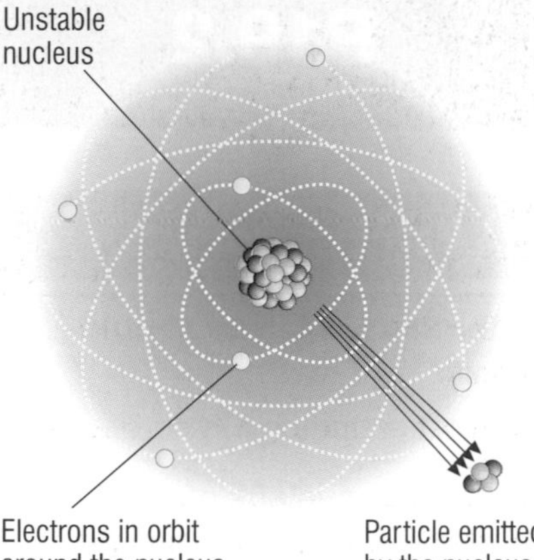

Figure 4 Radioactive decay

A radioactive puzzle

Why are some substances radioactive? Every atom has a nucleus made up of protons and neutrons. Electrons move about in energy levels (or shells) surrounding the nucleus.

Most atoms each have a stable nucleus that doesn't change. But the atoms of a radioactive substance each have a nucleus that is unstable. An unstable nucleus becomes stable by emitting alpha, beta or gamma radiation. We say an unstable nucleus **decays** when it emits radiation.

We can't tell when an unstable nucleus will decay. It is a **random** event that happens without anything being done to the nucleus.

The origins of background radiation

A Geiger counter clicks even when it is not near a radioactive source. This effect is caused by **background radiation**. This is ionising radiation from radioactive substances:

- in the environment (e.g. in the air or the ground or in building materials)
- from space (cosmic rays)
- from man-made sources such as 'fallout' (leftover radioactive substances in the air) from nuclear weapons testing and nuclear accidents at some power stations.

Background radiation is mostly from naturally occurring substances in the Earth. For example, radon gas is radioactive and is a product of the decay of uranium found in the rocks in certain areas. Medical sources of background radiation include X-ray tubes and radioactive substances used in hospitals.

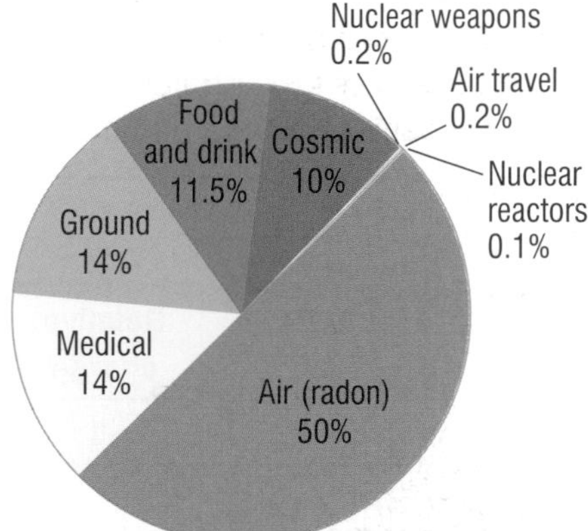

Figure 5 The origins of background radiation

links

Look back at 8.5 'X-rays in medicine' for more about X-rays.

Summary questions

1. a State two differences between the radiation from uranium and the radiation from a lamp.
   b State two differences between radioactive atoms compared with the atoms in a lamp filament.
2. a The radiation from a radioactive source is stopped by paper. What type of radiation does the source emit?
   b The radiation from a different source goes through paper. What can you say about this radiation?
3. a Explain why some substances are radioactive.
   b State two sources of background radioactivity.
   c A Geiger counter clicks very rapidly when a certain substance is brought near it. After the substance is taken away, the Geiger counter still clicks, but much less often.
      i What can you say about the substance that made the Geiger counter click?
      ii Why did the counter click after the source had been moved away?

Key points

- A radioactive substance contains unstable nuclei that become stable by emitting radiation.
- There are three main types of radiation from radioactive substances – alpha, beta and gamma radiation.
- Radioactive decay is a random event – we cannot predict or influence when it will happen.
- Background radiation is mostly from radioactive substances occurring naturally in rocks or space or from man-made sources such as nuclear fallout.

P19.2 Nuclear reactions

Learning objectives

After this topic, you should know:

- what an isotope is
- how the nucleus of an atom changes when it emits an alpha particle or a beta particle
- how to represent the emission of an alpha or a beta particle from a nucleus.

Table 1

	Relative mass	Relative charge
proton	1	+1
neutron	1	0
electron	$\approx\frac{1}{2000}$	–1

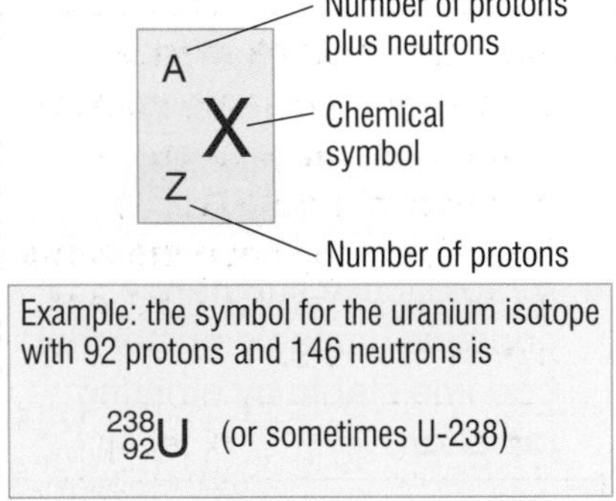
Number of protons plus neutrons
A
X
Chemical symbol
Z
Number of protons
Example: the symbol for the uranium isotope with 92 protons and 146 neutrons is
$^{238}_{92}U$ (or sometimes U-238)

Figure 1 Representing an isotope

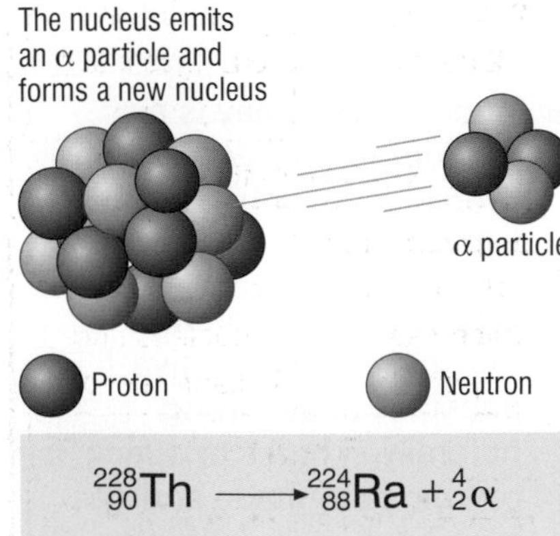
The nucleus emits an α particle and forms a new nucleus
α particle
Proton
Neutron
$^{228}_{90}Th \longrightarrow {}^{224}_{88}Ra + {}^{4}_{2}\alpha$

Figure 2 α emission

In α (alpha) or β (beta) decay, the number of protons in a nucleus changes. In α decay, the total number of neutrons and protons also changes. We will now look at the changes that happen in α and β decay and how we can represent these changes.

Table 1 gives the relative masses and the relative electric charges of a proton, a neutron and an electron.

Atoms are uncharged. They have equal numbers of protons (+) and electrons (–). A charged particle, called an **ion**, is formed when an atom gains or loses one or more electrons. Then there are unequal numbers of protons and electrons in the ion.

The atoms of the same element each have the same number of protons. The number of protons in a nucleus is given the symbol *Z*. It is called the **atomic number** (or **proton number**).

Isotopes are atoms of the same element with different numbers of neutrons. The isotopes of an element have nuclei with the same number of protons but a different number of neutrons.

The number of protons plus neutrons in a nucleus is called its **mass number**. We give it the symbol *A*.

Figure 1 shows how to represent an isotope of an element X, which has *Z* protons and *A* protons plus neutrons. For example, the uranium isotope $^{238}_{92}U$ contains 92 protons and 146 neutrons (= 238 – 92) in each nucleus. So, its mass number is 238 and the relative charge of the nucleus is +92.

Radioactive decay

An unstable nucleus becomes more stable by emitting an α (alpha) or a β (beta) particle or by emitting γ (gamma) radiation.

α emission

An α particle consists of two protons plus two neutrons. Its relative mass is 4 and its relative charge is +2. So we can represent it by the symbol $^{4}_{2}\alpha$.

When an unstable nucleus emits an α particle, its atomic number goes down by 2 and its mass number goes down by 4.

For example, the thorium isotope $^{228}_{90}Th$ decays by emitting an α particle. So it forms the radium isotope $^{224}_{88}Ra$.

Figure 2 shows an equation to represent this decay.

- The numbers along the top represent the mass number, which is the number of protons and neutrons in each nucleus and in the α particle.
- The equation shows that the total number of protons and neutrons after the change (= 224 + 4) is equal to the total number of neutrons and protons before the change (= 228).
- The numbers along the bottom represent the atomic number, which is the number of protons in each nucleus and in the α particle.
- The equation shows that the total number of protons after the change (= 88 + 2) is equal to the total number of protons before the change (= 90).

β emission

- A β particle is an electron created and emitted by a nucleus which has too many neutrons compared with its protons. A neutron in the nucleus changes into a proton and a β particle. This is instantly emitted at high speed by the nucleus.
- The relative mass of a β particle is effectively zero and its relative charge is –1. So we can represent a β particle by the symbol ${}^{0}_{-1}\beta$.
- When an unstable nucleus emits a β particle, the atomic number of the nucleus goes up by 1 but its mass number stays the same (because a neutron changes into a proton).
- For example, the potassium isotope ${}^{40}_{19}K$ decays by emitting a β particle. So it forms a nucleus of the calcium isotope ${}^{40}_{20}Ca$.
- The numbers along the top represent the mass number which is the number of protons and neutrons for each nucleus and zero for the β particle, as explained above.
- The equation shows that the total number of protons and neutrons after the change (= 40 + 0) is equal to the total number of neutrons and protons before the change (= 40).
- The numbers along the bottom represent the atomic number. This is the number of protons for each nucleus and –1 for the β particle, as explained below.
- The equation shows that the total charge (in relative units) after the change (= 20 – 1) is equal to the total charge before the change (= 19). (Note the relative charge of the β particle is –1 so we represent its atomic number as –1 in these nuclear equations, even though it has no protons at all.)

A β particle is created in the nucleus and instantly emitted
A neutron in the nucleus changes into a proton

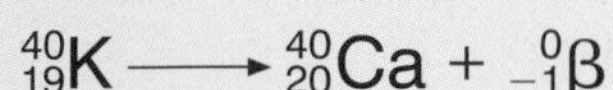

$${}^{40}_{19}K \longrightarrow {}^{40}_{20}Ca + {}^{0}_{-1}\beta$$

Figure 3 β emission

γ emission

γ radiation is emitted by some unstable nuclei after an α particle or a β particle has been emitted. γ radiation is uncharged and has no mass. So it does not change the number of protons or the number of neutrons in a nucleus.

Examiner's tip

Make sure you know the changes to mass number and to atomic number that occur in alpha decay and in beta decay.

Summary questions

1 How many protons and how many neutrons are there in the nucleus of each of the following isotopes:
   a ${}^{12}_{6}C$ **b** ${}^{60}_{27}Co$ **c** ${}^{235}_{92}U$?
   d How many more protons and how many more neutrons are in ${}^{238}_{92}U$ compared with ${}^{224}_{88}Ra$?

2 A substance contains the radioactive isotope ${}^{238}_{92}U$, which emits alpha radiation. The product nucleus X emits beta radiation and forms a nucleus Y. How many protons and how many neutrons are present in:
   a a nucleus of ${}^{238}_{92}U$ **b** a nucleus of X **c** a nucleus of Y?

3 **a** Copy and complete the following equations for α and β decay.
   i ${}^{235}_{92}U \rightarrow {}^{?}_{?}Th + {}^{4}_{2}\alpha$ **ii** ${}^{64}_{29}Cu \rightarrow {}^{?}_{?}Zn + {}^{0}_{-1}\beta$
   b A radioactive isotope of polonium (Po) has 84 protons and 126 neutrons.
   i The isotope is formed from the decay of a radioactive isotope of bismuth, which emits a β particle in the process. Copy and complete the equation below with the correct values of *A* and *Z* to represent this decay.

$$Bi \rightarrow Po + \beta$$

   ii The polonium isotope decays by emitting an α particle to form a stable isotope of lead (Pb). Copy and complete the equation below with the correct values of *A* and *Z* to represent this decay.

$$Po \rightarrow Pb + \alpha$$

Key points

- **Isotopes of an element are atoms with the same number of protons but different numbers of neutrons. Therefore they have the same atomic number but different mass numbers.**

α decay	β decay
Change in the nucleus	
Nucleus loses 2 protons and 2 neutrons	A neutron in the nucleus changes into a proton
Particle emitted	
2 protons and 2 neutrons emitted as an α particle	An electron is created in the nucleus and instantly emitted
Equation	
${}^{A}_{Z}\mathbf{X} \rightarrow {}^{A-4}_{Z-2}\mathbf{Y} + {}^{4}_{2}\alpha$	${}^{A}_{Z}\mathbf{X} \rightarrow {}^{A}_{Z+1}\mathbf{Y} + {}^{0}_{-1}\beta$

P19.3 More about alpha, beta and gamma radiation

Learning objectives

After this topic, you should know:

- how far each type of radiation can travel in air and what stops it
- what alpha, beta and gamma radiation is
- how to separate a beam of alpha, beta and gamma radiation
- why alpha, beta and gamma radiation is dangerous.

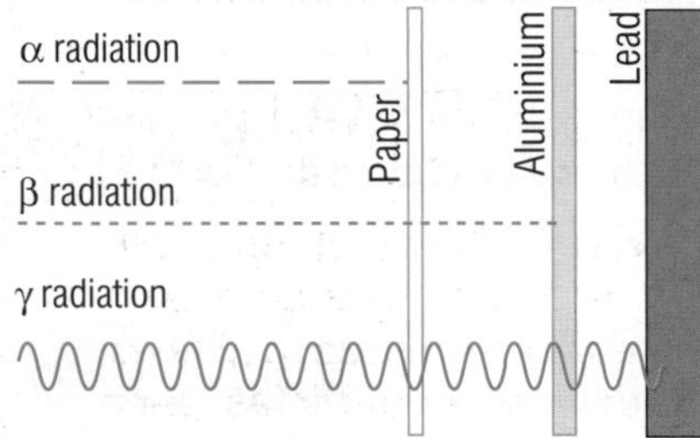

α radiation
β radiation
γ radiation
Paper
Aluminium
Lead

Figure 2 The penetrating powers of α, β and γ radiation

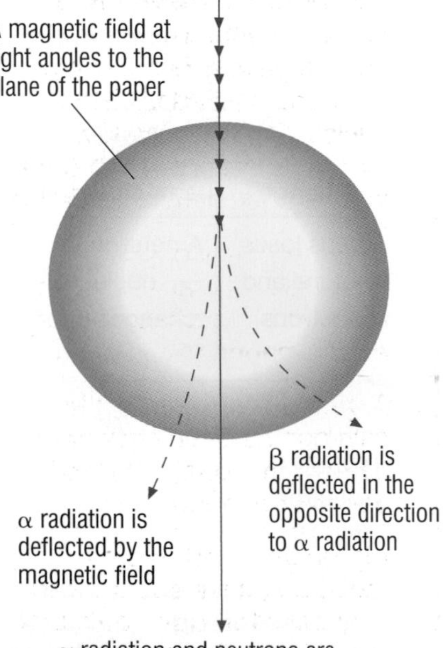

Beam of radiation enters a magnetic field
A magnetic field at right angles to the plane of the paper
α radiation is deflected by the magnetic field
β radiation is deflected in the opposite direction to α radiation
γ radiation and neutrons are undeflected by the magnetic field

Figure 3 Radiation in a magnetic field

Penetrating power

Alpha radiation can't penetrate paper. But what stops beta and gamma radiation? And how far can each type of radiation travel through air? We can use a Geiger counter to find out, but we must take account of background radiation. To do this we should:

1. Measure the count rate (which is the number of counts per second) without the radioactive source present. This is the background count rate.
2. Measure the count rate with the source in place. Subtracting the background count rate from this gives the count rate from the source alone.

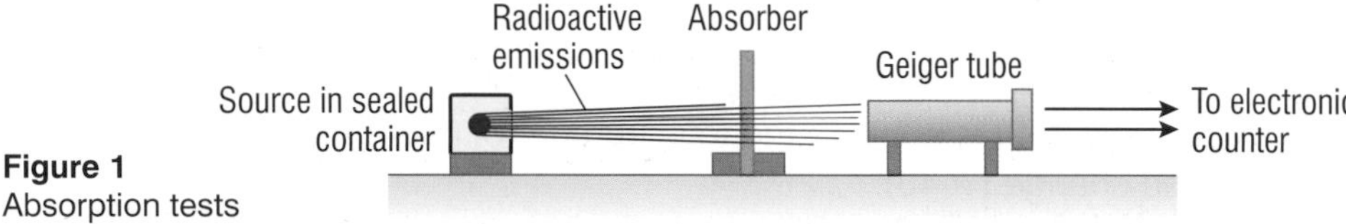

Radioactive emissions
Absorber
Geiger tube
Source in sealed container
To electronic counter

Figure 1 Absorption tests

We can then test absorber materials and the range in air.

- To test different materials, we need to place each material between the tube and the radioactive source. Then we measure the count rate. We can add more layers of material until the count rate from the source is zero. The radiation from the source has then been stopped by the absorber material.
- To test the range in air, we need to move the tube away from the source. When the tube is beyond the range of the radiation, the count rate from the source is zero.

The table here shows the results of the two tests.

Type of radiation	Absorber materials	Range in air
alpha (α)	Thin sheet of paper	about 5 cm
beta (β)	Aluminium sheet (about 5 mm thick) Lead sheet (2–3 mm thick)	about 1 m
gamma (γ)	Thick lead sheet (several cm thick) Concrete (more than 1 m thick)	unlimited

Gamma radiation spreads out in air without being absorbed. It does get weaker as it spreads out.

The nature of alpha, beta and gamma radiation

We can separate these radiations using a magnetic field or an electric field.

Deflection by a magnetic field

- β radiation is easily deflected, in the same way as electrons. So the radiation consists of negatively charged particles. In fact, a β particle is a fast-moving electron. It is emitted by an unstable nucleus that contains too many neutrons.
- α radiation is deflected in the opposite direction to β radiation. So α radiation is made up of positively charged particles. α particles are harder to deflect than β radiation. This is because an α particle has a much greater mass than a β particle has. An α particle is two protons and two neutrons stuck together, the same as a helium nucleus.
- γ radiation is not deflected by a magnetic field or by an electric field. This is because γ radiation is electromagnetic radiation so is uncharged.

Deflection by an electric field

α and β particles passing through an electric field are deflected in opposite directions, as shown in Figure 4.

- The α particles are attracted towards the negative plate because they are positively charged.
- The β particles are attracted towards the positive plate because they are negatively charged,

In Figures 3 and 4, an alpha particle is deflected much less than a beta particle. The charge of an alpha particle is double the charge of a beta particle, so the force is twice as great. But the mass of an alpha particle is about 8000 times the mass of a beta particle, so the deflection of the alpha particle is much less.

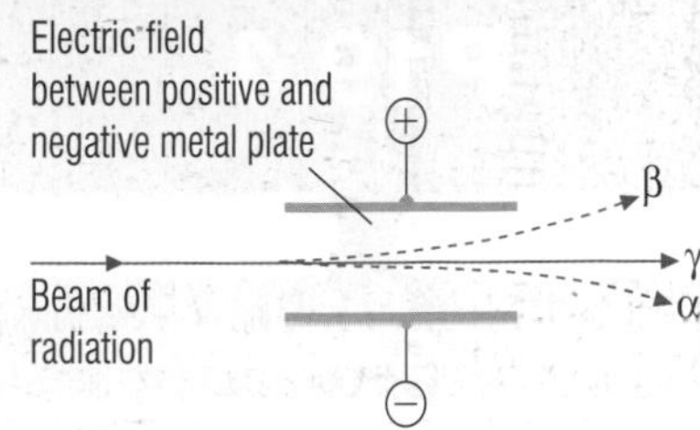

Figure 4 Radiation passing through an electric field

Figure 5 Radioactive warnings

Radioactivity dangers

The radiation from a radioactive substance can knock electrons out of atoms. The atoms become charged because they lose electrons. The process is called **ionisation**. (Remember that a charged particle is called an ion.)

X-rays also cause ionisation. Ionisation in a living cell can damage or kill the cell. Damage to the genes in a cell can be passed on if the cell generates more cells. Strict safety rules must always be followed when radioactive substances are used.

Alpha radiation is more dangerous in the body than beta or gamma radiation. This is because it ionises substances much more than beta radiation, which is more ionising than gamma radiation. In other words, the ionising power of alpha radiation is much greater than the ionising power of beta or gamma radiation.

Examiner's tip

Make sure you can explain the different paths taken by alpha, beta and gamma radiation in magnetic and electric fields.

Summary questions

1 a Why is a radioactive source stored in a lead-lined box?
  b How do we know that gamma radiation is **not** made up of charged particles?
  c Why should long-handled tongs be used to move a radioactive source?
  d What type or types of radiation from a radioactive source is stopped by a thick aluminium plate?

2 a Which type of radiation is:
    i uncharged
    ii positively charged
    iii negatively charged?
  b A narrow beam of α, β and γ radiation is directed into a magnetic field.
    i Explain why the γ radiation is not deflected although the α and β particles are deflected.
    ii Explain why the α and β particles are deflected in opposite directions.
    iii Explain why the α particles are deflected much less than the β particles are deflected.

3 a Explain why ionising radiation is dangerous.
  b Explain how you would use a Geiger counter to find the range of the radiation from a source of α radiation.

Key points

- **α radiation** is stopped by paper, has a range of a few centimetres in air and consists of particles, each composed of two protons and two neutrons. It has the greatest ionising power.
- **β radiation** is stopped by a thin sheet of metal, has a range of about a metre in air and consists of fast-moving electrons emitted from the nucleus. It is less ionising than alpha radiation and more ionising than gamma radiation.
- **γ radiation** is stopped by thick lead, has an unlimited range in air and consists of electromagnetic radiation.
- A magnetic or an electric field can be used to separate a beam of alpha, beta and gamma radiation.
- Alpha, beta and gamma radiation ionise substances they pass through. Ionisation in a living cell can damage or kill the cell.

P19.4 Half-life

Learning objectives

After this topic, you should know:

- what is meant by the 'half-life' of a radioactive source
- what is meant by the count rate from a radioactive source
- what happens to the count rate from a radioactive isotope as it decays.

Every atom of an element always has the same number of protons in its nucleus. However, the number of neutrons in the nucleus can differ. Each type of atom is called an isotope. (Isotopes of an element contain the same number of protons but different numbers of neutrons.)

The **activity** of a radioactive isotope is the number of atoms that decay per second. As the nucleus of each unstable atom (the 'parent' atom) decays, the number of parent atoms goes down. So the activity of the sample decreases.

We can use a Geiger counter to monitor the activity of a radioactive sample. We need to measure the **count rate** from the sample. This is the number of counts per second (or per minute). The graph below shows how the count rate of a sample decreases.

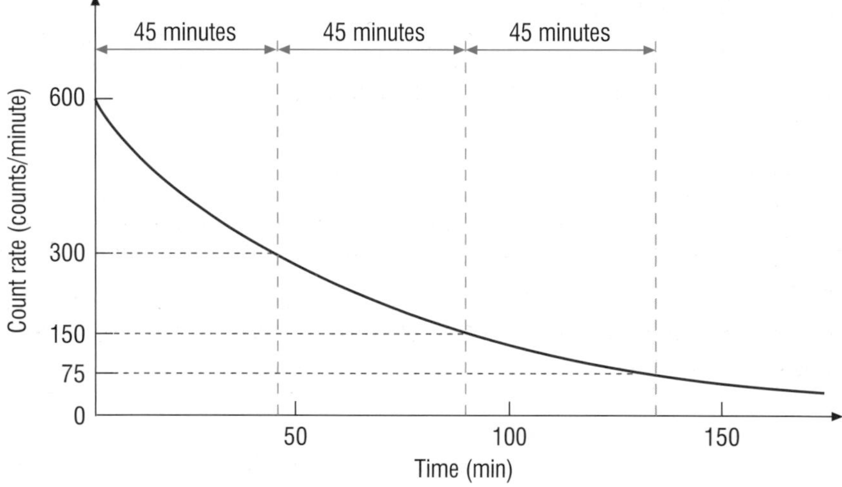

Figure 1 Radioactive decay: a graph of count rate against time

The graph shows that the count rate decreases with time. The count rate falls from:

- 600 counts per minute (c.p.m.) to 300 c.p.m. in the first 45 minutes
- 300 counts per minute (c.p.m.) to 150 c.p.m. in the next 45 minutes.

The average time taken for the count rate (and therefore the number of parent atoms) to fall by half is always the same. This time is called the **half-life**. The half-life shown on the graph is 45 minutes.

The half-life of a radioactive isotope is the average time it takes:

- **for the number of nuclei of the isotope in a sample (and therefore the mass of parent atoms) to halve**
- **for the count rate from the isotope in a sample to fall to half its initial value.**

Examiner's tip

Remember that the half-life of a radioactive isotope is the time taken for the number of nuclei to halve AND for the count rate to halve.

Did you know ...?

Some radioactive isotopes have half-lives of a fraction of a second, whereas others have half-lives of more than a billion years. The nitrogen isotope N-12 has a half-life of 0.0125 seconds. The uranium isotope U-238 has a half-life of 4.5 billion years.

The random nature of radioactive decay

Radioactive decay is a random process. We can't predict *when* an individual atom will suddenly decay. But we *can* predict how many atoms will decay in a certain time – because there are so many of them. This is a bit like throwing dice. You can't predict what number you will get with a single throw. But if you threw 1000 dice, you would expect one-sixth to come up with a particular number.

Suppose we start with 1000 unstable atoms. Look at the graph on the right:

If 10% decay every hour:

- 100 atoms will decay in the first hour, leaving 900
- 90 atoms (= 10% of 900) will decay in the second hour, leaving 810.

The table below shows what you get if you continue the calculations. The results are plotted as a graph in Figure 2.

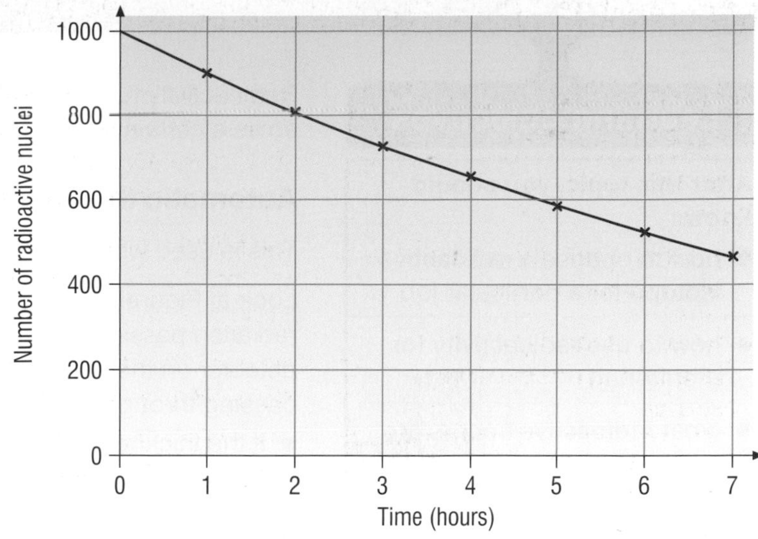

Figure 2 Half-life

Time from start (hours)	0	1	2	3	4	5	6	7
No. of unstable atoms present	1000	900	810	729	656	590	531	478
No. of unstable atoms that decay in the next hour	100	90	81	73	66	59	53	48

Did you know ... ?

Next time you help someone choose numbers for the lottery, think about whether this is something you can predict. The balls come out of the machine at random; is there any way of predicting what they will be?

Summary questions

1 a What is meant by the half-life of a radioactive isotope?

b What will the count rate in Figure 1 be after 135 minutes from the start?

c Use the graph in Figure 2 to work out the half-life of the radioactive isotope.

2 A radioactive isotope has a half-life of 15 hours. A sealed tube contains 8 milligrams of this isotope.

a What mass of the isotope is in the tube:

i 15 hours later?

ii 45 hours later?

b Estimate how long it would take for the mass of the isotope to decrease to less than 5% of the initial mass.

3 a A sample of a radioactive isotope contains 320 million atoms of the isotope. How many atoms of the isotope are present after:

i one half-life **ii** five half-lives?

b In Figure 1, estimate how long it would take for the count rate to decrease to less than 40 counts per minute.

Key points

- The half-life of a radioactive isotope is the average time it takes for the number of nuclei of the isotope in a sample to halve.
- The count rate of a Geiger counter due to a radioactive source decreases as the activity of the source decreases.
- The number of atoms of a radioactive isotope and the count rate both decrease by half every half-life.

P19.5 Radioactivity at work

Learning objectives

After this topic, you should know:

- **how to choose a radioactive isotope for a particular job**
- **how to use radioactivity for monitoring**
- **what radioactive tracers are**
- **what radioactive dating is.**

Radioactivity has many uses. For each use, we need a radioactive isotope that emits a certain type of radiation and has a suitable half-life.

Automatic thickness monitoring

This is used when making metal foil.

Look at Figure 1. The radioactive source emits β radiation. The amount of radiation passing through the foil depends on the thickness of the foil. A detector on the other side of the metal foil measures the amount of radiation passing through it.

- If the thickness of the foil increases too much, the detector reading drops.
- The detector sends a signal to the rollers to increase the pressure on the metal sheet.

This makes the foil thinner again.

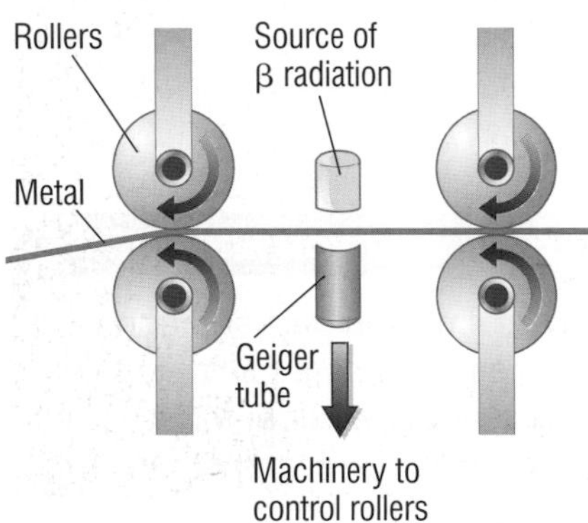

Figure 1 Thickness monitoring using a radioactive source

Radioactive tracers

These are used to trace the flow of a substance through a system. For example, doctors use radioactive iodine to find out if a patient's kidney is blocked.

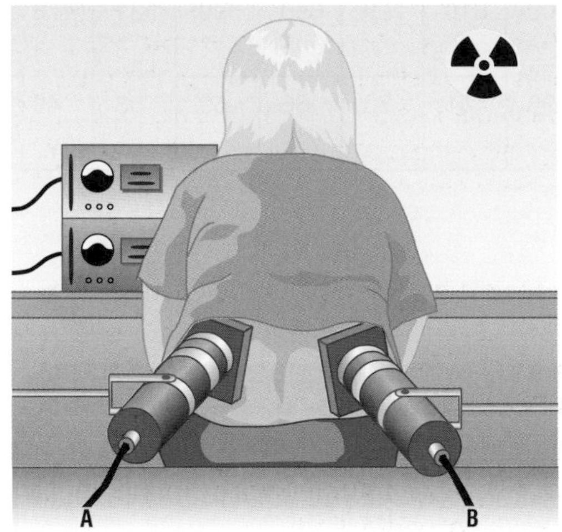

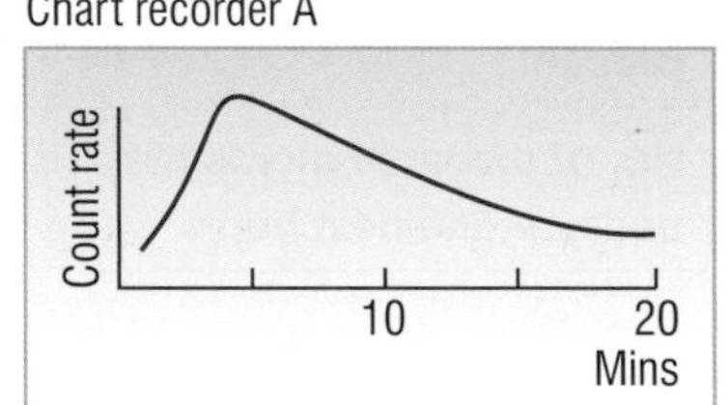

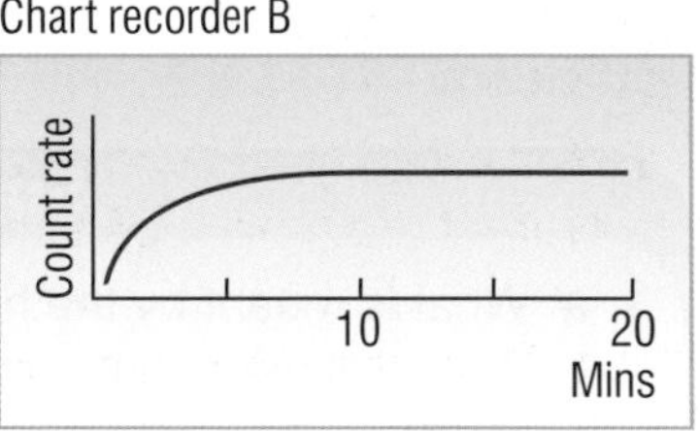

Figure 2 Using a tracer to monitor a patient's kidneys

Before the test, the patient drinks water containing a tiny amount of the radioactive substance. A detector is then placed against each kidney. Each detector is connected to a chart recorder.

- The radioactive substance flows in and out of a normal kidney. So the detector reading goes up then down (see Chart recorder A).
- For a blocked kidney, the reading goes up and stays up. This is because the radioactive substance goes into the kidney but doesn't flow out again (see Chart recorder B).

Radioactive iodine is used for this test because:

- Its half-life is 8 days, so it lasts long enough for the test to be done but decays almost completely after a few weeks.
- It emits gamma radiation, so it can be detected outside the body.
- It decays into a stable product.

Reducing risk

Workers who are at risk from ionising radiations cut down their exposure to the radiation by:

- keeping as far as possible from the source of radiation, using special handling tools with long handles
- spending as little time as possible in 'at-risk' areas
- shielding themselves from the radiation by staying behind thick concrete barriers and/or using thick lead plates.

Radioactive dating

This is used to find the age of ancient material. We can use:

- **Carbon dating** – this is used to find the age of ancient wood and other organic material. Living wood contains a tiny proportion of radioactive carbon. This has a half-life of 5600 years. When a tree dies, it no longer absorbs any carbon. So the amount of radioactive carbon in it decreases. To find the age of a sample, we need to measure the count rate from the wood. This is compared with the count rate from the same mass of living wood. For example, suppose the count rate in a sample of wood is half the count rate of an equal mass of living wood. Then the sample must be 5600 years old.
- **Uranium dating** – this is used to find the age of igneous rocks. These rocks contain radioactive uranium, which has a half-life of 4500 million years. Each uranium atom decays into an atom of lead. We can work out the age of a sample by measuring the number of atoms of uranium and lead. For example, if a sample contains 1 atom of lead for every atom of the uranium, the age of the sample must be 4500 million years. This is because there must have *originally* been 2 atoms of uranium for each atom of uranium now present.

Examiner's tip

Make sure you can decide on the appropriate radioactive isotope for a particular task.

Did you know ... ?

Smoke alarms save lives. A radioactive source inside the alarm sends out alpha particles into a gap in a circuit in the alarm. The alpha particles ionise the air in the gap so it conducts a current across the gap. In a fire, smoke absorbs the ions created by the alpha particles so they don't cross the gap. The current across the gap drops and the alarm sounds. The battery in a smoke alarm needs to be checked regularly – to make sure it is still working!

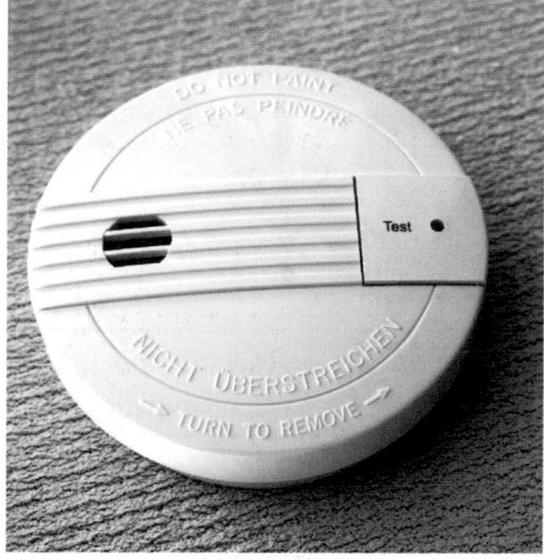

Figure 3 A smoke alarm

Summary questions

1 Radiation from radioactive sources is used for different purposes. Which type of radiation, alpha, beta or gamma, is used in the examples **a** to **c** below? Give a reason for your choice in each example.
  - **a** Monitoring the continuous production of thin metal sheets.
  - **b** Finding out whether a kidney in a patient is blocked.
  - **c** Monitoring a leak in an underground pipeline.

2 **a** Explain why γ radiation is not suitable for monitoring the thickness of metal foil.
  b When a radioactive tracer is used, why is it best to use a radioactive isotope that decays into a stable isotope?

3 **a** What are the ideal properties of a radioactive isotope used as a medical tracer?
  b **i** A sample of old wood was carbon dated and found to have 25% of the count rate measured in an equal mass of living wood. The half-life of the radioactive carbon is 5600 years. How old is the sample of wood?
  ii When the count rate measurements were made, they needed to be corrected to take account of background radiation. Explain why this correction is necessary, and describe how it is made.

Key points

- The use we can make of a radioactive isotope depends on:
  - **a** its half-life
  - **b** the type of radiation it gives out.
- For monitoring, the isotope should have a long half-life.
- Radioactive tracers should be β or γ emitters that last long enough to monitor but not too long.
- For radioactive dating of a sample, we need a radioactive isotope that is present in the sample which has a half-life about the same as the age of the sample.

Summary questions

1 **a** How many protons and how many neutrons are in a nucleus of each of the following isotopes:
  i $^{14}_{6}C$? **ii** $^{228}_{90}Th$?

b $^{14}_{6}C$ emits a β particle and becomes an isotope of nitrogen (N).
  i How many protons and how many neutrons are in this nitrogen isotope?
  ii Write down the symbol for this isotope.

c $^{228}_{90}Th$ emits an α particle and becomes an isotope of radium (Ra).
  i How many protons and how many neutrons are in this isotope of radium?
  ii Write down the symbol for this isotope.

2 Copy and complete the following table about the properties of alpha, beta and gamma radiation.

	α	β	γ
Identity		electrons	
Stopped by			thick lead
Electric field deflection	towards the negative plate		
Range in air		about 1 m	
Relative ionisation			weak

3 **a** The table below gives information about four radioactive isotopes **A**, **B**, **C** and **D**.

Isotope	Type of radiation emitted	Half-life
A californium-241	alpha	4 minutes
B cobalt-60	gamma	5 years
C hydrogen-3	beta	12 years
D strontium-90	beta	28 years

Match each statement **1** to **4** with **A**, **B**, **C** or **D**.
1. The isotope that gives off radiation with an unlimited range.
2. The isotope that has the longest half-life.
3. The isotope that decays the fastest.
4. The isotope with the smallest mass of each atom.

b **i** Why would none of the isotopes in the table be suitable for use in a smoke alarm?
  ii Which entry in each of the last two columns in the table above would be most suitable for a smoke alarm? Give reasons for your choice from each column.

4 The following measurements were made of the count rate from a radioactive source.

Time (hours)	0	0.5	1.0	1.5	2.0	2.5
Count rate due to the source (counts per minute)	510	414	337	276	227	188

a Plot a graph of the count rate (on the vertical axis) against time.

b Use your graph to find the half-life of the source.

5 In a carbon dating experiment of ancient wood, a sample of the wood gave a corrected count rate of 0.4 counts per minute. The same mass of living wood gave a corrected count rate of 1.6 counts per minute.

a How many half-lives did the count rate take to decrease from 1.6 to 0.4 counts per minute?

b The half-life of the radioactive carbon in the wood is 5600 years. What is the age of the sample?

6 In an investigation to find out what type of radiation was emitted from a given source, the following measurements were made with a Geiger counter.

Source	Average count rate (in counts per minute)
No source present	29
Source at 20 mm from tube with no absorber between	385
Source at 20 mm from tube with a sheet of metal foil between	384
Source at 20 mm from tube with a 10 mm thick aluminium plate between	32

a What caused the count rate when no source was present?

b What was the count rate from the source with no absorbers present?

c What type of radiation was emitted by the source? Explain how you arrive at your answer.

AQA Examination-style questions

1 The diagram shows two atoms, **X** and **Y**, of the same element.

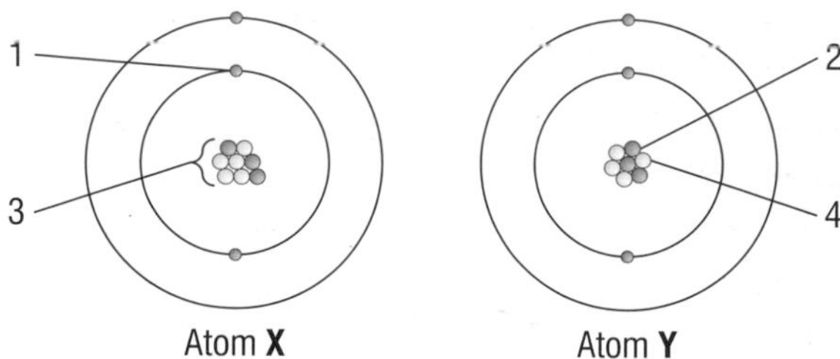

a i Match words **A**, **B**, **C** and **D**, with the numbers, **1–4**, on the diagram. (4)

A electron
B neutron
C nucleus
D proton

ii Atoms **X** and **Y** are isotopes of the element. What are *isotopes*? (2)

iii An atom of sodium can be represented as shown:

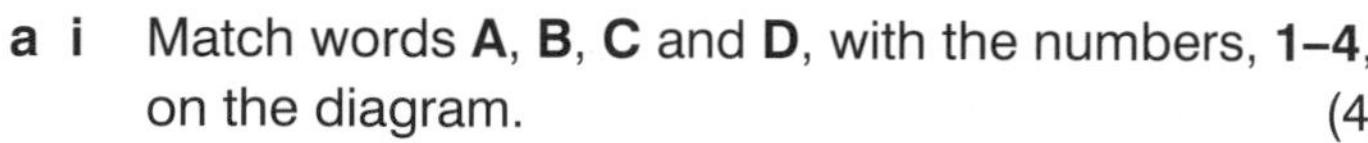

$^{23}_{11}\mathbf{Na}$

Add suitable numbers to represent the atom **Y**. (2)

b Some isotopes are radioactive.

What is meant by *radioactive*? (2)

2 Radioactive materials emit three different types of radiation.

Some years ago, newspapers reported that a former spy had been poisoned with the radioactive isotope polonium-210.

Scientists carried out many tests at restaurants, hotels and airports. Some of the spy's friends were found to be contaminated with polonium-210. Scientists reassured them that they were safe unless they had taken some of the polonium-210 into their bodies.

a From the information above, deduce what type of radiation is emitted by polonium-210, explain why the friends should have been reassured and why the scientists found that it was difficult to detect the radiation outside the spy's body. (6)

b Another isotope of polonium is polonium-208.

How is a nucleus of polonium-208 different from a nucleus of polonium-210, and how is it the same? (2)

3 a The graph shows how the count rate of a radioactive isotope, $^{238}_{92}\mathbf{X}$, changes with time.

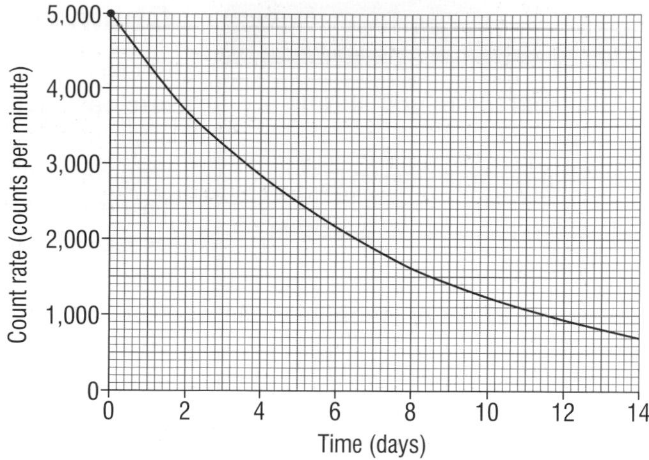

i Use the graph to determine the half-life of the radioactive isotope. (2)

ii What would you expect the count rate to have been 10 hours before the graph starts? (3)

iii The radioactive isotope $^{238}_{92}\mathbf{X}$ decays by alpha emission to an isotope of element **Y**.

What is:

the mass number of the isotope of **Y**?

the atomic number of the isotope of **Y**? (2)

b A hospital patient is thought to have a blood circulation problem. The doctors investigate the problem by injecting a radioactive isotope into the patient's bloodstream to act as a tracer.

Explain the properties that the radioactive isotope should have for it to be suitable as a tracer. (5)

c The diagram shows a section through a smoke alarm fitted to the ceiling.

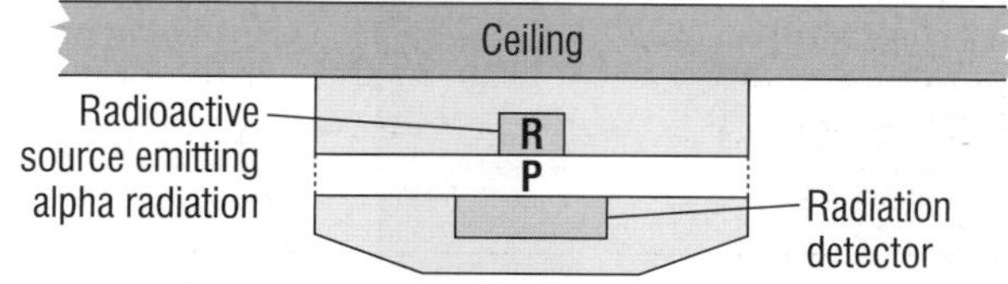

The radioactive isotope, **R**, used in the smoke alarm, emits alpha particles and has a half-life of 432 years.

i If smoke enters the smoke alarm at **P**, the alarm sounds.
Explain why. (4)

ii Give three reasons why **R** is a suitable radioactive isotope to use in the smoke alarm. (3)

P20.1 Nuclear fission

Learning objectives

After this topic, you should know:

- what nuclear fission is
- which radioactive isotopes undergo fission
- what a chain reaction is
- how a chain reaction in a nuclear reactor is controlled.

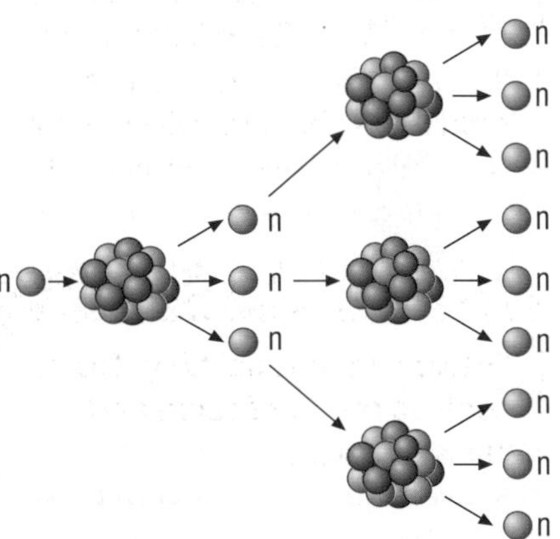

Figure 2 A chain reaction in a nuclear reactor

Figure 3 Ernest Rutherford

Chain reactions

Energy is released in a nuclear reactor as a result of **nuclear fission**. In this process, the nucleus of an atom of a fissionable substance splits into two smaller 'fragment' nuclei as a result of absorbing a neutron. This event can release several neutrons, which can cause other fissionable nuclei to split. This then produces a **chain reaction** of fission events.

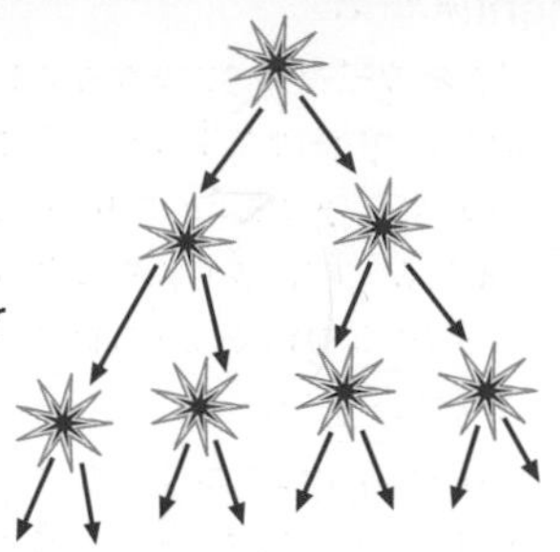

In a chain reaction, each reaction causes more reactions which cause more reactions, etc.

Figure 1 A chain reaction

Fission neutrons

When a nucleus undergoes fission, it releases:

- two or three neutrons (called 'fission' neutrons) at high speeds
- energy, in the form of radiation, plus kinetic energy of the fission neutrons and the fragment nuclei.

The fission neutrons may cause further fission resulting in a chain reaction. In a **nuclear fission reactor**, on average, exactly one fission neutron from each fission event goes on to produce further fission. This ensures energy is released at a steady rate in the reactor.

Did you know ...?

Ernest Rutherford was awarded the Nobel Prize in 1908 for his discoveries on radioactivity. His famous discovery of the nucleus was made in 1913. He was knighted in 1914 and made a member of the House of Lords in 1931. He hoped that no one would discover how to release energy from the nucleus until people learned to live at peace with their neighbours. He died in 1937 before the discovery of nuclear fission.

Fissionable isotopes

The fuel in a nuclear reactor must contain fissionable isotopes.

- Most reactors at the present time are designed to use 'enriched uranium' as the fuel. This consists mostly of the non-fissionable uranium isotope $^{238}_{92}U$ (U-238) and about 2–3% of the uranium isotope $^{235}_{92}U$ (U-235), which *is* fissionable. In comparison, natural uranium is more than 99% U-238.
- The U-238 nuclei in a nuclear reactor do not undergo fission but they change into other heavy nuclei, including plutonium-239. The isotope $^{239}_{94}Pu$ is fissionable. It can be used in a different type of reactor, but not in a uranium-235 reactor, which is the most common type of reactor.

Inside a nuclear reactor

A nuclear reactor consists of uranium fuel rods spaced evenly in the reactor core. Figure 4 shows a cross-section of a pressurised water reactor.

- The reactor core contains the fuel rods, control rods and water at high pressure. The fission neutrons are slowed down by collisions with the atoms in the water molecules. This is needed because fast neutrons do not cause further fission of U-235. We say the water acts as a **moderator** because it slows down the fission neutrons.

- **Control rods** in the core absorb surplus neutrons. This keeps the chain reaction under control. The depth of the rods in the core is adjusted to maintain a steady chain reaction.
- The water acts as a **coolant**. Its molecules gain kinetic energy from the neutrons and the fuel rods. The water is pumped through the core. Then it goes through sealed pipes to and from a heat exchanger outside the core. The water transfers energy from the core to the heat exchanger.
- The **reactor core** is made of thick steel to withstand the very high temperature and pressure in the core. The core is enclosed by thick concrete walls. These absorb radiation that escapes through the walls of the steel vessel.

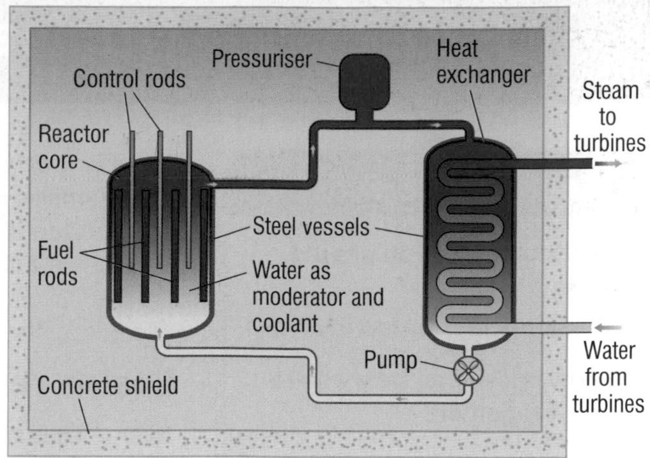

Figure 4 A nuclear reactor

Summary questions

1 Natural uranium consists mainly of uranium-238. Uranium fuel is produced from natural uranium by increasing the proportion of uranium-235 in it.

 a What happens to a uranium-235 nucleus when a neutron collides with it and causes it to undergo fission?

 b What happens to a uranium-238 nucleus when a neutron collides with it?

2 a Put the statements **A** to **D** in the list below into the correct sequence, starting with B, to describe a steady chain reaction in a nuclear reactor.

 A a U-235 nucleus splits **C** neutrons are released

 B a neutron hits a U-235 nucleus **D** energy is released

 b i In a nuclear reactor, what is the purpose of the control rods?

 ii If the control rods in a nuclear reactor are pushed further into the reactor core, state and explain what would happen to the number of fission neutrons in the reactor.

3 a Look at the chain reaction shown in the figure.

 i Which of the nuclei A to F have been hit by a neutron?

 ii What has happened to these nuclei?

 iii Which two of the other nuclei A to F could undergo fission from a fission neutron shown?

 b In a chain reaction, a neutron causes a fission event X that releases three neutrons, two of which go on to produce further fission events Y and Z that each cause two further fission events.

 i Complete the figure by adding 'neutron' arrows to represent this chain reaction.

 ii Give one reason why one of the three neutrons released by event X did not cause further fission.

Did you know ... ?

A nuclear bomb is two lumps of $^{235}_{92}U$ or $^{239}_{94}Pu$. Each lump loses too many fission neutrons to produce a chain reaction. But if you bring the two together ...!

Examiner's tip

'Fission' means splitting. Don't confuse nuclear fission and nuclear fusion.

Key points

- Nuclear fission is the splitting of an atomic nucleus into two smaller nuclei and the release of two or three neutrons and energy.
- **Nuclear fission** occurs when a neutron is absorbed by a uranium-235 nucleus or a plutonium-239 nucleus and the nucleus splits.
- A **chain reaction** occurs in a nuclear reactor when each fission event causes further fission events.
- In a **nuclear reactor**, control rods absorb fission neutrons to ensure that, on average, only one neutron per fission goes on to produce further fission.

P20.2 Nuclear fusion

Learning objectives

After this topic, you should know:

- what nuclear fusion is
- how nuclei can be made to fuse together
- where the Sun's energy comes from
- why it is difficult to make a nuclear fusion reactor.

Imagine if we could get energy from water. Stars release energy as a result of fusing small nuclei such as hydrogen to form larger nuclei. Water contains lots of hydrogen atoms. A glass of water could provide the same amount of energy as a tanker full of petrol. But only if we could make a fusion reactor here on Earth.

Fusion reactions

Two small nuclei release energy when they are fused together to form a single larger nucleus. This process is called **nuclear fusion**. It releases energy only if the relative mass of the nucleus formed is no more than about 55 (about the same as an iron nucleus). Energy must be supplied to create bigger nuclei.

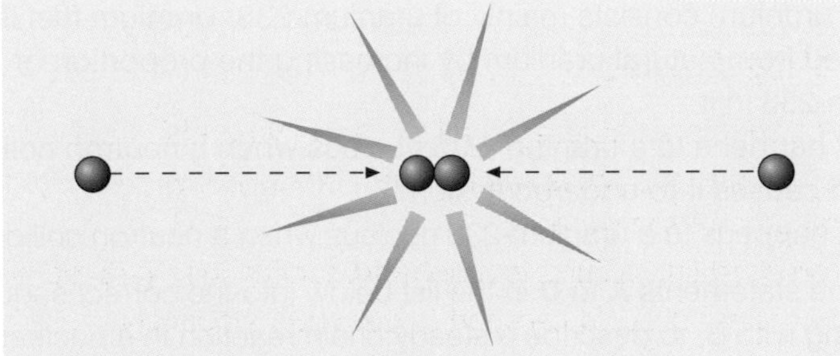

Figure 1 A nuclear fusion reaction

Examiner's tip

'Fusion' means joining together. Don't confuse fusion with fission.

The Sun is about 75 per cent hydrogen and 25 per cent helium. The core is so hot that it consists of a 'plasma' of bare nuclei with no electrons. These nuclei move about and fuse together when they collide. When they fuse, they release energy. Figure 2 shows how protons fuse together to form a $^{4}_{2}$He nucleus. Energy is released at each stage.

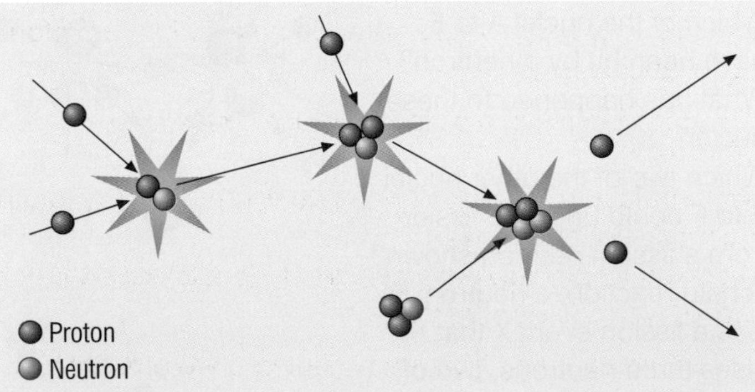

Figure 2 Fusion reactions in the Sun

- When two protons (i.e. hydrogen nuclei) fuse, they form a 'heavy hydrogen' nucleus, $^{2}_{1}$H. Other particles are created and emitted at the same time.
- Two more protons collide separately with two $^{2}_{1}$H nuclei and turn them into heavier nuclei.
- The two heavier nuclei collide to form the helium nucleus $^{4}_{2}$He.
- The energy released at each stage is carried away as kinetic energy of the product nucleus and other particles emitted.

Did you know ... ?

A hydrogen bomb is a uranium bomb surrounded by the hydrogen isotope, $^{2}_{1}$H. When the uranium bomb explodes, it makes the surrounding hydrogen fuse and release even more energy. A single hydrogen bomb could completely destroy London.

Fusion reactors

There are enormous technical difficulties with making fusion a useful source of energy. The plasma of light nuclei must be heated to very high temperatures before the nuclei will fuse. This is because two nuclei approaching each other will repel each other due to their positive charges. If the nuclei are moving fast enough, they can overcome the force of repulsion and fuse together.

In a fusion reactor:

- the plasma is heated by passing a very large electric current through it
- the plasma is contained by a magnetic field so it doesn't touch the reactor walls. If it did, it would go cold and fusion would stop.

Scientists have been working on these problems since the 1950s. A successful fusion reactor would release more energy than it uses to heat the plasma. At the present time, scientists working on experimental fusion reactors are able to do this by fusing heavy hydrogen nuclei to form helium nuclei – but only for a few minutes!

Figure 3 An experimental fusion reactor

A promising future

Practical fusion reactors could meet all our energy needs.

- The fuel for fusion reactors is readily available as heavy hydrogen and is naturally present in sea water.
- The reaction product, helium, is a non-radioactive inert gas, so is harmless.
- The energy released could be used to generate electricity.

In comparison, fission reactors mostly use uranium, which is only found in certain parts of the world. Also, they produce nuclear waste that has to be stored securely for many years. However, fission reactors have been in operation for over 50 years, unlike fusion reactors, which are still under development.

Summary questions

1 a What is meant by nuclear fusion?

b Look at Figure 2 and work out what is formed when a proton collides with a $^{2}_{1}H$ nucleus.

2 a i Why does the plasma of light nuclei in a fusion reactor need to be very hot?

ii Why would a fusion reactor that needs more energy than it produces not be much use?

b State one advantage and one disadvantage a fusion reactor has compared with a fission reactor.

3 a How many protons and how many neutrons are present in a $^{2}_{1}H$ nucleus?

b Write down an equation to represent the fusion of a proton and a $^{2}_{1}H$ nucleus when they form a helium $^{3}_{2}He$ nucleus. The symbol for a proton is $^{1}_{1}p$ (because its proton number (the lower number) is 1 and its mass number (the top number) is 1).

c Copy and complete the equation below to show the reaction in Figure 2 that takes place when two $^{3}_{2}He$ nuclei fuse together to form a $^{4}_{2}He$ nucleus.

$$^{3}_{2}He + ^{3}_{2}He \rightarrow ^{4}_{2}He + \text{..........} + \text{..........}$$

Key points

- Nuclear fusion is the process of forcing two atomic nuclei close enough together so they form a single larger nucleus.
- Nuclear fusion can be brought about by making two light nuclei collide at very high speed.
- Energy is released when two light nuclei are fused together. Nuclear fusion in the Sun's core releases energy.
- A fusion reactor needs to be at a very high temperature before nuclear fusion can take place. The nuclei to be fused are difficult to contain.

P20.3 Nuclear issues

Learning objectives

After this topic, you should know:

- what radon gas is and why it is dangerous
- how safe nuclear reactors are
- what happens to nuclear waste.

 links

For more information on ionising radiation, look back at 19.3 'More about alpha, beta and gamma radiation'.

Did you know ...?

Nuclear waste

Used fuel rods are very hot and very radioactive.

- After removal from a reactor, they are stored in large tanks of water for up to a year. The water cools the rods down.
- Remote-control machines are then used to open the fuel rods. The unused uranium and plutonium are removed chemically from the used fuel. These are stored in sealed containers so they can be used again.
- The remaining material contains many radioactive isotopes with long half-lives. This radioactive waste must be stored in secure conditions for many years.

Figure 2 Storage of nuclear waste

Radioactivity all around us

When we use a Geiger counter, it clicks even without a radioactive source near it. This is due to background **radiation**. Radioactive substances are found naturally all around us.

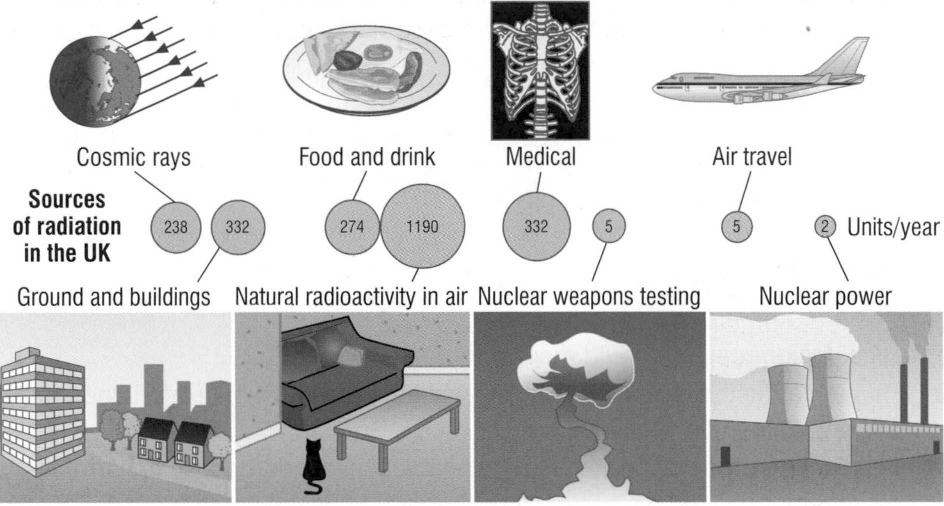

Figure 1 Radioactivity

Figure 1 shows the sources of background radiation. The radiation from radioactive substances is hazardous because it ionises substances it passes through. The numbers in Figure 1 tell you the **radiation dose**, which is how much radiation on average each person gets in a year from each source.

- Medical sources include X-rays as well as radioactive substances, because X-rays have an ionising effect. People who work in jobs that involve the use of ionising radiation have to wear personal radiation monitors to ensure they are not exposed to too much ionising radiation.
- Background radiation in the air is caused mostly by radon gas that seeps through the ground from radioactive substances in rocks deep underground. Radon gas emits alpha particles, so radon is a health hazard if it is breathed in. It can seep into homes and other buildings in certain locations. In homes and buildings where people are present for long periods, methods need to be taken to reduce exposure to radon gas. For example, pipes under the building can be installed and fitted to a suction pump to draw the gas out of the ground before it seeps into the building.

Chernobyl

In 1986, a nuclear reactor in Ukraine exploded. Emergency workers and scientists struggled for days to contain the fire. A cloud of radioactive material from the fire drifted over many parts of Europe, including Britain. More than 100 000 people were evacuated from Chernobyl and the surrounding area. Over 30 people died in the accident. More have developed leukaemia or cancer since then. It was and still is (up to now) the world's worst nuclear accident.

Could it happen again?

- Most nuclear reactors are of a different design. There are thousands of nuclear reactors in the world that have been working safely for many years.
- The Chernobyl accident did not have a high-speed shutdown system like most reactors have. The operators at Chernobyl ignored safety instructions.
- The lessons learned from Chernobyl were put into practice at Fukushima in Japan after three nuclear reactors were crippled in March 2011 by an earthquake and a tsunami. The entire population living within 20 kilometres of the reactors was evacuated from their homes, and they are unlikely to be allowed to return for many years. Radiation levels and health effects over a much wider area will need to be monitored. Food and milk production in the entire area will also need to be monitored and controlled for many years. Nearby reactors with greater protection from tsunamis were much less affected than the three crippled reactors. Major lessons from Fukushima will need to be learned about how to minimise the effect of natural disasters on nuclear reactors and the local people.

Radioactive risks

The effect of radiation on living cells depends on:

- the type and the amount of radiation received (the dose)
- whether the source of the radiation is inside or outside the body
- how long the living cells are exposed to the radiation.

The larger the dose of radiation someone gets, the greater the risk of cancer. High doses kill living cells.

	Alpha radiation	Beta radiation	Gamma radiation
source inside the body	**very dangerous** – affects all the surrounding tissue	**dangerous** – reaches cells throughout the body	
source outside the body	**some danger** – absorbed by skin; damages skin cells, retinal cells		

The smaller the dose, the less the risk – but it is never zero. So there is a very low level of risk to each of us because of background radioactivity.

Summary questions

1 a Why does radioactive waste need to be stored:
 i securely, and ii for many years?
 b Why is a source of alpha radiation very dangerous inside the human body but not as dangerous outside it?

2 In some locations, the biggest radiation hazard comes from radon gas that seeps up through the ground and into buildings. The dangers of radon gas can be minimised by building new houses that are slightly raised on brick pillars and modifying existing houses. Radon gas is an α-emitting isotope.
 a Why is radon gas dangerous in a house?
 b Describe one way of making an existing house safe from radon gas.

3 Should the UK government replace our existing nuclear reactors with new reactors, either fission or fusion or both? Answer this question by discussing the benefits and drawbacks of new fission and fusion reactors.

 Did you know ... ?

New improved nuclear reactors

Most of the world's nuclear reactors in use now will need to be replaced in the next 20 years. New improved 'third generation' nuclear reactors will replace them. The new types of reactors have:

- a standard design to cut down costs and construction time
- a longer operating life – typically 60 years
- more safety features, such as convection of outside air through cooling panels along the reactor walls
- much less effect on the environment.

Figure 3 Chernobyl

Key points

- **Radon gas is an α-emitting isotope that seeps into houses in certain areas through the ground.**
- **There are thousands of fission reactors safely in use in the world. None of them is of the same type as the Chernobyl reactors that exploded.**
- **Nuclear waste is stored in safe and secure conditions for many years after unused uranium and plutonium (to be used in the future) are removed from it.**

P20.4 The early universe

Learning objectives

After this topic, you should know:

- what a galaxy is
- what the universe was like in the billions of years before stars and galaxies were formed
- the force that is responsible for the formation of stars and galaxies.

The Big Bang that created the universe was about 13 thousand million (13 billion) years ago. Space, time and radiation were created in the Big Bang. At first, the universe was a hot glowing ball of radiation and matter. As it expanded, its temperature fell. Now the universe is cold and dark, except for hot spots we call stars.

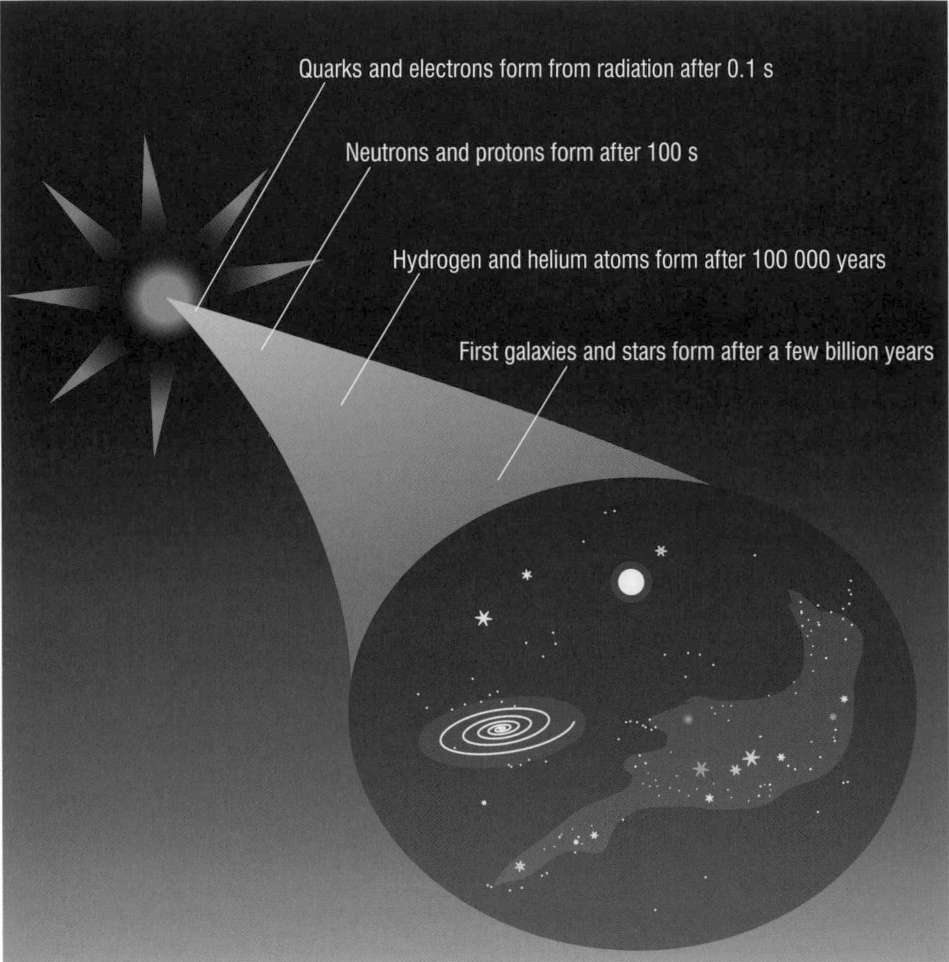

Quarks and electrons form from radiation after 0.1 s
Neutrons and protons form after 100 s
Hydrogen and helium atoms form after 100 000 years
First galaxies and stars form after a few billion years

Figure 1 Timeline for the universe

Examiner's tip

Make sure you know how stars are formed.

Did you know ... ?

In the Cold War, US satellites detected bursts of gamma radiation from space. At first, the US military thought nuclear weapons were being tested in space by Russia. Then astronomers found the bursts were from violent events long ago in distant galaxies – maybe stars being sucked into black holes!

The stars we see in the night sky are all in the Milky Way galaxy, our home galaxy. The Sun is just one of billions of stars in the Milky Way galaxy. Using powerful telescopes, we can see many more stars in the Milky Way galaxy. We can also see individual stars in other galaxies.

We now know there are billions of galaxies in the universe. There is vast empty space between them. Light from the furthest galaxies that we can see has taken billions of years to reach us.

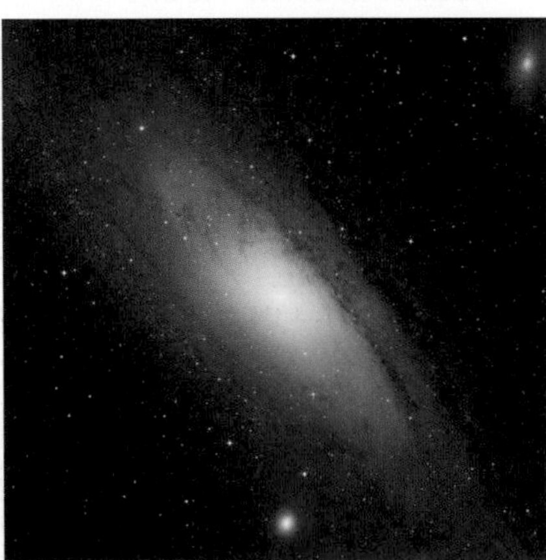

Figure 2 Andromeda – the nearest big galaxy to the Milky Way

The Dark Age of the universe

As the universe expanded, it became transparent as radiation passed through the empty space between its atoms. The microwave background radiation that causes the spots on an untuned analogue television was released at this stage. The Dark Age of the universe had begun!

For the next few billion years, the universe was a completely dark, patchy, expanding cloud of hydrogen and helium. Then the stars and galaxies formed and lit up the universe!

The force of gravity takes over

Uncharged atoms don't repel each other. But they can attract each other. During the Dark Age of the universe, the force of gravitational attraction was at work without any opposition from repulsive forces.

As the universe continued to expand, it became more patchy as the denser parts attracted nearby matter. Gravity pulled more matter into the denser parts and turned them into gigantic clumps.

Eventually, the force of gravity turned the clumps into galaxies and stars. A few billion years after the Big Bang, the Dark Age came to an end, as the stars lit up the universe.

Figure 4 The force of gravity takes over

links

See 12.2 'The Big Bang' for more about the cosmic microwave background radiation.

Figure 3 Arno Allan Penzias and Robert Woodrow Wilson standing on the radio antenna that unexpectedly discovered the universe's microwave background radiation

Summary questions

1 **a** Why do powerful telescopes give us a picture of the universe long ago?
  b How long, to the nearest billion years, has cosmic microwave background radiation been travelling for?
  c Why would the force of gravity between two helium nuclei be unable to pull the nuclei together?

2 **a** **i** Why can't we take a photo of the Milky Way galaxy from outside?
  ii Why can't we take photos of a distant galaxy at different stages in its formation?
  b **i** Why do the stars in a galaxy not drift away from each other?
  ii Why are there vast spaces between the galaxies?

3 **a** Put these events in the correct sequence with the earliest event first:
  1 Cosmic microwave background radiation was released.
  2 Hydrogen nuclei were first fused to form helium nuclei.
  3 The Big Bang took place.
  4 Neutrons and protons formed.
  b The stars were formed from clouds of dust and gas.
  i What force can cause dust and gas particles to attract each other?
  ii Where did the energy that heated the stars come from?
  iii The stars in a galaxy revolve about the centre of the galaxy. Why do the stars in a galaxy not pull each other into a large single massive object at the centre?

Key points

- **A galaxy is a collection of billions of stars held together by their own gravity.**
- **Before galaxies and stars formed, the universe was a dark patchy cloud of hydrogen and helium.**
- **The force of gravity pulled matter into galaxies and stars.**

P20.5 The life history of a star

Learning objectives

After this topic, you should know:
- what a protostar is
- the stages in the life of a star
- what will eventually happen to the Sun
- what a supernova is.

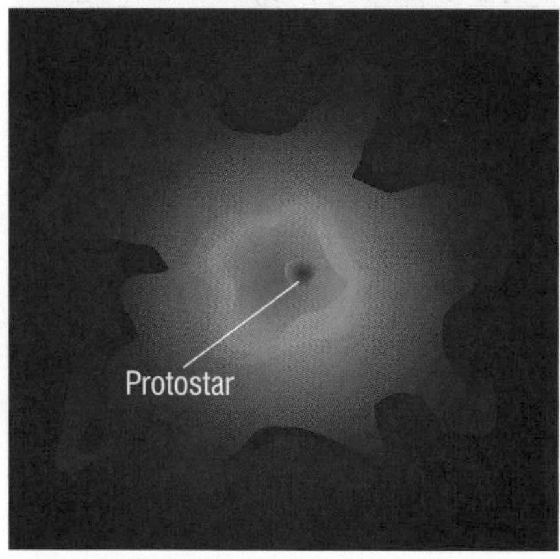

Figure 1 Star birth

The birth of a star

Stars form out of clouds of dust and gas.

- The particles in the clouds are pulled together by their own gravitational attraction. The clouds merge together. They become more and more concentrated to form a **protostar**, which is a star-to-be.
- As a protostar becomes denser, it gets hotter. If it becomes hot enough, the nuclei of hydrogen atoms and other light elements fuse together. Energy is released in this fusion so the core gets hotter and brighter and starts to shine. A star is born!
- Objects may form that are too small to become stars. Such objects may be attracted by a protostar to become **planets**.

Shining stars

Stars like the Sun radiate energy because of hydrogen fusion in the core. They are called **main sequence** stars because this is the main stage in the life of a star. It can maintain its energy output for millions of years until the star runs out of hydrogen nuclei to fuse together.

- Energy released in the core keeps the core hot so the process of fusion continues. Radiation flows out steadily from the core in all directions.
- The star is stable because the forces within it are balanced. The force of gravity that makes a star contract is balanced by the outward force of the radiation from its core. These forces stay in balance until most of the hydrogen nuclei in the core have been fused together.

The end of a star

When a star runs out of hydrogen nuclei to fuse together, it reaches the end of its main sequence stage and it swells out.

Stars about the same size as the Sun (or smaller) swell out, cool down and turn red.

- The star is now a **red giant**. At this stage, helium and other light elements in its core fuse to form heavier elements.
- When there are no more light elements in its core, fusion stops and no more radiation is released. Because of its own gravity, the star collapses in on itself. As it collapses, it heats up and turns from red to yellow to white. It becomes a **white dwarf**. This is a hot, dense white star much smaller in diameter than it was. Stars such as the Sun then fade out, go cold and become **black dwarfs**.

Stars much bigger than the Sun end their lives after the main sequence stage much more dramatically.

- This type of star swells out to become a **red supergiant**, which then collapses.
- In the collapse, the matter surrounding the star's core compresses the core more and more. Then the compression suddenly reverses in a cataclysmic explosion called a **supernova**. This event can outshine an entire galaxy for several weeks!

Examiner's tip

Make sure you can recall the life cycle of a star.

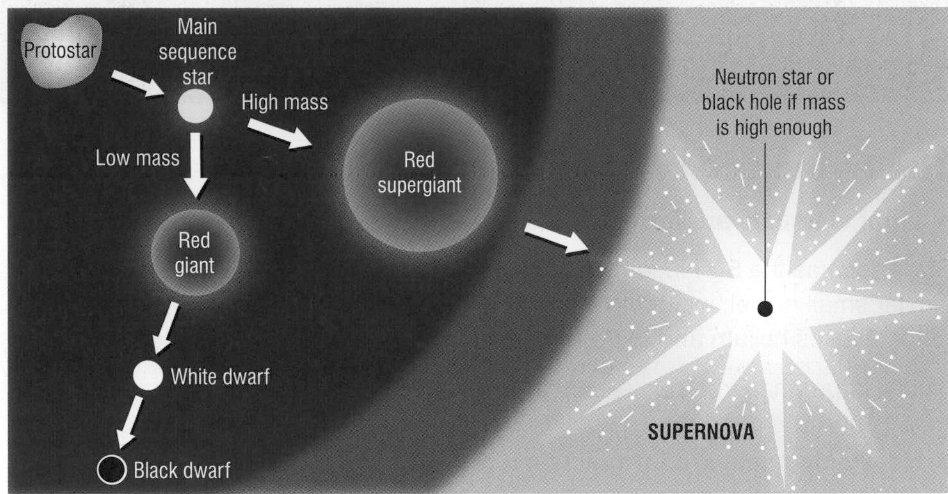

Figure 2 The life cycle of a star

What's left after a supernova?

The explosion compresses the core of the star into a **neutron star**. This is an extremely dense object made up only of neutrons. If the star is massive enough, it becomes a **black hole** instead of a neutron star. The gravitational field of a black hole is so strong that nothing can escape from it. Not even light, or any other form of electromagnetic radiation, can escape.

Summary questions

1 a The list below shows some of the stages in the life of a star such as the Sun. Put the stages in the correct sequence.

- **A** main sequence
- **B** protostar
- **C** red giant
- **D** white dwarf

b i Which stage in the above list is the Sun at now?

ii What will happen to the Sun after it has gone through the above stages?

2 a Copy and complete **i** and **ii** using the words below. Each word can be used more than once.

collapse expand explode

i The Sun will eventually .... then ....

ii A red supergiant will .... then ....

b i What is the main condition needed for a red supergiant to form a black hole?

ii Why is it not possible for light to escape from a black hole?

c i What is a supernova?

ii What happens to a red supergiant star that explodes if it doesn't become a black hole?

3 a i What force makes a red supergiant collapse?

ii What force prevents a main sequence star from collapsing?

b i Why does a white dwarf eventually become a black dwarf?

ii What type of radiation is emitted by a black dwarf that is still warm?

Did you know ... ?

- The Sun is about 5000 million years old and will probably continue to shine for another 5000 million years.
- The Sun will turn into a red giant bigger than the orbit of Mercury. By then, the human race will probably have long passed into history. But will intelligent life still exist?

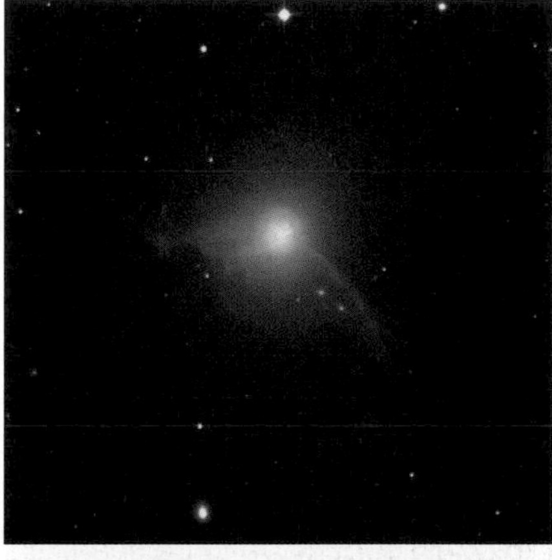

Figure 3 M87 is a galaxy that spins so fast at its centre that it is thought to contain a black hole with a billion times more mass than the Sun

Key points

- A protostar is a gas and dust cloud in space that can go on to form a star.
- Stars with about the same mass as the Sun: Protostar → main sequence star → red giant → white dwarf → black dwarf
- Stars much more massive than the Sun: Protostar → main sequence star → red supergiant → supernova → neutron star or black hole if enough mass
- The Sun will eventually become a black dwarf.
- A supernova is the explosion of a red supergiant after it collapses.

P20.6 How the elements formed

Learning objectives

After this topic, you should know:

- which elements are formed inside stars
- which elements are formed in supernovas
- why the Earth contains heavy elements.

The birthplace of the elements

- **Light elements are formed from fusion in stars.**

Stars such as the Sun fuse hydrogen nuclei (i.e. protons) into helium and similar small nuclei, including carbon nuclei. When the star becomes a red giant, it fuses helium and the other small nuclei into larger nuclei.

Nuclei larger than iron nuclei cannot be formed by this process because too much energy is needed.

- **Heavy elements are formed when a massive star collapses then explodes as a supernova.**

The enormous force of the collapse fuses small nuclei into nuclei larger than iron nuclei. The explosion scatters the star into space.

The debris from a supernova contains all the known elements, from the lightest to the heaviest. Eventually, new stars form as gravity pulls the debris together.

Planets form from debris surrounding a new star. As a result, such planets will be composed of all the known elements too.

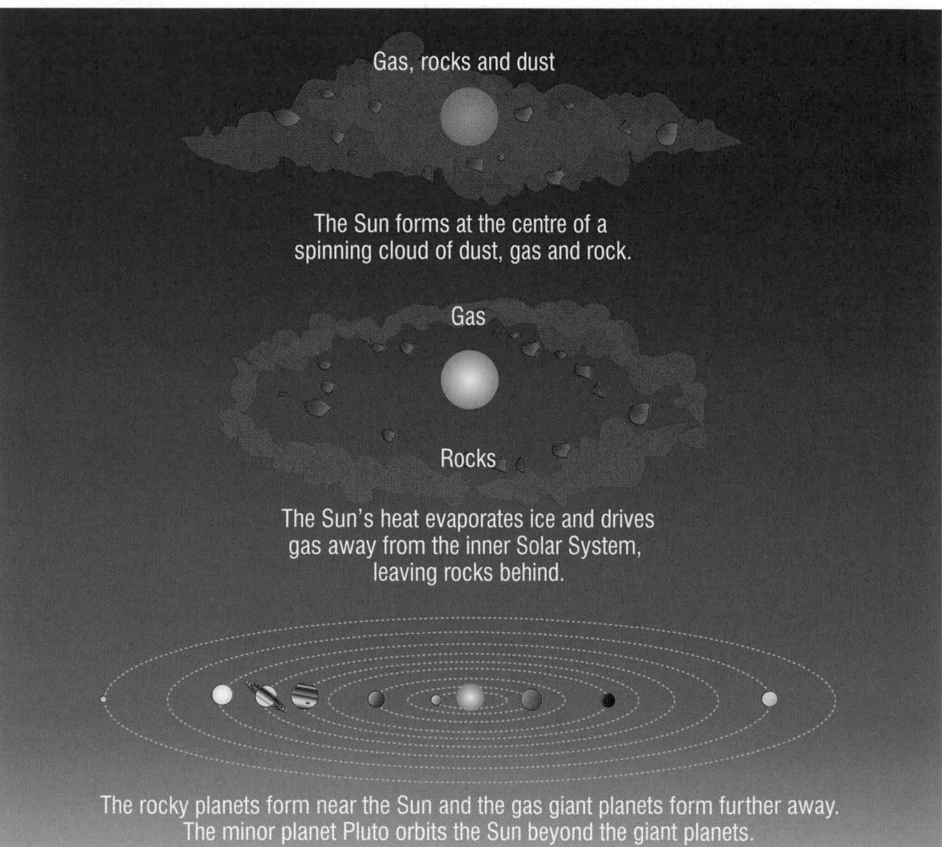

Gas, rocks and dust
The Sun forms at the centre of a spinning cloud of dust, gas and rock.
Gas
Rocks
The Sun's heat evaporates ice and drives gas away from the inner Solar System, leaving rocks behind.
The rocky planets form near the Sun and the gas giant planets form further away. The minor planet Pluto orbits the Sun beyond the giant planets.

Figure 2 Formation of the Solar System

Did you know ... ?

The Crab Nebula is the remnants of a supernova explosion that was observed in the 11th century. In 1987, a star in the southern hemisphere exploded and became the biggest supernova to be seen for four centuries. Astronomers realised that it was Sandaluk II, a star in the Andromeda galaxy millions of light years from Earth.

If a star near the Sun exploded, the Earth would probably be blasted out of its orbit. We would see the explosion before the shock wave hit us.

Figure 1 The Crab Nebula

Did you know ... ?

Molecules of carbon-based chemicals are present in space. Life on Earth probably developed from chemicals reacting in lightning storms.

So are we looking for any scientific evidence about life on other planets, either in our own Solar System or around other stars?

- ***Space probes sent to Mars*** have tested the atmosphere, rocks and soil on Mars looking for microbes or chemicals that might indicate life was once present on Mars. Water is necessary for life. Astronomers now have strong evidence of the presence of 'underground' water breaking through to the surface of Mars.
- ***The search for extra-terrestrial intelligence***, called SETI, has gone on for more than 40 years using radio telescopes. Signals from space would indicate the existence of living beings with technologies at least as advanced as our own. No signals have been detected – yet!

Figure 3 The NASA Exploration Rovers looked for signs of life on Mars

Planet Earth

The heaviest known natural element is uranium. It has a half-life of 4500 million years. The presence of uranium on the Earth is evidence that the Solar System must have formed from the remnants of a supernova.

Elements such as plutonium are heavier than uranium. Scientists can make these elements by bombarding heavy elements such as uranium with high-speed neutrons. They would have been present in the debris that formed the Solar System. Elements heavier than uranium formed then have long since decayed.

Examiner's tip

Make sure you know how the heavier elements were formed and that they were **not** formed during the Big Bang.

Summary questions

1 Match each statement below with an element or elements in the list.

helium hydrogen iron uranium

- **a** Helium nuclei are formed when nuclei of this element are fused.
- **b** This element is formed in a supernova explosion.
- **c** Stars form nuclei of these two elements (and others not listed) by fusing smaller nuclei.
- **d** The early universe mostly consisted of this element.
- **e** This element is formed when a supergiant star collapses.

2 In which astronomical objects can each of the following processes occur:

- **a** the creation of light elements from hydrogen and helium?
- **b** the splitting of heavy nuclei?
- **c** the scattering of elements into space?
- **d** the gathering of debris to form a star?

3 Uranium-238 is a radioactive isotope found naturally in the Earth. It has a half-life of about 4500 million years. It was formed from lighter elements.

- **a i** What is the name of the physical process in which this isotope is formed?
  - **ii** What is the name for the astronomical event in which the above process takes place?
- **b i** Why has all the uranium in the Earth not decayed by now?
  - **ii** Plutonium-239 has a half-life of 24 000 years. It is formed in a nuclear reactor from uranium-238. Why is plutonium-239 not found naturally?

Key points

- Elements as heavy as iron are formed inside stars as a result of nuclear fusion.
- Elements heavier than iron are formed in supernovas as well as light elements.
- The Sun and the rest of the Solar System were formed from the debris of a supernova explosion.

Summary questions

1 **a** Copy and complete **i** to **iv** using the words below.

decreases increases stays the same

When energy is released at a steady rate in a nuclear reactor:

i the number of fission events each second in the core ....

ii the amount of uranium-235 in the core ....

iii the number of radioactive isotopes in the fuel rods ....

iv the number of fission neutrons in the core ....

b Explain what would happen in a nuclear reactor if:

i the coolant fluid leaked out of the core

ii the control rods were pushed further into the reactor core.

2 **a** **i** What do we mean by nuclear fusion?

ii Why do two nuclei repel each other when they get close?

iii Why do they need to collide at high speed to fuse together?

b Give two reasons why nuclear fusion is difficult to achieve in a reactor.

3 **a** Copy and complete **i** to **iv** using the words below. Each word can be used more than once.

fission fusion

i In a .... reactor, two small nuclei join together and release energy.

ii In a .... reactor, a large nucleus splits and releases energy.

iii The fuel in a .... reactor contains uranium-235.

iv A very large electric current is passed through the plasma in a .... reactor in order to heat the plasma.

b State **two** advantages that nuclear fusion reactors would have in comparison with nuclear fission reactors.

4 **a** **i** What physical process causes energy to be released in the Sun?

ii Which element is used in the physical process named in part **i** to release energy in the Sun?

b How will the Sun change in the next stage of its life cycle when it has used up all the element named in part **a ii**?

5 Copy and complete **a** to **d** using the words below. Each word can be used more than once.

galaxy planet stars

a A .... isn't big enough to be a star.

b The Sun is inside a ....

c .... became hot after they formed from matter pulled together by the force of gravity.

d The force of gravity keeps .... together inside a ....

6 Describe the main differences between a supergiant star and a giant star in terms of the changes that take place after all the light elements in their cores have undergone fusion.

7 **a** The stages in the development of the Sun are listed below. Put the stages in the correct sequence.

A dust and gas
B main sequence
C protostar
D red giant
E white dwarf

b State **two** differences other than colour between the Sun at its present stage and:

i a red giant star

ii a white dwarf star.

c **i** After the white dwarf stage, what will happen to the Sun?

ii What will happen to a star that has much more mass than the Sun?

8 **a** **i** What is a supernova?

ii How could we tell the difference between a supernova and a distant star like the Sun at present?

b **i** What is a black hole?

ii What would happen to stars and planets near a black hole?

iii What is a neutron star, and how is it formed?

9 **a** **i** Which element as well as hydrogen was formed in the early universe?

ii Which of the two elements is formed from the other one in a star?

b **i** Which two of the elements listed below are *not* formed in a star that gives out radiation at a steady rate?

carbon iron lead uranium

ii How would the two elements given in your answer to part **i** have been formed?

iii How do we know that the Sun formed from the debris of a supernova?

AQA Examination-style questions

1 Different energy sources are used in power stations to generate electricity. Each type of power station in the box below uses either a renewable or a non-renewable energy source.

a Copy and complete the table by writing each type of power station in the correct column.

coal-fired   gas-fired   nuclear   solar-powered
tidal   wind farm

Non-renewable	Renewable

(5)

b Nuclear power stations contain nuclear reactors.

In a nuclear reactor, neutrons are used to bombard the nuclei of uranium-235.

This is represented in the diagram.

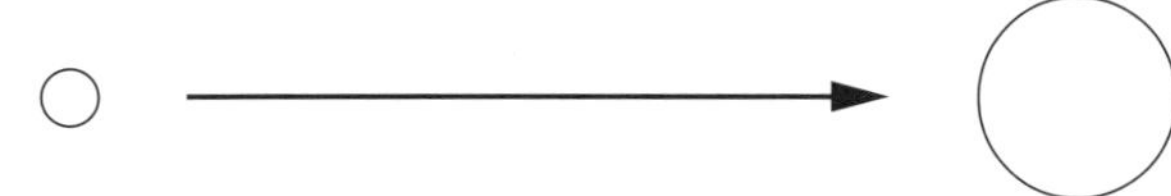

i Describe what happens when the neutron hits the nucleus. (QWC) (6)

ii What is the purpose of a *moderator* in a nuclear reactor? (2)

iii What is the purpose of the *control rods* in a nuclear reactor? (2)

2 Nuclear fission and nuclear fusion produce energy. Both processes have advantages and disadvantages.

a The table shows a list of statements.

Decide whether each statement is related to **fission** or **fusion**.

Statement	Fission or fusion
Fuel readily available in sea water	i)
Waste product of the reaction is radioactive	ii)
Has been used in power stations for over 50 years	iii)
Fuel has to be mined and is only found in certain areas	iv)
Reaction product is a harmless inert gas	v)

(5)

b Nuclear fusion in the Sun releases large amounts of energy.

Explain what is meant by nuclear fusion. (3)

c i Complete the equation below to give the mass number and the atomic number of He.

$${}^{2}_{1}\mathrm{H} + {}^{2}_{1}\mathrm{H} = \mathrm{He}$$ (2)

ii Describe the nucleus of ${}^{2}_{1}\mathrm{H}$ (2)

iii Explain why it is difficult to fuse two nuclei together. (4)

3 The chart represents part of the life cycle of a star much bigger than the Sun.

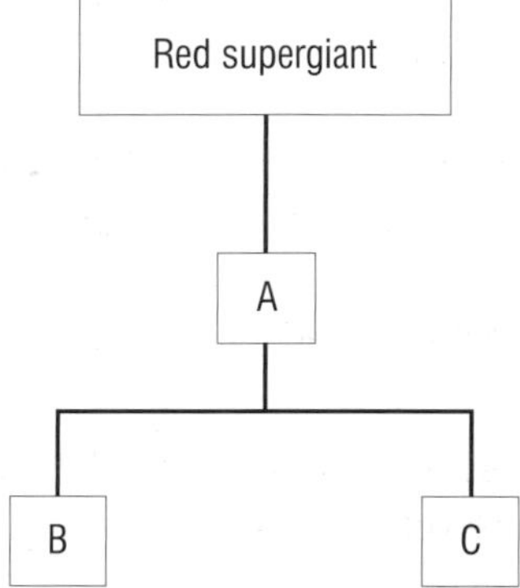

a Identify the labels A, B and C above to show the sequence after the red supergiant stage.

A ....

B ....

C .... (3)

b i Describe how a star forms. (4)

ii The Sun is at the stable stage of its life.
Describe and explain what this means. (3)

iii At the end of the stable stage of its life, a star will change.
Describe how a star about the same size as the Sun changes. (QWC) (6)

Investigations

Learning objectives

After this topic, you should know:

- what 'continuous' and 'categoric variables' are
- what is meant by 'repeatable evidence', 'reproducible evidence' and 'valid evidence'
- what the link is between the independent and dependent variable
- what a 'hypothesis' and a 'prediction' are
- how to reduce risks in hazardous situations.

Science works for us all day, every day. Working as a scientist you will have knowledge of the world around you and particularly about the subject you are working with. You will observe the world around you. An enquiring mind will then lead you to start asking questions about what you have observed.

Science usually moves forward by slow steady steps. Each small step is important in its own way. It builds on the body of knowledge that we already have.

Thinking scientifically

Deciding on what to measure

Variables can be one of two different types:

- A **categoric variable** is one that is best described by a label (usually a word). The type of material is a categoric variable, e.g. metal or plastic.
- A **continuous variable** is one that we measure, so its value could be any number. Temperature (as measured by a thermometer or temperature sensor) is a continuous variable, e.g. 37.6 °C, 45.2 °C. Continuous variables can have values (called a quantity) that can be given by any measurements made (e.g. light intensity, voltage, etc.).

When designing your investigation you should always try to measure continuous data whenever you can. If this is not always possible, you should then try to use ordered data. If there is no other way to measure your variable then you have to use a label (categoric variable).

Making your investigation repeatable, reproducible and valid

When you are designing an investigation you must make sure that others can repeat any results you get – this makes it **reproducible**. You should also plan to make each result **repeatable**. You can do this by getting consistent sets of repeat measurements.

You must also make sure you are measuring the actual thing you want to measure. If you don't, your data can't be used to answer your original question. This seems very obvious but it is not always quite so easy. You need to make sure that you have controlled as many other variables as you can, so that no-one can say that your investigation is not **valid**.

How might an independent variable be linked to a dependent variable?

The **independent variable** is the one you choose to vary in your investigation.

The **dependent variable** is used to judge the effect of varying the independent variable.

These variables may be linked together. If there is a pattern to be seen (for example as one thing gets bigger the other also gets bigger), it may be that:

- changing one has caused the other to change
- the two are related, but one is not necessarily the cause of the other.

Starting an investigation

Observation

As scientists we use observations to ask questions. We can only ask useful questions if we know something about the observed event. We will not have all of the answers, but we know enough to start asking the correct questions.

When you are designing an investigation you have to observe carefully which variables are likely to have an effect.

What is a hypothesis?

A hypothesis is an idea based on observation that has some really good science to try to explain it.

When making hypotheses you can be very imaginative with your ideas. However, you should have some scientific reasoning behind those ideas so that they are not totally bizarre.

Remember, your explanation might not be correct, but you think it is. The only way you can check out your hypothesis is to make it into a prediction and then test it by carrying out an investigation.

observation + knowledge → hypothesis → prediction → investigation

Starting to design an investigation

An investigation starts with a question, followed by a prediction. You, as the scientist, predict that there is a relationship between two variables.

You should think about a preliminary investigation to find the most suitable range and interval for the independent variable.

Making your investigation safe

Remember that when you design your investigation, you must:

- look for any potential hazards
- decide how you will reduce any risk.

In the 'practical' questions in the examination, you may need to:

- write down your plan
- make a risk assessment
- make a prediction
- draw a blank table ready for the results.

Examiner's tip

Observations, backed up by creative thinking and good scientific knowledge can lead to a hypothesis.

Key points

- **Continuous data can give you more information than other types of data.**
- **You must design investigations that produce repeatable, reproducible and valid results if you are to be believed.**
- **Be aware that just because two variables are related, does not mean that there is a causal link.**
- **Hypotheses can lead to predictions and investigations.**
- **You must make a risk assessment, make a prediction and write a plan.**

Setting up investigations

Learning objectives

After this topic, you should know:
- what a 'fair test' is
- how a survey is set up
- what a 'control' group is
- how to decide on the variables, range and intervals
- how to ensure accuracy and precision
- the causes of error and anomalies.

Examiner's tip

Trial runs will tell you a lot about how your investigation might work out. They should get you to ask yourself:
- Do you have the correct conditions?
- Have you chosen a sensible range?
- Have you got enough readings that are close together?
- Will you need to repeat your readings?

Examiner's tip

A word of caution!

Just because your results show precision does not mean your results are accurate.

Imagine you carry out an investigation into the energy value of a type of fuel. You get readings of the amount of energy released that are all about the same. This means that your data will have precision, but it doesn't mean that they are necessarily accurate.

Fair testing

A fair test is one in which only the independent variable affects the dependent variable. All other variables are controlled.

This is easy to set up in the laboratory, but almost impossible in fieldwork. Investigations in the environment are not that simple and easy to control. There are complex variables that are changing constantly.

So how can we set up the fieldwork investigations? The best you can do is to make sure that all of the many variables change in much the same way, except for the one you are investigating.

If you are investigating two variables in a large population then you will need to do a survey. Again, it is impossible to control all of the variables. Imagine scientists were investigating the effect of mobile phone usage on health. They would have to choose people of the same age and same family history to test. The larger the sample size tested, the more valid the results will be.

Control groups are used in these investigations to try to make sure that you are measuring the variable that you intend to measure. This would involve monitoring the health of similar groups of people who do not use mobile phones

Designing an investigation

Accuracy

Your investigation must provide accurate data. Accurate data is essential if your results are going to have any meaning.

How do you know if you have accurate data?

It is very difficult to be certain. Accurate results are very close to the true value. It is not always possible to know what that true value is.

- Sometimes you can calculate a theoretical value and check it against the experimental evidence. Close agreement between these two values could indicate accurate data.
- You can draw a graph of your results and see how close each result is to the line of best fit.
- Try repeating your measurements with a different instrument and see if you get the same readings.

How do you get accurate data?

- Using instruments that measure accurately will help.
- The more carefully you use the measuring instruments, the more accuracy you will get.

Precision

Your investigation must provide data with sufficient precision. If it doesn't then you will not be able to make a valid conclusion.

How do you get precise and repeatable data?

- You have to repeat your tests as often as necessary to improve repeatability.
- You have to repeat your tests in exactly the same way each time.
- Use measuring instruments that have the appropriate scale divisions needed for a particular investigation. Smaller scale divisions have better resolution.

Making measurements

Using instruments

You cannot expect perfect results. When you choose an instrument you need to know that it will give you the accuracy that you want, i.e. it will give you a true reading.

When you choose an instrument you need to decide how precise you need to be. Some instruments have smaller scale divisions than others. Instruments that measure the same thing can have different sensitivities. The resolution of an instrument refers to the smallest change in a value that can be detected. Choosing the wrong scale can cause you to miss important data or make silly conclusions.

You also need to be able to use an instrument properly.

Errors

Even when an instrument is used correctly, the results can still show differences. Results may differ because of a random error. This is most likely to be due to a poor measurement being made. It could be due to not carrying out the method consistently.

The error may be a systematic error. This means that the method was carried out consistently but an error was being repeated.

Anomalies

Anomalies are results that are clearly out of line. They are not those that are due to the natural variation that you get from any measurement. These should be looked at carefully. There might be a very interesting reason why they are so different. If they are simply due to a random error then they should be ignored.

If anomalies can be identified while you are doing an investigation, then it is best to repeat that part of the investigation. If you find anomalies after you have finished collecting the data for an investigation, then they must be discarded.

Did you know ...?

Imagine measuring the temperature after a set time when a fuel is used to heat a fixed volume of water.

Two students repeated this experiment, four times each. Their results are marked on the thermometer scales below:

- A precise set of results is grouped closely together.
- An accurate set of results will have a mean (average) close to the true value.

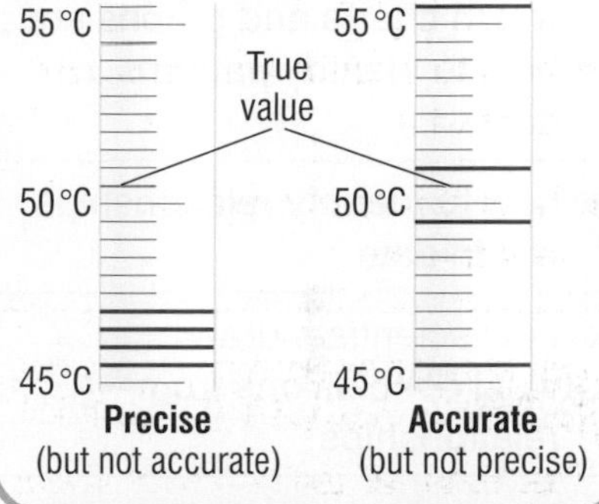

Key points

- Care must be taken to ensure fair testing.
- You can use a trial run to make sure that you choose the best values for your variables.
- Careful use of the correct equipment can improve accuracy.
- If you repeat your results carefully you can improve precision.
- Results will nearly always vary. Better instruments give more accurate results.
- Resolution in an instrument is the smallest change that it can detect.
- Human error can produce random and systematic errors.
- We must examine anomalies.

Using data

Learning objectives

After this topic, you should know:

- what is meant by the 'range' and the 'mean' of a set of data
- how data should be displayed
- which charts and graphs are best to identify patterns in data
- how to identify relationships within data
- how scientists draw valid conclusions from relationships
- how to evaluate the reproducibility of an investigation.

Presenting data

Tables

Tables are really good for getting your results down quickly and clearly. You should design your table before you start your investigation.

The range of the data

Pick out the maximum and the minimum values and you have the range. You should always quote these two numbers when asked for a range. For example, the range is between … (the lowest value) and … (the highest value) and don't forget to include the units!

The mean of the data

Add up all of the measurements and divide by how many there are.

Bar charts

If you have a categoric independent variable and a continuous dependent variable then you should use a bar chart.

Line graphs

If you have a continuous independent and a continuous dependent variable then use a line graph.

Using data to draw conclusions

Identifying patterns and relationships

Now you have a bar chart or a graph of your results you can begin looking for patterns in your results. You must have an open mind at this point.

Firstly, there could still be some anomalous results. You might not have picked these out earlier. How do you spot an anomaly? It must be a significant distance away from the pattern, not just within normal variation.

A line of best fit will help to identify any anomalies at this stage. Ask yourself – do the anomalies represent something important or were they just a mistake?

Secondly, remember a line of best fit can be a straight line or it can be a curve – you have to decide from your results.

The line of best fit will also lead you into thinking what the relationship is between your two variables. You need to consider whether your graph shows a linear relationship. This simply means can you be confident about drawing a straight line of best fit on your graph? If the answer is yes, then is this line positive or negative?

A directly proportional relationship is shown by a positive straight line that goes through the origin (0, 0).

Your results might also show a curved line of best fit. These can be predictable, complex or very complex!

Scatter graphs

These are used in much the same way as a line graph, but you might not expect to be able to draw such a clear line of best fit. For example, if you want to see if the maximum frequency of sound that is audible to people is related to their age, you might draw a scatter graph of your results.

Note that an **inversely proportional relationship** gives a graph as in the margin. This shows how the current I through a resistor varies according to the resistance R when there is a fixed pd V across the resistor. As explained on p166 , the relationship between I and R is given by the equation $I = \frac{V}{R}$. The graph opposite obeys this relationship if $I \times R$ always has the same value. So for example, I would be ten times smaller if resistance R was *10* times bigger. See also p27.

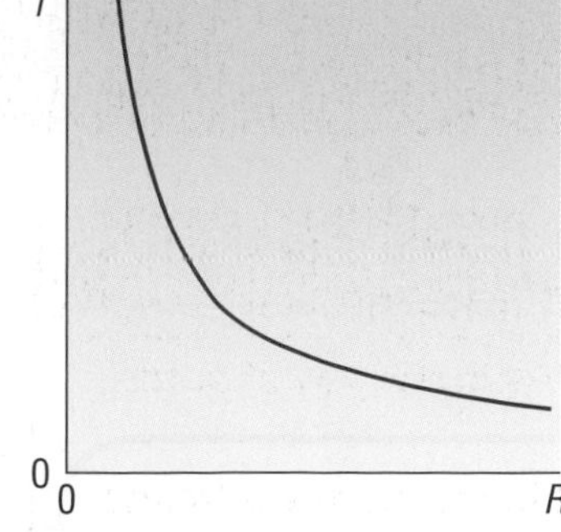

Drawing conclusions

Your graphs are designed to show the relationship between your two chosen variables. You need to consider what that relationship means for your conclusion. You must also take into account the repeatability and the validity of the data you are considering.

You will continue to have an open mind about your conclusion.

You will have made a prediction. This could be supported by your results, it might not be supported, or it could be partly supported. It might suggest some other hypothesis to you.

You must be willing to think carefully about your results. Remember it is quite rare for a set of results to completely support a prediction and be completely repeatable.

Look for possible links between variables. It may be that:

- changing one has caused the other to change.
- the two are related, but one is not necessarily the cause of the other.

You must decide which is the most likely. Remember a positive relationship does not always mean a causal link between the two variables.

Your conclusion must go no further than the evidence that you have. Any patterns you spot are only strictly valid in the range of values you tested. Further tests are needed to check whether the pattern continues beyond this range.

The purpose of the prediction was to test a hypothesis. The hypothesis can:

- be supported,
- be refuted, or
- lead to another hypothesis.

You have to decide which it is on the evidence available.

Evaluation

If you are still uncertain about a conclusion, it might be down to the repeatability, reproducibility and the validity of the results. You could check reproducibility by:

- looking for other similar work on the Internet or from others in your class,
- getting somebody else to redo your investigation,
- trying an alternative method to see if you get the same results.

Key points

- The range states the maximum and the minimum value.
- The mean is the sum of the values divided by how many values there are.
- Tables are best used during an investigation to record results.
- Bar charts are used when you have a categoric independent variable and a continuous dependent variable.
- Line graphs are used to display data that are continuous.
- Drawing lines of best fit help us to study the relationship between variables. The possible relationships are linear, positive and negative; directly proportional; predictable and complex curves.
- Conclusions must go no further than the data available.
- The reproducibility of data can be checked by looking at other similar work done by others, perhaps on the Internet. It can also be checked by using a different method or by others checking your method.

The correct control variables have been ticked.

The candidate has correctly stated what a zero error is and given the way of correcting the meter reading if the zero error is positive. They could have said that it is necessary to add the zero error to each reading when the meter has a negative reading when it should read 0.

1 Some students were asked to investigate the factors that determine the resistance of a piece of wire.

One group of students decided to find out how the resistance depends on the length of the wire.

1 (a) Which of the following variables should be controlled?

Tick **three** boxes.

colour of wire	
diameter of wire	✓
length of wire	
temperature of wire	✓
type of wire	✓

(3)

1 (b) The students set up the circuit below.

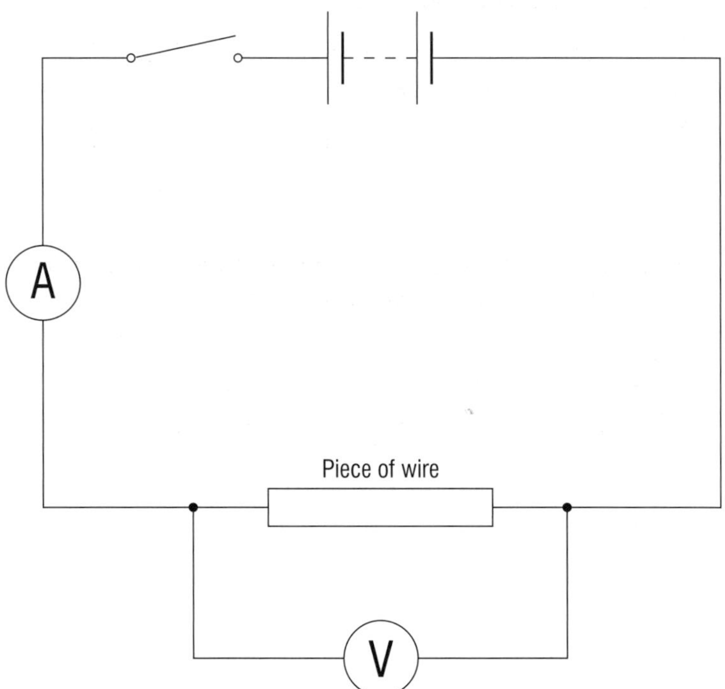

One of the meters had a zero error.

What is a *zero error* and how would you correct readings taken from the meter with the zero error?

A zero error is when the pointer on a meter does not return to 0 when there is no current. If the meter has a reading when it should read zero, this value should be subtracted from every reading.

(2)

1 (c) The students cut six different lengths from a reel of wire. They measured the length of each piece of wire.

Then they used crocodile clips to connect a length of wire in the circuit.

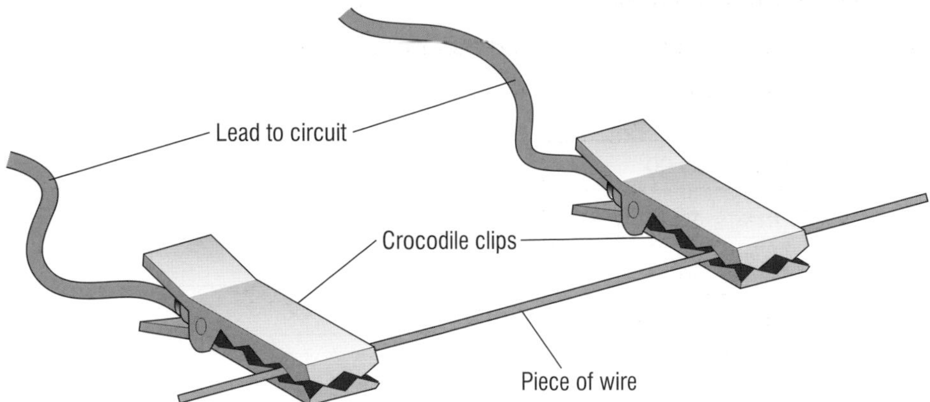

1 (c) (i) Identify a fault in their technique and suggest how the measurement of length could be improved.

The length of wire in the circuit is less than the measured length. The measurement could be improved by measuring the distance between the points of contact of the crocodile clips with the wire.

(2)

The candidate has given the correct answer – this is a case where a diagram, marking exactly what should be measured, would help.

1 (c) (ii) Suggest reasons why they should not use pieces of wire less than 5 cm long or pieces of wire more than 1 m long.

If the wire is too short, its resistance will be low and the current may be high enough to melt some wires. If the wire is long it will be cumbersome and in fact it could short out.

(5)

The candidate would be awarded five marks, since they have made five relevant points, but a better answer would explain what a 'short' is, especially since we have a different meaning to the word 'short' already in the answer. Other points could gain credit: if the wire gets hot, one of the control variables has not been kept constant and the results will not be valid; the percentage error in measuring length will be higher for shorter wires: 1 mm in 5 cm = 2%; 1 mm in 1 m = 0.1%.

1 (d) The students obtained the data they needed and repeated the procedure with the other pieces of wire. They then calculated the resistance of each piece of wire.

Their results are given in the table.

Length of wire in cm	Resistance in Ω
40	0.8
50.00	1.0
60.0	1.2
70	0.4
80.0	1.6
90	1.8

Some candidates may put $V = I \times R$ or put the equation in words rather than letters and still score the mark.

1 (d) (i) What equation should the students use to calculate resistance?

R = V ÷ I

(1)

The answer could have been improved by pointing out the inconsistencies – some lengths to the nearest cm, others to the nearest mm and one to 0.01 cm, but both marks would be scored.

1 (d) (ii) Comment on the recorded readings of *length of wire* in the table.

The readings are inconsistent. A normal ruler can measure to the nearest mm so all results should be recorded to the first decimal place.

(2)

1 (d) (iii) The results have been plotted on the grid below.
Draw a line of best fit.

A straight line, through (0, 0), has been drawn with the aid of a ruler and the anomalous result has been ignored.

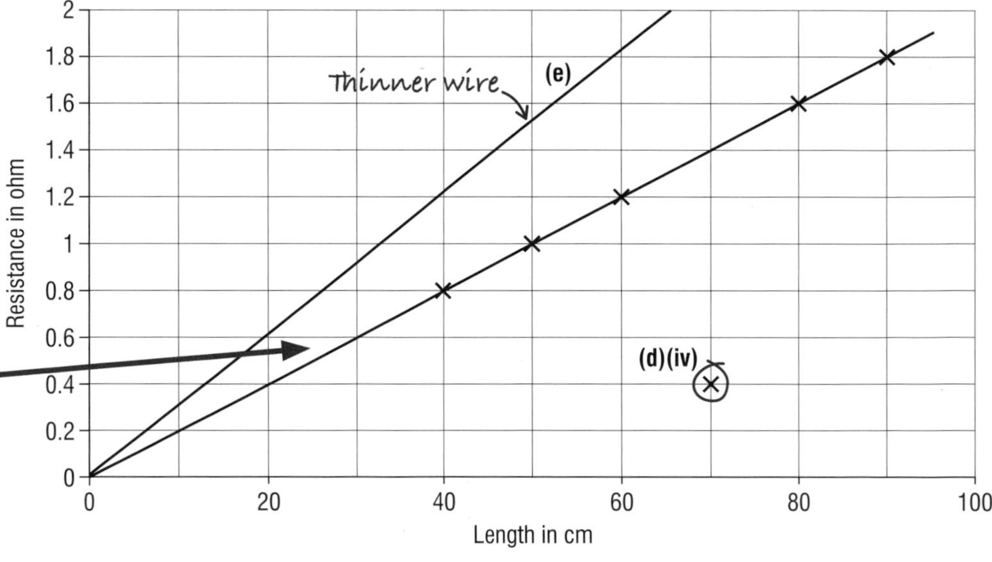

(2)

1 (d) **(iv)** One of the results is anomalous.
Put a ring around the anomalous result on the graph.

Ring round (70, 0.4)

(1)

The anomalous point has been correctly identified.

1 (d) **(v)** Describe the relationship between the length of a wire and its resistance.

As the length is doubled, the resistance is doubled

(2)

The candidate could have said that the two quantities are directly proportional. This is indicated by the straight line through the origin of the graph.

1 (e) Another group of students carried out the same investigation. They used a reel of thinner wire.

Draw a line on the graph to show how their results were different to those of the first group of students. Label this line '**Thinner wire**'.

Graph line with greater gradient

(1)

Thinner wires have a higher resistance per unit length so the line has a greater slope.

Answers

1 Motion

1.1

1 a i The distance travelled each second does not change.
ii The gradient of the graph is constant.
b i 30 m/s
ii 500 s
iii 13.3 m/s
2 a 30 m/s
b 9000 m
c 110 s
3 d = 7560 m, speed = 18 m/s

1.2

1 a Speed is distance travelled ÷ time taken regardless of direction. Velocity is speed in a given direction.
b 2400 m
2 1.25 m/s²
3 a i As it left the motorway.
ii When it travelled at constant velocity.
b 27 m/s

1.3

1 1 B
2 A
3 D
4 C
2 a i A
ii C
b B
3 a Distance = velocity × time = 8 × 20 = 160 m
b C
c 40 m
d 100 m

1.4

1 a 15 m/s
b i The speed is zero at time = 0.
ii The speed increases gradually.
2 a The cyclist accelerates at a constant acceleration from rest to 8 m/s for 40 s then decelerates at constant deceleration for the last 20 s.
b i 0.20 m/s², 160 m.
ii −0.40 m/s², 80 m.
c 4.0 m/s
3 a Student's graph, accurately drawn.
b 2.0 m/s²
c i 400 m
ii 400 m

Answers to end of chapter summary questions

1 Use the stopwatch to measure the time taken to complete 10 complete laps. Repeat the timing several times to obtain a mean value, then divide this mean value by 10 to give the time for one complete lap.
Use the tape measure to measure the diameter by π of the circle made by the centre line of the track then multiply the diameter to obtain a value for the circumference (or lay a long string along the centre line of the track exactly once round the track then mark the start and end of the string on the track; the distance between the two marks can be measured using the tape measure. This equals the circumference.
The speed of the car is the circumference divided by the time for one lap.
2 a A to B
b i 20 m/s
ii 10 m/s
c 125 s
3 a The speed decreased then became constant.
b i 17 m/s
ii 7.5 m/s
4 a 2.5 m/s²
b 175 m
c 17.5 m/s

5 a

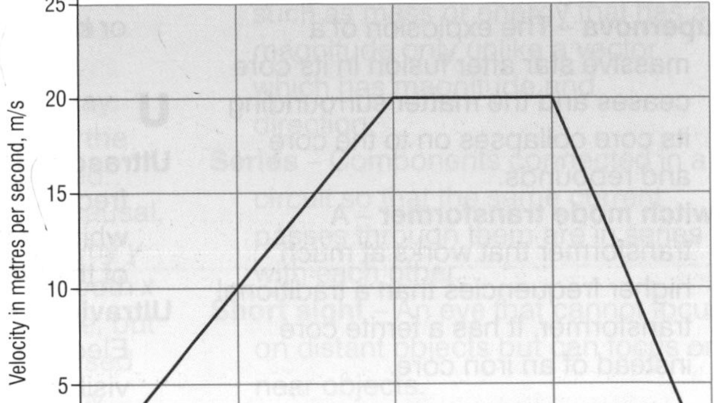

b 0.25 m/s², 0, −0.50 m/s²
c 2000 m
d Average speed = $\frac{\text{distance}}{\text{time}} = \frac{2000}{160}$ = 12.5 m/s.

6 a

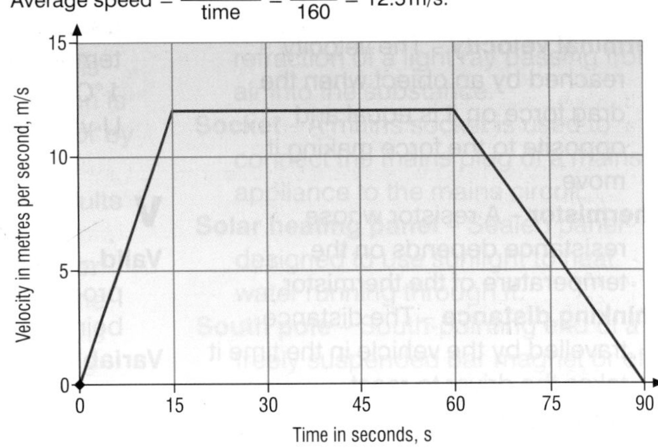

b 0.80 m/s²
c −0.40 m/s²
d 810 m

Answers to end of chapter examination-style questions

1 a i Deceleration/slowing down
ii Constant speed
iii Accelerating/speeding up (3)
b 5 drops = 5 seconds
Speed = 100/5 = 20 m/s (3)
c Change in velocity = 5 − 25 = −20 m/s
Acceleration = −20/10 = −2 m/s²
(1 mark for the correct unit; 1 mark for the minus sign) (5)
2 a i stationary
ii travelling at constant speed (2)
b i 0.7 s (1)
ii Speed = 24 m/s
Distance = speed × time = 24 × 0.7 = 16.8 m (3)
c i Change in velocity = 24 − 0 = 24 m/s
Time = 4.7 − 0.7 = 4 s
Deceleration = 24/4 = 6 m/s² (4)
ii Distance = area = ½ base × height
= ½ × 4 × 24 = 48 m (3)
3 a i Marks for this answer will be determined by the Quality of Written Communication (QWC) as well as the standard of scientific response. Measure out a distance; one student at either end; student gives signal when a vehicle passes; second student starts timing when sees the signal; stops timing when vehicle passes; calculate speed as distance/time.
Equipment: metric tape or trundle wheel; stopwatch (6)
ii any *three* of: as large a distance as possible; extra students timing; take average time; as many vehicles as possible; use sensors and electronic timers. (3)

b i bar chart
pie chart
One variable categoric; one variable discrete; can calculate percentage of total number at each speed. (5)
ii Time needs to be long enough to give a large sample ideally a morning/afternoon/day; a bar chart would need 'the number of vehicles per ....' (2)

4 a i acceleration
ii speed
iii velocity–time (3)
b X starts after Y (0.4 s); X completes race in a shorter time (X 9.6 s – Y 10.8 s); X wins the race; gradients of both graphs increase throughout; both X and Y accelerate throughout; X's acceleration > Y's; 100 m race (6)

2 Resultant forces

2.1

1 a The car decelerates
b The gravitational force (i.e. your weight), the support force on you from the cushion.

2 a i 50 N upwards ii 200 N
b i equal, opposite
ii downwards, upwards
iii upwards

3 a 500 N downwards
b 500 N upwards
c 500 N upwards

2.2

1 a The glider decelerates and stops. Without the air blower on, the glider is in contact with the track and friction acts on it so its velocity decreases to zero and it stops.
b They are equal and opposite.

2 a It is in the opposite direction to the velocity.
b It is zero.

3 a The force of the mud on the car is greater than the force on the car from the tractor.
b 50 N

2.3

1 a 10 N to the left.
b 50 N vertically upwards.
c 500 N up the slope.

2 a 5.0 N
b 6.1 N
c 6.5 N

3 5400 N (to 2 s.f.)

2.4

1 a 640 N
b 4.0 m/s^2

2 a 16 N
b 40 kg
c 12 m/s^2
d 2.4 N
e 25 000 kg

3 a 3000 N
b i 600 N
ii 2400 N

Answers to end of chapter summary questions

1 a i 1.6 N vertically downwards.
ii 1.6 N
b i 0.4 N vertically downwards.
ii 0.4 N vertically upwards.

2 a i It is zero.
ii The upthrust acting on the balloon is equal to the sum of the gravitational force on the balloon and the downward pull of the thread on the balloon. The upthrust is therefore greater than the gravitational force on the balloon.
b The balloon would move upwards because there is no downward pull on it from the thread. The upthrust is greater than the gravitational force on the balloon so the resultant force on the balloon is vertically upwards.

3 a increases, stays the same
b decreases
c stays the same

4 a 960 N
b i 1.1 m/s^2
ii 77 N

5 a i 7200 N
ii 0
b 13 300 N

6 b 9.57 kN

Answers to end of chapter examination-style questions

1 a acceleration; force; velocity (3)
b Acceleration is rate of change of velocity; velocity is a vector quantity – it has direction; train is changing direction; so although at constant speed, it is accelerating. (4)
c The tension in the towrope is the resultant force; it is the diagonal in a scaled parallelogram drawing; the component (part) of the force along the river will be longer (force larger) when the diagonal is longer. (3)

2 a 1600 N
b Resultant force is 4000 – 1600 = 2400 N
Acceleration = F/m = 2400/1200 = 2 m/s^2
(1 mark for answer; 1 mark for correct unit) (4)
c Marks for this answer will be determined by the Quality of Written Communication (QWC) as well as the standard of scientific response. As speed increases, so does force A; resultant force is less; acceleration is reduced; speed still increases but at a reducing rate; eventually, force A = 4000 N; resultant force then zero; acceleration is zero; speed then remains constant. (6)
d As fuel is used the mass of the car becomes less; for the same force, the acceleration is greater; average velocity will be higher; so the time taken for one lap will be less. (4)

3 a i To the right. (1)
ii To the left. (1)
b The force on Y causes it to move; its acceleration is 800/200; acceleration is 4 m/s^2; the force on X causes it to slow down; its deceleration is 800/1200; deceleration is 0.67 m/s^2. (6)

4 a Choose a scale for the force diagram; draw a line 100 units long; construct an angle of 30° to the line; draw a second line, at this angle, 100 units long; complete the parallelogram; measure the length of the diagonal; convert to size of force using the scale; measure the angle of the diagonal from one of the force vectors. (6)
b He would need to make the angle between his rope and the other rope larger; so that the diagonal of the force parallelogram is still in the same direction. (2)

3 Momentum and force

3.1

1 a Momentum = mass × velocity, kg m/s.
b 240 kg m/s
c 0.48 m/s

2 a 400 kg m/s
b 0.5 m/s
c 1000 m/s

3 a 5000 kg m/s
b 2.0 m/s

3.2

1 a They exert equal and opposite forces on each other.
b They have equal and opposite momentum just after they separate.
c Just after they separate, the velocity of the 80 kg skater is three-quarters the velocity of the 60 kg skater and in the opposite direction.
d Their total momentum is zero just after they separate.

2 a 120 kg m/s
b 1.5 m/s

3 a 25 m/s
b It would have been less.

3.3

1 a The seat belt increases the time taken to stop the person so the change of momentum per second is less, and therefore the force on the person is less.
b –7200 N

2 a i 4000 N
ii 800 N
b Force = change of momentum divided by time taken. The change of momentum would be the same but the time taken would be much less. So the force would be much greater.

3 a Initial momentum = 2000 kg × 12 m/s = 24 000 kg m/s = final momentum. This is equal to the total mass × the velocity after impact which is therefore equal to 24 000 kg m/s ÷ 12 000 kg = 2 m/s.
b i –33 m/s^2
ii –20 000 kg m/s
iii 67 000 N

3.4

1 In an accident where the car suddenly stopped, the child would press against the back of the car seat spreading out the force. This would prevent the chid from being thrown forwards.

2 The air bag increases the time taken to stop the person it acts on. This reduces the force of the impact. Also, the force is spread out across the chest by the air bag so its effect is lessened again.

3 a 26100 kg m/s b 35 m/s c Yes

Answers to end of chapter summary questions

1 a i 45000 kg m/s ii 3750 N
  b It is reduced to zero.
  c The car would probably have skidded as there is an upper limit on how much friction the road can exert on the tyres.

2 a i 115 N
   ii The force acts horizontally backwards from the seat belt.
  b The child would not have stopped when the car stops and would hit the back of the front seats or be thrown through the windscreen.

3 a The force of the student's foot on the boat pushes the boat away.
  b i 37.5 kg m/s ii 0.75 m/s

4 a i 36000 kg m/s ii 20000 kg m/s
  b i 16000 kg m/s ii 13.3 m/s

5 a i Acceleration = change in $\frac{\text{velocity}}{\text{time}}$, since weight starts at rest.

   Speed = $\frac{10}{0.63}$ = 6.3 m/s.
   ii 44 kg m/s
  b 20000 N
  c The impact force would probably have been the same because the increase of the speed and hence the momentum of the weight would have been over a longer impact time.

6 a 8.4 kg m/s
  b Impact force = $\frac{\Delta p}{t} = \frac{8.4}{0.0384}$ = 218.75 = 220 N (2 s.f.)

Answers to end of chapter examination-style questions

1 a Momentum is mass × velocity; velocity is speed in a given direction; so momentum has magnitude and direction. (3)
  b i Momentum of P = mass × velocity OR 20 000 × 14
   = 280 000 kgm/s
   (1 mark for answer; 1 mark for correct unit) (3)
   ii momentum of Q = 600 000 kgm/s (1)
   iii total momentum before collision = 880 000 kgm/s
   momentum after collision = 880 000 kgm/s
   = 50 000 × v
   v = 17.6 m/s (4)

2 a i kgm/s (1)
   ii **Similarities:** both have same *magnitude* of momentum.
   Differences: they have momentum in opposite directions and since the coach has a larger mass, he has a smaller velocity. (3)
  b momentum of dancer = 50 × 1.5
   momentum of coach = 75 kgm/s
   = 90 × v
   v = 0.83 m/s (3)

3 a Marks for this answer will be determined by the Quality of Written Communication (QWC) as well as the standard of scientific response. Physics points: seatbelts they stop drivers/passengers continuing forward when car stops suddenly; preventing them hitting the windscreen/seat in front; time of impact is increased; so deceleration is reduced; therefore the force of impact is reduced; seatbelts also spread the force; airbags inflate on impact; spread the force; increase time of impact; reducing the deceleration; also reducing the force. (6)
  b The batsman wants the impact force to be large; therefore the impact time should be as short as possible; the fielder wants the force on his hands to be as small as possible; therefore the impact time should be long. (4)

4 a The crumple zone 'gives'; making the impact time longer than it would be without the crumple zone; this reduces the deceleration; thus reducing the force and the damage to the car. (4)
  b Acceleration = F/m OR 60/0.2
   = 300 m/s^2
   = change in velocity/time OR change in velocity/0.008 s
   change in velocity = 300 × 0.008 = 2.4 m/s (5)

5 a i 8 m/s; 9600 kg m/s (2)
   ii Impact time = 2 milliseconds (1);
   Impact force = $\frac{1200 \times -8}{0.002}$ = –4800000 N = –4800 kN (3)
  b The decrease in velocity does not take place at a constant rate; as shown by the graph being a curve/line has a changing gradient; so momentum is not lost at a steady rate; therefore the impact force is not constant and is least at the end of the impact. (4)

4 More about forces

4.1

1 a Braking distance
  b Thinking distance
  c Braking distance

2 a i 6.0 m ii 24.0 m iii 30.0 m
  b 12 m

3 a i The thinking distance is proportional to the speed as the reaction time is constant.
   ii When the speed is twice as large and the braking force is constant, the braking time is greater, so the braking distance more than doubles (think about the area under the velocity–time graph).
  b Yes; the braking distance divided by the square of the speed is the same for all three speeds. So the braking distance is proportional to the square of the speed.

4.2

1 a The initial resultant force is equal to its weight.
  b The frictional force is less than the weight.
  c Zero
  d Zero

2 a 500 N
  b 80 N
  c 48 N

3 a The frictional force due to the parachute increases with speed so the resultant force on the parachutist decreases. When the frictional force becomes equal to the weight, the resultant force becomes zero and the parachutist moves at terminal velocity.
  b i 900 N
   ii 900 N upwards

4.3

1 a i The extension of a spring is directly proportional to the force applied, as long as its limit of proportionality is not exceeded.
   ii 2.5 N
  b i It does not return to its original length when it is released.
   ii The rubber band does return to its original length when it is released whereas the polythene strip does not.

2 a The limit beyond which the tension is no longer proportional to the extension.
  b The force per unit extension as long as the limit of proportionality is not reached.
  c The increase of its length from its unstretched length.

3 a i 80 mm
   ii 54 mm
   iii 10 mm
  b i 60 mm
   ii 50 N/m
   iii 1/the spring constant

Answers to end of chapter summary questions

1 a 25.5 m
  b i –4.0 m/s^2 ii 94.5 m

2 a i The braking distance is increased because friction between the tyres and the road is reduced
   ii The reaction time is increased so the distance travelled in this time (the thinking distance) is increased.
  b i 12.6 m
   ii 3.4 m
   iii Stopping distance = $\frac{\text{distance}}{\text{speed}} = \frac{24}{18}$ = 1.33 s

   Deceleration = $\frac{0-18}{1.33}$ = –13.5 m/s^2

   Braking force = 1200 × –13.5 = 16200 N

3 a 320 N b 80 N

4 a For an object of mass m, the gravitational force on it = m × g. Since this is the only force acting on the object, the resultant force on the object = m × g. The acceleration of the object = resultant force/mass = m × g/m = g.
  b 17 m/s
  c i The acceleration of X is constant and equal to 10 m/s^2
   ii Object accelerates at first. The frictional force on it increases with speed so the resultant force on it and its acceleration decreases. When the frictional force is equal to the weight of the object, the resultant force is zero. The acceleration is then zero so the velocity is constant.

5 a i 225 N
   ii 450 N

b The cyclist exerts a constant force driving her forward. Crouching reduces the force of air resistance (the frictional force). The frictional force increases with speed. So the cyclist can get to a higher speed before the frictional force becomes equal to the driving force.

6 a i 0.048 m ii 25 N/m
b 1.0 N

7 a 79 mm, 121 mm, 160 mm, 201 mm, 239 mm
b

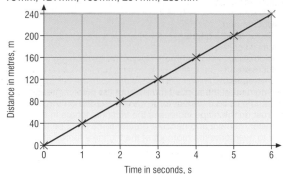

Distance in metres, m
240
200
160
120
80
40
0
0 1 2 3 4 5 6
Time in seconds, s

c 280 mm
d i 25 N/m ii 3.5 N

Answers to end of chapter examination-style questions

1 a The distance travelled during the reaction/thinking time. (1)
b i Alcohol slows reactions; this increases the reaction time; which increases the thinking distance. (3)
ii The thinking distance increases with increasing speed; they are directly proportional. (2)
c i Deceleration = change in velocity/time
= 30/4.8
= 6.25 m/s^2 (2)
ii Braking force = 900 × 6.25
= 5825 N (2)
iii distance = area
= ½ × 4.8 × 30
= 72 m (3)
d Speed of vehicle; braking force; mass of vehicle; condition of road; condition of brakes/tyres. (5)

2 a i C (1)
ii zero error (1)
b i Gravity (1)
ii Drag of oil/viscosity of oil (1)
c i Speed increasing; but with decreasing acceleration; force Y increases with speed; so resultant force decreases. (4)
ii Steady/constant speed; eventually force Y = force X; resultant force zero; acceleration zero. (4)

3 a Marks for this answer will be determined by the Quality of Written Communication (QWC) as well as the standard of scientific response. Measure the initial length of spring with only weight hanger attached; add one weight and measure new length; subtract initial length to find the extension; repeat with further weights; each time removing weight to check spring returns to previous length. (6)
b i Plot extension against stretching force; straight line through origin indicates that they are directly proportional. (2)
ii Calculate the extension for each force; then doubling force from 1 N to 2 N doubles extension from 0.5 to 1.0 cm; doubling again from 2 N to 4 N doubles 1.0 cm to 2.0 cm. Therefore, extension is directly proportional to stretching force. (3)
c When the stretching force is removed; the material returns to original shape/size. (2)

5 Forces and energy

5.1

1 a i Energy is transferred into kinetic energy of the boat and the water and thermal energy of the surroundings.
ii Energy is transferred into gravitational potential energy of the barrier and thermal energy due to friction and sound energy.
b 80 000 J

2 a The kinetic energy of the car is transferred by heating to the disc pads by friction.
b 140 000 J

3 a i 96 J
ii 96 J
b 200 N

5.2

1 a i A mains-connected filament lamp.
ii 10 000 W electric cooker
b 600 000 kW (= 600 MW)

2 a 800 J
b 800 J
c 160 W

3 a i 1800 m
ii 9.0 MJ
b Force $= \frac{\text{work done}}{\text{distance}} = \frac{9000000}{1800} = 500\text{ N}$

5.3

1 a On descent, gravitational potential energy of the ball is transferred to kinetic energy of the ball. On impact, the kinetic energy of the ball is transferred into elastic energy of the ball and some of the elastic energy is transferred back to kinetic energy as it rebounds. After the impact, the kinetic energy of the ball is transferred to gravitational potential energy of the ball as it rises.
b i 1.1 J
ii Energy transfer to the surroundings due to air resistance as the ball moves through the air; energy transfer by heating to the ball when the ball is deformed.

2 a 90 J
b 4500 J

3 a 450 J
b 375 J

4 Energy must be supplied to keep the biceps muscle in the arm contracted. No work is done on the object, because it doesn't move. The energy supplied heats the muscles and is transferred by heating to the surroundings.

5.4

1 a i 36 kJ
ii 88 J
b 17 m/s

2 a i Work done by the muscles transfer chemical energy from the muscles to elastic potential energy of the catapult.
ii Elastic potential energy of the catapult is transferred to kinetic energy of the object.
b i 10 J
ii 10 m/s

3 a 3600 N
b 800 kg

Answers to end of chapter summary questions

1 a i 210 MJ
ii 6900 m
iii Resistive force $= \frac{\text{work done}}{\text{distance}} = \frac{210000000}{6900} = 30345 = 30000\text{ N}$ (2 s.f.)
iv The acceleration of the train is zero so the resultant force on it is zero. Therefore, the driving force and the resistive force must be equal and opposite to each other.
b The train gains gravitational energy as it travels up the incline. The rate at which it transfer energy to the surroundings is unchanged as its speed is the same and the resistive forces acting on it are unchanged. So the output power of the engine needs to be greater as energy must be transferred to the train as gravitational potential energy as well as to the surroundings.

2 a 180 J
b work done = force × distance in the direction of the force = 11 N × 20 m = 220 J.
c The trolley did not gain kinetic energy as its speed was constant. The trolley gained 180 J of gravitational potential energy. Resistive forces such as friction at the trolley wheels must have transferred 40 J of energy to the surroundings as waste energy.

3 a i 530 kJ
ii 7100 kN
iii The car would skid.
b No; the kinetic energy of cars moving at 80 mph is much greater than that of cars moving at 70 mph. Impact forces would therefore be much greater and so injuries would be more severe. In addition, motorists have less time to act to avoid an impact at high speed.

4 a 2.0 m/s
b i 9.6 kJ
ii 4.0 kJ
iii 2.2 kJ
c i The change of momentum of each wagon occurs over a longer time so the change of momentum per second and hence the impact force is less.
ii Energy is transferred to the surroundings as sound and heat in the impact and energy is stored in the compressed spring.

5 a Energy is initially stored in the stretched cord as elastic potential energy. This energy is transferred to the arrow as kinetic energy when the cord is released. As the arrow gains height, its kinetic energy decreases and its gravitational potential energy increases. At maximum height, the arrow has maximum gravitational potential energy and minimum kinetic energy. As it travels through the air, some of its energy is transferred to the air due to air resistance.
  b i 4.7 J
   ii 3.0 J
   iii 15 m/s
6 a 135 kJ
  b i 940 J
   ii 675 kJ
  c 810 kJ

Answers to end of chapter examination-style questions

1 a joule; kilojoule; kilowatt-hour (3)
  b i $W = m \times g$ OR $W = 58 \times 10$ (1)
   $= 580$ N (1)
   ii Work = weight × height OR work = 580 × 12 (1)
   = 6960 J (1)
   iii Power = work done/time taken OR power = 6960/120 (1)
   = 58 W (1 mark for 58, 1 mark for the unit)
2 a i chemical energy from food (1); transferred to kinetic as the jumper runs (1); to gravitational potential as he rises above ground (1)
   ii Gravitational potential energy $= m \times g \times h = 65 \times 10 \times 1.25$ (1)
   = 812.5 J (1)
  b i Kinetic energy $= 812.5 = \frac{1}{2} \times m \times v^2$ (1)
   $v^2 = 2 \times 812.5/65$ (1)
   $= 25$ (1)
   $v = 5$ m/s (1)
   ii Energy is lost (1); due to drag along the track (1); and in rising (1)
3 a Marks for this answer will be determined by the Quality of Written Communication (QWC) as well as the standard of scientific response. Equipment needed: stopwatch; scales/balance; tape measure. They need to measure: their mass; the vertical height of the stairs (they may measure the rise and number of steps and multiply together – in which case a tape measure would not be needed, just a ruler); and the time taken to climb the stairs – this would need co-operation and some form of signalling to indicate starting and stopping of the stopwatch. (6)
  b Work done = 450 × 4 (1)
  power = work/time = 1800/2.5 (1)
  = 720 W (1)
4 a i gravitational potential (1)
   ii Loss in height = 0.5 m (1)
   percentage loss = 0.5/2.0 × 100 (1)
   = 25% (1)
   iii Transferred to thermal; warms the ground; spreads out. (3)
  b i Equal to GPE $= m \times g \times h$ (1)
   $= 0.2 \times 10 \times 2$ (1)
   $= 4$ J (1)
   ii $\frac{1}{2} \times m \times v^2 = 4$ (1)
   $= 8/0.2$ (1)
   $= 40$ (1)
   $v = 6.3$ m/s (1)
   iii Reaction force of the floor changes the motion (1); speed changes (1); direction is reversed (1); acceleration is the rate of change of the vector velocity. (1)

6 Forces in action

6.1

1 **a** and **c** The centre of mass is where the two diagonal lines from the corners cross.
  b The centre of mass is found by drawing two diametric lines at right angles. The centre of mass is where the two line cross.
2 The centre of mass of the child is then directly below the midpoint M of the points of suspension of the swing. At this position, the moment of the child about M is zero.
3 See the practical instructions and Figure 4 on p 51.

6.2

1 a i It decreases. ii It is unchanged.
  b i 1.4 s ii 0.71 Hz
2 a 37.93 s
  b 0.53 Hz
3 a Similarity: They both move repeatedly along a line or they both move repeatedly through the equilibrium position.
  Difference: Their time period differs or the amplitude of the swing decreases faster than the amplitude of the simple pendulum.
  b The relevant length that determines the time period is from the point of suspension to the centre of mass. This is shorter in the swing than in the pendulum as the effect of the child sitting on the swing raises the centre of mass, so the swing time period is less.

6.3

1 a i Increased
   ii Unchanged
   iii Reduced to a quarter
  b 18 N m
2 a Anticlockwise
  b i Increased
   ii Decreased
3 a The moment of the applied force about the pivot is greater the longer the handle is, so a greater force can be exerted on the nail.
  b The rust on the hinge increases the frictional forces in the hinge, so a greater moment and hence a greater force must be applied to the door to overcome the moment of the frictional forces at the hinge.
4 72 N

6.4

1 a i 3 N
   ii 1.2 N
  b In both examples, the line of action of the effort is at a greater perpendicular distance from the pivot than the corresponding distance for the load. A smaller effort therefore gives an equal and opposite moment about the pivot to the load's moment.
2 a Dawn
  b 340 N, 1.84 m
  c Dawn needs to move 0.66 m towards the pivot so she is 1.84 m from the pivot.
3 1.5 N

6.5

1 a i It would be less stable as its centre of mass would be higher.
   ii Without stabilisers, when the child leans to one side, the moment of the rider's weight (about the line between the points where the cycle wheels are on the ground) makes the bicycle fall over. The stabiliser wheel on that side touches to ground and an upward force from the ground acts on it. This upward force provides a moment (about the line between the points where the cycle wheels are on the ground) which counterbalances the moment of the rider's weight and stops the bicycle falling over.
  b A supermarket trolley, a tall electric kettle, etc.
2 a The chair would topple over if the baby in the chair leans too far sideways.
  b The lower the centre of mass, the harder it is to topple it over.
3 a When it is empty, its centre of mass is approximately halfway up the bottle. When it is standing upright and is less than half full, its centre of mass is approximately halfway between its base and the water level. This position of the centre of mass will always be lower than the position when it is empty.
  b The cone has a wide base which is attached to a heavy square board. The centre of mass of the cone is therefore much lower than it would be if the base was narrow, and therefore more stable.

6.6

1 a B, C
  b C, D
2 a friction
  b pull (tension)
  c gravity
  d electrostatic force
3 a i The car would skid off the bend because the centripetal force needed would be greater at a higher speed and the friction on the tyres providing the centripetal force would be unchanged.
   ii The car would skid off the bend as the centripetal force needed increases as the radius of the circle is decreased.
  b If the track was not banked, the track would not be able to exert enough centripetal force on the train to make it stay on the track when it travels round the curve. With a banked track, the weight of the train would contribute towards the necessary centripetal force in addition to the force of the track on the train.

6.7

1 a The area of your hands in contact with the ground when you do a handstand is smaller than the area of your feet on the ground when you are upright. Since the force (i.e. your weight) is the same in both cases and pressure = force divided by area, the pressure on your hands in a handstand is greater than the pressure on your feet when you are upright.

b When in use, a sharp knife has a smaller contact area than a blunt knife has. For the same force, the pressure of a sharp knife is greater so it cuts more easily than a blunt knife does.

2 a A crane, a digger, vehicle brakes, etc.
b i The pressure of the compressed air forces the piston in X upwards, making the two outer parts of the arm move up.
ii The bucket moves in a downward scoop towards the cab.

3 a 18 000 N b 8800 N

Answers to end of chapter summary questions

1 a The effort acts further from the fulcrum than does the force of the bottle opener on the top. So the force of the bottle opener on the top is greater than the effort.
b 75 N; the effort is 3 times further from the fulcrum than edge of the cap is. So an effort of 25 N causes three times as much force to be exerted on the edge of the cap.

2 a It would be less stable as it would be easier to disturb.
b 0.06 N

3 a The distance from the wheel axle to force *F* is much greater than the distance from the axle to the centre of mass. The weight of the sand and the wheelbarrow causes a certain moment about the wheel axle. To lift the wheelbarrow legs off the ground, force *F* must create a greater moment about the wheel axle. Because the distance from the wheel axle to force *F* is much greater than the distance from the axle to the centre of mass, force *F* can be much smaller than the weight to give an greater moment than that of the weight.
b i 149 N ii 84 N

4 Friction between the footwear and the floor provides the necessary centripetal force to enable the person to revolve with the floor. The floor is too slippy to provide such friction so anyone stepping on the floor would probably slide towards the edge and be thrown off it as it revolves.

5 a The centre of the brake pedal is about 4 times further from the pivot that the piston rod. A force of 20 N on the piston could therefore be achieved by applying a force of 5 N to the brake pedal. This would give a moment sufficient to cause a force of 20 N on the piston.
b i 33 kPa
ii The pressure in the master cylinder is transmitted without loss to each brake cylinder. The force on each brake cylinder is equal to the pressure × its cross-sectional area. As each brake cylinder has a much greater cross-sectional area than the master cylinder has, the force exerted by the brake cylinder is much greater than 20 N.

6 a The time period is the time for the pendulum bob to swing from one extreme to the opposite extreme and back (or the time between successive passes through the centre in the same direction).
b i 3.03 s
ii The time period would become less and the frequency would increase.
c Displace the pendulum by a measured distance from the centre and measure the time for 10 complete oscillations. Repeat the procedure several times for the same initial displacement to obtain an average time for 10 oscillations and hence calculate the mean value of the time period. Repeat the test for different measured amplitudes. Plot a graph of the time period on the y-axis against the amplitude on the x-axis to see if the time period varies with amplitude.

Answers to end of chapter examination-style questions

1 a Marks for this answer will be determined by the Quality of Written Communication (QWC) as well as the standard of scientific response. Points to be made: put a pin through one hole; suspend the sheet from the pin; hang a plumb-line from the pin; draw a vertical line along the plumb-line; repeat hanging the sheet from the other hole; where the two lines cross is the centre of mass. (6)
b i Moment = force × (perpendicular) distance from pivot OR = 2.5 × 30 (1) = 75 N cm (1)
ii Anticlockwise moment less (1); since perpendicular distance is less (1); therefore clockwise moment is less (1); so tension in spring is less. (1)

2 a i Two from: track; wheel base; position of centre of mass (2)
ii The government test should be unbiased/manufacturers' test could be biased. (1)
b i Weight = 12 000 N (1) moment = weight × distance from pivot OR = 12 000 × 0.5 (1) = 6 000 Nm (1 for answer; 1 for the unit).
ii Low centre of mass (1); clockwise moment returns vehicle to the horizontal (1); line of action of weight passes through base. (1)
iii Centre of mass raised (1); vehicle tilts less (1); before line of action of weight passes outside base. (1)

3 a centripetal (1)
b Electrostatic attraction (1); gravity. (1)
c Towards the centre of the circle. (1)
d Mass (1); velocity (1); radius of circle. (1)

4 a Liquids are almost incompressible (1); pressure transmitted equally in all directions. (1)
b Pressure acts equally on both sides of rim (1); brake blocks have same area. (1)
c Force = pressure × area OR = 250 × 2 (1) = 500 N (1) Two blocks, so total force = 1000 N. (1)
d Master piston has small area (1); large pressure transmitted (1); slave piston has larger area so F (P × A) is larger. (1)

7 General properties of waves

7.1

1 a The oscillations in a transverse wave are perpendicular to the direction of energy transfer. The oscillations of a longitudinal wave are parallel to the direction of energy transfer.
b i An electromagnetic wave or waves on a stretched string or wire.
ii Sound waves.
c The particles are displaced so they are closer together.

2 a Transverse
b i Along the rope from one end to the other.
ii It oscillates in a direction perpendicular to the energy transfer.

3 a Stretch the slinky out with each person holding one end. To send transverse waves along the slinky, move one end so it oscillates at right angles to the slinky. To send longitudinal waves along the slinky, move one end so it oscillates parallel to the slinky.
b The red coil moves to and fro in a direction parallel to the slinky axis about a fixed point along the axis.

7.2

1 a amplitude = 9 mm, wavelength = 37 mm
b The number of wavecrests passing a point in one second or the number of cycles of the waves that pass a point in one second.

2 a **i** and **iii** see 7.2 Figure 1.
b Point P will oscillate at right angles to the wave moving from a maximum as the wave peak passes down to a minimum as the wave trough passes.

3 a 6.0 m/s
b i 6.0 m
ii 360 m

7.3

1 a They are equal.
b The angle of each refracted wavefront to the boundary becomes greater than the angle of each incident wave front to the boundary.

2 See 7.3 Figure 3

3 a The slopes prevent reflection of the waves at the sides of the tank.
b Reflection of waves from the sides would occur and these reflected waves would spoil the pattern of the waves in the tank.

7.4

1 a The wavelength is unchanged.
b i The waves spread out (or diffract) more.
ii The waves spread out (or diffract) less.

2 a Diffraction is the spreading of waves when and after they pass through a gap or pass by an obstacle.
b i The radio waves carrying the TV signal from the transmitter are short compared with obstacles such as the hills so the waves do not diffracted much. Therefore, fewer radio waves would reach a TV receiver on the other side of a hill to the transmitter.
ii The longer wavelength radio waves are diffracted more than the waves carrying the TV signal and so they spread out more when the pass over a hill and can reach radio receivers at some locations which TV signals cannot reach.

3 The sound waves from the radio diffract when they reach the doorway so they spread out and travel along the corridor.

7.5

1 The tea tray reflects some of the radio waves carrying the TV signal. The reflected waves and waves directly from the transmitter produce an interference pattern. If the aerial is at a point where the waves cancel each other out, the TV signal becomes very weak.

2 The waves from each slit arrive at the same time at this point because they travel equal distances. Therefore they always reinforce each other at this point and the detector signal is stronger.

3 a The interference fringes would be further apart.
b The interference fringes would be green and their spacing would be less than the spacing of red fringes and more than the spacing of blue fringes.

Answers to end of chapter summary questions

1 a See 7.2 Figure 1
b In a transverse wave, the particles oscillate at right angles to the direction in which the wave travels. In a longitudinal wave, the particles oscillate along the direction in which the wave travels.
c Transverse wave; waves on a string or a rope, electromagnetic waves Longitudinal waves; sound waves

2 a 0.05 Hz
b 0.40 m/s
c 8.0 m

3 a i Decreases
ii Unchanged
b i Unchanged
ii Unchanged
iii Unchanged

4 a See Figure 1a
b See Figure 1b

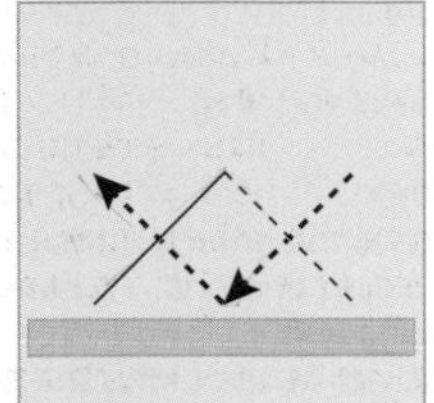
Figure 1a

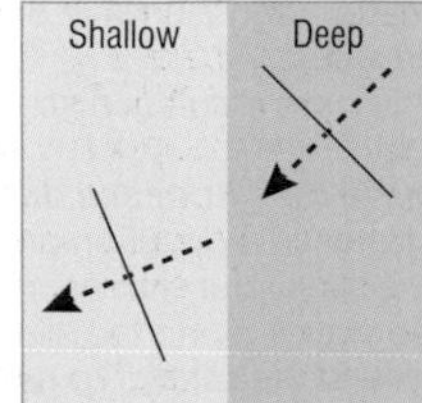

Figure 1b

5 a 100 MHz
b The waves would travel across the top of a hill without diffracting if their wavelength is much less than the height of the hill. As a result, no waves would spread down the hill so a receiver on the far side of the hill would not receive a signal.

6 a

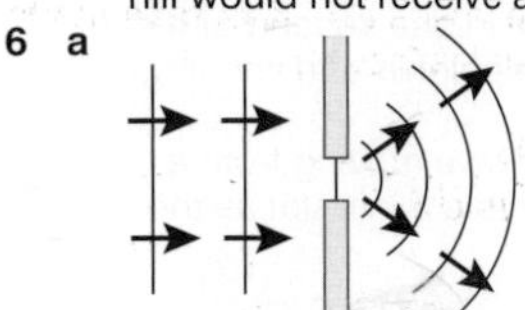

i Diffraction
ii The waves would be shorter (at the same distance apart), diffracted less.

8 a i Diffraction
ii Interference
iii Cancellation
iv and v reinforcement
b i The points of cancellation and reinforcement would be closer together.
ii The waves would be further apart. The points of cancellation and reinforcement would be further apart.

Answers to end of chapter examination-style questions

1 a i C ii D
iii A iv B (4)
b i There are two sets of radio waves; travelling in opposite directions; they overlap/interfere at the car; where crest meets trough it is soft; where crest meets crest/trough meets trough it is loud. (5)
ii Only sound waves from speakers; conditions not right for interference. (2)

2 a i X – transverse (1)
ii Y – longitudinal (1)
iii Perpendicular to the direction of energy transfer. (1)
iv Parallel to the direction of energy transfer. (1)
b Marks for this answer will be determined by the Quality of Written Communication (QWC) as well as the standard of scientific response.
Similarities: all travel in the form of waves; all transfer energy; light & radio have the same wave speed.
Differences: light & radio are transverse waves/sound is longitudinal; wavelength of radio longer than that of light for same frequency; sound has a much lower wave speed than light and radio; sound cannot travel through a vacuum/needs a medium. (6 – for full marks, there must be at least 2 similarities)

3 a i R
ii Q (2)
b $\lambda = 0.03$ m (1)
$f = c/\lambda$ OR $f = 3 \times 10^8/0.03$ (1)
$= 1 \times 10^{10}$ (1) Hz/hertz (1)
c i Waves from the two slits come together; crest to trough; cancel/subtract. (3)
ii Waves come together crest to crest/trough to trough; add/reinforce. (2)
iii higher than N (1)

4 a Diffraction increases with decreasing gap width; greatest diffraction when gap width = wavelength. (2)
b Sound waves diffract through doorway; door width similar to wavelength; light waves have much shorter wavelengths and so do not diffract significantly through doorway. (3)
c i Radio 4 carrier wave has a much greater wavelength than BBC1 television carrier wave; it is 3000 times as great. (2)
ii Radio 4 carrier waves diffract round the hill; they have a similar wavelength to the width of the hill. (2)
iii BBC1 television carrier wave has a much smaller wavelength; the carrier wave does not diffract round the hill. (2)

8 Electromagnetic waves

8.1

1 a Radio waves
b The speed is the same for all electromagnetic waves.
c X-rays
d Microwaves

2 radio microwaves infrared visible light ultraviolet X-rays gamma rays

3 a 0.50 m
b 1000 MHz

4 a Gamma radiation
b All electromagnetic waves travel at the same speed in space. Since both types of waves travel the same distance and they are emitted at the same time, they reach the Earth at the same time.

8.2

1 a i Radio waves
ii Light waves
b i Microwaves
ii Radio waves

2 a Mobile phone calls would not be clear as the phones would detect handset signals as well as mobile phone signals.
b If other radio wave users operated in the same wavelength range as the emergency services, their signals would be detected by the emergency services and might 'mask' the emergency services signals making conversations carried by the emergency services signals difficult to listen to.

3 a i Radio waves
ii Microwaves
iii Infrared radiation
iv Light
b 0.125 m

8.3

1 a i Radio waves or microwaves
ii Infrared radiation
b i The two signals would interfere where they cross and there would be points where they cancel each other
ii The signals cannot escape from the fibre so they cannot be detected except by the detector at the receiver end. Radio signals travel through the air so can be detected by any radio detector in the path of the waves.

2 a The skull of a child is thinner than that of an adult which means that mobile phone radiation can pass more easily through the skull of a child into the brain and cause a greater heating effect
b Light waves have a much higher frequency and a much smaller wavelength in air than radio waves so can carry many more pulses per second than radio waves can.

3 a Microwaves are absorbed less by the atmosphere than radio waves and are not diffracted as much so they spread out less making them suitable for satellite TV. Terrestrial TV uses radio waves as diffraction as it helps to prevent signal problems.
b Microwaves from such a transmitter dish are directed in a beam at the other dish so they travel in a straight line towards the other dish. If the other dish is visible from the first transmitter, it can detect the microwaves directed at it. The atmosphere does not absorb the beam much so the received signal is strong enough to be detected.

8.4

1 a X-rays pass through the crack but not through the surrounding metal. On the X-ray picture, the crack appears as a break in the shadow of the metal object.
b Yes
c A metal case would stop the X-rays so the X-rays would not reach the film inside the case.

2 a It harms the skin and can cause skin cancer. It damages the eyes and can cause blindness.
b i It absorbs most of the ultraviolet radiation from the Sun.
ii Ultraviolet radiation causes sunburn. Suncreams stop UV radiation reaching the skin. Suncreams absorbs the UV radiation that passes through the ozone layer.
3 a X-rays and gamma rays
b Lead
c i X-rays and gamma rays
ii Ultraviolet radiation, X-rays and gamma rays

8.5

1 a The contrast medium absorbs X-rays. Without it, the X-rays would pass through the stomach so no image of the stomach will be seen on the X-ray photograph.
b X-ray therapy can be used to destroy cancerous tissue.
2 a Dense material such as bone in the patient absorb X-rays from the tube and stop them reaching the film cassette. X rays that reach the film cassette blacken the film and do not pass through such absorbing materials. When the film is developed, clear images of the bones and other absorbing materials in the patient are seen on the film because X-rays did not reach these areas.
b If the film was not in a lightproof cassette, light from the room would blacken the entire film.
c X-rays ionise substances they pass through. Ionisation in healthy cells can damage or kill the cells or cause cell mutation and cancerous growth. The shielding prevents X-rays from reaching and damaging cells in parts of the patient not under investigation.
3 a X-rays
b Advantage = higher dose; disadvantage = higher cost.

Answers to end of chapter summary questions

1 a D E A B C
b i Microwaves
ii Gamma rays
iii Infrared rays
2 a i speed = wavelength × frequency
ii 103 MHz
b As the radio waves travel away from the transmitter, their amplitude is gradually reduced due to absorption by the air. At a certain distance *d*, the amplitude is just large enough for the waves to be detected. Reducing the power of the transmitter reduces the amplitude at that distance so the range is reduced.
3 a Mobile phones signals are carried by microwaves. Microwaves can heat substances which absorb them. If a mobile phone emits too much microwave radiation, the radiation absorbed by tissues in the head (e.g. brain tissue) may be adversely damaged by the heating effect of the microwaves.
b A; it emits less microwave energy per second so it would not affect the organs in the head (e.g. the brain or the ear) as much.
c Microwave radiation penetrates their skulls more than older skills because their skulls are thinner. Also, smaller heads heat up more easily than bigger heads.
4 a i Bone absorbs X-rays so a 'shadow' image is formed on the film.
ii X-rays pass through the fracture but not through the bones.
b i Barium absorbs X-rays so an image of the stomach is formed on the film.
ii The stomach movements would blur the images.
iii X-rays ionise substances they pass through. The amount of ionising radiation the patient is exposed to is reduced by stopping the X-rays reaching the patient. The quality of the image is unaffected because the low energy X-rays would not reach the film anyway.
c Ultrasound waves from a scanner do not harm the baby because they are non-ionising. X-rays are ionising and would harm the baby.
5 a Ionisation is the process of creating ions, which are charged atoms from uncharged atoms.
b X rays, gamma rays
c Ionising radiation can damage or kill living cells and can cause cell mutation and cancerous growth.
6 a When ultraviolet radiation is directed at invisible ink, the radiation is absorbed by atoms in the ink which then emit light so the ink glows and becomes visible.
b The further infrared radiation travels through air, the more it is absorbed by air molecules so a beam of infrared radiation would be too weak to detect after more than a few metres.
c Local radio signals are carried by electromagnetic waves of a much longer wavelength than microwaves so they spread out much more from a transmitter and the amplitude decreases with distance more than for microwaves which spread out enough to reach a wide area but not so much as to become too weak to detect. In addition, radio waves are absorbed more by the atmosphere than microwaves because microwaves are much higher in frequency and are not affected as much by air molecules.

Answers to end of chapter examination-style questions

1 a i X-rays (1)
ii radio waves (1)
iii X-rays (1)
iv ultraviolet (1)
b i They penetrate tissue (1); and clothing (1); but not bone (1); or metal. (1)
ii They carry a lot of energy (1); they cause ionisation (1); can cause cancer (1); and kill cells. (1)
2 a Gamma: Prolonging the shelf-life of fruit (1);
Infrared: In a TV remote control (1);
Radio: Carrying TV programmes (1);
Ultraviolet: Security marking of TV sets. (1)
b i They can pass through the atmosphere. (1)
ii Marks for this answer will be determined by the Quality of Written Communication (QWC) as well as the standard of scientific response. Points to be made: phones use microwaves; microwaves deliver energy to cells; can heat them up; phones are held near the brain; skull is thinner in young children; brain cells may be damaged. (6)
3 a i Can distinguish between different types of tissue (1); produce 3D images. (1)
ii Larger doses of radiation are used (1); much more expensive. (1)
b X-rays can damage cells (1); fetus has developing cells which can mutate. (1)
c Any six from: the overall dose has more than doubled (1); dose from background radiation is unchanged (1) dose from medical uses has increased by a large amount (1); other man-made radiation has also increased (1) more medical procedures involving radiation in 2010 (1); some, such as CT scans, deliver large doses (1); other man-made due to nuclear accidents (1); and weapons testing. (1)
4 a Infrared (1); light. (1)
b i Any wavelength greater than 100 m. (1)
ii Any wavelength between 1 m and 100 m. (1)
iii Any wavelength less than 1 m. (1)
c Frequency = 2.4×10^9 Hz (1)
$\lambda = c/f$ OR $= 3 \times 10^8/2.4 \times 10^9$ (1) = 0.125 m (1)

9 Sound and ultrasound

9.1

1 a Thick felt or a similar material.
b The bushes absorb some sound and also scatter it. Sound from traffic that reaches the fence panels is reflected back towards the motorway by the panels.
2 a 20 000 Hz
b When the whistle is blown, the ball inside the whistle revolves at high speed pushing the air in and out of the gaps in the case of the whistle. The vibrations of the air at the gaps causes sound waves to spread out from the whistle. The frequency of the sound is constant because the ball revolves at constant speed inside the whistle.
3 a i The cliff face would reflect sound from the horn and create an echo.
ii distance = 340 m/s × 5.0 s/2 = 850 m
b The person creates a sound which spreads out in all directions. The echoes are due to sound reflected from different parts of the cavern walls.

9.2

1 a The amplitude decreases; the frequency does not change.
b The loudness of the sound decreases because the amplitude of the sound waves decreases. This happens because the amplitude of the vibrations of the wire decreases.
2 a The amplitude of the waves would be taller but the horizontal spacing between the peaks and troughs would be unchanged.
b The horizontal spacing between the peaks and troughs would be greater but the amplitude of the waves would be unchanged.
3 a i and ii The pitch or frequency is raised.
iii The pitch is lowered.
b The sound of a violin (played correctly) lasts as long as the violin bow is in contact with a string. The sound of a drum dies away after the drum skin has been struck. A drum note is less rhythmical than a violin note.
c The vibrating tuning fork makes the table surface vibrate. The vibrating table surface creates sound waves in a much greater volume of air than the tips of the vibrating tuning fork does.

9.3

1 a The organs have a different density to the surrounding tissue. So ultrasound is reflected at the tissue/organ boundaries.
b Ultrasound is not ionising radiation whereas X-rays are. Ionising radiation is harmful to living tissue. Ultrasound is reflected at the boundaries between different types of tissue whereas X-rays are not.
c The reflected pulses would be weaker if there is more diffraction because the waves would spread out more and become weaker. Also, the pulses would be reflected from a wider area of each boundary so the position of the boundary would be more difficult to locate.
2 a 3 if the last pulse is due to the other side of the body.
b i 96 millionths of a second
ii 0.144 m
3 a 12 mm
b +2–3 mm

Answers to end of chapter summary questions

1 a i As the surface of the object vibrates, it alternately pushes air particles away as it moves into the air then allows them to return as it retreats from the air, in effect pulling them back. The air particles pushed away from the surface push on other air particles further away then allow them to retreat as they retreat. These further particles in turn alternately push and pull on particles further away. In this way, waves of compressions and rarefactions pass through the air.
ii The sound waves spread out as they travel away from the loudspeaker so the sound becomes fainter and the amplitude becomes smaller.
b i The waves on the screen become taller (higher amplitude).
ii The waves on the screen become more stretched out across the screen so fewer waves appear on the screen.
c The signal generator is connected to the loudspeaker and to the oscilloscope. The signal generator should be adjusted so the subject can hear the sound from the loudspeaker comfortably. The frequency of the signal generator should then be increased gradually until the subject can no longer hear the sound. The frequency at this point can then be determined by measuring the time period of the waveform on the oscilloscope screen. The upper limit frequency is equal to 1/the measured time period.
2 a reflected, smooth
b rough, scattered
c soft, absorbed
d The speed of sound in air increases with increasing air temperature. Refraction takes place at the boundaries between layers of air at different temperatures. At night the air near the ground is colder than air higher up so you can hear sound a long way from its source because sound waves refract back to the ground.
3 a Approximately 20 000 Hz.
b Keep the frequency and the loudness of the sound from the loudspeaker the same throughout. Keep the loudspeaker, the board or cushion and the sound meter in the same positions throughout. With the board in position, measure the sound meter reading. Replace the board with the cushion and measure the sound meter reading again. If the reading for the board is higher than the reading for the cushion, the board reflects more sound than the cushion.
4 a Sound waves created by clapping her hands together travel through the air to the wall where they reflect from it. Some of the reflected waves travel back to the person who hears the echo when the reflected sound waves reach her.
b 51 m
5 270 m
6 a 8.5 mm
b If the bat detects echoes directly ahead, the time delay between each pulse being emitted and being detected enables the bat to sense the distance to the reflecting object. The difference in the intensity of the echo at each ear enables the bat to sense the direction of the reflecting object.
7 a 0.75 mm
b i They could not be detected because they would be absorbed by the tissue.
ii The reflected pulses would be much weaker. Also, if the pulses spread out, it is difficult to tell which boundary a reflected pulse is from.
c Ultrasound as it is non-ionising unlike X-rays. Ionising radiation can damage or kill cells in living tissue.

Answers to end of chapter examination-style questions

1 a i Signal generator (1); loudspeaker (1); microphone (1); cathode ray oscilloscope. (1)
ii A is louder than B (1); A is lower in pitch than B. (1)
b i An echo. (1)
ii Measure the distance to the wall (1); start a stopwatch when they hear the first sound (1); stop the stopwatch when they hear the echo (1); double the distance to the wall to find total distance travelled(1); divide the total distance by the time. (1)
iii Each student should measure the time and then find the average. (1)
2 a i longitudinal; transverse (1) (both correct for mark)
ii slower (1)
iii cannot; can (1) (both correct for mark)
b i 1 cm (1)
ii f = 1/T = 1/0.002 (1) = 500 Hz (1)
iii λ = c/f = 340/500 (1) = 0.68 m (1)
iv Diffraction most marked when gap width similar to wavelength (1); 0.68 m is of the same order as a doorway (1); so waves would be diffracted. (1)
3 a i Longitudinal wave (1); series of compressions in water (1); and rarefactions. (1)
ii There is nothing to be compressed. (1)
iii λ = c/f = 1400/2000 (1) = 0.7 m (1)
b i Sound/longitudinal waves (1); frequency above the range of the human ear. (1)
ii Distance = speed × time = 1400 × 0.1 (1) = 140 m (1)
This is twice the depth – answer 70 m (1)
iii One from: pre-natal scans; dispersing kidney stones; detecting flaws in metals; removing plaque; cleaning surgical instruments (1)
4 a 30 000 Hz (1)
b Marks for this answer will be determined by the Quality of Written Communication (QWC) as well as the standard of scientific response. Points to be made: transducer transmits ultrasound pulses into body; ultrasound can travel through solids and liquids; ultrasound travels through the body; partially reflected at boundaries between different types of tissue/baby/foetus; reflected ultrasound returns to the transducer; where it is detected; the computer processes the information to give a visual image on the screen. (6)

10 Reflection and refraction of light

10.1

1 a i 20° ii 40°
b 42°
2 a, b i

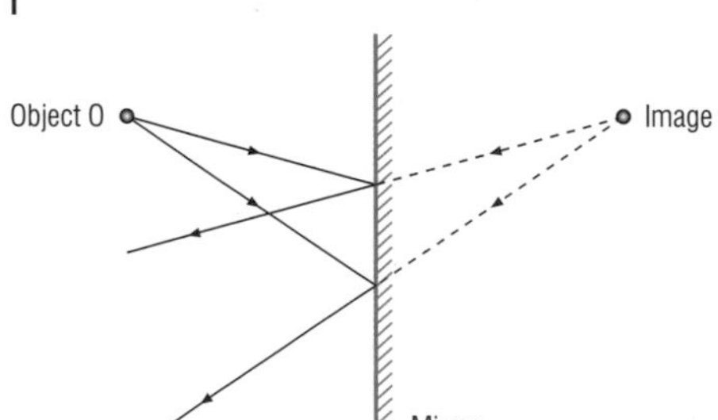

ii Use a millimetre ruler to measure the perpendicular distance from O to the mirror and from the image to the mirror.
3 a

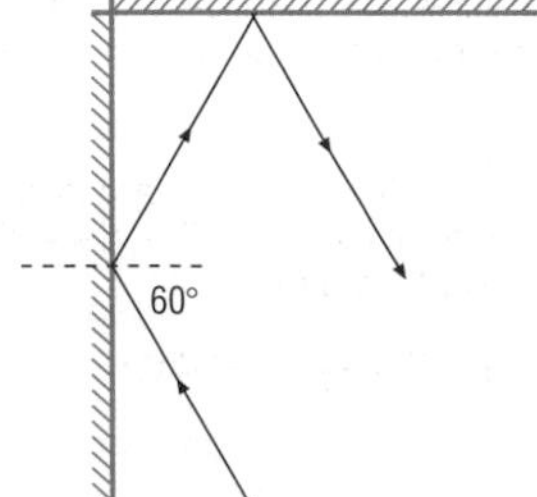

b i 180°
ii As the two mirrors are perpendicular to each other, the angle of incidence for the second reflection is always 90° – first angle of incidence. Therefore, adding both angles of incidences always equals 90° and therefore both reflected rays also equal 90° giving a total of 180°.

10.2

1 a Decrease
b Zero
c Smaller

2 a

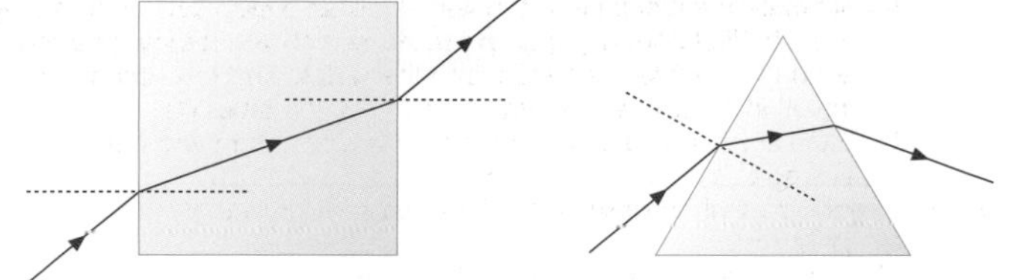

b i Blue

ii In glass, blue light travels slower than red light.

3 a

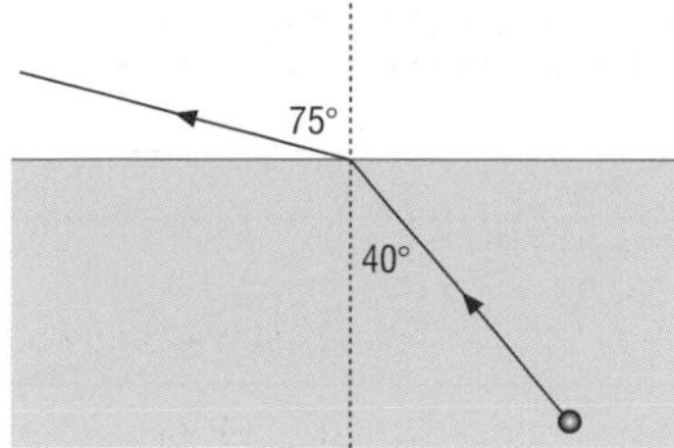

b All the light rays from a point on the bottom of the pool that refract at the surface appear to travel straight from a point above the bottom.

10.3

1 a 1.54

b 1.53

2 a 1.47

b The measurement in Q2 was a single pair of measurements and three pairs of measurements were made in Q1 so the result in Q2 is less reliable than that in Q1; the refractive index of glass of the second block might have been different.

3 a 25.5°

b 70.1°

c 1.52

10.4

1 a The angle of incidence must be greater than the critical angle.

b 90°

c 1.47

2 a

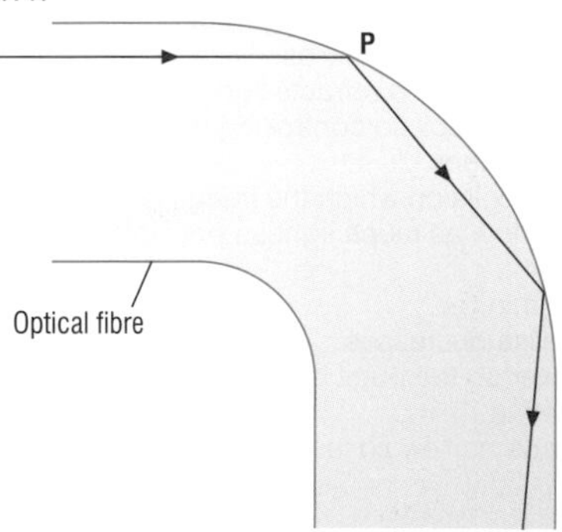

b Any two advantages:

1. The endoscope uses light which is non-ionising (unlike X-rays).
2. Movement of the fragments can be seen with an endoscope.
3. Fragments may be hidden by other fragments on an X-ray picture.

3 a 48.8°

b i 1.49

ii Range of critical angle = 41.5° – 42.5°. At 41.5°, the refractive index = 1.51. At 42.5°, the refractive index = 1.48. Therefore, the largest difference to the answer in part **i** is 0.02.

Answers to end of chapter summary questions

1 a i They are the same.

ii

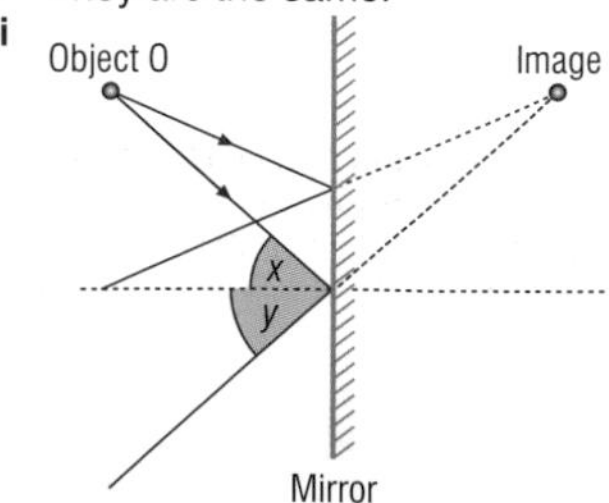

iii They are the same.

b Draw a straight line XY on a sheet of white paper and use a protractor to draw a 'normal' line perpendicular to XY. Place the mirror exactly on XY and use the ray box to direct a light ray at the point P where the normal intersects XY. Adjust the direction of the light ray so the angle of incidence is about 10°. Use a pencil to mark the direction of the incident and reflected rays. Remove the mirror and use a protractor to measure the angles of incidence and reflection. Repeat the text for several different angles of incidence. Record all your results in a table. Plot a straight line graph of the angle of reflection against the angle of incidence. The line should show that the angles of incidence and reflection are always equal to one another.

2 a i

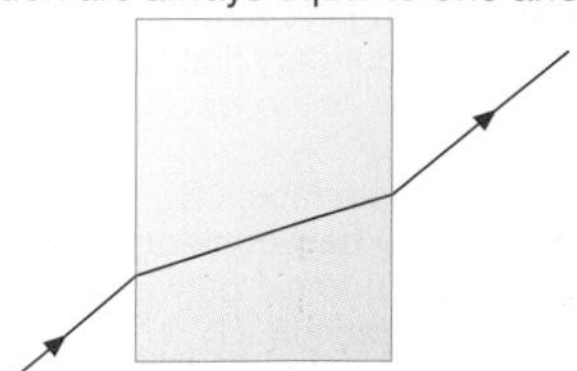

ii The change of direction at the second refraction is exactly equal and opposite to the change at the first refraction. Since the opposite sides of the block are parallel, the light ray that emerges is therefore exactly parallel to the incidence light ray.

b i

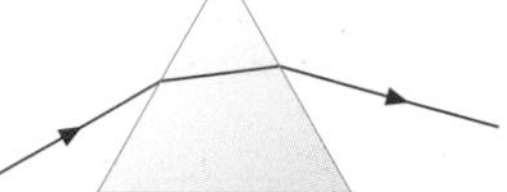

ii A continuous spectrum of colour is seen on the screen with blue light refracted most and red light least. This happens because the refractive index of the glass varies with the wavelength of the light and is greatest for blue light and least for red light.

3 a i 1.53

ii 196 000 km/s

b i 19.5°

ii 80°

4 a

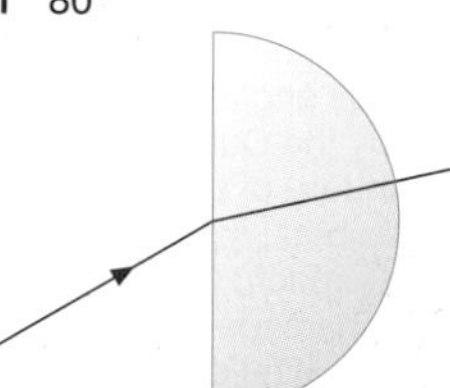

b Draw an outline of the block on a sheet of white paper and use a ruler to locate the centre C of the flat side of the outline. Mark point C on the sheet and use a protractor to draw the normal to the flat side at C. Place the block exactly on the outline and direct a light ray at C so the light ray passes into the block at C. Mark the path of the light ray before it enters the block and where it leave the block as point D. Remove the block and draw the path of the incident light ray and the path of the light ray from C to D. Use a protractor to measure the angle of incidence and the angle of refraction at C.
Calculate the refractive index n using the formula $n = \sin i/\sin c$ from C to D. Repeat the test for different angles of incidence and calculate a mean value for the refractive index from the individual values.

5 a i Total internal reflection is the total reflection of a light ray in a transparent medium at a boundary between the medium and a less refractive medium.

ii The angle of incidence at the boundary should be greater than the critical angle of the boundary.

iii 1.56

b i 41°

ii

iii One bundle takes light into the cavity. The other bundle is used to observe an image formed by a lens near the end of this bundle in the cavity.

6 a $\sin r = \frac{\sin i}{n}$; $\sin r = \frac{\sin 40}{1.59} = 0.404$; $r = 24°$

b i 39°

ii The angles in the triangle formed by the two normals at P and Q and the line PQ add up to 180°. The angle between the two normals is 90°. If x is the angle of incidence at Q, $x + 25° + 90° = 180°$ so $x = 65°$.

iii As angle x is greater than the critical angle of the block, the light ray undergoes total internal reflection at Q so it does not enter the air at Q.

Answers to end of chapter examination-style questions

1 a i Rays only appear to come from it/rays do not pass through it (1); cannot be formed on a screen. (1)
ii It is 'the wrong way round' or words to that effect BUT NOT upside down. (1)
b i Image 1 is 1 m behind mirror A (1); image 1 is 2 m behind mirror B (1); distance = 6 m. (1)
ii Image 1 in mirror B acts as virtual object for mirror A (1); image 1 in mirror A acts as virtual object for mirror B, whose image acts as object for mirror A etc. (1)

2 a i Light waves slow down on entering the other medium (1); the end X of the wavefront reaches the boundary first and so slows down first (1); this changes the direction of the wavefront downwards/towards the normal. (1)
ii If the wavefront is parallel to the interface. (1)
b i Normal correctly drawn (1); angle between normal and incident ray marked angle of incidence (1); angle between normal and refracted ray marked angle of refraction. (1)
ii A protractor (1)
iii Calculate the sines of all the angles (1); divide sin(i) by sin(r) for each pair of values (1); take the average of sin(i)/sin(r). (1)
iv Refractive index = sin 35/sin 22 (1)
= 1.53 (1)
sin C = 1/1.53 (1)
C = 41 degrees (1)

3 a i total internal (1); reflection (1)
ii endoscope; in phone cables; etc. (2)
b i The normal (1)
ii Ray bends away from the normal (1); with arrow to show direction. (1)
iii Critical angle (1)
iv Total internal reflection with angle of reflection equal to angle of incidence, judged by eye. (1)

4 a i Correct refraction at the first surface – towards the normal (1); correct refraction at the second surface – away from the normal. (1)
ii Orange is refracted/slowed down more than red (1); violet refracted most (1); so you would see a spectrum/dispersion. (1)
b Light must be travelling into a less dense medium (1); and the angle of incidence must be greater than the critical angle. (1)
c Marks for this answer will be determined by the Quality of Written Communication (QWC) as well as the standard of scientific response. Points to be made: two bundles of optical fibres; inserted through the throat; one bundle to shine light into the stomach; the other to carry light back to the observer; the lens forms an image on the end of the fibres; the process involved is total internal reflection; surgery is invasive; X-rays pose health risks. (6)

11 Lenses and the eye

11.1

1 a A real image is formed where light rays from an object meet. A virtual image is formed where light rays from an object appear to originate from.
b i A real image
ii A virtual image
iii A virtual image

2 a Upright, enlarged and virtual.
b i Inverted, magnified and real.
ii The slide must be moved towards the screen.
c i ×3
ii The magnification would increase until the flower is at the focal point of the lens when no image is seen.

3 a The image is real, inverted and enlarged. Magnification ×3.
b The image would be smaller than it was and would still be upside down.

11.2

1 a

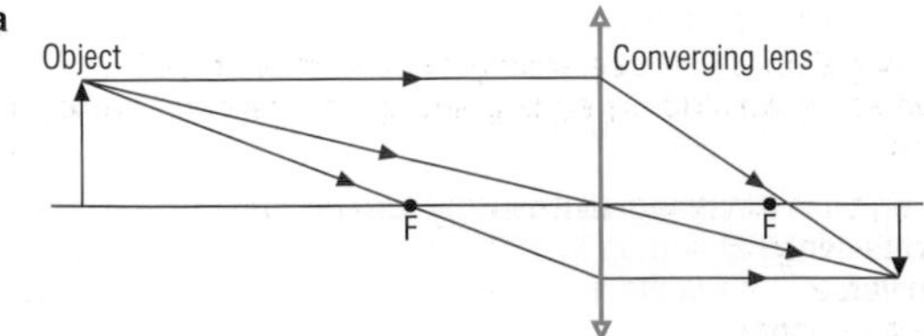

b i Real
ii Diminished
iii Inverted

2 a

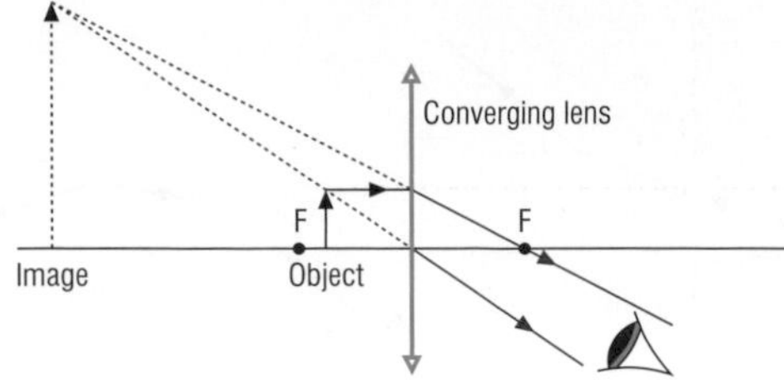

b i Virtual
ii Magnified
iii Upright
c A diverging lens produces images smaller than the object.

3 a

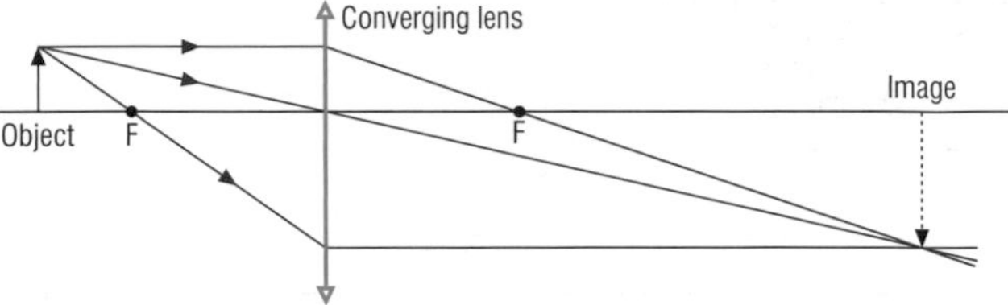

b f = 1.8 cm
c The nearer the object is to the focal point, the further the image would be from the lens and the larger it would be. At the focal point, no image would be formed (because the rays from it that pass through the lens would be parallel).

11.3

1 a +0.220 m
b i +0.033 m
ii Real

2 –0.204 m

3 a –0.017 m
b Virtual

11.4

1 a i Alters the thickness of the eye lens to alter its power.
ii Focuses light onto the retina.
iii Allows light to enter the eye after passing through the cornea.
iv Joins the eye lens to the ciliary muscles.
v Protects the front of the eye and refracts light.
vi Controls the width of the pupil so controlling the amount of light passing through the eye lens.
vii Layer of light-sensitive cells on which the image is formed.
b It widens in darkness to allow as much light as possible to pass through the eye lens.

2 a Each eye lens becomes thinner.
b The power of each eye lens decreases.

3 a The iris becomes narrower so the pupil is not as wide and less light passes through to the retina.
b The aperture stop is made narrow so less light passes through it to the camera film or CCD.

11.5

1 a Short sight.
b A diverging lens.

2 a The lens is a converging lens with a focal length of 50 cm.
b The sight defect is long sight. It may be caused by an eyeball that is too short or an eye lens that is not strong enough.
c The eye lens does not have enough focusing power to focus a near object on the retina. Making the cornea flatter would decrease the effective focusing power of the lens. This would worsen the sight defect.

3 a The lens with the higher refractive index would be flatter.
b i +2.0 D
ii –2.5 D

Answers to end of chapter summary questions

1 a i converging
ii

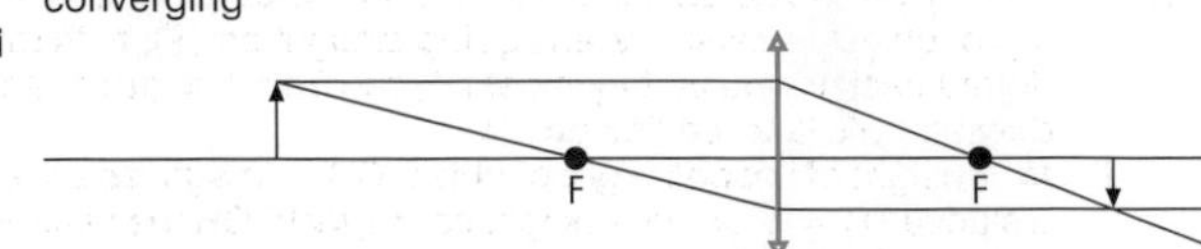

b Real, inverted and smaller than the object; camera.

2 a

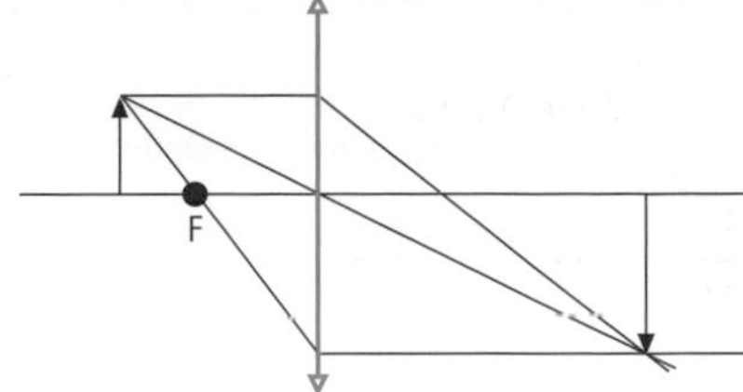

b i Real
ii Inverted
c 2.0
d 300 mm

3 a See 10.2 Figure 4
b i Virtual
ii Inverted
c 53 mm

4 a

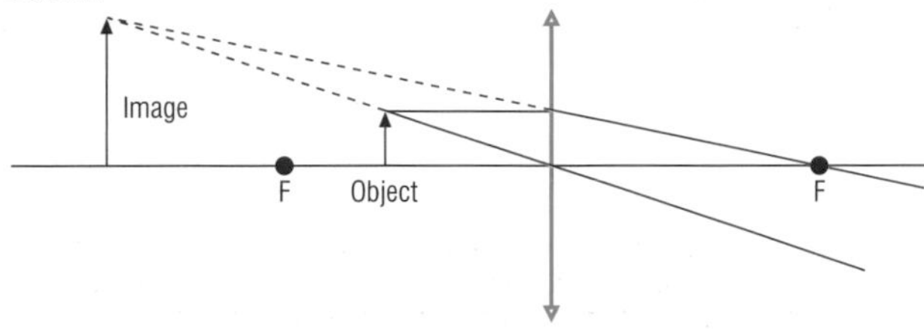

b i 12.5 cm
ii 0.50 m from the lens on the same side as the object.
c i Virtual
ii Upright

5 a i Short-sight is where a distant object can not be seen clearly but a nearby object can.
ii

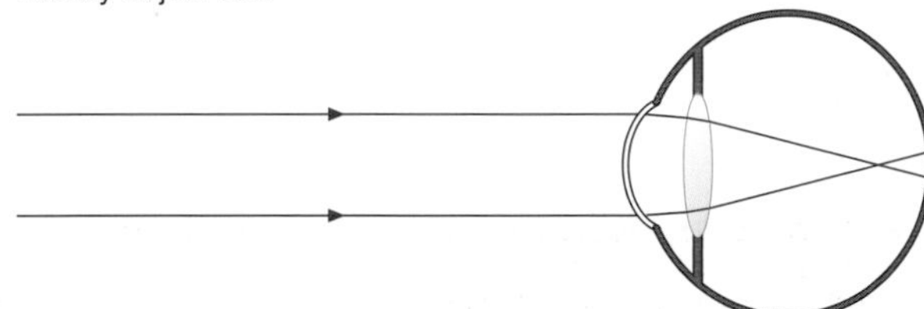

b i Diverging
ii –1.25 D
c i The cornea. It is made slightly thinner so it becomes flatter at the front surface.
ii Laser light entering the eye damages the retina.

6 a i

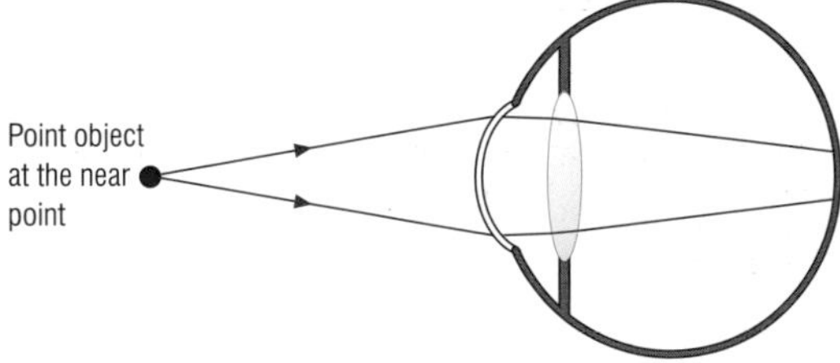

ii When a long-sighted eye views a near object, the eye lens is unable to focus the light rays on the retina. The image would be formed behind the retina. The eye lens is too weak to focus light from the object onto the retina. A blurred image is therefore seen.
b i A converging lens is needed
ii +0.50 D

Answers to end of chapter examination-style questions

1 a i Diagram showing rays parallel to the principal axis (1); brought to a point on the axis (1); distance from point to the lens marked 'focal length'. (1)
ii Diagram showing rays parallel to the principal axis (1); diverging from a point behind the lens (1); distance from point to lens marked 'focal length'. (1)
b i The ray parallel to principal axis passing through F (1); ray from top of object to centre of lens going straight on (1); both rays dotted back to where they meet (1); line from this point vertically down to axis labelled 'image'. (1)
ii M = height of image/height of object OR = image distance/object distance (1) = 2 OR their height of image/10 OR their image distance/5 (1)
iii magnified (1); upright (1); virtual (1)
c i Two (1 mark each) from: both have light-sensitive detectors; both form real images; both can focus objects at different distances; both form diminished images; both have inverted images.
ii Camera moves the lens (1) away from the film for near objects (1); eye changes the curvature/focal length/power of lens (1); more curved/shorter focal length/more powerful for near objects. (1)
iii Two (1 mark each) from: camera has a film or CCD ; eye has light sensitive retina; camera has an adjustable aperture; eye has an iris.

2 a

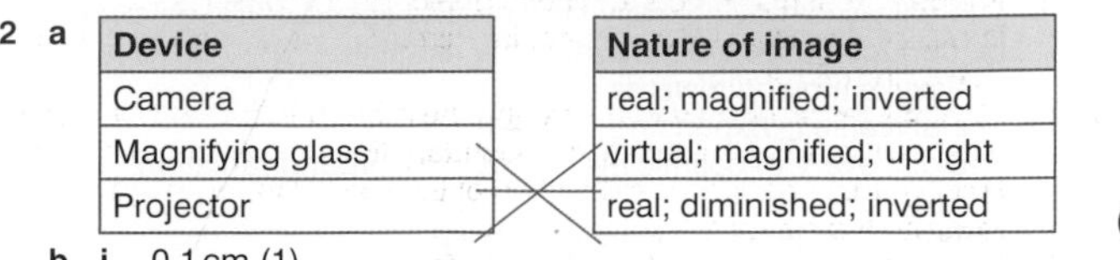

Device
Camera
Magnifying glass
Projector
Nature of image
real; magnified; inverted
virtual; magnified; upright
real; diminished; inverted

(3)

b i 0.1 cm (1)
ii mean v = 13.3 cm (1)
1/f = 1/u + 1/v OR 1/f = 1/40 + 1/13.5 (1)
= 0.099 (1)
f = 10.1 cm (1)
iii Calculate f for each pair of u and v values (1); take the average. (1)
iv Object inside F (1); virtual image formed (1); cannot be formed on a screen/rays do not pass through the image. (1)

3 a A = iris (1); B = retina (1); C = optic nerve (1); D = cornea (1); E = pupil (1)
b Marks for this answer will be determined by the Quality of Written Communication (QWC) as well as the standard of scientific response. Points to be made: iris controls the size of the pupil; in dark conditions, pupil has larger diameter OR the converse for light conditions; ciliary muscles alter the shape of the lens; making it more curved for nearer objects; increasing the power of the lens; making the focal length shorter; so that diverging rays from object are brought to a focus on the retina; eye at rest/muscles relaxed the eye lens can focus parallel light on the retina; i.e. light from a distant object. (6)
c i Short sight (1)
ii Concave/diverging (1)
iii f = 1/D OR f = 1/–2.5 (1)
= [100/2.5] cm (1)
= 40 cm (1)

12 Red-shift

12.1

1 a i Receding
ii Approaching
b The light from Andromeda shows a blue-shift which means Andromeda must be moving towards us.

2 a Earth, Sun, Andromeda galaxy, universe.
b i Their red-shift is of the same order of magnitude as that of the distant galaxies. Since red-shift depends on distance, this means that quasars can be as far away as the distant galaxies.
ii The power of a quasar is the same as that of billions of stars in a galaxy but a quasar is much smaller object than a galaxy so the power of a quasar is much greater.

3 a The light from a light source (e.g. galaxy) that is moving away from us is increased in wavelength due to the motion of the source moving away from us. This increase in wavelength is called a red-shift.
b i Y
ii X

12.2

1 a The Big Bang theory holds that the universe was created in a massive explosion about 13 billion years ago.
b They had no evidence for a massive explosion and they could explain Hubble's finding that the universe is expanding by assuming that the universe has always existed and is expanding because matter is entering it and pushing the galaxies apart.
c Cosmic background microwave radiation provided evidence that the universe was created in a massive explosion.

2 C D A B

3 a The distant galaxies are accelerating away from each other.
b The universe would stop expanding and go into reverse, ending in a Big Crunch.

Answers to end of chapter summary questions

1 a galaxy, wavelengths
b away, universe
c wavelength, shorter

2 a i the Big Bang
ii away from each other
iii billion

- **b** **i** Electromagnetic radiation created as gamma radiation just after the Big Bang.
  - **ii** The expansion of the universe discovered by Hubble is due to the Big Bang, a massive explosion in which the universe was created.

3 **a** **i** An increase.
  - **ii** Red light has a longer wavelength than any other colour of light. The wavelength of the light is made longer by the motion of the galaxy and is shifted towards the red part of the spectrum.
  - **iii** The galaxy is moving away from us. The speed of the galaxy can be deduced from the amount of the red-shift.
- **b** The galaxy is moving towards us.
- **c** **i** The universe is expanding.
  - **ii** The discovery of cosmic microwave background radiation.

4 **a** **i** Galaxy **A**.
  - **ii** Galaxy **C** is further away than galaxy **A**.
- **b** **i** It is expanding.
  - **ii** We are not in any special place.

5 **a** **i** **X**, because it appears smaller than **Y** as seen from the Earth.
  - **ii** **X**, because it is further away than **Y** so it is moving faster and has a larger red-shift than **Y**.
- **b** **Z** is moving away faster than **X** is because **Z** has a larger red-shift. **Z** must be a larger galaxy than **X**.

6 **a** 0.05 metres per second.
- **b** 0.50 metres per second.

Answers to end of chapter examination-style questions

1 **a** **i** Sound gets louder as car approaches (1); when car going away it gets softer (1); and lower pitch/frequency. (1)
  - **ii** Travelling at same speed as police car (1); in same direction (1); no relative motion. (1)
- **b** Marks for this answer will be determined by the Quality of Written Communication (QWC) as well as the standard of scientific response. Points to be made: source moving relative to observer; waves produced at constant rate/frequency; on approach, waves 'squashed'; wavelength reduced; frequency heard is higher than that emitted; velocity the same; opposite happens when receding; waves 'stretched'; wavelength increased; frequency heard is higher than that emitted; volume changes because waves spread out; less far when approaching; further when receding. (6)

2 **a** **i** Light waves stretched out so wavelength shifted to red part of spectrum. (1)
  - **ii** Doppler effect of galaxies moving away from our galaxy. (1)
  - **iii** M99 (1)
- **b** **i** Three of (1 mark each): there was an explosion; from very small initial point; billions of years ago; universe has been expanding ever since.
  - **ii** Four of (1 mark each): red-shift means galaxies are moving away; the further away the bigger the red-shift; the bigger the red-shift the faster it is moving; most distant galaxies moving fastest; suggests universe is expanding; from a point.

3 **a** **i** blue-shift (1)
  - **ii** D (1)
  - **iii** B (1)
  - **iv** Speed: stayed the same (1); Frequency: decreased (1)
- **b** The other astronomers used a larger range of distances/galaxies at a greater distance (1); and greater range of speeds/galaxies travelling at higher speeds (1); data revealed a clearer pattern/definite relationship(1); suggests that the speed is directly proportional to distance. (1)
- **c** **i** Straight line drawn on graph passing through (0, 0) (1) gradient = $\Delta y/\Delta x$ OR substitution (1) = answer in the range 55 to 65 km/s per megaparsec. (1)
  - **ii** Points much closer to a straight line (1); bigger range of galaxies (1); more accurate value for the Hubble constant. (1)

13 Kinetic theory

13.1

1 **a** Vaporisation
- **b** Freezing
- **c** Melting

2 **a** Condensation
- **b** Evaporation/vaporisation
- **c** Melting
- **d** Freezing

3 **a** The particles start to move about each other at random and are no longer in fixed positions.
- **b** The particles in water vapour are not in contact with each other except when they collide and they move about at random. When water vapour condenses on a cold surface, the vapour particles lose energy when they collide with the surface and they stick to the surface as a film of liquid. The particles in film move about at random in contact with each other.

13.2

1 The small bucket warms up faster because the mass of water in it is much less than in the large bucket.

2 **a** Lead has a lower specific heat capacity than aluminium. Less energy is needed by lead for a given temperature rise.
- **b** **i** 4500 J
  - **ii** 42 000 J
  - **iii** 46.5 kJ
- **c** 25.6

3 A storage heater contains bricks or concrete that are heated by the heater element. A radiant heater does not contain bricks or concrete.
A storage heater transfers energy to the surroundings gradually. A radiant heater transfers heat instantly.

13.3

1 Boiling takes place at a certain temperature whereas evaporation occurs from a liquid at any temperature; boiling takes place throughout a liquid whereas evaporation is from the surface only; evaporation can cause a liquid to cool whereas boiling can never have this effect.

2 **a** **i**

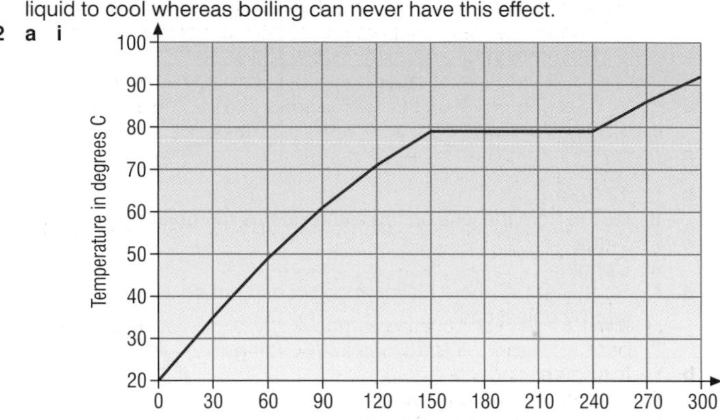

  - **ii** 79 °C
- **b** At 60 °C the substance is solid. Once it reachers 79 °C it begins to melt. After 90 seconds it has all melted and the liquid then increases in temperature to 90 °C.

3 Salt and water on the road forms a solution which will not freeze on the road unless the temperature drops below the freezing point of the solution. So no ice forms on the road unless the temperature drops below the freezing point of the solution. If the solution does freeze, grit helps to stop vehicles sliding as it provides friction between the tyres and the ice.

13.4

1 **a** 0.044 kg
- **b** 340 kJ/kg

2 **a** 2.3 MJ/kg
- **b** Energy was transferred from beaker to the surroundings. Therefore not all the energy supplied to the heater was used to boil the water as some was transferred by heating to the surroundings. The specific latent heat value obtained from the data would have been less as the energy needed to boil away the water was less than 18 400 J.

3 **a** 3020 J
- **b** $E = mC\theta = 0.008 \times 4200 \times 9 = 302.4$ J = 300 J (2 s.f.)
- **c** 340 kg/kg

Answers to end of chapter summary questions

1 **a** **i** The substance was a solid from A to B and its temperature increased towards its melting point as it was supplied with energy.
  - **ii** The substance melted from B to C and its temperature did not changed until all of it had melted.
  - **iii** The substance was liquid from C to D and its temperature increased as it was supplied with energy.
- **b** 78 °C
- **c** From A to B the particles are in contact with each other and they vibrate about fixed positions. As the temperature increases the vibrations increase. From B to C, more and more of the particles break away from the fixed positions and move about at random. From C to D, the particles have all broken free and they move about at random in contact with each other.

2 **a** **i** 101 MJ
  - **ii** 2 MJ/s
- **b** If the water was pumped at a slower rate, the temperature increase would be greater.

3 **a** 13 kJ

b The temperature of the air leaving the heater would decrease as the mass of air flowing through it each second would be greater and the energy supplied to it each second is unchanged.

4 **a** 6300 J
b 14 J/s

5 **a** 90 kJ
b 0.039 kg

6 **a** $E_k = \frac{1}{2}mv^2 = \frac{1}{2} \times 1200 \times (30)^2 = 540000\ J = 0.54\ MJ$
b 60 °C

Answers to end of chapter examination-style questions

1 **a** **i** Boiling point (1)
ii Any three (1 mark each) from: some escapes into the air; some is used to warm the gauze; some is used to warm the beaker; it spreads out.
iii Marks for this answer will be determined by the Quality of Written Communication (QWC) as well as the standard of scientific response. Points to be made: during OA the molecules gain energy; they vibrate more; some have sufficient energy to break free of the structure; the ice melts; during AB the molecules of liquid gain energy to move about faster; some gain enough energy to escape; the water evaporates; BC all the molecules have enough energy to escape; the water boils. (6)
iv Data is recorded continuously/frequently (1); greater resolution. (1)

2 **a** Energy needed depends on the mass (1); half the mass, half the energy needed/energy proportional to the mass. (1)
b $E = m \times c \times \theta$ OR $= 8 \times 4200 \times 20$ (1)
$= 672\ 000$ (1)
$= 672\ kJ$ (1)

3 **a** **i** large mass per unit volume (1); large specific heat capacity. (1)
ii $E = m \times c \times \theta$ (1)
$\theta = E/(m \times c)$ OR $= 540\ 000/(12 \times 900)$. (1)
$= 50\ °C$ (1)
iii It will be less (1); because some energy is not absorbed by the bricks (1); some is lost to the surroundings. (1)
b **i** It is lighter/portable (1)
ii It stores more energy (1)

4 **a** **i** Mass evaporated = 16 g (1)
= 0.016 kg (1)
$L = E/m$ OR $= 36\ 800/0.016$ (1)
$= 230\ 000\ J/kg$ (1)
ii Put lagging round the beaker. (1)

14 Energy transfer by heating

14.1

1 **a** Plastic and wood do not conduct by heating, so a plastic or wooden handle would not become hot when the pan was hot. A steel handle would become as hot as the pan as steel is a good conductor.
b Felt because it contains fibres that trap layers of air and dry air is a good insulator.

2 **a** Felt or synthetic fur could be used, because they are good insulators.
b Student's plan. Look for design of a fair test.

3 **a** The free electrons that gain kinetic energy diffuse through the metal quickly, passing on energy to other electrons and ions in the metal.
b When part of an insulator is heated, the atoms there vibrate more than elsewhere and they make atoms in adjacent parts vibrate so these parts become hot. The atoms in these parts make the atoms in adjacent colder parts vibrate so these colder parts become hot. Energy is therefore transferred through the non-metal.

14.2

1 Hot gases from the flame heat the base of the pan. Energy is transferred by conduction through the base of the pan to heat the water in contact with the base. The water at the base rises because it becomes less dense when it is heated. The rising water makes the water throughout the pan circulate through convection currents and colder water sinks to the base where the colder water is heated so it rises and causes the circulation to continue until the water throughout the pan is hot.

2 **a** It heats it reducing its density so it rises.
b The hot air passes through the grille into the room.
c Cold air flows into the heater at the bottom.

3 **a** Drop the crystal into a beaker of water through a tube. Heat gently under one corner. The colour rises above point of heating and travels across the top and falls at opposite side of beaker (where density of cooler water is greater). The colour then travels across the bottom of the beaker to replace lower density warmer water that rises above the Bunsen flame.
b Air in contact with the radiator is heated so it rises and circulates in the room. The air in the room becomes warmer as a result. The rising air against the radiator is replaced by cold air so the cold air is then warmed and it circulates. All parts of the room therefore become warm. If the radiator was elsewhere, warm air from the radiator that circulates and reaches the top of the window would become cold and move down the window, becoming colder as it transferred energy by heating to the cold window. People near the window would feel colder than elsewhere in the room.

14.3

1 **a** Water particles in the surrounding air collide with atoms on the cold surface and lose energy as a result. They are held on the surface by the surface atoms to form a film of liquid.
b The more energetic particles in the water escape from the liquid at the surface. The average energy of the remaining liquid particles becomes lower as a result. So the temperature of the liquid decreases.

2 **a** The air in the bus becomes damp as everyone breathes out warm water vapour. The water vapour condenses on the inside of the windows.
b When the door is opened, warm air carrying water vapour enters the refrigerator. The water vapour now in the refrigerator condenses on the cold walls of the inside of the refrigerator and runs down the walls to the drip tray. If the door is opened too often, water vapour keeps entering the refrigerator and condensing so filling the drip tray.

3 **a** Water evaporates faster from the wet clothes on a hot day than on a cold day because more energy is transferred to the clothes by the warmer air leading to a faster rate of evaporation.
b Evaporation of water from the wet clothes on a windy day transfers more energy from the skin, which makes the wearer colder than someone wearing dry clothes.

14.4

1 **a** Electromagnetic radiation emitted from the surface of objects due to their temperature.
b The city is hotter than the rural areas surrounding it because the hotter an area of a surface is the more infrared radiation it emits. This may be due to the greater amount of energy being used in urban areas.

2 **a**

Object	Infrared	Light
A hot iron	✓	✗
A light bulb	✓	✓
A TV screen	✗	✓
The Sun	✓	✓

b Put your hand near it and see if it gets warm due to radiation from the iron.

3 **a** They lose less heat through radiation when they huddle together because they radiate energy to each other.
b The wavelength is short enough to enable the radiation to pass through the prism and lies just below the red part of the visible spectrum.

14.5

1 **a** The sand grains provide a rougher and darker surface than ice and can therefore absorb more infrared radiation from the Sun. They therefore warm up and melt the surrounding ice.
b A matt black surface absorbs infrared radiation from the Sun better than any other type of surface.

2 **a** The black surface absorbs more infrared radiation from the Sun than the silver surface.
b As the cars are identical except for their colour, the black car would cool faster because it radiates more infrared radiation than the silver car. However, the temperature in both cars would probably decrease to the same value which would be the temperature of the surroundings.

3 **a** To make the test fair. The temperature recorded will differ at different distances from the cube as the radiation spreads out.
b **i** B
ii D
c Greater accuracy, collects multiple sets of data at whatever time intervals you choose.

14.6

1 Energy transfer from the hot water to the outer surface of the radiator takes place due to conduction. Air in contact with the radiator surface is heated by infrared radiation and conduction. The hot air near the radiator rises and circulates causing energy transfer to the air in the room by convection.

2 a i To prevent the component overheating.
ii Metal is a good conductor. The heat sink is plate-shaped to increase its surface area, so it transfers energy to the surrounding air as effectively as possible.
b Plan must have a fair system that compares a single plate of glass to a pair of plates, ideally with a sealed air gap between.
3 a Student's explanation to include the role played by the plastic cap, double-walled plastic container, silvered inside surfaces, vacuum layer.
b Water vapour from the warm water condenses on the frosted surfaces in the freezer and releases energy in the process which transfers by conduction to the frost and causes it to melt.

14.7

1 When the oven heats up, the brass tube expands more than the Invar rod. When the oven overheats, the difference in the expansion of the brass tube and the Invar rod is sufficient to move the valve so it closes the large opening between the two parts of the chamber.
2 a Without expansion gaps between sections of concrete, adjacent sections would make contact and push against each other and the concrete would crack.
b Rubber in the expansion gaps prevents rubble falling into the gap. If rubble fell into the gap, the concrete sections either side of the gap would be unable to expand and the sections would push via the rubble on each other.
3 a The bimetallic strip consists of two different metals fixed to each other. One of the metals expands more than the other when the temperature of the strip is increased. As a result the strip bends.
b The bimetallic strip should be reversed so it bends away from the contact screw when its temperature increases instead of bending towards it. The contact screw should be adjusted so it remains in contact with bimetallic strip until the required 'switch off' temperature is reached.

Answers to end of chapter summary questions

1 a i The temperature variations causes the roofing material to expand and contract. If the temperature variations are great enough, this repeated expansion and contraction would cause small cracks to develop.
ii A smooth shiny surface is better because it would reflect sunlight and would therefore not get as hot in sunlight. It would also radiate less energy to the surroundings at night.
b The panel with the transparent cover would reflect sunlight and the fluid in the panel would absorb some radiation so not as much radiation would be absorbed by the matt black surface. However, the matt black surface would heat the fluid in the panel directly. The panel with the matt black cover would absorb sunlight very effectively so it would become warmer in sunlight than the base of the other panel. However, it would need to be an effective conductor to heat the fluid underneath effectively and it would also emit radiation into the surrounding air. The panel with the matt black cover would probably be more effective further form the equator as the Sun is lower in the sky.
2 a i By conduction through the plate.
ii By radiation and convection in the air.
b The fins increase the surface area of the heat sink. The larger the surface area, the greater the energy loss due to radiation and convection from the plate.
c The greater the density of the material, the larger the mass of the heat sink will be. The greater the mass and specific heat capacity of the material, the lower the increase of temperature will be for a given amount of energy transferred by heating to the heat sink.
3 a i Energy transfer from the hot water in the radiator takes place due to convection. Energy transfer through the radiator metal takes place due to conduction. Energy transfer from the outside of the radiator takes place due to convection in the air and radiation from the radiator surface.
ii Air between the panels becomes hotter than the air near the panels on the outside of the radiator. The hot air in the gap rises and is replaced by cooler air drawn in to the gap at the bottom of the panels. The hot air from the radiator circulates in the room.
b Radiation from the heater element rapidly heats the outer surface of the bricks. The inside of the bricks slowly become warmer due to conduction and therefore store energy by heating. When the heater is switched off, the outer surface of the bricks emits radiation to the surroundings so it becomes cooler than the interior. Conduction from the hot interior to the surface takes place gradually so the interior gradually cools down.
4 a Wool fibres is a good insulator as the fibres are made of insulating material and they trap dry air which is a good insulator. The inside of the clothing becomes warm due to radiation from the body. The body inside stays warm because the clothing does not conduct energy away from the inside.
b In cold weather, radiation from exposed skin causes energy transfer from the head. Hair is a insulator and it contains some trapped air so it does reduce some conduction. Wearing a hat cuts out radiation from exposed parts of the scalp and reduces conduction by providing extra insulation.
c The surface area of the ear is relatively large in relation to its mass. In normal conditions, radiation from your ears is balanced by radiation received from the surroundings by the ears. In very cold weather, energy received is significantly less so the ears radiate more energy than they receive. Because their surface area is so large in relation the their mass, they soon cool down.
5 a Their clothing becomes damp due to sweat and cooling by evaporation occurs so the clothing and hence the skin becomes cold.
b i Infrared radiation
ii The reflective coating traps infrared radiation in the space between the body and the blanket so the space becomes warmer. The warm air in the space keeps the body warm.
6 a i The water heated at the bottom rose to the top causing convection in the tube and melting the ice cube at the top.
ii The water was warmed at the top and stayed there as it is less dense than cold water. Conduction through the water eventually made the water at the bottom warm, and then the ice cube melted.
b 2 Energy transfer in water is mainly due to convection.

Answers to end of chapter examination-style questions

1 a i diameter of rods (1); length of rods. (1)
ii Energy makes the wax melt (1); the first pin to drop was on the best conductor. (1)
b i Marks for this answer will be determined by the Quality of Written Communication (QWC) as well as the standard of scientific response. Points to be made: heated water expands; becomes less dense; heated water rises; the colder water at the top is denser; colder water falls; setting up a convection current (6)
ii Any five of (1 mark each): metal is a good heat conductor; because there are free electrons in its structure; the free electrons near the inside surface gain KE; they move faster; and collide with electrons and ions nearer the outside; transferring some energy; outer surface warms up.
c i For example in bridges/roads (1); by leaving a small gap for expansion to take place safely. (1)
ii A fire causes the temperature of the strip to rise (1); the metals in the strip expand (1); brass expands more than steel (1); top of strip bends to the right (1); making contact at the contact screw (1); completes circuit/bell rings. (1)
2 a absorbers (1)
b reflectors (1)
c Large surface area; facing south; angled at 45 degrees to horizontal (1)
3 a i nature of the surface of the mug (1); surface area of the mug (1); temperature of the water (1); temperature of the surroundings. (1)
ii The mass of the water (1); the specific heat capacity of water. (1)
b The petrol evaporates (1); the most energetic molecules escape (1); the mean kinetic energy of the molecules is reduced (1); temperature is proportional to the mean kinetic energy. (1)
c i Larger area (1); warmer temperature (1); both increase the rate of evaporation. (1)
ii Particles of water experience forces of attraction (1); closer together than in vapour (1); have less energy than in the vapour. (1)

15 Energy transfers and efficiency

15.1

1 a The brake pads becomes hot due to friction. Energy transfer from the brake pads to the surroundings by heating. Sound waves created by braking also transfers energy to the surroundings.
b Kinetic energy of the roller coaster is transferred to gravitational potential energy of the roller coaster and to kinetic energy of the air as the roller coaster goes up the hill. Gravitational potential energy is transferred to kinetic energy and the air as the roller coaster descends.
2 a **On descent:** Gravitational potential energy $\rightarrow$ kinetic energy + energy heating the surroundings due to air resistance.
On impact: Kinetic energy $\rightarrow$ elastic energy of trampoline + energy heating the surroundings due to impact + sound.

On ascent: Elastic energy of trampoline → kinetic energy → gravitational potential energy + energy heating the surroundings due to air resistance.

b The ball has less energy at the top of its bounce than at the point of release.

c Use a clamp to hold a metre ruler vertically over the middle of the trampoline surface. Hold the ball next to the metre ruler with its lowest point level with the top of the ruler. Release the ball so it rebounds vertically and observe the highest level of the bottom of the ball against the metre ruler after the rebound. Repeat the same test several times to obtain the average rebound position of the ball. Repeat the test with the same ball for the other two trampolines. The one with the highest rebound position is the bounciest.

3 Elastic energy of the rubber straps is transferred to kinetic energy of the capsule. This kinetic energy is transferred to gravitational potential energy as the capsule rises to the top of its flight etc.

15.2

1 a Wasted: sound, kinetic energy of the air.
b Useful: light and sound. Wasted: heat.
c Useful: boils the water. Wasted: heat loss through surfaces, sound.
d Useful: sound. Wasted: heat loss.

2 a The gear box would heat up due to energy transfer through friction between the gears. The hotter the gear box gets, the less efficient the gears will work.
b The shoes would heat up due to energy transfer by conduction and infrared radiation from the feet. The feet would transfer less energy as the shoes warm up so the feet would become hotter.
c The drill would heat up and smoke if it burns the wood.
d The discs would heat up due to energy transfer by friction between the discs and the brake pads from the kinetic energy of the moving parts of the car.

3 a As the pendulum swings towards the middle, its gravitational potential energy decreases and its kinetic energy increases. As it moves from the middle to the highest position on the opposite side, its kinetic energy transfers back to gravitational potential energy. Air resistance acting causes some of its kinetic energy to be transferred to the surrounding as heat.
b Air resistance causes friction as the pendulum swings. This produces heat and so the pendulum transfers energy to the surroundings and stops.

15.3

1 a 85 J
b It is transferred by conduction to the surroundings
c

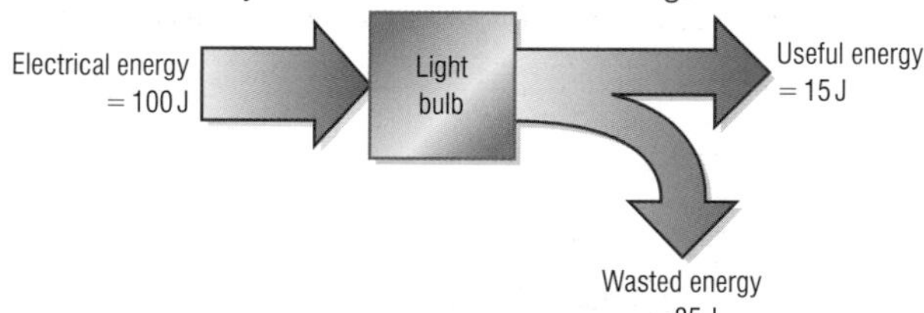

2 a 36 J
b 40%

3 a 800 J
b 50 W

15.4

1 a Cavity wall insulation conducts much less energy than air especially if the air is damp. It prevents energy transfer by radiation and convection across the cavity.
b The foil reflects infrared radiation from the radiator so preventing absorption of radiation by the surface of the wall behind the foil.

2 a Plastic is a poor conductor. Metal is a good conductor. Energy transfer through a metal frame would therefore be greater than through a plastic frame.
b Energy transfer due to conduction and convection takes place in the space between the panes if the space is filled with air but not if there is a vacuum there.
c The window which has the lower U-value is better because less energy per second passes through it for the same temperature difference.

3 a £180
b £60
c 3 years

Answers to end of chapter summary questions

1 a electrical, light, useful, wasted
b i 18%
ii 369 kJ

2 a i 1200 J
ii 12%
b i 8800 J
ii

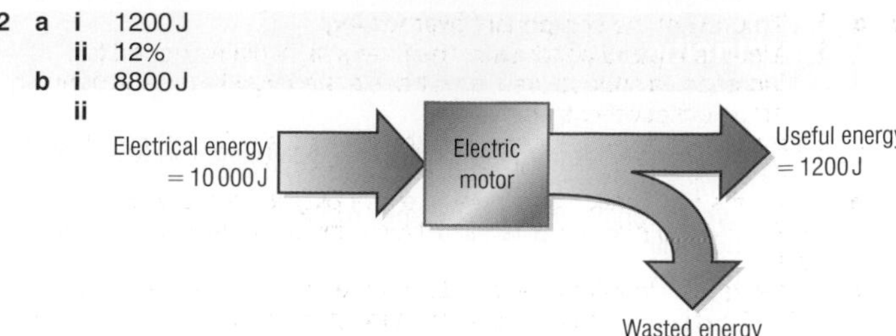

3 a i 960 J
ii 240 J
iii

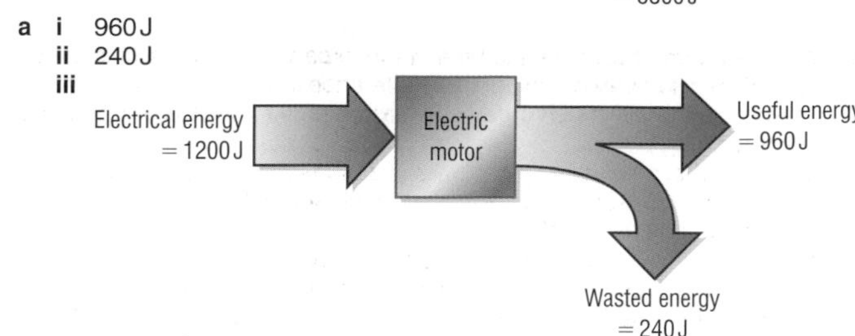

b 5040 J

4 a Gravitational potential energy is transferred to kinetic energy of the block as the block falls. On impact, some of the energy of the block is transferred to kinetic energy of the girder and some is transferred to the surroundings as sound energy. In addition, some of the energy of the block is transformed in the block and the girder into energy by heating.
b i 9000 J
ii 1800 W

5 a i 1500 J
ii 13 500 J
iii 10%
b i Apply oil to the bearings of the motor and the pulley to reduce friction.
ii Friction or air resistance can never be completely eliminated from the motor. In addition, the motor becomes warm due to the heating effect of the electric current passing through it.

6 a U-value is the energy per second that passes through each square metre of material when the temperature difference across it is 1 °C.
b Energy transfer through each square metre is 6.4 times greater through the window than through the wall. The walls are better insulators than the windows due to a combination of the substances used, design and construction as well as the thickness. However the wall area is 7 times that of the window so more energy passes through the walls than through the window.
c i Cavity wall insulation is when the cavity between the two layers of bricks in an outer wall is filled with an insulating foam which traps air in small pockets reducing convection.
ii The payback time is the time taken for the cost of the cavity wall insulation to be repaid from the reduction of the heating costs.

Answers to end of chapter examination-style questions

1 a A = 4; B = 2; C = 3; D = 1 (4)
b Marks for this answer will be determined by the Quality of Written Communication (QWC) as well as the standard of scientific response. Points to be made: at the start, the ball has gravitational potential energy; as it falls, this transfers to kinetic; when it hits the table, some is transferred to sound; and by heating; warming the table; this energy spreads out/is dissipated; as the ball bounces up, kinetic is transferred back to gravitational potential; but since some has been lost in the impact; it does not regain its original height. (6)

2 a i light (1)
ii electrical (1)
iii kinetic (1)
b Energy cannot be created or destroyed/the total amount of energy before and after a transfer is the same. (1)
c i 38 J (1)
ii 2 J (1)
iii 60 J (1)
iv 0.38 or 38% (1)

3 a i Conduction (1)
ii (3000/7000) × 100 (1)
= 42.6% (1)
iii To maintain the temperature, energy must be supplied at the same rate at which it is being lost (1); 7000 W. (1)
b i Loft insulation (1)
ii Loft insulation (1)
iii Payback time = 1100/400 (1) = 2.75 years (1)

16 Electricity

16.1

1 a i Electrons transfer from the cloth to the polythene rod when the rod is rubbed with the cloth.
ii Electrons transfer from the perspex rod to the cloth when the rod is rubbed with the cloth.
b Glass loses electrons.
2 a Attraction
b Attraction
c Repulsion
3 a X and Y have the same type of charge.
b Suspend R horizontally on the end of a thread and then charge R by rubbing it with a dry cloth. Charge X and hold it near R. If it repels R, X is also positive. If X attracts R, X is negative. Y has the same type of charge to X.

16.2

1 1 = cell; 2 = switch; 3 = indicator; 4 = fuse
2 a

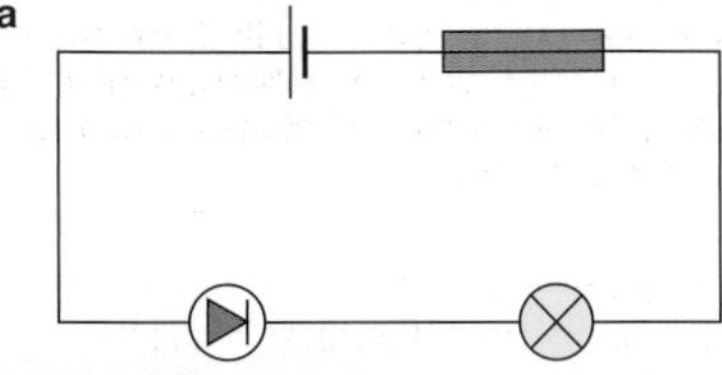

b A variable resistor.
c 15C
3 a A light-emitting diode is a diode that emits light when current passes through it.
b A variable resistor is used to change the current in a circuit.

16.3

1 a 8.0Ω
b 10.0Ω
2 W: 6.0Ω; X: 80 V; Y: 2.0 A
3 a 50Ω
b i 18C
ii 54J

16.4

1 a i Thermistor
ii Diode
iii Filament bulb
b i 5Ω
ii 10Ω
2 a 15Ω
b The ammeter reading increases because the resistance of the thermistor decreases.
3 a When the LDR is covered, its resistance increases. The current decreases because the resistance of the LDR increases and the potential difference across the LDR is still 3.0 V.
b i The current is zero until the potential difference is about 0.7V then the current increases rapidly.
ii The resistance is very large until about 0.7V then it decreases rapidly.

16.5

1 a 0.4V
b 0.20A, 0.5V
2 a

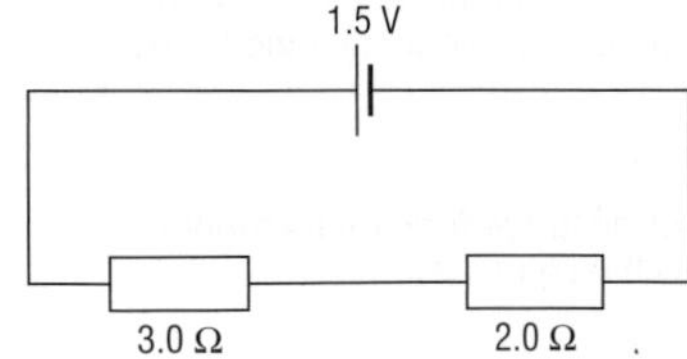

b i 5.0Ω
ii 0.3A
3 a i 12Ω
ii 3.0V
b $\frac{3\text{V}}{12\Omega} = 0.25\text{A}$
c P = 0.5 V, Q = 2.5 V
d i 15Ω
ii 0.20A
iii P 0.40V, Q 2.00V, R 0.60V

16.6

1 a 0.30A
b The 3Ω resistor.
c 0.60Ω
2 a

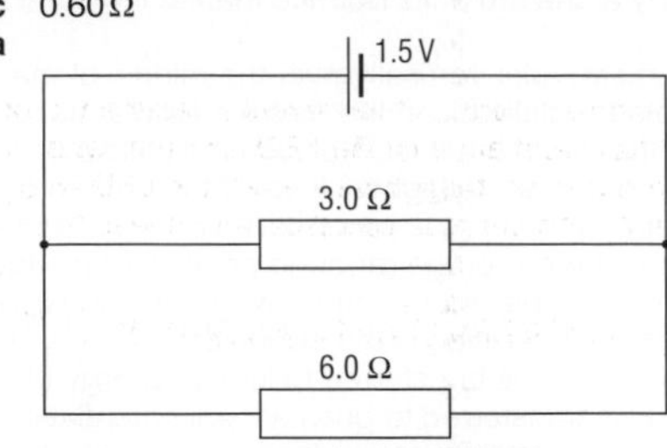

b i Current = 1.5 V/3Ω = 0.50A
ii Current = 1.5 V/6Ω = 0.25A
c Cell current = 0.5 + 0.25 = 0.75 A
3 a i I_1 = 3.0A; I_2 = 2.0A; I_3 = 1.0A
ii Current through the battery = 6.0A
b 6.5A

Answers to end of chapter summary questions

1 The resistance increases when the current is increased. This is because the increase of current makes the bulb hotter. As a result, the metal ions of the filament vibrate more, so they resist the passage of electrons through the filament more.
2 a Filament bulb
b Resistor
c Thermistor
d Diode
3 a

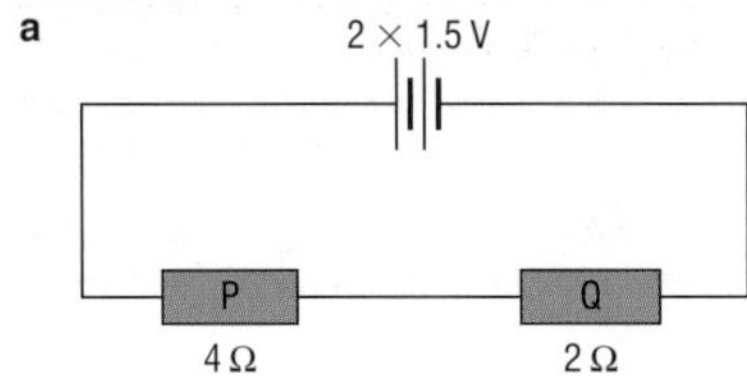

b i 3.0V
ii 6Ω
iii 0.5A
iv P: 2.0 V; Q: 1.0 V
4 a

R
S

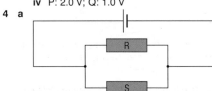

b i 1.0A
ii 0.5A
iii 1.5A
5 a Different from, equal to
b Equal to, less than
6 a i 2.0V
ii Potential difference across LDR = 3.0 − 2.0 = 1.0V
iii 100Ω
b i Ammeter reading decreases when LDR is covered as resistance increases.
ii The potential difference across the LDR = $V - (I \times R)$ so the LDR resistance = potential difference across LDR ÷ current I
7 a

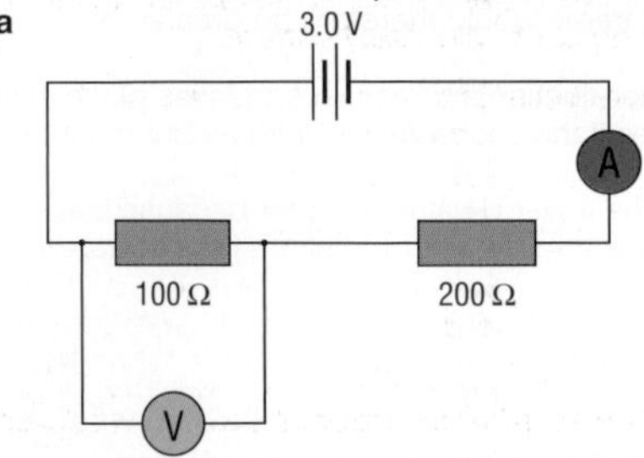

b i 300Ω
ii 0.01A
iii 1.0V
iv 100Ω 1.0V; 200Ω 2.0V

8 a i The battery pd of 3.0 V is shared between the LED and the resistor. Since the potential difference across the LED is 0.6 V when it emits light, the potential difference across the resistor is 3.0 – 0.6 = 2.4 V.
ii 0.0024 A
b 200 Ω
c The current would be (almost) zero as the 'reverse' resistance of the LED is very high. The total resistance of the LED and the resistor would therefore be much greater than it was when the LED was in its 'forward' direction so the current would be much less than 0.0024 A.

Answers to end of chapter examination-style questions

1 a i negative
ii uncharged
iii positive
b Electrons are transferred to surface atoms of ruler from the duster (1); ruler has an excess of negative charge (1); duster has a deficiency of electrons (1); so is positively charged. (1)
c Marks for this answer will be determined by the Quality of Written Communication (QWC) as well as the standard of scientific response. Points to be made: friction at the nozzle/connection to + terminal of a supply; causes paint molecules to lose electrons; paint droplets have the same type of charge; so repel each other; causing droplets to spread out forming a fine spray; the opposite charge on the car door; attracts the droplets; to give an even coating of paint. (6)

2 a i Correct symbols for battery, switch, variable resistor, resistor (piece of wire), ammeter (2); in series (1); with correct symbol for voltmeter in parallel with resistance wire. (1)
ii So that current only flows when readings are to be taken (1); if current flows all the time, the piece of wire will heat up (1); increasing its resistance. (1)
iii So that a series of results can be obtained (1); and a mean value for resistance calculated/graph plotted. (1)
b i 60 Ω (1)
ii 115 V (1)
c i 230 V (1)
ii 30 Ω (1)
iii 15.4 A (1)

3 a 3 kΩ (1)
b Total R = 5.5 kΩ (1)
I = V/R OR = 6/5500 (1)
= 1.09 mA (1)
c i V = I × R OR = 0.00109 × 2500 (1)
= 2.73 V (1)
ii R at 0 °C = 17.5 kΩ (1)
V = (2.5/20) × 6 (1)
= 0.75 V (1)
iii The potential difference across R increases with temperature (1) so could be used to switch on/off a system when temperature rises (1) thermostat (1); e.g. for cooling system. (1)

17 Household electricity

17.1

1 a 12 V
b 230 V
c 1.5 V
d 325 V

2 The number of cycles on the screen would: **a** increase **b** decrease.

3 25 Hz

4 a Direct current is in one direction only. Alternating current repeatedly reverses.
b The diode only allows current to pass in one direction, its direction. So it rectifies the alternating current to direct current.
c i

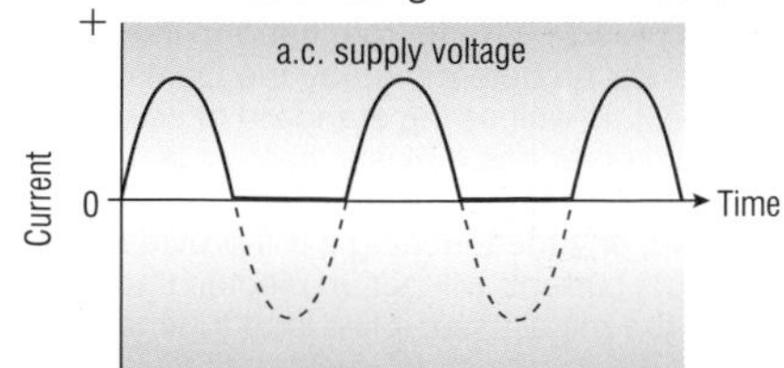

ii The peaks would not be as tall; the horizontal spacing would be unchanged

17.2

1 a i The neutral wire
ii Yellow/green
b i The sockets are in parallel so each of the appliances connected to the sockets can be switched on and off without affecting the other appliances.
ii Brass is a good conductor and doesn't oxidise like copper does. Brass is harder than copper and doesn't deform as easily as copper.
iii The live wire could be exposed where the cable is worn away or damaged.

2 a 1 C; 2 D; 3 A; 4 B
b 1 Rubber is flexible and is an insulator.
2 Stiff plastic is an insulator, it doesn't wear and it can't be squashed.
3 Brass is a good conductor and doesn't deteriorate.
4 Copper is an excellent conductor and copper wires bend easily.

3 a The three wires must be insulated from each other otherwise there would be a dangerously large current in the cable due to the very low resistance between the live wire and the other wires where they touch.
b The earth wire of the cable is connected to a terminal fixed to the metal case. The other end of the earth wire is connected to the earth pin in the three-pin plug attached to the cable. When the plug is connected to a three-pin wall socket, the metal case is therefore connected via the earth wire to the ground.
c The cables to the wall sockets need to be thicker so their resistance is lower and more current passes through them than through the lighting cables. If they were not thicker, the heating effect of the current would be greater and the cables would overheat.

17.3

1 a A fuse protects an appliance or a circuit.
b So it cuts off the live wire if too much current passes through it.
c It is faster than a fuse and doesn't need to be replaced after it 'trips'.

2 a Yes.
b The element is live.
c

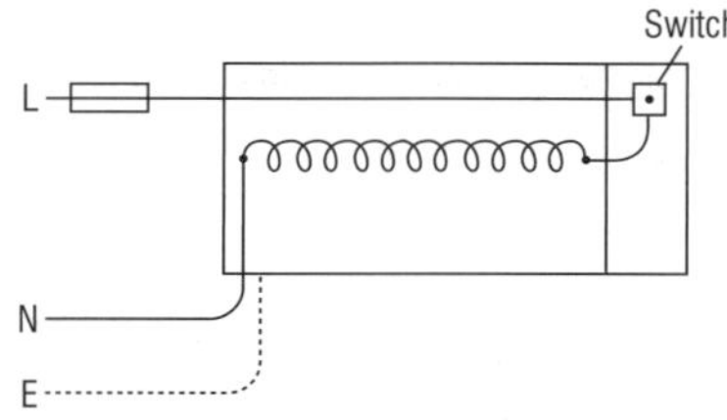

3 a i An ordinary circuit-breaker switches the current in the live wire off if the current is greater than a certain value. An RCCB switches the current in the live wire if the current in the live wire and the neutral wire differ.
ii The current in the live wire might be too small to operate an ordinary circuit breaker. An RCCB would operate with a small current in current in the neutral wire and in the live wire differ.
b A RCCB acts faster than a circuit breaker and a fuse and can be used when there is no earth connection.

17.4

1 a 1 W
b 1150 W
c The current through the lamp in normal operation is 0.4 A. A 13 A fuse would not melt if a current greater than 0.4 A passed through it.

2 a i 36 W
ii 460 W
b i 3 A
ii 5 A

3 c i 6.5 V, 169 W
ii 2.8%

17.5

1 a 150 C
b 120 J
c 180 J

2 a i 80 C
ii 720 C
b i 120 J
ii 300 J
c i 150 C
ii 12 J/C from the battery; 8 J/C to the lamp; 4 J/C to the variable resistor.
iii 1800 J from the battery = 1200 J to the lamp + 600 J to the variable resistor.

3 a 12.0 Ω
b 0.50 A
c 30 C
d 4 Ω: 2.0 V; 8.0 Ω: 4.0 V
e 4 Ω: 60 J (= 30 C × 2.0 V); 8.0 Ω: 120 J (= 30 C × 4.0 V)
f 180 J

17.6

1 a 2.4 kWh
b 15 kJ
c £177.80

2 a i 1.5 kWh
ii 0.5 kWh
iii 0.8 kWh

3 a i 4 kW
ii 43.2 million joules (4000 × 3 × 60 × 60)
b i 390 W
ii 51 kWh
iii £6.10

17.7

1 An example of each possible electrical hazard is given in the table.

Appliance	Hazard
Electric drill	The drill might 'hit' a live wire in a cable in the wall.
Electric saw	The saw might cut the cable (or cut a limb).
Hairdryer	Anyone with wet hands using a hairdryer would be at risk.
Vacuum cleaner	The vacuum cleaner might run over and damage its cable.

2 a i The fault needs to be put right or the appliance replaced otherwise a new fuse will melt as soon as the appliance that caused the fault is switched on.
ii Three-core as an iron has a metal base.
b i 30
ii 11
iii 3000 kWh at 10p per kWh = £300
iv Cost of 30 bulbs + electricity = £315; cost of 11 LEDs + electricity = £83; saving = £232

3 a 4.8 A
b The metal case must be 'earthed'. The 3 core cable includes an earth wire for this purpose. A 2 core cable does not have an earth wire.
c i 5 A
ii If a fault develops and the current is much greater than 4.8 A, a higher current fuse such as a 13 A fuse would not blow if the current was less than the fuse rating. Too much current would pass through the appliance and the cables and either the appliance or the cables would overheat.

17.8

1 a i Step-up
ii Step-down
b The grid voltage would be lower than if a transformer was connected. The current through the grid cables would be much greater and a much greater percentage of the power supplied to the grid system would be wasted.

2 a To reduce the energy wasted in transmitting the electricity.
b To reduce the voltage to a safer level for cables inside towns and cities.

3 a i It increases the voltage.
ii It reduces the current.
b i 190 A
ii 10 kW
c Mains devices operate at 230 V. The grid voltage needs to be stepped down by transformers from 132 000 V to 230 V for safe use in our homes.

Answers to end of chapter summary questions

1 a i The neutral wire.
ii The live wire.
b i The waves would be taller as the amplitude would increase.
ii The waves would be closer together as the time for each cycle would be less.

2 a If a live wire touches the case, the case would become live. Anyone touching the case would be electrocuted as an electric current would pass through their body to earth.
b Live – brown, neutral – blue, earth – green/yellow

3 a i parallel
ii series, live
b i A fuse is a thin wire that overheats and melts if too much current passes through it; a circuit breaker is an electromagnetic switch that opens and stays open if too much current passes through it.
ii A circuit breaker works faster than a fuse and can be reset more quickly.

4 a i 11 A
ii 13 A fuse
iii 35 kWh
b i The kettle.
ii 64p

5 a

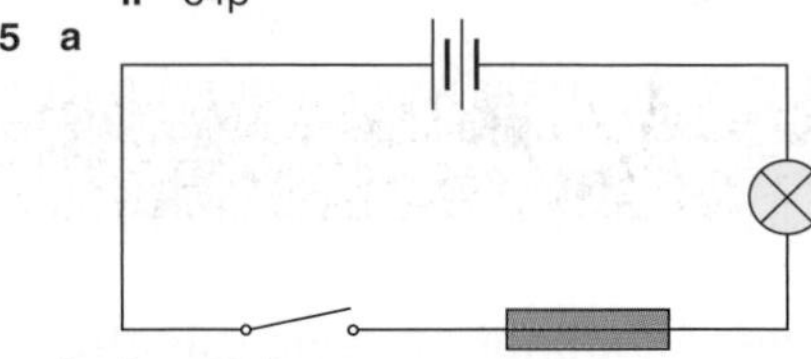

b i 432 J
ii 108 J
iii 324 J
c i 30 Ω
ii 0.4 A
iii battery 4.8 W; 5 Ω resistor 0.8 W; 25 Ω resistor 4.0 W.

6 a i 3.0 A
ii 600 C
b i $E = P \times t$ = 36 W × 200 s = 7200 J
ii 12 J/C
c i 3.0 A through each bulb; 6.0 A through the battery.
ii Energy supplied per second to each bulb = 36 W = 36 J/s; energy supplied per second by the battery = 12 V × 6.0 A = 72 J/s. Therefore energy supplied per second to the two bulbs = the energy supplied per second by the battery.

7 a 28.7 A
b i D because the maximum safe current through D is greater than the current that would pass through it when the oven operates at full power. So D would not overheat. E would not overheat either but it would be more expensive than D.
ii Cables A, B and C would overheat as their maximum safe current is less than the current that would pass through them when the oven is at full power. The overheated cable might cause a fire. Also, the cable insulation could melt and cause a short-circuit that may start a fire.

8 a i To change the voltage from the power station generator to a suitably high grid voltage and reducing the grid voltage to a suitable mains voltage for our homes.
ii A step-up transformer.
b i The grid voltage is much higher.
ii The current supplied to the grid is much smaller.
iii Power is wasted in the cables due to the heating effect of the current. The less the current, the less the power that is wasted.

Answers to end of chapter examination-style questions

1 a It needs an ac supply (1); needs a potential difference of 230V (1); frequency 50 Hz (1); so mains (1); When on hottest setting, with maximum fan speed it takes 1200 joules of energy per second. (1)
b i No. of kilowatt-hours used = 7198.5 – 6471.5 = 727.0 (1)
Cost = 727 × 0.15 (1)
= £109.05 (1)
ii 2000 W = 2 kW (1)
Cost = 2 × 3 × 0.15 (1)
= £0.90 (1)
c i P = V × I OR 60 = 230 × I
I = 60/230 (1)
= 0.26 A (1)
ii 30 hours = 30 × 3600 s (1)
Q = I × t OR = 0.26 × 30 × 3600 (1)
= 28 080 (1) coulomb/C (1)

2 a One lead (brown/live) is not connected (1); cable grip tightened on leads not outer cable (1) neutral (blue) lead connected to live pin. (1)
b Water conducts electricity/wet hands have lower resistance than dry hands (1); water can provide a route from hand to live pin. (1)
c Marks for this answer will be determined by the Quality of Written Communication (QWC) as well as the standard of scientific response. Points to be made: hairdryer has a plastic case; it is double insulated; if there is a fault and the live lead touches the metal case of the kettle, the case becomes live; anyone touching it will provide a route to earth; they will conduct current; will get an electric shock; the earth lead is connected to the metal case; if live lead touches the earthed kettle, a large current will flow to earth; melting the wire in the fuse; thus breaking the circuit; and rendering the kettle unusable until fault rectified. (6)

3 a LED (1)
b filament lamp (1)
c LED (1)

4 a Time period = 1 cm = 0.02 s (1)
F = 1/T = 1/0.02 (1)
= 50 Hz (1)
b peak potential difference = 1.5 cm (1)
= 3 V (1)

18 Motors, generators and transformers

18.1

1 a i N
ii S
b P is a N-pole; P repels X because it has like polarity and it attracts Y because it has unlike polarity.
2 a N
b S
c Unmagnetised
3 a See 18.1 Figure 4
b i X = N, Y = S
ii The needle of the compass would also rotate in the same direction as the bar magnet.

18.2

1 a See 18.2 Figure 2
b Although both iron and steel can be magnetised, steel does not lose its magnetism when the current is switched off. Iron does lose its magnetism when the current is switched off.
2 C; B; E; D; A
3 a The current through the electromagnet coil magnetises the core of the electromagnet. The armature is pulled on to the core. This opens the make-and-break switch which cuts the current. The electromagnet loses its magnetism and the make-and-break switch closes so the cycle repeats itself.
b The armature of the buzzer has a much lower mass so it moves faster than the bell's armature and it therefore has a higher frequency of vibration.

18.3

1 a When a current passes through the coil of the electric motor, a force acts on each side of the coil due to the magnetic field of the magnet in the motor. The force on each side has a turning effect on the coil and because the current on each side is in opposite directions, the forces on each side are always in opposite directions so the motor turns. Each time the coil passes the position where the coil is at right angles to the magnetic field, the split-ring commutator reverses the connections to the battery so the current round the coil reverses direction. Without the split-ring commutator, the forces would reverse and so the coil would turn back. The action of the split-ring commutator allows the forces to continue to turn the coil in the same direction.
b The force on the loudspeaker coil would be in one direction only with a direct current so the coil would not vibrate.
2 a The current is in the opposite direction to what it would have been so the force on each side is in the opposite direction to what it would have been. The coil therefore rotates in the opposite direction.
b i Faster because the coil is lighter.
ii Faster because the field is much stronger due to the presence of the iron.
3 a The force decreases gradually as the wire is turned and becomes zero when the wire is at right angles to the field lines.
b A force acts on the coil when a current passes through it because it is in a magnetic field. An alternating current causes an alternating force to act on the coil. The coil therefore vibrates because it is acted on by an alternating force. The vibration of the coil makes the diaphragm vibrate which produces sound waves.

18.4

1 a A potential difference is induced in a wire when it cuts across the magnetic field lines of the magnet. The induced potential difference causes a current to pass through the wire and the ammeter while the wire is cutting the field lines.
b The ammeter would show a smaller reading in the opposite direction because the wire cuts across the field lines more slowly and in the opposite direction so the induced potential difference is less and in the reverse direction.
2 a There would be no deflection of the pointer.
b The pointer deflection would be bigger.
3 a The current in X creates a magnetic field which passes through coil Y. The increase of the magnetic field in Y induced a potential difference in Y.
b The magnetic field does not change. A potential difference can only be induced when the magnetic field is changing.

18.5

1 a A potential difference is induced in the coil when the sides of the coil cut across the field lines. The potential difference reverses direction each time the coil is at the position where its sides are moving parallel to the field lines. This happens every half-turn of the coil so one full turn of the coil corresponds to one full cycle of the alternating voltage.
b The alternating voltage would have a greater peak value (i.e. amplitude) and its time period would be less (i.e. its frequency would be greater).
2 a The peak value would be smaller. The waves would be stretched more across the screen.
b The peak value is less because the sides of the coil cut more slowly across the field lines so the potential difference at any position of the coil is less than when the coil spins faster. The waves are more stretched out across the screen because the time for each cycle would be longer.
3 a The split-ring commutator reconnects the coil the opposite way round in the circuit every half-turn each time the coil is perpendicular to the magnetic field lines. As a result, the induced potential difference changes its polarity.
b See 18.5 Figure 4b

18.6

1 a An alternating current is passed through the primary coil. This coil creates an alternating magnetic field that passes through the secondary coil. As a result, an alternating potential difference is induced in the secondary coil.
b i The 4000-turn coil
ii A steel core would not be easily magnetised and demagnetised. When an alternating current passes through the primary coil, a steel core would not produce as strong a magnetic field as the iron core would, so the induced potential difference in the secondary coil would be much smaller.
2 a Direct current in the primary coil would not produce an alternating magnetic field so no potential difference would be induced in the secondary coil.
b The current would short-circuit across the wires instead of passing through them. This would cause the coil to overheat if it did not cause a fuse to blow.
c Iron is a magnetic material so it makes the magnetic field much stronger. It is easily magnetised and demagnetised when the current alternates.
3 a i If the mains supply fails, the battery takes over.
ii The transformer steps the potential difference down.
b It has a ferrite core, which is much lighter than an iron core of the same size.

18.7

1 a 1200 turns
b 1150 turns
c i 6.0 A
ii 0.26 A
2 a 2000 turns
b i 3 A
ii 0.15 A
3 a The current in A is less than the current in B.
b The cables have the same resistance and the current in A is less than in B. So the heating effect of the current in A is less than that in B.

Answers to end of chapter summary questions

1 a i See 18.1 Figure 6a
ii The compass points in a direction parallel to the axis of the magnets to the left or right according to whether the magnet with the N-pole at the gap is on the left or the right of the gap.
b i current, force
ii current, lines, field
2 a When a current passes through the coil of the electromagnet, the core of the electromagnet becomes magnetised and attracts the iron armature. The iron armature turns about the pivot and its lower end pushes against one side of the switch and makes the switch close.
b When the ignition switch is closed, the core of the relay coil becomes magnetised so the relay switch closes. The motor is switched on as a result of the relay switch closing.
3 a Upwards
b The force is zero.
c The force on the sides make the coil turn.
4 a i See 18.5 Figure 4
ii The split-ring commutator would need to be replaced by two separate slip rings with a connecting brush at each ring.

- **b** Direct current through the primary coil does not produce an alternating magnetic field. No potential difference is induced in the secondary coil as the magnetic field through it does not change.

5 **a** **i** 10A
- **ii** 100A
- **b** The higher the potential difference, the less the current needed to transfer a certain amount of electric power. The smaller the current through the cables, the less power is wasted in the cables due to their resistance and the heating effect of the current.

6 **a** 12V
- **b** 0.5A
- **c** 5A

7 **a** 150 turns
- **b** 0.15A

Answers to end of chapter examination-style questions

1 **a** **i** strength of magnetic field (1)
- **ii** If you double or treble the current, you double or treble the force (1); the force is directly proportional to the current. (1)
- **b** **i** Force on AD is down (1); force on BC is up (1); so coil turns (1) anticlockwise. (1)
- **ii** Force on BC is still up with force on AD is still down (1); so coil turns clockwise. (1)
- **iii** Reverse the current (1)

2 **a** Marks for this answer will be determined by the Quality of Written Communication (QWC) as well as the standard of scientific response. Points to be made: the coil spins in a magnetic field; the coil cuts the magnetic field lines; the coil is effectively in a changing magnetic field; a potential difference is induced across the coil; since the coil is part of a circuit, a current flows; the slip rings carry the current to the brushes; which are connected to the external circuit. (6)
- **b** **i** The current varies in magnitude (1); and reverses at regular intervals. (1)
- **ii** One complete cycle in 0.04s (1); f = 1/t = 1/0.04 (1); f = 25 Hz (1)

3 **a** iron (1)
- **b** **i** 5000 (1)
- **ii** $n_s/n_p = V_s/V_p$ OR $n_s/5000 = 110/230$ (1)
  $n_s = (5000 \times 110)/230$ (1)
  $n_s = 2391$ (1)
- **iii** An alternating current passes through the primary coil (1); this produces an alternating magnetic field in the core (1); the secondary coil is therefore in a changing magnetic field (1); an alternating potential difference is induced across the secondary coil (1); this drives an alternating current through the shaver. (1)
- **c** The car battery provides direct current (1); so there is no changing magnetic field. (1)
- **d** $V_s \times I_s = V_p \times I_p$ OR $230 \times I_s = 48\,000$ (1)
  $I_s = 48\,000/230$ (1)
  $I_s = 209$ A (1)

19 Radioactivity

19.1

1 **a** Radiation from uranium consists of particles whereas the radiation from a lamp is electromagnetic waves; radiation from uranium is ionising whereas radiation from a lamp is non-ionising.
- **b** Radioactive atoms have unstable nuclei whereas the atoms in a lamp filament do not. The decay of a radioactive atom cannot be stopped whereas the atoms in a lamp filament stop emitting radiation when the filament current is switched off.

2 **a** Alpha radiation.
- **b** Beta or gamma radiation.

3 **a** There are atoms in the substance that have nuclei that are unstable. These nuclei become stable by emitting radiation.
- **b** Any two from radioactive isotopes in the air, the ground or in building materials; X ray machines; cosmic radiation.
- **c** **i** The substance is radioactive.
- **ii** The Geiger counter continues to detect background radiation.

19.2

1 **a** 6p + 6n
- **b** 27p + 33n
- **c** 92p + 143n
- **d** 4 protons, 10 neutrons

2 **a** 92p + 146n
- **b** 90p + 144n
- **c** 91p + 143n

3 **a** **i** $^{235}_{92}X \rightarrow {}^{231}_{90}Th + {}^{4}_{2}\alpha$
- **ii** $^{64}_{29}Cu \rightarrow 6^{4}_{30}Zn + {}^{0}_{-1}\beta$
- **b** **i** $^{210}_{83}Bi \rightarrow {}^{210}_{84}Po + {}^{0}_{-1}\beta$
- **ii** $^{210}_{84}Po \rightarrow {}^{206}_{82}Pb + {}^{4}_{2}\alpha$

19.3

1 **a** To stop the radiation so it can't affect objects or people nearby.
- **b** Charged particles are deflected by an electric or magnetic field. Gamma radiation is not deflected by an electric or a magnetic field so gamma radiation is not made up of charged particles.
- **c** To keep the source out of range.
- **d** α, β radiation

2 **a** **i** Gamma
- **ii** Alpha
- **iii** Beta
- **b** **i** The magnetic field deflects charged particles and γ radiation is uncharged whereas α and β particles are charged.
- **ii** α and β particles are oppositely charged so they are deflected in opposite directions.
- **iii** The mass of an α particle is much greater than that of a β particle and so it is much harder to deflect an alpha particle than to deflect a beta particle.

3 **a** Radiation can knock electrons from atoms. This ionisation damages the genes in a cell which can be passed on if the cell generates more cells.
- **b** Place the Geiger tube in a holder so the tube can be moved horizontally. Move the holder and tube so the end of the tube is close to the source and the Geiger counter detects radiation from the source. Move the tube and holder gradually away from the source until the count rate from the counter decreases significantly. The distance from the end of the tube to the source is the range of the α radiation from the source.

19.4

1 **a** The half-life is the average time it takes for the number of nuclei of the isotope in a sample to halve.
- **b** 75 cpm
- **c** 6.5 hours

2 **a** **i** 4 milligrams
- **ii** 1 milligram
- **b** About 65 hours (= just over 4 half lives)

3 **a** **i** 160 million atoms
- **ii** 10 million atoms
- **b** Just less than 180 minutes (= just less than 4 half lives)

19.5

1 **a** β; thin metal stops α radiation completely and does not stop γ radiation. The amount of β radiation passing through a thin metal sheet depends on the thickness of the sheet.
- **b** γ; α radiation would be wholly absorbed by the body so could not be used. β radiation would be partly absorbed but γ radiation is absorbed much less so γ radiation is more reliable.
- **c** γ; α radiation would be wholly absorbed by the pipe wall so could not be used. β radiation would be partly absorbed by the ground but γ radiation would much less affected so γ radiation is more reliable.

2 **a** γ-radiation would hardly be absorbed by the foil as it would all pass straight through the foil.
- **b** A stable isotope in the body (or elsewhere) would not be dangerous whereas an unstable isotope would be harmful as it is radioactive.

3 **a** It needs to be detectable outside the body, non-toxic, have a short half-life (1–24 hours) and decay into a stable product.
- **b** 11 200 years old.
- **c** The count rate measurements would be due to background radiation as well as the wood. The count rate due to background radiation is measured by measuring the count rate without the wood present. This is then subtracted from the count rate with the wood present to give the count rate due to the wood only.

Answers to end of chapter summary questions

1 a i 6p + 8n
ii 90p + 138n
b i 7p + 7n
ii $^{14}_{7}N$
c i 88p + 136n
ii $^{224}_{88}Ra$

2

	α	β	γ
Identity	helium nuclei	electrons	electromagnetic radiation
Stopped by	paper	5 mm aluminium	thick lead
Electric field deflection	towards the positive plate	towards the negative plate	no deflection
Range in air	about 5 cm	about 1 m	unlimited
Relative ionisation	very strong	strong	weak

3 a **1** B, **2** D, **3** A, **4** C.
b i Smoke alarms use alpha radiation. However, californium-241 has too short a half-life to be useful in a smoke alarm.
ii 2nd column – alpha because α radiation creates enough ions in the air to give an ionisation current in the detector without smoke present. Smoke absorbs the ions and stops the ionisation current which triggers the alarm. 3rd column – 28 years – the longer the half-life, the longer the smoke alarm will continue to operate (provided the battery is changed when necessary).
4 a Student graph
b 1 hour 40 minutes
5 a 2 half-lives
b 11 200 years
6 a Background radioactivity.
b 356 cpm
c Beta radiation, because it penetrates thin foil and is stopped by an aluminium plate. Alpha radiation would be stopped by the foil. Gamma radiation would pass through the foil and the plate.

Answers to end of chapter examination-style questions

1 a i A: 1 B: 4 C: 3 D: 2 (4)
ii Atoms with the same number of protons/same atomic number (1); but with a different number of neutrons/different mass number. (1)
iii $^{7}_{3}Y$ (1) (1)
b Their nuclei give out radiation (1); which is a random event occurring without anything being done. (1)
2 a Marks for this answer will be determined by the Quality of Written Communication (QWC) as well as the standard of scientific response. The radiation is alpha particles (1); it is relatively safe if the source is outside the body (1); because it has a range of only a few centimetres in air; (1); and it is stopped by clothing/skin (1); if the source is inside the body the radiation can affect living cells (1); the radiation cannot penetrate through the body to detectors outside (1)
b It has 2 fewer neutrons (1); and the same number of protons. (1)
3 a i Divide the initial count rate in two (2500 cpm) and find the x-axis figure at this point (1); 5 hours (1)
ii 10 hours = 2 × half-life (1); so count rate is 4 times as great (1); 20 000 cpm (1)
iii mass number = 234 (1); atomic number = 90 (1)
b It should emit gamma radiation (1); for the radiation to be detectable outside the body (1); the half-life should be a few hours (1); long enough to do the investigation (1); but short enough for the isotope not to remain in the body for long. (1)
c i Normally the alpha particles ionise the air (1); the air conducts a current (1); if smoke enters at P, the smoke absorbs ions (1); the drop in current triggers the alarm. (1)
ii It emits alpha particles which are highly ionising (1); the alpha particles have a short range so do not reach people in the room (1); the half-life is long enough for it not to need replacing. (1)

20 Energy from the nucleus

20.1

1 a The nucleus splits into two fragments and releases energy and several neutrons in the process.
b The nucleus absorbs a neutron without undergoing fission.
2 a (In order) B, A, C, D, B …
b i The control rods absorb fission neutrons and keep the chain reaction under control, maintaining an even rate of fission.
ii More fission neutrons will be absorbed so the number of fission neutrons in the reactor core will decrease and the rate of release of energy due to fission will therefore decreases.
3 a i A and D
ii They have undergone fission and released neutrons and energy.
iii C and E
b i

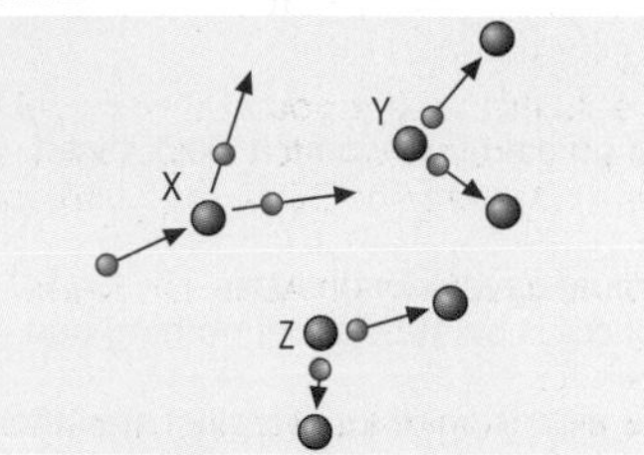

ii Either, the third neutron released by X was absorbed by a control rod, or slowed by the moderator, or absorbed by a non-fissionable nucleus, or escaped from the reactor.

20.2

1 a Nuclear fusion is the formation of a nucleus when two smaller nuclei collide and fuse together.
b A helium nucleus with 2 protons and a single neutron is formed, $^{3}_{2}He$.
2 a i So the nuclei have enough kinetic energy to overcome the force of repulsion between them and fuse.
ii The energy output would be less than the energy input so it would not produce any energy overall.
b *Advantage* – the fuel is readily available or, the reaction products are less harmful than fission products or, the reactions would stop if the plasma touches the sides of the reactor.
Disadvantage – the reactions cannot be maintained for long periods of time or, strong magnetic fields are needed to control the plasma.
3 a 1 proton and 1 neutron.
b $^{2}_{1}H + ^{1}_{1}p \rightarrow ^{3}_{2}He$
c $^{3}_{2}He + ^{3}_{2}He \rightarrow ^{4}_{2}He + ^{1}_{1}p + ^{1}_{1}p$

20.3

1 a i It needs to be stored securely because it is hazardous and would be a danger to people and animals if it escaped.
ii It needs to be stored for a long time because it contains radioactive isotopes with long half-lives.
b The α-radiation from the source will be absorbed by the surrounding tissues and it could damage or kill cells in the body or cause cancer. Outside the body, it is less dangerous as α-radiation has no penetrating power, but it can damage skin cells if within range of them or retinal cells if near the eye.
2 a Radon gas in a house may be more concentrated than outdoors and people in the house would breathe it in. The lungs would be exposed to α-radiation from radon gas atoms that enter the lungs. The ionising effect of the α-particles in the tissue cells would damage or kill the cells or cause cancer.
b Install pipes under the house and connect them to a suction pump to draw radon gases out of the ground before it seeps into the house. The top of the outlet pipe from the pump would need to be high up outside the house.
3 Benefits to building either type of reactor should include no greenhouse gas emissions, reliable and secure electricity supplies, and large-scale generation from small sites compared with renewable supplies that would take up much larger areas etc. Drawbacks should include long-term storage of nuclear waste, possible escape of radioactive substances into the environment, impracticality of fusion reactors, etc.

20.4

1 a When we use a powerful telescope to see a distant galaxy, we are seeing the galaxy as it was billions of years ago because the light from it has taken billions of years to reach us.
b About 13 billion years.
c They are both positively charged, so they repel each other. The force of repulsion is much greater than the force of gravity between them.

2 a i We could not send a probe far enough to be outside the Milky Way.
ii As galaxies take millions of years to form, any sequence of photos would not span this timescale.
b i Gravitational forces hold the stars together.
ii The universe has expanded leaving these vast spaces.
3 a 3, 4, 1, 2
b i The force of gravity between them.
ii Gravitational potential energy is released and transferred into kinetic energy as dust and gas clouds pull together. As the clouds of gas and dust become denser and denser, the particles in the clouds move faster and faster and so the clouds heat up.
iii The force of gravitational attraction towards the centre of the galaxy acts as the centripetal force to keep the stars revolving about the centre of the galaxy.

20.5

1 a B, A, C, D.
b i A
ii It will fade out and go cold to become a black dwarf.
2 a i expand, collapse
ii collapse, explode
b i The neutron star must have enough mass.
ii The gravitational field is so strong that nothing can escape from it.
c i A supernova is the explosion of a supergiant star after it collapses on itself.
ii It becomes a neutron star.
3 a i The force of attraction due to its gravity acting on its own mass.
ii The force of the radiation flowing outwards to its surface from its core.
b i A white dwarf cools down and when it no longer emits light it has become a black dwarf because it can no longer be seen.
ii Infrared radiation.

20.6

1 a hydrogen
b uranium
c helium, iron
d hydrogen
e iron
2 a A star
b A supernova
c A supernova
d A galaxy
3 a i Nuclear fusion
ii A supernova event
b i The Sun and the rest of the Solar System formed from the debris of a supernova. Much of the uranium-238 formed from the debris of the supernova still exists because has it has a half-life which is comparable with the age of the Earth.
ii Some plutonium-239 would have been created in the supernova from which the Sun was formed. Since this event was at least 4500 million years ago, any plutonium-239 created then would have long since decayed into other elements.

Answers to end of chapter summary questions

1 a i stays the same
ii decreases
iii increases
iv stays the same
b i The reactor would overheat and the materials in it might melt. In the meltdown the reactor pressure might be high enough to cause an explosion releasing radioactive material into the atmosphere. The coolant fluid that leaked out would be radioactivity and would need to be contained in secure storage.
ii The excess neutrons would be absorbed and the reaction would slow down releasing less energy.
2 a i The process where two small nuclei fuse together to form a single larger nucleus.
ii Because they are both positively charged.
iii To overcome the force of repulsion between them due to their charge.
b The plasma needs to be very hot. The plasma is difficult to control.
3 a i fusion
ii fission
iii fission
iv fusion
b The fuel is readily available. The products of fusion are not radioactive.
4 a i Nuclear fusion
ii Hydrogen
b The Sun will cool down and swell out to become a red giant.
5 a planet
b galaxy
c stars
d stars, galaxy
6 A giant star collapses and becomes a white dwarf which is a star that is hotter, smaller and more dense. The white dwarf loses energy by radiation and eventually cools to become a black dwarf which is cold and invisible. A supergiant star collapses more rapidly than a giant star and then explodes throwing matter in all directions into the surrounding space and emitting so much radiation that is becomes much brighter than the supergiant. The core of the supergiant is compressed further in the explosion and forms a neutron star or, if its mass is large enough, it forms a black hole.
7 a **A**, **C**, **B**, **D**, **E**.
b i A red giant is much larger in diameter and cooler than the Sun. It is less dense than the Sun.
ii A white dwarf is much smaller in diameter and hotter than the Sun. It is more dense than the Sun.
c i It will fade out.
ii It will explode as a supernova, leaving a neutron star at its core. If the mass of the neutron star is large enough, it will be a black hole.
8 a i A large star that explodes.
ii A star that becomes a supernova suddenly becomes much brighter then it fades. A star like the Sun has a constant brightness.
b i A massive object, from which nothing can escape.
ii They would be pulled in by the force of gravity and then disappear.
iii A neutron star is composed entirely of neutrons. It is formed at the core of a supernova if there is not enough matter to form a black hole.
9 a i Helium
ii Helium
b i lead, uranium
ii The two elements would have been formed in a supernova explosion.
iii Heavy elements can only have formed in a supernova. The presence of heavy elements in the Earth tells us that the Solar System formed from the debris of a supernova.

Answers to end of chapter examination-style questions

1 a

Non-renewable	Renewable
coal-fired	solar-powered
gas-fired	tidal
nuclear	wind farm

(5)

b i Marks for this answer will be determined by the Quality of Written Communication (QWC) as well as the standard of scientific response. Points to be made: the neutron is absorbed by the nucleus; which makes the nucleus unstable; the nucleus splits into two fragments; releasing a lot of energy; and 2 or 3 neutrons; this is called nuclear fission; the neutrons can split further nuclei; setting up a chain reaction. (6)
ii To slow down the neutrons (1); so that they can cause fission. (1)
iii To absorb neutrons (1); stopping the fission process. (1)
2 a i fusion (1)
ii fission (1)
iii fission (1)
iv fission (1)
v fusion. (1)
b Nuclei (1); of smaller/hydrogen atoms (1); join together to form larger/helium atoms. (1)
c i mass number 4 (1); atomic number 2 (1)
ii 1 proton (1); 1 neutron (1)
iii Nuclei contain protons (1); protons have a positive electric charge (1); therefore protons repel each other (1); with a force that gets larger the closer they are. (1)

3 a A – supernova (1); B – neutron star OR black hole (1); C – black hole OR neutron star (1)

b i Dust and gas (1); from space (1); are pulled together (1); by gravitational attraction. (1)

ii The two forces acting on it balance (1); one is the force of gravitational attraction (1); the other the expansion force due to its radiation. (1)

iii Marks for this answer will be determined by the Quality of Written Communication (QWC) as well as the standard of scientific response. Points to be made: when the star runs out of hydrogen nuclei to fuse together; it expands; cools down; becomes a red giant; its own gravity causes the star to collapse in on itself; causing it to heat up; it turns from red to yellow to white; becomes a white dwarf; it then fades out; goes cold and becomes a black dwarf. (6)

Index

T

U

V

W

X

Photo acknowledgements

P1.1.1 Keith Kent/Science Photo Library; P1.1.4 Martyn Chillmaid; P1.2.2 iStockphoto; P1.3.2T Data Harvest; P1.3.2B Martyn Chillmaid; P2.3.2 Topfoto; P2.4.3 Rob Melnychuk/Getty Images; P3.1.1 Getty Images; P3.2.3 AFP/Getty Images; P3.3.2 Copyright 2010 photolibrary.com; P3.4.1 Fstop/Getty Images; P3.4.2 iStockphoto; P4.1.3 iStockphoto; P4.3.2 Martyn F. Chillmaid/Science Photo Library; P5.1.1 iStockphoto; P5.1.2 AFP/Getty Images; P5.2.1 Getty Images; P5.2.2 AFP/Getty Images; P5.4.2 iStockphoto; P6.1.1L Getty Images; P6.1.1R AFP/Getty Images; P6.2.1 Blend Images/Alamy; P6.5.1 cscredon/iStockphoto; P6.5.4 Optare plc; P6.6.1R AFP/Getty Images; P6.6.3a Getty Images; P6.6.3b Cordelia Molloy/Science Photo Library; P6.7.1 bikeitup/iStockphoto; P6.7.3 dr3amer/iStockphoto; P7.1.1 istockphoto; P7.4.2 NASA/ESA/STSCI/Hubble Heritage Team/Science Photo Library; P7.4.3 istockphoto; P7.5.4 Berenice Abbott/Science Photo Library; P7.5.8 Jim Breithaupt; P8.3.1 iStockphoto; P8.3.2 iStockphoto; P8.4.1 Mauro Fermariello/Science Photo Library; P8.4.2 Image 100 22 (NT); P8.4.3 Martyn F. Chillmaid/Science Photo Library; P8.5.1a AJ Photo/Hop Americain/Science Photo Library; P8.5.1b czardases/iStockphoto; P8.5.2 emmy-images/iStockphoto; P9.1.1 Fotolia; P9.2.1 Photolibrary/Imagebroker.net; P9.3.2 iStockphoto; P10.1.1 Photolibrary; P10.1.4 Shout/Rex Features; P10.2.3 Pasieka/Science Photo Library; P10.2.DYK iStockphoto; P10.3.1 GIPhotostock/Science Photo Library; P10.4.5 David M. Martin, MD/Science Photo Library; P11.1.7 AlexTyum/Fotolia; P11.5.2 Ian Hooton/Science Photo Library; P11.5.4 Adam Gault/Science Photo Library; P12.1.1 NASA/ESA/Getty Images; P12.2.1 Mark Garlick/Science Photo Library; P12.2.2 NASA/Science Photo Library; P13.1.1 Charles D. Winters/Science Photo Library; P13.2.3 G&D Images/Alamy; P13.3.3 Brian Stevenson/Getty Images; P14.1.1 Fotolia; P14.1.3 Gary Ombler/Getty Images; P14.2.1 iStockphoto; P14.3.2 Spohn Matthieu/Getty Images; P14.3.5 iStockphoto; P14.4.1 Ted Kinsman/Getty Images; P14.4.3 Tony Craddock/Science Photo Library; P14.4.4 Photolibrary/Tsuneo Nakamura; P14.5.1 AP/PA Photos; P14.6.1 Cordelia Molloy/Science Photo Library; P14.6.2 iStockphoto; P14.6.3 iStockphoto; P14.6.SQ1 iStockphoto; P14.6.5a Fotolia; P14.6.5b Fotolia; P14.7.1 David Taylor/Science Photo Library; P14.7.4 Mark Burnett/Science Photo Library; P14.ESQ2 Fotolia; P15.1.1 Fotolia; P15.1.3 iStockphoto; P15.2.1 iStockphoto; P15.2.2a iStockphoto; P16.1.1 SSPL/Science Museum/Getty Images; P16.4.3a Martyn F. Chillmaid/Science Photo Library; P16.4.3b Martyn F. Chillmaid/Science Photo Library; P17.2.3 iStockphoto; P17.3.1 iStockphoto; P17.3.3 ia_64/Fotolia.com; P17.4.1 SSPL/Science Museum/Getty Images; P17.4.2 Cordelia Molloy/Science Photo Library; P17.6.1 Jim Breithaupt; P17.6.2 iStockphoto; P17.8.2 Fotolia; P17.8.4 Tony Gwynne/Alamy; P18.1.1 Peter Zijlstra/iStockphoto; P18.1.3a Cordelia Molloy/Science Photo Library; P18.2.4 Alex Bartel/Science Photo Library; P18.4.1 B. Boissonnet/Science Photo Library; P18.5.3 Science Photo Library; P18.5.4 Science Photo Library; P18.7.1 ImageBroker.net/Photolibrary; P19.1.2 Popperfoto/Getty Images; P19.5.3 PascalR/Fotolia.com; P20.1.3 SSPL/Science Museum/Getty; P20.2.3 Copyright 2010 photolibrary.com; P20.3.2 Getty Images; P20.3.3 Getty Images; P20.4.2 NOAO/AURA/NSF/T. Rector and B.A. Wolpa; P20.4.3 Physics Today Collection/American Insitute of Physics/Science Photo Library; P20.4.4 NASA Image of the Day Collection; P20.5.3 X-ray: NASA/CXC/CfA/W. Forman et al.; Optical: DSS; P20.6.1 NASA/ESA/JPL/Arizona State University; P20.6.3 NASA/JPL/Cornell University